UNION
DES GRANDS
CRUS DE
BORDEAUX

Union des Grands Crus de Bordeaux

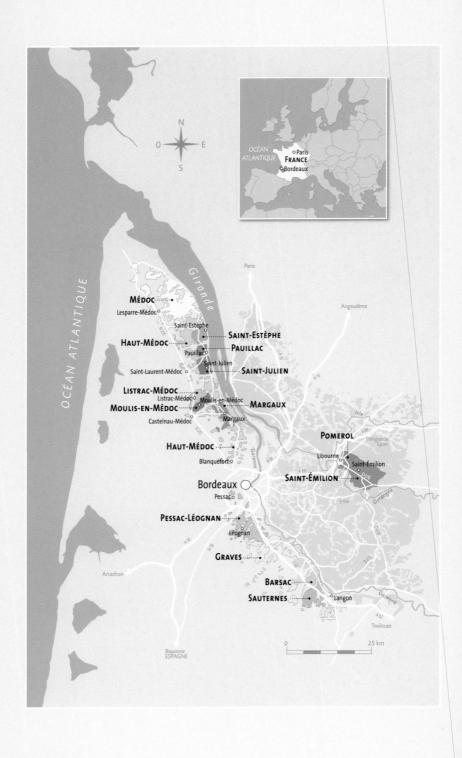

The Union des Grands Crus de Bordeaux

Founded in 1973, the Union des Grands Crus de Bordeaux is an association consisting of 132 grands crus estates with the same high standards of quality. These are located exclusively in the finest appellations in the Gironde department: Médoc, Haut-Médoc, Saint-Estèphe, Pauillac, Saint-Julien, Margaux, Moulis, Listrac, Graves, Pessac-Léognan, Sauternes, Barsac, Saint-Émilion, and Pomerol.

As professional, devoted producers, Union des Grands Crus members not only make great wine, but also enjoy sharing it and the centuries-old culture behind it. Along with their fellow producers, the men and women in charge of these estates travel all over the world to personally present their recent vintages to the media, local importers and distributors, and wine enthusiasts.

The Union des Grands Crus de Bordeaux: Reflecting a culture thousands of years old

The history of the most famous vineyards on earth goes back hundreds of years, and winemaking in Bordeaux can trace its roots back two thousand years.

The Celtic *Bituriges Vivisques* tribe settled on the banks of the Garonne in the 3rd century B.C. and founded the city of *Burdigala* (present-day Bordeaux). They made wine there from a very early date and, influenced by the Romans, planted and adapted Biturica, a variety originally from the Pyrenees. This evolved into Vidure, then Carmenet, and finally into Cabernet. In the 4th century AD, the famous orator and Bordeaux winegrower, Ausonious (Ausone), described his native region as "the birthplace of Bacchus, well-known thanks to its rivers and great men".

Records from the Middle Ages show the constant growth of winegrowing, which is hardly surprising in light of the number of churches and monasteries where wine was consumed for religious and cultural reasons.

The birth of a large vineyard region turned toward international trade dates from the mid-12th century at a time when Aquitaine was English, owing allegiance to Henry Plantagenet, one of the wealthiest princes in Europe, who went on to become King of England in 1154. This was the beginning of a long and extraordinary history of commercial exchanges. A huge market for Bordeaux wines developed. Exports represented an impressive amount of money and the Bordeaux trade became one of the most thriving businesses in medieval Europe.

Many foreign merchants from Holland, Germany, Ireland, and other countries settled in Bordeaux in the 15th and 16th centuries, contributing considerably to wine sales to their native country and beyond...

The 17th and 18th centuries were marked by an impressive improvement in quality of the best crus (or "growths") thanks to the demands of discerning customers in France and abroad. Wealthy landowners, aristocrats, and merchants invested massively in winegrowing estates that soon took on the name of "château". The wines they produced were shipped by Bordeaux *négociants* to a similar class of wealthy foreign consumers.

The notion of *cru* or *château* became the norm for the elite estates. Today's grands crus reflect an ancient tradition and most of them date from this period. They are the elite of Bordeaux wines.

The privileged location of the grands crus does not alone account for their quality. At that level, a natural predisposition and potential is not enough. In fact, remarkable advances in scientific research and winemaking expertise explain the huge success of the finest Bordeaux wines in the 19th and 20th centuries.

From their very origin, the grands crus of Bordeaux have always targeted the world's most demanding wine enthusiasts.

People who love such wines are, above all, hedonists. They are able to appreciate great wines like works of art. In fact the château owner, or artist, creates his fine wine for other artists, i.e. knowledgeable and perceptive tasters who enjoy discovering, analysing, identifying, and above all appreciating subtle flavours and balance. Like every artistic domain (painting, music, etc.), great wine can only be created when the appropriate techniques have been mastered. And this mastery must also be accompanied by the artist's natural talent and love for what he does. Meeting the artist-winegrower is unquestionably a tremendous way of introducing a new dimension to his work.

In this spirit, discovering Bordeaux – the city, the wine country, the grands crus, and the people who make the wine – is a tremendously worthwhile experience and a unique way of learning. Visiting the grands crus has never been easier, and their châteaux and cellars are located on the most famous *terroirs* in Bordeaux.

A trip to Bordeaux will create a special link between you and the people who produce the wine, because French hospitality is not just a myth. It is very much a reality as far as the members of the Union des Grands Crus are concerned.

Above and beyond the traditional week of en *primeur* barrel tastings – a veritable baptism for the new vintage, attracting some 5,000 professionals from the media and the wine trade – the Union des Grands Crus also organises a "Week-end des Grands Crus" in the month of May. This enables enthusiasts from all over the world to enjoy the wines they love at the source and talk to the people who make them.

Editorial

Sylvie Cazes
President of the Union des Grands Crus de Bordeaux

Viticulture, winemaking, and wine appreciation have given rise since time immemorial to expertise, exchanges, traditions, and a philosophy of life.

Wine is meant to share, and knowledge about it something to pass on. This unique beverage is produced by men and women who have inherited know-how thousands of years old. In keeping with wine's universal values, the team at the Union des Grands Crus de Bordeaux are keen to meet you and show you the rich diversity of wines produced by member estates.

Throughout the year, Union des Grands Crus members travel around the world to pour their wines, explain their fascinating background, and illustrate the quality of their terroir to people just starting to enjoy wine as well as connoisseurs, critics, journalists, merchants and brokers.

They are always very happy to help you discover or rediscover their region's heritage – because wine in Bordeaux has also shaped landscapes, given rise to beautiful buildings, and created many fascinating places of interest. Indeed, Bordeaux, the heart of the wine country and a beautiful, historic city, is now a UNESCO World Heritage Site.

We are sure that our tastings will leave you with fine memories of enjoyable wines, enhanced still further by a trip to our region.

You will always be welcome in Bordeaux!

Sylvie Cazes

Contents

Château Angélus	p 46	Château d'Yquem	p 16
Château Angludet	p 110	Château Dassault	p 53
Château Balestard La Tonnelle	p 47	Château Dauzac	p 113
Château Bastor-Lamontagne	p 166	Château de Camensac	p 99
Château Batailley	p 144	Château de Chantegrive	p 40
Château Beau-Séjour Bécot	p 48	Domaine de Chevalier	p 24
Château Beaumont	p 94	Château de Fargues	p 169
Château Beauregard	p 70	Château de Fieuzal	p 25
Château Belgrave	p 95	Château de France	p 26
Château Berliquet	p 49	Château de Lamarque	p 100
Château Beychevelle	p 132	Château de Malle	p 170
Château Bouscaut	p 22	Château de Pez	p 159
Château Branaire-Ducru	p 133	Château de Rayne Vigneau	p 171
Château Brane-Cantenac	p 111	Château Desmirail	p 114
Château Canon	p 50	Château Doisy Daëne	p 172
Château Canon La Gaffelière	p 51	Château Doisy-Védrines	p 173
Château Cantemerle	p 96	Château du Tertre	p 115
Château Cantenac-Brown	p 112	Château Durfort-Vivens	p 116
Château Cap de Mourlin	p 52	Château Ferrande	p 41
Château Carbonnieux	p 23	Château Ferrière	p 117
Vieux Château Certan	p 71	Château-Figeac	p 54
Château Chasse-Spleen	p 88	Château Fonréaud	p 83
Château Cheval Blanc	p 14	Château Fourcas Dupré	p 84
Château Citran	p 97	Château Fourcas Hosten	p 85
Château Clarke	p 82	Clos Fourtet	p 55
Château Clerc Milon	p 145	Château Franc Mayne	p 56
Château Climens	p 167	Château Gazin	p 73
Château Clinet	p 72	Château Giscours	p 118
Château Cos Labory	p 158	Château Gloria	p 134
Château Coufran	p 98	Château Grand Mayne	p 57
Château Coutet	p 168	Château Grand-Puy Ducasse	p 148
Château Croizet-Bages	p 146	Château Grand-Puy-Lacoste	p 149
Château d'Armailhac	p 147	Château Greysac	p 106
		Château Gruaud Larose	p 135

Contents

List in Alphabetical Order

Château Guiraud	p 174	Château Lynch-Moussas	p 152
Château Haut-Bages Libéral	p 150	Château Malartic-Lagravière	p 33
Château Haut-Bailly	p 27	Château Malescasse	p 103
Château Haut-Bergey	p 28	Château Malescot Saint-Exupéry	p 122
Château Kirwan	p 119	Château Marquis de Terme	p 123
Château L'Évangile	p 74	Château Maucaillou	p 89
Château La Cabanne	p 75	Château Monbrison	p 124
Château La Conseillante	p 76	Château Mouton Rothschild	p 18
Château La Couspaude	p 58	Château Nairac	p 177
Château La Croix de Gay	p 77	Château Olivier	p 34
Château La Dominique	p 59	Château Ormes de Pez	p 161
Château La Gaffelière	p 60	Château Pape Clément	p 35
Château La Lagune	p 101	Château Pavie	p 64
Château La Louvière	p 29	Château Pavie-Macquin	p 65
Château La Pointe	p 78	Château Petit-Village	p 79
Château La Tour Blanche	p 175	Château Phélan Ségur	p 162
Château La Tour Carnet	p 102	Château Pichon-Longueville	p 153
Château La Tour de By	p 107	Château Pichon Longueville Comtesse de Lalande	p 154
Château La Tour Figeac	p 61	Château Picque Caillou	p 36
Château Labégorce	p 120	Château Poujeaux	p 90
Château Lafaurie-Peyraguey	p 176	Château Prieuré-Lichine	p 125
Château Lafon-Rochet	p 160	Château Rahoul	p 42
Château Lagrange	p 136	Château Rauzan-Gassies	p 126
Château Langoa Barton	p 137	Château Rauzan-Ségla	p 127
Château Larcis Ducasse	p 62	Château Saint-Pierre	p 140
Château Larmande	p 63	Château Sigalas Rabaud	p 178
Château Larrivet Haut-Brion	p 30	Château Siran	p 128
Château Lascombes	p 121	Château Smith Haut Lafitte	p 37
Château Latour-Martillac	p 31	Château Suduiraut	p 179
Château Léoville Barton	p 138	Château Talbot	p 141
Château Léoville Poyferré	p 139	Château Troplong Mondot	p 66
Château Les Carmes Haut-Brion	p 32	Château Trottevieille	p 67
Château Lynch-Bages	p 151		

Contents

List by Appellation

Pessac-Léognan

Château Bouscaut — p 22
Château Carbonnieux — p 23
Domaine de Chevalier — p 24
Château de Fieuzal — p 25
Château de France — p 26
Château Haut-Bailly — p 27
Château Haut-Bergey — p 28
Château La Louvière — p 29
Château Larrivet Haut-Brion — p 30
Château Latour-Martillac — p 31
Château Les Carmes Haut-Brion — p 32
Château Malartic-Lagravière — p 33
Château Olivier — p 34
Château Pape Clément — p 35
Château Picque Caillou — p 36
Château Smith Haut Lafitte — p 37

Graves

Château de Chantegrive — p 40
Château Ferrande — p 41
Château Rahoul — p 42

Saint-Emilion Grand Cru

Château Angélus — p 46
Château Balestard La Tonnelle — p 47
Château Beau-Séjour Bécot — p 48
Château Berliquet — p 49
Château Canon — p 50
Château Canon La Gaffelière — p 51
Château Cap de Mourlin — p 52
Château Cheval Blanc — p 14
Château Dassault — p 53
Château-Figeac — p 54
Clos Fourtet — p 55
Château Franc Mayne — p 56
Château Grand Mayne — p 57
Château La Couspaude — p 58
Château La Dominique — p 59

Château La Gaffelière — p 60
Château La Tour Figeac — p 61
Château Larcis Ducasse — p 62
Château Larmande — p 63
Château Pavie — p 64
Château Pavie-Macquin — p 65
Château Troplong Mondot — p 66
Château Trottevieille — p 67

Pomerol

Château Beauregard — p 70
Vieux Château Certan — p 71
Château Clinet — p 72
Château Gazin — p 73
Château L'Évangile — p 74
Château La Cabanne — p 75
Château La Conseillante — p 76
Château La Croix de Gay — p 77
Château La Pointe — p 78
Château Petit-Village — p 79

Listrac-Médoc

Château Clarke — p 82
Château Fonréaud — p 83
Château Fourcas Dupré — p 84
Château Fourcas Hosten — p 85

Moulis-en-Médoc

Château Chasse-Spleen — p 88
Château Maucaillou — p 89
Château Poujeaux — p 90

Haut-Médoc

Château Beaumont — p 94
Château Belgrave — p 95
Château Cantemerle — p 96
Château Citran — p 97
Château Coufran — p 98
Château de Camensac — p 99

Contents

LIST BY APPELLATION

Château de Lamarque   p 100
Château La Lagune   p 101
Château La Tour Carnet   p 102
Château Malescasse   p 103

MÉDOC
Château Greysac   p 106
Château La Tour de By   p 107

MARGAUX
Château Angludet   p 110
Château Brane-Cantenac   p 111
Château Cantenac-Brown   p 112
Château Dauzac   p 113
Château Desmirail   p 114
Château du Tertre   p 115
Château Durfort-Vivens   p 116
Château Ferrière   p 117
Château Giscours   p 118
Château Kirwan   p 119
Château Labégorce   p 120
Château Lascombes   p 121
Château Malescot Saint-Exupéry   p 122
Château Marquis de Terme   p 123
Château Monbrison   p 124
Château Prieuré-Lichine   p 125
Château Rauzan-Gassies   p 126
Château Rauzan-Ségla   p 127
Château Siran   p 128

SAINT-JULIEN
Château Beychevelle   p 132
Château Branaire-Ducru   p 133
Château Gloria   p 134
Château Gruaud Larose   p 135
Château Lagrange   p 136
Château Langoa Barton   p 137
Château Léoville Barton   p 138
Château Léoville Poyferré   p 139
Château Saint-Pierre   p 140
Château Talbot   p 141

PAUILLAC
Château Batailley   p 144
Château Clerc Milon   p 145
Château Croizet-Bages   p 146
Château d'Armailhac   p 147
Château Grand-Puy Ducasse   p 148
Château Grand-Puy-Lacoste   p 149
Château Haut-Bages Libéral   p 150
Château Lynch-Bages   p 151
Château Lynch -Moussas   p 152
Château Mouton Rothschild   p 18
Château Pichon-Longueville   p 153
Château Pichon Longueville   p 154
    Comtesse de Lalande

SAINT-ESTÈPHE
Château Cos Labory   p 158
Château de Pez   p 159
Château Lafon-Rochet   p 160
Château Ormes de Pez   p 161
Château Phélan Ségur   p 162

SAUTERNES OR BARSAC
Château Bastor-Lamontagne   p 166
Château Climens   p 167
Château Coutet   p 168
Château d'Yquem   p 16
Château de Fargues   p 169
Château de Malle   p 170
Château de Rayne Vigneau   p 171
Château Doisy Daëne   p 172
Château Doisy-Védrines   p 173
Château Guiraud   p 174
Château La Tour Blanche   p 175
Château Lafaurie-Peyraguey   p 176
Château Nairac   p 177
Château Sigalas Rabaud   p 178
Château Suduiraut   p 179

Château Cheval Blanc

Premier Grand Cru Classé "A"

Background

Once upon a time, Cheval Blanc was a modest tenant farm (that nevertheless had a long winegrowing history) called Le Barrail des Cailloux. However, starting in the 19th century, the estate took on an aura of romanticism and greatness. From the time the château was created in 1834 until its present-day boundaries were fixed in 1871, Cheval Blanc became a legend.

Since it takes two parents to have children, it can be said that Cheval Blanc was born of the marriage between Merlot, the traditional grape variety in Saint-Émilion and Pomerol, and Cabernet Franc.

Helped by the fact that phylloxera spared the estate in the late 19th century, the château's reputation grew and grew. In fact, the wine was in strong demand in port cities and trading posts around the world... London, Paris, Antwerp, etc. The 20th century brought truly international recognition.

In 1954, Cheval Blanc was classified a *Premier Grand Cru Classé A*, and this supreme distinction has been confirmed in every subsequent classification.

A special spirit

Since 1998, Bernard Arnault and Baron Frère have perpetuated Cheval Blanc's tradition of excellence, while introducing elegant modern influences. Baron Frère is a member of the board of directors of some of the most powerful financial and industrial groups in Europe. A true connoisseur, he is passionate, respectful and curious about fine wine.

As for Bernard Arnault, his name is forever linked with that of LVMH, the world's leading luxury goods group, with such fabulous brands as Dior, Krug, Moët-Hennessy, Louis Vuitton, and Château d'Yquem. By serving Cheval Blanc to his guests and making sure that it graces fine tables around the world, he added even more lustre to the wine.

THE FUTURE

Planned for quite some time, the construction of new buildings and a new cellar became a reality in 2011.

The owners of Cheval Blanc wanted to create a "wine workshop" that also makes a strong architectural statement in tune with the 21st century, while reflecting its status as a famous great growth. This challenge was met by the 1994 Pritzker Prize winning architect, Christian de Portzamparc, who designed a winery totally integrated with its surroundings.

Château Cheval Blanc 33330 Saint-Émilion
Tel. +33 (0)5 57 55 55 55 - Fax +33 (0)5 57 55 55 50
contact@chateau-chevalblanc.com - **www.chateau-chevalblanc.com**

Château d'Yquem

Premier Cru Supérieur Classé en 1855

Dating back to the 15th century, an impressive manor house – more of a fortified farm than a château – overlooks the Sauternes countryside from a hill forty kilometres south of the city of Bordeaux.

This building was famous as long ago as the Enlightenment. Its name: Château d'Yquem.

The wine, a miracle of nature, owes its exquisite quality not only to a unique *terroir* and the professionalism of the Yquem team in the vineyard and the cellar, but also to a microscopic fungus (*Botrytis cinerea*) found in the Sauternes region and especially at Yquem. This divine nectar with a fabulous golden colour is famous from Moscow to Washington, by way of Seoul, London, Hong Kong, Tokyo, etc.

In the autumn, morning mists give way to sunny afternoons. If accompanied by an easterly wind, conditions are just right to send pickers out to harvest the hundred hectares of vines, seeking only the finest Sémillon and Sauvignon Blanc grapes affected by "noble rot," which concentrates both sweetness and flavour.

The sweet, botyrtised gapes are carefully removed with small secateurs in order not to harm the remaining grapes that have not yet reached 20 degrees potential alcohol.

In an average year, pickers go over each vineyard plot six different times – as things have been here done since the 19th century...

The grapes are pressed as soon as they arrive at the cellar and the juice is immediately put into new oak barrels for fermentation.

The wine is then aged in these same barrels for the next thirty months, during which it is regularly topped up and racked.

Since 1999, the L.V.M.H (Moët Hennessy - Louis Vuitton) group have been majority shareholders of this estate rated a *Premier Cru Supérieur* in the 1855 classification, and Pierre Lurton is the manager.

Yquem's philosophy has been the same for the past five centuries: to cooperate with nature to produce an average of just one glass of this famous wine per vine.

If the quality is not worthy of the estate's reputation in a given year, it is not sold under the château name. Nine vintages were thus not marketed by Yquem in the 20th century.

Quality comes at this price!

Managing Director: Pierre Lurton
Technical Director: Francis Mayeur
Cellar Master: Sandrine Garbay - Vineyard Manager: Antoine Depierre

Château d'Yquem - 33210 Sauternes
GPS: latitude: 44.5445174 - Longitude: -0.3292862
Tel. +33 (0)5 57 98 07 07 - Fax +33 (0)5 57 98 07 08
info@yquem.fr - **www.chateau-yquem.fr**

Château
Mouton Rothschild

Premier Cru Classé

A first growth since 1973, Château Mouton Rothschild is one of the world's greatest wines.

Owned by Baroness Philippine de Rothschild, the only child of the legendary Baron Philippe, Château Mouton Rothschild has 84 hectares of vines in Pauillac, consisting of 84% Cabernet Sauvignon, 13% Merlot, and 3% Cabernet Franc. The *terroir* is outstanding, with well-drained soil and great sun exposure.

The greatest care and attention are lavished on Mouton Rothschild at every step of the way, from the vine to the bottle, combining both age-old methods and state-of-the-art techniques: hand picking, ageing in new oak barrels, etc.

In 1853, Baron Nathaniel de Rothschild, from the English branch of the famous banking family, acquired Château Brane-Mouton, which he renamed Mouton Rothschild.

In 1922, his great-grandson, Baron Philippe de Rothschild (1902-1988), decided to take over management of the estate. He oversaw winemaking there for some sixty-five years, leaving a strong mark on the estate and introducing many innovations.

He bottled the entire 1924 vintage at the château, a revolutionary practice at the time.

In 1926, he built the famous *grand chai* (100 metres long), one of the major attractions during a visit to Mouton.

1945, the year the Second World War ended, marked the beginning of a painting by a famous artist on the label of every vintage of Mouton.

Located next to the *grand chai* and inaugurated in 1962, a Museum of Wine in Art, displaying three millennia of works of art revolving around the theme of wines and vines, attracts thousands of visitors.

In 1991, Aile d'Argent, a white wine made from 4 hectares of vines (57% Sauvignon Blanc, 42% Sémillon, and 1% Muscadelle) was made for the first time.

In 1994, Mouton also began to produce a second wine for the first time: le Petit Mouton de Mouton Rothschild.

Since 1988, Baronne Philippine has followed in her father's footsteps not only by guaranteeing the quality of wine from this famous estate, but also by creating the *Art et l'Étiquette* ("Paintings for the Labels") exhibition devoted to artists whose works have illustrated labels of Mouton Rothschild.

Supervisory Board chaired by Baroness Philippine de Rothschild
Managing Director and Estates Winemaker: Philippe Dhalluin
Managing Director and Commercial Director Châteaux: Hervé Berland

Château Mouton Rothschild BP 117 - 33250 Pauillac
Tel. +33 (0)5 56 73 20 20 - Fax +33 (0)5 56 73 20 33
pjean@bphr.com - **www.bpdr.com**

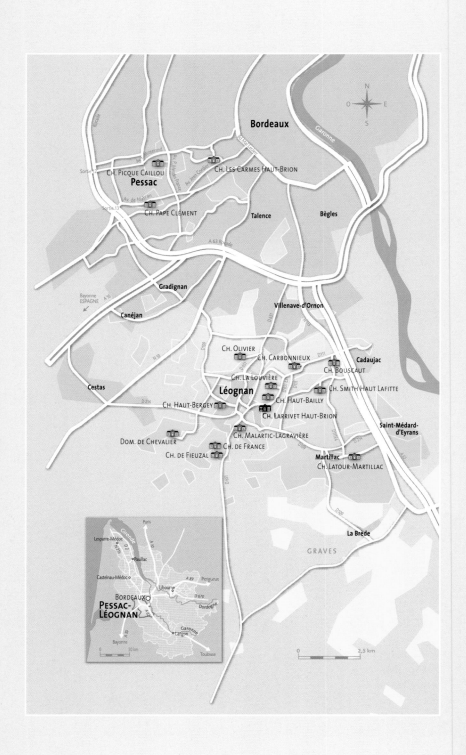

CRUS DE PESSAC-LÉOGNAN

Although Pessac-Léognan is the youngest appellation in Bordeaux (1987), it is paradoxically the cradle of winegrowing in the Gironde department. From the time they were first planted to the present day, i.e. for some 21 centuries, the vineyards of Pessac-Léognan have contributed to the prestige and development of Bordeaux wine.

The first diocesan records, dating back to 1382, mention wine production here, including the estate belonging to Bertrand de Goth (elected Pope under the name of Clément V in 1305) that was later given to the archbishops of Bordeaux. Since then, many well-known people have lived or stayed in the region. The Black Prince had a hunting lodge in Léognan, and Montesquieu, not only a famous philosopher and author of "The Spirit of Laws", but also a winegrower, was undoubtedly inspired by the wines of the Graves – which also guaranteed him financial independence.

The very notion of *cru* and production of the first great Bordeaux wines can be traced back to Château Haut-Brion in the late 17th century. This prestigious estate is now in the forefront of the Graves Great Growths, all of which are located in the Pessac-Léognan appellation.

These estates, members of the Union des Grands Crus de Bordeaux, bear witness to an outstanding history.

p 22	Château Bouscaut
p 23	Château Carbonnieux
p 24	Domaine de Chevalier
p 25	Château de Fieuzal
p 26	Château de France
p 27	Château Haut-Bailly
p 28	Château Haut-Bergey
p 29	Château La Louvière
p 30	Château Larrivet Haut-Brion
p 31	Château Latour-Martillac
p 32	Château Les Carmes Haut-Brion
p 33	Château Malartic-Lagravière
p 34	Château Olivier
p 35	Château Pape Clément
p 36	Château Picque Caillou
p 37	Château Smith Haut Lafitte

CHÂTEAU BOUSCAUT
CRU CLASSÉ DE GRAVES

PESSAC-LÉOGNAN — *Owners: Sophie Lurton-Cogombles and Laurent Cogombles*

Both the red and white wines of Château Bouscaut are classed growths. Vines were first planted there in the 17th century. Located close to the city of Bordeaux, the vineyard is in a single block on a beautiful gravelly rise facing due south. The attractive 18th century château is made of honey-coloured stone. It is surrounded by rose bushes and shaded by century-old oak trees.

Lucien Lurton, a passionate winegrower and owner of several great growths in the Médoc, purchased Bouscaut in 1979 from North American owners. In 1992, he handed over management to his daughter, Sophie Lurton, who has been assisted by her husband, Laurent Cogombles, since 1997.

They are committed to producing wine that is fully in keeping with Bouscaut's rank thanks to the greatest of care and attention in both the vineyard and cellars. For this reason, the cellars and vat rooms were entirely renovated in September 2010, and a new barrel cellar built. Decorated with barrel staves, this epitomises their philosophy of natural winemaking and respect for the environment.

Area under vine	42 hectares
Production	Red wine: 100,000 bottles - White wine: 20,000 bottles
Soil	Gravel and clay on a limestone platform
Grape varieties	Red wine: 55% Merlot, 40% Cabernet Sauvignon, 5% Malbec
	White wine: 50% Sémillon, 50% Sauvignon
Barrel ageing	Red wine: 18 months - White wine: 12 months - New barrels: 40%
Second wine	Les Chênes de Bouscaut

Consulting Oenologist: Édouard Massie - Cellar Master: Patrice Grandjean - Vineyard Manager: Manuel da Paixao

Château Bouscaut 1477, avenue de Toulouse - 33140 Cadaujac
GPS: Latitude: 44.7464892 - Longitude: -0.5477121
Tel. +33 (0)5 57 83 12 20 - Fax +33 (0)5 57 83 12 21
cb@chateau-bouscaut.com - **www.chateau-bouscaut.com**

CHÂTEAU CARBONNIEUX
CRU CLASSÉ DE GRAVES

Owner: the Perrin family

One of the most ancient winegrowing estates in Bordeaux, Château Carbonnieux has made wine without interruption since the 13th century. The château itself is an impressive building dating from the 14th century that had as many as twelve towers at one time.

The first owners – and accomplished winegrowers – were the Benedictine monks of Sainte-Croix abbey in Bordeaux, who made internationally-renowned red and white wines centuries ago. They also succeeded in introducing their pale-coloured, crystal-clear white wine to the palace of the Sultan of Constantinople by labelling it "Mineral Water of Carbonnieux" to get around the prohibition against alcoholic beverages...

For over fifty years, Carbonnieux has belonged to the Perrin family, winegrowers from father to son since the early 19th century.

Located on the highest point in the commune of Léognan, on soil that is perfectly drained by a stream called L'Eau Blanche, Carbonnieux's *terroir* is especially conducive to producing fine quality red and white wines.

Area under vine	92 hectares
Production	Red wine: 200,000 bottles - White wine: 180,000 bottles
Soil	Deep gravel on slopes with clay soil
Grape varieties	Red wine: 60% Cabernet Sauvignon, 30% Merlot, 7% Cabernet franc, 3% Petit Verdot and Carmenère - White wine: 65% Sauvignon, 35% Sémillon
Barrel ageing	Red wine: 15-18 months - White wine: 10 months - New barrels: Red wine: 35-40% - White wine: 30%
Second wine	La Croix de Carbonnieux - Château Tour Léognan

Co-Managers: Éric Perrin and Philibert Perrin

Château Carbonnieux 33850 Léognan
GPS: Latitude: 44.745183 - Longitude: -0.566477
Tel. +33 (0)5 57 96 56 20 - Fax +33 (0)5 57 96 59 19
info@chateau-carbonnieux.fr - **www.carbonnieux.com**

DOMAINE DE CHEVALIER

CRU CLASSÉ DE GRAVES

PESSAC-LÉOGNAN

Owner: the Bernard family

Located in Léognan, capital of the Graves, Domaine de Chevalier is a very ancient estate. It was designated as "Chibaley" (the Gascon word for *chevalier*) on the famous 1763 map produced by engineer Pierre de Belleyme.

The fact that Chevalier has never abandoned the name of "domaine" in favour of the more recent appellation "château" is proof of the estate's long history.

In 1983, Domaine de Chevalier was acquired by the Bernard family, leading French producers of industrial alcohol and major Bordeaux wine merchants.

Chevalier has been managed since then by Olivier Bernard, who perpetuates the spirit of harmony and quest for perfection that has long characterized this superb wine.

Domaine de Chevalier rouge is one of the leading wines in the Pessac-Léognan appellation and one of the finest classed growths of Bordeaux. Domaine de Chevalier blanc is recognized as one of the greatest dry white wines in the world.

Area under vine	45 hectares
Production	Red wine: 100,000 bottles - White wine: 15,000 bottles
Soil	Gravel, with clay-gravel subsoil
Grape varieties	Red wine: 65% Cabernet Sauvignon, 30% Merlot, 3% Petit Verdot, 2% Cabernet franc
	White wine: 70% Sauvignon, 30% Sémillon
Barrel ageing	Red wine and White wine: 18 months - New barrels: 35%
Second wine	L'Esprit de Chevalier

Managing Director: Olivier Bernard - Assistant Manager: Rémi Edange - Technical Director: Thomas Stonestreet

Domaine de Chevalier 102 chemin de Mignoy - 33850 Léognan
GPS: Latitude: 44.721969 - Longitude: -0.6195552
Tel. +33 (0)5 56 64 16 16 - Fax +33 (0)5 56 64 18 18
olivierbernard@domainedechevalier.com - **www.domainedechevalier.com**

CHÂTEAU DE FIEUZAL

CRU CLASSÉ DE GRAVES

PESSAC-LÉOGNAN   *Owners: Brenda and Lochlann Quinn*

GRAND CRU CLASSÉ DE GRAVES

CHATEAU
DE FIEUZAL
2008
Pessac-Léognan

MIS EN BOUTEILLE AU CHATEAU

Located in the heart of the Graves, the cradle of Bordeaux winemaking, Château de Fieuzal takes its name from the family to which it belonged until 1851. This Graves great growth, now owned by Brenda and Lochlann Quinn, is famous for its elegant white wines and opulent red wines.

Great care is taken to make the most of Château de Fieuzal's *terroir* in order to produce excellent wines as well as to protect the remarkable diverse natural environment. In keeping with demanding French standards of luxury craftsmanship, all work in the vineyard and cellar is done both meticulously and traditionally. The vines are looked after on an individual basis and closely followed in order to obtain fruit that reflects the excellence of this unique *terroir*.

Winemaking takes into account vintage characteristics and the profile of each different grape variety.

Fieuzal's demanding criteria are devoted to pleasing wine lovers everywhere...

Area under vine	75 hectares
Production	Red wine: 114,000 bottles - White wine: 18,000 bottles
Soil	Günz gravel from the Quaternary Period washed down from the Pyrenees, and clay-limestone sand
Grape varieties	Red wine: 50% Cabernet Sauvignon, 40% Merlot, 6% Cabernet franc, 4% Petit Verdot
	White wine: 70% Sauvignon, 30% Sémillon
Barrel ageing	Red wine: 12-16 months - White wine: 8-12 months
	New barrels: Red wine: 60% - White wine: 40%
Second wine	L'Abeille de Fieuzal

Technical Director: Stephen Carrier - Consultant: Hubert de Boüard

Château de Fieuzal 124, avenue de Mont de Marsan - 33850 Léognan
GPS: Latitude: 44,712464 - Longitude: -0,606608
Tel. +33 (0)5 56 64 77 86 - Fax +33 (0)5 56 64 18 88
infochato@fieuzal.com

CHÂTEAU DE FRANCE

PESSAC-LÉOGNAN

Owner: the Thomassin family

GRAND VIN DE GRAVES

MIS EN BOUTEILLE AU CHÂTEAU

CHÂTEAU DE FRANCE
PESSAC-LÉOGNAN

Château de France is cited in reference books as early as 1874. The vineyard is located on the highest slopes in the commune of Léognan, on the tallest of four gravelly terraces deposited by the Garonne River when it overflowed its banks in centuries past. The sunny microclimate and the unusual soil account for Château de France's unique *terroir*.

Bernard Thomassin acquired the estate in 1971 and has made numerous investments ever since. The vineyard was entirely replanted and the vat room and cellars were renovated and restructured. This was all done with one goal in mind: to make very great wine.

Arnaud Thomassin came to work at the estate in 1996 and now manages it in the same spirit as his father, Bernard.

Château de France is distributed in France and around the world. Its fine reputation is an acknowledgement of its quality as well as the major efforts made by the Thomassin family for over forty years.

Both the *grand vin*, Château de France, and the second wine, Château Coquillas, are produced in red and white versions.

Area under vine	40 hectares
Production	Red wine: 170,000 bottles - White wine: 18,000 bottles
Soil	Deep gravel
Grape varieties	Red wine: 60% Cabernet Sauvignon, 40% Merlot
	White wine: 80% Sauvignon, 20% Sémillon
Barrel ageing	Red wine: 12-14 months - White wine: 9 months
	New barrels: Red wine: 40% - White wine: 40%
Second wine	Château Coquillas

Chief Executive Officer: Bernard Thomassin - Managing Director: Arnaud Thomassin

Château de France 98, route de Mont de Marsan - 33850 Léognan
GPS: Latitude: 44.716093 - Longitude: -0.604999
Tel. +33 (0)5 56 64 75 39 - Fax +33 (0)5 56 64 72 13
contact@chateau-de-france.com - **www.chateau-de-france.com**

Château Haut-Bailly

CRU CLASSÉ DE GRAVES

Owner: Robert G. Wilmers

GRAND VIN DE BORDEAUX

CHÂTEAU HAUT-BAILLY

GRAND CRU CLASSÉ
PESSAC-LÉOGNAN

2005

MIS EN BOUTEILLE AU CHATEAU

For over four centuries, Château Haut-Bailly has overlooked a 30 hectare vineyard in a single block. The soil consists of sand and gravel from the Quaternary Period and the subsoil has a high proportion of fossils (shell marl).

Haut-Bailly's reputation as one of the great wines of Bordeaux dates from the 19th century, and the word "outstanding" most often associated with the château reflects its superb quality.

Robert G. Wilmers, owner since 1998, and the current manager, Véronique Sanders, have very demanding standards that entail using the best of traditional and modern methods, with full respect for the environment.

A quarter of the vines at Haut-Bailly are a hundred years old, and the estate has a unique terroir that accounts for wines of amazing regularity. These great wines have an inimitable style, finesse, and elegance, whatever the vintage.

Area under vine	30 hectares
Production	80,000 bottles
Soil	Sand and gravel
Grape varieties	64% Cabernet Sauvignon, 30% Merlot, 6% Cabernet franc
Barrel ageing	16 months - New barrels: 50-65%
Second wine	La Parde de Haut-Bailly

Chief Executive Officer: Véronique Sanders

Château Haut-Bailly 103, avenue de Cadaujac - 33850 Léognan
GPS: Latitude: 44.73587 - Longitude: -0.580623
Tel. +33 (0)5 56 64 75 11 - Fax +33 (0)5 56 64 53 60
mail@chateau-haut-bailly.com - **www.chateau-haut-bailly.com**

CHÂTEAU HAUT-BERGEY

Owner: Sylviane Garcin-Cathiard

2008

CHATEAU
HAUT-BERGEY

PESSAC-LÉOGNAN
GRAND VIN DE BORDEAUX

Château Haut-Bergey, with its bartizans topped by conical slate towers, is reminiscent of Sleeping Beauty's castle... an impression reinforced by the pink cellars. The estate dates back to the 15th century. Owner of Haut Bergey since 1991, Sylviane Garcin Cathiard was determined to lavish the same care and attention on her estate as the greatest châteaux in Bordeaux.

This charming property now applies rigorous standards and the necessary technical means to achieve the vineyard's full potential. Soil surveys were done on every plot, enabling each one to receive tailor-made treatment using natural, traditional methods. The grapes are meticulously handpicked and optical sorting retains only perfectly ripe, healthy fruit. Small stainless steel vats are propitious to precision winemaking adapted to grapes from each plot. The ageing cellar houses barrels that are either new or used for one previous vintage. The proportion varies from year to year.

Château Haut-Bergey produces well-structured, elegant red wines of outstanding character, as well as fine, delicate white wines.

28

Area under vine	40 hectares
Production	120,000 bottles
Soil	Gravel with a clay-siliceous subsoil
Grape varieties	Red wine: 60% Cabernet Sauvignon, 40% Merlot
	White wine: 80% Sauvignon, 20% Sémillon
Barrel ageing	Red wine: 15-18 months - White wine: 12 months
	New barrels: Red wine: 50% - White wine: 30%
Second wine	Étoile de Bergey

Château Haut-Bergey 69, cours Gambetta - B.P. n°2 - 33850 Léognan
GPS: Latitude: 44.726659 - Longitude: -0.610342
Tel. +33 (0)5 56 64 05 22 - Fax +33 (0)5 56 64 06 98
info@vignoblesgarcin.com - **www.vignoblesgarcin.com**

CHÂTEAU LA LOUVIÈRE

Owner: André Lurton

Located fourteen kilometres south of the city of Bordeaux, in the heart of the Pessac-Léognan appellation, Château La Louvière's history goes back seven centuries. Records show that wine was already made here in 1310.

However, the vineyard as we know it today dates from the early 16th century. In 1620, the Carthusian monks who inherited the estate contributed their experience and expertise to producing wines that acquired an international reputation. Jean-Baptiste Mareilhac, a rich *négociant*, purchased the property during the French Revolution and built the present-day château in a pure neoclassical style. It is now a listed historic monument. André Lurton became the owner of La Louvière in 1965 and has worked tirelessly to restore the estate's former splendour.

Terroir-based vineyard management, environmentally-friendly viticultural practices, and traditional winemaking methods coupled with the judicious use of modern techniques enable La Louvière to produce dry white and red wines of great character.

Area under vine	61 hectares
Production	Red wine: 150,000 bottles - White wine: 60,000 bottles
Soil	Gravel and silica with limestone at the bottom of the slope
Grape varieties	Red wine: 64% Cabernet Sauvignon, 30% Merlot, 3% Cabernet franc, 3% Petit Verdot,
	White wine: 85% Sauvignon, 15% Sémillon
Barrel ageing	Red wine: 12-18 months - White wine: 9-10 months
	New barrels: Red wine: 50% - White wine: 30%
Second wine	L de La Louvière

Château La Louvière 149, avenue de Cadaujac - 33850 Léognan
GPS: Latitude: 44.7360925 - Longitude: -0.5778971
Tel. +33 (0)5 56 64 75 87 - Fax +33 (0)5 56 64 71 76
lalouviere@andrelurton.com - **www.andrelurton.com**

PESSAC-LÉOGNAN

Owner: Philippe Gervoson

CHATEAU
LARRIVET HAUT-BRION

PESSAC-LÉOGNAN
•••
2008

Château Larrivet Haut-Brion was cited as one of the leading wines in the commune of Léognan as early as 1840. The Gervoson family acquired the estate in 1987 and have worked hard ever since to restore this wine's illustrious reputation.

Larrivet Haut-Brion is an immensely charming 100-hectare property. The superb 19th century château also has thirteen hectares of attractive grounds. The vines grow on high and medium-size rises of Garonne gravel. The estate also features woods and meadows.

An ambitious modernisation programme in the cellar (pneumatic winepress using inert gas, optical sorting of grapes, etc.) and vineyard (detailed soil survey for improved plot-by-plot management) has resulted in wines reputed for their elegance and character.

Representing the upcoming generation of her family, Émilie Gervoson tirelessly promotes Château Larrivet Haut-Brion around the world.

30

Area under vine	72.5 hectares
Production	Red wine: 180,000 bottles - White wine: 25,000 bottles
Soil	Gravel
Grape varieties	Red wine: 45% Cabernet Sauvignon, 50% Merlot, 5% Cabernet franc
	White wine: 80% Sauvignon, 20% Sémillon
Barrel ageing	Red wine: 14-18 months - White wine: 11 months
	New barrels: Red wine: 40% - White wine: 100%
Second wine	Les Demoiselles de Larrivet Haut-Brion - Les Hauts de Larrivet Haut-Brion

Managing Director: Bruno Lemoine - Communication/PR: Émilie Gervoson

Château Larrivet Haut-Brion 84, avenue de Cadaujac - 33850 Léognan
GPS: Latitude: 44,731229 - Longitude: -0,585210
Tel. +33 (0)5 56 64 75 51 - Fax +33 (0)5 56 64 53 47
contact@larrivethautbrion.fr - **www.larrivethautbrion.fr**

CHÂTEAU LATOUR-MARTILLAC

CRU CLASSÉ DE GRAVES

PESSAC-LÉOGNAN

Owner: G.F.A. Château Latour-Martillac

GRAND CRU CLASSÉ DE GRAVES
PESSAC-LÉOGNAN

Designated a Graves classed growth in 1953, Château Latour-Martillac owes its name to the tower in the courtyard, the vestige of a fortress built in the 12th century by the ancestors of the famous winegrower and philosopher, Montesquieu.

Located on an outstanding rise of Pyrenean gravel, this estate caught the eye of Édouard Kressmann, a Bordeaux *négociant*, as early as 1871. He was particularly impressed with the quality of the white wines. His elder son, Alfred, finally bought the estate in 1930. He expanded the red wine vineyard and, in 1934, designed with his son, Jean, the label with gold and sand-coloured diagonal stripes that is still used today.

Today, Jean Kressmann's sons, Tristan and Loïc, assisted by the best consulting oenologists in Bordeaux, perpetuate the family tradition in order to extract the quintessence of the superb Graves *terroir*.

Thanks to their elegant structure and balance, the red and white wines of Latour-Martillac (both of which are classed) are widely recognized as among the most reliable in Pessac-Léognan.

Area under vine	45 hectares
Production	Red wine: 150,000 - White wine: 36,000
Soil	Pyrenean gravel
Grape varieties	Red wine: 60% Cabernet Sauvignon, 35% Merlot, 5% Petit Verdot
	White wine: 40% Sauvignon, 55% Sémillon, 5% Muscadelle
Barrel ageing	Red wine: 18 months - White wine: 12-15 months - New barrels: 30%
Second wine	Lagrave-Martillac

Managing Director: Tristan Kressmann - Technical Director: Loïc Kressmann

Château Latour-Martillac 8, chemin de la Tour - 33650 Martillac
GPS: Latitude: 44,7091002 - Longitude: -0,5431261
Tel. +33 (0)5 57 97 71 11 - Fax +33 (0)5 57 97 71 17
latourmartillac@latourmartillac.com - **www.latourmartillac.com**

CHÂTEAU LES CARMES HAUT-BRION

Owner: Patrimoniale du Groupe PICHET

One of the jewels of the Bordeaux wine country, Château Les Carmes Haut-Brion has nearly five hectares of vines in the Pessac-Léognan appellation. It is located just southwest of the city of Bordeaux, like its neighbour, Château Haut-Brion.

From 1584 to 1789, Les Carmes Haut Brion belonged to the Carmelite religious order, which accounts for the origin of its name. After the French Revolution, the property was acquired by Bordeaux *négociants*, the Chantecaille family, and then sold in late 2010 to Patrimoniale du Groupe Pichet, who were seeking to diversify. They have already planned major investments: installing new vats, renovating the cellar, and building an extension for holding receptions and special events.

The château was built in the early 19th century and the three hectares of beautiful grounds designed by the landscape artist Fischer date from the same period. Château Les Carmes Haut Brion is a haven of peace and tranquillity in the historic heart of the Bordeaux wine country. It has an astonishingly warm microclimate that protects the vines from spring frosts and is conducive to early ripening.

32

Area under vine	4.7 hectares
Production	25,000 bottles
Soil	Large Günz gravel, sand, and clay on a limestone platform
Grape varieties	55% Merlot, 30% Cabernet franc, 15% Cabernet Sauvignon
Barrel ageing	18 months - New barrels: 50%
Second wine	Le Clos des Carmes

Director: Delphine Stein - Estate Manager: Aurélie Carreau - Manager: Patrice Pichet
Consulting oenologist: Stéphane Derenoncourt

SCEA Château les Carmes Haut-Brion 197 avenue Jean Cordier - 33600 Pessac
GPS: Latitude 44.8202121 - Longitude: -0.6107926 - Entrance: 20 rue des Carmes 33000 Bordeaux
Tel. + 33 (0)5 56 93 23 40 - Fax + 33 (0)5 56 93 10 71
chateau@les-carmes-haut-brion.com - **www.les-carmes-haut-brion.com**

Château Malartic-Lagravière
CRU CLASSÉ DE GRAVES

PESSAC-LÉOGNAN

Owner: Alfred-Alexandre Bonnie

GRAND CRU CLASSÉ DE GRAVES
PESSAC-LÉOGNAN

Domaine de Lagravière has been famous since time immemorial for its excellent *terroir* and famous "hillock" of gravel. In honour of Count Hippolyte de Malartic, an admiral of the Kings of France and owner of the estate in the 18th century, the château was renamed Malartic-Lagravière.

Bought by Michèle and Alfred-Alexandre Bonnie in late 1996, the estate has been completely renovated. It features: a first-class *terroir* and vineyard tended according to the principles of sustainable agriculture, innovative and efficient facilities making use of gravity flow with which to enhance traditional winemaking, and a committed, energetic team.

Château Malartic-Lagravière is one of only six estates in Bordeaux classified for both its white and red wines. These are well-known all over the world over for their complexity, elegance, intensity, and balance.

Area under vine	53 hectares
Production	210,000 bottles
Soil	Gravel with a clay and shell limestone subsoil
Grape varieties	Red wine: 45% Cabernet Sauvignon, 45% Merlot, 8% Cabernet franc, 2% Petit Verdot
	White wine: 80% Sauvignon, 20% Sémillon
Barrel ageing	Red wine: 15-22 months - White wine: 10-15 months - New barrels: 50-70%
Second wine	La Réserve de Malartic

Château Malartic-Lagravière 43, avenue de Mont de Marsan - 33850 Léognan
GPS: Latitude: 44.7245035 - Longitude: -0,6002992
Tel. +33 (0)5 56 64 75 08 - Fax +33 (0)5 56 64 99 66
malartic-lagraviere@malartic-lagraviere.com - **www.malartic-lagraviere.com**

CHÂTEAU OLIVIER
CRU CLASSÉ DE GRAVES

PESSAC-LÉOGNAN

Owner: Jean-Jacques de Bethmann

2007

Château Olivier
Grand Cru Classé
PESSAC-LÉOGNAN

Château Olivier emerges in a vast clearing in the middle of a large estate consisting of forest, meadows, and vines. The château's distinctive architecture, ponds, attractive outbuildings, and beautiful natural setting just eleven kilometres from the city of Bordeaux make this an outstanding property.

Olivier is a very ancient seigneury, whose history goes back to the early Middle Ages, and it is said that the Black Prince (the eldest son of King Edward III of England) liked to hunt here. The estate has belonged to the de Bethmann family since the 19th century.

They have invested heavily in renovating the estate in recent years. A detailed soil survey has revealed new potential for the *terroir* and led to the same vineyard configuration as in the 18th century.

Six different grape varieties are grown on gravelly soil atop clay-limestone bedrock. These are all picked by hand into small crates and sorted first in the vineyard and again in the cellar.

Château Olivier was classified in 1953 for both its red and white wines.

34

Area under vine	58 hectares
Production	Red wine: 100,000 bottles - White wine: 25,000 bottles
Soil	Deep, compact gravel on marl, clay, and limestone from the Miocene epoch
Grape varieties	Red wine: 50% Cabernet Sauvignon, 48% Merlot, 2% Petit Verdot
	White wine: 70% Sauvignon, 28% Sémillon, 2% Muscadelle
Barrel ageing	12 months - New barrels: 35%
Second wine	Le Dauphin d'Olivier - La Seigneurerie d'Olivier

Managing Director: Laurent Lebrun - Cellar Master: Damien Bielle - Vineyard Manager: Miguel Fisac

Château Olivier 175 avenue de Bordeaux - 33850 Léognan
GPS: Latitude: 44.7497523 - Longitude: -0.588383
Tel. +33 (0)5 56 64 73 31 - Fax +33 (0)5 56 64 54 23
mail@chateau-olivier.com - **www.chateau-olivier.com**

CHÂTEAU PAPE CLÉMENT

CRU CLASSÉ DE GRAVES

PESSAC-LÉOGNAN   *Owner: Bernard Magrez*

Few great wines can boast seven centuries of history and trace their origins back to a pope. Elected supreme pontiff during the reign of King Philip the Handsome in 1305, Clement V gave his name to Château Pape Clément.

The present owner does his utmost to perpetuate the ancient tradition of quality. Among other innovations, this was the first estate in Bordeaux to destem the entire crop by hand. The grapes are transported by gravity flow into small oak fermentation vats adapted to the yield of each plot. The entire winemaking process is conducted with minute attention to detail. Combining traditional and state-of-the-art techniques, Pape Clément is made according to the highest standards.

Everything is done in the vineyard to let the *terroir* express itself fully. As part of an environmentally-friendly approach, chemical weed killers have been abandoned in favour of ploughing.

Area under vine	46 hectares
Production	120,000 bottles (Red wine and White wine)
Soil	Pyrenean gravel from the late Pliocene and early Quaternary periods
Grape varieties	Red wine: 50% Cabernet Sauvignon, 45% Merlot, 3% Petit Verdot, 2% Cabernet franc
	White wine: 40% Sauvignon, 35% Sémillon, 16% Sauvignon gris, 9% Muscadelle
Barrel ageing	Red wine: 18-22 months - White wine: 15 months
Second wine	Le Clémentin de Pape Clément

Vineyard Manager: Patrice Hateau

Château Pape Clément 216 avenue du Docteur Nancel Pénard - 33600 Pessac
GPS: Latitude: 44,8067903 - Longitude:-0,6460475
Tel. + 33 (0)5 57 26 38 38 - Fax + 33 (0)5 57 26 38 39
contact@pape-clement.com - **www.pape-clement.com**

CHÂTEAU PICQUE CAILLOU

PESSAC-LÉOGNAN　　　　　　　　　*Owners: Isabelle and Paulin Calvet*

Built in 1755, Château Picque Caillou is located on the outskirts of the city of Bordeaux, in the historic Pessac-Léognan appellation, the cradle of regional winegrowing.

A close neighbour of the prestigious châteaux Haut-Brion and Pape Clément, Picque Caillou has stony soil deposited by the Garonne River over centuries (as reflected by its name, since *caillou* means "pebble" in French). Consisting of fine gravel, the well-drained subsoil is responsible for wines of great finesse, elegance, and ageing potential.

In 2007, Paulin Calvet took over management and breathed new life into the estate, which quickly gained recognition from wine professionals, who acknowledged its fine, reliable quality. That same year, consulting oenologists Professor Denis Dubourdieu and Madame Valérie Lavigne began providing technical assistance to the new team. Their combined efforts have resulted in first-class wines of remarkable balance and delicacy that are highly representative of the famous Pessac-Léognan appellation.

36

Area under vine	21 hectares
Production	Red wine: 70,000 bottles - White wine: 5,000 bottles
Soil	Gravel
Grape varieties	Red wine: 50% Merlot, 50% Cabernet Sauvignon
	White wine: 60% Sauvignon, 40% Sémillon
Barrel ageing	Red wine: 12 months - White wine: 8 months - New barrels: Red wine: 35% - White wine: 20%
Second wine	La Réserve de Picque Caillou

Vineyard Manager: Jean-Pierre Maillard - Cellar Master: Amandine Capella

Château Picque Caillou 93 avenue Pierre Mendès France - 33700 Mérignac
GPS: Latitude: 44.8296013 - Longitude: -0.6395475
Tel. +33 (0)5 56 47 37 98 - Fax +33 (0)5 56 97 99 37
chateaupicquecaillou@wanadoo.fr

CHÂTEAU SMITH HAUT LAFITTE

CRU CLASSÉ DE GRAVES

Owner: Florence and Daniel Cathiard

This great growth owes its reputation as "the quintessential Graves" to its superb Günz gravel *terroir* in a single block. The estate's history dates back to the Crusades. The Scottish navigator Georges Smith acquired the château in the 18th century and Monsieur Duffour-Dubergier, a Mayor of Bordeaux from a famous family of *négociants*, was a subsequent owner.

Since its purchase by Florence and Daniel Cathiard in 1990, Smith Haut Lafitte has become one of the leading lights of Bordeaux thanks to its elegant, powerful red and white wines.

In twenty years, the owners have not only brought the wine of Smith Haut Lafitte up to the very highest level, but also restored the château's 16th century tower, completely renovated two underground cellars, built their own cooperage, and introduced such organic methods as horse-drawn ploughing, home-made compost, the use of plant extracts, etc. The château is located next to the Sources de Caudalie and its famous spa, open seven days a week all year round.

Area under vine	67 hectares
Production	Red wine: 120,000 bottles - White wine: 30,000 bottles
Soil	Günz gravel
Grape varieties	Red wine: 59% Cabernet Sauvignon, 30% Merlot, 10% Cabernet franc, 1% Petit Verdot
	White wine: 90% Sauvignon Blanc, 5% Sauvignon Gris, 5% Sémillon
Barrel ageing	Red wine: 18 months - White wine: 12 months
	New barrels: Red wine: 60% - White wine: 50%
Second wine	Les Hauts de Smith

Oenologist and Technical Director: Fabien Teitgen

Château Smith Haut Lafitte 33650 Martillac
GPS: Latitude: 44.733183 - Longitude: -0.559638
Tel. +33 (0)5 57 83 11 22 - Fax +33 (0)5 57 83 11 21
f.cathiard@smith-haut-lafitte.com - **www.smith-haut-lafitte.com**

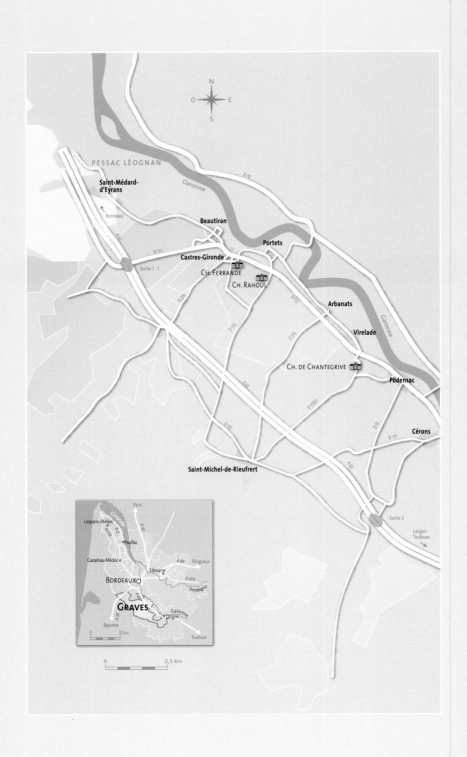

CRUS DE GRAVES

The Graves region, stretching south from the city of Bordeaux to Langon and beyond, produces a wide range of excellent wines. The Graves were famous for their dry and semi-sweet white wines, as well as their red wines, as early as the 13th and 14th centuries. These were very popular with the English and Dutch, who spread their reputation worldwide.

The appellation is the only one in the world whose name identifies the nature of its *terroir*: *graves* = gravel. The soil is ideal for winegrowing, and virtually unsuited to any other crop.

p 40 | Château de Chantegrive
p 41 | Château Ferrande
p 42 | Château Rahoul

CHÂTEAU DE CHANTEGRIVE

GRAVES   *Owner: the Lévêque family*

Françoise and Henri Lévêque acquired the first plots of Château de Chantegrive in the commune of Podensac, south of Bordeaux, in 1966.

Forty-five years later, Chantegrive now has 96 hectares of vines and has become one of the most important and prestigious estates in the Graves appellation. Combining modern techniques with traditional viticultural and winemaking methods, Château de Chantegrive has state-of-the-art equipment to produce wine that regularly receives medals at international competitions.

Château de Chantegrive has gone from strength to strength, and the new generation of the Lévêque family is closely involved in managing the estate. Since 2006, they are assisted by Hubert de Boüard de Laforest, owner of Château Angélus in Saint-Émilion.

The wine is marketed via brokers to the Bordeaux *négociants*, who export 40% of total production.

Area under vine	96 hectares
Production	Red wine: 200,000 bottles - White wine: 65,000 bottles
Soil	coarse gravel with layers of fine or medium-grain sand (according to the depth) on a clay-limestone subsoil
Grape varieties	Red wine: 50% Merlot, 50% Cabernet Sauvignon - White wine: 50% Sémillon, 50% Sauvignon
Barrel ageing	Red wine: 12 months - White wine: 9 months - New barrels: Red wine: 50% - White wine: 50%
Second wine	Benjamin de Chantegrive

President: Françoise Lévêque - Managing Director: Hélène Lévêque - Director: François Lévêque

Château de Chantegrive 44, cours Georges Clémenceau - 33720 Podensac
GPS: Latitude: 44.6529498 - Longitude: -0.3593362
Tel. +33 (0)5 56 27 17 38 - Fax. +33 (0)5 56 27 29 42
courrier@chateau-chantegrive.com - **www.chantegrive.com**

CHÂTEAU FERRANDE

| GRAVES | *Owner: Châteaux et Domaines Castel* |

Château Ferrande is located in the commune de Castres-Gironde, in the heart of the Graves. The beautiful manor house, restored in the late 19th century, overlooks a vineyard that is much older.

Ferrande is located near the town of Castres on the Bordeaux-Toulouse road. The known presence of Romans in the commune as early as the 1st century B.C. makes it more than likely that wine was produced here at a very early date. A manor house has existed on the estate since the late 15th century. According to land records, the vineyard has expanded significantly over the centuries.

Rich owners and major *négociants* succeeded one another at Ferrande. In the 1960s, Admiral Delnaud, a lover of both fine wine and horse racing, purchased the château.

The Castel family acquired Ferrande in 1992. They have made many investments in the vineyard and cellars since then, and Château Ferrande's former lustre is being increasingly restored with each passing year.

Area under vine	98 hectares
Production	450,000 bottles
Soil	Gravel
Grape varieties	Red wine: 50% Merlot, 50% Cabernet
	White wine: 60% Sauvignon, 40% Sémillon
Barrel ageing	12 months - New barrels: 50%

Public Relations for Châteaux et Domaines Castel: Véréna Raoux

Château Ferrande Route du bois de Savi - 33640 Castres
GPS: Latitude: 43.6052913 - Longitude: 2.241007
Tel. +33 (0)5 56 95 54 00
contact@chateaux-castel.com - **www.chateau-ferrande.com**

Château Rahoul

Owner: Alain Thiénot

In 1646, Chevalier Guillaume Rahoul built a lovely manor house which he named after himself. The vineyards were expanded in the late 18th century by Pierre Balguerie, at which time Rahoul grew to its present boundaries.

Thanks to English, Australian, and Danish owners, Château Rahoul attained international recognition starting in the 1970s.

Alain Thiénot, from Champagne, who already possessed vineyards in Bordeaux, bought Rahoul in 1986 and undertook an ambitious modernisation programme. 2007 was a benchmark year in his uncompromising approach to quality during which sizeable investments were made in renovating the vineyard and equipping the cellars, relying of state-of-the-art techniques.

Unusual in that it is made predominantly from Sémillon, the white wine faithfully reflects the finesse and elegance of Rahoul's *terroir*. The attractive red wine features a very refined style, silky tannin, and a full, rich flavour.

42

Area under vine	42 hectares
Production	Red wine: 100,000 bottles - White wine: 8,000 bottles
Soil	Sandy-gravel and clay-gravel
Grape varieties	Red wine: 79% Merlot, 19% Cabernet Sauvignon, 2% Petit Verdot
	White wine: 76% Sémillon, 24% Sauvignon
Barrel ageing	Red wine: 12-15 months - White wine: 8-10 months - New barrels: 20-30%
Second wine	L'Orangerie de Rahoul

Manager: Guillaume Pouthier

Château Rahoul 4 route du Courneau - 33640 Portets
GPS: Latitude: 44.687950 - Longitude: -0.425884
Tel. +33 (0)5 56 35 53 00 - Fax +33 (0)5 56 35 53 29
contact@cvbg.com - **www.chateau-rahoul.com**

CRUS DE SAINT-ÉMILION

Edward I, King of England, delimited the Jurisdiction of Saint-Émilion, consisting of nine parishes, in 1289. Since then, only wines produced in one of these communes is entitled to the Saint-Émilion appellation. Saint-Émilion's superb reputation is due primarily to wines from the *côtes*, plateau, and *graves* areas.

The picturesque medieval village of Saint-Émilion is an architectural jewel, built in a half circle on hills opposite the Dordogne. The steep, narrow streets, Romanesque and Gothic churches, monasteries, and cloisters make this one of the loveliest villages in France. Listed as a World Heritage Site by UNESCO, Saint-Émilion is an outstanding location which the members of the Union des Grands Crus will be delighted to help you discover.

p 46	Château Angélus
p 47	Château Balestard La Tonnelle
p 48	Château Beau-Séjour Bécot
p 49	Château Berliquet
p 50	Château Canon
p 51	Château Canon La Gaffelière
p 52	Château Cap de Mourlin
p 53	Château Dassault
p 54	Château-Figeac
p 55	Clos Fourtet
p 56	Château Franc Mayne
p 57	Château Grand Mayne
p 58	Château La Couspaude
p 59	Château La Dominique
p 60	Château La Gaffelière
p 61	Château La Tour Figeac
p 62	Château Larcis Ducasse
p 63	Château Larmande
p 64	Château Pavie
p 65	Château Pavie-Macquin
p 66	Château Troplong Mondot
p 67	Château Trottevieille

CHÂTEAU ANGÉLUS
PREMIER GRAND CRU CLASSÉ

SAINT-ÉMILION GRAND CRU
Owner: the de Boüard de Laforest family

Located less than a kilometre from the steeple of the church in Saint-Émilion, on the famous *pied de côte* (or "foot of the slope") with south-facing sun exposure, Château Angélus reflects the winemaking passion of eight generations of the de Boüard de Laforest family.

The property takes its name from a plot of very old vines from which vineyard workers could hear the Angelus ringing simultaneously in three different churches. This three-hectare plot was acquired in the early 20th century by Maurice de Boüard de Laforest. The original small vineyard holding was gradually expanded by his sons, Jacques and Christian, who bought several contiguous plots to form a superb estate in the 1960s that is currently managed by Hubert de Boüard de Laforest and his cousin, Jean-Bernard Grenié.

Promoted to Premier Grand Cru Classé status, and recognized around the world as one of the jewels of Saint-Émilion, Château Angélus' success is due to the dedication of a family to their *terroir*.

46

Area under vine	23.4 hectares
Production	80-90,000 bottles
Soil	Clay-limestone on the upper part and clay-sand-limestone on the hillside
Grape varieties	50% Merlot, 47% Cabernet franc, 3% Cabernet Sauvignon
Barrel ageing	18-24 months - New barrels: 100%
Second wine	Le Carillon de l'Angélus

Managers: Hubert de Boüard de Laforest - Jean-Bernard Grenié

Château Angélus Mazerat - 33330 Saint-Émilion
GPS: Latitude: 44.8928817 - Longitude: -0,1704865
Tel. +33 (0)5 57 24 71 39 - Fax +33 (0)5 57 24 68 56
chateau-angelus@chateau-angelus.com - **www.chateau-angelus.com**

Château Balestard La Tonnelle

Grand Cru Classé

Saint-Émilion Grand Cru

Owner: Jacques Capdemourlin

The name of this estate has two different origins. "Balestard" was a former canon of the Chapter of Saint-Émilion, and "La Tonnelle" refers to the 15th-century stone watchtower that still stands in the heart of the vineyard.

The château's reputation dates back to François Villon who cited it in a poem that is reproduced on the label of the *grand vin*.

Located a stone's throw from the medieval town of Saint-Émilion, atop a slope on a clay-limestone plateau, the charming vineyard has a superb *terroir*. The present owner, Jacques Capdemourlin, manages the estate with the greatest care and attention.

The wine is fermented the traditional way and then aged in oak barrels, half of which are new every year. Combining respect for the *terroir*, tradition, and the best modern techniques, Balestard La Tonnelle produces full-bodied wine of extreme elegance, one of the finest *grands crus classés* in Saint-Émilion.

Area under vine	10.6 hectares
Production	55,000 bottles
Soil	clay-limestone plateau
Grape varieties	70% Merlot, 25% Cabernet franc, 5% Cabernet Sauvignon
Barrel ageing	15-18 months - New barrels: 50%
Second wine	Chanoine de Balestard

Château Balestard La Tonnelle D 243 - 33330 Saint-Émilion
GPS: Latitude: 44.89953 - Longitude: -0.14621
Tel. +33 (0)5 57 74 62 06 - Fax +33 (0)5 57 74 59 34
info@vignoblescapdemourlin.com - **www.vignoblescapdemourlin.com**

CHÂTEAU BEAU-SÉJOUR BÉCOT
PREMIER GRAND CRU CLASSÉ

SAINT-ÉMILION GRAND CRU

Located immediately west of the magical town of Saint-Émilion on the Saint-Martin de Mazerat limestone plateau, Beau-Séjour Bécot is in the heart of the appellation. The estate has been devoted to winemaking since the Gallo-Roman period. In 1787, General Jacques de Carles, wishing to commemorate for all time the pleasure that he enjoyed staying there, named the estate "Beau-Séjour" (meaning "lovely stay").

In 1969, Michel Bécot acquired the château and brought the area under vine up to 18.50 hectares thanks to the purchase of neighbouring vineyard plots with the same *terroir*. He also turned seven hectares of former underground limestone quarries into a storage cellar where tens of thousands of bottles age under ideal conditions. His work in improving and embellishing the estate went on until his retirement in 1985.

His two sons, Gérard and Dominique, have followed in their father's footsteps while introducing numerous technical innovations to both the cellars and the vineyard. Only the ripest, healthiest grapes are now harvested, and then sorted one by one. Gérard's daughter, Juliette, started working at the château in 2001 in order to market wines from the family estate.

48

Area under vine	16.50 hectares
Production	65,000 bottles
Soil	clay and asteriated limestone
Grape varieties	70% Merlot, 24% Cabernet franc, 6% Cabernet Sauvignon
Barrel ageing	16-18 months - New barrels: 80%
Second wine	Tournelle de Beau-Séjour Bécot

Co-manager (cellar): Gérard Bécot - Co-manager (vineyard): Dominique Bécot - Sales: Juliette Bécot

Château Beau-Séjour Bécot 33330 Saint-Émilion
GPS: Latitude: 44.8960129 - Longitude: -0.1554754
Tel. +33 (0)5 57 74 46 87 - Fax +33 (0)5 57 24 66 88
contact@beausejour-becot.com - **www.beausejour-becot.com**

CHÂTEAU BERLIQUET
GRAND CRU CLASSÉ

SAINT-ÉMILION GRAND CRU

Owner: Viscount Patrick de Lesquen

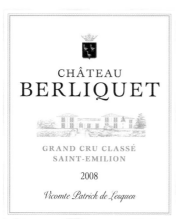

Berliquet is one of the oldest vineyards in Saint-Émilion and appears on Belleyme's map dating back to 1768. In his 1828 classification, Paguierre lists Berliquet as one of the appellation's five first growths. Belonging to the de Sèze, and then the Pérès families, it was acquired in 1918 by Count de Carles, the current owner's grandfather. Château Berliquet was accorded its rightful place among the greatest wines of Saint-Émilion in the 1986 classification.

The estate is located on the Magdelaine plateau, a few hundred metres from the town of Saint-Émilion. The vines have south and southwest-facing sun exposure and border on several *Premiers Grands Crus Classés*. The wine is aged in magnificent underground cellars hewn out of solid rock.

The arrival of Nicolas Thienpont and Stéphane Derenoncourt in July 2008 made it possible to define the needs of each vineyard plot and achieve optimum ripeness to reflect the full elegance of the *terroir*.

Area under vine	9 hectares
Production	30,000 bottles
Soil	Limestone and clay-limestone
Grape varieties	70% Merlot, 25% Cabernet franc, 5% Cabernet Sauvignon
Barrel ageing	12-16 months - New barrels: 50%
Second wine	Les Ailes de Berliquet

Manager: Nicolas Thienpont - Consultant: Stéphane Derenoncourt - Co-Manager: Jérôme de Lesquen

Château Berliquet 33330 Saint-Émilion
GPS: Latitude: 44.8894515 - Longitude: -0.1650495
Tel. +33 (0)5 57 24 70 48 - Fax +33 (0)5 57 24 70 24
chateau.berliquet@wanadoo.fr

CHÂTEAU CANON
PREMIER GRAND CRU CLASSÉ

SAINT-ÉMILION GRAND CRU

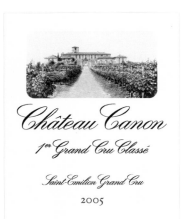

Jacques Kanon acquired this estate in 1760 thanks to the substantial profits he made as a privateer capturing English ships for King Louis XV. Improvements made to the property over the years revealed its winegrowing potential and enhanced its reputation.

In 1996, the House of Chanel purchased Canon and undertook an ambitious renovation in keeping with the château's prestigious classification. Over half the vines were replanted, a new sorting table was introduced in 2002, fermentation vats were replaced in 2005, an extension was built to the vat room in 2009, etc.

Château Canon's silky, velvety texture is due to the magical relationship between the soil and ideally-adapted grape varieties. Both Merlot and Cabernet Franc benefit from *terroir* that enables them to fully express their finest qualities. The subtle combination of asteriated limestone and a thin layer of clay produces wines that are both fresh and elegant.

Classified a *premier grand cru classé*, Château Canon is widely recognized as a distinguished, superlative wine often requiring patience to reach its peak.

50

Area under vine	22 hectares
Production	55-65,000 bottles
Soil	Clay-limestone plateau
Grape varieties	70% Merlot, 30% Cabernet franc
Barrel ageing	18 months - New barrels: 50-70%
Second wine	Clos Canon

Manager: John Kolasa

Château Canon BP 22 - 33330 Saint-Émilion
GPS: Latitude: 44.893701 - Longitude: -0.162392
Tel. +33 (0)5 57 55 23 45 - Fax +33 (0)5 57 24 68 00
contact@chateau-canon.com - **www.chateau-canon.com**

CHÂTEAU CANON LA GAFFELIÈRE

SAINT-ÉMILION GRAND CRU

Owners: Counts von Neipperg

Located on the famous slope (and the foot of the slope) south of the medieval village of Saint-Émilion, Château Canon La Gaffelière has belonged to the Counts von Neipperg since 1971. The *terroir* consists of clay-limestone and clay-sand soil that is particularly efficient at capturing and retaining heat. The choice of grape varieties is rather atypical for the appellation in light of the soil: almost a perfect 50/50 divide between Merlot and Cabernet.

Thanks to the intrinsic balance between the natural parameters, enhanced by a deep respect for the environment, Château Canon La Gaffelière produces elegant wines year in and year out. Remarkably well-structured and complex, Canon La Gaffelière is pure and unfailingly elegant, reflecting the uncompromising way in which it is made.

Representing some eight centuries of family winegrowing tradition, Count Stephan von Neipperg has succeeded in placing Château Canon La Gaffelière among the top *Grands Crus Classés* of Saint-Émilion thanks to a winegrowing philosophy that gives priority not only to quality, but also respect for the environment.

Area under vine	19.5 hectares
Production	65,000 bottles
Soil	clay-limestone and clay-sand soil at the foot of the slope
Grape varieties	55% Merlot, 40% Cabernet franc, 5% Cabernet Sauvignon
Barrel ageing	15-20 months - New barrels: 80-100%
Second wine	Les Hauts de Canon La Gaffelière

Manager: Count Stephan von Neipperg

Château Canon La Gaffelière 33330 Saint-Émilion
GPS: Latitude: 44.880931 - Longitude: -0,160718
Tel. +33 (0)5 57 24 71 33 - Fax +33 (0)5 57 24 67 95
info@neipperg.com - **www.neipperg.com**

CHÂTEAU CAP DE MOURLIN

GRAND CRU CLASSÉ

SAINT-ÉMILION GRAND CRU   *Owner: Jacques Capdemourlin*

The Capdemourlin family has owned vineyards in Saint-Émilion for nearly four centuries, as attested by a wine sales contract dating from 1647. In an unusual departure from practices at the time, this document mentions the place name of the vineyard and the name of the wine, one of the oldest in Saint-Émilion.

In 1983, Jacques Capdemourlin, the present owner, reunited this estate that had been divided between his father and his uncle for many years. He also undertook a major renovation in order to introduce modern fermentation and ageing techniques (a new vat room, new air-conditioned area for malolactic fermentation, and new barrel ageing cellar).

The vineyard is ideally situated on slopes north of the town of Saint-Émilion and receives meticulous care all year round. Château Cap de Mourlin's *grand vin* is both generous and extremely elegant, with a very expressive bouquet. It is one of the most highly-reputed wines of Saint-Émilion.

52

Area under vine	14 hectares
Production	70,000 bottles
Soil	Clay-limestone and clay-siliceous
Grape varieties	65% Merlot, 25% Cabernet franc, 10% Cabernet Sauvignon
Barrel ageing	15-18 months - New barrels: 50%
Second wine	Capitan de Mourlin

Château Cap de Mourlin 33330 Saint-Émilion
GPS: Latitude: 44.9076845 - Longitude: -0.1540661
Tel. +33 (0)5 57 74 62 06 - Fax +33 (0)5 57 74 59 34
info@vignoblescapdemourlin.com - **www.vignoblescapdemourlin.com**

CHÂTEAU DASSAULT
GRAND CRU CLASSÉ

SAINT-ÉMILION GRAND CRU *Owner: S.A.S Château Dassault*

SAINT-ÉMILION GRAND CRU

CHATEAU DASSAULT
2005
GRAND CRU CLASSÉ

Château Dassault was born thanks to the determination of the famous aeronautical engineer Marcel Dassault. He acquired Château Couperie in Saint-Émilion in 1955 "on a calculated impulse" as he liked to say. Château Couperie was initially created in 1862 by Victor Beylot.

Marcel Dassault rechristened the estate Château Dassault. He introduced the finest winemaking equipment and gradually improved quality over the years. In 1969, Château Dassault was promoted to *Grand Cru Classé* status. The winemaking team who have worked tirelessly alongside three generations of the Dassault family deserve to be congratulated for making Château Dassault one of the jewels of the Saint-Emilion appellation.

Today, Laurent Dassault is in charge of the estate. Together with Laurence Brun, he oversees the estate's ongoing commitment to quality. Laurent Dassault enjoys welcoming wine professionals to his château and for the past several several years his *Déjeuner sur l'Herbe* ("Luncheon on the Grass") is a major event for friends and enthusiasts of Château Dassault.

Area under vine	24 hectares
Production	80,000 bottles
Soil	Glacis (wash pediment)
Grape varieties	65% Merlot, 30% Cabernet franc, 5% Cabernet Sauvignon
Barrel ageing	14-18 months - New barrels: 70%-90%
Second wine	Le D de Dassault

President: Laurent Dassault - Managing Director: Laurence Brun

Château Dassault 33330 Saint-Émilion
GPS: Latitude: 44.908399 - Longitude: -0.141599
Tel. +33 (0)5 57 55 10 00 - Fax +33 (0)5 57 55 10 01
lbv@chateaudassault.com - **www.chateaudassault.com**

CHÂTEAU-FIGEAC

PREMIER GRAND CRU CLASSÉ

SAINT-ÉMILION GRAND CRU — *Owner: the Manoncourt family*

Figeac is a very ancient estate. Its history can be dated back to the Gallo-Roman period, during the 2nd century AD, when the Figeacus family gave their name to the "villa" they built on this location.

Château-Figeac has belonged to the family of the present owners since 1892. Thierry Manoncourt, later assisted by his wife, Marie-France, began restructuring the vineyard in 1947 in order to make Figeac one of the greatest wines of Bordeaux. Perpetuating the family tradition, his daughter, Laure, and son-in-law, Count Éric d'Aramon, have since taken over managing the estate.

Figeac has an outstanding *terroir* consisting of three gravelly rises. In keeping with the nature of this soil, Figeac is the Right Bank estate with the highest percentage of Cabernet. This atypical combination accounts for wines that are elegant, long-lived, and extremely well-reputed.

54

Area under vine	40 hectares
Production	100,000 bottles
Soil	Three gravelly rises
Grape varieties	35% Cabernet Sauvignon, 35% Cabernet franc, 30% Merlot
Barrel ageing	18 months - New barrels: 100%
Second wine	La Grange Neuve de Figeac

Co-Owner: Countess Laure d'Aramon Manoncourt - Manager: Count Éric d'Aramon

Château de Figeac 33330 Saint-Émilion
GPS: Latitude: 44.546407 - Longitude: -0,116494
Tel. +33 (0)5 57 24 72 26 - Fax +33 (0)5 57 74 45 74
chateau-figeac@chateau-figeac.com - **www.chateau-figeac.com**

CLOS FOURTET
PREMIER GRAND CRU CLASSÉ

SAINT-ÉMILION GRAND CRU

Owner: Philippe Cuvelier

1ᵉʳ *Grand Cru Classé*

Clos Fourtet
SAINT-ÉMILION

2008

Philippe CUVELIER
PROPRIÉTAIRE

Clos Fourtet owes its initial reputation to the Rulleau and Carles families, Lords of Figeac. In the 18th century, they were the first to make the most of this land with only a thin layer of arable soil, but blessed with outstanding natural drainage. Clos Fourtet has abundantly proved its standing as a Premier Grand Cru Classé, helped in this respect by hard work and major investments by the Cuvelier family, owners since 2001.

Located atop the limestone plateau well-known for producing some of the greatest wines in Saint-Émilion, Clos Fourtet has one of the appellation's best and most famous *terroirs*.

The vineyard is in a single block surrounding a country house dating from just before the French Revolution. Clos Fourtet is a stone's throw from the medieval village and the wine ages in impressive underground quarries.

Winemaking is very traditional, but complemented by the most up-to-date techniques. In keeping with Clos Fourtet's inherently strong personality, it is aged entirely in new oak barrels. The wine is extremely elegant, with incomparable minerality and freshness.

Area under vine	18.7 hectares
Production	55,000 bottles
Soil	Clay-limestone
Grape varieties	85% Merlot, 10% Cabernet Sauvignon, 5% Cabernet franc
Barrel ageing	15-18 months - New barrels: 75%
Second wine	Closerie de Fourtet

Manager: Matthieu Cuvelier - Director: Tony Ballu

Clos de Fourtet 1 Châtelet Sud - 33330 Saint-Émilion
GPS: Latitude: 44.8953455 - Longitude: -0.1634372
Tel. +33 (0)5 57 24 70 90 - Fax +33 (0)5 57 74 46 52
closfourtet@closfourtet.com - **www.closfourtet.com**

CHÂTEAU FRANC MAYNE
GRAND CRU CLASSÉ

SAINT-ÉMILION GRAND CRU *Owners: Griet Van Malderen-Laviale and Hervé Laviale*

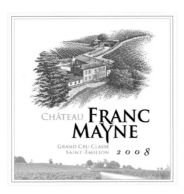

One reaches Château Franc Mayne by going along a long drive with Merlot vines on either side. Located on the Côte de Franc, which gave its name to the estate, part of the vineyard is steep and part is on the limestone plateau. The topsoil consists of a thin layer of clay with limestone outcrops. Traces of an ancient Gallo-Roman road run alongside the property and a former coaching inn bears witness to the steady flow of pilgrims on their way to Santiago de Compostela.

The owners felt that the grapes needed a worthy architectural and technological showcase so they built a new vat room (with small stainless steel and oak vats to ferment fruit from each plot separately) as well as a new first year cellar in 2005. The wines finish ageing in former underground quarries. These magical cellars, spread out over more than two hectares, are visited by thousands of wine enthusiasts every year.

The château also features a 12-room boutique hotel and a natural swimming pool. Franc Mayne epitomises everything that has made Saint-Émilion world-famous!

56

Area under vine	7 hectares
Production	23,000 bottles
Soil	Clay-limestone on the plateau and slope, clay-sand at the foot of the slope
Grape varieties	90% Merlot, 10% Cabernet franc
Barrel ageing	18 months - New barrels: 60-80%
Second wine	Les Cèdres de Franc Mayne

Manager: Kurt De Varé

Château Franc Mayne 14 La Gomerie (RD243) - 33330 Saint-Émilion
GPS: Latitude: 44.899344 - Longitude: -0,171710
Tel. +33 (0)5 57 24 62 61 - Fax +33 (0)5 57 24 68 25
info@chateaufrancmayne.com - **www.chateaufrancmayne.com**

CHÂTEAU GRAND MAYNE

GRAND CRU CLASSÉ

SAINT-ÉMILION GRAND CRU

Owner: the Nony family

With a prime location on one of the finest slopes in Saint-Émilion, (and at the foot of this slope), Grand Mayne – historically referred to as "Le Mayne" – is one of the most prestigious vineyards in the appellation. The château is a superb 16th century manor house that bears witness to the property's long history.

Thanks to a fine *terroir* – famous for over three centuries – as well as exemplary work in the vineyard, precision winemaking, and careful ageing, Grand Mayne produces wines that have won numerous distinctions and earned glowing reviews in the press for their exceptional bouquet and great finesse.

Grand Mayne has belonged to the Jean Nony family since 1934. Jean-Pierre and Marie-Françoise Nony managed the estate from 1977 to 2001. Marie-Françoise has continued the family tradition, assisted by her oldest son, Jean-Antoine, since the death of her husband.

Area under vine	17 hectares
Production	55,000 bottles
Soil	Slope: limestone and clay. Foot of the slope: clay and sand on clay
Grape varieties	80% Merlot, 15% Cabernet franc, 5% Cabernet Sauvignon
Barrel ageing	16-18 months - New barrels: 60-70%
Second wine	Les Plantes du Mayne

Manager: Marie-Françoise Nony

Château Grand Mayne BP 64 - 33330 Saint-Émilion
GPS: Latitude: 44.8996737 - Longitude: -0,1752124
Tel. +33 (0)5 57 74 42 50 - Fax +33 (0)5 57 74 41 89
contact@grand-mayne.com - **www.grand-mayne.com**

CHÂTEAU LA COUSPAUDE
GRAND CRU CLASSÉ

SAINT-ÉMILION GRAND CRU
Owner: S.C.E. Vignobles Aubert

Château La Couspaude is located in the heart of Saint-Émilion, near the famous monolithic church carved out of solid rock. La Couspaude has been the pride and joy of the Aubert family (who also own other estates in the region) for over a century. In fact, the Auberts have been making fine wine in Bordeaux for over two centuries and have unquestionably maintained the family tradition of quality and respect for the *terroir* to the present day.

La Couspaude, was called "La Croix Paute" in the Middle Ages in reference to the cross that still marks the intersection of two roads in front of the estate, and which served as a meeting point for pilgrims on their way to Santiago de Compostela.

This magnificent estate is on the Saint-Émilion limestone plateau, entirely surrounded by walls like all the village's most ancient vineyards. Château La Couspaude also has underground cellars where the wine is fermented and aged in barrels, as well as an impressive reception room that serves as venue for important functions.

58

Area under vine	7 hectares
Production	36,000 bottles
Soil	limestone plateau with a clay-limestone subsoil
Grape varieties	75% Merlot, 20% Cabernet franc, 5% Cabernet Sauvignon
Barrel ageing	18-20 months - New barrels: 100%
Second wine	Junior de la Couspaude

Managers: Héloïse Aubert - Vanessa Aubert - Yohann Aubert

Château la Couspaude BP 40 - 33330 Saint-Émilion
GPS: Latitude: 44.896979 - Longitude: -0.1490804
Tel. +33 (0)5 57 40 15 76 - Fax +33 (0)5 57 40 10 14
vignobles.aubert@wanadoo.fr - **www.aubert-vignobles.com**

CHÂTEAU LA DOMINIQUE
GRAND CRU CLASSÉ

SAINT-ÉMILION GRAND CRU   *Owner: Clément Fayat*

CHÂTEAU
LA DOMINIQUE

GRAND CRU CLASSÉ
SAINT-ÉMILION GRAND CRU

Vignobles Clément Fayat

Located in the western part of the Saint-Émilion appellation, bordering on Pomerol, the estate takes its name from the Caribbean island where the first owner made his fortune.

The vineyard is surrounded by other illustrious estates such as Châteaux Cheval Blanc and Figeac to the west, and La Conseillante and L'Évangile to the north.

Clément Fayat came away utterly enchanted from a visit to La Dominique and eventually acquired the château in 1969.

Consisting of deep gravel and sand, the superb *terroir* is planted with Merlot and Cabernet Franc vines. The combination of these grape varieties, accompanied by meticulous work in the vineyard and cellar, accounts for a wine whose balance and fruity exuberance impress even the most demanding of connoisseurs.

An inveterate entrepreneur, Clément Fayat decided to initiate a particularly ambitious renovation programme in 2010 (in conjunction with architect Jean Nouvel) to go along with the improvements being made to his wine. Visitors will soon be able to discover one of the most striking estates in Bordeaux!

Area under vine	23 hectares
Production	80,000 bottles
Soil	Clay, gravel, and sand
Grape varieties	85% Merlot, 15% Cabernet franc
Barrel ageing	16-18 months - New barrels: 60%
Second wine	Saint-Paul de Dominique

Managing Director: Yannick Evenou - Technical Director: Pierre Meylheuc - Cellar Master: Romain Sapet

Château La Dominique 33330 Saint-Émilion
GPS: Latitude: 44.920023 - Longitude: -0.185866
Tel. +33 (0)5 57 51 31 36 - Fax +33 (0)5 57 51 63 04
contact@vignobles.fayat.com - www.vignobles.fayat.com

CHÂTEAU LA GAFFELIÈRE

PREMIER GRAND CRU CLASSÉ

SAINT-ÉMILION GRAND CRU   *Owner: Count Léo de Malet Roquefort*

Vines have been grown at Château La Gaffelière since the Gallo-Roman period, as proved by the remains of a villa discovered on the property in 1969 by Count Léo de Malet Roquefort. Perhaps it is just a coincidence, but the poet Ausone is known to have had a vineyard in this area at about the same time the villa was built, in the 4th century AD. A recent study by the National Centre for Scientific Research showed that the villa definitely produced wine. It had more than ten rooms decorated with multi-coloured mosaics and the owner was clearly prosperous. The location is still called Le Palat, meaning "the Palace".

The unbroken presence of the Malet Roqueforts at La Gaffelière for some four centuries makes them the oldest winegrowing family in Saint-Émilion. This confers a unique status to Count Léo de Malet Roquefort, the current owner. He focuses his passion and considerable experience on his vineyard in order to perpetuate the traditions that have earned La Gaffelière a fine reputation in France and around the world.

The Malet Roquefort family's very identity, as well as their future, is devoted to the art of making unforgettable wines.

60

Area under vine	16 hectares
Production	60,000 bottles
Soil	Clay-limestone on the slope, siliceous at the foot of the slope
Grape varieties	90% Merlot, 10% Cabernet franc
Barrel ageing	12-14 months - New barrels: 50%
Second wine	Clos La Gaffelière

President: Alexandre de Malet Roquefort - Consultants: Stéphane Derenoncourt - Philippe Gard

Château La Gaffelière 1, La Gaffelière - 33330 Saint-Émilion
GPS: Latitude: 44.884884 - Longitude: -0.157757
Tel. +33 (0)5 57 24 72 15 - Fax +33 (0)5 57 24 69 06
contact@chateau-la-gaffeliere.com - **www.chateau-la-gaffeliere.com**

CHÂTEAU LA TOUR FIGEAC

GRAND CRU CLASSÉ

SAINT-ÉMILION GRAND CRU

Located on the famous *terroir* of the graves de Saint-Émilion bordering on Pomerol, this estate was separated from Château Figeac in 1879. La Tour Figeac was included as a Grand Cru Classé starting with the very first classification of Saint-Émilion in 1955.

The Rettenmaier family has owned and managed the estate since the early 1970s. The vines are tended and the wine made according not only to time-honoured Bordeaux traditions, but also to environmental protection and biodynamic principles. The estate produces its own compost, *pigeage* (punching down the cap) is practised, and many other natural methods are used.

Winemaking is adapted to the particularities of each vintage and benefits from the expertise of an experienced team, assisted by advice from Christine and Stéphane Derenoncourt, in order to fully reflect the fine *terroir*. La Tour Figeac is elegant, fruity, and attractively spicy, with hints of mint, eucalyptus, and violet.

Area under vine	14.5 hectares
Production	45,000 bottles
Soil	Gravel and sand with a clay subsoil
Grape varieties	65% Merlot, 35% Cabernet franc
Barrel ageing	15-18 months - New barrels: 50-80%
Second wine	L'Esquisse de La Tour Figeac

Managing Director: Otto Rettenmaier

Château La Tour Figeac BP 007 - 33330 Saint-Émilion
GPS: Latitude: 44.9169843 - Longitude: -0.2011028
Tel. +33 (0)5 57 51 77 62 - Fax +33 (0)5 57 25 36 92
latourfigeac@wanadoo.fr - **www.latourfigeac.com**

CHÂTEAU LARCIS DUCASSE
GRAND CRU CLASSÉ

SAINT-ÉMILION GRAND CRU   *Owner: the Gratiot-Attmane family*

Château Larcis Ducasse, a Saint-Émilion Grand Cru Classé, has belonged to the Gratiot-Attmane family since 1893. Starting in 2002, Nicolas Thienpont has perpetuated the family's efforts to produce quality wines, assisted by consultant Stéphane Derenoncourt.

Larcis Ducasse's character is defined by its clay-limestone soil and south-facing sun exposure conducive to ripeness. The wines have a fresh, mineral flavour. Their complexity and structure are due to the varied nature of the parent rock, which goes from asteriated limestone on the plateau to feldspathic, iron-rich sandy soil at the foot of the slope.

Merlot and Cabernet Franc vines are planted according to the profile of each part of the vineyard. The final blend features well-balanced, characterful flavours and fine tannin. Sustainable viticultural practices coupled with low yields, gentle fermentation, and barrel ageing adapted to each vintage reflect all the elegance and personality of this great *terroir*.

62

Area under vine	11 hectares
Production	30-35,000 bottles
Soil	Clay-limestone fossiliferous soil on the southern slope
Grape varieties	78% Merlot, 22% Cabernet franc
Barrel ageing	16-18 months - New barrels: 60%

Estate Manager: Nicolas Thienpont - Technical Manager: David Suire

Château Larcis Ducasse 33330 Saint-Laurent-des-Combes
GPS: Latitude: 44.881129 - Longitude: -0.144989
Tel. +33 (0)5 57 24 70 84 - Fax +33 (0)5 57 24 64 00
larcis-ducasse@nicolas-thienpont.com - **www.larcis-ducasse.com**

CHÂTEAU LARMANDE

GRAND CRU CLASSÉ

SAINT-ÉMILION GRAND CRU

Owner: Groupe AG2R La Mondiale

CHÂTEAU
LARMANDE
GRAND CRU CLASSÉ
SAINT-ÉMILION

2008
•
GRAND VIN DE BORDEAUX

Located 1,200 metres from the medieval village of Saint-Émilion, Château Larmande is one of the oldest estates in the appellation. The local archives contain references going as far back as 1585.

Larmande now has a very modern cellar with small vats making it possible to fine-tune winemaking by fermenting grapes on a plot-by-plot basis.

Thanks to a subtle combination of age-old methods and state-of-the-art technology, Larmande makes superb wine in every vintage.

Gentle, traditional-style fermentation retains fresh, fruity aromas and leads to round, attractive wines that reflect the finesse of the *terroir*.

Larmande is particularly well-balanced, delicate wine, with a great deal of elegance.

Area under vine	22 hectares
Production	80,000 bottles
Soil	Clay-limestone, clay-siliceous, and sand
Grape varieties	65% Merlot, 30% Cabernet franc, 5% Cabernet Sauvignon
Barrel ageing	16-18 months - New barrels: 65%
Second wine	Le cadet de Larmande

Manager and oenologist: Claire Thomas-Chenard

Château Larmande Larmande BP 4 - 33330 Saint-Émilion
GPS: Latitude: 44.906104 - Longitude: -0.149174
Tel. +33 (0)5 57 24 71 41 - Fax +33 (0)5 57 74 42 80
contact@soutard-larmande.com - **www.chateau-larmande.com**

CHÂTEAU PAVIE
PREMIER GRAND CRU CLASSÉ

SAINT-ÉMILION GRAND CRU

Owner: Gérard Perse

Vines were first grown in Saint-Émilion on the Pavie slope in the 4th century. The name comes from small vine peaches, called "pavies" that once grew there. A winegrowing estate was painstakingly consolidated there, plot by plot, under the name of Château Pavie. It was included among the Premier Grand Cru Classés in the first classification of Saint-Émilion wines.

Today, this vineyard in a single block on Saint-Émilion's southern slope is one of the largest of the Premiers Grands Crus Classés. The *terroir* is on three different levels (slightly gravelly soil at the foot of the slope, clay-limestone soil on the middle of the slope, and limestone soil on the plateau). The estate took a giant leap forward in terms of quality with the arrival of Chantal and Gérard Perse in March 1998.

Enhanced by low yields (30 hectolitres per hectare) and the separate fermentation of grapes from each individual plot in temperature-controlled oak vats, the blend from the varied *terroirs* is a unique wine of immense complexity. Its marvellous structure and elegance benefit from an ageing cellar that is probably the most audacious and modern in Bordeaux, featuring large stone archways and a monumental fresco by Michel Pourteyron entitled *Grappe Symphonie*.

Area under vine	35 hectares
Production	80,000 bottles
Soil	Clay limestone plateau, clay midway up the slope, and gravel at the foot of the slope
Grape varieties	70% Merlot, 20% Cabernet franc, 10% Cabernet Sauvignon
Barrel ageing	24 months - New barrels: 70-100%
Second wine	Arômes de Pavie

Château Pavie 33330 Saint-Émilion
GPS: Latitude: 44.883204 - Longitude: -0.151309
Tel. +33(0)5 57 55 43 43 - Fax +33 (0)5 57 24 63 99
contact@vignoblesperse.com - www.vignoblesperse.com

Château Pavie Macquin

Premier Grand Cru Classé

Saint-Émilion Grand Cru

Owner: the Corre-Macquin family

PREMIER GRAND CRU CLASSÉ

Famille Corre-Macquin
propriétaire

This estate was founded by Albert Macquin (1852-1911), who studied viticulture at Paris-Grignon and Montpellier, and became a specialist in grafting and root stocks. Saint-Émilion can be grateful to him for introducing grafted vines, which saved the vineyards from ruin by phylloxera in the late 19th century.

Owned by the Corre-Macquin family, the vineyard has a prime location atop the plateau overlooking the limestone ledge of the Côte de Saint-Émilion. Facing westward, opposite the medieval town, Pavie Maquin overlooks the small Fongaban Valley.

The clay-limestone soil on asteriated limestone bedrock provides superb natural drainage and regular water supply. The high concentration of clay makes the wine strong, full-bodied, and generous.

One of Saint-Émilion's model châteaux, this beautiful estate uses traditional methods in the vineyard and cellar as well as selected modern techniques.

This is because, however noble the origin, it takes infinite care and attention to make great wine...

Area under vine	15 hectares
Production	50,000 bottles
Soil	Clay-limestone plateau
Grape varieties	85% Merlot, 14% Cabernet franc, 1% Cabernet Sauvignon
Barrel ageing	14-18 months - New barrels: 60%
Second wine	Les chênes de Macquin

Estate Manager: Nicolas Thienpont - Consultant: Stéphane Derenoncourt

Château Pavie Macquin Peygenestau - 33330 Saint-Émilion
GPS: Latitude: 44.889952 - Longitude: -0.1465585
Tel. +33 (0)5 57 24 74 23 - Fax +33 (0)5 57 24 63 78
contact@pavie-macquin.com - **www.pavie-macquin.com**

65

CHÂTEAU TROPLONG MONDOT

PREMIER GRAND CRU CLASSÉ

SAINT-ÉMILION GRAND CRU   *Owners: Christine and Xavier Pariente*

Domaine de Mondot belonged to Father de Sèze, who had the present-day château built in 1745. Under his management, the wine of Mondot became one of the most sought-after in Saint-Émilion.

Very much taken by the estate, Raymond Troplong purchased it in 1850 and constituted the vineyard as we know it today. Troplong was a French peer, famous lawyer, lover of art and literature, close friend of Théophile Gautier, and President of the French Senate from 1852 until his death in 1869. He succeeded in making the most of Mondot's fine *terroir* to produce superb wine that the 1868 edition of the famous Cocks and Féret (the "Bordeaux Bible") rated second best in Saint-Émilion. Before selling the estate, his nephew and heir, Édouard Troplong, added the family name.

Alexandre Valette, a wine merchant from Paris, acquired the property in the early 20th century. He already owned Château La France in Fronsac, another château of the same name in Quinsac, and acquired Château Pavie shortly thereafter. Alexandre's son, Bernard, followed by his grandson, Claude, followed in his footsteps as managers of the estate. Christine Valette-Pariente and her husband, Xavier Pariente, now own and operate Troplong Mondot.

66

Area under vine	33 hectares
Production	80,000 bottles
Soil	Clay-limestone
Grape varieties	90% Merlot, 5% Cabernet franc, 5% Cabernet Sauvignon
Barrel ageing	12-24 months - New barrels: 100%
Second wine	Mondot

Communication: Margaux Pariente

Château Troplong Mondot 33330 Saint-Émilion
GPS: Latitude: 44.888895 - Longitude:-0.141445
Tel. +33 (0)5 57 55 32 05 - Fax +33 (0)5 57 55 32 07
contact@chateau-troplong-mondot.com - **www.chateau-troplong-mondot.com**

CHÂTEAU TROTTEVIEILLE
PREMIER GRAND CRU CLASSÉ

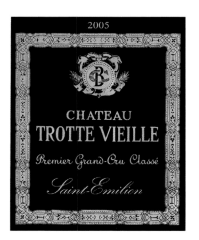

Château Trottevieille is a very old estate. Its name comes from a legend having to do with an old lady who lived there centuries ago. A coach stop was located at the intersection of two roads just outside her house. Whenever a carriage stopped there, the old woman (*la vieille*) "trotted out" to hear the latest news.

The present-day château is surrounded by attractive grounds as well as vines. The vineyard overlooks a small south-facing valley, and the vines have remarkable sun exposure. The *terroir* consists of a thin layer (thirty centimetres) of clay soil on a limestone shelf. Visible in former quarries found on the estate, vine roots have pushed through in search of nourishment. There is also a small plot of pre-phylloxera vines approximately 120 years old.

Château Trottevieille is known for its elegance, roundness, and very long aftertaste. These characteristics are partly due to the large percentage of Cabernet Franc. The wine is fruity and well-balanced even when young, but fills out and develops beautifully after several years in bottle. This explains why Trottevieille is much sought after by connoisseurs around the world.

Area under vine	10 hectares
Production	36,000 bottles
Soil	Clay-limestone
Grape varieties	50% Merlot, 45% Cabernet franc, 5% Cabernet Sauvignon
Barrel ageing	18 months - New barrels: 100%
Second wine	La Vieille Dame de Trottevieille

Château Trottevieille 33330 Saint-Émilion
GPS: Latitude: 44.894522 - Longitude: -0.14544
Tel. +33 (0)5 56 00 00 70 - Fax +33 (0)5 57 87 48 61
domaines@borie-manoux.fr - **www.trottevieille.com**

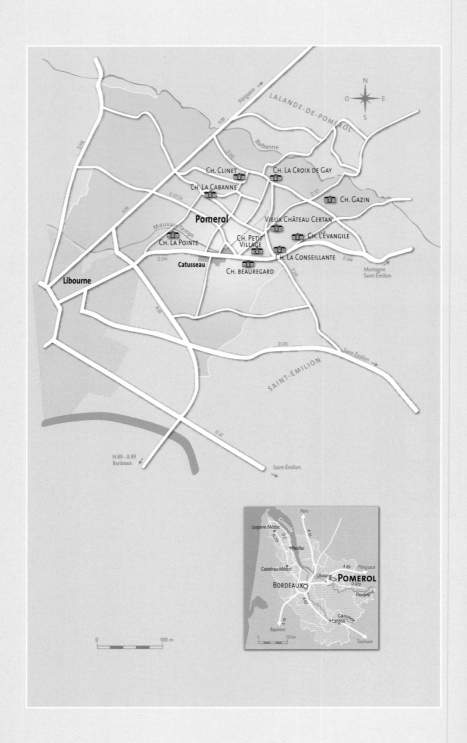

CRUS DE POMEROL

Located on the pilgrim road to Santiago de Compostela, the vineyards of Pomerol, which date back to Roman times, were developed by the Knights Templar. Although the Hundred Years' War brought only poverty and misery to the region, the vineyards once again thrived in the 15th and 16th centuries, and the reputation of their wines grew steadily.

In the 18th and 19th centuries, Pomerol's borders became more clearly defined, and the rarest wines were much sought after by buyers from around the world.

The major crises of the 20th century were overcome thanks to the devotion and commitment of winegrowers. The reputation of wines from this appellation has increased from year to year. Pomerol produces only a small quantity of wine so, historically, *négociants* and importers had to go there to sample and buy wines of the most recent vintage as soon as these were blended. This tradition has been maintained at the major tasting organised by the Union des Grands Crus de Bordeaux.

p 70   Château Beauregard
p 71   Vieux Château Certan
p 72   Château Clinet
p 73   Château Gazin
p 74   Château L'Évangile
p 75   Château La Cabanne
p 76   Château La Conseillante
p 77   Château La Croix de Gay
p 78   Château La Pointe
p 79   Château Petit-Village

CHÂTEAU BEAUREGARD

POMEROL

Château Beauregard is in an ideal location on the southern side of the famous Catusseau plateau in Pomerol, with a magnificent gravel and clay *terroir*.

Beauregard's history dates back to the 12th century. The Knights of Saint John of Jerusalem (the former name of the Knights of Malta) had a small manor house here which served as a stopover for pilgrims on the road to Santiago de Compostela. The Beauregard family built an impressive villa in the 17th century. This was in turn replaced by the present-day château designed by a student of Victor Louis and built during the Napoleonic period. This elegant 18th century building personifies Beauregard's history and universally acknowledged charm.

Beauregard has an unusual blend of grape varieties, including some 30% Cabernet Franc. This variety is often discreet when young, but adds considerable freshness and elegance over time. Brilliantly fruity when young, Château Beauregard displays all the depth and smoothness of the great wines of Pomerol over time.

70

Area under vine	17.5 hectares
Production	60,000 bottles
Soil	Mixed gravel and clay, sand, and gravel
Grape varieties	70% Merlot, 30% Cabernet franc
Barrel ageing	18-22 months - New barrels: 60%
Second wine	Le Benjamin de Beauregard

Managing Director: Michel Garat - Manager: Vincent Priou

Château Beauregard 33500 Pomerol
GPS: Latitude: 44.922527 - Longitude: -0.202003
Tel. +33 (0)5 57 51 13 36 - Fax +33 (0)5 57 25 09 55
beauregard@chateau-beauregard.com - **www.chateau-beauregard.com**

VIEUX CHÂTEAU CERTAN

POMEROL   *Owner: the Thienpont family*

Vieux Château Certan is the oldest known wine estate in Pomerol. It was founded in the 16th century by the Demay family of Scotland. Acquired in 1924 by Georges Thienpont, a wine merchant from Etikhove in Belgium, the estate has been owned and managed by a *société civile* (family-owned company) established by his heirs since 1957.

The vineyard is in a single block on the middle of the Pomerol plateau internationally renowned for its great wines. The proportion of Cabernet Franc and Cabernet Sauvignon is extremely high for the Pomerol appellation. This old tradition has been maintained even though neighbouring estates now have almost exclusively Merlot, which produces wine that is more flattering in its youth.

Like the great Médocs, Vieux Château Certan is best enjoyed ten to fifteen years after the vintage, at which time it displays unequalled finesse and elegance. Distributed exclusively by Bordeaux brokers and *négociants*, the wine is sold all over the world.

Area under vine	14 hectares
Production	50,000 bottles
Soil	Clay and gravel
Grape varieties	60% Merlot, 30% Cabernet franc, 10% Cabernet Sauvignon
Barrel ageing	18-22 months - New barrels: 90%
Second wine	La Gravette de Certan

Vieux Château Certan 1, route de Lussac - 33500 Pomerol
GPS: Latitude: 44.9269211 - Longitude: -0.1977539
Tel. +33 (0)5 57 51 17 33 - Fax +33 (0)5 57 25 35 08
info@vieuxchateaucertan.com - **www.vieuxchateaucertan.com**

CHÂTEAU CLINET

Owner: the Laborde family

2008

CHÂTEAU

CLINET

Pomerol

Located on the highest part of the famous Pomerol plateau, Château Clinet has an outstanding *terroir* – a Günz gravel terrace that is home to the appellation's most prized estates. Clinet was acquired in 1998 by Jean-Louis Laborde.

Using sustainable methods in the vineyard and the most natural possible winemaking methods, the Laborde family has worked hard ever since to make the most of this exceptional *terroir*.

An ambitious restructuring programme took place in part of the vineyard and infinite care is taken in day-to-day operations: ploughing, training to just the right height, pruning, leaf thinning, etc.

Inaugurated in time for the 2004 vintage, the cellar was designed in such a way as to make maximum use of gravity flow. The wine ages in oak barrels and is neither fined nor filtered before bottling.

Château Clinet is an elegant, intense, refined wine with complex aromas of red fruit, blackberry, and truffle.

Area under vine	8.64 hectares
Production	40,000 bottles
Soil	Gravel and clay with a great deal of *crasse de fer*
Grape varieties	87% Merlot, 10% Cabernet Sauvignon, 3% Cabernet franc
Barrel ageing	18-22 months - New barrels: 60%
Second wine	Fleur de Clinet

Managing Director: Ronan Laborde

Château Clinet 16 chemin de Feytit - 33500 Pomerol
GPS: Latitude: 44.9353841 - Longitude: -0.2114823
Tel. +33 (0)5 57 25 50 00 - Fax +33 (0)5 57 25 70 00
contact@chateauclinet.com - **www.chateauclinet.com**

CHÂTEAU GAZIN

POMEROL   *Owner: G.F.A. Château Gazin*

Château Gazin formerly belonged to the Knights of Saint John of Jerusalem (the Order of Malta) and is one of the largest estates in its appellation. The vineyard is in a single block on the upper part of the famous Pomerol plateau.

Gazin is currently owned by the Bailliencourt family. Descended from the Lords of Landas, the Bailliencourt dit Courcol family is one of the oldest in the province of Artois. The name Courcol (meaning "short collar") was given to an ancestor by Philippe Auguste, King of France in 1214 due to his bravery in time of war. Louis Soualle, the great-grandfather of the present owners, acquired Château Gazin in the early 20th century and the estate continues to be carefully managed by his descendants.

The grapes are fermented in concrete vats and malolactic fermentation takes place in barrel, after which the wine is also aged in oak. It is then fined with egg whites and, if need be, lightly filtered before bottling at the château. Annual production (80% exported) can attain up to 100,000 bottles (including 30,000 for the second wine). Château Gazin belongs to the Académie du Vin de Bordeaux.

Area under vine	24.24 hectares
Production	100,000 bottles
Soil	Clay-gravel with Günz gravel
Grape varieties	90% Merlot, 7% Cabernet Sauvignon, 3% Cabernet franc
Barrel ageing	18 months - New barrels: 50%
Second wine	L'Hospitalet de Gazin

Managing Directors: Christophe and Nicolas de Bailliencourt dit Courcol - Director: Mickaël Obert

Château Gazin Chemin de Chantecaille - 33500 Pomerol
GPS: Latitude: 44.931896 - Longitude: -0.1864528
Tel. +33 (0)5 57 51 07 05 - Fax +33 (0)5 57 51 69 96
contact@gazin.com - **www.gazin.com**

CHÂTEAU L'ÉVANGILE

| POMEROL | Owner: Domaines Barons de Rothschild (Lafite) |

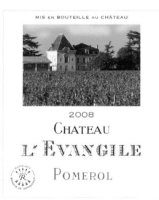

Due to a curious geological anomaly, a long strip of gravel was formed on the southeastern part of the Pomerol plateau. Three vineyards, including L'Évangile, share this rare *terroir*. The estate is bordered to the north by Pétrus, and is only separated from Cheval Blanc to the south (in the Saint-Émilion appellation) by a country road.

The property was constituted in the 18th century by the Léglise family and was renamed L'Évangile at the turn of the 19th century.

In 1862, L'Évangile was acquired by Paul Chaperon, whose heirs, the Ducasse family, were owners until 1990. As early as 1868, it was considered the *Premier Cru du Haut Pomerol* (2nd edition of Cocks and Féret).

Domaines Barons de Rothschild acquired Château L'Évangile in 1990. The first manifestation of their influence was a more rigorous selection for the *grand vin* and the creation of a second wine, Blason de l'Évangile. A vineyard replanting programme was also initiated in 1998. The new configuration was finalised in 2004 with the renovation of the vat room and cellars. These efforts have been conducive to a decade of remarkable vintages.

Area under vine	16 hectares
Production	24-36,000 bottles
Soil	Sand and clay with pure gravel and *crasse de fer* (ironpan)
Grape varieties	80% Merlot, 20% Cabernet franc
Barrel ageing	18 months - New barrels: 70%
Second wine	Blason de L'Évangile

Château L'Évangile 33500 Pomerol
GPS: Latitude: 44.9261571 - Longitude: -0.1921797
Tel. +33 (0)5 57 55 45 55 - Fax +33 (0)5 57 55 45 56
levangile@lafite.com - **www.lafite.com**

CHÂTEAU LA CABANNE

Owner: the Jean-Pierre Estager family

POMEROL

ChateauLaCabanne®

2005

Owned by the Jean-Pierre Estager family, Château La Cabanne is located in the heart of Pomerol.

Although vines have been grown here since Gallo-Roman times, the name goes back to the 14th century, when serfs lived in *cabanes*, or huts.

Château La Cabanne is a dynamic estate. The vineyard is gradually being restructured and investments are regularly made in new equipment. The vines are tended according to the best of both traditional and modern methods, and in keeping with the appellation's highest standards.

Château La Cabanne is well-balanced and has a bouquet of red fruit and cocoa. It is round and velvety on the palate with soft, unaggressive tannin. After careful blending, during which only the best wines are kept aside for the *grand vin*, this is one of the greatest wines of Pomerol.

Château La Cabanne also produces a second wine, Domaine de Compostelle, from young vines.

Area under vine	10 hectares
Production	36,000 bottles
Soil	Clay-gravel with a subsoil rich in *crasse de fer* (ironpan)
Grape varieties	92% Merlot, 8% Cabernet franc
Barrel ageing	15 months - New barrels: 60%
Second wine	Domaine de Compostelle

Manager: Michèle Estager - Director: François Estager - Oenologist: Florent Faure

Château La Cabanne 2, chemin de la Cabanne - 33500 Pomerol
GPS: Latitude: 44.93194 - Longitude: -0.21
Tel. +33 (0)5 57 51 04 09 - Fax +33 (0)5 57 25 13 38
estager@estager.com - **www.estager.com**

CHÂTEAU LA CONSEILLANTE

Owner: S.C. des Héritiers Nicolas

The first recorded history of La Conseillante's name appears in the mid-18th century. It was bequeathed by an influential woman who owned the estate almost 300 years ago: Catherine Conseillan.

The Nicolas family bought the château in 1871, and its size and configuration have not changed ever since. Exemplifying the Nicolas family's continued commitment to this great wine, the fifth generation is currently at the helm.

Located on the heart of the famous Pomerol plateau next to its renowned neighbours, Pétrus and Cheval Blanc, La Conseillante has an outstanding *terroir*. Its full potential has been achieved, and the wine has gained a well-deserved reputation for power and elegance.

La Conseillante's silky tannin, aromatic complexity, and regularity year in and year out account for its loyal following around the world.

Area under vine	11.8 hectares
Production	50,000 bottles
Soil	Clay and gravel over *crasse de fer* (ironpan) in the subsoil
Grape varieties	80% Merlot, 20% Cabernet franc
Barrel ageing	18 months - New barrels: 80-100%
Second wine	Duo de Conseillante

Director: Jean-Michel Laporte - Co-Manager: Bertrand Nicolas - Co-Manager: Valmy Nicolas

Château La Conseillante 33500 Pomerol
GPS: Latitude: 44.924247 - Longitude: -0.194814
Tel. +33 (0)5 57 51 15 32 - Fax +33 (0)5 57 51 42 39
contact@la-conseillante.com - **www.la-conseillante.com**

Château La Croix de Gay

Owner: Chantal Lebreton

Château La Croix de Gay has been in the Raynaud family for five generations and their history is intimately linked with that of Pomerol.

Located on a part of the Pomerol plateau with ideal sun exposure, (along with the other finest châteaux in the appellation), La Croix de Gay is carefully managed by its owners, who use the best of both age-old traditions and modern techniques.

Visitors to the estate are able to enjoy tasting this generous wine with a bouquet of vanilla, almond, and red fruit in one of the region's few underground cellars. Château La Croix de Gay is aged in stave wood oak barrels, which add complexity to this intrinsically elegant wine. It has received numerous medals and distinctions, and satisfies even the most demanding of connoisseurs.

Area under vine	10 hectares
Production	35-45,000 bottles
Soil	Clay-gravel and sandy-gravel
Grape varieties	95% Merlot, 5% Cabernet franc
Barrel ageing	18 months - New barrels: 80%

Château La Croix de Gay 8, chemin de Saint-Jacques de Compostelle - 33500 Pomerol
GPS: Latitude: 44,9349982 - Longitude: -0,1997938
Tel. +33 (0)5 57 51 19 05 - Fax. +33 (0)5 57 51 81 81
contact@chateau-lacroixdegay.com

77

Château La Pointe

Owner: S.C.E. Château La Pointe

Château La Pointe's lovely 2 hectares of grounds and centuries-old trees have made this an outstandingly beautiful property for over a century and a half. It gained recognition as an important winegrowing estate in the 19th century.

One of the largest vineyards in Pomerol, La Pointe underwent a major renovation starting in 2008 in order to enhance its image and achieve the *terroir*'s full potential.

A detailed soil survey made it possible to maximise drainage and restructure the vineyards in the interest of quality. The Cabernet Sauvignon vines were uprooted and the yields of Cabernet Franc adapted in order to express the finesse and elegance that make La Pointe one of the mostly highly-reputed wines on the Right Bank.

A major renovation of the cellars was also undertaken. This makes it possible to ferment grapes from each plot separately to fine-tune winemaking, as well as respect stringent environmental standards.

The internationally respected consultant, Hubert de Boüard de Laforest, co-owner of Château Angélus, now shares his expertise with the Château La Pointe team.

78

Area under vine	22 hectares
Production	100,000 bottles
Soil	Gravel and river stones deposited by the Isle River, clay limestone soil, sand on clay, and clay on gravel
Grape varieties	Red wine: 85% Merlot, 15% Cabernet franc
Barrel ageing	12 months - New barrels: 50%
Second wine	La Pointe Riffat

Managing Director: Éric Monneret - Consultant: Hubert de Boüard de Laforest - Technical Director: Émilie Faniest

Château La Pointe 33500 Pomerol
GPS: Latitude: 44.92555 - Longitude: -0.21685
Tel. +33 (0)5 57 51 02 11 - Fax +33 (0)5 57 51 42 33
contact@chateaulapointe.com - **www.chateaulapointe.com**

CHÂTEAU PETIT-VILLAGE

POMEROL   *Owner: AXA Millésimes*

Château Petit-Village is located on the highest point of the gravel plateau in the heart of the Pomerol appellation. The 10.5 hectares vineyard is in a single triangular-shaped plot.

Combining age-old vine-growing traditions with modern facilities of the highest standard to optimise all that enormous potential without hindering nature in any way whatsoever – that is the challenge we set ourselves at Petit-Village. Today, the vast labours of restructuring the vineyard and renovating the winery facilities are bearing fruit.

Each and every action in the process that leads through to bottling, from picking the grapes by hand to allowing the wine to rest in oak casks, is guided by our sense of values and the fullest expression of the terroir.

Château Petit-Village wines are powerful, yet soft and well-balanced. They have all the incomparable richness and finesse of the greatest wines of Pomerol.

GRAND VIN DU

Château
Petit-Village

2008

POMEROL

Area under vine	10.5 hectares
Production	30,000 bottles
Soil	Deep gravel with light sandy clay on *crasse de fer* (iron hardpan)
Grape varieties	75% Merlot, 18% Cabernet franc, 7% Cabernet Sauvignon
Barrel ageing	15 months - New barrels: 60-70%
Second wine	Le Jardin de Petit-Village

Managing Director: Christian Seely - Technical Director: Serge Ley

Château Petit-Village 33500 Pomerol
GPS: Latitude: 44.923913 - Longitude: -0.200393
Tel. +33 (0)5 57 51 21 08   - Fax +33 (0)5 57 51 87 31
contact@petit-village.com - **www.petit-village.com**

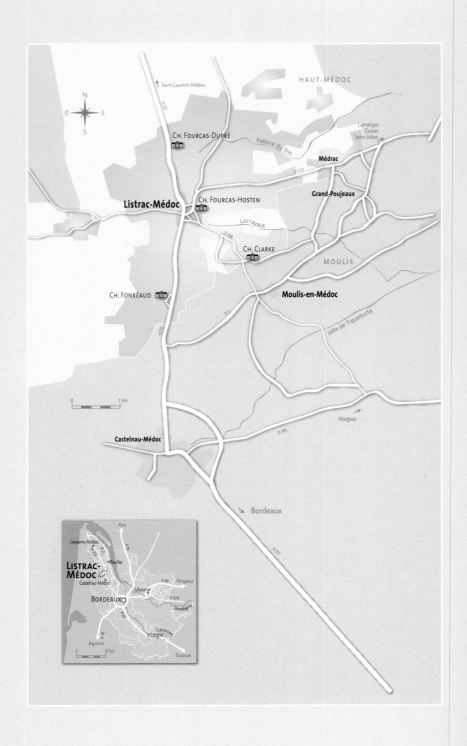

CRUS DE LISTRAC-MÉDOC

This wine-producing commune has been famous since the late 18th century. *Le Producteur*, a publication targeting the Bordeaux wine industry, noted as early as 1838 that vineyard owners in Listrac were able to overcome numerous challenges to make a name for themselves thanks to the unique quality of their wines.

This quality was acknowledged in the early 20th century when the *appellation contrôlée* system was first established, although separate status was granted somewhat later than other Médoc communes, in June 1957, when Listrac-Médoc was officially entitled to its own appellation. Three years after Margaux, it became the youngest communal appellation in Bordeaux.

p 82   Château Clarke
p 83   Château Fonréaud
p 84   Château Fourcas Dupré
p 85   Château Fourcas Hosten

CHÂTEAU CLARKE
BARON EDMOND DE ROTHSCHILD

LISTRAC-MÉDOC　　　　　*Owner: Baron Benjamin de Rothschild*

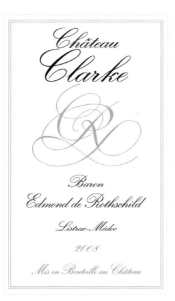

Château Clarke is named after an Irish family who acquired the estate in the 18th century. Clarke was purchased by Baron Edmond de Rothschild in 1973 and entirely renovated. The vineyard currently consists of fifty-four hectares of clay-limestone rises ideally suited to Merlot, which is by far the most widely-planted variety (a fairly rare situation in the Médoc).

Methods such as hand picking into small crates, meticulous sorting in the cellar, and the use of gravity flow are perfectly adapted to recently-constructed winemaking facilities and an unfailing emphasis on quality.

The magnificent 4-hectare gardens surrounding Château Clarke feature an amazingly diverse selection of plants and trees which are looked after with the same care and attention as the vines and wine.

Since 1997, Baron Benjamin de Rothschild and his wife, Ariane, have been in charge of the estate, helping to motivate a dynamic winemaking team with their quest for excellence in keeping with the vision of the late Baron Edmond de Rothschild.

Area under vine	54 hectares
Production	250,000 bottles
Soil	Clay-limestone
Grape varieties	70% Merlot, 30% Cabernet Sauvignon
Barrel ageing	16-18 months - New barrels: 60-80%
Second wine	Les Granges des Domaines Edmond de Rothschild

Managing Director: Georges Alnot - Technical Director: Yann Buchwalter
Commercial Director: Hélène Combabessouse

Château Clarke 33480 Listrac-Médoc
GPS: Latitude: 45.0661156 - Longitude: -0.7735646
Tel. +33 (0)5 56 58 38 00 - Fax +33 (0)5 56 58 26 46
contact@cver.fr - **www.cver.fr**

Château Fonréaud

Owner: the Chanfreau family

Château Fonréaud is well-known for its historic vineyard and the quality of its wines. The estate is unusual in that its name comes from a legend and also because of its privileged location on the highest point in the Médoc.

Fonréaud, was formerly called Font-réaux, meaning "royal fountain". A legend tells us that in the 12th century, the King of England (probably Henry II Plantagenet, the husband of Eleanor of Aquitaine) quenched his thirst from a spring he found on the grounds.

Thanks to a subtle blend of grape varieties, the *terroir* comes through beautifully in round wines with ripe tannin, fine structure and a velvety texture that develops beautifully on the palate.

The vat room houses small temperature-controlled vats that allow grapes from each plot to express their nuances, and also make it possible to fine-tune the final blend. Aged in barrel, the elegance and charm of this fine wine reflect the spirit of the Chanfreau family.

Area under vine	38 hectares
Production	150,000 bottles
Soil	Gravel with a clay-limestone subsoil
Grape varieties	52% Cabernet Sauvignon, 44% Merlot, 4% Petit Verdot
Barrel ageing	12 months - New barrels: 33%
Second wine	La Légende de Fonréaud

Château Fonréaud 33480 Listrac-Médoc
GPS: Latitude: 45.05775 - Longitude: -0.797389
Tel. +33 (0)5 56 58 02 43 - Fax +33 (0)5 56 58 04 33
contact@vignobles-chanfreau.com - **www.chateau-fonreaud.com**

83

CHÂTEAU FOURCAS DUPRÉ

LISTRAC-MÉDOC

Owner: S.C.E. du Château Fourcas Dupré

Vines have grown in "Fourcas" since the early 18th century, as proved by royal cartographers Masse, Robert, Belleyme, etc. Situated at an altitude of 42 metres, the Fourcas plateau is called the "roof of the Médoc" and features the oldest geological stratum in the region. Formerly called "cru Roullet", Fourcas Dupré took on its present name in 1843 when Jean-Antoine Baptiste Dupré, a Bordeaux solicitor, acquired the estate.

In 1970, Guy Pagès bought the château and undertook a major renovation, transforming Fourcas Dupré in the process into one of the finest wines in its appellation. His son, Patrice Pagès, took over in 1985, perpetuating the same spirit of meticulousness, expertise, and passion. Château Fourcas Dupré's *terroir* is an unusual blend of gravel, clay, and limestone. It is one of the rare estates in the Médoc with more than 80% Pyrenean gravel, which accounts for the wine's strong personality.

Thanks to this soil and carefully-studied proportions of grape varieties, the wines of Fourcas Dupré reflect their *terroir* with great success. Mineral, complex, and very expressive on the palate, they also have tremendous ageing potential.

84

Area under vine	46 hectares
Production	220,000 bottles
Soil	Pyrenean gravel, with a clay-limestone subsoil
Grape varieties	44% Merlot, 10% Cabernet franc, 44% Cabernet Sauvignon, 2% Petit Verdot
Barrel ageing	12 months - New barrels: 33%
Second wine	Bellevue de Fourcas Dupré

Manager: Patrice Pagès

Château Fourcas Dupré Le Fourcas - 33480 Listrac-Médoc
GPS: Latitude: 45,0750997 - Longitude: -0,7901877
Tel. +33 (0)5 56 58 01 07 - Fax +33 (0)5 56 58 02 27
info@fourcasdupre.com - **www.fourcasdupre.com**

CHÂTEAU FOURCAS HOSTEN

LISTRAC-MÉDOC

Owners: Renaud and Laurent Momméja

Thanks to a highly unusual *terroir* that accounts for the wine's subtle balance, Château Fourcas Hosten has enjoyed a fine reputation for nearly two hundred years.

Located in the heart of the village of Listrac, in the middle of 3-hectare English-style grounds, the 18th century manor house overlooks a clay-limestone plain where Merlot grapes express all their goodness. Further north, Cabernet Sauvignon and Cabernet Franc vines are very much at home on the gravel soil of the plateau de Fourcas.

While making sure to respect centuries-old traditions and longstanding Médoc winemaking expertise, the new owners, Renaud and Laurent Momméja, are also committed to providing the most up-to-date facilities and techniques. Everything possible is done to express the character and elegance of Fourcas Hosten.

Area under vine	47 hectares
Production	220,000 bottles
Soil	60% Pyrenean gravel and 40% clay-limestone
Grape varieties	45% Merlot, 45% Cabernet Sauvignon, 10% Cabernet franc
Barrel ageing	12 months - New barrels: 40%
Second wine	Les Cèdres d'Hosten

Château Fourcas Hosten 2 place de l'Église - 33480 Listrac-Médoc
GPS: Latitude: 45.0750997 - Longitude: -0.7901877
Tel. +33 (0)5 56 58 01 15 - Fax +33 (0)5 56 58 06 73
contact@fourcas-hosten.com - **www.fourcas-hosten.com**

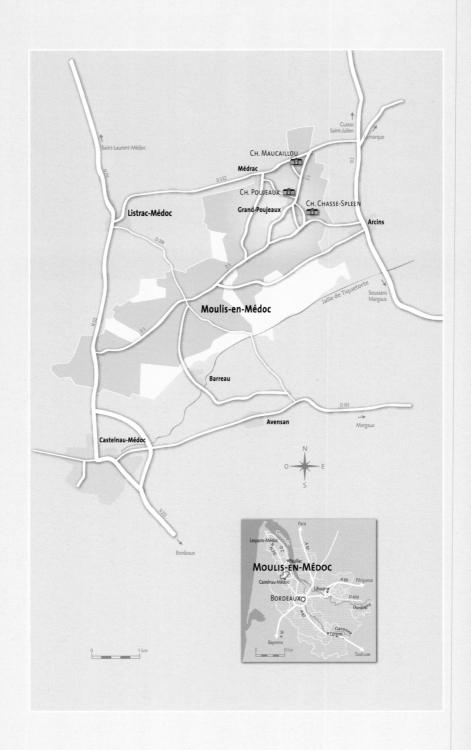

CRUS DE MOULIS-EN-MÉDOC

The commune of Moulis, and thus the wine appellation, are named after the numerous *moulins*, or mills (both water and wind-powered) found there at one time. Moulis is a deformation of the words *molinis* and *mola* of Latin origin. While this name proves that grain was grown in the region, we also know that vines were cultivated here as far back as the Middle Ages by several vineyard owners and a large religious community. The winegrowing commune of Moulis is probably one of the oldest in the Médoc. Bearing witness to a prestigious past, the town also has one of the most beautiful Romanesque churches in the entire region.

The vineyards of Moulis and the reputation of its wines greatly developed during the 18th and 19th centuries, at the same time as other neighbouring communes.

p 88   Château Chasse-Spleen

p 89   Château Maucaillou

p 90   Château Poujeaux

CHÂTEAU CHASSE-SPLEEN

MOULIS-EN-MÉDOC

Owner: Céline Villars-Foubet

"C'est toi qui dors dans l'ombre, ô sacré souvenir."
Les rayons et les ombres, Victor Hugo.

CHÂTEAU
CHASSE-SPLEEN
Moulis en Médoc
APPELLATION MOULIS-EN-MÉDOC CONTRÔLÉE
2008
CÉLINE VILLARS FOUBET
MIS EN BOUTEILLE AU CHÂTEAU

Some people attribute the name of this château to Lord Byron during a trip he made to France, whereas others credit Charles Baudelaire while visiting his artist friend Odilon Redon, a neighbour of Chasse Spleen and illustrator of *Spleen et Idéal*.

The estate has been managed by women for the past thirty years: Jacques Merlaut's daughter, Bernadette Villars, starting in 1976, followed by her daughter, Claire, beginning in 1992, and now her sister, Céline.

The vineyard is located in Moulis, the smallest appellation in the Médoc, just off the Route des Châteaux, halfway between Margaux and Saint-Julien. Its extraordinarily varied *terroir* consists of complementary soil types going from pure Garonne and Pyrenean gravel to a mixture of clay and limestone.

Chasse-Spleen reflects this diversity and the best of its appellation thanks to the fresh, mineral qualities of Cabernet Sauvignon grown on a thick layer of gravel and the roundness and smoothness of Merlot planted on largely clay-limestone soil.

88

Area under vine	90 hectares
Production	300-400,000 bottles
Soil	80% Garonne gravel, 20% clay-limestone
Grape varieties	55% Cabernet Sauvignon, 40% Merlot, 5% Petit Verdot
Barrel ageing	16-18 months - New barrels: 40%
Second wine	Oratoire de Chasse-Spleen

President: Céline Villars-Foubet - Managing Director: Jean-Pierre Foubet
Technical Manager: Dominique Lafuge

Château Chasse-Spleen 32 chemin de la raze - 33480 Moulis-en-Médoc
GPS: Latitude: 45.0754529 - Longitude: -0.7410965
Tel. +33 (0)5 56 58 02 37 - Fax +33 (0)5 57 88 84 40
info@chasse-spleen.com - **www.chasse-spleen.com**

CHÂTEAU MAUCAILLOU

MOULIS-EN-MÉDOC

Owner: S.A.R.L. Château Maucaillou

2008

CHATEAU

MAUCAILLOU

MOULIS

APPELLATION MOULIS CONTRÔLÉE

MIS EN BOUTEILLE AU CHATEAU

13% vol.   S.A.R.L. CHÂTEAU MAUCAILLOU   75 cl
PROPRIÉTAIRE A MOULIS-EN-MÉDOC · GIRONDE · FRANCE

PRODUCT OF FRANCE   BORDEAUX WINE

Coinciding with a veritable family saga, Château Maucaillou's history reflects both patience and passion. The château was built in 1875 in a very Baroque style that was popular at the time. It was surrounded by five hectares of vines.

The Dourthe brothers, Roger and André, devoted their efforts to expanding the vineyard when they arrived at the estate in 1929, succeeding in attaining twenty hectares in 1967. At this point, Roger's son, Philippe, became manager. He added a further 67 hectares over a forty-year period, including vines on the three finest rises in Moulis. In 2007, Philippe Dourthe handed over management to his children Caroline, Pascal, and Magali. A fully-qualified team respectful of the Dourthe winemaking philosophy is now in control. A draconian selection at harvest time, precision winemaking in temperature-controlled vats, and careful ageing in barrel produce wines with a sumptuous colour, as well as rich, concentrated aromas, subtle tannin, and an astonishingly long aftertaste.

Château Maucaillou has won numerous medals and regularly receives good reviews from critics.

Area under vine	87 hectares
Production	300,000 bottles
Soil	75% Günz gravel and 25% clay-limestone
Grape varieties	52% Cabernet Sauvignon, 41% Merlot, 7% Petit Verdot
Barrel ageing	18-21 months - New barrels: 30-40%
Second wine	Numéro 2 de Maucaillou

Manager: Pascal Dourthe - Technical Director: Magali Dourthe - Public relations: Caroline Dourthe

Château Maucaillou 33480 Moulis-en-Médoc
GPS: Latitude: 45.0857059 - Longitude: -0.7447877
Tel. +33 (0)5 56 58 01 23 - Fax +33 (0)5 56 58 00 88
chateau@maucaillou.com - **www.chateau-maucaillou.com**

CHÂTEAU POUJEAUX

MOULIS-EN-MÉDOC   *Owner: Philippe Cuvelier*

Winegrowing at Château Poujeaux dates from the 19th century, although it was a seigneury owing allegiance to Latour Saint Mambert, the future Château Latour, in the Middle Ages... A period of prosperity was followed by an unsettled time with many different owners, and the vineyard was broken up in the early 20th century. Fortunately, it was reconsolidated by the Theil family, who did much to give the wine a fine reputation.

Château Poujeaux was purchased by the Cuvelier family (who were already the proud owners of Clos Fourtet, a Premier Grand Cru Classé in Saint-Émilion) in January 2008. This was the beginning of a new chapter in Poujeaux's history. Philippe Cuvelier and his son, Matthieu, asked Nicolas Thienpont and Stéphane Derenoncourt to advise them, while retaining the existing winemaking team. This is headed by Christophe Labenne, the grandson of the former owners.

While perpetuating the wine's generous, yet delicate style, the new orientation is toward better focus in order to bring Poujeaux up to its ultimate potential. The vines grow in a single block on a great *terroir* in the heart of the Médoc: a beautiful gravelly rise in Grand-Poujeaux.

90

Area under vine	70 hectares
Production	300,000 bottles
Soil	Günz gravel
Grape varieties	50% Cabernet Sauvignon, 40% Merlot, 5% Cabernet franc, 5% Petit Verdot
Barrel ageing	12 months - New barrels: 30%
Second wine	La Salle de Château Poujeaux

Estate Manager: Matthieu Cuvelier - Directors: Christophe Labenne - Nicolas Thienpont

Château Poujeaux 33480 Moulis-en-Médoc
GPS: Latitude: 45.0658658 - Longitude: -0.7736866
Tel. +33 (0)5 56 58 02 96 - Fax +33 (0)5 56 58 01 25
contact@chateau-poujeaux.com - **www.chateau-poujeaux.com**

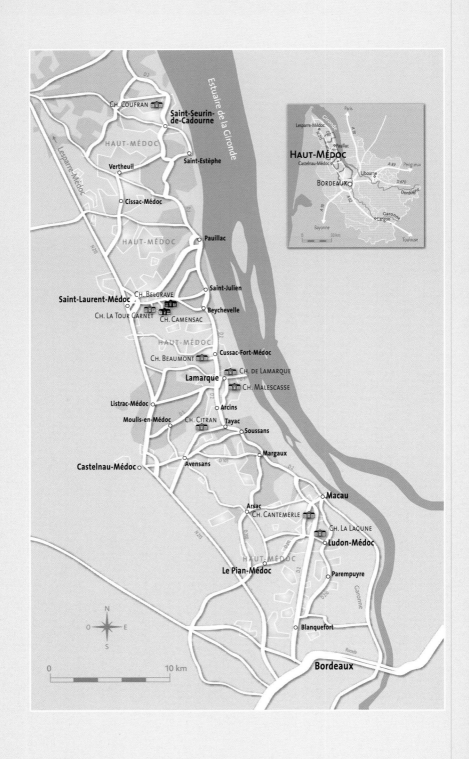

CRUS DE HAUT-MÉDOC

The Haut-Médoc stretches northwest of Bordeaux, from a stream called the Jalle de Blanquefort to the commune of Saint-Seurin-de-Cadourne. These boundaries had been defined for many years, and wines from this region have a long-established reputation. The part of the Médoc located closest to the city of Bordeaux, its vast *terroir* has produced fine wine since the 17th century. The owners of large estates made the most of their privileged location close to the port of Bordeaux and major transportation routes to export their wines all over the world. The northernmost vineyards were mostly created in the latter half of the 19th century.

p 94	Château Beaumont
p 95	Château Belgrave
p 96	Château Cantemerle
p 97	Château Citran
p 98	Château Coufran
p 99	Château de Camensac
p 100	Château de Lamarque
p 101	Château La Lagune
p 102	Château La Tour Carnet
p 103	Château Malescasse

CHÂTEAU BEAUMONT

| HAUT-MÉDOC | Owner: Grands Millésimes de France |

Winegrowing at Château Beaumont dates back to 1824. The present château, a pure jewel of Mansart-style architecture, was built in 1854. Its exotic history includes an unusual collection of characters: a Breton aristocrat, a Honduran minster, a Parisian industrialist, a lieutenant-colonel from Caracas, a Venezuelan senator, etc. – twelve different owners who ensured that Beaumont was enjoyed around the world.

Currently owned by Grands Millésimes de France, Château Beaumont produces an elegant, concentrated, well-balanced wine with beautiful colour, extreme finesse, an exquisite bouquet, and a silky texture.

Committed to sustainable viticulture for several years, Château Beaumont obtained certification to this effect from the Terra Vitis organization in 2004 after conforming to a set of stringent specifications.

Area under vine	114 hectares
Production	480,000 bottles
Soil	A rise consisting of Günz gravel and sand
Grape varieties	54% Cabernet Sauvignon, 42% Merlot, 4% Petit Verdot
Barrel ageing	14 months - New barrels: 30%
Second wine	Château d'Arvigny

President: Aymar de Baillenx - Director: Étienne Priou - Manager: Philippe Blanc

Château Beaumont 33460 Cussac-Fort-Médoc
GPS: Latitude: 45.108643 - Longitude: -0.73088
Tel. +33 (0)5 56 58 92 29 - Fax +33 (0)5 56 58 90 94
beaumont@chateau-beaumont.com - **www.chateau-beaumont.com**

CHÂTEAU BELGRAVE
CRU CLASSÉ EN 1855

HAUT-MÉDOC

Included as a 5th growth in the 1855 classification thanks to the quality of its deep gravel soil, Château Belgrave has been managed by the *négociant* firm of Dourthe since 1979. An attractive 18th century hunting lodge surrounded by sixty hectares of vines in a single block, Belgrave is located in the commune of Saint-Laurent, separated from the Saint-Julien appellation only by a small stream.

A great deal of work, passion, and energy have gone into producing wines worthy of one of the finest *terroirs* in the Médoc. The vineyard has been entirely renovated and is looked after with great care and attention.

Benefiting from experience acquired by Dourthe at their various estates, the ripe, healthy grapes are fermented in a vat room featuring the latest technological advances.

The ageing cellar was also refurbished in 2007 in an unabashedly mordern style epitomising the rebirth of the estate. Thanks to this in-depth modernisation and expert care, Château Belgrave is now among the elite of Médoc great growths.

Area under vine	59 hectares
Production	250,000 bottles
Soil	Three deep gravelly rises with a clay subsoil
Grape varieties	46% Merlot, 46% Cabernet Sauvignon, 4% Cabernet franc, 4% Petit Verdot
Barrel ageing	12-15 months - New barrels: 35-45%
Second wine	Diane de Belgrave

Estate Manager: Patrick Jestin - Administrative Manager: Frédéric Bonnaffous

Château Belgrave 33112 Saint-Laurent Médoc
GPS: Latitude: 45.151545 - Longitude: -0.780239
Tel. +33 (0)5 56 35 53 00   - Fax +33 (0)5 56 35 53 29
contact@dourthe.com - **www.dourthe.com**

CHÂTEAU CANTEMERLE
CRU CLASSÉ EN 1855

Owner: Groupe SMABTP

Located in the communes of Macau and Ludon, Château Cantemerle, designated a great growth in the famous 1855 classification, has deep fine gravel soil. Thanks to its unique *terroir*, Cantemerle produces complex, well-balanced, and refined wines.

After belonging to the Villeneuve (1576-1892) and Dubos (1892-1980) families, the château was acquired in 1981 by the SMABTP, a large mutual insurance company in the construction and civil engineering sector. The estate's long history is reflected in the château's distinctive architecture and the magnificent grounds that surround it. Cantemerle exudes romantic charm and the vineyard has a magical feel to it.

Attractive even when quite young, the wine is rich, powerful, and smooth. It is made by an experienced and enthusiastic team using a careful blend of traditional and state-of-the-art techniques.

Area under vine	90 hectares
Production	400,000 bottles
Soil	Siliceous and deep gravel from the Quaternary Period
Grape varieties	60% Cabernet Sauvignon, 30% Merlot, 6% Cabernet franc, 4% Petit Verdot
Barrel ageing	12-14 months - New barrels: 40%
Second wine	Allées de Cantemerle

Managing Director: Philippe Dambrine

Château Cantemerle 33460 Macau
GPS: Latitude: 44,9931576 - Longitude: -0.6241741
Tel. +33 (0)5 57 97 02 82 - Fax +33 (0)5 57 97 02 84
cantemerle@cantemerle.com - **www.cantemerle.com**

CHÂTEAU CITRAN

HAUT-MÉDOC

Owner: S.A. Château Citran

Included in the 1932 classification of crus bourgeois, Château Citran is one of the oldest winegrowing estates in the Médoc. It is mentioned in records dating as far back as 1235, at which time it belonged to the Marquis de Donissan. His descendants owned the estate for six centuries but, as time went on, there were only a few remaining vines growing on small, scattered plots. Fortunately, Monsieur Clauzel restructured the vineyard in the 19th century.

Both the Miailhe brothers and their successors, the Cesselin family, were responsible for the estate's impressive development. After nine years of Japanese ownership, Citran became French once again in 1996 when it was acquired by the Merlaut family, well known for their expertise and passion for making fine wine.

Citran now reflects the full potential of its *terroir*. Its hundred hectares of beautiful gravel soil and excellent winemaking facilities make Citran worthy of holding its head high among the great growths and finest wines of Bordeaux.

Area under vine	100 hectares
Production	450,000 bottles
Soil	Gravel and sand on asteriated limestone and clay-limestone soil
Grape varieties	50% Merlot, 48.5% Cabernet Sauvignon, 1.5% Cabernet franc
Barrel ageing	15-18 months - New barrels: 30%
Second wine	Moulins de Citran

Chief Executive Officer: Antoine Merlaut

Château Citran Chemin de Citran - 33480 Avensan
GPS: Latitude: 45.0491048 - Longitude: -0.7489337
Tel. +33 (0)5 56 58 21 01   - Fax +33 (0)5 57 88 84 60
info@citran.com - **www.citran.com**

CHÂTEAU COUFRAN

Owner: the Miailhe family

Château Coufran was acquired in 1924 by Louis Miailhe, the grandfather of the present owners. The Miailhe family were well-known wine brokers at the time, with experience in the profession going back to 1793. As time went on, they came to own a number of well-known Médoc wine châteaux. Jean Miailhe's children, Marie-Cécile Vicaire and Éric Miailhe, now manage the family estates: Château Coufran and Château Verdignan.

Often called the "Pomerol of the Médoc" because it is made nearly entirely from Merlot, Château Coufran has a fine location overlooking the Gironde estuary, with a mild microclimate and fine sun exposure.

This large estate produces in excess of 400,000 bottles of generous, concentrated wine that ages very well. Furthermore, Château Coufran specialises in selling wines that are ready to drink. Modern storage facilities house large quantities of wines from the previous ten years. This makes it possible to appreciate mature wines with an excellent quality/price ratio, and whose provenance one can be assured of.

Area under vine	76 hectares
Production	420,000 bottles
Soil	Garonne gravel
Grape varieties	85% Merlot, 15% Cabernet Sauvignon
Barrel ageing	12-18 months - New barrels: 25%
Second wine	N°2 de Coufran

Château Coufran 33180 Saint-Seurin-de-Cadourne
GPS: Latitude: 45.302437 - Longitude: -0.788913
Tel. Château +33 (0)5 56 59 31 02 - Office +33 (0)5 56 44 90 84 - Fax +33 (0)5 56 81 32 35
contact@chateau-coufran.com - **www.chateau-coufran.com**

CHÂTEAU DE CAMENSAC
CRU CLASSÉ EN 1855

Owners: Jean Merlaut and Céline Villars-Foubet

Château de Camensac is located on the perimeter of the Médoc's great growths, bordering on the Saint-Julien appellation. The 75-hectare vineyard consists of Cabernet Sauvignon and Merlot vines on slopes with deep gravel soil over a mix of clay and hardpan.

It is a very old estate that was cited on Belleyme's famous 18th century map. Camensac means "on the water's way", and comes from the words *camens*, which means "path" or "way" and *ac*, which means "water" in local dialect. In the 17th century, monks dug ditches along the bottom of the gravelly rises. These contributed to the quality of the *terroir* by draining off excess rainwater.

The Merlaut family acquired Camensac in time for the 2005 vintage. Céline Villars and Jean Merlaut are now in charge of the estate. The niece and uncle are also the respective owners of Chasse-Spleen and Gruaud-Larose. Éric Boissenot is the consulting oenologist. Cabernet Sauvignon now plays a greater role at Camensac. This variety is ideally suited to the deep gravel soil, producing wines with depth, fruit, elegance, and minerality. The old Merlot vines are totally complementary, yielding wines that add volume and body to the final blend.

Area under vine	75 hectares
Production	260-270,000 bottles
Soil	Deep, fine gravel on a clay-limestone substratum
Grape varieties	60% Cabernet Sauvignon, 40% Merlot
Barrel ageing	15-18 months - New barrels: 40%
Second wine	La Closerie de Camensac

Executive Board: Jean Merlaut - Jean-Pierre Foubet - Céline Villars-Foubet

Château de Camensac Route de Saint-Julien - 33112 Saint-Laurent-Médoc
GPS: Latitude:45.1466044 - Longitude: -0.7862808
Tel. +33 (0)5 56 59 41 69 - Fax +33 (0)5 56 59 41 73
chateaucamensac@wanadoo.fr - **www.chateaucamensac.com**

CHÂTEAU DE LAMARQUE

Owner: S.C. Gromand d'Evry

The seigneury of Lamarque takes its name from *la marche* (meaning "the marches", reflecting its location on the border of the province of Guyenne). The fortified château was built to defend the Médoc against Vikings invading from the Gironde estuary and was also subject to fierce assaults by the English during the Hundred Years' War.

Thalésie de Lamarque, who owned the château in 1247, was a very charming, happy person who left her mark on the castle and its surrounding vineyard. In fact, her presence is part of the vineyard's soul and can still be felt on evenings when a strong wind blows over the castle battlements.

Her spirit continues to accompany the talented men and women who take care of this superb *terroir*, giving the wines of Lamarque their brilliance, freshness, sensuality, and long aftertaste.

763 years later, another Thalésie - Thalésie d'Everlange - the granddaughter of Marie-Hélène and Pierre-Gilles Gromand-Brunet d'Evry, embodies the same virtues as her distinguished 13th century predecessor.

Area under vine	35 hectares
Production	160,000 bottles
Soil	85% Garonne gravel, 5% clay-limestone soil, 10% other
Grape varieties	45% Cabernet Sauvignon, 40% Merlot, 10% Cabernet franc, 5% Petit Verdot
Barrel ageing	18 months - New barrels: 35-40%
Second wine	✎ de Lamarque

Directors: Pierre-Gilles Gromand-Brunet d'Evry - Marie-Hélène Gromand-Brunet d'Evry

Château de Lamarque rue Principale - 33460 Lamarque
GPS: Latitude: 45.096074 - Longitude: -0.717636
Tel. +33 (0)5 56 58 90 03 - Fax +33 (0)5 56 58 93 43
lamarque@chateaudelamarque.fr - **www.chateaudelamarque.fr**

CHÂTEAU LA LAGUNE
CRU CLASSÉ EN 1855

Owner: the Frey family

Château La Lagune is located on a terrace of alluvial gravel parallel to the *palus* (rich soil that is productive, but not for quality wine) bordering the river. The "Village de La Lagune" was built here in 1525. Circa 1587, a certain Monsieur Eyral built a tenant farm in its place and gradually invested in transforming several modest leaseholds into a major winegrowing estate.

He was succeeded by numerous owners and the lovely château we know today was built between 1730 and 1734. In 1855, La Lagune joined the select club of *grands crus classés* as a third growth. The Sèze family acquired La Lagune in 1886 and it stayed with them until 1956. They sold to Georges Brunet, who gave an important new impetus to the estate before in turn selling it to the family who owned Champagne Ayala in 1964.

The Frey family arrived in 2000. They have made large-scale investments in the vineyard, cellars, and château aiming for excellence at all levels.

Area under vine	82 hectares
Production	150,000 bottles
Soil	Gravel
Grape varieties	60% Cabernet Sauvignon, 30% Merlot, 10% Petit Verdot
Barrel ageing	18 months - New barrels: 50%
Second wine	Moulin de La Lagune

Manager and oenologist: Caroline Frey

Château La Lagune 33290 Ludon-Médoc
GPS: Latitude: 44.9774613 - Longitude: -0.6182981
Tel. +33 (0)5 57 88 82 77 - Fax +33 (0)5 57 88 82 70
contact@chateau-lalagune.com - www.chateau-lalagune.com

CHÂTEAU LA TOUR CARNET

CRU CLASSÉ EN 1855

HAUT-MÉDOC　　　　　　　　*Owner: Bernard Magrez*

Dating from the 12th century, La Tour Carnet is a genuine medieval castle with a moat. The oldest château in the Médoc, it owes its name to the equerry Carnet, who fought valiantly beside Lord Jean de Foy. Carnet's courage and devotion were such that he ended up inheriting the estate. Éléonore, the sister of Michel de Montaigne, was one of several illustrious owners during the 16th century.

The current owner, Bernard Magrez, has expended an enormous amount of time and energy in renovating the estate. His efforts have concerned the vineyard, the cellars, and the château.

Care is taken during pruning, leaf thinning, and green harvesting to reduce yields in the interest of quality. The grapes are hand picked into small crates and sorted by hand before being transferred by gravity flow into wooden fermentation vats and then into barrel. These are just a few of the practices that contribute to the excellence of this estate that was included in the prestigious 1855 classification.

102

Area under vine	75 hectares
Production	250,000 bottles
Soil	Slopes facing south by southwest with gravel from the Günz glaciation period on a clay and limestone platform
Grape varieties	51% Merlot, 40% Cabernet Sauvignon, 6% Cabernet franc, 3% Petit Verdot
Barrel ageing	18 months - New barrels: 60%
Second wine	Cuvées les Douves Château La Tour Carnet

Technical Director: Frédéric Chabaneau

Château La Tour Carnet Route de Beychevelle - 33112 Saint-Laurent-Médoc
GPS: Latitude: 45.1472778 - Longitude: -0,7937662
Tel. +33 (0)5 56 73 30 90 - Fax +33 (0)5 56 59 48 54
latour@latour-carnet.com - **www.bernard-magrez.com**

CHÂTEAU MALESCASSE

Owner: S.A.S. Château Malescasse

Malescasse has had an important part to play on the Médoc wine scene since the estate was created, in 1824. The château has eight windows with eight panes whose perfect balance is maintained by frames in eight parts. Each window affords a view of the beautiful, perfectly proportioned garden. Everything at Malescasse emanates a feeling of peace and harmony with its surroundings.

The vines grow on one of the most beautiful gravelly rises between Margaux and Saint-Julien. Thanks to this deep, well-drained soil, the vineyard is able to produce delicious, subtle wines. Furthermore, the temperate microclimate is softened by its proximity to the Gironde estuary. A well-equipped cellar and experienced winemaking team take full advantage of these natural blessings.

From the very first, Château Malescasse has always fit in seamlessly with its natural setting – a must in order to produce great wine.

Area under vine	40 hectares
Production	200,000 bottles
Soil	Siliceous with Garonne gravel on a limestone substratum
Grape varieties	45% Cabernet Sauvignon, 45% Merlot, 6% Cabernet franc, 4% Petit Verdot
Barrel ageing	14 months - New barrels: 25%
Second wine	La Closerie de Malescasse

Cellar Master: Bertrand Chemin - Vineyard Manager: Antonio Flores

Château Malescasse 6 chemin du Moulin Rose - 33460 Lamarque
GPS: Latitude: 45.0885168 - Longitude: -0.1763979
Tel. +33 (0)5 56 58 90 09 - Fax +33 (0)5 56 58 97 89
chateaumalescasse@wanadoo.fr - **www.chateau-malescasse.com**

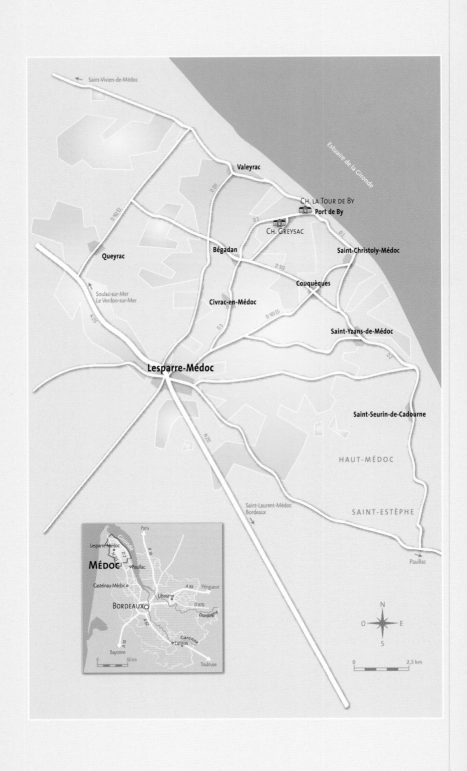

CRUS DE MÉDOC

The Médoc is a huge triangular peninsula starting northwest of the city of Bordeaux, at a stream called the Jalle de Blanquefort, and going as far north as the Pointe de Grave. It is bordered by the Atlantic Ocean on the west and the Gironde estuary on the east. Located off the northern tip of this peninsula, Cordouan, "the King of Lighthouses", reflects the long history of the Bordeaux wine trade and the necessity for merchant ships to have safe access up and down the Gironde estuary.

Wine from the Médoc appellation comes mainly from vineyards located in the northern part of the peninsula, bordering the estuary, on a strip of land two to five km. wide, and 20 km. long, starting from Ordonnac in the south and going as far north as Vensac. The western boundary is limited at the drainage divide by a pine forest which serves as a natural windbreak against ocean gales.

| p 106 | Château Greysac |
| p 107 | Château La Tour de By |

Château Greysac

MÉDOC

Owner: Greysac S.A.S.

2008

MÉDOC

APPELLATION MÉDOC CONTRÔLÉE

It was love at first sight when a group of friends led by Baron François de Gunzburg visited Château Greysac in 1973. Supported by the IFINT group (presided by Giovanni Agnelli), they ended up buying the estate. Greysac has made remarkable progress since then, and was accepted as a member of the very select Union des Grands Crus de Bordeaux in 1982.

Produced from an outstanding *terroir* with one of the finest gravelly rises in the hamlet of By, Château Greysac is elegant, extremely well-structured, full-bodied, flavoursome, and voluptuous. The wine is carefully fermented the traditional way, and standards for the final blend are so rigorous that the *grand vin* rarely represents more than 70% of total production.

Château Greysac is marketed worldwide via a network of exclusive agents and sold via the traditional wine trade.

Area under vine	60 hectares
Production	400,000 bottles
Soil	Gravel and clay-limestone
Grape varieties	50% Merlot, 45% Cabernet Sauvignon, 3% Cabernet franc, 2% Petit Verdot
Barrel ageing	12 months - New barrels: 25%
Second wine	Château de By

Chief Executive Officer: Brandino Brandolini D'Adda - Managing Director: Philippe Dambrine
Manager: Stéphane Pariaud

Château Greysac 18 route de By - 33340 Bégadan
GPS: Latitude: 45.3736 - Longitude: -0.8650
Tel. +33(0)5 56 73 26 56 - Fax +33(0)5 56 73 26 58
info@greysac.com - **www.greysac.com**

CHÂTEAU LA TOUR DE BY

MÉDOC   *Owner: the Marc Pagès family*

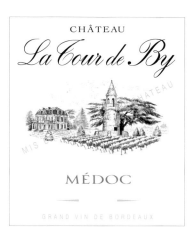

Vines have been grown at La Tour de By since the 16th century, and records show that the château was acquired by Pierre Tizon, lord of the fiefdom of By, in 1599. The *tour*, or tower, symbolising the estate is a former lighthouse built in the middle of the vines in 1825 to guide sailors navigating the Gironde estuary on foggy nights.

Marc Pagès, an agricultural engineer from Tunisia, purchased this beautiful estate in the northern Médoc in 1965 and was responsible for its rebirth. He was assisted by advice from Professor Émile Peynaud, who contributed enormously to making the most of the remarkable *terroir*.

A tank commander in General Leclerc's 2nd armoured division that liberated Strasbourg, Marc Pagès unquestionably brought this Médoc estate up to its full potential in the four decades during which he managed it.

His grandson, Frédéric Le Clerc, is now in charge of La Tour de By, which he runs according to a philosophy combining quality, precision winemaking, and respect for tradition.

Area under vine	94 hectares
Production	480,000 bottles
Soil	Gravel with iron hardpan subsoil
Grape varieties	60% Cabernet Sauvignon, 35% Merlot, 5% Petit Verdot
Barrel ageing	12 months - New barrels: 30%
Second wine	La Roque de By

Owner-Manager: Frédéric Le Clerc - Owner-Commercial Director: Benjamin Richer de Forges

Château La Tour de By 5 rue de la Tour de By - 33340 Bégadan
GPS: Latitude: 45.3770901 - Longitude: -0.8511275
Tel. +33 (0)5 56 41 50 03   - Fax +33 (0)5 56 41 36 10
info@la-tour-de-by.com - **www.la-tour-de-by.com**

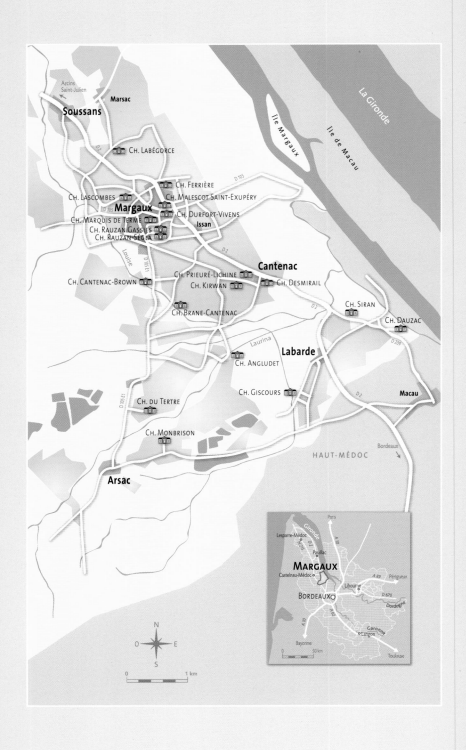

Arcins
Saint-Julien

Marsac

Soussans

Ch. Labégorce

Ch. Ferrière
Ch. Lascombes
Ch. Malescot Saint-Exupéry
Margaux
Ch. Marquis de Terme
Ch. Durfort-Vivens
Ch. Rauzan Gassies
Issan
Ch. Rauzan-Ségla

La Gironde
Île Margaux
Île de Macau

Cantenac
Ch. Prieuré-Lichine
Ch. Cantenac-Brown
Ch. Desmirail
Ch. Kirwan

Ch. Brane-Cantenac

Ch. Siran

Ch. Dauzac

Laurina
Labarde
Ch. Angludet

Ch. du Tertre
Ch. Giscours
Macau

Ch. Monbrison
Bordeaux

HAUT-MÉDOC

Arsac

N
O   E
S

0   1 km

Paris
Lesparre-Médoc
Gironde
Pauillac
MARGAUX
Castelnau-Médoc
Libourne
Périgueux
Dordogne
BORDEAUX
Garonne
Bayonne
Langon
Toulouse

0   50 km

CRUS DE MARGAUX

The name Margaux is magical and reflects a history of winemaking going back a thousand years. As with most vineyard areas close to the city of Bordeaux, wine production began during the Gallo-Roman period.

Records from the early 18th century refer to numerous winegrowing estates. While the château whose name is eponymous with the appellation already had a long history of selling their wines, it was only in the late 18th century that other vineyard owners became aware of the value of their land and introduced the production and ageing methods that gave rise to the grands crus of Margaux.

It took more than a century after the famous classification of 1855 for this large, complex region to put conflicts between communes behind it and for the rigorously delimited Margaux appellation to be recognized.

p 110	Château Angludet
p 111	Château Brane-Cantenac
p 112	Château Cantenac-Brown
p 113	Château Dauzac
p 114	Château Desmirail
p 115	Château du Tertre
p 116	Château Durfort-Vivens
p 117	Château Ferrière
p 118	Château Giscours
p 119	Château Kirwan
p 120	Château Labégorce
p 121	Château Lascombes
p 122	Château Malescot Saint-Exupéry
p 123	Château Marquis de Terme
p 124	Château Monbrison
p 125	Château Prieuré-Lichine
p 126	Château Rauzan-Gassies
p 127	Château Rauzan-Ségla
p 128	Château Siran

CHÂTEAU ANGLUDET

Château Angludet belongs to the Sichel family, Bordeaux wine merchants for six generations. It is one of the oldest estates in the Médoc. Records going back to the year 1150 mention a "noble residence" in Angludet, a name which means "Angle of High Land". The first lord of the manor, referred to in a deed dated 1273, was the knight Bertrand d'Angludet. The vineyard has had practically the same configuration since 1758 – thus for over 250 years – which is exceedingly rare.

Diana and Peter Sichel fell in love with Angludet and acquired it 1961. They undertook a major renovation and Peter Sichel made constant improvements during the 40 years he was in charge. It is now one of the finest wines in Margaux. After Peter Sichel's death in 1998, his wife, Diana, and their six children have continued his efforts to make the best possible wine.

Since 1989, Benjamin Sichel manages the estate and oversees all aspects of viticulture and winemaking. He is also attentive to using natural, sustainable practices in the vineyard.

110

Area under vine	32 hectares
Production	100,000 bottles
Soil	Graves dating from the first Mindel glacial period
Grape varieties	55% Cabernet Sauvignon, 35% Merlot, 10% Petit Verdot
Barrel ageing	12 months - New barrels: 30%
Second wine	Moulin d'Angludet

Manager: Benjamin Sichel - Financial and Commercial Director: Allan Sichel

Château Angludet 33460 Cantenac
GPS: Latitude: 45.014946 - Longitude: -0.66168
Tel. +33 (0)5 57 88 71 41 - Fax. +33 (0)5 57 88 72 52
contact@chateau-angludet.fr - **www.chateau-angludet.fr**

CHÂTEAU BRANE-CANTENAC
CRU CLASSÉ EN 1855

MARGAUX

Owner: Henri Lurton

Founded in the 18th century (when it was known as "Gorce") and considered one of the best second growths at the time of 1855 Médoc classification, this estate is located on one of the finest gravelly hillocks in Cantenac. Indeed, Brane-Cantenac was often sold at first growth prices!

The estate was acquired in 1833 by Baron de Brane, known as "Napoleon of the Vines," who renamed it Brane-Cantenac. In 1925, Léonce Récapet, owner of Château Margaux, purchased the property. His grandson, Lucien Lurton, took over the reins in 1956. In 1992, Lucien's son Henri, oenologist and ampelographer, followed in his father's footsteps after having gained experience in South Africa and Chile.

From the moment he arrived, Henri Lurton has done his utmost to make this great Margaux reflect the brilliance and complexity of its outstanding *terroir* year in and year out, always seeking a balance between vintage character and the wine's intrinsic elegance. Brane-Cantenac now has a state-of-the-art cellar with sophisticated equipment such as a new optical sorting system, and its owner is totally dedicated to producing the best possible wines!

Area under vine	75 hectares
Production	150,000 bottles
Soil	Deep gravel from the Quaternary Period
Grape varieties	55% Cabernet Sauvignon, 40% Merlot, 4.5% Cabernet franc, 0.5% Carmenère
Barrel ageing	18 months - New barrels: 60-70%
Second wine	Baron de Brane

Estate Manager: Christophe Capdeville - Vineyard Manager: Charles de Ravinel
Marketing and Communication Manager: Corinne Conroy

Château Brane-Cantenac 33460 Cantenac
GPS: Latitude: 45.024008 - Longitude: -0.674243
Tel. +33 (0)5 57 88 83 33   - Fax +33 (0)5 57 88 72 51
contact@brane-cantenac.com - **www.brane-cantenac.com**

CHÂTEAU CANTENAC-BROWN

CRU CLASSÉ EN 1855

MARGAUX

Owner: the Simon Halabi family

John Lewis Brown, an animal painter of Scottish descent, purchased the vineyard in the early 19th century and commissioned the construction of a Tudor-style château. A *bon vivant*, he soon acquired a reputation for hospitality thanks to the brilliant celebrations he hosted at his château. He sold the estate in 1843 to a banker named Gromard who was the owner in 1855 when Château Cantenac-Brown was granted a grand cru classification.

One hundred fifty years later, the Simon Halabi family have given a new impetus to the estate, which they are determined to raise to the very highest level. Winegrowing methods have been changed accordingly.

Work in the vineyard has become much more respectful of the environment and yields are kept quite low. A return to more natural practices at Cantenac Brown includes ploughing to enhance the vineyard's intrinsic physical, chemical, and biological properties.

112

Area under vine	48 hectares
Production	130,000 bottles
Soil	Gravel
Grape varieties	65% Cabernet Sauvignon, 30% Merlot, 5% Cabernet franc
Barrel ageing	15 months - New barrels: 50%
Second wine	Brio de Cantenac Brown

Managing Director/Winemaker: José Sanfins

Château Cantenac Brown 33460 Cantenac
GPS: Latitude: 45.0208177 - Longitude: -0.6793229
Tel. +33 (0)5 57 88 81 81 - Fax +33 (0)5 57 88 81 90
contact@cantenacbrown.com - **www.cantenacbrown.com**

CHÂTEAU DAUZAC
CRU CLASSÉ EN 1855

MARGAUX

Owner: M.A.I.F.

Château Dauzac has 42 hectares of vines in a single block on deep gravel soil. Thomas Michel Lynch acquired Dauzac in 1740 and is responsible for establishing the reputation of this beautiful, large estate included in the 1855 classification. In 1885, Ernest David, manager of both Dauzac and Ducru Beaucaillou, perfected Bordeaux mixture (copper sulphate and hydrated lime) here in conjunction with Professor Alexis Millardet in order to fight mildew and other fungi.

The M.A.I.F. purchased this fine estate in 1988 and handed over management to André Lurton, who became President of the Executive Board in 1992. His daughter, Christine Lurton de Caix took over from him in 2005. The cellars were totally renovated in 2004 and now feature state-of-the-art winemaking equipment. The grapes are hand picked into small crates and sorted twice (before and after destemming). The wine is aged in new barrels.

Area under vine	42 hectares
Production	120,000 bottles
Soil	Deep gravel
Grape varieties	60% Cabernet Sauvignon, 40% Merlot
Barrel ageing	16-18 months - New barrels: 60-70%
Second wine	Labastide Dauzac

President of the Executive Board: Christine Lurton-de-Caix

Château Dauzac 1 avenue Johnston - 33460 Labarde
GPS: Latitude: 45.0188395 - Longitude: -0.624448
Tel. +33 (0)5 57 88 32 10 - Fax +33 (0)5 57 88 96 00
chateaudauzac@chateaudauzac.com - **www.chateaudauzac.com**

113

CHÂTEAU DESMIRAIL
CRU CLASSÉ EN 1855

MARGAUX

Owner: Denis Lurton

GRAND CRU CLASSÉ

CHÂTEAU
DESMIRAIL
MARGAUX

2008

DENIS LURTON

Château Desmirail, included among the third growths in the 1855 classification, has an outstanding *terroir* bordering on the Route des Châteaux. The elegant 18th century manor house is located behind a majestic gate made of pink marble. The cellar features a vat room typical of those from the late 19th century Médoc.

Visitors can admire the magnificent roof structure and new wooden vats first used for the 2010 vintage.

Jean Desmirail gave his name to the château after marrying an heiress from the Rausan family in the late 17th century.

The current owner and manager, Denis Lurton, took over from his father, Lucien, in 1992. He has invested in modernising the estate on a regular basis ever since. Château Desmirail produces smooth, elegant wines in the classic Margaux style.

Area under vine	37 hectares
Production	100,000 bottles
Soil	Deep gravel from the Quaternary Period
Grape varieties	60% Cabernet Sauvignon, 37.5% Merlot, 2.5% Petit Verdot
Barrel ageing	14 months - New barrels: 40%
Second wine	Initial de Desmirail

Château Desmirail 28 avenue de la Vᵉ République - 33460 Cantenac
GPS: Latitude: 45.0286229 - Longitude: -0.6542153
Tel. +33 (0)5 57 88 34 33   - Fax +33 (0)5 57 88 96 27
contact@desmirail.com - **www.desmirail.com**

CHÂTEAU DU TERTRE
CRU CLASSÉ EN 1855

MARGAUX   *Owner: Éric Albada Jelgersma*

Located on one of the highest and most beautiful gravelly rises in the Margaux appellation, Château du Tertre has a very interesting history. It was created in the 18th century by an important Irish *négociant*, Pierre Mitchell, who had fallen in love with the Bordeaux region and its wines. The founder of the first glassworks in Bordeaux, this refined, innovative man realized one of his fondest dreams by establishing his own fine wine estate.

Other famous families followed in his footsteps: the de Brezets and Vallandés, as well as the Koenigswarters, rich bankers close to Emperor Napoleon III. The quality of the wine was such that it was included among the great growths of Margaux in the 1855 classification.

Éric Albada Jelgersma acquired the estate in 1997. Thanks to major investments and careful management, Château du Tertre now expresses its intrinsically elegant personality year after year.

Area under vine	52 hectares
Production	150,000 bottles
Soil	Günz gravel and sand
Grape varieties	43% Cabernet Sauvignon, 33% Merlot, 19% de Cabernet franc, 5% Petit Verdot
Barrel ageing	15-17 months - New barrels: 45%
Second wine	Les Hauts du Tertre

Managing Director: Alexander Van Beek - Technical Director: Frédéric Ardouin

Château du Tertre 33460 Arsac
GPS: Latitude: 45.02210 - Longitude: -0.405207
Tel. +33 (0)5 57 88 52 52 - Fax +33 (0)5 57 97 09 00
tertre@chateaudutertre.fr - **www.chateaudutertre.fr**

Château Durfort-Vivens

Cru Classé en 1855

MARGAUX

Owner: Gonzague Lurton

Founded in the 14th century by the Durfort de Duras family, the estate stayed in their hands until the 19th century. In 1824, Viscount de Vivens added his name to that of Durfort. Already a famous wine by the time Thomas Jefferson cited it in the late 18th century, the estate was included among the first of the second growths in the famous 1855 classification. Lucien Lurton acquired Durfort-Vivens in 1961. His son, Gonzague, presently manages the estate.

His excellent understanding of the *terroir* and ecologically-responsible winegrowing practices are conducive to growing perfectly ripe grapes that produce wines of character.

The environmentally-friendly facilities and techniques used at Durfort-Vivens result in the optimum expression of grapes from each separate plot. Furthermore, the different-size oak and cement fermentation vats are adapted to the yields of every plot. The wine is aged in cellars that have an ideal natural temperature and humidity.

A superb *terroir*, state-of-the-art technology, and respect for the environment make Château Durfort-Vivens a truly unique wine.

Area under vine	55 hectares
Production	150,000 bottles
Soil	Gravel from the Quaternary Period, with varying proportions of sand and clay
Grape varieties	70% Cabernet Sauvignon, 25% Merlot, 5% Cabernet franc
Barrel ageing	18-22 months - New barrels: 40-50%
Second wine	Vivens / Relais de Durfort-Vivens

Château Durfort-Vivens 33460 Margaux
GPS: Latitude: 45.0411142 - Longitude: -0.6761154
Tel. +33 (0)5 57 88 31 02 - Fax +33 (0)5 57 88 60 60
infos@durfort-vivens.com - **www.durfort-vivens.com**

CHÂTEAU FERRIÈRE
CRU CLASSÉ EN 1855

MARGAUX

Owner: Claire Villars Lurton

Gabriel Ferrière, a well-known broker in Bordeaux in the 18th century, was the founder of this estate. Château Ferrière was classified a third growth in 1855. The Villars family bought the vineyards and the château in 1988, and took over viticulture and winemaking.

With its 10 hectares, Château Ferrière is one of the smallest classified growths. The vineyard is mainly located in Margaux, and the soil consists of very deep gravel on limestone marl. The size of the vineyard, combined with its beautiful *terroir*, make Château Ferrière a rare and highly-valued wine.

Claire Villars Lurton is responsible for the revival of this estate. Year after year, she has done her best to bring out the unique terroir of Château Ferrière in the wine, to restore the vineyard to its original splendour, and to make it fully worth of its prestigious classification.

Area under vine	10 hectares
Production	40,000 bottles
Soil	Deep gravel
Grape varieties	70% Cabernet Sauvignon, 30% Merlot
Barrel ageing	18-20 months - New barrels: 40%
Second wine	Les Remparts de Ferrière

Production Manager: Gérard Fenouillet

Château Ferrière 33 bis rue de la Trémoille - 33460 Margaux
GPS: Latitude: 45.0427866 - Longitude: -0.6775218
Tel. +33 (0)5 57 88 76 65 - Fax +33 (0)5 57 88 98 33
chateau@ferriere.com - **www.ferriere.com**

CHÂTEAU GISCOURS
CRU CLASSÉ EN 1855

MARGAUX

The history of Château Giscours goes back to the 14th century, at which time an impressive keep protected the estate from potential attacks. However, the true creation of the estate can be considered to date from the purchase of the "maison noble de Guyscoutz" by Pierre de Lhomme, a rich cloth merchant, in 1552. This marked the beginning of Château Giscours' winegrowing tradition.

The estate underwent a golden age in the 19th century thanks to wealthy and influential owners such as the Promis, Pescatore, and Cruse families. This is also when Giscours underwent a number of important changes: the château was transformed into a neoclassic palace, the grounds were landscaped by Eugène Bülher, rare tree species were planted, and immense outbuildings were built, including the famous Ferme Suzanne...

In 1995, a Dutch businessman, Éric Albada Jelgersma, took over management and set about meticulously renovating the vineyard and buildings to make this prestigious estate fully worthy of its third growth ranking in the 1855 classification.

118

Area under vine	90 hectares
Production	280,000 bottles
Soil	Deep Garonne gravel
Grape varieties	60% Cabernet Sauvignon, 32% Merlot, 5% Cabernet franc, 3% Petit Verdot
Barrel ageing	15-17 months - New barrels: 50%
Second wine	La Sirène de Giscours

Chief Executive Officer: Éric Albada Jelgersma - Managing Director: Alexander Van Beek
Technical Director: Didier Forêt

Château Giscours 10 route de Giscours - 33460 Labarde
GPS: Latitude: 45.0084998 - Longitude: -0.6454524
Tel. +33 (0)5 57 97 09 09 - Fax +33 (0)5 57 97 09 00
giscours@chateau-giscours.fr - **www.chateau-giscours.fr**

CHÂTEAU KIRWAN
CRU CLASSÉ EN 1855

Kirwan is an infinitely charming estate. The late 18th century château was built by Mark Kirwan, a prosperous Irish businessman who combined two small adjoining vineyards in the village of Cantenac and gave his name to the new entity. He did much to enhance the wine's reputation, and the book "Thomas Jefferson on Wine" tells us that the third American president praised the wine greatly during a trip to Bordeaux in 1787, noting that "Château de Quirouen" was in the 2nd category, along with "Ségur", "Lynch", etc.

Château Kirwan was listed as the first of the third growths in 1855, when a classification of Médoc wines was made for the universal exhibition during the reign of Napoleon III. The Godard family acquired Kirwan in the latter half of the 19th century. They expanded the vineyards and designed beautiful grounds and gardens with a fish pond and rose arbour.

The Schÿler family purchased Kirwan in 1926. Originating from cities belonging to the Hanseatic League, the Schÿlers came to Bordeaux in 1739 to establish a wine business. They made major investments at Kirwan starting in the 1970s and are closely identified with this great wine. In 2007, Sophie, Nathalie and Yann Schÿler's expertise was complemented by the appointment of a new managing director, the experienced oenologist Philippe Delfaut.

Area under vine	37 hectares
Production	90,000 bottles
Soil	Pyrenean gravel on the Cantenac plateau and sand and gravel on the clay subsoil
Grape varieties	45% Cabernet Sauvignon, 30% Merlot, 15% Cabernet franc, 10% Petit Verdot
Barrel ageing	18-22 months - New barrels: 50%
Second wine	Charmes de Kirwan

Managing Director: Philippe Delfaut
Marketing and Communication: Sophie Schÿler-Thierry
Tourism and Special Events: Nathalie Schÿler

Château Kirwan 33460 Cantenac
GPS: Latitude: 45.0263838 - Longitude: -0.6571677
Tel. +33 (0)5 57 88 71 00 - Fax +33 (0)5 57 88 77 62
mail@chateau-kirwan.com - **www.chateau-kirwan.com**

CHÂTEAU LABÉGORCE

MARGAUX   *Owner: the Perrodo family, represented by Nathalie Perrodo Samani*

This elegant neoclassical château is located on the famous Route des Châteaux. Seventy hectares of the 250-hectare estate are devoted to viticulture. Bordering on châteaux Margaux and Lascombes, this property is mentioned in the 1868 edition of Cocks and Feret ("Bordeaux and its Wines"), which tells us of the existence of "a vineyard belonging to the Noble de la Bégorce family". The château is described as "... one of the most beautiful and best situated in the commune of Margaux".

The Perrodo family acquired Labégorce in 1989 and renovated not only the château building, but also the vineyard. They also improved winemaking, and Labégorce is now a charming wine with beautiful structure, bright fruit, and great finesse. The Perrodo family also acquired Château Marquis d'Alesme, a third growth Margaux, which they aim to transform into one of the jewels of the appellation.

Area under vine	70 hectares
Production	100-130,000 bottles
Soil	70% sand and gravel, 30% sand and silt
Grape varieties	50% Cabernet Sauvignon, 45% Merlot, 3% Cabernet franc, 2% Petit Verdot
Barrel ageing	14 months - New barrels: 40%
Second wine	Zédé de Labégorce

Managing Director: Marjolaine Maurice de Coninck - Commercial Director: Delphine Dariol Kolasa

Château Labégorce Lieu-dit Labégorce - 33460 Margaux
GPS: Latitude: 45.05198 - Longitude: -0,688148
Tel. +33 (0)5 57 88 71 32 - Fax +33 (0)5 57 88 35 01
mpoupard@chateau-marquis-dalesme.fr - **www.chateau-labegorce.fr**

CHÂTEAU LASCOMBES
CRU CLASSÉ EN 1855

With one hundred eighteen hectares of vines (including one hundred twelve in the Margaux appellation and six in the Haut-Médoc appellation) Château Lascombes is one of the largest estates in the Médoc. Included among the second growths in the 1855 classification, the estate has a prestigious history going back to Chevalier de Lascombes, born in 1625. The *terroir* consists of forty of the finest plots in the Margaux appellation. The wine is extremely well-known and much-appreciated on export markets.

The best traditional and modern techniques are used in the vineyard and cellar to produce powerful, concentrated, fruity, and elegant wine. The fact that the various plots are widely scattered gives Lascombes remarkable complexity, balance, and ageing potential.

Colony Capital acquired the estate in April 2001 and a new era began under the management of Dominique Befve. Since then, the cellars and vineyard have been entirely restructured in order to produce wine worthy of Lascombes' classification and appellation.

Area under vine	118 hectares
Production	300,000 bottles
Soil	Clay-limestone, clay-gravel, and gravel
Grape varieties	50% Merlot, 47% Cabernet Sauvignon, 2% Petit Verdot, 1% Cabernet franc
Barrel ageing	18 months - New barrels: 80-100%
Second wine	Chevalier de Lascombes

Managing Director: Dominique Befve

Château Lascombes 1 cours de Verdun - BP 4 - 33460 Margaux
GPS: Latitude: 45.0402218 - Longitude: -0.6836185
Tel. +33 (0)5 57 88 70 66 - Fax +33 (0)5 57 88 72 17
visite.lascombes@chateau-lascombes.fr - **www.chateau-lascombes.com**

CHÂTEAU MALESCOT ST-EXUPÉRY

CRU CLASSÉ EN 1855

MARGAUX   *Owner: Jean-Luc Zuger*

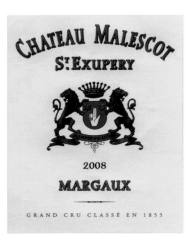

Château Malescot St-Exupéry owes its name to two former owners: Simon Malescot, a royal councillor to the Bordeaux parliament, who acquired the estate in 1697, and Count Jean-Baptiste de Saint-Exupéry, who owned it from 1827 to 1853.

Paul Zuger and his son, Roger, purchased the château, located in the middle of the town of Margaux, in June 1955. After more than thirty years of unstinting efforts, Malescot St-Exupéry's coat of arms has never been truer: *Semper Ad Altum* ("Ever Higher"). The 45-hectare estate has 23.5 hectares of vines on a fine terroir that "overlooks the river" – indicative of the best vineyard sites according to an old local saying.

Connoisseurs very much appreciate the outstanding bouquet of this great growth, whose fruitiness and body go together beautifully with meat dishes and cheeses.

122

Area under vine	28 hectares
Production	120,000 bottles
Soil	Pyrenean gravel
Grape varieties	50% Cabernet Sauvignon, 35% Merlot, 10% Cabernet franc, 5% Petit Verdot
Barrel ageing	12-14 months - New barrels: 100%
Second wine	Dame de Malescot

Château Malescot St-Exupéry 33460 Margaux
GPS: Latitude: 45.0411142 - Longitude: -0.6761154
Tel. +33 (0)5 57 88 97 20 - Fax +33 (0)5 57 88 97 21
jeanluczuger@malescot.com - **www.malescot.com**

CHÂTEAU MARQUIS DE TERME
CRU CLASSÉ EN 1855

MARGAUX   *Owners: Pierre-Louis and Philippe Sénéclauze*

GRAND VIN DE BORDEAUX

CHATEAU
MARQUIS DE TERME

2009

MARGAUX

GRAND CRU CLASSÉ EN 1855

In December 1762, Élisabeth de Ledoux d'Emplet, great niece of Pierre des Mesures de Rauzan, married a Gascon gentleman, François de Péguilhan de Larboust, otherwise known as Marquis de Terme, who gave his name to an estate consisting of several vineyard plots that were part of his wife's dowry.

The property went through rough times in the 19th century and had several owners. It was acquired in 1935 by Pierre Sénéclauze, father of the present owners.

The vineyard is located on gravelly rises in the communes of Margaux and Cantenac. Plot-by-plot management is not only conducive to quality, but also ecologically-friendly.

The grapes are entirely picked by hand, sorted in the vineyard and a second time – even more meticulously – in the cellar after destemming before being transferred into vat.

Château Marquis de Terme is aged in oak barrels from the finest French forests. Once bottled, it ages well for many years.

Area under vine	39 hectares
Production	130,000 bottles
Soil	Gravel typical of the Margaux appellation, with quartz and quartzite. Greater concentration of clay in the subsoil
Grape varieties	60% Cabernet Sauvignon, 35% Merlot, 5% Petit Verdot
Barrel ageing	16 months - New barrels: 50%
Second wine	La couronne de Marquis de Terme

Managing Director: Ludovic David

Château Marquis de Terme 3 route de Rauzan - BP 11 - 33460 Margaux
GPS: Latitude: 45.0364854 - Longitude: -0.6767923
Tel. +33 (0)5 57 88 30 01 - Fax +33 (0)5 57 88 32 51
mdt@chateau-marquis-de-terme.com - **www.chateau-marquis-de-terme.com**

CHÂTEAU MONBRISON

MARGAUX

Owner: Laurent Vonderheyden

Château Monbrison has a very long history. It was created when half of Château Desmirail, a third growth Margaux, was added to an existing vineyard as the result of an inheritance. The estate came into the hands of the eponymous Monsieur de Monbrison and was then acquired by Monsieur Chaix d'Est-Ange, a famous lawyer and President of the French Senate, who transformed it into a model vineyard.

Château Monbrison once again changed hands in 1887 when it was purchased by the *négociant* Jean Clanis. His family in turn sold Monbrison to Robert Meacham Davis in 1922, and the estate has since been managed by his children and grandchildren.

Laurent Vonderheyden has been in charge for the past twenty years, transforming Château Monbrison into one of the leading wines in its appellation. Well-received by critics, Monbrison has received prestigious medals and distinctions in France and abroad. The quality of its enchanting bouquet is equalled only by the elegance it displays on the palate. Incredibly refined, Monbrison brilliantly reflects its superb *terroir* and is the epitome of a great Margaux.

124

Area under vine	18.41 hectares
Production	50,000 bottles
Soil	Pyrenean gravel
Grape varieties	64% Cabernet Sauvignon, 21% Merlot, 12% Cabernet franc, 3% Petit Verdot
Barrel ageing	12-18 months - New barrels: 40%
Second wine	Bouquet de Monbrison

Château Monbrison 1 allée de Monbrison - 33460 Arsac
GPS: Latitude: 45.0004058 - Longitude: -0.6762237
Tel. +33 (0)5 56 58 80 04 - Fax +33 (0)5 56 58 85 33
lvdh33@wanadoo.fr - **www.chateaumonbrison.com**

CHÂTEAU PRIEURÉ-LICHINE
CRU CLASSÉ EN 1855

Owner: Groupe Ballande

2008

MARGAUX
APPELLATION MARGAUX CONTRÔLÉE

MIS EN BOUTEILLE AU CHÂTEAU

Founded in the 12th century by monks from Vertheuil Abbey, the *prieuré* (or "priory") of Cantenac produced well-reputed wines from the very beginning. The vineyard belonged to the Church until the French Revolution.

In 1951, Alexis Lichine, called "the Pope of Wine", took over the estate and added his name two years later. Thanks to his patient determination, he was able to add new vineyard plots, modernize the cellars, and renovate the monks' former living quarters. Château Prieuré-Lichine's fate was linked to that of the Lichine family for nearly half a century.

Now owned by the Ballande group, the château has entered a dynamic new phase of its history and is resolutely turned towards the future.

A new approach to managing far-flung vineyard plots has turned this diversity into a decided advantage, enabling Prieuré-Lichine to express the full complexity of its *terroir* thanks to an experienced and devoted winemaking team.

Area under vine	70 hectares
Production	180,000 bottles
Soil	Pyrenean gravel and gravel from the Günz glaciation period
Grape varieties	55% Cabernet Sauvignon, 40% Merlot, 5% Petit Verdot
Barrel ageing	18 months - New barrels: 50%
Second wine	Confidences de Prieuré-Lichine

Managing Director: Justin Onclin - Sales and Communication: Lise Latrille
Technical Manager: Étienne Charrier

Château Prieuré-Lichine 34 avenue de la Ve République - 33460 Cantenac
GPS: Latitude: 45.0286229 - Longitude: -0.6542153
Tel. +33 (0)5 57 88 36 28 - Fax +33 (0)5 57 88 78 93
contact@prieure-lichine.fr - **www.prieure-lichine.fr**

CHÂTEAU RAUZAN-GASSIES
CRU CLASSÉ EN 1855

MARGAUX   *Owner: Jean-Michel Quié*

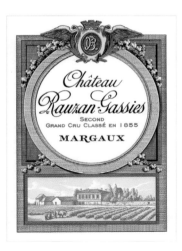

The origins of the noble house of Gassies in the Médoc go back to medieval times. The Lords of Gassies were considered knights, and owed allegiance to the owners of Château Margaux. Monsieur de Rauzan acquired the seigneury in 1661 and is responsible for establishing the reputation of its wine. The estate was divided into two parts in 1785. The name of one of these, Rauzan-Gassies, very much reflects its historic roots.

Since 1946, second growth Château Rauzan-Gassies has belonged to the Quié family, who also own châteaux Croizet-Bages and Bel Orme Tronquoy de Lalande.

Monsieur Paul Quié undertook a major renovation of the vineyard during the postwar period. This was finalised by his son, Jean-Michel, who took over management in 1968.
He is assisted by his children, Anne-Françoise and Jean-Philippe, in overseeing the three family châteaux.

Their passion for fine wine is very much in the tradition of the great growths of Bordeaux, and one of Jean-Michel Quié's greatest pleasures is to share his wine with people who are dear to him.

126

Area under vine	28.5 hectares
Production	90,000 bottles
Soil	Gravel
Grape varieties	65% Cabernet Sauvignon, 25% Merlot, 5% Petit Verdot, 5% Cabernet franc
Barrel ageing	18 months - New barrels: 55%
Second wine	Le Chevalier de Rauzan-Gassies

Technical and Commercial Director: Jean-Philippe Quié - Communication: Anne-Françoise Quié

Château Rauzan-Gassies 1 rue Alexis Millardet - 33460 Margaux
GPS: Latitude: 45.0411142 - Longitude: -0.6761154
Tel. +33 (0)5 57 88 71 88 - Fax +33 (0)5 57 88 37 49
rauzangassies@domaines-quie.com - **www.rauzangassies.fr**

CHÂTEAU RAUZAN-SÉGLA
CRU CLASSÉ EN 1855

MARGAUX

In 1661, Pierre Desmezures de Rauzan acquired an estate which he named after himself. Over the next two centuries, his successors succeeded remarkably well in enhancing the reputation of Château Rauzan-Ségla, which was one of the favourite wines of Thomas Jefferson.

Acquired by Chanel in 1994, this second growth has made major investments in order to be fully worthy of its reputation and rank.

Château Rauzan-Ségla currently has sixty-six hectares of vines. These are lovingly tended, with the greatest of respect for the environment: sustainable methods are used, the soil is ploughed, the vineyard is managed plot-by-plot, the grapes are hand picked into small crates, then sorted twice before fermentation, etc. These are just a few of the steps taken to ensure outstanding quality.

Rauzan-Ségla has a generous bouquet with a great deal of finesse. It epitomises the internationally recognized and much appreciated qualities of the finest wines of Margaux.

Area under vine	66 hectares
Production	130,000 bottles
Soil	Fine, deep gravel and clay
Grape varieties	60% Cabernet Sauvignon, 35% Merlot, 3.5% Petit Verdot, 1.5% Cabernet franc
Barrel ageing	18 months - New barrels: 50%
Second wine	Ségla

Managing Director: John Kolasa - Cellar Master: Henry de Ruffray
Production and quality control: Bénédicte Laborde-Huguet - Consulting oenologist: Éric Boissenot

Château Rauzan-Ségla 33460 Margaux
GPS: Latitude: 45.034819 - Longitude: -0.675262
Tel. +33 (0)5 57 88 82 10 - Fax +33 (0)5 57 88 34 54
contact@rauzan-segla.com - **www.rauzan-segla.com**

Château Siran

MARGAUX

Owner: S.C. Château Siran - the Miailhe family

Château Siran is located in Labarde, the southernmost commune in the Margaux appellation. Siran is undoubtedly one of the Médoc's great historic estates.

The 88-hectare property has 36 hectares of vines, of which 25 are in the Margaux appellation. The remarkable *terroir* consists of a plateau with siliceous gravel soil. Planted essentially with Cabernet Sauvignon and Merlot, this vineyard nevertheless has an unusually large percentage of Petit Verdot (11 %) – a variety that contributes finesse, concentration and, above all, a spicy aftertaste typical of Château Siran. Siran is also one of the rare estates in Bordeaux to have belonged to the same family for over 150 years (the château was acquired in 1859 by the family who presently own it).

Representing the fifth generation, Édouard Miailhe has been at the helm of this unique estate since 2007. Helped by a new, young winemaking team, he is determined to perpetuate and enhance the château's fine reputation.

Château Siran produces from 130 to 150,000 bottles of their *grand vin* and second wine, S de Siran, every year.

Area under vine	25 hectares
Production	80,000 bottles
Soil	Deep gravel
Grape varieties	48% Merlot, 40% Cabernet Sauvignon, 11% Petit Verdot, 1% Cabernet franc
Barrel ageing	12 months - New barrels: 35%
Second wine	S de Siran

Co-Manager: Édouard Miailhe - Co-Manager: Brigitte Miailhe

Château Siran 13 avenue Comte JB de Lynch - 33460 Labarde-Margaux
GPS: Latitude: 42.021855 - Longitude: -0.634375
Tel. +33 (0)5 57 88 34 04 - Fax +33 (0)5 57 88 70 05
info@chateausiran.com - **www.chateausiran.com**

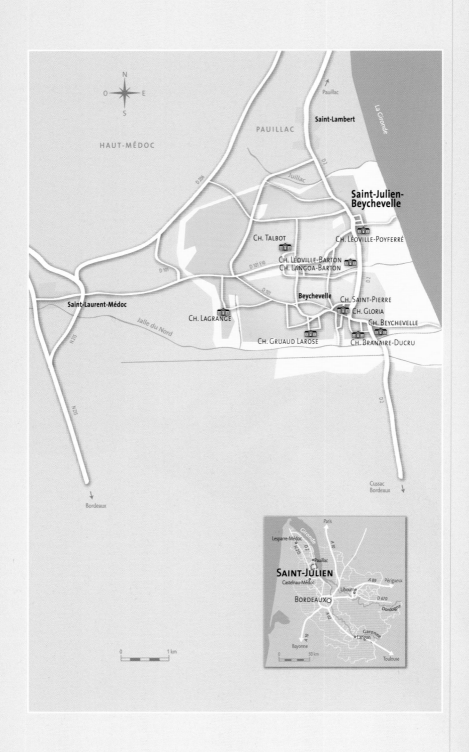

CRUS DE SAINT-JULIEN

The parish of Saint-Julien dates back to the 7th century. Originally named Saint-Julien-de-Reignac, the town became known as Saint-Julien-Beychevelle in the early 20th century, combining the name of the small port and that of the hamlet famous for its fine wines.

Starting in the 17th century, aristocrats and other land owners made the most of the winegrowing potential of their outstanding *terroir*. They were responsible for creating the great estates included in the 1855 classification.

p 132	Château Beychevelle
p 133	Château Branaire-Ducru
p 134	Château Gloria
p 135	Château Gruaud Larose
p 136	Château Lagrange
p 137	Château Langoa Barton
p 138	Château Léoville Barton
p 139	Château Léoville Poyferré
p 140	Château Saint-Pierre
p 141	Château Talbot

CHÂTEAU BEYCHEVELLE
CRU CLASSÉ EN 1855

SAINT-JULIEN   *Owner: Grands millésimes de France*

This spirit of this prestigious great growth was forged over three centuries.

During the reign of Henri III, Beychevelle was the fief of the Dukes of Épernon, including the first of that name, Jean-Louis Nogaret de La Valette, an admiral in the French navy. According to legend, ships passing in front of his château lowered their sails as a sign of allegiance to this powerful man. In fact, the name Beychevelle comes from the Old French *Baisse-Voile*, meaning "lowered sails", as reflected in the château's emblem. This depicts a ship with a griffin – the guardian of Dionysos' wine crater in Greek mythology – on the prow.

Built in the 17th century and reconstructed by Marquis de Brassier in 1757, "the Versailles of the Médoc" was restored to its original splendour in the late 20th century. The elegance of Beychevelle's architecture is reflected in its refined, well-balanced wine served at prestigious tables around the world.

The management is also very respectful of the environment, and the estate has been certified for sustainable viticulture by Terra Vitis.

Area under vine	78 hectares
Production	250-260,000 bottles
Soil	Deep Garonne gravel
Grape varieties	62% Cabernet Sauvignon, 31% Merlot, 5% Cabernet franc, 2% Petit Verdot
Barrel ageing	16-18 months - New barrels: 50%
Second wine	Amiral de Beychevelle

President: Aymar de Baillenx - Manager: Philippe Blanc

Château Beychevelle 33250 Saint-Julien-Beychevelle
GPS: Latitude: 42.145666 - Longitude: -0.735891
Tel. +33 (0)5 56 73 20 70 - Fax +33 (0)5 56 73 20 71
beychevelle@beychevelle.com - **www.beychevelle.com**

CHÂTEAU BRANAIRE-DUCRU

CRU CLASSÉ EN 1855

SAINT-JULIEN

Co-Owner: Patrick Maroteaux

Jean-Baptiste Braneyre, the first person to own the estate in 1680, was well aware of the superb winegrowing potential of the gravelly soil located a stone's throw from the Gironde estuary. The 1855 classification was later to confirm the quality of our *terroir*. Branaire-Ducru and its prestigious neighbours form a group of châteaux that are famous the world over for their excellent wines.

In 1988, our family group asked me to write a new page in the history of this great growth. We defined the spirit in which we wanted to do this from the very first: to make quality an absolute priority and to do everything possible to express Branaire-Ducru's intrinsic personality and complexity.

Composed primarily of Cabernet Sauvignon, our wines express their character year in, year out with great regularity, displaying an enormous amount of fruit, freshness, and subtlety. The winemaking team is fully devoted to highlighting these characteristics in every vintage, and Branaire-Ducru is invariably an elegant wine and a quintessential Saint-Julien.

We are delighted whenever we think about the pleasure and emotions Branaire-Ducru provides to wine enthusiasts around the world.

Area under vine	60 hectares
Soil	Deep gravel from the Quaternary Period overlaying clay soil
Grape varieties	70% Cabernet Sauvignon, 22% Merlot, 5% Cabernet franc, 3% Petit Verdot
Barrel ageing	18 months - New barrels: 60%
Second wine	Duluc de Branaire-Ducru

President: Patrick Maroteaux - Manager: Jean-Dominique Videau

Château Branaire-Ducru 33250 Saint-Julien
GPS: Latitude: 45.145401 - Longitude: -0.738364
Tel. +33 (0)5 56 59 25 86 - Fax +33 (0)5 56 59 16 26
branaire@branaire.com - **www.branaire.com**

CHÂTEAU GLORIA

Owner: Françoise Triaud

Despite his training and success as a cooper, Henri Martin's heart was not in barrelmaking. So, starting in 1939, he left to become a winegrower.

His lifelong ambition was to create a new estate, Château Gloria — a monumental undertaking! Plot by plot, vine row after vine row, he patiently and systematically purchased vineyard land from his friends and neighbours in the commune of Saint-Julien to form Château Gloria. This included many vines from classified growth estates.

Indeed, this was quite a feat considering that Saint-Julien has only 900 hectares of vines, consisting almost entirely of land belonging to the appellation's eleven great growths.

Henri Martin's new estate was created in the 1970s, attaining an area of 50 hectares.

Château Gloria is therefore the story of one man's passion for vines and wine. Although the history of famous châteaux of Bordeaux generally goes back hundreds of years, Gloria is an exception. Its existence is due to the determination of one man in the late 20th century, and it has already established a sterling reputation.

134

Area under vine	50 hectares
Production	250,000 bottles
Soil	Deep Garonne gravel from the Günz period
Grape varieties	65 % Cabernet Sauvignon, 25 % Merlot, 5 % Cabernet franc, 5 % Petit Verdot
Barrel ageing	14 months - New barrels: 40 %
Second wine	Château Peymartin

Manager: Françoise Triaud - Managing Director: Jean-Louis Triaud - Commercial Director: Jean Triaud

Château Gloria Domaines Martin - 33250 Saint-Julien
GPS: Latitude: 45.147683 - Longitude: -0.743012
Tel. +33 (0)5 56 59 08 18 - Fax +33 (0)5 56 59 16 18
contact@domaines-martin.com - **www.domaines-henri-martin.com**

CHÂTEAU GRUAUD LAROSE

CRU CLASSÉ EN 1855

SAINT-JULIEN *Owner: Jean Merlaut*

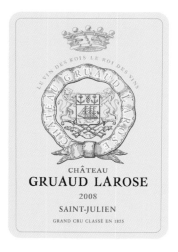

Gruaud Larose is named after the two people who were responsible for creating the estate. In 1725, an abbot, Father Gruaud, bought 50 hectares of land and planted vines there. His nephew, Chevalier de Larose, inherited the property in 1781 and the vineyard grew to 80 hectares under his ownership. Seeing as he had no heirs, Gruaud Larose was jointly purchased by two families at auction in 1812. However, their relations soured and the vineyard was divided into two parts in 1865. In 1934, the Cordier family reunited the estate.

It has belonged to the Merlaut family since 1997. They have introduced sustainable development and organic farming methods in the vineyard. The *terroir* consists of rises of deep Garonne gravel from the Quaternary Period (about 700,000 years ago) where Cabernet Sauvignon is king – as befits a wine whose motto is "The King of Wines and the Wine of Kings".

Château Gruaud Larose is one of the most historic estates in the Médoc. Its size has hardly changed through the centuries and it now deserves its second growth status in the 1855 classification more than ever.

Area under vine	80 hectares
Production	200,000 bottles
Soil	Garonne gravel from the first and second Mindel glacial stages
Grape varieties	61% Cabernet Sauvignon, 29% Merlot, 5% Cabernet franc, 5% Petit Verdot
Barrel ageing	18 months - New barrels: 65%
Second wine	Sarget de Gruaud Larose

Vineyard Manager: Patrick Frédéric - Cellar Master: Philippe Carmagnac
Sales Director: David Launay - Oenologist: Éric Boissenot

Château Gruaud Larose 33250 Saint-Julien-Beychevelle
GPS: Latitude: 45.1640718 - Longitude: -0.7382187
Tel. +33 (0)5 56 73 15 20 - Fax +33 (0)5 56 59 64 72
gl@gruaud-larose.com - **www.gruaud-larose.com**

CHÂTEAU LAGRANGE
CRU CLASSÉ EN 1855

SAINT-JULIEN

Owner: Château Lagrange S.A.S.

The history of Lagrange dates back to 1796, when it was acquired by Count Jean Valère Cabarrus, Napoleon's Finance Minister in Spain. He expanded the estate by purchasing numerous vineyards plots and remained the owner until 1825. Château Lagrange was classified a third growth in 1855.

In 1983, the Suntory group, the leading Japanese wine and spirits firm, acquired Lagrange and invested heavily in a spectacular renovation. Priority was given to the vineyard, followed by refurbishing and modernising the vat room and cellars.

Today, Lagrange has 117 hectares of vines. Efforts undertaken since the 1980s include plot-by-plot vineyard management and separate fermentation of grapes from each of these plots in order to fine tune the final blend. This results in a powerful, elegant wine with great ageing potential year in, year out. Château Lagrange is also one of the rare estates in the Médoc to produce a white wine: Les Arums de Lagrange.

Above and beyond their focus on quality, Bruno Eynard and his team also show great respect for the environment in everything they do.

Area under vine	117 hectares
Production	300,000 bottles
Soil	Günz gravel rises
Grape varieties	65% Cabernet Sauvignon, 28% Merlot, 7% Petit Verdot
Barrel ageing	21 months - New barrels: 60%
Second wine	Les Fiefs de Lagrange

Managing Director: Bruno Eynard - Assistant Manager: Matthieu Bordes
Public Relations: Charlotte Denjean

Château Lagrange 33250 Saint-Julien-Beychevelle
GPS: Latitude: 45.1534152 - Longitude: -0.7792606
Tel. + 33 (0)5 56 73 38 38 - Fax +33 (0)5 56 59 26 09
chateau-lagrange@chateau-lagrange.com - **www.chateau-lagrange.com**

CHÂTEAU LANGOA BARTON

CRU CLASSÉ EN 1855

SAINT-JULIEN   *Owner: the Barton family*

Château Langoa Barton was bought by Hugh Barton in 1821. This was some 30 years before the classification of 1855 and Hugh was not to know that Langoa would be classified as a 3rd growth.

It was perhaps the architecture and the beautiful façade that attracted him. Since then the property has remained in the family and today the shares are divided between Anthony Barton, his daughter Lilian Barton Sartorius and her two children Mélanie and Damien, thus reaching out to the 8th generation.

The vineyards are situated at the southern end of the appellation Saint Julien and the style of the wine is best described as typical Saint Julien. This means a wine of great elegance and finesse with subtle flavours rather than over-extracted wines not strictly the produce of this magnificent area.

The Château itself is in excellent condition and the improvement of the economic situation has enabled the necessary refurbishing to be completed.

Area under vine	18 hectares
Production	95,000 bottles
Soil	Gravel on clay
Grape varieties	72% Cabernet Sauvignon, 25% Merlot, 3% Cabernet franc
Barrel ageing	18 months - New barrels: 60%

President of the limited liability company: Lilian Barton-Sartorius - President of the Supervisory Council: Anthony Barton
Vice-President of the Supervisory Council: Eva Barton

Château Langoa Barton 33250 Saint-Julien-Beychevelle
GPS: Latitude: 45.1805867 - Longitude: -0.751923
Tel. +33 (0)5 56 59 06 05 - Fax +33 (0)5 56 59 14 29
chateau@leoville-barton.com - **www.leoville-barton.com**

CHÂTEAU LÉOVILLE BARTON

CRU CLASSÉ EN 1855

SAINT-JULIEN   *Owner: the Barton family*

In 1826 Hugh Barton, already proprietor of Château Langoa Barton, purchased part of the big Léoville estate which then became Château Léoville Barton. The property still belongs to the Barton family; it is classified as a second growth and is situated in the centre of the appellation Saint Julien.

The current owners believe very much in the importance of "terroir" and consequently produce a true Saint Julien wine of great finesse and perfect balance avoiding the trend of excessive extraction and extreme alcohol. Twice in the history of Léoville Barton, the proprietor has been obliged to flee from France.

Hugh in 1793 during the French Revolution returned to Ireland after a short stay in prison in Bordeaux. It was some years later that he bought Léoville Barton. Ronald Barton also had to abandon his home in 1940 just before the arrival of the German forces. He returned in 1945 to make one of the finest vintages ever.

Area under vine	50 hectares
Production	300.000 bottles
Soil	Gravel on clay
Grape varieties	74% Cabernet Sauvignon, 23% Merlot, 3% Cabernet franc
Barrel ageing	18 months - New barrels: 60%
Second wine	La réserve de Léoville Barton

President of the limited liability company: Lilian Barton-Sartorius - President of the Supervisory Council: Anthony Barton
Vice-President of the Supervisory Council: Eva Barton

Château Léoville Barton 33250 Saint-Julien-Beychevelle
GPS: Latitude: 45.1805867 - Longitude: -0.751923
Tel. +33 (0)5 56 59 06 05 - Fax. +33 (0)5 56 59 14 29
chateau@leoville-barton.com - **www.leoville-barton.com**

CHÂTEAU LÉOVILLE POYFERRÉ

CRU CLASSÉ EN 1855

SAINT-JULIEN | *Owner: the Cuvelier family, G.F.A. des Domaines de St Julien*

Léoville Poyferré came into existence in 1840 as the result of a division of a larger estate, and was included among the second growths in the famous 1855 classification. The Poyferré family kept the château until 1865, but had to sell due to the oidium crisis. Related to the Lawtons, the new owners were the Erlanger and Lalande families.

The Cuvelier family, important *négociants* in northern France since the 19th century, acquired the estate in 1920.

In 1979, Didier Cuvelier took over management and transformed the château into one of the leading great growths.

He has made major investments, both in terms of equipment and human resources, ever since. The many improvements have always been in synergy with Léoville Poyferré's outstanding *terroir*, and all efforts are focused on faithfully reflecting this in the wine. Constant care and attention have resulted in a very great wine that is distributed around the world.

Léoville Poyferré has perfect balance, great finesse, elegance, and remarkable ageing potential.

Area under vine	80 hectares
Production	220,000 bottles
Soil	Garonne gravel
Grape varieties	65% Cabernet Sauvignon, 25% Merlot, 8% Petit Verdot, 2% Cabernet franc
Barrel ageing	18-20 months - New barrels: 80%
Second wine	Pavillon de Léoville Poyferré

Manager: Didier Cuvelier

Château Léoville Poyferré 38 rue de Saint-Julien - 33250 Saint-Julien
GPS: Latitude: 45.1640718 - Longitude: -0.7382187
Tel. +33 (0)5 56 59 08 30 - Fax +33 (0)5 56 59 60 09
lp@leoville-poyferre.fr - **www.leoville-poyferre.fr**

CHÂTEAU SAINT-PIERRE
CRU CLASSÉ EN 1855

SAINT-JULIEN   *Owner: S.C. Domaines Martin*

GRAND CRU CLASSÉ EN 1855

CHATEAU SAINT-PIERRE
SAINT-JULIEN

DOMAINES MARTIN

Château Saint-Pierre's history dates back to the 16th century. Records from 1693 prove the existence of an estate named "Serançan" belonging to Marquis de Cheverry. Baron de Saint-Pierre bought the property in 1767, during the reign of Louis XV and, in keeping with the custom of the time, gave his name to it. His two daughters inherited the estate in 1832. Saint-Pierre was included among the fourth growths in the famous 1855 classification.

In 1892, Madame de Luetkens sold her share of the vineyard to Léon Sevaistre, after which Saint-Pierre was sold under two separate labels: Saint-Pierre-Sevaistre and Saint-Pierre-Bontemps-Dubarry.

In 1922, Belgian wine merchants reunified the estate except for the buildings, which were retained by the previous owners. The Baron's last descendent sold them to Henri Martin in 1981, who completed his purchase by buying the vineyard in 1982. Château Saint-Pierre, which had become a patchwork of vineyard plots over the centuries, was finally reunited.

Today, Françoise and Jean-Louis Triaud, assisted by their children, Vanessa and Jean, continue the family tradition with passion.

140

Area under vine	17 hectares
Production	70,000 bottles
Soil	Deep Garonne gravel
Grape varieties	75% Cabernet Sauvignon, 15% Merlot, 10% Cabernet franc
Barrel ageing	14 months - New barrels: 50%-60%

Manager: Françoise Triaud - Managing Director: Jean-Louis Triaud - Commercial Director: Jean Triaud

Château Saint-Pierre 33250 Saint-Julien-Beychevelle
GPS: Latitude: 45.1484543 - Longitude: -0.7470501
Tel. +33 (0)5 56 59 08 18 - Fax +33 (0)5 56 59 16 18
contact@domaines-martin.com - **www.domaines-henri-martin.com**

CHÂTEAU TALBOT
CRU CLASSÉ EN 1855

SAINT-JULIEN   *Owners: Lorraine Cordier and Nancy Bignon-Cordier*

This imposing estate owes its name to Connétable Talbot, the English general and governor of the province of Guyenne who was defeated at the famous Battle of Castillon in 1453.

Talbot's vines grow in an ideal location bordering the estuary, on some of the region's most highly prized gravelly rises which alone produce great wine. Talbot is one of the oldest estates in the Médoc, and its reputation has been unfailingly fine through the years. That is because the château has been in the hands of experienced managers, and always shown itself to be worthy of its inclusion in the 1855 classification.

Owners of Talbot since the early 20th century, the Cordier family have perpetuated the commitment to quality of their predecessors. At Talbot, wine is very much past, present, and future. Therefore, tradition and technical innovations both count a great deal.

Thanks to an alliance between man and nature, and generations of experience, this outstanding *terroir* produces wine that may vary depending on the vintage, but is always well-balanced and complex. Five hectares are given over to the production of a dry white wine, Caillou Blanc, which is crisp and well-balanced. It likewise reflects its noble *terroir*.

Area under vine	109 hectares
Production	360,000 bottles
Soil	Médoc gravel
Grape varieties	67% Cabernet Sauvignon, 27% Merlot, 5% Petit Verdot, 1% Cabernet franc
Barrel ageing	12-14 months - New barrels: 50%
Second wine	Connétable Talbot

Château Talbot 33250 Saint-Julien-Beychevelle
GPS: Latitude: 45.1576355 - Longitude: -0.75815714
Tel. +33 (0)5 56 73 21 50 - Fax. +33 (0)5 56 73 21 51
chateau-talbot@chateau-talbot.com - **www.chateau-talbot.com**

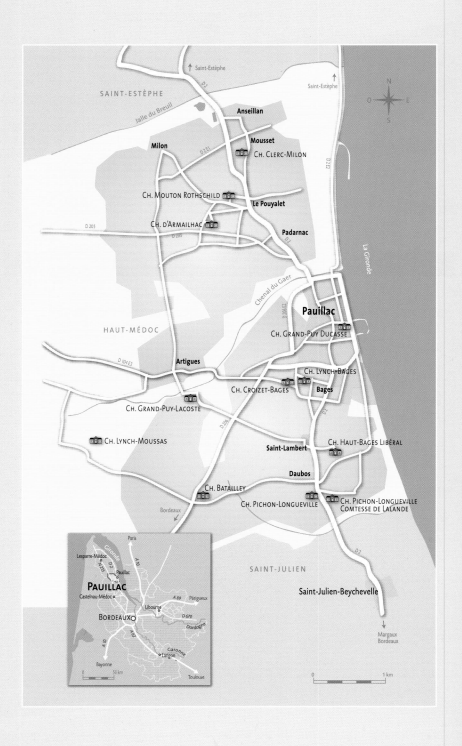

CRUS DE PAUILLAC

Pauillac had a busy port from the dawn of history until the 21st century thanks to its privileged location halfway between the mouth of the Gironde estuary and the city of Bordeaux. Many ships stopped over before going upriver to Bordeaux or else out to sea.

Winegrowing in Pauillac dates back to the Late Middle Ages and developed significantly over the centuries. However, it was the creation of large estates from the early 17th century to the late 19th century that gave Pauillac the importance it has today. It is also the commune with the greatest number of first growths in the 1855 classification.

p 144	Château Batailley
p 145	Château Clerc Milon
p 146	Château Croizet-Bages
p 147	Château d'Armailhac
p 148	Château Grand-Puy Ducasse
p 149	Château Grand-Puy-Lacoste
p 150	Château Haut-Bages Libéral
p 151	Château Lynch-Bages
p 152	Château Lynch-Moussas
p 153	Château Pichon-Longueville
p 154	Château Pichon Longueville Comtesse de Lalande

CHÂTEAU BATAILLEY
CRU CLASSÉ EN 1855

Owners: Héritiers Castéja

The name Batailley comes from the word for "battle", in reference to a conflict that took place towards the end of Hundred Years' War, before English troops were forced to withdraw from the Médoc.

Owned since the 1920s by the Borie family, Batailley belonged to the Saint-Martins in the 18th century and the Guestiers in the 19th century.

In 1961, the estate was inherited by the Castéja family (as were châteaux Beau-Site in Saint-Estèphe, Trottevieille in Saint-Émilion and, at a later date, Lynch Moussas in Pauillac). Philippe Castéja is currently in charge of this superb property. Batailley has 58 hectares of vineyards with pure gravel soil. The vines are an average of 40 years old.

Château Batailley has a remarkably fresh flavour and a unique bouquet of red flowers. It is fruity and straightforward on the palate with plenty of body. With age, it becomes very smooth and displays black pepper, tobacco, and graphite nuances, at which stage it is ideal with peppered and lightly-spiced red meats.

144

Area under vine	58 hectares
Production	300,000 bottles
Soil	Gravel
Grape varieties	70% Cabernet Sauvignon, 25% Merlot, 3% Cabernet franc, 2% Petit Verdot
Barrel ageing	18 months - New barrels: 50%

Château Batailley 33250 Pauillac
GPS: Latitude: 45.1767988 - Longitude: -0.7732238
Tel. +33 (0)5 56 00 00 70 - Fax +33 (0)5 57 87 48 61
domaines@borie-manoux.fr - **www.batailley.com**

CHÂTEAU CLERC MILON
CRU CLASSÉ EN 1855

Owner: Baronne Philippine de Rothschild G.F.A.

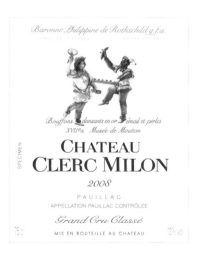

Included in the famous 1855 classification, Château Clerc Milon has 41 hectares of vines overlooking the Gironde estuary in the commune of Pauillac. The vineyard borders on two of the greatest estates in the Médoc, Mouton and Lafite. It has a superb *terroir*, both in terms of soil and sun exposure.

Baron Philippe de Rothschild purchased Château Clerc Milon in 1970, at which time it was much in need of refurbishing. Thanks to the dynamism of his daughter, Baroness Philippine de Rothschild, and a devoted winemaking team, Château Clerc Milon is gaining in quality year after year. The vineyard was entirely restructured and many technical improvements instituted. The construction of a new vat room in 2007 and introduction of innovative winemaking equipment rounded out an ambitious renovation programme. The various changes have borne fruit, and Clerc Milon has become one of the finest wines in the Médoc.

It is now one the most sought-after in its appellation, and has acquired a nobility and richness comparable to the very best great growths.

Area under vine	41 hectares
Soil	Gravel and clay-limestone
Grape varieties	49% Cabernet Sauvignon, 37% Merlot, 11% Cabernet franc, 2% Petit Verdot, 1% Carmenère
Barrel ageing	16 months - New barrels: 30%

Managing Director and Estates Winemaker: Philippe Dhalluin
Managing Director and Commercial Director Châteaux: Hervé Berland - Director: Jean-Emmanuel Danjoy

Château Clerc Milon 33250 Pauillac
GPS: Latitude: 45.1992039 - Longitude: -0.7488862
Tel. +33 (0)5 56 73 20 20
webmaster@bpdr.com - **www.bpdr.com**

CHÂTEAU CROIZET-BAGES
CRU CLASSÉ EN 1855

PAUILLAC   *Owner: Jean-Michel Quié*

In the early 18th century, the Croizet brothers, both members of the Bordeaux parliament, consolidated a number of small vineyard plots in order to form a wine estate in the famous hamlet of Bages, in Pauillac. This estate was included among the fifth growths in the famous 1855 classification under the name of Château Croizet-Bages.

Jean-Baptiste Monnot, an American citizen and owner of the famous Klaxon brand, acquired Croizet Bages soon after the First World War. He in turn sold it to Paul Quié, owner of châteaux Rauzan-Gassies and Bel Orme Tronquoy de Lalande, in 1942.

Monsieur Quié undertook a renovation of the vineyard during the postwar period. This was completed by his son, Jean-Michel, who took over management in 1968.

Jean-Michel Quié is now assisted by his children, Anne-Françoise and Jean-Philippe, in overseeing the three family châteaux.

Their passion for fine wine is very much in the tradition of the great growths of Bordeaux, and one of Jean-Michel Quié's greatest pleasures is to share his wine with people who are dear to him.

Area under vine	28.5 hectares
Production	90,000 bottles
Soil	Gravel
Grape varieties	60% Cabernet Sauvignon, 32% Merlot, 6% Cabernet franc, 2% Petit Verdot
Barrel ageing	18 months - New barrels: 50%
Second wine	La Tourelle de Croizet-Bages

Technical Director: Jean-Philippe Quié - Communication: Anne-Françoise Quié

Château Croizet-Bages rue du Port de la Verrerie - 33250 Pauillac
GPS: Latitude: 45.1915223 - Longitude: -0.7601589
Tel. +33 (0)5 56 59 01 62 - Fax +33 (0)5 56 59 23 39
croizetbages@domaines-quie.com - **www.domaines-quie.com**

CHÂTEAU D'ARMAILHAC
CRU CLASSÉ EN 1855

PAUILLAC
Owner: Baronne Philippine de Rothschild G.F.A.

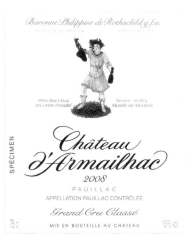

Classified a fifth growth in 1855, Château d'Armailhac, a neighbour of Mouton Rothschild in Pauillac, has 69 hectares of vines planted with the finest premium grape varieties: Cabernet Sauvignon, Merlot, Cabernet Franc, and Petit Verdot.

Aged in oak barrels, the wine combines finesse, power, and the superb tannin of a fine Pauillac. Widely recognized for the quality of its wine, Château d'Armailhac benefits from centuries of innovations such as those described by Armand d'Armailhacq in his 1867 treatise entitled *La Culture des vignes, de la Vinification et des vins dans le Médoc*.

In 1933, Baron Philippe de Rothschild acquired this estate – also well-known for its grounds (among the most beautiful in the Médoc), front courtyard, and château – which had belonged to the d'Armailhacq family since the 18th century.

Known as Mouton d'Armailhacq between 1956 and 1989, the château was then successively named Mouton Baronne Philippe and Mouton Baron Philippe. However, since 1989, Baronne Philippine de Rothschild has revived the historic link with the original owner by renaming the estate Château d'Armailhac.

Area under vine	69 hectares
Soil	80% gravel, 20% clay-limestone
Grape varieties	53% Cabernet Sauvignon, 34% Merlot, 11% Cabernet franc, 2% Petit Verdot
Barrel ageing	15 months - New barrels: 25%

Managing Director and Estates Winemaker: Philippe Dhalluin
Managing Director and Commercial Director Châteaux: Hervé Berland

Château d'Armailhac 33250 Pauillac
GPS: Latitude: 45.1992039 - Longitude: -0.7488862
Tel. +33 (0)5 56 73 20 20
webmaster@bpdr.com - **www.bpdr.com**

CHÂTEAU GRAND-PUY DUCASSE

CRU CLASSÉ EN 1855

PAUILLAC

Owner: CA Grands Crus

CHATEAU
GRAND-PUY DUCASSE

CRU CLASSÉ EN 1855
PAUILLAC
APPELLATION PAUILLAC CONTRÔLÉE

2008

MIS EN BOUTEILLE AU CHATEAU

This classified growth consists of three large plots with some of the finest *terroir* in Pauillac: the northern plot is a neighbour of Mouton and Lafite, the central plot is located in a part of the commune called Grand-Puy, and the southern plot is on the Saint-Lambert plateau. This unusual configuration was due to the estate's founder, Pierre Ducasse, an eminent lawyer who pieced together this splendid vineyard with land he inherited or purchased in the 18th century.

Grand-Puy Ducasse has recently entered a new phase of its history with a decided upswing in quality. This is largely thanks to a study of the potential of each vineyard plot and a change in vineyard management. The vines are now trained higher and each different grape variety has been perfectly matched to the most suitable *terroir*.

Ripe, healthy Cabernet Sauvignon and Merlot grapes, coupled with rigorous production methods, account for Grand Puy Ducasse's reputation for aromatic complexity, beautiful structure, and excellent ageing potential. It is the epitome of a fine Pauillac.

Area under vine	40 hectares
Production	120,000 bottles
Soil	Garonne gravel and a mixture of silica and gravel
Grape varieties	60% Cabernet Sauvignon, 40% Merlot
Barrel ageing	18-24 months - New barrels: 30-40%
Second wine	Prélude à Grand-Puy Ducasse

Managing Director: Thierry Budin

Château Grand-Puy Ducasse 4 quai Antoine Ferchaud - 33250 Pauillac
GPS: Latitude: 45.1997883 - Longitude: -0.7461077
Tel. +33 (0)5 56 59 00 40 - Fax +33 (0)5 56 59 36 47
contact@cagrandscrus.com - **www.cagrandscrus.com**

CHÂTEAU GRAND-PUY-LACOSTE

CRU CLASSÉ EN 1855

Owner: François-Xavier Borie

The name Grand-Puy ("puy" comes from the Latin word *podium*, meaning hill) describes this vineyard's privileged location overlooking Pauillac, where the château reigns over a sea of vines.

Included in the famous 1855 classification, Grand-Puy-Lacoste has had an important role to play in the history of Bordeaux wine since the early 16th century. It previously belonged to a family who contributed several members to the Bordeaux parliament. They fell in love with the magnificent gravel *terroir* and were responsible for establishing the wine's fine reputation. They were followed by several other families: the Lacostes (who gave the estate its definitive name), the Saint-Guirons, and the Saint-Legiers.

In 1930, the château's history was marked by the arrival of Raymond Dupin, an unusual character and bon vivant who remained the owner until 1978. Shortly before his death, he sold Grand-Puy-Lacoste to the Borie family because he appreciated their rigour and devotion to producing fine great growth wine in the Médoc.

François-Xavier Borie, the present owner, is behind this superb estate's renaissance. He has made major investments and constantly improved the quality of Grand-Puy-Lacoste in order to reflect all the finesse of its great Pauillac *terroir*.

Area under vine	55 hectares
Production	180,000 bottles
Soil	Deep gravel
Grape varieties	75 % Cabernet Sauvignon, 20 % Merlot, 5 % Cabernet franc
Barrel ageing	16-18 months
Second wine	Lacoste-Borie

Public relations: Emeline Borie

Château Grand-Puy-Lacoste Domaines François-Xavier Borie - BP 82 - 33250 Pauillac
GPS: Latitude: 45.189545 - Longitude: -0.766758
Tel. +33 (0)5 56 59 06 66 - Fax +33 (0)5 56 59 22 27
dfxb@domainesfxborie.com - **www.grand-puy-lacoste.com**

CHÂTEAU HAUT-BAGES LIBÉRAL
CRU CLASSÉ EN 1855

PAUILLAC	Owner: Claire Villars Lurton

The Libéral family founded the estate at the beginning of the 18th century. Generation after generation, they succeeded in forming a vineyard consisting of some of the best soil in Pauillac. Château Haut-Bages Libéral was included among the fifth growths in the 1855 classification. Since the arrival of the Villars family in 1983, Haut-Bages Libéral has gradually recovered its formal glory.

Château Haut-Bages Libéral has 30 hectares of vines overlooking the Gironde River. Half of this area, located right next to Château Latour, features gravel on limestone, and the other part, on the plateau of Bages, has deep gravel soil.

Today, the property is run by Claire Villars Lurton who modernised the winemaking facilities and introduced new, environmentally-friendly methods. She is committed to making the most of the *terroir* thanks to a very quality-oriented approach devoted to restoring the estate's prestige.

150

Area under vine	30 hectares
Production	100,000 bottles
Soil	Deep gravels, gravels on clay and limestone
Grape varieties	75% Cabernet Sauvignon, 25% Merlot
Barrel ageing	16-18 months - New barrels: 40%
Seconds vins	La Chapelle de Bages - La Fleur de Haut-Bages Libéral

Operation Manager: Stefano Ruini

Château Haut-Bages Libéral Chemin des Balogues - 33250 Pauillac
GPS: Latitude: 45.1822763 - Longitude: -0.7477769
Tel. +33 (0)5 57 88 76 65 - Fax +33 (0)5 57 88 98 33
infos@hautbagesliberal.com - **www.hautbagesliberal.com**

CHÂTEAU LYNCH-BAGES
CRU CLASSÉ EN 1855

| PAUILLAC | *Owner: the Cazes family* |

Overlooking the Gironde estuary, Château Lynch-Bages is located on the outskirts of Pauillac, on the plateau de Bages, one of the most beautiful gravelly rises in the appellation. The estate formerly belonged to the Lynch family, originally from Ireland, and was purchased by Jean-Charles Cazes in 1934. His successors, André, Jean-Michel, Sylvie, and Jean-Charles Cazes, have worked tirelessly to develop and promote this well-known château included in the 1855 classification. Starting in 1980, Jean-Michel Cazes undertook an in-depth modernisation of Lynch-Bages, while preserving the former 19th century vat room – as well as the reputation of this outstanding wine... Convinced that wine is part of a certain culture and life style, and a way of being and sharing, he created Château Cordeillan Bages. This Relais & Châteaux hotel-restaurant welcomes guests from around the world and features fine cuisine prepared by chef Jean-Luc Rocha. In 2001, Jean-Michel handed over management of Lynch Bages to his son, Jean-Charles, and took on the project of breathing new life into the adjacent Village de Bages. The wines of Lynch Bages reflect the family tradition of generosity and excellence. Furthermore, the entire family wishes to welcome you to the estate, so that their wine is something more than just a beautiful label, and to share their passion for Lynch Bages.

Area under vine	100 hectares
Production	350,000 bottles
Soil	Garonne gravel
Grape varieties	72% Cabernet Sauvignon, 20% Merlot, 5% Cabernet franc, 3% Petit Verdot
Barrel ageing	12-18 months - New barrels: 70%
Second wine	Écho de Lynch Bages

Manager: Jean-Charles Cazes

Château Lynch Bages 33250 Pauillac
GPS: Latitude: 45.19164 - Longitude: -0.754119
Tel. +33 (0)5 56 73 24 00 - Fax +33 (0)5 56 59 26 42
infochato@lynchbages.com - **www.lynchbages.com**

CHÂTEAU LYNCH-MOUSSAS

CRU CLASSÉ EN 1855

PAUILLAC

Owners: Héritiers Castéja

Lynch Moussas was originally part of an estate in Pauillac owned by Count Lynch in the 18th century. This was later divided into two separate entities, Lynch Bages and Lynch Moussas. Consisting of more than two hundred hectares of woods, grounds, and vines, Lynch Moussas was included in the 1855 classification of the finest wines in the Médoc.

Purchased by Jean Castéja in 1919 (at a time when he was co-owner of Duhart-Milon), Lynch Moussas was acquired by Émile Castéja and his family in 1970. This marked the beginning of an important new phase in the château's history. The vineyard was restructured, the cellars and vat room rebuilt, and winemaking modernised. Meticulous care is taken of the vines in order to express the multi-faceted *terroir*: bud pruning, leaf thinning, green harvesting, and picking by hand produce grapes of optimum quality. In 2001, Émile and Philippe Castéja created a second wine, Les Hauts de Lynch Moussas, which is the name of plots located on the butte overlooking the château.

Lynch Moussas is much-appreciated today for its deep, dark colour, red fruit bouquet, round, ripe tannin, and overtones of blackcurrant typical of the finest wines of Pauillac. It is also full-bodied, with a beautiful, long aftertaste.

152

Area under vine	57 hectares
Production	180,000 bottles
Soil	Gravel
Grape varieties	70% Cabernet Sauvignon, 30% Merlot
Barrel ageing	18 months - New barrels: 55%
Second wine	Les Hauts de Lynch-Moussas

Château Lynch-Moussas 33250 Pauillac
GPS: Latitude: 45.2022481 - Longitude: -0.8349154
Tel. +33 (0)5 56 00 00 70 - Fax +33 (0)5 57 87 48 61
domaines@borie-manoux.fr - **www.lynch-moussas.com**

CHÂTEAU PICHON-LONGUEVILLE

PAUILLAC

Owner: AXA Millésimes

Château Pichon-Longueville features among the top Bordeaux wines, and was ranked as a *Deuxième Cru* in the historic 1855 classification.

Since 2001, we have intensified our selection policy, focusing essentially on the historic *terroir* of Pichon-Longueville Baron (only 40 out of a total of 73 hectares are used to make the *Grand Vin*) and choosing only the quintessence of the vineyard when making the blends.

The wine reflects this attention to the tiniest detail, combining power and finesse with exceptional elegance and length, while keeping the tannic structure that is characteristic of the great Pauillac wines.

The château was built in 1851. It boasts a superb view over the Gironde estuary and fairytale architecture with slender turrets and a reflecting waterpond. Opening the Château up to wine lovers from the four corners of the world is one of our priorities. The quality of our events organisation has just been rewarded by a Golden Trophy at the Best of Wine Tourism Awards 2011.

Area under vine	73 hectares
Production	180,000 bottles
Soil	Garonne gravel
Grape varieties	65% Cabernet Sauvignon, 35% Merlot
Barrel ageing	20 months - New barrels: 80%
Second wine	Les Tourelles de Longueville

Managing Director: Christian Seely - Technical Director: Jean-René Matignon

Château Pichon-Longueville BP 112 - 33250 Pauillac
GPS: Latitude: 45.176667 - Longitude: -0.751111
Tel. +33 (0)5 56 73 17 17 - Fax +33 (0)5 56 59 64 62
contact@pichonlongueville.com - **www.pichonlongueville.com**

CHÂTEAU PICHON-LONGUEVILLE
COMTESSE DE LALANDE CRU CLASSÉ EN 1855

PAUILLAC *Owner: Champagne Louis Roederer*

Pichon Longueville's history can be traced back to 1688-1689. In 1850, Virginie de Pichon Longueville, Comtesse de Lalande, and her two sisters inherited three fifths of the vineyard that was named Château Pichon Longueville Comtesse de Lalande a few years later.

In 1978, May-Éliane de Lencquesaing, daughter of Édouard Miailhe, in turn inherited this fine estate and became totally devoted to it. She was largely responsible for maintaining the wine's superb quality and fine international reputation.

A neighbour of Château Latour, this second growth Pauillac borders on the Saint-Julien appellation. Its unusual blend of grape varieties gives the wine a unique personality whose hallmarks are elegance, balance, and finesse. Traditional and modern techniques complement one another to express the character of the prestigious *terroir*.

The Champagne firm of Louis Roederer acquired this great growth in January 2007. They aim to perpetuate the excellent work done by their predecessor and to attain the ultimate in quality and prestige.

154

Area under vine	89 hectares
Production	200,000 bottles
Soil	Gravel on clay from the Günz glaciation period
Grape varieties	45% Cabernet Sauvignon, 35% Merlot, 12% Cabernet franc, 8% Petit Verdot
Barrel ageing	18 months - New barrels: 50%
Second wine	Réserve de la Comtesse

President: Frédéric Rouzaud - Managing Director: Sylvie Cazes - Technical Director: Thomas Dô Chi Nam

Château Pichon-Longueville Comtesse de Lalande 33250 Pauillac
GPS: Latitude: 45.1765615 - Longitude: -0.7505894
Tel. +33 (0)5 56 59 19 40 - Fax +33 (0)5 56 59 26 56
pichon@pichon-lalande.com - **www.pichon-lalande.com**

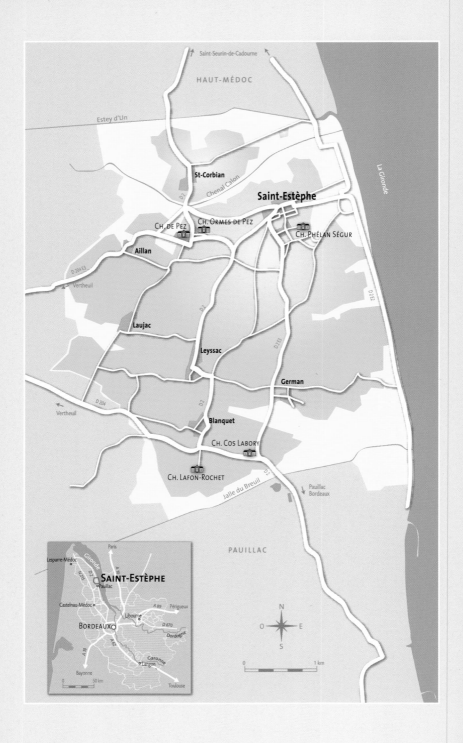

CRUS DE SAINT-ESTÈPHE

Saint-Estèphe is the northernmost appellation in the Haut-Médoc. It benefits from an outstanding location along the Gironde estuary, which can be seen from most of the commune's gravelly rises.

The first known inhabitants date back to the Bronze Age, and vines were planted here during the Roman occupation at the beginning of the Common Era.

The 17th, 18th and 19th centuries saw the development of grands crus which, as in the other famous communal appellations in the Médoc and helped by the Bordeaux *négociants* who aged and sold the wines, contributed greatly to the reputation of Saint-Estèphe around the world.

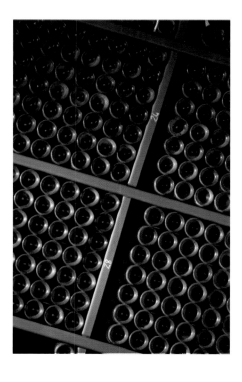

p 158	Château Cos Labory
p 159	Château de Pez
p 160	Château Lafon-Rochet
p 161	Château Ormes de Pez
p 162	Château Phélan Ségur

CHÂTEAU COS LABORY

CRU CLASSÉ EN 1855

Owner: the Audoy family

Château Cos Labory owes its name to the word "caux", meaning "stony hill," and to François Labory, who owned the estate from 1820 to 1840. Purchased in 1845 by Monsieur d'Estournel, Cos Labory was sold in 1852 to Charles Martyns, an English banker. Included in the famous 1855 classification, this great growth has belonged to the Audoy family for over half a century.

Located on the famous gravelly rise of Cos, the eighteen-hectare vineyard benefits from remarkable sun exposure. It is planted with traditional grape varieties.

Major investments have been made over the past several years and Château Cos Labory now relies on the latest technology to produce their great wines.

Great attention is paid during fermentation and ageing, which are adapted to the character of each vintage. Cos Labory combines power, elegance, and the structure typical of a great Saint-Estèphe.

158

Area under vine	18 hectares
Production	80,000 bottles
Soil	Günz gravel on a marl and limestone platform
Grape varieties	60% Cabernet Sauvignon, 35% Merlot, 5% Cabernet franc
Barrel ageing	18 months - New barrels: 50%
Second wine	Charme de Cos Labory

Manager: Bernard Audoy

Château Cos Labory 33180 Saint-Estèphe
GPS: Latitude: 45.230717 - Longitude: -0.777014
Tel. +33 (0)5 56 59 30 22 - Fax +33 (0)5 56 59 73 52
contact@cos-labory.com - www.cos-labory.com

CHÂTEAU DE PEZ

Owner: Champagne Louis Roederer

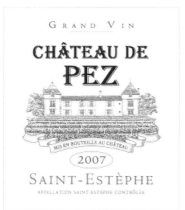

The Champagne house of Louis Roederer bought this beautiful, historic estate in June 1995.

Château de Pez is one of the oldest winegrowing properties in the appellation. Created in the 15th century, it achieved fame in the 16th century when it was acquired by the Pontac family, who also founded Haut Brion. Initially a hunting lodge, the property was enlarged and transformed exclusively into a wine producing estate over time. Its architecture was also significantly modified in the 18th century. Two wings and two towers were added to the main building, which definitely took on the appearance of a château as a result. It was entirely renovated in 2000, as were the outbuildings and winemaking facilities.

Located west of the town of Saint-Estèphe, the vineyard consists of 38 hectares of gravelly soil on clay-limestone bedrock. The wines of château de Pez have wonderful tannic structure, power, a long aftertaste, a great deal of finesse, and excellent ageing potential.

Area under vine	38 hectares
Production	160,000 bottles
Soil	Limestone gravel and clay
Grape varieties	47% Cabernet Sauvignon, 44% Merlot, 6% Cabernet franc, 3% Petit Verdot
Barrel ageing	12-18 months - New barrels: 40%

President: Frédéric Rouzaud - Manager: Sylvie Cazes - Managing Director: Philippe Moureau

Château de Pez Lieu-dit Pez - 33180 Saint-Estèphe
GPS: Latitude: 45.2602074 - Longitude: -0.7898998
Tel. +33 (0)5 56 59 30 26 - Fax +33 (0)5 56 59 39 25
pmoureau@chateaudepez.com - **www.chateaudepez.com**

CHÂTEAU LAFON-ROCHET
CRU CLASSÉ EN 1855

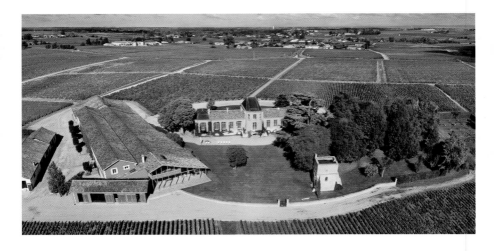

This estate can trace its history back to the latter 16th century. For over two hundred years, it belonged to the Lafon family, who managed to keep hold of it through the turmoil of the French Revolution. They also lived to see its ultimate recognition in the 1855 classification, when Lafon-Rochet was admitted to the very select club of great growths, one of only five in Saint-Estèphe. Ideally situated, between Cos d'Estournel and Lafite-Rothschild to the south, Lafon-Rochet features some of the finest vineyard land in the world. It is not hard to see why Guy Tesseron, well-known for the quality of his old Cognac, became interested in acquiring the estate over forty years ago.

He soon came to the conclusion that the existing buildings were not worthy of saving. He thus completely demolished them, going on to build a new cellar as well as a château based on the plans of a 17th century *chartreuse*, or manor house, that is unique in Bordeaux.

Thanks to unceasing care and attention, Lafon-Rochet is one of the finest wines in Saint-Estèphe, France, and the whole world.

160

Area under vine	45 hectares
Production	140,000 bottles
Soil	Gravel from the Quaternary Period with a clay-limestone subsoil
Grape varieties	55% Cabernet Sauvignon, 40% Merlot, 3% Cabernet franc, 2% Petit Verdot
Barrel ageing	15 months - New barrels: 50%
Second wine	Les Pèlerins de Lafon Rochet

Manager: Basile Tesseron

Château Lafon-Rochet - 33180 Saint-Estèphe
GPS: Latitude: 45,2292655 - Longitude: -0,7833726
Tel. +33 (0)5 56 59 32 06 - Fax +33 (0)5 56 59 72 43
lafon@lafon-rochet.com - **www. lafon-rochet.com**

CHÂTEAU ORMES DE PEZ

SAINT-ESTÈPHE

Owner: the Cazes family

2003

CHÂTEAU
ORMES DE PEZ
SAINT-ESTÈPHE

CRU BOURGEOIS EXCEPTIONNEL

J.M. CAZES PROPRIÉTAIRE À SAINT-ESTÈPHE

This estate is located in the hamlet of Pez, whose name comes from the Old French word for "peace". At one time, the château also had very old elm trees (or *ormes* in French) dating back to the 18th century. Born in 1880, Marie Cazes married the owner of Les Ormes de Pez in the late 19th century. Widowed, she took on the task of managing the estate, which was highly unusual for a woman at that time. Château les Ormes de Pez has always had great sentimental value for the family, and was purchased just before the Second World War by Marie's brother, Jean-Charles, owner of Château Lynch Bages in Pauillac. The Cazes family's link with this *cru exceptionnel* thus goes back more than a century.

The two main plots are located either side of the hamlet of Pez. They have a very homogeneous *terroir* that produces dependably fine wines year in, year out. Many investments have been made in the cellars, vat room, château, etc. since the early 1980s as part of an ambitious renovation programme. However, the most important change from the Cazes family's point of view was opening up the estate to wine enthusiasts, who can now stay in charming guest rooms in order to enjoy the unique setting and lifestyle.

Area under vine	40 hectares
Production	250,000 bottles
Soil	Garonne gravel
Grape varieties	52% Cabernet Sauvignon, 34% Merlot, 12% Cabernet franc, 2% Petit Verdot
Barrel ageing	12-18 months - New barrels: 45%

Manager: Jean-Charles Cazes

Château Ormes de Pez 29 route des Ormes - 33180 Saint-Estèphe
GPS: Latitude: 45.26011595 - Longitude: -0.7893041
Tel. +33 (0)5 56 73 24 00 - Fax +33 (0)5 56 59 26 42
infochato@ormesdepez.com - **www.ormesdepez.com**

CHÂTEAU PHÉLAN SÉGUR

SAINT-ESTÈPHE

Owners: Xavier Gardinier and sons

MIS EN BOUTEILLE AU CHÂTEAU

Château
Phélan Ségur
2005
Saint-Estèphe

X. GARDINIER & FILS

Located in the village of Saint-Estèphe, Château Phélan Ségur has proudly overlooked the Gironde estuary since the early 19th century. Its history is intimately linked with that of the Médoc. Founded by Irishman Bernard Phelan when he united Clos de Garramey and Domaine Ségur de Cabanac, the estate was developed by his son, Frank, and renamed Phélan Ségur in the early 20th century.

Consisting of seventy hectares of vines divided into four distinct parts, the great diversity of the *terroir* accounts for Phélan Ségur's complexity. The cellar and vat room are integrated into the château in a highly unusual architectural ensemble. The wines are aged with the greatest of care and Phélan Ségur is famous for its elegance, finesse, and balance.

Belonging to the family-owned Gardinier group specialised in luxury hotels and restaurants, Château Phélan Ségur has raised the art of hospitality to new heights.

162

Area under vine	70 hectares
Production	200,000 bottles
Soil	Gravel and clay
Grape varieties	53% Cabernet Sauvignon, 47% Merlot
Barrel ageing	16-18 months - New barrels: 60%
Second wine	Frank Phélan

Managing Director: Véronique Dausse

Château Phélan Ségur 33180 Saint-Estèphe
GPS: Latitude : 45.261808 - Longitude : -0.769708
Tel. +33 (0)5 56 59 74 00 - Fax +33 (0)5 56 59 74 10
phelan@phelansegur.com - **www.phelansegur.com**

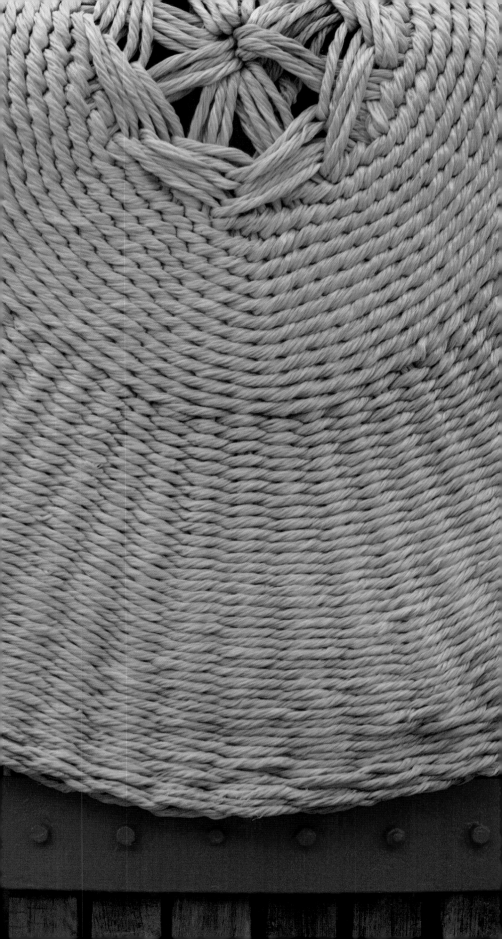

CÉRONS

Ch. Nairac   **Barsac**

Ch. Coutet

Ch. Climens   Ch. Doisy-Daëne

Ch. Doisy-Védrines

Preignac

SAINTE-CROIX-DU-MONT

GRAVES

le Ciron

Ch. de Malle

Ch. Bastor-Lamontagne

Ch. Suduiraut

Ch. Sigalas-Rabaud

Ch. de Rayne-Vigneau   Ch. Lafaurie-Peyraguey

Bommes

Ch. d'Yquem

Ch. La Tour-Blanche

Fargues

Sauternes

Ch. Guiraud

Ch. de Fargues

GRAVES

le Brion

Sortie 2

Bordeaux

La Garonne

Langon

Langon

Sortie 3

Bordeaux

Paris

Lesparre-Médoc   Médoc   Gironde

Pauillac

Castelnau-Médoc

Libourne

Périgueux

BORDEAUX

Dordogne

BARSAC

Garonne

Langon

SAUTERNES

Bayonne

Toulouse

N
O   E
S

0   1 km

0   50 km

CRUS DE SAUTERNES ET DE BARSAC

The Sauternes appellation consists of five communes: Sauternes, Fargues, Bommes, Preignac, and Barsac. Barsac has its own separate appellation as well.

Sauternes produces precious nectar that is known all over the world and considered the finest white wine in the world by many connoisseurs. Furthermore, the jewel of Sauternes, Château d'Yquem, was the only estate in either the Médoc or Sauternes to be classified a "Premier Cru Supérieur" in 1855.

The appellation is separated from the Graves on its western side by the Ciron valley. The river Ciron is responsible for the microclimate particularly conducive to *Botrytis cinerea*, a fungus that concentrates the grapes and produces outstanding wines.

p 166	Château Bastor-Lamontagne
p 167	Château Climens
p 168	Château Coutet
p 169	Château de Fargues
p 170	Château de Malle
p 171	Château de Rayne Vigneau
p 172	Château Doisy Daëne
p 173	Château Doisy-Védrines
p 174	Château Guiraud
p 175	Château La Tour Blanche
p 176	Château Lafaurie-Peyraguey
p 177	Château Nairac
p 178	Château Sigalas Rabaud
p 179	Château Suduiraut

Château Bastor-Lamontagne

Sauternes

Located in Preignac, one of the five communes in the Sauternes appellation, Château Bastor-Lamontagne has 56 hectares of vineyards in a single block on siliceous-gravel soil. The estate takes its name from Chevalier de la Montaigne, a councillor of the Bordeaux Parliament who became the owner in 1711.

Today, critics often emphasise the wine's fine, dependable quality. The *grand vin*, Château Bastor-Lamontagne, is often described as a "modern Sauternes" thanks to its freshness, finesse, and balance. It is enjoyable both as an aperitif and with food. Although it can age very well, Bastor-Lamontagne is also delicious young thanks to its vivaciousness and elegance. The second wine, Les Remparts de Bastor-Lamontagne, is also particularly fruity and well-balanced. Caprice de Bastor-Lamontagne is an exuberant, easy-to-drink, and quintessential Sauternes thanks to the blend of 50% Sémillon and 50% Sauvignon blanc.

All the wines of have good acidity and a floral bouquet with overtones of honey and acacia.

166

Area under vine	56 hectares
Production	60-80,000 bottles
Soil	Siliceous-gravel and clay-gravel
Grape varieties	80% Sémillon, 20% Sauvignon
Barrel ageing	16 months - New barrels: 30%
Second wine	Les Remparts de Bastor-Lamontagne

Managing Director: Michel Garat

Château Bastor-Lamontagne 33210 Preignac
GPS: Latitude: 44.584982 - Longitude: -0.2954852
Tel. +33 (0)5 56 63 27 66 - Fax +33 (0)5 56 76 87 03
bastor@bastor-lamontagne.com - www.bastor-lamontagne.com

CHÂTEAU CLIMENS
PREMIER CRU CLASSÉ EN 1855

BARSAC   *Owner: Bérénice Lurton*

2007

Château Climens

1ᵉʳ CRU · BARSAC
GRAND VIN DE SAUTERNES

BÉRÉNICE LURTON

A first growth Sauternes since 1855, Château Climens has long been called the "Lord of Barsac" because of the incomparable elegance of its wines.

Climens' strong personality is derived above all from its unique limestone *terroir* whose outlines have not changed since the estate was established in the 16th century. Sémillon is the exclusive grape variety at Climens, where it achieves outstanding aromatic complexity and freshness.

However, it still takes human know-how to cut a rough diamond. And Château Climens has been blessed with a series of committed, professional, and highly-demanding owners and managers. They have given Climens a reputation for unfailingly purity and reliability in all vintages that make this one of the greatest sweet white wines in Bordeaux.

Lucien Lurton, an emblematic winegrowing figure, fell in love with Chateau Climens and purchased it in 1971. The youngest of his ten children, Bérénice Lurton, took over management in 1992, devoting all her energy to creating magical wines, vintage after vintage.

Area under vine	30 hectares
Production	25-30,000 bottles
Soil	Red ferruginous-clay and sand on a limestone shelf with fissured asteriated rock
Grape varieties	100% Sémillon
Barrel ageing	20-24 months - New barrels: 35-45%
Second wine	Cyprès de Climens

Technical Director: Frédéric Nivelle - Commercial development and communication: Virginie Achou-Lepage

Château Climens 33720 Barsac
GPS: Latitude: 44.5896355 - Longitude: -0.3345215
Tel. +33 (0)5 56 27 15 33 - Fax +33 (0)5 56 27 21 04
contact@chateau-climens.fr - **www.chateau-climens.fr**

Château Coutet
Premier Cru Classé en 1855

| BARSAC | Owners: Philippe Baly - Dominique Baly |

Recognised as among the finest wines in its appellation, Château Coutet was classed a First Growth in 1855. One of the oldest estates in the Sauternes region, Coutet has an outstanding *terroir* and architectural heritage. Its origins date back to the late 13th or early 14th century, as evidenced by a tower similar in style to those built at forts during the English occupation of Aquitaine.

Château Coutet belonged to the de Lur Saluces family for over a century and is currently owned and managed by Philippe and Dominique Baly, with technical and commercial assistance from Baron Philippe de Rothschild S.A., who have exclusive distribution rights.

The name Coutet comes from the Gascon word for *couteau*, or knife, in reference to the wine's fresh, vibrant acidity and unique crispness. When young, Château Coutet has aromas of white flowers, citrus, honey, and vanilla. With age, the botrytis character comes through in a deep, delicate bouquet with hints of spice and candied fruit.

168

Area under vine	38.5 hectares
Production	42,000 bottles
Soil	Clay on a limestone subsoil
Grape varieties	75% Sémillon, 23% Sauvignon Blanc, 2% Muscadelle
Barrel ageing	18 months - New barrels: 100%
Second wine	La Chartreuse de Coutet

Château Coutet 33720 Barsac
GPS: Latitude: 44.5945998 - Longitude: -0.3251383
Tel. +33 (0)5 56 27 15 46 - Fax +33 (0)5 56 27 02 20
info@chateaucoutet.com - www.chateaucoutet.com

CHÂTEAU DE FARGUES

Owner: Alexandre de Lur Saluces

Built in 1306 par by cardinal Raymond Guilhem de Fargues, Château de Fargues came into the de Lur family in 1472 via marriage, and has been owned by the de Lur Saluces family since 1586. The solid walls of the former fortified château, greatly damaged by fire in 1687, proudly overlook the vines of one of the finest estates in Sauternes. Although the estate is quite large (170 hectares), only the magnificent clay-gravel rise next to the old castle is devoted to winegrowing.

Owners for over five centuries, the Lur Saluces family have perfected winemaking in complete harmony with noble rot. Absolute perfection is sought at all cost in every vintage, and the wine is not estate-bottled or sold under the château name if quality is not up to scratch (for example, there were no 1972, 1974, or 1992 vintages of Château de Fargues).

The grapes are picked meticulously in several waves and the wine is aged in barrel for three years to produce a wine of rare complexity with remarkably long ageing potential. It is thus hardly surprising that connoisseurs like to compare Château de Fargues to Yquem... and sometimes end up not knowing which is which.

Area under vine	15 hectares
Production	15,000 bottles
Soil	Gravel and clay
Grape varieties	80% Sémillon, 20% Sauvignon
Barrel ageing	30-36 months - New barrels: 15-20%

Manager: François Amirault

Château de Fargues 33210 Fargues de Langon
GPS: Latitude: 44.535843 - Longitude: -0.295317
Tel. +33 (0)5 57 98 04 20 - Fax +33 (0)5 57 98 04 21
fargues@chateau-de-fargues.com - **www.chateau-de-fargues.com**

Château de Malle
Cru Classé en 1855

Sauternes

Château de Malle, which dates back to 1540, has always remained in the same family: five generations of de Malle, six of de Lur Saluces and three of de Bournazel. The château and its Italian gardens embody all that is noble about wine. A visit to this beautiful historic monument, like no other in Southwest France, is strongly recommended. Few other places evoke tradition, an enviable lifestye, and refinement as perfectly as Château de Malle.

Comprising some two hundred hectares, the estate is unusual in that it straddles both the Sauternes and Graves (red and white) appellations.

Château de Malle was included in the 1855 classification. Its light sandy and gravelly soil produces wines of great fruitiness. Very aromatic when young, with hints of ripe apricot, lime blossom, and acacia honey, Château de Malle is rich, distinguished, and relatively light. It is very open for the first five or six years after the vintage before shutting down, at which point it generally takes ten more years to reach its peak.

170

Area under vine	27 hectares
Production	40-50,000 bottles
Soil	Sandy and clay-gravel, with a siliceous subsoil
Grape varieties	69% Sémillon, 28% Sauvignon, 3% Muscadelle
Barrel ageing	15-18 months - New barrels: 33%
Second wines	Sainte-Hélène du Château de Malle - Les Fleurs de Malle

Manager: Countess de Bournazel

Château de Malle 33210 Preignac
GPS: Latitude: 44.565 - Longitude: 0.2966667
Tel. +33 (0)5 56 62 36 86 - Fax +33 (0)5 56 76 82 40
chateaudemalle@wanadoo.fr - **www.chateau-de-malle.fr**

CHÂTEAU DE RAYNE VIGNEAU

PREMIER GRAND CRU CLASSÉ EN 1855

SAUTERNES

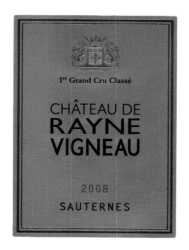

Located near the commune of Bommes, atop a magnificent gravelly rise overlooking the Sauternes region, Château Rayne Vigneau is the third highest point in the region.

There have been generations of owners since this estate was founded in the early 17th century by Gabriel de Vigneau. The most famous was probably the Pontac family, whose name is inseparable from the creation of great Bordeaux wines. They acquired the property in 1834. Albert de Pontac, great-nephew of Madame de Rayne, née Catherine de Pontac, named the château Rayne Vigneau.

It was during his family's ownership that the estate was included among the first growths in the famous 1855 classification.

Château Rayne Vigneau is a unique and rare wine. According to legend, its soil contains gemstones that account for its incredible golden hue.

Area under vine	62 hectares
Production	80,000 bottles
Soil	Gravel and sand on a clay subsoil
Grape varieties	80% Sémillon, 20% Sauvignon
Barrel ageing	12-18 months - New barrels: 40%
Second wine	Madame de Rayne

Managing Director: Thierry Budin

Château de Rayne Vigneau 33210 Bommes
GPS: Latitude: 44.5467126 - Longitude: -0.3570709
Tel. +33 (0)5 56 76 61 63 - Fax +33 (0)5 56 59 36 47
contact@cagrandscrus.com - **www.cagrandscrus.com**

CHÂTEAU DOISY DAËNE
CRU CLASSÉ EN 1855

BARSAC   Owner: Denis Dubourdieu

Château Doisy Daëne, included among the second growths in the 1855 classification, is located on the Barsac limestone plateau in the Sauternes appellation. It has belonged to the Dubourdieu family since 1924. Four generations have made fine white wine here from father to son: Georges (1924-1948), Pierre (1949-1999) and Denis Dubourdieu since the 2000 vintage – assisted by his sons, Fabrice and Jean-Jacques. The family is committed to defending and promoting Doisy Daëne's image around the world. Denis Dubourdieu is also a professor of oenology at Bordeaux University and an internationally renowned consultant.

Château Doisy Daëne's 17.2 hectares of vines (87% Sémillon and 13% Sauvignon Blanc) are over 40 years old.

The wines have their own special style, with bright fruit concentrated by "noble rot" as well as lively acidity, excellent balance, and delicate flavours. Doisy Daëne's much-appreciated personality reflects both its excellent limestone *terroir* and a long family tradition of quality.

172

Area under vine	17.2 hectares
Production	40,000 bottles
Soil	Clay-limestone
Grape varieties	87% Sémillon, 13% Sauvignon
Barrel ageing	18 months - New barrels: 33%

Château Doisy Daëne 10 Gravas - 33720 Barsac
GPS: Latitude: 44.6093681 - Longitude: -0.3139061
Tel. +33 (0)5 56 62 96 51 - Fax +33 (0)5 56 62 14 89
reynon@wanadoo.fr - **www.denisdubourdieu.com**

CHÂTEAU DOISY-VÉDRINES

CRU CLASSÉ EN 1855

Owners: Héritiers Pierre Castéja

SAUTERNES

The Chevaliers de Védrines owned this estate for centuries and gave their name to it. Included in the 1855 classification, it was acquired by the present owners in the mid-19th century.

Doisy-Védrines is located on the clay-limestone rise in Haut Barsac. The soil is ploughed the traditional way and the grapes are picked by hand in several waves (up to 6 or 8). Fermentation and ageing take place in barrels (exclusively French oak).

The combination of modern and traditional techniques gives Château Doisy-Védrines its trademark richness and finesse typical of the finest wines of Sauternes. Annual production amounts to 36,000 bottles.

When young, the wine is well-balanced and very delicious, especially as an aperitif. Older vintages are a delight at the end of a meal.

Area under vine	35 hectares
Production	36,000 bottles
Soil	Clay-limestone
Grape varieties	80% Sémillon, 15% Sauvignon, 5% Muscadelle
Barrel ageing	18 months - New barrels: 40-60%
Second wine	Château Petit Védrines

Manager: Olivier Castéja

Château Doisy-Védrines 1 Védrines - 33720 Barsac
GPS: Latitude: 44.58797 - Longitude: -0.321093
Tel. +33 (0)5 56 27 15 13 - Fax +33 (0)5 56 27 26 76
doisy-vedrines@orange.fr

CHÂTEAU GUIRAUD
PREMIER CRU CLASSÉ EN 1855

Owner: Financière Guiraud

Château Guiraud takes its name from a Bordeaux *négociant*, Pierre Guiraud, who purchased the estate in 1766. Included among the first growths in the 1855 classification, Château Guiraud has more than a hundred hectares of vines.

This magnificent property is well-known for their natural approach to viticulture. This includes the construction of insect hotels, planting five kilometres of hedges, developing genetic diversity, studying and propagating vines in a conservatory, etc.

Château Guiraud is currently the only first growth in the 1855 classification to be officially certified for organic viticulture.

The estate's ecological orientation helps to produce great wines with a strong personality and tremendous finesse. Château Guiraud is profound and well-focused with fruity and mineral flavours of extreme freshness.

174

Area under vine	100 hectares
Production	100,000 bottles
Soil	Gravel with sand and clay
Grape varieties	65% Sémillon, 35% Sauvignon
Barrel ageing	18-24 months - New barrels: 100%
Second wine	Le Dauphin de Guiraud

Owners: Financière Guiraud (Xavier Planty - Olivier Bernard - Stephan Von Neipperg
Robert Peugeot representing FFP)

Château Guiraud 33210 Sauternes
GPS: Latitude: 44.5328926 - Longitude: -0.3322452
Tel. +33 (0)5 56 76 61 01 - Fax +33 (0)5 56 76 67 52
xplanty@chateauguiraud.com - **www.chateauguiraud.com**

CHÂTEAU LA TOUR BLANCHE

PREMIER CRU CLASSÉ EN 1855

SAUTERNES

Founded in the 18th century, Château La Tour Blanche is located in the commune of Bommes, in the heart of the prestigious Sauternes appellation. A previous owner, Daniel "Osiris" Iffla, left the estate to the French government in 1907, on the condition that a tuition-free School of Viticulture and Oenology be created there.

The estate overlooks the Ciron river (a tributary of the Garonne), which is responsible for the unique microclimate that gives rise to the famous "noble rot".

Rigorous management in the vineyard (sustainable viticulture, traceability, waste water treatment, etc.) and the cellar (new barrels, temperature control, etc.) reflect the harmony that has been found between traditional and modern methods. This is essential for making a wine worthy of First Growth status.

La Tour Blanche's style achieves a perfect balance between concentration and freshness, with impressive finesse and elegance. For all these reasons, Château La Tour Blanche unquestionably deserves its rank as the first of the First Growths in the 1855 classification.

Area under vine	37 hectares
Production	50,000 bottles
Soil	Gravel with a clay-limestone subsoil
Grape varieties	80% Sémillon, 15% Sauvignon, 5% Muscadelle
Barrel ageing	16-18 months - New barrels: 100%
Second wine	Les Charmilles de Tour Blanche

Director: Alex Barrau - Communication and Sales: Didier Fréchinet
Cellar Master: Jean-Pierre Faure

Château La Tour Blanche 33210 Bommes
GPS: Latitude: 44.543010 - Longitude: -0.348030
Tel. +33 (0)5 57 98 02 73 - Fax +33 (0)5 57 98 02 78
tour-blanche@tour-blanche.com - **www.tour-blanche.com**

CHÂTEAU LAFAURIE-PEYRAGUEY
PREMIER CRU CLASSÉ EN 1855

SAUTERNES   *Owner: S.P.F.F.*

Château Lafaurie-Peyraguey was built in an astonishing Byzantine-Hispanic style in the 18th century. However, the main gate and outer wall (which the cellars adjoin) date from the 13th century.

The diversity of soils and sun exposures produces Sémillon grapes of great complexity and regularity, as well as Sauvignon Blanc and Muscadelle grapes that contribute vivacity, finesse, and elegance.

The vines are tended meticulously, with the greatest of respect for the *terroir*, the environment and, above all, the vineyard workers. The soil is ploughed instead of using herbicides and the frequency of treating the vines with chemical sprays has been severely reduced (minus 35% in the past two years).

The wine is fermented and aged in entirely renovated, air-conditioned cellars with controlled humidity. This enables Château Lafaurie-Peyraguey to reach its full potential of a first growth Sauternes.

Area under vine	36 hectares
Production	50,000 bottles
Soil	Clay and gravel as well as clay and sand
Grape varieties	90% Sémillon, 8% Sauvignon, 2% Muscadelle
Barrel ageing	18 months - New barrels: 35-50%
Second wine	La Chapelle de Lafaurie-Peyraguey

Manager: Éric Larramona

Château Lafaurie-Peyraguey 33210 Bommes
GPS: Latitude: 44.549167 - Longitude: -0.337222
Tel. +33 (0)5 56 76 60 54 - Fax +33 (0)5 56 76 61 89
info@lafaurie-peyraguey.com - **www.lafaurie-peyraguey.com**

CHÂTEAU NAIRAC

CRU CLASSÉ EN 1855

Owner: Nicole Tari-Heeter

Built at the end of the Ancien Régime by Jean Mollié, a disciple of Victor Louis, Château Nairac is named after a family of Huguenot ship owners who bought the property in 1777. The courtyard is flanked by outbuildings and cellars dating from the 17th century. As for the vineyard, records mention vines having grown here going back to the 16th century...

Included among the second growths in the 1855 classification, Nairac was noted as one of the finest wines in the region in the second edition of Cocks & Féret ("Bordeaux and its Wines") in 1868. After a series of crises, the estate was considerably renovated and rejuvenated in the 1970s. Thanks to owner Nicole Tari-Heeter and her three children, Nairac has since regained its former glory. Her son, Nicolas, has managed the estate with rigour and passion since 1993. Nairac is one of the finest wines of Barsac. As rich as the best châteaux in Sauternes, it displays a subtle difference due to its minerality, unique flavour profile, and elegant mouth feel. Everything possible is done to retain vintage character, respect nature, and reflect the *terroir*. The entire crop has been known to be declassified in vintages when there was no "noble rot".

Very much aware of their role as stewards of this historic estate, each member of the family exemplifies, in their own way, Nairac's motto: *Inséparable d'une culture* ("exemplifying a certain culture").

Area under vine	17 hectares
Production	0-15,000 bottles
Soil	Grave and sand as well as clay and sand on asteriated limestone bedrock
Grape varieties	90% Sémillon, 6% Sauvignon, 4% Muscadelle
Barrel ageing	18-36 months - New barrels: 10-100%
Second wine	Esquisse de Nairac

Estate Manager: Nicolas Heeter-Tari - Contact: Nicolas or Éloïse Heeter-Tari

Château Nairac 81 avenue Aristide Briand - 33720 Barsac
GPS: Latitude: 44.6098571 - Longitude: -0.3144207
Tel. +33 (0)5 56 27 16 16 - Fax +33 (0)5 56 27 26 50
chateau.nairac@wanadoo.fr - **www.chateaunairac.com**

177

CHÂTEAU SIGALAS RABAUD

PREMIER CRU CLASSÉ EN 1855

SAUTERNES

The configuration of Domaine de Rabaud, created in 1660, changed significantly in 1903 when Monsieur de Sigalas combined various vineyard plots with excellent sun exposure and gravelly soil from among those purchased by his father forty years beforehand. These fourteen hectares formed a jewel of a vineyard, the smallest of the first growths in the 1855 classification.

Six generations later, the grandchildren of the last representative of the older branch of the Sigalas family, Marquise de Lambert des Granges, now look after viticulture and winemaking with the same passion.

They produce a fine, fresh, elegant Sauternes whose structure is conferred by 85% Sémillon and charm by 15% Sauvignon Blanc. Sigalas-Rabaud is subtle and understated, a true connoisseur's wine that is enjoyable when young thanks to a bouquet of lime blossom and white fruit, although it is frequently able to age for over a century.

The second wine, Lieutenant de Sigalas, is the first growth's "little brother," made after a strict selection. The estate also produces an aromatic dry white wine, La Demoiselle de Sigalas. All the wines reflect a unique *terroir*.

Area under vine	14 hectares
Production	25,000 bottles
Soil	Gravel with sand and clay
Grape varieties	85% Sémillon, 15% Sauvignon
Barrel ageing	20 months - New barrels: 33%
Second wine	Lieutenant de Sigalas

President and Managing Director: Marquis de Lambert des Granges - Deputy Manager: Laure de Lambert Compeyrot
Oenologist: Éric Boissenot

Château Sigalas Rabaud 33210 Bommes
GPS: Latitude: 44.553808 - Longitude: -0.341295
Tel. +33 (0)5 56 21 31 43 - Fax +33 (0)5 56 78 71 55
contact@chateau-sigalas-rabaud.com - www.chateau-sigalas-rabaud.fr

CHÂTEAU SUDUIRAUT

PREMIER CRU CLASSÉ EN 1855

| SAUTERNES | Owner: AXA Millésimes |

The team of Château Suduiraut are striving towards a unique goal: to make one of the world's truly great wines.

Today, Château Suduiraut is acknowledged to be one of the finest Sauternes, thanks to a commitment to quality that is uncompromising in the extreme: tailored selection of the plots of vines, grape-by-grape harvesting and faultless control over the fermentation process in each individual barrel. Nowhere is this meticulous approach more evident than in the drastic selection process when the time comes to make the blend of the different wines.

Château Suduiraut is made with a selection of grapes from the most prestigious terroirs. This great wine boasts exceptional ageing capacity and offers a most harmonious alliance between aromas of flowers and fruit candied and *rôti* grapes. Above all else, he embodies perfect balance and elegance.

The château is a perfect example of 17th century architecture: noble, stately, and full of light. It is surrounded by magnificent gardens designed by Le Nôtre, which make the estate even more attractive.

Area under vine	92 hectares
Production	Variable according to the vintage
Soil	Sand and gravel
Grape varieties	90% Sémillon, 10% Sauvignon
Barrel ageing	18-24 months - New barrels: 50%
Second wine	Castelnau de Suduiraut

Managing Director: Christian Seely - Technical Director: Pierre Montégut

Château Suduiraut 33210 Preignac
GPS: Latitude: 44.557084 - Longitude: -0.318689
Tel. +33 (0)5 56 63 61 90 - Fax +33 (0)5 56 63 61 93
contact@suduiraut.com - **www.suduiraut.com**

Le Week-end des Grands Crus

The Union des Grands Crus attracts Bordeaux wine enthusiasts from all over the world to enjoy an outstanding weekend in the heart of the the region's finest appellations. Over two days, you will be able to take taste exceptional wines, meet château owners and winemakers, share meals with them, and visit their prestigious estates.

Information & booking at

www.ugcb.net

Saturday
TASTING
HANGAR 14 - QUAI DES CHARTRONS BORDEAUX

From 10:30 am
to 5 pm

Located in the historic port of Bordeaux, designated a World Heritage Site by UNESCO, more than a hundred château owners will welcome you and pour two vintages of their wines.

You will have a rare chance to be on an equal footing with Bordeaux wine professionals and to learn the secrets and subtleties of this type of tasting. This is a unique opportunity to discover the amazing diversity of these great wines, appreciate their impressive quality, and speak with the people who make them. According to your preference, you can enjoy lunch at the tasting or at one of the many restaurants in close proximity.

Starting at
8 pm.

"DÎNER PASSION" AT A WINE ESTATE
AND "SOIREE DES GRANDS CRUS"

"Dîner Passion" at a famous wine château: The Union des Grands Crus de Bordeaux organises a series of warm, friendly dinners in the wine country. Various UGC members will be glad to welcome you in the most prestigious appellations in Bordeaux. This is an ideal opportunity to discover the wine and food combinations that have made French cuisine and the French lifestyle so famous. Dining with château owners or people in charge of their estates, you can take advantage of this rare occasion to learn from professionals who make the finest dry white, red, and sweet white wines of Bordeaux.

Soirée des Grands Crus: Another, more relaxed and less formal evening has been planned in Bordeaux for people aged 18 to 35. This will consist of a wine bar and light buffet dinner with the estate owners and managers from prestigious châteaux to the tune of music played by a well-known DJ.

For prices and booking: www.ugcb.net

SUNDAY

VINEYARD TOURS AND OPEN DAY
IN THE WINE COUNTRY

All day
long

There is nothing like a day in the wine country to learn about the importance of *terroir*. The great appellations of Bordeaux are all represented: Saint-Estèphe, Pauillac, Saint-Julien, Margaux, Haut-Médoc, Moulis, Listrac ,Pessac-Léognan, Graves, Sauternes and Barsac, Saint-Émilion, and Pomerol.

Vineyard tours: Three coach tours are offered for people who wish to visit famous estates. One is to the Médoc, the second to Saint-Émilion and Pomerol, and the third to the Graves and Sauternes.

Detailed programme available at www.ugcb.net.

Open Day: Many estates belonging to the Union des Grands Crus de Bordeaux will welcome visitors on theme tours all day long.

To see the list of estates open and the terms, please go to www.ugcb.net

All day
long

GOLF TOURNAMENT
GARDEN GOLF DE MARGAUX

Golfers are also invited to participate in the Union des Grands Crus de Bordeaux Cup, a competition involving wine lovers and owners of Grands Crus taking place at the Golf du Médoc.

Designed by architect Olivier Dongradi in 2005, the Garden Golf de Margaux has 45 hectares of beautiful grounds bordering the Gironde estuary. Located in the heart of the famous Margaux appellation, and close to prestigious wine châteaux, the course features ponds as well as fairways lined with elm and ash trees, and is right along the estuary in places.

For prices and booking: www.ugcb.net

"Bordeaux Grand Cru"

by Riedel

This glass, first created in 1959 by Claus Riedel in the handmade Sommelier collection, and by Georg Riedel in 1986 in its machine-made version Vinum, is not a design gimmick but a precision instrument, developed to highlight the unique characteristics of the great wines of Bordeaux. The large bowl brings out the full depth of contemporary wines made from Cabernet Sauvignon, Cabernet Franc and Merlot.

Modern vinification techniques enable wine-makers to concentrate the fruit to such an extent that young wines may seem one-dimensional, tannic and over-oaked if served in smaller glasses.

The Bordeaux Grand Cru glasses give breathing space to both young and more mature wines, unpacking the various layers of bouquet and delivering a full spectrum of aromas. On the palate, the texture of the wine - soft, silky, velvety - is intensified and the finish prolonged, gently blending acidity with supple, sweet tannins. This is a glass that showcases these majestically structured red wines in all their complexity and finesse.

RIEDEL
THE WINE GLASS COMPANY

www.riedel.com

Château Angelus: © Château Angelus. Château Angludet: Claude Lada - Agence Class (photo family) and Franck Brunet d'Aubiac (photo château). Château Balestard La Tonnelle: Vignobles Capdemourlin (on the left) and Thierry Durandau (on the right). Château Bastor Lamontagne: Twin. Château Batailley: © Château Batailley. Château Beaumont: Guilène Proust. Château Beauregard: Studio Deepix (on the left), Twin (on the right). Château Beau-Séjour Bécot: Hervé Lefèbvre - Twin. Château Belgrave: Twin. Château Berliquet: Anna Lanta - Kréaphoto. Château Beychevelle: Loïc Bordaz. Château Bouscaut: Hervé Lefebvre - Twin. Château Branaire-Ducru: © Château Branaire-Ducru. Château Brane-Cantenac: François Poincet (photo Henri Lurton) and Guy Charneau (cellar). Château Canon: Twin. Château Canon La Gaffelière: François Poincet. Château Cantemerle: Vinexia.fr. Château Cantenac-Brown: © Château Cantenac-Brown. Château Cap de Mourlin: Thierry Durandau. Château Carbonnieux: Deepix. Vieux Château Certan: Philippe Roy. Château Chasse Spleen: Jean-Marc Palisse. Château Cheval Blanc: Alain Benoît - Deepix. Château Citran: Patrick Cronenberger. Château Clarke: Olivier Seignette (on the left), Hervé Lefebvre (on the right). Château Clerc Milon: © Château Clerc Milon. Château Climens: © Château Climens. Château Clinet: Patrick Cronenberger. Château Cos Labory: © Château Cos Labory. Château Coufran: François Poincet. Château Coutet: © Château Coutet. Château Croizet-Bages: Guy Charneau. Château d'Armailhac: © Château d'Armailhac. Château d'Yquem: Patrick Durand (photo P. Lurton) and Jean-Pierre Bost (photo château). Château Dassault: © Château Dassault. Château Dauzac: Alain Benoît - Deepix. Château de Camensac: Sabine Delcour. Château de Chantegrive: F. Vaysse. Domaine de Chevalier: Jean-Pierre Lamarque. Château de Fargues: M. Le Collen (aerial photo) and © Château de Fargues (cellar). Château de Fieuzal: Alain Benoît - Deepix. Château de France: © Château de France. Château de Lamarque: © Château de Lamarque. Château de Malle: Vincent Bengold. Château de Pez: Michel Jolyot. Château de Rayne Vigneau: Furax Jacques Péré. Château Desmirail: Gilles Arroyo. Château Doisy Daëne: Michel Geney. Château Doisy-Védrines: © Château Doisy-Védrines. Château du Tertre: © Château du Tertre. Château Durfort-Vivens: © Château Durfort-Vivens. Château Ferrande: Castel. Château Ferrière: © Château Ferrière. Château-Figeac: © Château-Figeac. Château Fonréaud: © Château Fonréaud. Château Fourcas Dupré: © Château Fourcas Dupré. Château Fourcas Hosten: Jean-Pierre Lamarque. Clos Fourtet: Anaka (portrait) and Klein (château). Château Franc Mayne: Twin. Château Gazin: Sarah Mattews. Château Giscours: © Château Giscours. Château Gloria: © Château Gloria. Château Grand Mayne: Mathieu Drouet - Agence Take a sip. Château Grand-Puy Ducasse: © Château Grand-Puy Ducasse. Château Grand-Puy-Lacoste: © Château Grand-Puy Lacoste. Château Greysac: S. Cottereau (on the right) and © Château Greysac (on the left). Château Gruaud Larose: © Château Gruaud Larose. Château Guiraud: François Poincet. Château Haut-Bages Libéral: © Château Haut-Bages Libéral. Château Haut-Bailly: Laurent Chartier. Château Haut-Bergey: © Château Haut-Bergey. Château Kirwan: V. Nadalié - www.toutenart.fr. Château L'Évangile: © DBR (Lafite). Château La Cabanne: © Château La Cabanne. Château La Conseillante: © Château La Conseillante. Château La Couspaude: © Château La Couspaude. Château La Croix de Gay: Philippe Viaud. Château La Dominique: © Château La Dominique. Château La Gaffelière: Anaka (portrait) and Anne Lanta (château). Château La Lagune: Twin (on the left) - © Ch. La Lagune. Château La Louvière: Alain Benoît. Château La Pointe: © Château La Pointe. Château La Tour Blanche: Hervé Lefebvre - Twin. Château La Tour Carnet: © Château La Tour Carnet. Château La Tour de By: © Château La Tour de By. Château La Tour Figeac: © Château La Tour Figeac. Château Labégorce: Catherine Poinson. Château Lafaurie-Peyraguey: © Château Lafaurie Peyraguey. Château Lafon-Rochet: © Château Lafon Rochet. Château Lagrange: Studio Deepix. Château Langoa Barton: Studio Pistolet Bleu. Château Larcis Ducasse: Anna Lanta. Château Larmande: Maitetxu Etcheverri. Château Larrivet Haut-Brion: Hervé Lefebvre - Twin. Château Lascombes: Guilène Proust. Château Latour-Martillac: Alain Benoît - Deepix. Château Léoville Barton: Hervé Lefebvre - Agence Pistolet Bleu. Château Léoville Poyferré: Anaka - Studio Pistolet Bleu. Château Les Carmes Haut-Brion: © Château Les Carmes Haut-Brion. Château Lynch-Bages: © Château Lynch-Bages. Château Lynch Moussas: © Château Lynch Moussas. Château Malartic-Lagravière: © Château Malartic-Lagravière. Château Malescasse: Alain Proust. Château Malescot Saint-Exupéry: Hervé Lefebvre - Twin. Château Marquis de Terme: Sébastien Cottereau. Château Maucaillou: APC Viaud. Château Monbrison: © Ch. Monbrison. Château Mouton Rothschild: Guy Charneau (photo at the bottom on the left) and © Château Mouton Rothschild. Château Nairac: Vincent Bengold - Pixels Grains d'Argent. Château Olivier: Studio Deepix. Château Ormes de Pez: © Château Ormes de Pez. Château Pape Clément: Alain Benoît - Deepix. Château Pavie: © Château Pavie. Château Pavie-Macquin: © Château Pavie-Macquin. Château Petit Village: © Château Petit-Village, photo A. Benoît - Deepix. Château Phélan Ségur: Twin. Château Pichon Longueville: © Château Pichon Longueville, photo A. Benoît - Deepix. Château Pichon Longueville Comtesse de Lalande: Sébastien Cottereau. Château Picque Caillou: François Poincet. Château Poujeaux: Anaka. Château Prieuré Lichine: Guy Charneau. Château Rahoul: Claude Prigent (photo château) and Yann Pandaris (Thiénot family photo). Château Rauzan-Gassies: Guy Charneau. Château Rauzan-Ségla: Michel Geney. Château Saint-Pierre: © Château Saint-Pierre. Château Sigalas-Rabaud: © Château Sigalas-Rabaud. Château Siran: © Château Siran. Château Smith Haut Lafitte: Pekka Nuikki. Château Suduiraut: © Ch. Suduiraut. Château Talbot: Vinexia.fr. Château Troplong Mondot: © Château Troplong Mondot. Château Trottevieille: © Château Trottevieille.

Notice

In keeping with French law, the publishers cannot be held liable in instances of involuntary errors or omissions despite the considerable attention and quality control measures that went into producing this guide.
The guide is co-published by:
The Union des Grands Crus de Bordeaux
10, cours du XXX Juillet
33000 Bordeaux - France.
&
Les éditions Féret
24 allées de Tourny
33000 Bordeaux - France

Editors:
Union des Grands Crus de Bordeaux – *Manager*, Jean-Marc Guiraud
Nicolas Mestre

Coordination
Éditions Féret – *Manager*, Bruno Boidron
Assistant, Véronique Garrouste

Production
Vinexia.fr – *Manager*, Lison Braastad

Translation
Aquitaine Traduction – *Manager*, Alexandre Rychlewski

Technical assistance and printing
Perfecto, Bordeaux

General remarks

The list of members belonging to the Union des Grands Crus dates from February 2011. The updated list can be found at www.ugcb.net.

Please note that there is no classification for the wines of Pomerol.

Furthermore, seeing as the size of the crop varies from one year to the next, the production figures cited in this guide are only an indication, and represent an average annual figure. They also only relate to the *grand vin*.

Likewise, the surface area mentioned reflects not the total size of the estate, but the area under vine.

The GPS coordinates are expressed in decimals.

Printed on 31 March 2011 in the EU

THE

QUOTABLE
BIBLE

compiled by
Martin H. Manser

Checkmark Books®
An imprint of Facts On File, Inc.

The Quotable Bible

First U.S. edition 2001

Copyright © 1999 Martin H. Manser

Checkmark Books
An imprint of Facts On File, Inc.
132 West 31st Street
New York NY 10001

Library of Congress Cataloging-in-Publication Data

Manser, Martin H.
   [Lion Bible quotation collection]
   The quotable Bible / Martin H. Manser
     p.cm.
   Originally published: The Lion Bible quotation collection. London, England: Lion Pub., 1999.
    Includes index.
    ISBN 0-8160-4655-7 (pbk. : alk. paper)
    1. Bible—Quotations. I. Title.
   BS391.3 .M36 2001
   220.5'2   2001023257

Original edition published in English under the title *The Lion Bible Quotation Collection* by Lion Publishing plc, Oxford, England

Published simultaneously in hardcover by Facts On File as *Biblical Quotations: A Reference Guide*.

Checkmark Books are available at special discounts when purchased in bulk quantities for businesses, associations, institutions or sales promotions. Please call our Special Sales Department in New York at (212) 967-8800 or (800) 322-8755.

You can find Facts On File on the World Wide Web at http://www.factsonfile.com

Printed in the United States of America

MP FOF 10 9 8 7 6 5 4 3 2

CONTENTS

Introduction   7

BOOKS OF THE BIBLE, INCLUDING THE APOCRYPHA   8

The Quotable Bible   9

Appendix   311

SPECIAL OCCASIONS   311

SELECTED HOLIDAYS AND FESTIVALS   315

Index of Themes   321

Index of Bible References   328

Index of Key Words   376

ACKNOWLEDGMENTS

I would like to acknowledge the invaluable help of the following: my wife Yusandra, my children Ben and Hannah, Rosalind Desmond (particularly for help on the indexes), Lynda Drury, Lynn Elias, Frank Harper and Gloria Wren; and of the publishers Angela Handley and Philip Law. I would also like to acknowledge the permission of HarperCollins Publishers in allowing me to adapt certain extracts from my book, *Amazing Book of Bible Facts*.

INTRODUCTION

Quotations from the Bible are among the best-known of all quotations in the English language. This book has been compiled to make a wide selection of quotations accessible to those who want to know what the Bible has to say on a particular subject, and also for those who simply want to browse.

The quotations in this collection are arranged under nearly 300 main themes, which are arranged in alphabetical order. Under each main theme heading, the quotations are arranged in the order in which they appear in the Bible. Certain main themes, e.g. **God**, **Holy Spirit**, **Jesus**, and **Prayer** have secondary theme headings. Each quotation has its own paragraph number, Bible reference and Bible version, so that readers can look up the quotations in a Bible to see their fuller context. Three indexes are also provided, listing themes, references in alphabetical order of Bible books, and key words used in the quotations.

The quotations have been cited from a range of different translations. Often the words are most familiar in the Authorized or King James Version. The words of the New Revised Standard Version, the New International Version, the Revised English Bible and the New Jerusalem Bible echo the older language but are more easily understood today. Other renderings, such as the Good News Bible and the Contemporary English Version, have been quoted to communicate the text in a simpler and fresher way.

In addition to the main text, over sixty feature panels look at words, phrases and allusions, such as 'the salt of the earth' and 'the powers that be', that have been formative in the development of the English language. Several other special features list different aspects of Christian teaching, e.g. parables and miracles. The Appendix gives additional Bible texts that might prove useful on special occasions, such as birthdays or weddings, and also at selected holidays and festivals.

This book has been compiled with the intention that it will lead to a greater reading of the Bible, and a response to its message. It is hoped that this selection will serve not only as a useful reference and resource tool, but also as a source of helpful encouragement and fresh inspiration.

BOOKS OF THE BIBLE, INCLUDING THE APOCRYPHA

The Old Testament

Genesis
Exodus
Leviticus
Numbers
Deuteronomy
Joshua
Judges
Ruth
1 Samuel
2 Samuel
1 Kings
2 Kings
1 Chronicles
2 Chronicles
Ezra
Nehemiah
Esther
Job
Psalms
Proverbs
Ecclesiastes
Song of Songs
Isaiah
Jeremiah
Lamentations
Ezekiel
Daniel
Hosea
Joel
Amos
Obadiah
Jonah
Micah
Nahum
Habakkuk
Zephaniah
Haggai
Zechariah
Malachi

The Apocrypha

1 Esdras
2 Esdras
Tobit
Judith
Additions to Esther*
Wisdom of Solomon
Ecclesiasticus
Baruch
Letter of Jeremiah*
Prayer of Azariah and the
      Song of the Three
      Jews*
History of Susanna*
Bel and the Dragon*
Prayer of Manasseh
1 Maccabees*
2 Maccabees

* Not quoted in this Bible quotation collection

The New Testament

Matthew
Mark
Luke
John
Acts
Romans
1 Corinthians
2 Corinthians
Galatians
Ephesians
Philippians
Colossians
1 Thessalonians
2 Thessalonians
1 Timothy
2 Timothy
Titus
Philemon
Hebrews
James
1 Peter
2 Peter
1 John
2 John
3 John
Jude
Revelation

ABBREVIATIONS

BCP	Book of Common Prayer
CEV	Contemporary English Version
GNB	Good News Bible
KJV	King James Version
NIV	New International Version
NJB	New Jerusalem Bible
NRSV	New Revised Standard Version
REB	Revised English Bible
RSV	Revised Standard Bible

The Quotable

Bible

Abilities

1.1 And you shall speak to all who have ability, whom I have endowed with skill, that they make Aaron's vestments to consecrate him for my priesthood.

Exodus 28:3 NRSV

1.2 The Lord has given to Bezalel, Oholiab, and others the skills needed for building a place of worship, and they will follow the Lord's instructions.

Exodus 36:1–2 CEV

1.3 Now therefore command thou that they hew me cedar trees out of Lebanon… for thou knowest that there is not among us any that can skill to hew timber like unto the Sidonians.

1 Kings 5:6 KJV

1.4 You have an abundance of workers: stonecutters, masons, carpenters, and all kinds of artisans without number, skilled in working gold, silver, bronze, and iron.

1 Chronicles 22:15–16 NRSV

1.5 Shemaiah… was the father of sons who had authority in their family, for they were men of great ability.

1 Chronicles 26:6 REB

1.6 [David to Solomon] The Lord my God will help you do everything needed to finish the temple, so it can be used for worshipping him. The priests and Levites have been assigned their duties, and all the skilled workers are prepared to do their work. The people and their leaders will do anything you tell them.

1 Chronicles 28:20–21 CEV

1.7 To one he gave five talents, to another two, to a third one, each in proportion to his ability.

Matthew 25:15 NJB

1.8 [On the day of Pentecost] All of them were filled with the Holy Spirit and began to speak in other languages, as the Spirit gave them ability.

Acts 2:4 NRSV

1.9 Let us use the different gifts allotted to each of us by God's grace.

Romans 12:6 REB

1.10 There is nothing I cannot do in the One who strengthens me.

Philippians 4:13 NJB

1.11 I thank Christ Jesus our Lord. He has given me the strength for my work because he knew that he could trust me.

1 Timothy 1:12 CEV

1.12 As every man hath received the gift, even so minister the same one to another, as good stewards of the manifold grace of God… if any man minister, let him do it as of the ability which God giveth: that God in all things may be glorified through Jesus Christ, to whom be praise and dominion for ever and ever. Amen.

1 Peter 4:10–11 KJV

See also **Gift**

Accepting the will of God

2.1 Moses said, 'No, Lord, don't send me. I have never been a good speaker, and I haven't become one since you began to speak to me. I am a poor speaker, slow and hesitant.' The Lord said to him, 'Who gives man his mouth? Who makes him deaf or dumb? Who gives him sight or makes him blind? It is I, the Lord. Now, go! I will help you to speak, and I will tell you what to say.'

Exodus 4:10–12 GNB

2.2 Though he slay me, yet will I trust in him: but I will maintain mine own ways before him.

Job 13:15 KJV

2.3 How good for me to have been chastened, so that I might be schooled in your statutes!

Psalm 119:71 REB

2.4 My child, do not despise the Lord's discipline or be weary of his reproof, for the Lord reproves the one he loves, as a father the son in whom he delights.

Proverbs 3:11–12 NRSV

2.5 Thy kingdom come. Thy will be done, in earth as it is in heaven.

Matthew 6:10 BCP

2.6 Going a little farther, he threw himself on the ground and prayed, 'My Father, if it is possible, let this cup pass from me; yet not what I want but what you want.'

Matthew 26:39 NRSV

2.7 One of you will say to me, 'If this is so, how can God find fault with anyone? Who can resist God's will?' But who are you, my friend, to answer God back? A clay pot does not ask the man who made it, 'Why did you make me like this?' After all, the man who makes the pots has the right to use the clay as he wishes, and to make two pots from the same lump of clay, one for special occasions and the other for ordinary use.

Romans 9:19–21 GNB

2.8 He said to me, 'My grace is sufficient for you, for power is made perfect in weakness.' So, I will boast all the more gladly of my weaknesses, so that the power of Christ may dwell in me.

2 Corinthians 12:9 NRSV

2.9 My dear friends, do not be taken aback at the testing by fire which is taking place among you, as though something strange were happening to you; but in so far as you share in the sufferings of Christ, be glad, so that you may enjoy a much greater gladness when his glory is revealed.

1 Peter 4:12–13 NJB

See also **Comfort; Contentment; Submission; Will of God**

Access

3.1 Who may go up the mountain of the Lord? Who may stand in his holy place? One who has clean hands and a pure heart, who has not set his mind on what is false or sworn deceitfully.

Psalm 24:3–4 REB

3.2 Jesus saith unto him, I am the way, the truth, and the life: no man cometh unto the Father, but by me.

John 14:6 KJV

3.3 Father, I desire that those also, whom you have given me, may be with me where I am, to see my glory, which you have given me because you loved me before the foundation of the world.

John 17:24 NRSV

3.4 By whom [Jesus Christ] also we have access by faith into this grace wherein we stand, and rejoice in hope of the glory of God.

Romans 5:2 KJV

3.5 Once you were far off, but now in union with Christ Jesus you have been brought near through the shedding of Christ's blood… for through him we both alike have access to the Father in the one Spirit.

Ephesians 2:13, 18 REB

3.6 In union with Christ and through our faith in him we have the boldness to go into God's presence with all confidence.

Ephesians 3:12 GNB

3.7 My friends, the blood of Jesus gives us courage to enter the most holy place by a new way that leads to life! And this way takes us through the curtain that is Christ himself. We have a great high priest who is in charge of God's house. So let's come near God with pure hearts and a confidence that comes from having faith. Let's keep our hearts pure, our consciences free from evil, and our bodies washed with clean water.

Hebrews 10:19–22 CEV

3.8 Draw near to God, and he will draw near to you.

James 4:8 NRSV

3.9 For Christ also suffered for sins once for all, the righteous for the unrighteous, in order to bring you to God. He was put to death in the flesh, but made alive in the spirit.

1 Peter 3:18 NRSV

See also **Adoption; Assurance; Confidence; Prayer, Promises in prayer**

Adam

4.1 So God created man in his own image, in the image of God created he him; male and female created he them.

Genesis 1:27 KJV

4.2 The Lord God formed man of the dust of the ground, and breathed into his nostrils the breath of life; and man became a living soul… And the Lord God said, It is not good that the man should be alone; I will make him an help meet for him.

Genesis 2:7, 18 KJV

4.3 As by one man sin entered into the world, and death by sin… so death passed upon all men, for that all have sinned.

Romans 5:12 KJV

4.4 So then, as the one sin condemned all people, in the same way the one righteous act sets all people free and gives them life. And just as the mass of people were made sinners as the result of the disobedience of one man, in the same way the mass of people will all be put right with God as the result of the obedience of the one man.

Romans 5:18–19 GNB

4.5 As in Adam all die, so in Christ all will be brought to life.

1 Corinthians 15:22 REB

4.6 Thus it is written, 'The first man, Adam, became a living being'; the last Adam became a life-giving spirit.

1 Corinthians 15:45 NRSV

See also **Eden, Garden of; Fall, the; Human beings; Life; Sin; Sinful nature**

Adoption

5.1 Now I tell you: love your enemies and pray for those who persecute you, so that you may become the children of your Father in heaven.

Matthew 5:44–45 GNB

5.2 Our Father, which art in heaven…

Matthew 6:9 BCP

5.3 Therefore take no thought, saying, What shall we eat? or, What shall we drink? or, Wherewithal shall we be clothed? (For after all these things do the Gentiles seek:) for your heavenly Father knoweth that ye have need of all these things. But seek ye first the kingdom of

God, and his righteousness; and all these things shall be added unto you.

Matthew 6:31–33 KJV

5.4 As many as received him, to them gave he power to become the sons of God, even to them that believe on his name.

John 1:12 KJV

5.5 For all who are led by the Spirit of God are sons of God. The Spirit you have received is not a spirit of slavery, leading you back into a life of fear, but a Spirit of adoption, enabling us to cry 'Abba! Father!' The Spirit of God affirms to our spirit that we are God's children; and if children, then heirs, heirs of God and fellow-heirs with Christ; but we must share his sufferings if we are also to share his glory.

Romans 8:14–17 REB

5.6 I will be your father, and you shall be my sons and daughters, says the Lord Almighty.

2 Corinthians 6:18 GNB

5.7 God sent his Son… in order to redeem those who were under the law, so that we might receive adoption as children. And because you are children, God has sent the Spirit of his Son into our hearts, crying, 'Abba! Father!'

Galatians 4:4–6 NRSV

5.8 Marking us out for himself beforehand, to be adopted sons, through Jesus Christ. Such was his purpose and good pleasure.

Ephesians 1:5 NJB

5.9 You have forgotten the exhortation that addresses you as children – 'My child, do not regard lightly the discipline of the Lord, or lose heart when you are punished by him; for the Lord disciplines those whom he loves, and chastises every child whom he accepts.' Endure trials for the sake of discipline. God is treating you as children; for what child is there whom a parent does not discipline?

Hebrews 12:5–7 NSRV

5.10 Think how much the Father loves us. He loves us so much that he lets us be called his children, as we truly are. But since the people of this world did not know who Christ is, they don't know who we are. My dear friends, we are already God's children, though what we will be hasn't yet been seen. But we do know that when Christ returns, we will be like him, because we will see him as he truly is.

1 John 3:1–2 CEV

See also **Access**; **Assurance**; **Confidence**; **God, Father**

Ambition

GODLY

6.1 One thing I ask of the Lord, it is the one thing I seek: that I may dwell in the house of the Lord all the days of my life, to gaze on the beauty of the Lord and to seek him in his temple.

Psalm 27:4 REB

6.2 Blessed are they which do hunger and thirst after righteousness: for they shall be filled.

Matthew 5:6 KJV

6.3 Strive to enter in at the strait gate: for many, I say unto you, will seek to enter in, and shall not be able.

Luke 13:24 KJV

6.4 Thus I [Paul] make it my ambition to proclaim the good news, not where Christ has already been named, so that I do not build on someone else's foundation.

Romans 15:20 NRSV

6.5 You are, I know, eager for gifts of the Spirit; then aspire above all to excel in those which build up the church.

1 Corinthians 14:12 REB

6.6 Because of the supreme advantage of knowing Christ Jesus my Lord, I count everything else as loss. For him I have accepted the loss of all other things, and look on them all as filth if only I can gain Christ and be given a place in him, with the uprightness I have gained not from the Law, but through faith in Christ, an uprightness from God, based on faith, that I may come to know him and the power of his resurrection, and partake of his sufferings by being moulded to the pattern of his death, striving towards the goal of resurrection from the dead. Not that I have secured it already, nor yet reached my goal, but I am still pursuing it in the attempt to take hold of the prize for which Christ Jesus took hold of me. Brothers, I do not reckon myself as having taken hold of it; I can only say that forgetting all that lies behind me, and straining forward to what lies in front, I am racing towards the finishing-point to win the prize of God's heavenly call in Christ Jesus.

Philippians 3:8–14 NJB

6.7 This is the Christ we are proclaiming, admonishing and instructing everyone in all wisdom, to make everyone perfect in Christ. And it is for this reason that I labour, striving with his energy which works in me mightily.

Colossians 1:28–29 NJB

6.8 It is true that anyone who desires to be a church official wants to be something worthwhile.

1 Timothy 3:1 CEV

See also **Christian life, Longing for God; Seeking God**

NEGATIVE

6.9 'Come,' they said, 'let us build ourselves a city and a tower with its top reaching heaven. Let us make a name for ourselves, so that we do not get scattered all over the world.'

Genesis 11:4 NJB

6.10 Some time later, Absalom got himself a chariot with horses to pull it, and he had fifty men to run in front. He would get up early each morning and wait by the side of the road that led to the city gate. Anyone who had a complaint to bring to King David would have to go that way, and Absalom would ask each of them, 'Where are you from?' If they said, 'I'm from a tribe in the north,' Absalom would say, 'You deserve to win your case. But the king doesn't have anyone to hear complaints like yours. I wish someone would make me the judge around here! I would be fair to everyone.'

2 Samuel 15:1–4 CEV

6.11 Do not wear yourself out in quest of wealth, stop applying your mind to this. Fix your gaze on it, and it is there no longer, for it is able to sprout wings like an eagle that flies off to the sky.

Proverbs 23:4–5 NJB

6.12 In the presence of the king do not give yourself airs, do not take a place among the great; better to be invited, 'Come up here', than be humiliated in the presence of the prince.

Proverbs 25:6–7 NJB

6.13 He that loveth silver shall not be satisfied with silver; nor he that loveth abundance with increase: this is also vanity. When goods increase, they are increased that eat them: and what good is there to the owners thereof, saving the beholding of them with their eyes?

Ecclesiastes 5:10–11 KJV

6.14 Bright morning star, how you have fallen from heaven, thrown to earth, prostrate among the nations! You thought to yourself: 'I shall scale the heavens to set my throne high above the mighty stars; I shall take my seat on the mountain where the gods assemble in the far recesses of the north. I shall ascend beyond the towering clouds and make myself like the Most High!'

Isaiah 14:12–14 REB

6.15 Seekest thou great things for thyself? seek them not.

Jeremiah 45:5 KJV

6.16 Though thou exalt thyself as the eagle, and though thou set thy nest among the stars, thence will I bring thee down, saith the Lord.

Obadiah 4 KJV

6.17 What will you gain, if you own the whole world but destroy yourself? What would you give to get back your soul?

Matthew 16:26 CEV

6.18 What is it you want me to do for you?' he asked. They [James and John] answered, 'Allow us to sit with you in your glory, one at your right hand and the other at your left.

Mark 10:36–37 REB

6.19 Among you, whoever wants to be great must be your servant, and whoever wants to be first must be the slave of all.

Mark 10:43–44 REB

6.20 Labour not for the meat which perisheth, but for that meat which endureth unto everlasting life, which the Son of man shall give unto you.

John 6:27 KJV

6.21 Leave no room for selfish ambition and vanity, but humbly reckon others better than yourselves.

Philippians 2:3 REB

6.22 Let your thoughts be on things above, not on the things that are on the earth.

Colossians 3:2 NJB

6.23 For all that is in the world, the lust of the flesh, and the lust of the eyes, and the pride of life, is not of the Father, but is of the world.

1 John 2:16 KJV

See also Desire, wrong; Pride; Riches

Angels

7.1 For he will charge his angels to guard you wherever you go.

Psalm 91:11 REB

7.2 Then Nebuchadnezzar spake, and said, Blessed be the God of Shadrach, Meshach, and Abednego, who hath sent his angel, and delivered his servants that trusted in him, and have changed the king's word, and yielded their bodies, that they might not serve nor worship any god, except their own God.

Daniel 3:28 KJV

7.3 At that time Michael will arise – the great Prince, defender of your people. That will be a time of great distress, unparalleled since nations first came into existence. When that time comes, your own people will be spared – all those whose names are found written in the Book.

Daniel 12:1 NJB

7.4 See that you don't despise any of these little ones. Their angels in heaven, I tell you, are always in the presence of my Father in heaven.

Matthew 18:10 GNB

7.5 When the Son of man shall come in his glory, and all the holy angels with him, then shall he sit upon the throne of his glory.
Matthew 25:31 KJV

7.6 In the sixth month the angel Gabriel was sent by God to a town in Galilee called Nazareth.
Luke 1:26 NRSV

7.7 In the same way, I tell you, there is joy among the angels of God over one sinner who repents.
Luke 15:10 REB

7.8 Angels gave you God's Law, but you still don't obey it.
Acts 7:53 CEV

7.9 Do you not know that we are to judge angels – to say nothing of ordinary matters?
1 Corinthians 6:3 NRSV

7.10 To make everyone see… that through the church the wisdom of God in its rich variety might now be made known to the rulers and authorities in the heavenly places.
Ephesians 3:9–10 NRSV

7.11 What are the angels, then? They are spirits who serve God and are sent by him to help those who are to receive salvation.
Hebrews 1:14 GNB

7.12 As I looked I heard, all round the throne and the living creatures and the elders, the voices of many angels, thousands on thousands, myriads on myriads. They proclaimed with loud voices: 'Worthy is the Lamb who was slain, to receive power and wealth, wisdom and might, honour and glory and praise!'
Revelation 5:11–12 REB

Anger

DIVINE

8.1 The Lord is merciful and gracious, slow to anger, and plenteous in mercy. He will not always chide: neither will he keep his anger for ever.
Psalm 103:8–9 KJV

8.2 As tongues of fire lick up the stubble and chaff shrivels in the flames, so their root will moulder away and their opening buds vanish like fine dust; for they have spurned the instruction of the Lord of Hosts and rejected the word of the Holy One of Israel. So the anger of the Lord is roused against his people, and he has stretched out his hand to strike them down; the mountains trembled, and corpses lay like refuse in the streets. Yet for all this his anger has not abated, and his hand is still stretched out.
Isaiah 5:24–25 REB

8.3 O Lord, revive thy work in the midst of the years, in the midst of the years make known; in wrath remember mercy.
Habakkuk 3:2 KJV

8.4 When he [John the Baptist] saw a number of Pharisees and Sadducees coming for baptism he said to them, 'Brood of vipers, who warned you to flee from the coming retribution?'
Matthew 3:7 NJB

8.5 Jesus was angry as he looked round at them, but at the same time he felt sorry for them, because they were so stubborn and wrong.
Mark 3:5 GNB

8.6 He that believeth on the Son hath everlasting life: and he that believeth not the Son shall not see life; but the wrath of God abideth on him.

John 3:36 KJV

8.7 For the wrath of God is revealed from heaven against all ungodliness and unrighteousness of men, who hold the truth in unrighteousness.

Romans 1:18 KJV

8.8 We too were once of their number: we were ruled by our physical desires, and did what instinct and evil imagination suggested. In our natural condition we lay under the condemnation of God like the rest of mankind.

Ephesians 2:3 REB

8.9 On the day of judgment Jesus will save us from God's anger.

1 Thessalonians 1:10 CEV

8.10 [They] said to the mountains and rocks, Fall on us, and hide us from the face of him that sitteth on the throne, and from the wrath of the Lamb: For the great day of his wrath is come; and who shall be able to stand?

Revelation 6:16 KJV

See also **Propitiation; Punishment**

HUMAN

8.11 If you stay calm, you are wise, but if you have a hot temper, you only show how stupid you are.

Proverbs 14:29 GNB

8.12 Hot tempers cause arguments, but patience brings peace.

Proverbs 15:18 GNB

8.13 Better be slow to anger than a fighter, better control one's temper than capture a city.

Proverbs 16:32 REB

8.14 You have heard that people were told in the past, 'Do not commit murder; anyone who does will be brought to trial.' But now I tell you: whoever is angry with his brother will be brought to trial.

Matthew 5:21–22 GNB

8.15 [Love] isn't quick-tempered.

1 Corinthians 13:5 CEV

8.16 Now the works of the flesh are obvious:… anger…

Galatians 5:19–20 NRSV

8.17 Be ye angry, and sin not: let not the sun go down upon your wrath: Neither give place to the devil… Let all bitterness, and wrath, and anger, and clamour, and evil speaking, be put away from you, with all malice.

Ephesians 4:26–27, 31 KJV

8.18 You must understand this, my beloved: let everyone be quick to listen, slow to speak, slow to anger; for your anger does not produce God's righteousness.

James 1:19–20 NRSV

See also **Bitterness**

Animals

9.1 God said, 'Let the earth produce every kind of living creature in its own species: cattle, creeping things and wild animals of all kinds.' And so it was. God made wild animals in their own species, and cattle in theirs, and every creature that crawls along the earth in its own species. God saw that it was good.

Genesis 1:24–25 NJB

9.2 The Lord took some soil and made animals and birds. He brought them to the man to see what names he would give each of them. Then the man named the tame animals and the birds and the wild animals. That's how they got their names.

Genesis 2:19–20 CEV

9.3 Of clean beasts, and of beasts that are not clean, and of fowls, and of every thing that creepeth upon the earth, there went in two and two unto Noah into the ark, the male and the female, as God had commanded Noah.

Genesis 7:8–9 KJV

9.4 These are the animals you may eat: ox, sheep, goat, deer, gazelle, roebuck, ibex, antelope, oryx, mountain sheep. You may eat any animal that has a divided and cloven hoof and that is a ruminant. Of those, however, that are ruminants and of those that have a divided and cloven hoof you may not eat the following: the camel, the hare and the coney... So also the pig, which though it has a cloven hoof is not a ruminant; you must class it as unclean. You must neither eat the meat of such animals nor touch their dead bodies.

Deuteronomy 14:4–8 NJB

9.5 [God to Job] Can you hunt prey for the lioness and satisfy the appetite of young lions, as they crouch in the lair or lie in wait in the covert... Do you know when the mountain goats give birth? Do you attend the wild doe when she is calving? Can you count the months that they carry their young or know the time of their delivery, when they crouch down to open their wombs and deliver their offspring, when the fawns growing and thriving in the open country leave and do not return? Who has let the Syrian wild ass range at will and given the Arabian wild ass its freedom?

Job 38:39–40, 39:1–5 REB

9.6 Is the wild ox willing to serve you or spend the night in your stall? Can you

harness its strength with ropes; will it harrow the furrows after you?... Do you give the horse his strength? Have you clothed his neck with a mane?

Job 39:9–10, 19 REB

9.7 Look at Behemoth, my creature, just as you are! He feeds on greenstuff like the ox, but what strength he has in his loins, what power in his stomach muscles!... Leviathan, too! Can you catch him with a fish-hook or hold his tongue down with a rope?

Job 40:15–16, 25 NJB

9.8 You let us rule everything your hands have made. And you put all of it under our power – the sheep and the cattle, and every wild animal, the birds in the sky, the fish in the sea, and all ocean creatures.

Psalm 8:6–8 CEV

9.9 Although you offer sacrifices and always bring gifts, I won't accept your offerings of bulls and goats. Every animal in the forest belongs to me, and so do the cattle on a thousand hills. I know all the birds in the mountains, and every wild creature is in my care.

Psalm 50:8–11 CEV

9.10 Then the wolf will live with the lamb, and the leopard lie down with the kid; the calf and the young lion will feed together, with a little child to tend them. The cow and the bear will be friends, and their young will lie down together; and the lion will eat straw like cattle. The infant will play over the cobra's hole, and the young child dance over the viper's nest. There will be neither hurt nor harm in all my holy mountain; for the land will be filled with the knowledge of the Lord, as the waters cover the sea.

Isaiah 11:6–9 REB

See also **Creation**; **Providence**

Antichrist

10.1 While I was staring at the horns, I saw a little horn coming up among the others. It tore out three of the horns that were already there. This horn had human eyes and a mouth that was boasting proudly.

Daniel 7:8 GNB

10.2 He will hurl defiance at the Most High and wear down the holy ones of the Most High. He will have it in mind to alter the festival seasons and religious laws; and the holy ones will be delivered into his power for a time, and times, and half a time.

Daniel 7:25 REB

10.3 For many shall come in my name, saying, I am Christ; and shall deceive many... For there shall arise false Christs, and false prophets, and shall shew great signs and wonders; insomuch that, if it were possible, they shall deceive the very elect.

Matthew 24:5, 24 KJV

10.4 Let no one deceive you in any way; for that day [the day of the Lord] will not come unless the rebellion comes first and the lawless one is revealed, the one destined for destruction. He opposes and exalts himself above every so-called god or object of worship, so that he takes his seat in the temple of God, declaring himself to be God.

2 Thessalonians 2:3–4 NRSV

10.5 And now you know what is holding him back, so that he may be revealed at the proper time. For the secret power of lawlessness is already at work; but the one who now holds it back will continue to do so till he is taken out of the way. And then the lawless one will be revealed, whom the Lord Jesus will overthrow with the breath of his mouth and destroy by the splendour of his coming. The coming of the lawless one will be in accordance with the work of Satan displayed in all kinds of counterfeit miracles, signs and wonders, and in every sort of evil that deceives those who are perishing. They perish because they refused to love the truth and so be saved.

2 Thessalonians 2:6–10 NIV

10.6 Children, this is the last hour! You were told that an antichrist was to come. Well, many antichrists have already appeared, proof to us that this is indeed the last hour.

1 John 2:18 REB

10.7 Anyone who denies that Jesus is the Christ is nothing but a liar. He is the antichrist, for he denies both the Father and the Son.

1 John 2:22 REB

10.8 No spirit which fails to acknowledge Jesus is from God; it is the spirit of Antichrist, whose coming you have heard of; he is already at large in the world.

1 John 4:3 NJB

10.9 Many deceivers have gone out into the world, people who do not acknowledge Jesus Christ as coming in the flesh. Any such person is the deceiver and antichrist.

2 John v. 7 REB

Apostles

11.1 Then he called his twelve disciples to him and gave them authority to drive out unclean spirits and to cure every kind of illness and infirmity. These are the names of the twelve apostles: first Simon, also called Peter, and his brother Andrew; James son of Zebedee, and his brother

John; Philip and Bartholomew, Thomas and Matthew the tax-collector, James son of Alphaeus, Thaddaeus, Simon the Zealot, and Judas Iscariot, the man who betrayed him.

Matthew 10:1–4 REB

11.2 Out of the men who have been with us the whole time that the Lord Jesus was living with us, from the time when John was baptising until the day when he was taken up from us, one must be appointed to serve with us as a witness to his resurrection.

Acts 1:21–22 NJB

11.3 When the apostles Barnabas and Paul heard of it, they tore their clothes and rushed into the crowd shouting.

Acts 14:14 REB

11.4 I am free. I am an apostle. I have seen the Lord Jesus and have led you to have faith in him. Others may think that I am not an apostle, but you are proof that I am an apostle to you.

1 Corinthians 9:1–2 CEV

11.5 Now you are the body of Christ and individually members of it. And God has appointed in the church first apostles…

1 Corinthians 12:27–28 NRSV

11.6 So then, you Gentiles are not foreigners or strangers any longer; you are now fellow-citizens with God's people and members of the family of God. You, too, are built upon the foundation laid by the apostles and prophets, the cornerstone being Christ Jesus himself.

Ephesians 2:19–20 GNB

11.7 Wherefore, holy brethren, partakers of the heavenly calling, consider the Apostle and High Priest of our profession, Christ Jesus.

Hebrews 3:1 KJV

11.8 [To the church at Ephesus] I know what you are doing, how you toil and endure. I know you cannot abide wicked people; you have put to the test those who claim to be apostles but are not, and you have found them to be false.

Revelation 2:2 REB

Assurance

12.1 All that the Father giveth me shall come to me; and him that cometh to me I will in no wise cast out.

John 6:37 KJV

12.2 I give unto them [my sheep] eternal life; and they shall never perish, neither shall any man pluck them out of my hand.

John 10:28 KJV

12.3 Therefore being justified by faith, we have peace with God through our Lord Jesus Christ: by whom also we have access by faith into this grace wherein we stand, and rejoice in hope of the glory of God. And not only so, but we glory in tribulations also: knowing that tribulation worketh patience; and patience, experience; and experience, hope: and hope maketh not ashamed; because the love of God is shed abroad in our hearts by the Holy Ghost which is given unto us.

Romans 5:1–5 KJV

12.4 Since we have now been justified by Christ's sacrificial death, we shall all the more certainly be saved through him from final retribution. For if, when we were God's enemies, we were reconciled to him through the death of his Son, how much more, now that we have been reconciled, shall we be saved by his life!

Romans 5:9–10 REB

12.5 Condemnation will never come to those who are in Christ Jesus.

Romans 8:1 NJB

12.6 What then are we to say about these things? If God is for us, who is against us? He who did not withhold his own Son, but gave him up for all of us, will he not with him also give us everything else? Who will bring any charge against God's elect? It is God who justifies. Who is to condemn? Is it Christ Jesus, who died, yes, who was raised, who is at the right hand of God, who indeed intercedes for us. Who will separate us from the love of Christ? Will hardship, or distress, or persecution, or famine, or nakedness, or peril, or sword?… No, in all these things we are more than conquerors through him who loved us. For I am convinced that neither death, nor life, nor angels, nor rulers, nor things present, nor things to come, nor powers, nor height, nor depth, nor anything else in all creation, will be able to separate us from the love of God in Christ Jesus our Lord.

Romans 8:31–35, 37–39 NRSV

12.7 So I am sure that God, who began this good work in you, will carry it on until it is finished on the Day of Christ Jesus.

Philippians 1:6 GNB

12.8 I am not ashamed! I know the one I have faith in, and I am sure that he can guard until the last day what he has trusted me with.

2 Timothy 1:12 CEV

12.9 Let us make our approach in sincerity of heart and the full assurance of faith, inwardly cleansed from a guilty conscience, and outwardly washed with pure water.

Hebrews 10:22 REB

12.10 If we walk in the light, as he is in the light, we have fellowship one with another, and the blood of Jesus Christ his Son cleanseth us from all sin… If we confess our sins, he is faithful and just to forgive us our sins, and to cleanse us from all unrighteousness.

1 John 1:7, 9 KJV

12.11 We are sure that we live in union with God and that he lives in union with us, because he has given us his Spirit.

1 John 4:13 GNB

12.12 He that hath the Son hath life; and he that hath not the Son of God hath not life.

1 John 5:12 KJV

See also **Access; Adoption; Comfort; Confidence; Doubt; Victory**

Atonement

13.1 He shall put his hand upon the head of the burnt offering; and it shall be accepted for him to make atonement for him.

Leviticus 1:4 KJV

13.2 Surely he hath borne our griefs, and carried our sorrows: yet we did esteem him stricken, smitten of God, and afflicted. But he was wounded for our transgressions, he was bruised for our iniquities: the chastisement of our peace was upon him; and with his stripes we are healed. All we like sheep have gone astray; we have turned every one to his own way; and the Lord hath laid on him the iniquity of us all… Yet it pleased the Lord to bruise him; he hath put him to grief: when thou shalt make his soul an offering for sin, he shall see his seed, he shall prolong his days, and the pleasure of the Lord shall prosper in his hand. He shall see of the travail of his soul, and shall be satisfied: by his knowledge shall my righteous servant justify many; for he shall bear their iniquities. Therefore will I divide him a portion with the great, and he shall divide the spoil with the strong; because he hath poured out his soul unto death: and he was numbered with the transgressors; and he bare the sin of many, and made intercession for the transgressors.

Isaiah 53:4–6, 10–12 KJV

13.3 For the Son of Man did not come to be served but to serve, and to give his life as a ransom for many.

Mark 10:45 REB

13.4 Being justified freely by his grace through the redemption that is in Christ Jesus: whom God hath set forth to be a propitiation through faith in his blood, to declare his righteousness for the remission of sins that are past, through the forbearance of God.

Romans 3:24–25 KJV

13.5 So it is proof of God's own love for us, that Christ died for us while we were still sinners.

Romans 5:8 NJB

13.6 For the love of Christ constraineth us; because we thus judge, that if one died for all, then were all dead.

2 Corinthians 5:14 KJV

13.7 For our sake he made him to be sin who knew no sin, so that in him we might become the righteousness of God.

2 Corinthians 5:21 NRSV

13.8 Your life must be controlled by love, just as Christ loved us and gave his life for us as a sweet-smelling offering and sacrifice that pleases God.

Ephesians 5:2 GNB

13.9 The Son is the radiance of God's glory and the exact representation of his being, sustaining all things by his powerful

word. After he had provided purification for sins, he sat down at the right hand of the Majesty in heaven.

Hebrews 1:3 NIV

13.10 He carried our sins in his own person on the gibbet, so that we might cease to live for sin and begin to live for righteousness. By his wounds you have been healed.

1 Peter 2:24 REB

13.11 Christ died once for our sins. An innocent person died for those who are guilty. Christ did this to bring you to God, when his body was put to death and his spirit was made alive.

1 Peter 3:18 CEV

13.12 He [Jesus Christ] is the propitiation for our sins: and not for ours only, but also for the sins of the whole world.

1 John 2:2 KJV

See also Blood; Forgiveness; Jesus Christ, Death; Justification; Propitiation; Reconciliation; Redemption; Salvation and Savior

Authority

14.1 For the lips of a priest should guard knowledge, and people should seek instruction from his mouth, for he is the messenger of the Lord of hosts.

Malachi 2:7 NRSV

14.2 He [Jesus] taught… as one having authority, and not as the scribes.

Matthew 7:29 KJV

14.3 The centurion answered and said, Lord, I am not worthy that thou shouldest come under my roof: but speak the word only, and my servant shall be healed. For I am a man under authority, having soldiers under me: and I say to this man, Go, and he goeth; and to another, Come, and he cometh; and to my servant, Do this, and he doeth it.

Matthew 8:8–9 KJV

Say the word
The expression *say the word*, to state one's intentions to someone who is willing to fulfill them immediately, has its basis in this verse. The centurion had such faith that he believed that Jesus only had to speak the word of healing and his servant would be completely well again.

14.4 'To prove to you that the Son of man has authority on earth to forgive sins,' – then he said to the paralytic – 'get up, pick up your bed and go off home.'

Matthew 9:6 NJB

14.5 Then Jesus summoned his twelve disciples and gave them authority over unclean spirits, to cast them out, and to cure every disease and every sickness.

Matthew 10:1 NRSV

14.6 They saw him and worshipped him, but some of them doubted. Jesus came to them and said: 'I have been given all authority in heaven and on earth…'

Matthew 28:17–18 CEV

14.7 They were all amazed and began to ask one another, 'What is this? A new kind of teaching! He speaks with authority. When he gives orders, even the unclean spirits obey.'

Mark 1:27 REB

14.8 I will show you whom to fear: fear him who, after he has killed, has authority to cast into hell. Believe me, he is the one to fear.

Luke 12:5 REB

14.9 As many as received him, to them gave he power to become the sons of God, even to them that believe on his name.

John 1:12 KJV

14.10 For as the Father hath life in himself; so hath he given to the Son to have life in himself; and hath given him authority to execute judgment also, because he is the Son of man.

John 5:26–27 KJV

14.11 No-one takes it [my life] from me, but I lay it down of my own accord. I have authority to lay it down and authority to take it up again. This command I received from my Father.

John 10:18 NIV

14.12 For you [the Father] gave him [the Son] authority over all humanity, so that he might give eternal life to all those you gave him.

John 17:2 GNB

14.13 Everyone must obey the state authorities, because no authority exists without God's permission, and the existing authorities have been put there by God.

Romans 13:1 GNB

See also **Jesus Christ, Authority; Power**

Baptism

15.1 [John the Baptist] I baptize you with water, for repentance; but the one who comes after me is mightier than I am, whose sandals I am not worthy to remove. He will baptize you with the Holy Spirit and with fire.

Matthew 3:11 REB

15.2 Jesus, when he was baptized, went up straightway out of the water: and, lo, the heavens were opened unto him, and he saw the Spirit of God descending like a dove, and lighting upon him.

Matthew 3:16 KJV

15.3 Go therefore and make disciples of all nations, baptizing them in the name of the Father and of the Son and of the Holy Spirit.

Matthew 28:19 NRSV

15.4 'You must repent,' Peter answered, 'and every one of you must be baptised in the name of Jesus Christ for the forgiveness of your sins, and you will receive the gift of the Holy Spirit'… They accepted what he said and were baptised. That very day about three thousand were added to their number.

Acts 2:38, 41 NJB

15.5 As they were going along the road, they came to some water; and the eunuch said, 'Look, here is water! What is to prevent me from being baptized?' He commanded the chariot to stop, and both of them, Philip and the eunuch, went down into the water, and Philip baptized him.

Acts 8:36, 38 NRSV

15.6 While it was still night, the jailer took them to a place where he could wash their cuts and bruises. Then he and everyone in his home were baptized.

Acts 16:33 CEV

15.7 Paul said, 'The baptism of John was for those who turned from their sins; and he told the people of Israel to believe in the one who was coming after him – that is, in Jesus.' When they [disciples in Ephesus] heard this, they were baptized in the name of the Lord Jesus.

Acts 19:4–5 GNB

15.8 Know ye not, that so many of us as were baptized into Jesus Christ were baptized into his death? Therefore we are buried with him by baptism into death: that like as Christ was raised up from the dead by the glory of the Father, even so we also should walk in newness of life.

Romans 6:3–4 KJV

15.9 For in the one Spirit we were all baptized into one body – Jews or Greeks, slaves or free – and we were all made to drink of one Spirit.

1 Corinthians 12:13 NRSV

15.10 There is one body, and one Spirit, even as ye are called in one hope of your calling; one Lord, one faith, one baptism.

Ephesians 4:4–5 KJV

Beauty

16.1 The Lord said to him [Samuel], 'Pay no attention to his outward appearance and stature, for I have rejected him. The Lord does not see as a mortal sees; mortals see only appearances but the Lord sees into the heart.'

1 Samuel 16:7 REB

16.2 Worship the Lord in the beauty of holiness.

1 Chronicles 16:29 KJV

16.3 On the seventh day, when he was merry with wine, the king ordered… the seven eunuchs who were in attendance on the king's person, to bring Queen Vashti into his presence wearing her royal diadem, in order to display her beauty to the people and to the officers; for she was indeed a beautiful woman.

Esther 1:10–11 REB

16.4 One thing have I desired of the Lord, that will I seek after; that I may dwell in the house of the Lord all the days of my life, to behold the beauty of the Lord, and to inquire in his temple.

Psalm 27:4 KJV

16.5 Out of Zion, the perfection of beauty, God hath shined.

Psalm 50:2 KJV

16.6 For the Lord taketh pleasure in his people: he will beautify the meek with salvation.

Psalm 149:4 KJV

16.7 Do not covet her [a married woman's] beauty in your heart or let her captivate you with the play of her eyes.

Proverbs 6:25 NJB

16.8 Charm can be deceiving, and beauty fades away, but a woman who honours the Lord deserves to be praised.

Proverbs 31:30 CEV

16.9 He hath made every thing beautiful in his time.

Ecclesiastes 3:11 KJV

16.10 How beautiful you are, my beloved, how beautiful you are! Your eyes are doves. How beautiful you are, my love, and how you delight me!

Song of Songs 1:15–16 NJB

16.11 Your heart has grown proud because of your beauty, your wisdom has been corrupted by your splendour.

Ezekiel 28:17 NJB

16.12 As it is written, How beautiful are the feet of them that preach the gospel of peace, and bring glad tidings of good things!

Romans 10:15 KJV

16.13 Now, my friends, all that is true, all that is noble, all that is just and pure, all that is lovable and attractive, whatever is excellent and admirable – fill your thoughts with these things.

Philippians 4:8 REB

16.14 Don't depend on things like fancy hair styles or gold jewellery or expensive clothes to make you look beautiful. Be beautiful in your heart by being gentle and quiet. This kind of beauty will last, and God considers it very special. Long ago those women who worshipped God and put their hope in him made themselves beautiful by putting their husbands first.

1 Peter 3:3–5 CEV

Bible

17.1 For as the rain cometh down, and the snow from heaven, and returneth not thither, but watereth the earth, and maketh it bring forth and bud, that it may give seed to the sower, and bread to the eater: So shall my word be that goeth forth out of my mouth: it shall not return unto me void, but it shall accomplish that which I please, and it shall prosper in the thing whereto I sent it.

Isaiah 55:10–11 KJV

17.2 Scripture says, 'Man is not to live on bread alone, but on every word that comes from the mouth of God.'

Matthew 4:4 REB

17.3 [To the Jews] You search the scriptures because you think that in them you have eternal life; and it is they that testify on my behalf. Yet you refuse to come to me to have life.

John 5:39–40 NRSV

17.4 The Holy Spirit will come and help you, because the Father will send the Spirit to take my place. The Spirit will teach you everything and will remind you of what I said while I was with you.

John 14:26 CEV

17.5 These [Jews at Berea] were more noble than those in Thessalonica, in that they received the word with all readiness of mind, and searched the scriptures daily, whether those things were so.

Acts 17:11 KJV

17.6 God trusted his message to the Jews.

Romans 3:2 GNB

17.7 And take the helmet of salvation, and the sword of the Spirit, which is the word of God.

Ephesians 6:17 KJV

17.8 Let the word of Christ dwell in you richly in all wisdom; teaching and admonishing one another in psalms and hymns and spiritual songs, singing with grace in your hearts to the Lord.

Colossians 3:16 KJV

17.9 We also constantly give thanks to God for this, that when you received the word of God that you heard from us, you accepted it not as a human word but as what it really is, God's word, which is also at work in you believers.

1 Thessalonians 2:13 NRSV

17.10 Make every effort to present yourself before God as a proven worker who has no need to be ashamed, but who keeps the message of truth on a straight path.

2 Timothy 2:15 NJB

17.11 How from childhood you have known the sacred writings that are able to instruct you for salvation through faith in Christ Jesus. All scripture is inspired by God and is useful for teaching, for reproof, for correction, and for training in righteousness, so that everyone who belongs to God may be proficient, equipped for every good work.

2 Timothy 3:15–17 NRSV

17.12 The word of God is alive and active, sharper than any double-edged sword. It cuts all the way through, to where soul and spirit meet, to where joints and marrow come together. It judges the desires and thoughts of the heart.

Hebrews 4:12 GNB

17.13 First note this: no prophetic writing is a matter for private interpretation. It was not on any human initiative that prophecy came; rather, it was under the compulsion of the Holy Spirit that people spoke as messengers of God.

2 Peter 1:20–21 REB

See also Law; Revelation; Will of God

Birth

18.1 The Lord God formed man of the dust of the ground, and breathed into his nostrils the breath of life; and man became a living soul.

Genesis 2:7 KJV

18.2 Unto the woman he said, I will greatly multiply thy sorrow and thy conception; in sorrow thou shalt bring forth children; and thy desire shall be to thy husband, and he shall rule over thee.

Genesis 3:16 KJV

18.3 From my birth I have been evil, sinful from the time my mother conceived me.

Psalm 51:5 REB

18.4 On you I have relied since my birth, since my mother's womb you have been my portion, the constant theme of my praise.

Psalm 71:6 NJB

18.5 You are the one who put me together inside my mother's body, and I praise you because of the wonderful way you created me. Everything you do is marvellous! Of this I have no doubt. Nothing about me is hidden from you! I was secretly woven together deep in the earth below, but with your own eyes you saw my body being formed. Even before I was born, you had written in your book everything I would do.

Psalm 139:13–16 CEV

18.6 To every thing there is a season, and a time to every purpose under the heaven: a time to be born, and a time to die.

Ecclesiastes 3:1–2 KJV

18.7 For unto us a child is born, unto us a son is given: and the government shall be upon his shoulder: and his name shall be called Wonderful, Counsellor, The mighty God, The everlasting Father, The Prince of Peace.

Isaiah 9:6 KJV

18.8 This word of the Lord came to me [Jeremiah]: 'Before I formed you in the womb I chose you, and before you were born I consecrated you; I appointed you a prophet to the nations.'

Jeremiah 1:4–5 REB

18.9 The time came for her to have her baby, and she gave birth to a son, her firstborn. She wrapped him in swaddling clothes, and laid him in a manger, because there was no room for them at the inn.

Luke 2:6–7 REB

18.10 As many as received him, to them gave he power to become the sons of God, even to them that believe on his name: which were born, not of blood, nor of the will of the flesh, nor of the will of man, but of God.

John 1:12–13 KJV

18.11 Jesus [said], 'I tell you for certain that you must be born from above before you can see God's kingdom!' Nicodemus asked, 'How can a grown man ever be born a second time?' Jesus answered: I tell you for certain that before you can get into God's kingdom, you must be born not only by water, but by the Spirit. Humans give life to their children. Yet only God's Spirit can change you into a child of God. Don't be surprised when I say that you must be born from above. Only God's Spirit gives new life.

John 3:3–8 CEV

18.12 A woman in childbirth suffers, because her time has come; but when she has given birth to the child she forgets the suffering in her joy that a human being has been born into the world.

John 16:21 NJB

18.13 Beloved, let us love one another: for love is of God; and every one that loveth is born of God, and knoweth God.

1 John 4:7 KJV

18.14 Whosoever believeth that Jesus is the Christ is born of God.

1 John 5:1 KJV

See also **New birth**

Bitterness

19.1 When Esau heard the words of his father, he cried with a great and exceeding bitter cry, and said unto his father, Bless me, even me also, O my father.

Genesis 27:34 KJV

19.2 She said unto them, Call me not Naomi, call me Mara: for the Almighty hath dealt very bitterly with me.

Ruth 1:20 KJV

19.3 I am sickened of life; I shall give free rein to my complaints, speaking out in the bitterness of my soul.

Job 10:1 REB

19.4 Fret not thyself because of evil-doers, neither be thou envious against the workers of iniquity. For they shall soon be cut down like the grass, and wither as the green herb.

Psalm 37:1–2 KJV

19.5 The heart knoweth his own bitterness; and a stranger doth not intermeddle with his joy.

Proverbs 14:10 KJV

19.6 A foolish son is a grief to his father, and bitterness to her that bare him.

Proverbs 17:25 KJV

19.7 He has given me my fill of bitterness, he has made me drunk with wormwood.

Lamentations 3:15 NJB

19.8 Laugh no man to scorn in the bitterness of his soul: for there is one which humbleth and exalteth.

Ecclesiasticus 7:11 KJV

19.9 I say unto you, Love your enemies, bless them that curse you, do good to them that hate you, and pray for them which despitefully use you, and persecute you.

Matthew 5:44 KJV

19.10 [Peter to Simon the Sorcerer] I see that bitter gall and the chains of sin will be your fate.

Acts 8:23 REB

19.11 Any bitterness or bad temper or anger or shouting or abuse must be far removed from you – as must every kind of malice.

Ephesians 4:31 NJB

19.12 The Lord's servant must not quarrel; instead, he must be kind to everyone, able to teach, not resentful.

2 Timothy 2:24 NIV

19.13 Take heed that there is no one among you who forfeits the grace of God, no bitter, noxious weed growing up to contaminate the rest.

Hebrews 12:15 REB

19.14 If at heart you have the bitterness of jealousy, or selfish ambition, do not be boastful or hide the truth with lies.

James 3:14 NJB

See also Anger; Envy; Jealousy

Blasphemy

20.1 Thou shalt not take the name of the Lord thy God in vain; for the Lord will not hold him guiltless that taketh his name in vain.

Exodus 20:7 KJV

20.2 My people carried off and no price paid, their rulers wailing, and my name reviled increasingly all day long, says the Lord.

Isaiah 52:5 REB

20.3 Therefore, son of man, speak to the people of Israel and say to them, 'This is what the Sovereign Lord says: In this also your fathers blasphemed me by forsaking me.'

Ezekiel 20:27 NIV

20.4 Wherefore I say unto you, All manner of sin and blasphemy shall be forgiven unto men: but the blasphemy against the Holy Ghost shall not be forgiven unto men.

Matthew 12:31 KJV

20.5 Again the High Priest spoke to him, 'In the name of the living God I now put you on oath: tell us if you are the Messiah, the Son of God.' Jesus answered him, 'So you say. But I tell all of you: from this time on you will see the Son of Man sitting on the right of the Almighty and coming on the clouds of heaven!' At this the High Priest tore his clothes and said, 'Blasphemy! We don't need any more witnesses! You have just heard his blasphemy!'

Matthew 26:63–65 GNB

20.6 [In the last days] Men shall be lovers of their own selves, covetous, boasters, proud, blasphemers...

2 Timothy 3:2 KJV

20.7 Is it not they [the rich] who blaspheme the excellent name that was invoked over you?

James 2:7 NRSV

See also **Vow**

Blessing

21.1 Now the Lord had said unto Abram, Get thee out of thy country, and from thy kindred, and from thy father's house, unto a land that I will shew thee: And I will make of thee a great nation, and I will bless thee, and make thy name great; and thou shalt be a blessing: And I will bless them that bless thee, and curse him that curseth thee: and in thee shall all families of the earth be blessed.

Genesis 12:1–3 KJV

21.2 He [the man who wrestled with Jacob] said, Let me go, for the day breaketh. And he said, I will not let thee go, except thou bless me.

Genesis 32:26 KJV

21.3 The Lord bless thee, and keep thee: The Lord make his face shine upon thee, and be gracious unto thee.

Numbers 6:24–26 KJV

21.4 And the following blessings will all come and light on you, because you obey the Lord your God.

Deuteronomy 28:2 REB

21.5 Bring the full tithe into the storehouse, so that there may be food in my house, and thus put me to the test, says the Lord of hosts; see if I will not open the windows of heaven for you and pour down for you an overflowing blessing.

Malachi 3:10 NRSV

21.6 [Jesus and young children] He took them up in his arms, put his hands upon them, and blessed them.

Mark 10:16 KJV

21.7 Bless those who persecute you; bless and do not curse.

Romans 12:14 NIV

21.8 Let us give thanks to the God and Father of our Lord Jesus Christ! For in our union with Christ he has blessed us by giving us every spiritual blessing in the heavenly world.

Ephesians 1:3 GNB

21.9 Never repay one wrong with another, or one abusive word with another; instead, repay with a blessing. That is what you are called to do, so that you inherit a blessing.

1 Peter 3:9 NJB

See also **Christian life, Character of the Christian; Obedience**

Blindness

22.1 The Lord answered, 'Who makes people able to speak or makes them deaf or unable to speak? Who gives them sight or makes them blind? Don't you know that I am the one who does these things?'

Exodus 4:11 CEV

22.2 You must not pervert the law; you must be impartial; you will take no bribes, for a bribe blinds the eyes of the wise and ruins the cause of the upright.

Deuteronomy 16:19 NJB

22.3 Cursed be he that maketh the blind to wander out of the way.

Deuteronomy 27:18 KJV

22.4 The Lord restores sight to the blind and raises those who are bowed down.

Psalm 146:8 REB

22.5 On that day the deaf will hear when a book is read, and the eyes of the blind will see out of impenetrable darkness.

Isaiah 29:18 REB

22.6 Then the eyes of the blind shall be opened, and the ears of the deaf shall be unstopped.

Isaiah 35:5 KJV

22.7 I the Lord have called thee in righteousness, and will hold thine hand, and will keep thee, and give thee for a covenant of the people, for a light of the Gentiles; to open the blind eyes, to bring out the prisoners from the prison, and them that sit in darkness out of the prison house.

Isaiah 42:6–7 KJV

22.8 They have not known nor understood: for he hath shut their eyes, that they cannot see; and their hearts, that they cannot understand.

Isaiah 44:18 KJV

22.9 The blind receive their sight, and the lame walk, the lepers are cleansed, and the deaf hear, the dead are raised up, and the poor have the gospel preached to them.

Matthew 11:5 KJV

22.10 Leave them [the Pharisees] alone. They are blind leaders of the blind; and if one blind person leads another, both will fall into a pit.

Matthew 15:14 NJB

The blind leading the blind
The saying *the blind leading the blind* refers to inexperienced people who try to guide others who are similarly inexperienced. The result is that neither group is helped. The expression derives from this comment by Jesus about his critics, the Pharisees.

22.11 Jesus said, 'It is for judgement that I have come into this world – to give sight to the sightless and to make blind those who see.' Some Pharisees who were present asked, 'Do you mean that we are blind?' 'If you were blind,' said Jesus, 'you would not be guilty, but because you claim to see, your guilt remains.'

John 9:39–41 REB

22.12 I shall rescue you from the people and from the nations to whom I send you to open their eyes, so that they may turn from darkness to light, from the dominion of Satan to God, and receive, through faith in me, forgiveness of their sins and a share in the inheritance of the sanctified.

Acts 26:17–18 NJB

22.13 If there is anything hidden about our message, it is hidden only to someone who is lost. The god who rules this world has blinded the minds of unbelievers. They cannot see the light, which is the good news about our glorious Christ, who shows what God is like.

2 Corinthians 4:3–4 CEV

22.14 You say, 'How rich I am! What a fortune I have made! I have everything I want.' In fact, though you do not realize it, you are a pitiful wretch, poor, blind, and naked.

Revelation 3:17 REB

See also Darkness

Blood

23.1 The life of a creature is in the blood, and I appoint it to make expiation on the altar for yourselves: it is the blood, which is the life, that makes expiation.

Leviticus 17:11 REB

23.2 This is my blood of the covenant, which is poured out for many for the forgiveness of sins.

Matthew 26:28 NRSV

23.3 [Christ Jesus] whom God hath set forth to be a propitiation through faith in his blood.

Romans 3:25 KJV

23.4 By his blood we are now put right with God; how much more, then, will we be saved by him from God's anger!

Romans 5:9 GNB

23.5 Christ sacrificed his life's blood to set us free, which means that our sins are now forgiven. Christ did this because God was so kind to us.

Ephesians 1:7 CEV

23.6 Having made peace through the blood of his cross.

Colossians 1:20 KJV

23.7 Indeed, under the law almost everything is purified with blood, and without the shedding of blood there is no forgiveness of sins.

Hebrews 9:22 NRSV

23.8 We have then, brothers, complete confidence through the blood of Jesus in entering the sanctuary.

Hebrews 10:19 NJB

23.9 Now the God of peace, that brought again from the dead our Lord Jesus, that great shepherd of the sheep, through the blood of the everlasting covenant.

Hebrews 13:20 KJV

23.10 You were rescued from the useless way of life that you learnt from your ancestors. But you know that you were not rescued by such things as silver or gold that don't last for ever. You were rescued by the precious blood of Christ, that spotless and innocent lamb.

1 Peter 1:18–19 CEV

23.11 If we walk in the light as he himself is in the light, we have fellowship with one another, and the blood of Jesus his Son cleanses us from all sin.

1 John 1:7 NRSV

23.12 Unto him that loved us, and washed us from our sins in his own blood, and hath made us kings and priests unto God and his Father; to him be glory and dominion for ever and ever. Amen.

Revelation 1:5–6 KJV

23.13 They overcame him by the blood of the Lamb, and by the word of their testimony; and they loved not their lives unto the death.

Revelation 12:11 KJV

See *also* Atonement; Sacrifice

Body

24.1 During supper Jesus took bread, and having said the blessing he broke it and gave it to the disciples with the words: 'Take this and eat; this is my body.'

Matthew 26:26 REB

24.2 I beseech you therefore, brethren, by the mercies of God, that ye present your bodies a living sacrifice, holy, acceptable unto God, which is your reasonable service.

Romans 12:1 KJV

24.3 Don't you know that your body is the temple of the Holy Spirit, who lives in you and who was given to you by God? You do not belong to yourselves but to God; he bought you for a price. So use your bodies for God's glory.

1 Corinthians 6:19–20 GNB

24.4 Now you are the body of Christ and individually members of it.

1 Corinthians 12:27 NRSV

24.5 As there are physical bodies, there are spiritual bodies. And our physical bodies will be changed into spiritual bodies.

1 Corinthians 15:44 CEV

24.6 He [Jesus] is the head of the body, the church. He is its origin, the first to return from the dead, to become in all things supreme.

Colossians 1:18 REB

Bribe

25.1 But you should search for capable, godfearing men among all the people, honest and incorruptible men, and appoint them over the people as officers over units of a thousand, of a hundred, of fifty, or of ten.

Exodus 18:21 REB

25.2 Do not accept a bribe, for a bribe makes people blind to what is right and ruins the cause of those who are innocent.

Exodus 23:8 GNB

25.3 If you try to make a profit dishonestly, you will get your family into trouble. Don't take bribes and you will live longer.

Proverbs 15:27 GNB

25.4 Corrupt judges accept secret bribes, and then justice is not done.

Proverbs 17:23 GNB

25.5 People co-operate to commit crime. Judges and leaders demand bribes, and rulers cheat in court.

Micah 7:3 CEV

Caring

26.1 The Lord God took the man and put him in the garden of Eden to till it and look after it.

Genesis 2:15 REB

26.2 The Lord is your protector, and he won't go to sleep or let you stumble.

Psalm 121:3 CEV

26.3 Can a woman forget her baby at the breast; feel no pity for the child she has borne? Even if these were to forget, I shall not forget you.

Isaiah 49:15 NJB

26.4 When you give a dinner or a banquet, don't invite your friends and family and relatives and rich neighbours. If you do, they will invite you in return, and you will be paid back. When you give a feast, invite the poor, the crippled, the lame, and the blind. They cannot pay you back. But God will bless you and reward you when his people rise from death.

Luke 14:12–13 CEV

26.5 You resisted any temptation to show scorn or disgust at my physical condition; on the contrary you welcomed me as if I were an angel of God, as you might have welcomed Christ Jesus himself.

Galatians 4:14 REB

26.6 Be careful for nothing; but in every thing by prayer and supplication with thanksgiving let your requests be made known unto God.

Philippians 4:6 KJV

26.7 This is a faithful saying, and these things I will that thou affirm constantly, that they which have believed in God might be careful to maintain good works.

Titus 3:8 KJV

26.8 Look after the flock of God whose shepherds you are; do it, not under compulsion, but willingly, as God would have it; not for gain but out of sheer devotion; not lording it over your charges, but setting an example to the flock.

1 Peter 5:2–3 REB

26.9 Casting all your care upon him; for he careth for you.

1 Peter 5:7 KJV

See also **Kindness; Mercy**

Celebration

27.1 The Lord told Moses to say to the Israelites: These are the appointed seasons of the Lord, and you are to proclaim them as sacred assemblies.

Leviticus 23:1 REB

27.2 Seven weeks after you start your grain harvest, go to the place where the Lord chooses to be worshipped and celebrate the Harvest Festival in honour of the Lord your God… After you have finished the grain harvest and the grape harvest… Celebrate the Festival of Shelters for seven days. Also invite the poor, including Levites, foreigners, orphans, and widows. The Lord will give you big harvests and make you successful in everything you do. You will be completely happy, so celebrate this festival in honour of the Lord your God.

Deuteronomy 16:9–10, 13–15 CEV

27.3 Josiah told the people of Judah, 'Celebrate Passover in honour of the Lord your God, just as it says in The Book of God's Law.' This festival had not been celebrated in this way since kings ruled Israel and Judah. But in Josiah's eighteenth year as king of Judah, everyone came to Jerusalem to celebrate Passover.

2 Kings 23:21–23 CEV

27.4 The Israelites – the priests, the Levites and the remainder of the exiles – joyfully celebrated the dedication of this Temple of God.

Ezra 6:16 NJB

27.5 The people started crying when God's Law was read to them. Then Nehemiah the governor, Ezra the priest and teacher, and the Levites who had been teaching the people all said, 'This is a special day for the Lord your God. So don't be sad and don't cry!' Nehemiah told the people, 'Enjoy your good food and wine and share some with those who didn't have anything to bring. Don't be sad! This is a special day for the Lord, and he will make you happy and strong.' The Levites encouraged the people by saying, 'This is a sacred day, so don't worry or mourn!' When the people returned to their homes, they celebrated by eating and drinking and by sharing their food with those in need, because they had understood what had been read to them.

Nehemiah 8:9–12 CEV

27.6 Let all those that put their trust in thee rejoice: let them ever shout for joy, because thou defendest them: let them also that love thy name be joyful in thee.

Psalm 5:11 KJV

27.7 In the same way, I tell you, there is rejoicing among the angels of God over one repentant sinner.

Luke 15:10 NJB

See also **Praise; Worship**

Celibacy

28.1 His disciples said to him, 'If this is how it is between a man and his wife, it is better not to marry.' Jesus answered, 'This teaching does not apply to everyone, but only to those to whom God has given it. For there are different reasons why men cannot marry: some, because they were born that way; others, because men made them that way; and others do not marry for the sake of the Kingdom of heaven. Let him who can accept this teaching do so.'

Matthew 19:10–12 GNB

28.2 I should like everyone to be as I myself am; but each person has the gift God has granted him, one this gift and another that.

1 Corinthians 7:7 REB

28.3 I would like you to be free from worry. An unmarried man concerns himself with the Lord's work, because he is trying to please the Lord.

1 Corinthians 7:32 GNB

Character

29.1 The Lord told him, 'Samuel, don't think Eliab is the one just because he's tall and handsome. He isn't the one I've chosen. People judge others by what they look like, but I judge people by what is in their hearts.'

1 Samuel 16:7 CEV

29.2 Lord, who shall abide in thy tabernacle? Who shall dwell in thy holy hill? He that walketh uprightly, and worketh righteousness, and speaketh the truth in his heart.

Psalm 15:1–2 KJV

29.3 A good name is more to be desired than great riches; esteem is better than silver or gold.

Proverbs 22:1 REB

29.4 Your light must shine in people's sight, so that, seeing your good works, they may give praise to your Father in heaven.

Matthew 5:16 NJB

29.5 Be ye therefore perfect, even as your Father which is in heaven is perfect.

Matthew 5:48 KJV

29.6 Here [Beroea] the Jews were more noble-minded than those in Thessalonica, and they welcomed the word very readily; every day they studied the scriptures to check whether it was true.

Acts 17:11 NJB

29.7 We gladly suffer, because we know that suffering helps us to endure. And endurance builds character, which gives us a hope that will never disappoint us.

Romans 5:3–5 CEV

29.8 Make no mistake: 'Bad company ruins good character.'

1 Corinthians 15:33 REB

29.9 As God's steward a bishop must be a man of unimpeachable character… hospitable, right-minded, temperate, just, devout, and self-controlled.

Titus 1:7–8 REB

29.10 Always set a good example for others. Be sincere and serious when you teach. Use clean language that no one can criticize. Do this, and your enemies will be too ashamed to say anything against you.

Titus 2:7–8 CEV

29.11 Giving all diligence, add to your faith virtue; and to virtue knowledge; and to knowledge temperance; and to temperance patience; and to patience godliness; and to godliness brotherly kindness; and to brotherly kindness charity. For if these things be in you, and abound, they make you that ye shall neither be barren nor unfruitful in the knowledge of our Lord Jesus Christ.

2 Peter 1:5–8 KJV

See also **Christian life, Character of the Christian**

Choice

30.1 You are a people holy to the Lord your God, and he has chosen you out of all peoples on earth to be his special possession.

Deuteronomy 7:6 REB

30.2 I summon heaven and earth to witness against you this day: I offer you the choice of life or death, blessing or curse. Choose life and you and your descendants will live.

Deuteronomy 30:19 REB

30.3 If it seem evil unto you to serve the Lord, choose you this day whom ye will serve… but as for me and my house, we will serve the Lord.

Joshua 24:15 KJV

30.4 Elijah stood in front of them and said, 'How much longer will you try to have things both ways? If the Lord is God, worship him! But if Baal is God, worship him!'

1 Kings 18:21 CEV

30.5 Let us then examine for ourselves what is right; let us together establish the true good.

Job 34:4 REB

30.6 I have chosen the path of faithfulness; I have set your decrees before me.

Psalm 119:30 REB

30.7 Let thine hand help me; for I have chosen thy precepts.

Psalm 119:173 KJV

30.8 Better gain wisdom than gold, choose understanding in preference to silver.

Proverbs 16:16 NJB

30.9 A good name is rather to be chosen than great riches, and loving favour rather than silver and gold.

Proverbs 22:1 KJV

30.10 The young woman is with child and will give birth to a son whom she will call Immanuel. On curds and honey will he feed until he knows how to refuse the bad and choose the good.

Isaiah 7:14–15 NJB

30.11 You did not choose me. I chose you and sent you out to produce fruit, the kind of fruit that will last.

John 15:16 CEV

30.12 God chose those who by human standards are fools to shame the wise; he chose those who by human standards are weak to shame the strong, those who by human standards are common and contemptible – indeed those who count for nothing – to reduce to nothing all those that do count for something, so that no human being might feel boastful before God.

1 Corinthians 1:27–29 NJB

30.13 By faith Moses, when he was come to years, refused to be called the son of Pharaoh's daughter; choosing rather to suffer affliction with the people of God, than to enjoy the pleasures of sin for a season.

Hebrews 11:24–25 KJV

30.14 Surely you know that love of the world means enmity to God? Whoever chooses to be the world's friend makes himself God's enemy.

James 4:4 REB

See also **Decisions**; **Election**

Christian life

CALLING OF THE CHRISTIAN

31.1 Now thus saith the Lord that created thee, O Jacob, and he that formed thee, O Israel, Fear not: for I have redeemed thee, I have called thee by thy name; thou art mine.

Isaiah 43:1 KJV

31.2 Ye are the salt of the earth: but if the salt have lost his savour, wherewith shall it be salted? it is thenceforth good for nothing, but to be cast out, and to be trodden under foot of men. Ye are the light of the world. A city that is set on a hill cannot be hid. Neither do men light a candle, and put it under a bushel, but on a candlestick; and it giveth light unto all that are in the house. Let your light so shine before men, that they may see your good works, and glorify your Father which is in heaven.

Matthew 5:13–16 KJV

The salt of the earth

Many of the expressions found in Jesus' Sermon on the Mount (Matthew 5–7) have become well-known idiomatic phrases in the English language. Such expressions include the following:
the salt of the earth, people thought to have an admirable character and to be of great value;
hide one's light under a bushel, to conceal or be modest about one's talents or abilities;
an eye for an eye, punishment or retaliation that is expressed in the same

way as the offense that was committed, originally a reference to Exodus 21:24; *turn the other cheek*, to refuse to retaliate when provoked, sometimes also to be ready to be humiliated further;
the left hand does not know what the right hand is doing, applied, for example, to the lack of communication between departments in a large organization;
cast pearls before swine, to waste something of quality or value on those who cannot appreciate it;
the straight and narrow, the upright, moral, and correct way to behave;
a wolf in sheep's clothing, someone who seems friendly and harmless but in reality is dangerous and ruthless.

31.3 But you will receive power when the Holy Spirit comes upon you; and you will bear witness for me in Jerusalem, and throughout all Judaea and Samaria, and even in the farthest corners of the earth.

Acts 1:8 REB

31.4 We know that all things work together for good for those who love God, who are called according to his purpose… And those whom he predestined he also called; and those whom he called he also justified; and those whom he justified he also glorified.

Romans 8:28, 30 NRSV

31.5 You can rely on God, who has called you to be partners with his Son Jesus Christ our Lord.

1 Corinthians 1:9 NJB

31.6 I therefore, the prisoner in the Lord, beg you to lead a life worthy of the calling to which you have been called.

Ephesians 4:1 NRSV

31.7 [God] Who hath saved us, and called us with an holy calling, not according to our works, but according to his own purpose and grace, which was given us in Christ Jesus before the world began.

2 Timothy 1:9 KJV

31.8 Be holy in all that you do, just as God who called you is holy.

1 Peter 1:15 GNB

31.9 You are God's chosen and special people. You are a group of royal priests and a holy nation. God has brought you out of darkness into his marvellous light. Now you must tell all the wonderful things that he has done.

1 Peter 2:9 CEV

31.10 For what credit is there if you endure the beatings you deserve for having done wrong? But if you endure suffering even when you have done right, God will bless you for it. It was to this that God called you, for Christ himself suffered for you and left you an example, so that you would follow in his steps.

1 Peter 2:20–21 GNB

31.11 Consider how great is the love which the Father has bestowed on us in calling us his children! For that is what we are.

1 John 3:1 REB

31.12 To those who are called, to those who are dear to God the Father and kept safe for Jesus Christ.

Jude v. 1 NJB

See also **Church; Disciples; Election**

CHARACTER OF THE CHRISTIAN

31.13 Happy is the one who does not take the counsel of the wicked for a guide, or follow the path that sinners tread, or take his seat in the company of scoffers. His delight is in the law of the Lord; it is his meditation day and night. He is like a tree planted beside water channels; it yields its fruit in season and its foliage never fades. So he too prospers in all he does.

Psalm 1:1–3 REB

31.14 Seeing the multitudes, he went up into a mountain: and when he was set, his disciples came unto him: And he opened his mouth, and taught them, saying, Blessed are the poor in spirit: for theirs is the kingdom of heaven. Blessed are they that mourn: for they shall be comforted. Blessed are the meek: for they shall inherit the earth. Blessed are they which do hunger and thirst after righteousness: for they shall be filled. Blessed are the merciful: for they shall obtain mercy. Blessed are the pure in heart: for they shall see God. Blessed are the peacemakers: for they shall be called the children of God. Blessed are they which are persecuted for righteousness' sake: for theirs is the kingdom of heaven. Blessed are ye, when men shall revile you, and persecute you, and shall say all manner of evil against you falsely, for my sake.

Matthew 5:1–11 KJV

31.15 The Spirit produces love, joy, peace, patience, kindness, goodness, faithfulness, humility, and self-control. There is no law against such things as these.

Galatians 5:22–23 GNB

31.16 We have everything we need to live a life that pleases God. It was all given to us by God's own power, when we learnt that he had invited us to share in his wonderful goodness. God made great and marvellous promises, so that his nature would become part of us. Then we could escape our evil desires and the corrupt influences of this world. Do your best to improve your faith. You can do this by

adding goodness, understanding, self-control, patience, devotion to God, concern for others, and love. If you keep growing in this way, it will show that what you know about our Lord Jesus Christ has made your lives useful and meaningful.

2 Peter 1:3–8 CEV

See also **Blessing; Character; Christlikeness; Sanctification**

COMING TO FAITH

31.17 Seek ye the Lord while he may be found, call ye upon him while he is near: Let the wicked forsake his way, and the unrighteous man his thoughts: and let him return unto the Lord, and he will have mercy upon him; and to our God, for he will abundantly pardon.

Isaiah 55:6–7 KJV

31.18 Come to me, all who are weary and whose load is heavy; I will give you rest.

Matthew 11:28 REB

31.19 Now large crowds were travelling with him; and he turned and said to them, 'Whoever comes to me and does not hate father and mother, wife and children, brothers and sisters, yes, and even life itself, cannot be my disciple. Whoever does not carry the cross and follow me cannot be my disciple.'

Luke 14:25–27 NRSV

31.20 As many as received him, to them gave he power to become the sons of God, even to them that believe on his name.

John 1:12 KJV

31.21 For God so loved the world, that he gave his only begotten Son, that whosoever believeth in him should not perish, but have everlasting life.

John 3:16 KJV

31.22 All that the Father giveth me shall come to me; and him that cometh to me I will in no wise cast out.

John 6:37 KJV

31.23 Jesus saith unto him, I am the way, the truth, and the life: no man cometh unto the Father, but by me.

John 14:6 KJV

31.24 When they heard this they were cut to the heart, and said to Peter and the other apostles, 'Friends, what are we to do?' 'Repent', said Peter, 'and be baptized, every one of you, in the name of Jesus the Messiah; then your sins will be forgiven and you will receive the gift of the Holy Spirit.'

Acts 2:37–38 REB

31.25 'Sirs, what must I do to be saved?' They told him, 'Become a believer in the Lord Jesus, and you will be saved, and your household too.'

Acts 16:30–31 NJB

31.26 In the past, God forgave all this because people did not know what they were doing. But now he says that everyone everywhere must turn to him. He has set a day when he will judge the world's people with fairness. And he has chosen the man Jesus to do the judging for him. God has given proof of this to all of us by raising Jesus from death.

Acts 17:30–31 CEV

31.27 For whosoever shall call upon the name of the Lord shall be saved.

Romans 10:13 KJV

31.28 So we are ambassadors for Christ, since God is making his appeal through us; we entreat you on behalf of Christ, be reconciled to God. For our sake he made him to be sin who knew no sin, so that in him we might become the righteousness of God.

2 Corinthians 5:20–21 NRSV

31.29 Christ too suffered for our sins once and for all, the just for the unjust, that he might bring us to God; put to death in the body, he was brought to life in the spirit.

1 Peter 3:18 REB

See also **Conversion**; **Salvation and Savior**

CONTINUING IN THE FAITH

31.30 Turning to the Jews who had believed him, Jesus said, 'If you stand by my teaching, you are truly my disciples… In very truth I tell you, if anyone obeys my teaching he will never see death.'

John 8:31, 51 REB

31.31 I am the vine, you are the branches. Whoever remains in me, with me in him, bears fruit in plenty; for cut off from me you can do nothing… I have loved you just as the Father has loved me. Remain in my love.

John 15:5, 9 NJB

31.32 Now I am no longer in the world, but they are in the world, and I am coming to you. Holy Father, protect them in your name that you have given me, so that they may be one, as we are one.

John 17:11 NRSV

31.33 They continued stedfastly in the apostles' doctrine and fellowship, and in breaking of bread, and in prayers.

Acts 2:42 KJV

31.34 [Paul and Barnabas] Strengthening the disciples and encouraging them to be true to the faith. They warned them that to enter the kingdom of God we must undergo many hardships.

Acts 14:22 REB

31.35 So I am sure that God, who began this good work in you, will carry it on until it is finished on the Day of Christ Jesus.

Philippians 1:6 GNB

31.36 Whom we preach, warning every man, and teaching every man in all wisdom; that we may present every man perfect in Christ Jesus.

Colossians 1:28 KJV

31.37 We must hold tightly to the hope that we say is ours. After all, we can trust the one who made the agreement with us.

Hebrews 10:23 CEV

31.38 Therefore, since we are surrounded by so great a cloud of witnesses, let us also lay aside every weight and the sin that clings so closely, and let us run with perseverance the race that is set before us, looking to Jesus the pioneer and perfecter of our faith, who for the sake of the joy that was set before him endured the cross, disregarding its shame, and has taken his seat at the right hand of the throne of God.

Hebrews 12:1–2 NRSV

31.39 [We] Who are kept by the power of God through faith unto salvation ready to be revealed in the last time.

1 Peter 1:5 KJV

31.40 Therefore, brothers and sisters, be all the more eager to confirm your call and election, for if you do this, you will never stumble.

2 Peter 1:10 NRSV

31.41 Keep yourselves in the love of God, looking for the mercy of our Lord Jesus Christ unto eternal life… Now unto him that is able to keep you from falling, and to present you faultless before the presence of his glory with exceeding joy.

Jude vv. 21, 24 KJV

31.42 I am coming soon; hold fast to what you have, and let no one rob you of your crown.

Revelation 3:11 REB

See also **Endurance**; **Perseverance**

LONGING FOR GOD

31.43 Moses prayed, 'Show me your glory.'

Exodus 33:18 REB

31.44 One thing have I desired of the Lord, that will I seek after; that I may dwell in the house of the Lord all the days of my life, to behold the beauty of the Lord, and to inquire in his temple.

Psalm 27:4 KJV

31.45 As the hart panteth after the water brooks, so panteth my soul after thee, O God. My soul thirsteth for God, for the living God: when shall I come and appear before God?

Psalm 42:1–2 KJV

31.46 God, you are my God; I seek you eagerly with a heart that thirsts for you and a body wasted with longing for you, like a dry land, parched and devoid of water. With such longing I see you in the sanctuary and behold your power and glory.

Psalm 63:1–2 REB

31.47 Whom have I in heaven but thee? And there is none upon earth that I desire beside thee.

Psalm 73:25 KJV

31.48 I pine and faint with longing for the courts of the Lord's temple; my whole being cries out with joy to the living God.

Psalm 84:2 REB

31.49 [Some Greeks] came therefore to Philip, which was of Bethsaida of Galilee, and desired him, saying, Sir, we would see Jesus.

John 12:21 KJV

31.50 For I delight in the law of God in my inmost self.

Romans 7:22 NRSV

31.51 Unto you therefore which believe he is precious.

1 Peter 2:7 KJV

See also **Ambition, Godly; Love, of humanity for God; Seeking God; Worship**

Christlikeness

32.1 As for me, I will behold thy face in righteousness: I shall be satisfied, when I awake, with thy likeness.

Psalm 17:15 KJV

32.2 Disciples are not better than their teacher, and slaves are not better than their master. It is enough for disciples to be like their teacher and for slaves to be like their master.

Matthew 10:24–25 CEV

32.3 And whosoever will be chief among you, let him be your servant: Even as the Son of man came not to be ministered unto, but to minister, and to give his life a ransom for many.

Matthew 20:27–28 KJV

32.4 For whom he did foreknow, he also did predestinate to be conformed to the image of his Son, that he might be the firstborn among many brethren.

Romans 8:29 KJV

32.5 Take me [Paul] as your pattern, just as I take Christ for mine.

1 Corinthians 11:1 NJB

32.6 We all see as in a mirror the glory of the Lord, and we are being transformed into his likeness with ever-increasing glory, through the power of the Lord who is the Spirit.

2 Corinthians 3:18 REB

32.7 My children, I am going through the pain of giving birth to you all over again, until Christ is formed in you.

Galatians 4:19 NJB

32.8 Let this mind be in you, which was also in Christ Jesus.

Philippians 2:5 KJV

32.9 My one desire is to know Christ and the power of his resurrection, and to share his sufferings in growing conformity with his death, in hope of somehow attaining the resurrection from the dead.

Philippians 3:10–11 REB

32.10 Be tolerant with one another and forgiving, if any of you has cause for complaint: you must forgive as the Lord forgave you.

Colossians 3:13 REB

32.11 You took us and the Lord as your model, welcoming the word with the joy of the Holy Spirit in spite of great hardship.

1 Thessalonians 1:6 NJB

32.12 My dear friends, we are already God's children, though what we will be hasn't yet been seen. But we do know that when Christ returns, we will be like him, because we will see him as he truly is.

1 John 3:2 CEV

32.13 This is how we know what love is: Christ gave his life for us. And we in our turn must give our lives for our fellow-Christians.

1 John 3:16 REB

See also **Christian life, Character of the Christian; Disciples**

Church

33.1 I say also unto thee, That thou art Peter, and upon this rock I will build my church; and the gates of hell shall not prevail against it.

Matthew 16:18 KJV

33.2 If the member refuses to listen to them [witnesses], tell it to the church; and if the offender refuses to listen even to the church, let such a one be to you as a Gentile and a tax-collector.

Matthew 18:17 NRSV

33.3 They continued stedfastly in the apostles' doctrine and fellowship, and in breaking of bread, and in prayers.

Acts 2:42 KJV

33.4 So it was that the church throughout Judea, Galilee, and Samaria had a time of peace. Through the help of the Holy Spirit it was strengthened and grew in numbers, as it lived in reverence for the Lord.

Acts 9:31 GNB

33.5 They also appointed for them elders in each congregation, and with prayer and fasting committed them to the Lord in whom they had put their trust.

Acts 14:23 REB

33.6 Be on your guard for yourselves and for all the flock of which the Holy Spirit has made you the guardians, to feed the Church of God which he bought with the blood of his own Son.

Acts 20:28 NJB

33.7 For the husband is the head of the wife just as Christ is the head of the church, the body of which he is the Saviour... Husbands, love your wives, just as Christ loved the church and gave himself up for her, in order to make her holy by cleansing her with the washing of water by the word, so as to present the church to himself in splendour, without a spot or wrinkle or anything of the kind – yes, so that she may be holy and without blemish.

Ephesians 5:23, 25–27 NRSV

33.8 Some people have got out of the habit of meeting for worship, but we must not do that. We should keep on encouraging each other, especially since you know that the day of the Lord's coming is getting closer.

Hebrews 10:25 CEV

Five portraits of the church

BODY OF CHRIST

All of you are Christ's body, and each one is a part of it.

1 Corinthians 12:27 GNB

See also Romans 12:4–5; 1 Corinthians 12:12–28; Ephesians 1:22–23, 4:1–16

BRIDE

And I saw the Holy City, the new Jerusalem, coming down out of heaven from God, prepared and ready, like a bride dressed to meet her husband.

Revelation 21:2 GNB

See also Ephesians 5:23–27.

BUILDING OR TEMPLE

Christ Jesus... is the one who holds the whole building together and makes it grow into a sacred temple dedicated to the Lord.

Ephesians 2:21 GNB

See also 1 Corinthians 3:9–17; 1 Peter 2:4–8

FAMILY OR HOUSEHOLD

God's household... is the church of the living God, the pillar and support of the truth.

1 Timothy 3:15 GNB

See also Galatians 6:10; Ephesians 2:19.

See also Christian life, Calling of the Christian

Circumcision

34.1 This is my covenant, which you shall keep, between me and you and your offspring after you: Every male among you shall be circumcised. You shall circumcise the flesh of your foreskins, and it shall be a sign of the covenant between me and you. Throughout your generations every male among you shall be circumcised when he is eight days old, including the slave born in your house and the one bought with your money from any foreigner who is not of your offspring.

Genesis 17:9–13 NRSV

34.2 The Lord says, 'The time is coming when I will punish the people of Egypt, Judah, Edom, Ammon, Moab, and the desert people, who have their hair cut short. All these people are circumcised, but have not kept the covenant it symbolizes. None of these people and none of the people of Israel have kept my covenant.'

Jeremiah 9:25–26 GNB

34.3 It is not externals that make a Jew, nor an external mark in the flesh that makes circumcision. The real Jew is one who is inwardly a Jew, and his circumcision is of the heart, spiritual not literal; he receives his commendation not from men but from God.

Romans 2:28–29 REB

34.4 For whether or not a man is circumcised means nothing; what matters is to obey God's commandments.

1 Corinthians 7:19 GNB

34.5 For when we are in union with Christ Jesus, neither circumcision nor the lack of it makes any difference at all; what matters is faith that works through love.

Galatians 5:6 GNB

34.6 For we are the circumcision, which worship God in the spirit, and rejoice in Christ Jesus, and have no confidence in the flesh.

Philippians 3:3 KJV

Comfort

WHEN AFRAID

35.1 After these things the word of the Lord came unto Abram in a vision, saying, Fear not, Abram: I am thy shield, and thy exceeding great reward.

Genesis 15:1 KJV

35.2 The Lord is my light and my salvation; whom shall I fear? the Lord is the strength of my life; of whom shall I be afraid?

Psalm 27:1 KJV

35.3 I sought the Lord's help; he answered me and set me free from all my fears.

Psalm 34:4 REB

35.4 God is our refuge and strength, a very present help in trouble. Therefore will not we fear, though the earth be removed, and though the mountains be carried into the midst of the sea.

Psalm 46:1–2 KJV

35.5 The Lord is a mighty tower where his people can run for safety.

Proverbs 18:10 CEV

35.6 Now thus saith the Lord that created thee, O Jacob, and he that formed thee, O Israel, Fear not: for I have redeemed thee, I have called thee by thy name; thou art mine. When thou passest through the waters, I will be with thee; and through the rivers, they shall not overflow thee: when thou walkest through the fire, thou shalt not be burned; neither shall the flame kindle upon thee.

Isaiah 43:1–2 KJV

35.7 When the disciples saw him walking on the sea they were terrified. 'It is a ghost,' they said, and cried out in fear. But at once Jesus called out to them, saying, 'Courage! It's me! Don't be afraid.'

Matthew 14:26–27 NJB

35.8 The angel said unto them [the shepherds] Fear not: for, behold, I bring you good tidings of great joy, which shall be to all people.

Luke 2:10 KJV

35.9 Fear not, little flock; for it is your Father's good pleasure to give you the kingdom.

Luke 12:32 KJV

35.10 Peace is what I leave with you; it is my own peace that I give you. I do not give it as the world does. Do not be worried and upset; do not be afraid.

John 14:27 GNB

35.11 [Christ] himself... shared the same things, so that through death he might destroy the one who has the power of death, that is, the devil, and free those who all their lives were held in slavery by the fear of death.

Hebrews 2:14–15 NRSV

See also **Courage; Fear**

WHEN ANXIOUS

35.12 Therefore I say unto you, Take no thought for your life, what ye shall eat, or what ye shall drink; nor yet for your body, what ye shall put on. Is not the life more than meat, and the body than raiment? Behold the fowls of the air: for they sow not, neither do they reap, nor gather into barns; yet your heavenly Father feedeth them. Are ye not much better than they? Which of you by taking thought can add one cubit unto his stature? And why take ye thought for raiment? Consider the lilies of the field, how they grow; they toil not, neither do they spin. And yet I say unto you, That even Solomon in all his glory was not arrayed like one of these. Wherefore, if God so clothe the grass of the field, which to day is, and to morrow is cast into the oven, shall he not much more clothe you, O ye of little faith? Therefore take no thought, saying, What shall we eat? or, What shall we drink? or, Wherewithal shall we be clothed? (For after all these things do the Gentles seek:) for your heavenly Father knoweth that ye have need of all these things. But seek ye first the kingdom of God, and his righteousness; and all these things shall be added unto you.

Matthew 6:25–33 KJV

35.13 But when you are arrested, do not worry about what you are to say, for when the time comes, the words you need will be given you.

Matthew 10:19 REB

35.14 Come to me, all you who labour and are overburdened, and I will give you rest.

Matthew 11:28 NJB

35.15 Carry one another's burdens, and in this way you will fulfil the law of Christ.

Galatians 6:2 REB

35.16 Do not worry about anything, but in everything by prayer and supplication with thanksgiving let your requests be made known to God. And the peace of God, which surpasses all understanding, will guard your hearts and your minds in Christ Jesus.

Philippians 4:6–7 NRSV

35.17 Casting all your care upon him; for he careth for you.

1 Peter 5:7 KJV

See also **Assurance; Doubt; Stress; Worry**

IN BEREAVEMENT AND SORROW

35.18 The Lord gives and the Lord takes away; blessed be the name of the Lord.

Job 1:21 REB

35.19 Yea, though I walk through the valley of the shadow of death, I will fear no evil: for thou art with me; thy rod and thy staff they comfort me. Thou preparest a table before me in the presence of mine enemies: thou anointest my head with oil; my cup runneth over. Surely goodness and mercy shall follow me all the days of my life: and I will dwell in the house of the Lord for ever.

Psalm 23:4–6 KJV

> **The valley of the shadow of death**
> Psalm 23 is among the best-known parts of the Bible and a number of idiomatic expressions derive from it: *the valley of the shadow of death* (verse 4), the dark circumstances in which one finds oneself facing death; *one's cup runneth over* (verse 5), one has full joys; *all the days of one's life* (verse 6), for as long as one lives.

35.20 Blessed are they that mourn: for they shall be comforted.

Matthew 5:4 KJV

35.21 Jesus said unto her [Martha], I am the resurrection, and the life: he that believeth in me, though he were dead, yet shall he live: and whosoever liveth and believeth in me shall never die. Believest thou this?

John 11:25–26 KJV

35.22 If I go and prepare a place for you, I will come again, and receive you unto myself; that where I am, there ye may be also.

John 14:3 KJV

35.23 Rejoice with those who rejoice; mourn with those who mourn.

Romans 12:15 NIV

35.24 Christ has been raised to life! And he makes us certain that others will also be raised to life.

1 Corinthians 15:20 CEV

35.25 For this corruptible must put on incorruption, and this mortal must put on immortality.

1 Corinthians 15:53 KJV

35.26 I would not have you to be ignorant, brethren, concerning them which are asleep, that ye sorrow not, even as others which have no hope… For the Lord himself shall descend from heaven with a shout, with the voice of the archangel, and with the trump of God: and the dead in Christ shall rise first: Then we which are alive and remain shall be caught up together with them in the clouds, to meet the Lord in the air: and so shall we ever be with the Lord. Wherefore comfort one another with these words.

1 Thessalonians 4:13, 16–18 KJV

See also **Death; Grief; Mourning; Sympathy**

IN DESPAIR

35.27 The Lord is near to those who are discouraged; he saves those who have lost all hope.

Psalm 34:18 GNB

35.28 Patiently I waited for the Lord; he bent down to me and listened to my cry. He raised me out of the miry pit, out of the mud and clay; he set my feet on rock and gave me a firm footing.

Psalm 40:1–2 REB

35.29 Why art thou cast down, O my soul? and why art thou disquieted in me? hope thou in God: for I shall yet praise him for the help of his countenance.
O my God, my soul is cast down within me: therefore will I remember thee.

Psalm 42:5–6 KJV

35.30 Cast me not away from thy presence; and take not thy holy spirit from me. Restore unto me the joy of thy salvation; and uphold me with thy free spirit.

Psalm 51:11–12 KJV

35.31 A bruised reed shall he [the Lord's servant] not break, and the smoking flax shall he not quench: he shall bring forth judgment unto truth.

Isaiah 42:3 KJV

35.32 This I call to mind, and therefore I have hope: The steadfast love of the Lord never ceases, his mercies never come to an end; they are new every morning; great is your faithfulness.

Lamentations 3:21–23 NRSV

35.33 We are subjected to every kind of hardship, but never distressed; we see no way out but we never despair.

2 Corinthians 4:8 NJB

See also **Depression; Despair**

WHEN LONELY

35.34 Turn to me, Lord, and be merciful to me, because I am lonely and weak.

Psalm 25:16 GNB

35.35 I lie awake and have become like a bird solitary on a rooftop.

Psalm 102:7 REB

35.36 Fear thou not; for I am with thee: be not dismayed; for I am thy God: I will strengthen thee; yea, I will help thee; yea, I will uphold thee with the right hand of my righteousness.

Isaiah 41:10 KJV

35.37 Zion said, The Lord hath forsaken me, and my Lord hath forgotten me. Can a woman forget her sucking child, that she should not have compassion on the son of her womb? yea, they may forget, yet will I not forget thee. Behold, I have graven thee upon the palms of my hands; thy walls are continually before me.

Isaiah 49:14–16 KJV

35.38 I will not leave you comfortless: I will come to you.

John 14:18 KJV

35.39 No one stood by me the first time I defended myself; all deserted me. May God not count it against them! But the Lord stayed with me and gave me strength, so that I was able to proclaim the full message for all the Gentiles to hear.

2 Timothy 4:16–17 GNB

See also **Loneliness**

IN SUFFERING

35.40 He [God] heard their groaning and called to mind his covenant with

Abraham, Isaac, and Jacob; he observed the plight of Israel and took heed of it.

Exodus 2:24–25 REB

35.41 The eternal God is thy refuge, and underneath are the everlasting arms.

Deuteronomy 33:27 KJV

35.42 Though he slay me, yet will I trust in him: but I will maintain mine own ways before him.

Job 13:15 KJV

35.43 My flesh and my heart faileth: but God is the strength of my heart, and my portion for ever.

Psalm 73:26 KJV

35.44 Comfort ye, comfort ye my people, saith your God. Speak ye comfortably to Jerusalem, and cry unto her, that her warfare is accomplished, that her iniquity is pardoned: for she hath received of the Lord's hand double for all her sins.

Isaiah 40:1–2 KJV

35.45 Surely he hath borne our griefs, and carried our sorrows: yet we did esteem him stricken, smitten of God, and afflicted.

Isaiah 53:4 KJV

35.46 Though the fig tree does not blossom, and no fruit is on the vines; though the produce of the olive fails and the fields yield no food; though the flock is cut off from the fold and there is no herd in the stalls, yet I will rejoice in the Lord; I will exult in the God of my salvation.

Habakkuk 3:17–18 NRSV

35.47 We know that all things work together for good for those who love God, who are called according to his purpose… Who will separate us from the love of Christ? Will hardship, or distress, or

persecution, or famine, or nakedness, or peril, or sword? As it is written, 'For your sake we are being killed all day long; we are accounted as sheep to be slaughtered.' No, in all these things we are more than conquerors through him who loved us. For I am convinced that neither death, nor life, nor angels, nor rulers, nor things present, nor things to come, nor powers, nor height, nor depth, nor anything else in all creation, will be able to separate us from the love of God in Christ Jesus our Lord.

Romans 8:28, 35–39 NRSV

35.48 Be joyful in hope, persevere in hardship; keep praying regularly.

Romans 12:12 NJB

35.49 So far you have faced no trial beyond human endurance; God keeps faith and will not let you be tested beyond your powers, but when the test comes he will at the same time provide a way out and so enable you to endure.

1 Corinthians 10:13 REB

35.50 Praise be to the God and Father of our Lord Jesus Christ, the Father of compassion and the God of all comfort, who comforts us in all our troubles, so that we can comfort those in any trouble with the comfort we ourselves have received from God.

2 Corinthians 1:3–4 NIV

35.51 We never give up. Our bodies are gradually dying, but we ourselves are being made stronger each day. These little troubles are getting us ready for an eternal glory that will make all our troubles seem like nothing. Things that are seen don't last for ever, but things that are not seen are eternal. That's why we keep our minds on the things that cannot be seen.

2 Corinthians 4:16–18 CEV

35.52 He said unto me, My grace is sufficient for thee: for my strength is made perfect in weakness. Most gladly therefore will I rather glory in my infirmities, that the power of Christ may rest upon me.

2 Corinthians 12:9 KJV

35.53 Let us therefore boldly approach the throne of grace, in order that we may receive mercy and find grace to give us timely help.

Hebrews 4:16 REB

35.54 Looking unto Jesus the author and finisher of our faith; who for the joy that was set before him endured the cross, despising the shame, and is set down at the right hand of the throne of God.

Hebrews 12:2 KJV

35.55 My dear friends, do not be surprised at the painful test you are suffering, as though something unusual were happening to you. Rather be glad that you are sharing Christ's sufferings, so that you may be full of joy when his glory is revealed.

1 Peter 4:12–13 GNB

35.56 And God shall wipe away all tears from their eyes; and there shall be no more death, neither sorrow, nor crying, neither shall there be any more pain: for the former things are passed away.

Revelation 21:4 KJV

See also Accepting the will of God; Help; Illness, Help in; Suffering

Communion

36.1 During supper Jesus took bread, and having said the blessing he broke it and gave it to the disciples with the words: 'Take this and eat; this is my body.' Then he took a cup, and having offered thanks to God he gave it to them with the words: 'Drink from it, all of you. For this is my blood, the blood of the covenant, shed for many for the forgiveness of sins.'

Matthew 26:26–28 REB

36.2 They continued stedfastly in the apostles' doctrine and fellowship, and in breaking of bread, and in prayers.

Acts 2:42 KJV

36.3 The cup of blessing that we bless, is it not a sharing in the blood of Christ? The bread that we break, is it not a sharing in the body of Christ? Because there is one bread, we who are many are one body, for we all partake of the one bread.

1 Corinthians 10:16–17 NRSV

36.4 I have already told you what the Lord Jesus did on the night he was betrayed. And it came from the Lord himself. He took some bread in his hands. Then after he had given thanks, he broke it and said, 'This is my body, which is given for you. Eat this and remember me.' After the meal, Jesus took a cup of wine in his hands and said, 'This is my blood, and with it God makes his new agreement with you. Drink this and remember me.' The Lord meant that when you eat this bread and drink from this cup, you tell about his death until he comes. But if you eat the bread and drink the wine in a way that isn't worthy of the Lord, you sin against his body and blood. That's why you must examine the way you eat and drink. If you fail to understand that you are the body of the Lord, you will condemn yourselves by the way you eat and drink. That's why many of you are sick and weak and why a lot of others have died.

1 Corinthians 11:23–30 CEV

See also Fellowship; Food and drink; Passover

Conceit

37.1 He [the wicked man] sees himself with too flattering an eye to detect and detest his guilt.

Psalm 36:2 NJB

37.2 Be not wise in thine own eyes: fear the Lord, and depart from evil.

Proverbs 3:7 KJV

37.3 You see someone who thinks himself wise? More to be hoped for from a fool than from him!

Proverbs 26:12 NJB

37.4 The rich man is wise in his own conceit; but the poor that hath understanding searcheth him out.

Proverbs 28:11 KJV

37.5 Woe betide those who are wise in their own sight and prudent in their own esteem.

Isaiah 5:21 REB

37.6 Do not think too highly of yourself, but form a sober estimate based on the measure of faith that God has dealt to each of you.

Romans 12:3 REB

37.7 Be of the same mind one toward another. Mind not high things, but condescend to men of low estate. Be not wise in your own conceits.

Romans 12:16 KJV

37.8 Knowledge makes us proud of ourselves, while love makes us helpful to others. In fact, people who think they know so much don't know anything at all.

1 Corinthians 8:1–2 CEV

37.9 If you think you are standing firm, take care, or you may fall.

1 Corinthians 10:12 REB

37.10 For it is not the one who recommends himself, but the one whom the Lord recommends, who is to be accepted.

2 Corinthians 10:18 REB

37.11 Don't be conceited or make others jealous by claiming to be better than they are.

Galatians 5:26 CEV

37.12 If anyone imagines himself to be somebody when he is nothing, he is deluding himself.

Galatians 6:3 REB

37.13 Let nothing be done through strife or vainglory; but in lowliness of mind let each esteem other better than themselves.

Philippians 2:3 KJV

See also Pride

Confession

38.1 For those who declare publicly that they belong to me, I will do the same before my Father in heaven.

Matthew 10:32 GNB

38.2 That if thou shalt confess with thy mouth the Lord Jesus, and shalt believe in thine heart that God hath raised him from the dead, thou shalt be saved. For with the heart man believeth unto righteousness; and with the mouth confession is made unto salvation.

Romans 10:9–10 KJV

38.3 Every tongue should confess that Jesus Christ is Lord, to the glory of God the Father.

Philippians 2:11 NRSV

38.4 If anyone acknowledges that Jesus is God's Son, God dwells in him and he in God.

1 John 4:15 REB

Of sin

38.5 When a person is guilty, he must confess the sin.

Leviticus 5:5 GNB

38.6 Happy is he to whom the Lord imputes no fault, in whose spirit there is no deceit. While I refused to speak, my body wasted away with day-long moaning. For day and night your hand was heavy upon me; the sap in me dried up as in summer drought. When I acknowledged my sin to you, when I no longer concealed my guilt, but said, 'I shall confess my offence to the Lord,' then you for your part remitted the penalty of my sin.

Psalm 32:2–5 REB

38.7 You will never succeed in life if you try to hide your sins. Confess them and give them up; then God will show mercy to you.

Proverbs 28:13 GNB

38.8 O Lord, thou art just, and all thy works and all thy ways are mercy and truth, and thou judgest truly and justly for ever. Remember me, and look on me, punish me not for my sins and ignorances, and the sins of my fathers, who have sinned before thee.

Tobit 3:2–3 KJV

38.9 I have sinned, Lord, I have sinned, and I acknowledge my transgressions.

Prayer of Manasseh 12 REB

38.10 Confess your faults one to another, and pray one for another, that ye may be healed. The effectual fervent prayer of a righteous man availeth much.

James 5:16 KJV

38.11 If we confess our sins, he who is faithful and just will forgive us our sins and cleanse us from all unrighteousness.

1 John 1:9 NRSV

See also **Repentance**

Confidence

39.1 Though an host should encamp against me, my heart shall not fear: though war should rise against me, in this will I be confident. One thing have I desired of the Lord, that will I seek after; that I may dwell in the house of the Lord all the days of my life, to behold the beauty of the Lord, and to inquire in his temple.

Psalm 27:3–4 KJV

39.2 In the fear of the Lord one has strong confidence.

Proverbs 14:26 NRSV

39.3 The righteous are bold as a lion.

Proverbs 28:1 KJV

39.4 Do not put your confidence in your money or say, 'With this I am self-sufficient.'

Ecclesiasticus 5:1 NJB

39.5 Observing that Peter and John were uneducated laymen, they were astonished at their boldness and took note that they had been companions of Jesus.

Acts 4:13 REB

39.6 Jesus understands every weakness of ours, because he was tempted in every way that we are. But he did not sin! So

whenever we are in need, we should come bravely before the throne of our merciful God. There we will be treated with undeserved kindness, and we will find help.
Hebrews 4:15–16 CEV

39.7 So now, my friends, the blood of Jesus makes us free to enter the sanctuary with confidence.
Hebrews 10:19 REB

39.8 So we can say with confidence: 'With the Lord on my side, I fear nothing: what can human beings do to me?'
Hebrews 13:6 NJB

39.9 Children, stay united in your hearts with Christ. Then when he returns, we will have confidence and won't have to hide in shame.
1 John 2:28 CEV

39.10 Beloved, if our hearts do not condemn us, we have boldness before God.
1 John 3:21 NRSV

39.11 This is how love has reached its perfection among us, so that we may have confidence on the day of judgement; and this we can have, because in this world we are as he is.
1 John 4:17 REB

39.12 Our fearlessness towards him consists in this, that if we ask anything in accordance with his will he hears us.
1 John 5:14 NJB

See also Access; Adoption; Assurance; Courage

Conscience

40.1 [David] got up stealthily and cut off a piece of Saul's cloak; but after he had cut it off, he was struck with remorse.
1 Samuel 24:4 REB

40.2 So I do my best always to have a clear conscience before God and human beings.
Acts 24:16 GNB

40.3 When Gentiles, who do not possess the law, do instinctively what the law requires, these, though not having the law, are a law to themselves. They show that what the law requires is written on their hearts, to which their own conscience also bears witness; and their conflicting thoughts will accuse or perhaps excuse them.
Romans 2:14–15 NRSV

40.4 This is the truth and I am speaking in Christ, without pretence, as my conscience testifies for me in the Holy Spirit.
Romans 9:1 NJB

40.5 Some people are still so accustomed to idols that when they eat such food they think of it as having been sacrificed to an idol, and since their conscience is weak, it is defiled.
1 Corinthians 8:7 NIV

40.6 Everything is pure for someone whose heart is pure. But nothing is pure for an unbeliever with a dirty mind. That person's mind and conscience are destroyed.
Titus 1:15 CEV

40.7 Let us draw near with a true heart in full assurance of faith, having our hearts sprinkled from an evil conscience, and our bodies washed with pure water.
Hebrews 10:22 KJV

40.8 If our conscience condemns us, we know that God is greater than our conscience and that he knows everything. And so, my dear friends, if our conscience does not condemn us, we have courage in God's presence.

1 John 3:20–21 GNB

See also **Guilt**

Contentment

41.1 Trust in the Lord and do good; settle in the land and find safe pasture.

Psalm 37:3 REB

41.2 If you offer your food to the hungry and satisfy the needs of the afflicted, then your light shall rise in the darkness and your gloom be like the noonday. The Lord will guide you continually, and satisfy your needs in parched places, and make your bones strong; and you shall be like a watered garden, like a spring of water, whose waters never fail.

Isaiah 58:10–11 NRSV

41.3 Some soldiers asked him [John the Baptist] in their turn, 'What about us? What must we do?' He said to them, 'No intimidation! No extortion! Be content with your pay!'

Luke 3:14 NJB

41.4 Jesus said unto them, I am the bread of life: he that cometh to me shall never hunger; and he that believeth on me shall never thirst.

John 6:35 KJV

41.5 Do not grumble, as some of them [children of Israel] did – and were killed by the destroying angel.

1 Corinthians 10:10 NIV

41.6 I am not complaining about having too little. I have learnt to be satisfied with whatever I have. I know what it is to be poor or to have plenty, and I have lived under all kinds of conditions. I know what it means to be full or to be hungry, to have too much or too little. Christ gives me the strength to face anything.

Philippians 4:11–13 CEV

41.7 Well, religion does make a person very rich, if he is satisfied with what he has. What did we bring into the world? Nothing! What can we take out of the world? Nothing! So then, if we have food and clothes, that should be enough for us.

1 Timothy 6:6–8 GNB

41.8 Do not live for money; be content with what you have, for God has said, 'I will never leave you or desert you.'

Hebrews 13:5 REB

See also **Accepting the will of God; Joy**

Conversion

42.1 Let all the ends of the earth remember and turn again to the Lord; let all the families of the nations bow before him.

Psalm 22:27 REB

42.2 Verily I say unto you, Except ye be converted, and become as little children, ye shall not enter into the kingdom of heaven.

Matthew 18:3 KJV

42.3 [The purpose of parables] So that they may look and look, but never perceive; listen and listen, but never understand; to avoid changing their ways and being healed.

Mark 4:12 NJB

42.4 [The Lord Jesus to Simon Peter] I have prayed for thee, that thy faith fail not: and when thou art converted, strengthen thy brethren.

Luke 22:32 KJV

42.5 We are here to announce the Good News, to turn you away from these worthless things to the living God, who made heaven, earth, sea, and all that is in them.

Acts 14:15 GNB

42.6 So that they may turn from darkness to light and from the power of Satan to God, so that they may receive forgiveness of sins and a place among those who are sanctified by faith in me.

Acts 26:18 NRSV

42.7 Other people tell us how we started the work among you, how you broke with the worship of false gods when you were converted to God and became servants of the living and true God.

1 Thessalonians 1:9 NJB

42.8 You had wandered away like sheep. Now you have returned to the one who is your shepherd and protector.

1 Peter 2:25 CEV

See also **Christian life, Coming to faith; Faith; New birth; Repentance; Salvation and Savior**

Conviction of sin

43.1 For well I know my misdeeds, and my sins confront me all the time. Against you only have I sinned and have done what displeases; you are right when you accuse me and justified in passing sentence.

Psalm 51:3–4 REB

43.2 I said, 'There is no hope for me! I am doomed because every word that passes my lips is sinful, and I live among a people whose every word is sinful. And yet, with my own eyes, I have seen the King, the Lord Almighty!'

Isaiah 6:5 GNB

43.3 When Simon Peter saw it, he fell down at Jesus' knees, saying, Depart from me; for I am a sinful man, O Lord.

Luke 5:8 KJV

43.4 When he [the Holy Spirit] comes, he will show the world how wrong it was, about sin, and about who was in the right, and about judgment: about sin: in that they refuse to believe in me.

John 16:8–9 NJB

43.5 When they heard this they were cut to the heart, and said to Peter and the other apostles, 'Friends, what are we to do?'

Acts 2:37 REB

See also **Guilt; Sin**

Counsel

44.1 Happy is the one who does not take the counsel of the wicked for a guide, or follow the path that sinners tread, or take his seat in the company of scoffers.

Psalm 1:1 REB

44.2 I shall instruct you and teach you the way to go; I shall not take my eyes off you. Be not like a horse or a mule; that does not understand bridle or bit.

Psalm 32:8–9 NJB

44.3 The Lord brings the counsel of the nations to nothing; he frustrates the plans of the peoples. The counsel of the Lord stands for ever, the thoughts of his heart to all generations.

Psalm 33:10–11 NRSV

44.4 Stupid people always think they are right. Wise people listen to advice.

Proverbs 12:15 GNB

44.5 Pay attention to advice and accept correction, so you can live sensibly.

Proverbs 19:20 CEV

44.6 For unto us a child is born, unto us a son is given: and the government shall be upon his shoulder: and his name shall be called Wonderful, Counsellor, The mighty God, The everlasting Father, The Prince of Peace.

Isaiah 9:6 KJV

44.7 O Lord, thou art my God; I will exalt thee, I will praise thy name; for thou hast done wonderful things; thy counsels of old are faithfulness and truth.

Isaiah 25:1 KJV

44.8 [Paul to the elders at Ephesus] I have kept back nothing; I have disclosed to you the whole purpose of God.

Acts 20:26–27 REB

See also Guidance; Way

Courage

45.1 [God to Joshua] Be strong and courageous; for you shall put this people in possession of the land that I swore to their ancestors to give them. Only be strong and very courageous, being careful to act in accordance with all the law that my servant Moses commanded you; do not turn from it to the right hand or to the left, so that you may be successful wherever you go. This book of the law shall not depart out of your mouth; you shall meditate on it day and night, so that you may be careful to act in accordance with all that is written in it. For then you shall make your way prosperous, and then you shall be successful. I hereby command you: Be strong and courageous; do not be frightened or dismayed, for the Lord your God is with you wherever you go.

Joshua 1:6–9 NRSV

45.2 [Hezekiah's encouragement] Be strong and courageous. Do not be afraid or discouraged because of the king of Assyria and the vast army with him, for there is a greater power with us than with him. With him is only the arm of flesh, but with us is the Lord our God to help us fight our battles.

2 Chronicles 32:7–8 NIV

45.3 Wait for the Lord; be strong and brave, and put your hope in the Lord.

Psalm 27:14 REB

45.4 Some people brought to him a paralysed man, lying on a bed. When Jesus saw how much faith they had, he said to the paralysed man, 'Courage, my son! Your sins are forgiven.'

Matthew 9:2 GNB

45.5 Jesus turned. He saw the woman and said, 'Don't worry! You are now well because of your faith.' At that moment she was healed.

Matthew 9:22 CEV

45.6 These things I have spoken unto you, that in me ye might have peace. In the world ye shall have tribulation: but be of good cheer; I have overcome the world.

John 16:33 KJV

45.7 Now, O Lord, mark their threats, and enable those who serve you to speak your word with all boldness.

Acts 4:29 REB

45.8 I will know that you stand firm in one spirit, contending as one man for the faith of the gospel without being frightened in any way by those who oppose you.

Philippians 1:27–28 NIV

45.9 For God hath not given us the spirit of fear; but of power, and of love, and of a sound mind.

2 Timothy 1:7 KJV

See also Comfort, when afraid; Confidence; Fear

Covenant

46.1 I will establish my covenant between me and you, and your offspring after you throughout their generations, for an everlasting covenant, to be God to you and to your offspring after you. And I will give to you, and to your offspring after you, the land where you are now an alien, all the land of Canaan, for a perpetual holding; and I will be their God... This is my covenant, which you shall keep, between me and you and your offspring after you: Every male among you shall be circumcised.

Genesis 17:7–8, 10 NRSV

46.2 Moses took the blood, and sprinkled it on the people, and said, Behold the blood of the covenant, which the Lord hath made with you concerning all these words.

Exodus 24:8 KJV

46.3 The Lord confides his purposes to those who fear him; his covenant is for their instruction.

Psalm 25:14 REB

46.4 This is my blood, which seals God's covenant, my blood poured out for many for the forgiveness of sins.

Matthew 26:28 GNB

46.5 [The Gentiles] Aliens with no part in the covenants of the Promise.

Ephesians 2:12 NJB

46.6 This means that Jesus guarantees us a better agreement with God.

Hebrews 7:22 CEV

46.7 This is the covenant that I will make with the house of Israel after those days, says the Lord: I will put my laws in their minds, and write them on their hearts, and I will be their God, and they shall be my people.

Hebrews 8:10 NRSV

46.8 For this reason he is the mediator of a new covenant, so that those who are called may receive the promised eternal inheritance, because a death has occurred that redeems them from the transgressions under the first covenant.

Hebrews 9:15 NRSV

46.9 Now the God of peace, that brought again from the dead our Lord Jesus, that great shepherd of the sheep, through the blood of the everlasting covenant.

Hebrews 13:20 KJV

46.10 I heard a great voice out of heaven saying, Behold, the tabernacle of God is with men, and he will dwell with them, and they shall be his people, and God himself shall be with them, and be their God.

Revelation 21:3 KJV

Creation

47.1 In the beginning God created the heaven and the earth.

Genesis 1:1 KJV

47.2 So God created man in his own image, in the image of God created he him; male and female created he them.

Genesis 1:27 KJV

47.3 When I consider thy heavens, the work of thy fingers, the moon and the stars, which thou hast ordained; what is man, that thou art mindful of him? and the son of man, that thou visitest him?

Psalm 8:3–4 KJV

47.4 The word of the Lord created the heavens; all the host of heaven was formed at his command.

Psalm 33:6 REB

47.5 O come, let us worship, and fall down, and kneel before the Lord our Maker.

Psalm 95:6 BCP

47.6 Lift up your eyes on high, and behold who hath created these things, that bringeth out their host by number: he calleth them all by names by the greatness of his might, for that he is strong in power; not one faileth... Hast thou not known? hast thou not heard, that the everlasting God, the Lord, the Creator of the ends of the earth, fainteth not, neither is weary? there is no searching of his understanding.

Isaiah 40:26, 28 KJV

47.7 Then he said to them: 'Go to every part of the world, and proclaim the gospel to the whole creation.'

Mark 16:15 REB

47.8 Ever since the creation of the world, the invisible existence of God and his everlasting power have been clearly seen by the mind's understanding of created things.

Romans 1:20 NJB

47.9 All of creation waits with eager longing for God to reveal his children. For creation was condemned to lose its purpose, not of its own will, but because God willed it to be so. Yet there was the hope that creation itself would one day be set free from its slavery to decay and would share the glorious freedom of the children of God. For we know that up to the present time all of creation groans with pain, like the pain of childbirth. But it is not just creation alone which groans; we who have the Spirit as the first of God's gifts also groan within ourselves, as we wait for God to make us his children and set our whole being free.

Romans 8:19–23 GNB

47.10 If anyone is in Christ, there is a new creation: everything old has passed away; see, everything has become new!

2 Corinthians 5:17 NRSV

47.11 For we are his workmanship, created in Christ Jesus unto good works, which God hath before ordained that we should walk in them.

Ephesians 2:10 KJV

47.12 Christ is exactly like God, who cannot be seen. He is the firstborn Son, superior to all creation. Everything was created by him, everything in heaven and on earth, everything seen and unseen, including all forces and powers, and all rulers and authorities. All things were created by God's Son, and everything was made for him.

Colossians 1:15–16 CEV

47.13 By faith we understand that the universe was formed by God's command, so that the visible came forth from the invisible.

Hebrews 11:3 REB

47.14 Thou art worthy, O Lord, to receive glory and honour and power: for thou hast created all things, and for thy pleasure they are and were created.

Revelation 4:11 KJV

See also Animals; Earth, the; God, Creator; Land; Providence; Revelation; World

Cruelty

48.1 I cry unto thee, and thou dost not hear me: I stand up, and thou regardest me not. Thou art become cruel to me: with thy strong hand thou opposest thyself against me.

Job 30:20–21 KJV

48.2 Come and save me, Lord God, from vicious and cruel and brutal enemies!

Psalm 71:4 CEV

48.3 Have respect unto the covenant: for the dark places of the earth are full of the habitations of cruelty.

Psalm 74:20 KJV

48.4 The merciful man doeth good to his own soul: but he that is cruel troubleth his own flesh.

Proverbs 11:17 KJV

48.5 A right-minded person cares for his beast, but one who is wicked is cruel at heart.

Proverbs 12:10 REB

48.6 You people are in for trouble! You have made cruel and unfair laws that let you cheat the poor and needy and rob widows and orphans.

Isaiah 10:1–2 CEV

48.7 Behold, the day of the Lord cometh, cruel both with wrath and fierce anger, to lay the land desolate: and he shall destroy the sinners thereof out of it.

Isaiah 13:9 KJV

48.8 Meanwhile the men who guarded Jesus were mocking and beating him. They blindfolded him and questioned him, saying, 'Prophesy! Who hit you then?' And they heaped many other insults on him.

Luke 22:63–65 NJB

48.9 Because they have not seen fit to acknowledge God, he has given them up to their own depraved way of thinking, and this leads them to break all rules of conduct. They are filled with every kind of wickedness, villainy, greed, and malice.

Romans 1:28–29 REB

48.10 Any bitterness or bad temper or anger or shouting or abuse must be far removed from you – as must every kind of malice.

Ephesians 4:31 NJB

48.11 You must stop being angry, hateful, and evil. You must no longer say insulting or cruel things about others.

Colossians 3:8 CEV

48.12 Others had trial of cruel mockings and scourgings, yea, moreover of bonds and imprisonment: They were stoned, they were sawn asunder, were tempted, were slain with the sword: they wandered about in sheepskins and goatskins; being destitute, afflicted, tormented.

Hebrews 11:36–37 KJV

See also Injustice; Oppression; Persecution

Darkness

49.1 In the beginning God created the heavens and the earth. The earth was a vast waste, darkness covered the deep, and the spirit of God hovered over the surface of the water. God said, 'Let there be light,' and there was light; and God saw the light was good, and he separated light from darkness. He called the light day, and the darkness night.

Genesis 1:1–5 REB

49.2 He unveils mysteries deep in obscurity and into thick darkness he brings light.

Job 12:22 REB

49.3 You, the Lord God, keep my lamp burning and turn darkness to light.

Psalm 18:28 CEV

49.4 If I say, Surely the darkness shall cover me; even the night shall be light about me. Yea, the darkness hideth not from thee; but the night shineth as the day: the darkness and the light are both alike to thee.

Psalm 139:11–12 KJV

49.5 The lifestyle of the wicked is like total darkness, and they will never know what makes them stumble.

Proverbs 4:19 CEV

49.6 Woe to those who call what is bad, good, and what is good, bad, who substitute darkness for light and light for darkness.

Isaiah 5:20 NJB

49.7 The people that walked in darkness have seen a great light: they that dwell in the land of the shadow of death, upon them hath the light shined.

Isaiah 9:2 KJV

49.8 Arise, shine, Jerusalem, for your light has come; and over you the glory of the Lord has dawned. Though darkness covers the earth and dark night the nations, on you the Lord shines and over you his glory will appear.

Isaiah 60:1–2 REB

49.9 The light shineth in darkness; and the darkness comprehended it not.

John 1:5 KJV

49.10 Walk while ye have the light, lest darkness come upon you: for he that walketh in darkness knoweth not whither he goeth.

John 12:35 KJV

49.11 The night is nearly over, daylight is on the way; so let us throw off everything that belongs to the darkness and equip ourselves for the light.

Romans 13:12 NJB

49.12 Take no part in the barren deeds of darkness, but show them up for what they are.

Ephesians 5:11 REB

49.13 He rescued us from the domain of darkness and brought us into the kingdom of his dear Son, through whom our release is secured and our sins are forgiven.

Colossians 1:13–14 REB

49.14 God has brought you out of darkness into his marvellous light. Now you must tell all the wonderful things that he has done.

1 Peter 2:9 CEV

49.15 God is light, and there is no darkness in him at all.

1 John 1:5 NJB

49.16 Whoever says, 'I am in the light,' but hates his fellow-Christian, is still in darkness. He who loves his fellow-Christian dwells in light: there is no cause of stumbling in him. But anyone who hates his fellow is in darkness; he walks in the dark and has no idea where he is going, because the darkness has made him blind.

1 John 2:9–11 REB

See also **Blindness**; **Light**

Deacons

50.1 During this period, when disciples were growing in number, a grievance arose on the part of those who spoke Greek, against those who spoke the language of the Jews; they complained that their widows were being overlooked in the daily distribution. The Twelve called the whole company of disciples together and said, 'It would not be fitting for us to neglect the word of God in order to assist in the distribution. Therefore, friends, pick seven men of good repute from your number, men full of the Spirit and of wisdom, and we will appoint them for this duty; then we can devote ourselves to prayer and to the ministry of the word.'

Acts 6:1–4 REB

50.2 Deacons likewise must be serious, not double-tongued, not indulging in much wine, not greedy for money; they must hold fast to the mystery of the faith with a clear conscience. And let them first be tested; then, if they prove themselves blameless, let them serve as deacons. Women likewise must be serious, not slanderers, but temperate, faithful in all things. Let deacons be married only once, and let them manage their children and their households well;

for those who serve well as deacons gain a good standing for themselves and great boldness in the faith that is in Christ Jesus.

1 Timothy 3:8–13 NRSV

See also **Elders**; **Leadership**; **Service**

Death

51.1 Of the tree of the knowledge of good and evil, thou shalt not eat of it: for in the day that thou eatest thereof thou shalt surely die.

Genesis 2:17 KJV

51.2 In the sweat of thy face shalt thou eat bread, till thou return unto the ground; for out of it wast thou taken: for dust thou art, and unto dust shalt thou return.

Genesis 3:19 KJV

51.3 Now the days of David drew nigh that he should die; and he charged Solomon his son, saying, I go the way of all the earth: be thou strong therefore, and shew thyself a man.

1 Kings 2:1–2 KJV

> **To go the way of all flesh**
> The expression *to go the way of all flesh* means to die or disappear finally. The phrase is in fact an alteration of the Bible narrative of David's dying words to Solomon. The actual phrase *go the way of all flesh* is not part of the Bible text.

51.4 Their soul abhorred all manner of meat: and they were even hard at death's door.

Psalm 107:18 BCP

51.5 A precious thing in the Lord's sight is the death of those who are loyal to him.

Psalm 116:15 REB

51.6 There is a way which seemeth right unto a man, but the end thereof are the ways of death.

Proverbs 14:12 KJV

51.7 For I have no pleasure in the death of anyone, says the Lord God. Turn, then, and live.

Ezekiel 18:32 NRSV

51.8 When he was at the last gasp, he said, Thou like a fury takest us out of this present life, but the King of the world shall raise us up, who have died for his laws, unto everlasting life.

2 Maccabees 7:9 KJV

51.9 I am telling you the truth: whoever obeys my teaching will never die.

John 8:51 GNB

51.10 Someone who has died, of course, no longer has to answer for sin. But we believe that, if we died with Christ, then we shall live with him too… In the same way, you must see yourselves as being dead to sin but alive for God in Christ Jesus.

Romans 6:7–8, 11 NJB

51.11 For the wages of sin is death; but the gift of God is eternal life through Jesus Christ our Lord.

Romans 6:23 KJV

51.12 Christ lives in you. So you are alive because God has accepted you, even though your bodies must die because of your sins. Yet God raised Jesus to life! God's Spirit now lives in you, and he will raise you to life by his Spirit.

Romans 8:10–11 CEV

51.13 If we live, we live for the Lord; and if we die, we die for the Lord. So whether we live or die, we belong to the Lord. This is why Christ died and lived again, to establish his lordship over both dead and living.

Romans 14:8–9 REB

51.14 For as all die in Adam, so all will be made alive in Christ.

1 Corinthians 15:22 NRSV

51.15 The last enemy that shall be destroyed is death.

1 Corinthians 15:26 KJV

51.16 So when this corruptible shall have put on incorruption, and this mortal shall have put on immortality, then shall be brought to pass the saying that is written, Death is swallowed up in victory. O death, where is thy sting? O grave, where is thy victory?

1 Corinthians 15:54–55 KJV

51.17 We are full of courage and would much prefer to leave our home in the body and be at home with the Lord.

2 Corinthians 5:8 GNB

51.18 As for you, you were dead in your transgressions and sins.

Ephesians 2:1 NIV

51.19 For me to live is Christ, and to die is gain.

Philippians 1:21 KJV

51.20 I am pulled in two directions. I want very much to leave this life and be with Christ, which is a far better thing.

Philippians 1:23 GNB

51.21 You must put to death, then, the earthly desires at work in you, such as sexual immorality, indecency, lust, evil passions, and greed (for greed is a form of idolatry).

Colossians 3:5 GNB

51.22 The Lord himself shall descend from heaven with a shout, with the voice of the archangel, and with the trump of God: and the dead in Christ shall rise first: Then we which are alive and remain shall be caught up together with them in the clouds, to meet the Lord in the air: and so shall we ever be with the Lord. Wherefore comfort one another with these words.

1 Thessalonians 4:16–18 KJV

51.23 Christ our Saviour defeated death and brought us the good news. It shines like a light and offers life that never ends.

2 Timothy 1:10 CEV

51.24 The saying is sure: If we have died with him, we will also live with him; if we endure, we will also reign with him.

2 Timothy 2:11–12 NRSV

51.25 Since the children share in flesh and blood, he too shared in them, so that by dying he might break the power of him who had death at his command, that is, the devil.

Hebrews 2:14 REB

51.26 It is appointed unto men once to die, but after this the judgment.

Hebrews 9:27 KJV

51.27 Then the desire conceives and gives birth to sin, and when sin reaches full growth, it gives birth to death.

James 1:15 NJB

51.28 Be thou faithful unto death, and I will give thee a crown of life.

Revelation 2:10 KJV

51.29 God shall wipe away all tears from their eyes; and there shall be no more death, neither sorrow, nor crying, neither shall there be any more pain: for the former things are passed away.

Revelation 21:4 KJV

See also **Comfort, in bereavement and sorrow; Jesus Christ, Death; Last things, Resurrection; Life**

Debt

52.1 Every seven years you must announce, 'The Lord says loans do not need to be paid back.' Then if you have loaned money to another Israelite, you can no longer ask for payment. This law applies only to loans you have made to other Israelites. Foreigners will still have to pay back what you have loaned them. No one in Israel should ever be poor. The Lord your God is giving you this land, and he has promised to make you very successful, if you obey his laws and teachings that I'm giving you today. You will lend money to many nations, but you won't have to borrow. You will rule many nations, but they won't rule you.

Deuteronomy 15:1–6 CEV

52.2 Some [Jews] complained that they had to give their sons and daughters as pledges for food to eat to keep themselves alive; others that they were mortgaging their fields, vineyards, and homes to buy grain during the famine; still others that they were borrowing money on their fields and vineyards to pay the king's tax. 'But', they said, 'our bodily needs are the same as other people's… yet here we are, forcing our sons and daughters into slavery… and there is nothing we can do, because our fields and vineyards now belong to others.'

Nehemiah 5:2–5 REB

52.3 The wicked borrows and will not repay, but the upright is generous in giving.

Psalm 37:21 NJB

52.4 What shall I render unto the Lord for all his benefits toward me?

Psalm 116:12 KJV

52.5 The rich ruleth over the poor, and the borrower is servant to the lender.

Proverbs 22:7 KJV

52.6 Do not be one of those who go guarantor, who go surety for debts: if you have no means of paying your bed will be taken from under you.

Proverbs 22:26–27 NJB

52.7 Consider the man who is righteous and does what is just and right… he oppresses no one, he returns the debtor's pledge, he never commits robbery; he gives his food to the hungry and clothes to those who have none. He never lends either at discount or at interest, but shuns injustice and deals fairly between one person and another.

Ezekiel 18:5, 7–8 REB

52.8 'Woe betide the person who amasses wealth that is not his and enriches himself with goods taken in pledge!' Will not your debtors suddenly start up? Will not those be roused who

will shake you till you are empty? Will you not fall a victim to them?

Habakkuk 2:6–7 REB

52.9 Before you are dragged into court, make friends with the person who has accused you of doing wrong. If you don't, you will be handed over to the judge and then to the officer who will put you in jail. I promise you that you will not get out until you have paid the last penny you owe.

Matthew 5:25–26 CEV

52.10 Forgive us our debts, as we forgive our debtors.

Matthew 6:12 KJV

52.11 Money paid to workers isn't a gift. It is something they earn by working.

Romans 4:4 CEV

52.12 Never pay back evil for evil. Let your aims be such as all count honourable.

Romans 12:17 REB

52.13 Pay to each one what is due to each: taxes to the one to whom tax is due, tolls to the one to whom tolls are due, respect to the one to whom respect is due, honour to the one to whom honour is due. The only thing you should owe to anyone is love for one another, for to love the other person is to fulfil the law.

Romans 13:7–8 NJB

See also Poverty

Decisions

53.1 I summon heaven and earth to witness against you this day: I offer you the choice of life or death, blessing or curse. Choose life and you and your descendants will live.

Deuteronomy 30:19 REB

53.2 Worshipping the Lord is sacred; he will always be worshipped. All of his decisions are correct and fair.
Psalm 19:9 CEV

53.3 The meek he will guide in judgment: and the meek will he teach his way.
Psalm 25:9 KJV

53.4 Put all your trust in the Lord and do not rely on your own understanding. At every step you take keep him in mind, and he will direct your path.
Proverbs 3:5–6 REB

53.5 We make our own decisions, but the Lord alone determines what happens.
Proverbs 16:33 CEV

53.6 The heart of the prudent getteth knowledge; and the ear of the wise seeketh knowledge.
Proverbs 18:15 KJV

53.7 Be sure you have sound advice before making plans or starting a war.
Proverbs 20:18 CEV

53.8 Daniel determined not to become contaminated with the food and wine from the royal table, and begged the master of the eunuchs to excuse him from touching it.
Daniel 1:8 REB

53.9 Multitudes, multitudes in the valley of decision: for the day of the Lord is near in the valley of decision.
Joel 3:14 KJV

53.10 No one can be the slave of two masters: he will either hate the first and love the second, or be attached to the first and despise the second. You cannot be the slave both of God and of money.'
Matthew 6:24 NJB

53.11 From one person God made all nations who live on earth, and he decided when and where every nation would be.
Acts 17:26 CEV

See also Choice; Guidance; Responsibility, human

Demons

54.1 When evening came, people brought to Jesus many who had demons in them. Jesus drove out the evil spirits with a word and healed all who were sick.
Matthew 8:16 GNB

54.2 The demons begged Jesus, 'If you are going to drive us out, send us into that herd of pigs.'
Matthew 8:31 GNB

54.3 Depart from me, ye cursed, into everlasting fire, prepared for the devil and his angels.
Matthew 25:41 KJV

54.4 The unclean spirits too, when they saw him, would fall at his feet and cry aloud, 'You are the Son of God.'
Mark 3:11 REB

54.5 Some teachers of the Law who had come from Jerusalem were saying, 'He has Beelzebul in him! It is the chief of the demons who gives him the power to drive them out.'
Mark 3:22 GNB

54.6 As Jesus stepped ashore, he was met by a man from the town who had demons in him. For a long time this man had gone without clothes and would not stay at home, but spent his time in the burial caves.
Luke 8:27 GNB

54.7 Jesus called the twelve together and gave them power and authority over all demons and to cure diseases.

Luke 9:1 NRSV

54.8 Jesus forced a demon out of a man who could not talk. And after the demon had gone out, the man started speaking, and the crowds were amazed.

Luke 11:14 CEV

54.9 For we wrestle not against flesh and blood, but against principalities, against powers, against the rulers of the darkness of this world, against spiritual wickedness in high places.

Ephesians 6:12 KJV

54.10 He disarmed the cosmic powers and authorities and made a public spectacle of them, leading them as captives in his triumphal procession.

Colossians 2:15 REB

54.11 Thou believest that there is one God; thou doest well: the devils also believe, and tremble.

James 2:19 KJV

See also **Devil; Occult**

Depression

55.1 Job spake, and said, Let the day perish wherein I was born.

Job 3:2–3 KJV

55.2 I am worn out with grief; every night my bed is damp from my weeping; my pillow is soaked with tears. I can hardly see; my eyes are so swollen from the weeping caused by my enemies.

Psalm 6:6–7 GNB

55.3 How much longer will you forget me, Lord? For ever? How much longer will

you hide yourself from me? How long must I endure trouble? How long will sorrow fill my heart day and night? How long will my enemies triumph over me?

Psalm 13:1–2 GNB

55.4 Day and night your hand lay heavy upon me; my heart grew parched as stubble in summer drought.

Psalm 32:4 NJB

55.5 My tears have been my meat day and night, while they continually say unto me, Where is thy God?... all thy waves and thy billows are gone over me.

Psalm 42:3, 7 KJV

55.6 A person's spirit sustains in sickness, but who can endure if the spirit is crushed?

Proverbs 18:14 REB

55.7 My soul is bereft of peace; I have forgotten what happiness is... The thought of my affliction and my homelessness is wormwood and gall! My soul continually thinks of it and is bowed down within me. But this I call to mind, and therefore I have hope: The steadfast love of the Lord never ceases, his mercies never come to an end; they are new every morning; great is your faithfulness. 'The Lord is my portion,' says my soul, 'therefore I will hope in him.'

Lamentations 3:17, 19–24 NRSV

See also **Comfort, in despair; Despair**

Desire, wrong

56.1 Thou shalt not covet thy neighbour's house, thou shalt not covet thy neighbour's wife, nor his manservant, nor his maidservant, nor his ox, nor his ass, nor any thing that is thy neighbour's.

Exodus 20:17 KJV

56.2 Give me the desire to obey your laws rather than to get rich. Keep me from paying attention to what is worthless; be good to me, as you have promised.

Psalm 119:36–37 GNB

56.3 If you try to make a profit dishonestly, you will get your family into trouble.

Proverbs 15:27 GNB

56.4 For all, high and low, are out for ill-gotten gain; prophets and priests are frauds, every one of them.

Jeremiah 6:13 REB

56.5 He said to them, 'Take care! Be on your guard against all kinds of greed; for one's life does not consist in the abundance of possessions.'

Luke 12:15 NRSV

56.6 You may be sure that no one who is immoral, indecent, or greedy (for greed is a form of idolatry) will ever receive a share in the Kingdom of Christ and of God.

Ephesians 5:5 GNB

56.7 Those who want to get rich fall into temptation and are caught in the trap of many foolish and harmful desires, which pull them down to ruin and destruction.

1 Timothy 6:9 GNB

56.8 You want something and you lack it; so you kill. You have an ambition that you cannot satisfy; so you fight to get your way by force.

James 4:2 NJB

56.9 Love not the world, neither the things that are in the world. If any man love the world, the love of the Father is not in him. For all that is in the world, the lust of the flesh, and the lust of the eyes,

and the pride of life, is not of the Father, but is of the world.

1 John 2:15–16 KJV

See also **Ambition, Negative; Greed; Riches; Selfishness**

Despair

57.1 When Moses repeated those words to the Israelites, they would not listen to him; because of their cruel slavery, they had reached the depths of despair.

Exodus 6:9 REB

57.2 Devotion is due from his friends to one who despairs and loses faith in the Almighty.

Job 6:14 REB

57.3 I am sick of life! And from my deep despair, I complain to you, my God.

Job 10:1 CEV

57.4 My God, my God, why hast thou forsaken me? why art thou so far from helping me, and from the words of my roaring?

Psalm 22:1 KJV

57.5 My body hurts all over because of your anger. Even my bones are in pain, and my sins are so heavy that I am crushed. Because of my foolishness, I am covered with sores that stink and spread. My body is twisted and bent, and I groan all day long. Fever has my back in flames, and I hurt all over. I am worn out and weak, moaning and in distress.

Psalm 38:3–8 CEV

57.6 Misfortunes beyond counting press on me from all sides; my iniquities have overtaken me, and I cannot see; they are more in number than the hairs of my head; my courage fails.

Psalm 40:12 REB

57.7 Wretched and close to death from my youth up, I suffer your terrors; I am desperate.

Psalm 88:15 NRSV

57.8 Out of the depths have I cried unto thee, O Lord.

Psalm 130:1 KJV

57.9 The enemy hath persecuted my soul; he hath smitten my life down to the ground; he hath made me to dwell in darkness, as those that have been long dead. Therefore is my spirit overwhelmed within me; my heart within me is desolate.

Psalm 143:3–4 KJV

57.10 A person's spirit sustains in sickness, but who can endure if the spirit is crushed?

Proverbs 18:14 REB

57.11 So I came to hate life, since everything that was done here under the sun was a trouble to me; for all is futility and a chasing of the wind… Then I turned and gave myself up to despair, as I reflected on all my labour and toil here under the sun. For though someone toils with wisdom, knowledge, and skill he must leave it all to one who has spent no labour on it. This too is futility and a great wrong.

Ecclesiastes 2:17, 20–21 REB

57.12 There will be only anguish, gloom, the confusion of night, swirling darkness. For is not everything dark as night for a country in distress?

Isaiah 8:22–23 NJB

57.13 Harvest is past, summer is over, and we are not saved.

Jeremiah 8:20 REB

57.14 When my soul fainted within me I remembered the Lord: and my prayer came unto thee, into thine holy temple.

Jonah 2:7 KJV

A Jonah

A *Jonah* is someone who brings bad luck – from the story of the biblical Jonah. God called him to preach against Nineveh but Jonah ran away from God and boarded a ship to Tarshish. He was then held responsible for the violent storm that struck the ship. Jonah was then swallowed by a great fish, and after praying to God was disgorged onto dry land. He then obeyed God's second call and after he had preached against Nineveh, the people repented.

57.15 We should like you to know how serious was the trouble that came upon us in the province of Asia. The burden of it was far too heavy for us to bear, so heavy that we even despaired of life.

2 Corinthians 1:8 REB

57.16 We are subjected to every kind of hardship, but never distressed; we see no way out but we never despair; we are pursued but never cut off; knocked down, but still have some life in us; always we carry with us in our body the death of Jesus so that the life of Jesus, too, may be visible in our body.

2 Corinthians 4:8–10 NJB

See also **Comfort, in despair; Depression; Grief**

Devil

58.1 Now the serpent was more subtil than any beast of the field which the Lord God had made. And he said unto the woman, Yea, hath God said, Ye shall not eat of every tree of the garden?

Genesis 3:1 KJV

58.2 When the Adversary left the Lord's presence, he afflicted Job with running sores from the soles of his feet to the crown of his head.

Job 2:7 REB

58.3 The Holy Spirit led Jesus into the desert, so that the devil could test him.

Matthew 4:1 CEV

58.4 When anyone hears the word of the kingdom without understanding, the Evil One comes and carries off what was sown in his heart: this is the seed sown on the edge of the path.

Matthew 13:19 NJB

58.5 You are from your father the devil, and you choose to do your father's desires. He was a murderer from the beginning and does not stand in the truth, because there is no truth in him. When he lies, he speaks according to his own nature, for he is a liar and the father of lies.

John 8:44 NRSV

58.6 Turn them from the darkness to the light and from the power of Satan to God, so that through their faith in me they will have their sins forgiven and receive their place among God's chosen people.

Acts 26:18 GNB

58.7 Lest Satan should get an advantage of us: for we are not ignorant of his devices.

2 Corinthians 2:11 KJV

58.8 In their case the god of this world has blinded the minds of the unbelievers, to keep them from seeing the light of the gospel of the glory of Christ, who is the image of God.

2 Corinthians 4:4 NRSV

58.9 Satan himself masquerades as an angel of light.

2 Corinthians 11:14 REB

58.10 As for you, you were dead in your transgressions and sins, in which you used to live when you followed the ways of this world and of the ruler of the kingdom of the air, the spirit who is now at work in those who are disobedient.

Ephesians 2:1–2 NIV

58.11 Put on the whole armour of God, that ye may be able to stand against the wiles of the devil.

Ephesians 6:11 KJV

58.12 We are people of flesh and blood. That is why Jesus became one of us. He died to destroy the devil, who had power over death.

Hebrews 2:14 CEV

58.13 Keep sober and alert, because your enemy the devil is on the prowl like a roaring lion, looking for someone to devour. Stand up to him, strong in faith.

1 Peter 5:8–9 NJB

58.14 The Son of God appeared for the very purpose of undoing the devil's work.

1 John 3:8 REB

58.15 We know that we are God's children, and that the whole world lies under the power of the evil one.

1 John 5:19 NRSV

58.16 Yes, that old snake and his angels were thrown out of heaven! That snake, who fools everyone on earth, is known as the devil and Satan. Then I heard a voice from heaven shout, 'Our God has shown his saving power, and his kingdom has come! God's own Chosen One has shown his authority. Satan accused our people in the presence of God day and night. Now he has been thrown out!'

Revelation 12:9–10 CEV

58.17 Then the Devil, who deceived them, was thrown into the lake of fire and sulphur, where the beast and the false prophet had already been thrown; and they will be tormented day and night for ever and ever.
Revelation 20:10 GNB

See also **Demons**; **Occult**; **Victory**

Dignity

59.1 So God created man in his own image, in the image of God created he him; male and female created he them.
Genesis 1:27 KJV

59.2 For your brother Aaron you will make sacred vestments to give dignity and magnificence.
Exodus 28:2 NJB

59.3 I am the Lord your God who brought you out of Egypt to be slaves there no longer; I broke the bars of your yoke and enabled you to walk erect.
Leviticus 26:13 REB

59.4 Terror after terror overwhelms me; my noble designs are swept away as by the wind.
Job 30:15 REB

59.5 She [the good wife] is clothed in strength and dignity and can afford to laugh at tomorrow.
Proverbs 31:25 REB

59.6 Folly is set in great dignity, and the rich sit in low place.
Ecclesiastes 10:6 KJV

59.7 The angel touched me a second time and said, 'Don't be frightened! God thinks highly of you, and he intends this

for your good, so be brave and strong.' At this, I regained my strength.
Daniel 10:18–19 CEV

59.8 Deacons, likewise, must be dignified, not indulging in double talk, given neither to excessive drinking nor to money-grubbing.
1 Timothy 3:8 REB

See also **Pride**; **Self-control**

Discernment

60.1 [Solomon's prayer] Give your servant therefore an understanding mind to govern your people, able to discern between good and evil; for who can govern this your great people?
1 Kings 3:9 NRSV

60.2 The spirit of the Lord shall rest upon him, the spirit of wisdom and understanding, the spirit of counsel and might, the spirit of knowledge and of the fear of the Lord.
Isaiah 11:2 KJV

60.3 The man without the Spirit does not accept the things that come from the Spirit of God, for they are foolishness to him and he cannot understand them, because they are spiritually discerned.
1 Corinthians 2:14 NIV

60.4 To yet another [the Spirit gives], the ability to tell the difference between gifts that come from the Spirit and those that do not.
1 Corinthians 12:10 GNB

60.5 Of the prophets, two or three may speak, while the rest exercise their judgement upon what is said.
1 Corinthians 14:29 REB

60.6 It is my prayer that your love for one another may grow more and more with… knowledge and complete understanding.

Philippians 1:9 NJB

60.7 For the word of God is quick, and powerful, and sharper than any two-edged sword, piercing even to the dividing asunder of soul and spirit, and of the joints and marrow, and is a discerner of the thoughts and intents of the heart.

Hebrews 4:12 KJV

60.8 Solid food is for the mature, for those whose faculties have been trained by practice to distinguish good from evil.

Hebrews 5:14 NRSV

See also **Examination; Knowledge; Self-examination; Wisdom**

Disciples

61.1 When he had called unto him his twelve disciples, he gave them power against unclean spirits, to cast them out, and to heal all manner of sickness and all manner of disease.

Matthew 10:1 KJV

61.2 Go, then, to all peoples everywhere and make them my disciples: baptize them in the name of the Father, the Son, and the Holy Spirit, and teach them to obey everything I have commanded you. And I will be with you always, to the end of the age.

Matthew 28:19–20 GNB

61.3 Whoever comes to me and does not hate father and mother, wife and children, brothers and sisters, yes, and even life itself, cannot be my disciple. Whoever does not carry the cross and follow me

cannot be my disciple… So therefore, none of you can become my disciple if you do not give up all your possessions.

Luke 14:26–27, 33 NRSV

61.4 Turning to the Jews who had believed him, Jesus said, 'If you stand by my teaching, you are truly my disciples.'

John 8:31 REB

61.5 By this shall all men know that ye are my disciples, if ye have love one to another.

John 13:35 KJV

61.6 It is to the glory of my Father that you should bear much fruit and be my disciples.

John 15:8 NJB

See also **Christian life, Calling of the Christian; Christlikeness; Self-denial**

Discipline

62.1 My son, do not spurn the Lord's correction or recoil from his reproof; for those whom the Lord loves he reproves, and he punishes the son who is dear to him.

Proverbs 3:11–12 REB

62.2 If one of my followers sins against you, go and point out what was wrong. But do it in private, just between the two of you. If that person listens, you have won back a follower. But if that one refuses to listen, take along one or two others. The Scriptures teach that every complaint must be proved true by two or more witnesses. If the follower refuses to listen to them, report the matter to the church. Anyone who refuses to listen to the church must be treated like an unbeliever or a tax collector. I promise you that God in heaven will allow whatever you allow on earth, but he will not allow anything you don't allow.

Matthew 18:15–18 CEV

62.3 Preach the word; be instant in season, out of season; reprove, rebuke, exhort with all longsuffering and doctrine.

2 Timothy 4:2 KJV

62.4 Endure trials for the sake of discipline. God is treating you as children; for what child is there whom a parent does not discipline? If you do not have that discipline in which all children share, then you are illegitimate and not his children. Moreover, we had human parents to discipline us, and we respected them. Should we not be even more willing to be subject to the Father of spirits and live? For they disciplined us for a short time as seemed best to them, but he disciplines us for our good, in order that we may share his holiness. Now, discipline always seems painful rather than pleasant at the time, but later it yields the peaceful fruit of righteousness to those who have been trained by it.

Hebrews 12:7–11 NRSV

62.5 As many as I love, I rebuke and chasten: be zealous therefore, and repent.

Revelation 3:19 KJV

See also Family, Children and the whole family; Punishment

Discouragement

63.1 They journeyed from mount Hor by the way of the Red sea, to compass the land of Edom: and the soul of the people was much discouraged because of the way.

Numbers 21:4 KJV

63.2 The Lord your God has now laid the land open before you. Go forward and occupy it in fulfilment of the promise which the Lord the God of your forefathers made you; do not be afraid or discouraged.

Deuteronomy 1:21 REB

63.3 The Lord himself goes at your head; he will be with you; he will not let you down or forsake you. Do not be afraid or discouraged.

Deuteronomy 31:8 REB

63.4 This is my command: be strong, be resolute; do not be fearful or discouraged, for wherever you go the Lord your God is with you.

Joshua 1:9 REB

63.5 David said to Solomon his son, Be strong and of good courage, and do it: fear not, nor be dismayed: for the Lord God, even my God, will be with thee; he will not fail thee, nor forsake thee, until thou hast finished all the work for the service of the house of the Lord.

1 Chronicles 28:20 KJV

63.6 Thus saith the Lord unto you, Be not afraid nor dismayed by reason of this great multitude; for the battle is not yours, but God's.

2 Chronicles 20:15 KJV

63.7 The people of the country then set about demoralising the people of Judah and deterring them from building.

Ezra 4:4 NJB

63.8 Remember how your words have guided and encouraged many in need. But now you feel discouraged when struck by trouble. You respect God and live right, so don't lose hope!

Job 4:3–6 CEV

63.9 Hope deferred makes the heart sick, desire fulfilled is a tree of life.

Proverbs 13:12 NJB

63.10 A bruised reed shall he not break, and the smoking flax shall he not quench: he shall bring forth judgment unto truth. He shall not fail nor be discouraged, till he have set judgment in the earth: and the isles shall wait for his law.

Isaiah 42:3–4 KJV

63.11 So, my friends, I don't think we should place burdens on the Gentiles who are turning to God.

Acts 15:19 CEV

63.12 Can anything separate us from the love of Christ? Can trouble, suffering, and hard times, or hunger and nakedness, or danger and death?… In everything we have won more than a victory because of Christ who loves us.

Romans 8:35, 37 CEV

63.13 Christ now gives us courage and confidence, so that we can come to God by faith. That's why you should not be discouraged when I suffer for you. After all, it will bring honour to you.

Ephesians 3:12–13 CEV

63.14 Fathers, do not exasperate your children, in case they lose heart.

Colossians 3:21 REB

See also **Comfort; Encouragement; Failure**

Dishonesty

64.1 Ye shall not steal, neither deal falsely, neither lie one to another.

Leviticus 19:11 KJV

64.2 The Lord is disgusted with anyone who cheats or is dishonest.

Deuteronomy 25:16 CEV

64.3 Samuel came to Saul: and Saul said unto him, Blessed be thou of the Lord: I have performed the commandment of the Lord.

1 Samuel 15:13 KJV

64.4 Don't trust in violence or depend on dishonesty or rely on great wealth.

Psalm 62:10 CEV

64.5 No good comes of ill-gotten wealth; uprightness is a safeguard against death.

Proverbs 10:2 REB

64.6 One whose life is pure lives in safety, but one whose ways are crooked is brought low.

Proverbs 10:9 REB

64.7 Money wrongly got will disappear bit by bit; money earned little by little will grow and grow.

Proverbs 13:11 CEV

64.8 A person whose conduct is upright fears the Lord; the double-dealer scorns him.

Proverbs 14:2 REB

64.9 Bread is sweet when it is got by fraud, but later the mouth is full of grit.

Proverbs 20:17 NJB

64.10 A double standard in weights is an abomination to the Lord, and false scales are unforgivable.

Proverbs 20:23 REB

64.11 As the partridge sitteth on eggs, and hatcheth them not; so he that getteth riches, and not by right, shall leave them in the midst of his days, and at his end shall be a fool.

Jeremiah 17:11 KJV

64.12 The master applauded the dishonest steward for acting so astutely. For in dealing with their own kind the children of this world are more astute than the children of light.

Luke 16:8 REB

64.13 Anyone who can be trusted in little matters can also be trusted in important matters. But anyone who is dishonest in little matters will be dishonest in important matters.

Luke 16:10 CEV

64.14 Anyone who was a thief must stop stealing; instead he should exert himself at some honest job with his own hands so that he may have something to share with those in need.

Ephesians 4:28 NJB

See also **Honesty; Lying**

Disobedience

65.1 If you will not obey the Lord your God by diligently observing all his commandments and statutes which I lay upon you this day, then all the following curses will come and light upon you.

Deuteronomy 28:15 REB

65.2 Your ancestors refused to listen. They were stubborn, and whenever I wanted them to go one way, they always went the other. Ever since your ancestors left Egypt, I have been sending my servants the prophets to speak for me. But you have ignored me and become even more stubborn and sinful than you ancestors ever were! Jeremiah... say to them: People of Judah, I am the Lord your God, but you have refused to obey me, and you didn't change when I punished you. And now, you no longer even pretend to be faithful to me.

Jeremiah 7:24–28 CEV

Jeremiah
The word *Jeremiah* has come to be used to refer to a pessimistic person who foresees a gloomy future or one who condemns the society he lives in.

65.3 Just as by one man's disobedience many were made sinners, so by one man's obedience are many to be made upright.

Romans 5:19 NJB

65.4 The ruler of the kingdom of the air, the spirit who is now at work in those who are disobedient.

Ephesians 2:2 NIV

65.5 [Jesus will appear] with a flaming fire, to punish those who reject God and who do not obey the Good News about our Lord Jesus.

2 Thessalonians 1:8 GNB

65.6 [In the last days] people will be lovers of themselves, lovers of money, boasters, arrogant, abusive, disobedient to their parents, ungrateful, unholy.

2 Timothy 3:2 NRSV

See also **Obedience; Punishment; Submission**

Doubt

66.1 So she laughed to herself and said, 'At my time of life I am past bearing children, and my husband is old.' The Lord said to Abraham, 'Why did Sarah laugh and say, "Can I really bear a child now that I am so old?" Is anything impossible for the Lord? In due season, at this time next year, I shall come back to you, and Sarah will have a son.'

Genesis 18:12–14 REB

66.2 I was afraid and thought that he had driven me out of his presence. But he heard my cry, when I called to him for help.

Psalm 31:22 GNB

66.3 Why sayest thou, O Jacob, and speakest, O Israel, My way is hid from the Lord, and my judgment is passed over from my God? Hast thou not known? hast thou not heard, that the everlasting God, the Lord, the Creator of the ends of the earth, fainteth not, neither is weary? there is no searching of his understanding.

Isaiah 40:27–28 KJV

66.4 Now John had heard in prison what Christ was doing and he sent his disciples to ask him, 'Are you the one who is to come, or are we to expect someone else?'

Matthew 11:2–3 NJB

66.5 Jesus at once reached out and caught hold of him [Peter]. 'Why did you hesitate?' he said. 'How little faith you have!'

Matthew 14:31 REB

66.6 Jesus said to them, 'If you have faith and don't doubt, I promise that you can do what I did to this tree. And you will be able to do even more. You can tell this mountain to get up and jump into the sea, and it will.'

Matthew 21:21 CEV

66.7 When they saw him, they worshipped him; but some doubted.

Matthew 28:17 NRSV

66.8 Thomas said to them, 'Unless I see the scars of the nails in his hands and put my finger on those scars and my hand in his side, I will not believe.'

John 20:25 GNB

> **A doubting Thomas**
> A *doubting Thomas* is a skeptical person, one who refuses to believe something until he or she has actually seen complete proof or evidence for it. The expression derives from Thomas, one of the twelve disciples who at first did not believe in Jesus' resurrection. Jesus then satisfied his doubts and Thomas in belief confessed Jesus to be his Lord and his God.

66.9 He who asks must ask in faith, with never a doubt in his mind; for the doubter is like a wave of the sea tossed hither and thither by the wind.

James 1:6 REB

66.10 Then I heard a loud voice in heaven, proclaiming, 'Now have come the salvation and the power and the kingdom of our God and the authority of his Messiah, for the accuser of our comrades has been thrown down, who accuses them day and night before our God.'

Revelation 12:10 NRSV

See also **Assurance; Comfort, when anxious; Unbelief**

Dreams

67.1 He [Jacob] dreamed, and behold a ladder set up on the earth, and the top of it reached to heaven: and behold the angels of God ascending and descending on it.

Genesis 28:12 KJV

67.2 Joseph had a dream, and when he told it to his brothers, their hatred of him became still greater.

Genesis 37:5 REB

67.3 Prophets or interpreters of dreams may promise a miracle or a wonder, in order to lead you to worship and serve gods that you have not worshipped before. Even if what they promise comes true, do not pay any attention to them. The Lord your God is using them to test you, to see if you love the Lord with all your heart. Follow the Lord and honour him; obey him and keep his commands; worship him and be faithful to him. But put to death any interpreters of dreams or prophets who tell you to rebel against the Lord, who rescued you from Egypt, where you were slaves. Such people are evil and are trying to lead you away from the life that the Lord has commanded you to live. They must be put to death, in order to rid yourselves of this evil.

Deuteronomy 13:1–5 GNB

67.4 When the Lord brought us back to Jerusalem, it was like a dream!

Psalm 126:1 GNB

67.5 I am against those prophets, says the Lord, who deal in false dreams and relate them to mislead my people with wild and reckless falsehoods. It was not I who sent them or commissioned them, and they will do this people no good service.

Jeremiah 23:32 REB

67.6 Facing the king, Daniel replied, 'None of the sages, soothsayers, magicians or exorcists has been able to tell the king the truth of the mystery which the king has propounded; but there is a God in heaven who reveals mysteries and who has shown King Nebuchadnezzar what is to take place in the final days. These, then, are the dream and the visions that passed through your head as you lay in bed...'

Daniel 2:27–28 NJB

67.7 It shall come to pass afterward, that I will pour out my spirit upon all flesh; and your sons and your daughters shall prophesy, your old men shall dream dreams, your young men shall see visions.

Joel 2:28 KJV

67.8 Just when he had resolved to do this, an angel of the Lord appeared to him in a dream and said, 'Joseph, son of David, do not be afraid to take Mary as your wife, for the child conceived in her is from the Holy Spirit.'

Matthew 1:20 NRSV

67.9 That night Paul had a vision in which he saw a Macedonian standing and begging him, 'Come over to Macedonia and help us!'

Acts 16:9 GNB

See also **Visions**

Drunkenness

68.1 Show me someone who drinks too much, who has to try out some new drink, and I will show you someone miserable and sorry for himself, always causing trouble and always complaining. His eyes are bloodshot, and he has bruises that could have been avoided. Don't let wine tempt you, even though it is rich red, though it sparkles in the cup, and it goes down smoothly.

Proverbs 23:29–31 GNB

68.2 You are doomed! You get up early in the morning to start drinking, and you spend long evenings getting drunk.

Isaiah 5:11 GNB

68.3 Let us eat and drink; for to morrow we shall die.

Isaiah 22:13 KJV

Eat, drink, and be merry

The saying *eat, drink, and be merry*, sometimes followed by the additional phrase *for tomorrow we die* expresses the philosophy that one should enjoy oneself fully with worldly pleasures at the present time, because the future is uncertain. The saying is derived from two verses, Ecclesiastes 8:15 and Isaiah 22:13.

68.4 These also lose their way through wine and are set wandering by strong drink: priest and prophet lose their way through strong drink and are befuddled with wine; they are set wandering by strong drink, lose their way through tippling, and stumble in judgement.

Isaiah 28:7 REB

68.5 Let us conduct ourselves properly, as people who live in the light of day – no orgies or drunkenness.

Romans 13:13 GNB

68.6 Now the works of the flesh are obvious… drunkenness, carousing, and things like these.

Galatians 5:19, 21 NRSV

68.7 Be not drunk with wine, wherein is excess; but be filled with the Spirit.

Ephesians 5:18 KJV

See also Food and drink; Temperance

Earth, the

69.1 In the beginning God created the heaven and the earth. And the earth was without form, and void; and darkness was upon the face of the deep. And the Spirit of God moved upon the face of the waters.

Genesis 1:1–2 KJV

69.2 As long as the earth lasts, seedtime and harvest, cold and heat, summer and winter, day and night, they will never cease.

Genesis 8:22 REB

69.3 For in six days the Lord made the heavens and the earth, the sea, and all that is in them, and on the seventh day he rested.

Exodus 20:11 REB

69.4 You alone are the Lord; you created the heavens, the highest heavens with all their host, the earth and all that is on it, the seas and all that is in them. You give life to them all, and the heavenly host worships you.

Nehemiah 9:6 REB

69.5 The earth is the Lord's, and the fulness thereof; the world, and they that dwell therein.

Psalm 24:1 KJV

69.6 God is our refuge and our stronghold, a timely help in trouble; so we are not afraid though the earth shakes and the mountains move in the depths of the sea.

Psalm 46:1–2 REB

69.7 Long ago you laid earth's foundations, the heavens are the work of your hands. They pass away but you remain; they all wear out like a garment... but you never alter, and your years never end.

Psalm 102:25–27 NJB

69.8 The heaven, even the heavens, are the Lord's: but the earth hath he given to the children of men.

Psalm 115:16 KJV

69.9 From the beginning, I [Wisdom] was with the Lord. I was there before he began to create the earth. At the very first, the Lord gave life to me.

Proverbs 8:22–23 CEV

69.10 The earth shall be full of the knowledge of the Lord, as the waters cover the sea.

Isaiah 11:9 KJV

69.11 I am creating new heavens and a new earth; everything of the past will be forgotten.

Isaiah 65:17 CEV

69.12 Thus saith the Lord, The heaven is my throne, and the earth is my footstool: where is the house that ye build unto me? and where is the place of my rest?

Isaiah 66:1 KJV

69.13 Thy kingdom come. Thy will be done in earth, as it is in heaven.

Matthew 6:10 KJV

69.14 Relying on his promise we look forward to new heavens and a new earth, in which justice will be established.

2 Peter 3:13 REB

69.15 Then I saw a new heaven and a new earth; the first heaven and the first earth had disappeared now, and there was no longer any sea.

Revelation 21:1 NJB

See also Creation; Land; World, Created universe

Eden, Garden of

70.1 The Lord God planted a garden eastward in Eden; and there he put the man whom he had formed. And out of the ground made the Lord God to grow every tree that is pleasant to the sight, and good for food; the tree of life also in the midst of the garden, and the tree of knowledge of good and evil... And the Lord God took the man, and put him into the garden of Eden to dress it and to keep it. And the Lord God commanded the man, saying, Of every tree of the garden thou mayest freely eat: But of the tree of the knowledge of good and evil, thou shalt not eat of it: for in the day that thou eatest thereof thou shalt surely die.

Genesis 2:8–9, 15–17 KJV

70.2 Therefore the Lord God sent him forth from the garden of Eden, to till the ground from whence he was taken. So he drove out the man; and he placed at the east of the garden of Eden Cherubims, and a flaming sword which turned every way, to keep the way of the tree of life.

Genesis 3:23–24 KJV

See also **Adam; Fall, the**

Elders

71.1 Go and assemble the elders of Israel; tell them that the Lord, the God of their forefathers, the God of Abraham, Isaac, and Jacob, has appeared to you.

Exodus 3:16 REB

71.2 The disciples decided to send relief, each to contribute what he could afford, to the brothers living in Judaea. They did this and delivered their contributions to the elders through the agency of Barnabas and Saul.

Acts 11:29–30 NJB

71.3 In each church they appointed elders, and with prayers and fasting they commended them to the Lord, in whom they had put their trust.

Acts 14:23 GNB

71.4 [Paul to the elders of the church at Ephesus] Take heed therefore unto yourselves, and to all the flock, over the which the Holy Ghost hath made you overseers, to feed the church of God, which he hath purchased with his own blood.

Acts 20:28 KJV

71.5 Now we ask you, brothers, to respect those who work hard among you, who are over you in the Lord and who admonish you. Hold them in the highest regard in love because of their work.

1 Thessalonians 5:12–13 NIV

71.6 This is a true saying: if a man is eager to be a church leader, he desires an excellent work. A church leader must be without fault; he must have only one wife, be sober, self-controlled, and orderly; he must welcome strangers in his home; he must be able to teach; he must not be a drunkard or a violent man, but gentle and peaceful; he must not love money; he must be able to manage his own family well and make his children obey him with all respect.

1 Timothy 3:1–4 GNB

71.7 Elders who give good service as leaders should be reckoned worthy of a double stipend, in particular those who work hard at preaching and teaching.

1 Timothy 5:17 REB

71.8 I left you behind in Crete for this reason, that you should put in order what remained to be done, and should appoint elders in every town, as I directed you.

Titus 1:5 NRSV

71.9 Don't forget about your leaders who taught you God's message. Remember what kind of lives they lived and try to have faith like theirs.

Hebrews 13:7 CEV

71.10 Obey your leaders and submit to their authority; for they are tireless in their care for you, as those who must render an account. See that their work brings them happiness, not pain and grief, for that would be no advantage to you.

Hebrews 13:17 REB

71.11 Is any sick among you? let him call for the elders of the church; and let them pray over him, anointing him with oil in the name of the Lord.

James 5:14 KJV

71.12 I, who am an elder myself, appeal to the church elders among you. I am a witness of Christ's sufferings, and I will share in the glory that will be revealed. I appeal to you to be shepherds of the flock that God gave you and to take care of it willingly, as God wants you to, and not unwillingly. Do your work, not for mere pay, but from a real desire to serve. Do not try to rule over those who have been put in your care, but be examples to the flock.

1 Peter 5:1–3 GNB

See also **Deacons; Leadership; Pastor**

Election

72.1 Everything is entrusted to me by my Father; and no one knows the Son but the Father, and no one knows the Father but the Son and those to whom the Son chooses to reveal him.

Matthew 11:27 REB

72.2 Then shall the King say unto them on his right hand, Come, ye blessed of my Father, inherit the kingdom prepared for you from the foundation of the world.

Matthew 25:34 KJV

72.3 All that the Father giveth me shall come to me; and him that cometh to me I will in no wise cast out.

John 6:37 KJV

72.4 No one can come to me unless drawn by the Father who sent me, and I will raise that person up on the last day.

John 6:44 NJB

72.5 You did not choose me, no, I chose you; and I commissioned you to go out and to bear fruit, fruit that will last.

John 15:16 NJB

72.6 You have given me some followers from this world, and I have shown them what you are like. They were yours, but you gave them to me, and they have obeyed you.

John 17:6 CEV

72.7 When the Gentiles heard this, they were glad and praised the Lord's message; and those who had been chosen for eternal life became believers.

Acts 13:48 GNB

72.8 For those whom he foreknew he also predestined to be conformed to the image of his Son, in order that he might be the firstborn within a large family. And those whom he predestined he also called; and those whom he called he also justified; and those whom he justified he also glorified… Who will bring any charge against God's elect?

Romans 8:29–30, 33 NRSV

72.9 The Lord told Moses that he has pity and mercy on anyone he wants to. Everything then depends on God's mercy and not on what people want or do.

Romans 9:15–16 CEV

72.10 Even before the world was made, God had already chosen us to be his through our union with Christ, so that we would be holy and without fault before him. Because of his love God had already decided that through Jesus Christ he would make us his sons and daughters – this was his pleasure and purpose.

Ephesians 1:4–5 GNB

72.11 You are the people of God; he loved you and chose you for his own. So then, you must clothe yourselves with compassion, kindness, humility, gentleness, and patience.

Colossians 3:12 GNB

72.12 We are always bound to thank God for you, my friends beloved by the Lord. From the beginning of time God chose you to find salvation in the Spirit who consecrates you and in the truth you believe.

2 Thessalonians 2:13 REB

72.13 Elect according to the foreknowledge of God the Father, through sanctification of the Spirit, unto obedience and sprinkling of the blood of Jesus Christ.

1 Peter 1:2 KJV

72.14 You are a chosen race, a royal priesthood, a holy nation, God's own people, in order that you may proclaim the mighty acts of him who called you out of darkness into his marvellous light.

1 Peter 2:9 NRSV

72.15 Instead of this, brothers, never allow your choice or calling to waver; then there will be no danger of your stumbling.

2 Peter 1:10 NJB

See also Choice; Christian life, Calling of the Christian

Encouragement

73.1 He [Peter] testified with many other arguments and exhorted them, saying, 'Save yourselves from this corrupt generation.'

Acts 2:40 NRSV

73.2 Joseph, surnamed by the apostles Barnabas (which means, 'Son of Encouragement'), a Levite and by birth a Cypriot.

Acts 4:36 REB

73.3 When he [Barnabas] arrived and saw the divine grace at work, he rejoiced and encouraged them all to hold fast to the Lord with resolute hearts.

Acts 11:23 REB

73.4 They [Paul and Barnabas] encouraged the followers and begged them to remain faithful. They told them, 'We have to suffer a lot before we can get into God's kingdom.'

Acts 14:22 CEV

73.5 Judas and Silas, being themselves prophets, spoke for a long time, encouraging and strengthening the brothers.

Acts 15:32 NJB

73.6 If it [a man's gift] is encouraging, let him encourage.

Romans 12:8 NIV

73.7 You know that we treated each one of you just as a father treats his own children. We encouraged you, we comforted you, and we kept urging you to live the kind of life that pleases God.

1 Thessalonians 2:11–12 GNB

73.8 We urge you, brothers, warn those who are idle, encourage the timid, help the weak, be patient with everyone.
1 Thessalonians 5:14 NIV

73.9 Proclaim the message; be persistent whether the time is favourable or unfavourable; convince, rebuke, and encourage, with the utmost patience in teaching.
2 Timothy 4:2 NRSV

73.10 Exhort one another daily, while it is called To day; lest any of you be hardened through the deceitfulness of sin.
Hebrews 3:13 KJV

73.11 Let us be concerned for one another, to help one another to show love and to do good. Let us not give up the habit of meeting together, as some are doing. Instead, let us encourage one another all the more, since you see that the Day of the Lord is coming nearer.
Hebrews 10:24–25 GNB

See also Comfort; Discouragement; Fellowship

Endurance

74.1 He that endureth to the end shall be saved.
Matthew 10:22 KJV

74.2 It strikes no root in him and he has no staying-power; when there is trouble or persecution on account of the word he quickly loses faith.
Matthew 13:21 REB

74.3 Endurance produces character, and character produces hope.
Romans 5:4 NRSV

74.4 None of the trials which have come upon you is more than a human being can stand. You can trust that God will not let you be put to the test beyond your strength, but with any trial will also provide a way out by enabling you to put up with it.
1 Corinthians 10:13 NJB

74.5 Put on the whole armour of God, that ye may be able to stand against the wiles of the devil... Praying always with all prayer and supplication in the Spirit, and watching thereunto with all perseverance and supplication for all saints.
Ephesians 6:11, 18 KJV

74.6 Fortified, in accordance with his glorious strength, with all power always to persevere and endure.
Colossians 1:11 NJB

74.7 As a good soldier of Christ Jesus you must endure your share of suffering.
2 Timothy 2:3 CEV

74.8 If we endure, we will also reign with him; if we deny him, he will also deny us.
2 Timothy 2:12 NRSV

74.9 Looking unto Jesus the author and finisher of our faith; who for the joy that was set before him endured the cross, despising the shame, and is set down at the right hand of the throne of God.
Hebrews 12:2 KJV

74.10 Happy are those who remain faithful under trials, because when they succeed in passing such a test, they will receive as their reward the life which God has promised to those who love him.
James 1:12 GNB

See also Christian life, Continuing in the faith; Patience; Victory; Waiting; Zeal

Enemy

75.1 Should you come upon your enemy's ox or donkey straying, you must take it back to him. Should you see the donkey of someone who hates you lying helpless under its load, however unwilling you may be to help, you must lend a hand with it.
Exodus 23:4–5 REB

75.2 When you please the Lord, you can make your enemies into friends.
Proverbs 16:7 GNB

75.3 Do not rejoice at the fall of your enemy; do not gloat when he is brought down.
Proverbs 24:17 REB

75.4 If your enemies are hungry, give them bread to eat; and if they are thirsty, give them water to drink; for you will heap coals of fire on their heads, and the Lord will reward you.
Proverbs 25:21–22 NRSV

75.5 Ye have heard that it hath been said, Thou shalt love thy neighbour, and hate thine enemy. But I say unto you, Love your enemies, bless them that curse you, do good to them that hate you, and pray for them which despitefully use you, and persecute you.
Matthew 5:43–44 KJV

75.6 For if, while we were enemies, we were reconciled to God through the death of his Son, how much more can we be sure that, being now reconciled, we shall be saved by his life.
Romans 5:10 NJB

Envy

76.1 Fret not thyself because of evildoers, neither be thou envious against the workers of iniquity.
Psalm 37:1 KJV

76.2 My feet were on the point of stumbling… envying the arrogant as I did, and seeing the prosperity of the wicked.
Psalm 73:2–3 NJB

76.3 I considered all toil and all achievement and saw that it springs from rivalry between one person and another.
Ecclesiastes 4:4 REB

76.4 For he [Pontius Pilate] knew that for envy they had delivered him.
Matthew 27:18 KJV

76.5 Now the works of the flesh are obvious… anger, quarrels, dissensions, factions, envy.
Galatians 5:19, 21 NRSV

76.6 Rid yourselves, then, of all evil; no more lying or hypocrisy or jealousy or insulting language.
1 Peter 2:1 GNB

See also Bitterness; Jealousy

Eternal life

77.1 These shall go away into everlasting punishment: but the righteous into life eternal.
Matthew 25:46 KJV

77.2 A certain ruler asked him, saying, Good Master, what shall I do to inherit eternal life?
Luke 18:18 KJV

77.3 God so loved the world that he gave his only Son, that everyone who has faith in him may not perish but have eternal life.

John 3:16 REB

77.4 He that believeth on the Son hath everlasting life: and he that believeth not the Son shall not see life; but the wrath of God abideth on him.

John 3:36 KJV

77.5 You [Jews] study the scriptures diligently, supposing that in having them you have eternal life; their testimony points to me, yet you refuse to come to me to receive that life.

John 5:39–40 REB

77.6 Simon Peter answered, 'Lord, to whom shall we go? You have the message of eternal life, and we believe; we have come to know that you are the Holy One of God.'

John 6:68–69 NJB

77.7 My sheep know my voice, and I know them. They follow me, and I give them eternal life, so that they will never be lost. No one can snatch them out of my hand.

John 10:27–28 CEV

77.8 He that loveth his life shall lose it; and he that hateth his life in this world shall keep it unto life eternal.

John 12:25 KJV

77.9 Eternal life is this: to know you, the only true God, and Jesus Christ whom you have sent.

John 17:3 NJB

77.10 To those who pursue glory, honour, and immortality by steady persistence in well-doing, he will give eternal life.

Romans 2:7 REB

77.11 For the wage paid by sin is death; the gift freely given by God is eternal life in Christ Jesus our Lord.

Romans 6:23 NJB

77.12 We shall not all die, but we shall all be changed in a flash, in the twinkling of an eye, at the last trumpet-call. For the trumpet will sound, and the dead will rise imperishable, and we shall be changed. This perishable body must be clothed with the imperishable, and what is mortal with immortality. And when this perishable body has been clothed with the imperishable and our mortality has been clothed with immortality, then the saying of scripture will come true: 'Death is swallowed up; victory is won!'

1 Corinthians 15:51–54 REB

77.13 Fight the good fight of faith and win the eternal life to which you were called and for which you made your noble profession of faith before many witnesses.

1 Timothy 6:12 NJB

77.14 God has also said that he gave us eternal life and that this life comes to us from his Son. And so, if we have God's Son, we have this life. But if we don't have the Son, we don't have this life.

1 John 5:11–12 CEV

See also **Jesus Christ**; **Last things**; **Life**; **New birth**

Evangelists

78.1 At that time the church in Jerusalem suffered terribly. All the Lord's followers, except the apostles, were scattered everywhere in Judea and Samaria… The Lord's followers who had been scattered went from place to place, telling the good news. Philip went to the city of Samaria and told the people about

Christ… When they believed what Philip was saying about God's kingdom and about the name of Jesus Christ, they were all baptized.

Acts 8:1–2, 4–5, 12 CEV

78.2 Then Philip began to speak; starting from this passage of scripture, he told him the Good News about Jesus.

Acts 8:35 GNB

78.3 On the following day we left and arrived in Caesarea. There we stayed at the house of Philip the evangelist.

Acts 21:8 GNB

78.4 It is he who has given some to be apostles, some prophets, some evangelists…

Ephesians 4:11 REB

78.5 As for you, always be sober, endure suffering, do the work of an evangelist, carry out your ministry fully.

2 Timothy 4:5 NRSV

See also Witness

Evil

79.1 For God doth know that in the day ye eat thereof, then your eyes shall be opened, and ye shall be as gods, knowing good and evil.

Genesis 3:5 KJV

79.2 For they have sown the wind, and they shall reap the whirlwind: it hath no stalk: the bud shall yield no meal: if so be it yield, the strangers shall swallow it up. Israel is swallowed up: now shall they be among the Gentiles as a vessel wherein is no pleasure.

Hosea 8:7–8 KJV

Sow the wind and reap the whirlwind
The expression *sow the wind and reap the whirlwind* means to do something that appears harmless but leads to the suffering of unforeseen disastrous consequences. The source of this expression lies in Hosea's prophecy: Israel had sown the wind of idolatry and would reap the whirlwind of an Assyrian invasion.

79.3 Shall there be evil in a city, and the Lord hath not done it?

Amos 3:6 KJV

79.4 Your eyes are too pure to look on evil; you cannot countenance wrongdoing.

Habakkuk 1:13 REB

79.5 Take therefore no thought for the morrow: for the morrow shall take thought for the things of itself. Sufficient unto the day is the evil thereof.

Matthew 6:34 KJV

79.6 Then he [Pontius Pilate] asked, 'Why, what evil has he done?' But they shouted all the more, 'Let him be crucified!'

Matthew 27:23 NRSV

79.7 For it is from within, from the heart, that evil intentions emerge.

Mark 7:21 NJB

79.8 The light has come into the world, and people who do evil things are judged guilty because they love the dark more than the light.

John 3:19 CEV

79.9 I don't do the good I want to do; instead, I do the evil that I do not want to do.

Romans 7:19 GNB

79.10 Love must be completely sincere. Hate what is evil, hold on to what is good.
Romans 12:9 GNB

79.11 See that none of you repays evil for evil, but always seek to do good to one another and to all.
1 Thessalonians 5:15 NRSV

79.12 Abstain from all appearance of evil.
1 Thessalonians 5:22 KJV

79.13 For the love of money is the root of all evil.
1 Timothy 6:10 KJV

79.14 I write to you, young men, because you have conquered the evil one.
1 John 2:13 REB

Examination

80.1 Search me, O God, and know my heart: try me, and know my thoughts: And see if there be any wicked way in me, and lead me in the way everlasting.
Psalm 139:23–24 KJV

80.2 [The Jews at Berea] were more noble than those in Thessalonica, in that they received the word with all readiness of mind, and searched the scriptures daily, whether those things were so.
Acts 17:11 KJV

80.3 God who searches our inmost being knows what the Spirit means.
Romans 8:27 REB

80.4 Prove all things; hold fast that which is good.
1 Thessalonians 5:21 KJV

80.5 My dear friends, not every spirit is to be trusted, but test the spirits to see whether they are from God.
1 John 4:1 NJB

See also **Discernment; Self-examination**

Failure

81.1 There failed not ought of any good thing which the Lord had spoken unto the house of Israel; all came to pass.

Joshua 21:45 KJV

81.2 Help, Lord; for the godly man ceaseth; for the faithful fail from among the children of men.

Psalm 12:1 KJV

81.3 My flesh and my heart faileth: but God is the strength of my heart, and my portion for ever.

Psalm 73:26 KJV

81.4 This I recall to my mind, therefore have I hope. It is of the Lord's mercies that we are not consumed, because his compassions fail not. They are new every morning: great is thy faithfulness.

Lamentations 3:21–23 KJV

81.5 You have been weighed in the balance and found wanting.

Daniel 5:27 REB

Weighed in the balance
One of the words that appeared on the wall of the royal palace of King Belshazzar was *Tekel,* interpreted by Daniel as referring to King Belshazzar's life, that it had been *weighed in the balance* and *found wanting.* This expression has passed into the language to stand for something that is judged and considered not to come up to a required standard. The expression *the writing on the wall* refers to the same incident and is now used in idiomatic English to refer to the existence of signs that warn of imminent failure or ruin, which alludes to the mysterious inscription interpreted as describing the king's downfall.

81.6 Last came forward the man who had the single talent. 'Sir,' said he, 'I had heard you were a hard man, reaping where you had not sown and gathering where you had not scattered; so I was afraid, and I went off and hid your talent in the ground. Here it is; it was yours, you have it back.'

Matthew 25:24–25 NJB

81.7 And it came to pass, as he sowed, some fell by the way side, and the fowls of the air came and devoured it up. And some fell on stony ground, where it had not much earth; and immediately it sprang up, because it had no depth of earth.

Mark 4:4–5 KJV

**Fall by the wayside;
fall on stony ground**
These two expressions come from the parable of the sower and the seed. To *fall by the wayside* is to give up or to fail in an activity because of weakness: 'The course started out with sixty students, but quite a number seem to have fallen by the wayside.' If something *falls on stony ground,* it is not received or listened to: 'The idea of expanding broadcasting of the arts fell on stony ground and was quickly abandoned.'

81.8 He came back and found them asleep; and he said to Peter, 'Asleep, Simon? Could you not stay awake for one hour?'

Mark 14:37 REB

81.9 Provide for yourselves purses that do not wear out, and never-failing treasure in heaven, where no thief can get near it, no moth destroy it. For where your treasure is, there will your heart be also.

Luke 12:33–34 REB

81.10 Simon, Simon, take heed: Satan has been given leave to sift all of you like wheat; but I have prayed for you, Simon, that your faith may not fail; and when you are restored, give strength to your brothers.

Luke 22:31–32 REB

81.11 The Lord turned and looked upon Peter. And Peter remembered the word of the Lord, how he had said unto him, Before the cock crow, thou shalt deny me thrice. And Peter went out, and wept bitterly.

Luke 22:61–62 KJV

81.12 Charity never faileth: but whether there be prophecies, they shall fail; whether there be tongues, they shall cease; whether there be knowledge, it shall vanish away.

1 Corinthians 13:8 KJV

81.13 Test yourselves and find out if you really are true to your faith. If you pass the test, you will discover that Christ is living in you. But if Christ isn't living in you, you have failed. I hope you will discover that we have not failed. We pray that you will stop doing evil things. We don't pray like this to make ourselves look good, but to get you to do right, even if we are failures.

2 Corinthians 13:5–7 CEV

81.14 For the high priest we have is not incapable of feeling our weaknesses with us, but has been put to the test in exactly the same way as ourselves, apart from sin. Let us, then, have no fear in approaching the throne of grace to receive mercy and to find grace when we are in need of help.

Hebrews 4:15–16 NJB

81.15 All of us do many wrong things. But if you can control your tongue, you are mature and able to control your whole body.

James 3:2 CEV

See also **Discouragement**

Faith

82.1 He [Abraham] believed in the Lord; and he counted it to him for righteousness.

Genesis 15:6 KJV

82.2 You are my mighty rock, my fortress, my protector, the rock where I am safe, my shield, my powerful weapon, and my place of shelter.

Psalm 18:2 CEV

82.3 Trust in the Lord and do good; settle in the land and find safe pasture. Delight in the Lord, and he will grant you your heart's desire. Commit your way to the Lord; trust in him, and he will act.

Psalm 37:3–5 REB

82.4 Trust in the Lord with all thine heart; and lean not unto thine own understanding.

Proverbs 3:5 KJV

82.5 The righteous live by their faith.

Habakkuk 2:4 NRSV

82.6 He saith unto them, Why are ye fearful, O ye of little faith?

Matthew 8:26 KJV

82.7 'Yes,' said Jesus, '… Everything is possible for the person who has faith.' The father at once cried out, 'I do have faith, but not enough. Help me to have more!'

Mark 9:23–24 GNB

82.8 Jesus answered them, 'Have faith in God… I tell you, whatever you ask for in prayer, believe that you have received it, and it will be yours.'

Mark 11:22, 24 NRSV

82.9 As many as received him, to them gave he power to become the sons of God, even to them that believe on his name.

John 1:12 KJV

82.10 For God so loved the world, that he gave his only begotten Son, that whosoever believeth in him should not perish, but have everlasting life.

John 3:16 KJV

82.11 No one who puts his faith in him comes under judgement; but the unbeliever has already been judged because he has not put his trust in God's only Son.

John 3:18 REB

82.12 Jesus gave them this answer, 'This is carrying out God's work: you must believe in the one he has sent.'

John 6:29 NJB

82.13 Let not your heart be troubled: ye believe in God, believe also in me.

John 14:1 KJV

82.14 These [miracles] are written so that you will put your faith in Jesus as the Messiah and the Son of God. If you have faith in him, you will have true life.

John 20:31 CEV

82.15 This proposal proved acceptable to the whole company. They elected Stephen, a man full of faith and of the Holy Spirit.

Acts 6:5 REB

82.16 They answered, 'Believe on the Lord Jesus, and you will be saved, you and your household.'

Acts 16:31 NRSV

82.17 [Christ Jesus] whom God hath set forth to be a propitiation through faith in his blood.

Romans 3:25 KJV

82.18 Therefore, since we have been justified through faith, we have peace with God through our Lord Jesus Christ.

Romans 5:1 NIV

82.19 If thou shalt confess with thy mouth the Lord Jesus, and shalt believe in thine heart that God hath raised him from the dead, thou shalt be saved. For with the heart man believeth unto righteousness; and with the mouth confession is made unto salvation.

Romans 10:9–10 KJV

82.20 So then, faith comes from hearing the message, and the message comes through preaching Christ.

Romans 10:17 GNB

82.21 Now abideth faith, hope, charity, these three; but the greatest of these is charity.

1 Corinthians 13:13 KJV

82.22 For we walk by faith, not by sight.

2 Corinthians 5:7 KJV

82.23 I have died, but Christ lives in me. And I now live by faith in the Son of God, who loved me and gave his life for me.

Galatians 2:20 CEV

82.24 For by grace are ye saved through faith; and that not of yourselves: it is the gift of God.

Ephesians 2:8 KJV

82.25 Above all, taking the shield of faith, wherewith ye shall be able to quench all the fiery darts of the wicked.

Ephesians 6:16 KJV

82.26 Now faith is the substance of things hoped for, the evidence of things not seen.

Hebrews 11:1 KJV

82.27 By faith we understand that the universe was formed by God's command, so that the visible came forth from the invisible.

Hebrews 11:3 REB

82.28 Without faith it is impossible to please him: for he that cometh to God must believe that he is, and that he is a rewarder of them that diligently seek him.

Hebrews 11:6 KJV

82.29 What good is it, my brothers and sisters, if you say you have faith but do not have works? Can faith save you?

James 2:14 NRSV

82.30 Can't you see? His faith and his actions worked together; his faith was made perfect through his actions…
So then, as the body without the spirit is dead, so also faith without actions is dead.

James 2:22, 26 GNB

82.31 Everyone who believes that Jesus is the Christ has been born of God.

1 John 5:1 NRSV

82.32 For whatever is born of God conquers the world. And this is the victory that conquers the world, our faith.

1 John 5:4 NRSV

See also Conversion; Justification; Repentance; Righteousness; Unbelief

Faithfulness

83.1 Know then that the Lord your God is God, the faithful God; with those who love him and keep his commandments he keeps covenant and faith for a thousand generations.

Deuteronomy 7:9 REB

83.2 Everyone talks about how loyal and faithful he is, but just try to find someone who really is!

Proverbs 20:6 GNB

83.3 It is of the Lord's mercies that we are not consumed, because his compassions fail not. They are new every morning: great is thy faithfulness.

Lamentations 3:22–23 KJV

83.4 Who, then, is the wise and trustworthy servant whom the master placed over his household to give them their food at the proper time?

Matthew 24:45 NJB

83.5 His lord said unto him, Well done, thou good and faithful servant: thou hast been faithful over a few things, I will make thee ruler over many things: enter thou into the joy of thy lord.

Matthew 25:21 KJV

83.6 Whoever is faithful in a very little is faithful also in much; and whoever is dishonest in a very little is dishonest also in much.

Luke 16:10 NRSV

83.7 God keeps faith and will not let you be tested beyond your powers, but when the test comes he will at the same time provide a way out and so enable you to endure.

1 Corinthians 10:13 REB

83.8 The fruit of the Spirit is… faithfulness.

Galatians 5:22 NRSV

83.9 You have often heard me teach. Now I want you to tell these same things to followers who can be trusted to tell others.

2 Timothy 2:2 CEV

83.10 If we are not faithful, he will still be faithful. Christ cannot deny who he is.
2 Timothy 2:13 CEV

83.11 For this reason he had to be made like his brothers in every way, in order that he might become a merciful and faithful high priest in service to God, and that he might make atonement for the sins of the people.
Hebrews 2:17 NIV

83.12 Behold, the devil shall cast some of you into prison, that ye may be tried; and ye shall have tribulation ten days: be thou faithful unto death, and I will give thee a crown of life.
Revelation 2:10 KJV

See also **God, Faithful; Love, of God; Loyalty; Mercy**

Fall, the

84.1 Now the serpent was more subtil than any beast of the field which the Lord God had made. And he said unto the woman, Yea, hath God said, Ye shall not eat of every tree of the garden?… And the serpent said unto the woman, Ye shall not surely die… And when the woman saw that the tree was good for food, and that it was pleasant to the eyes, and a tree to be desired to make one wise, she took of the fruit thereof, and did eat, and gave also unto her husband with her; and he did eat. And the eyes of them both were opened, and they knew that they were naked; and they sewed fig leaves together, and made themselves aprons… and Adam and his wife hid themselves from the presence of the Lord God amongst the trees of the garden.
Genesis 3:1, 4, 6–8 KJV

84.2 Unto the woman he said, I will greatly multiply thy sorrow and thy conception; in sorrow thou shalt bring forth children; and thy desire shall be to thy husband, and he shall rule over thee. And unto Adam he said, Because thou hast hearkened unto the voice of thy wife, and hast eaten of the tree, of which I commanded thee, saying, Thou shalt not eat of it: cursed is the ground for thy sake; in sorrow shalt thou eat of it all the days of thy life… In the sweat of thy face shalt thou eat bread, till thou return unto the ground; for out of it wast thou taken: for dust thou art, and unto dust shalt thou return.
Genesis 3:16–17, 19 KJV

84.3 As by one man sin entered into the world, and death by sin… so death passed upon all men, for that all have sinned.
Romans 5:12 KJV

84.4 God's act of grace is out of all proportion to Adam's wrongdoing. For if the wrongdoing of that one man brought death upon so many, its effect is vastly exceeded by the grace of God and the gift that came to so many by the grace of the one man, Jesus Christ. And again, the gift of God is not to be compared in its effect with that one man's sin; for the judicial action, following on the one offence, resulted in a verdict of condemnation, but the act of grace, following on so many misdeeds, resulted in a verdict of acquittal. If, by the wrongdoing of one man, death established its reign through that one man, much more shall those who in far greater measure receive grace and the gift of righteousness live and reign through the one man, Jesus Christ. It follows, then, that as the result of one misdeed was condemnation for all people, so the result of one righteous act is acquittal and life for all. For as through the disobedience of one man many were made sinners, so through the obedience of one man many will be made righteous.
Romans 5:15–19 REB

See also **Adam; Eden, Garden of; Sin; Sinful nature**

Falling away

85.1 The backslider in heart shall be filled with his own ways: and a good man shall be satisfied from himself.

Proverbs 14:14 KJV

85.2 But they did not listen; they paid no heed, and persisted in their own plans with evil and stubborn hearts; they turned their backs and not their faces to me.

Jeremiah 7:24 REB

85.3 Although our iniquities testify against us, act, O Lord, for your name's sake; our apostasies indeed are many, and we have sinned against you.

Jeremiah 14:7 NRSV

85.4 You, like your ancestors before you, have turned away from my laws and have not kept them. Turn back to me, and I will turn to you. But you ask, 'What must we do to turn back to you?'

Malachi 3:7 GNB

85.5 Then Jesus said to them, 'You will all fall away from me tonight, for the scripture says: "I shall strike the shepherd and the sheep of the flock will be scattered."'

Matthew 26:31 NJB

85.6 If you don't stay joined to me, you will be thrown away. You will be like dry branches that are gathered up and burnt in a fire.

John 15:6 CEV

85.7 I have said these things to you to keep you from stumbling.

John 16:1 NRSV

85.8 Now the Spirit expressly says that in later times some will renounce the faith by paying attention to deceitful spirits and teachings of demons.

1 Timothy 4:1 NRSV

85.9 For how can those who abandon their faith be brought back to repent again? They were once in God's light; they tasted heaven's gift and received their share of the Holy Spirit; they knew from experience that God's word is good, and they had felt the powers of the coming age. And then they abandoned their faith! It is impossible to bring them back to repent again, because they are again crucifying the Son of God and exposing him to public shame.

Hebrews 6:4–6 GNB

85.10 For if we deliberately persist in sin after receiving the knowledge of the truth, there can be no further sacrifice for sins.

Hebrews 10:26 REB

See also **Hardness; Rejection; Repentance; Unbelief**

Family

HUSBANDS AND WIVES

86.1 Therefore shall a man leave his father and his mother, and shall cleave unto his wife: and they shall be one flesh.

Genesis 2:24 KJV

86.2 A capable wife is her husband's crown; one who disgraces him is like a canker in his bones.

Proverbs 12:4 REB

86.3 He who finds a wife finds a good thing; he has won favour from the Lord.

Proverbs 18:22 REB

86.4 A capable wife who can find? She is far more precious than jewels.

Proverbs 31:10 NRSV

86.5 Your husband or wife who isn't a follower is made holy by having you as a partner. This also makes your children holy and keeps them from being unclean in God's sight.

1 Corinthians 7:14 CEV

86.6 I want you to understand that Christ is supreme over every man, the husband is supreme over his wife, and God is supreme over Christ.

1 Corinthians 11:3 GNB

86.7 Honour Christ and put others first. A wife should put her husband first, as she does the Lord. A husband is the head of his wife, as Christ is the head and the Saviour of the church, which is his own body. Wives should always put their husbands first, as the church puts Christ first. A husband should love his wife as much as Christ loved the church and gave his life for it... In the same way, a husband should love his wife as much as he loves himself. A husband who loves his wife shows that he loves himself.

Ephesians 5:21–25, 28 CEV

86.8 In the same way you wives must submit to your husbands, so that if any of them do not believe God's word, your conduct will win them over to believe. It will not be necessary for you to say a word, because they will see how pure and reverent your conduct is. You should not use outward aids to make yourselves beautiful, such as the way you do your hair, or the jewellery you put on, or the dresses you wear. Instead, your beauty should consist of your true inner self, the ageless beauty of a gentle and quiet spirit, which is of the greatest value in God's sight. For the devout women of the past who placed their hope in God used to make themselves beautiful by submitting to their husbands. Sarah was like that; she obeyed Abraham and called him her master. You are now her

daughters if you do good and are not afraid of anything. In the same way you husbands must live with your wives with the proper understanding that they are weaker than you. Treat them with respect, because they also will receive, together with you, God's gift of life. Do this so that nothing will interfere with your prayers.

1 Peter 3:1–7 GNB

See also **Human beings, Male and female; Marriage**

CHILDREN AND THE WHOLE FAMILY

86.9 Honour thy father and thy mother: that thy days may be long upon the land which the Lord thy God giveth thee.

Exodus 20:12 KJV

86.10 Repeat them [the Lord's commandments] to your children, and speak of them both indoors and out of doors, when you lie down and when you get up.

Deuteronomy 6:7 REB

86.11 [Joshua] As for me and my house, we will serve the Lord.

Joshua 24:15 KJV

86.12 Hannah made this vow: 'Lord of Hosts, if you will only take notice of my trouble and remember me, if you will not forget me but grant me offspring, then I shall give the child to the Lord for the whole of his life, and no razor shall ever touch his head.'

1 Samuel 1:11 REB

86.13 Out of the mouth of babes and sucklings hast thou ordained strength because of thine enemies, that thou mightest still the enemy and the avenger.

Psalm 8:2 KJV

Out of the mouth of babes
The comment *out of the mouths of babes and sucklings* is sometimes made when a young child or untaught person utters a wise and perceptive remark. The source of this quotation shows that the praise of God may come from even the youngest voice.

86.14 Lo, children are an heritage of the Lord: and the fruit of the womb is his reward. As arrows are in the hand of a mighty man; so are children of the youth. Happy is the man that hath his quiver full of them: they shall not be ashamed, but they shall speak with the enemies in the gate.
Psalm 127:3–5 KJV

86.15 A father who spares the rod hates his son, but one who loves his son brings him up strictly.
Proverbs 13:24 REB

Spare the rod
Spare the rod and spoil the child is a saying that comes from Proverbs. The expression is often used to support disciplined punishment so that a child will learn to behave properly and know the difference between right and wrong.

86.16 Children's children are a crown to the aged, and parents are the pride of their children.
Proverbs 17:6 NIV

86.17 Train up a child in the way he should go: and when he is old, he will not depart from it.
Proverbs 22:6 KJV

86.18 Those who love their father or mother more than me are not fit to be my disciples; those who love their son or daughter more than me are not fit to be my disciples.
Matthew 10:37 GNB

86.19 You teach that if a person has something he could use to help his father or mother, but says, 'This is Corban' (which means, it belongs to God), he is excused from helping his father or mother.
Mark 7:11–12 GNB

86.20 They brought young children to him, that he should touch them: and his disciples rebuked those that brought them. But when Jesus saw it, he was much displeased, and said unto them, Suffer the little children to come unto me, and forbid them not: for of such is the kingdom of God. Verily I say unto you, Whosoever shall not receive the kingdom of God as a little child, he shall not enter therein. And he took them up in his arms, put his hands upon them, and blessed them.
Mark 10:13–16 KJV

86.21 [Jesus and his parents] He went down with them then and came to Nazareth and lived under their authority. His mother stored up all these things in her heart. And Jesus increased in wisdom, in stature, and in favour with God and with people.
Luke 2:51–52 NJB

86.22 Children, you belong to the Lord, and you do the right thing when you obey your parents. The first commandment with a promise says, 'Obey your father and your mother, and you will have a long and happy life.'
Ephesians 6:1–2 CEV

86.23 Fathers, do not provoke your children to anger, but bring them up in the discipline and instruction of the Lord.
Ephesians 6:4 NRSV

86.24 Children, obey your parents in everything, for this is your acceptable duty in the Lord.

Colossians 3:20 NRSV

86.25 [A church leader] must be able to manage his own family well and make his children obey him with all respect.

1 Timothy 3:4 GNB

86.26 If anyone does not make provision for his relations, and especially for members of his own household, he has denied the faith and is worse than an unbeliever.

1 Timothy 5:8 REB

See also Discipline; Homes; Teachers and teaching; Youth

Fasting

87.1 The tenth day of this seventh month is the Day of Atonement. Hold a sacred assembly and deny yourselves, and present an offering made to the Lord by fire.

Leviticus 23:27 NIV

87.2 At that David and all the men with him took hold of their clothes and tore them. They mourned and wept, and they fasted till evening because Saul and Jonathan his son and the army of the Lord and the house of Israel had fallen in battle.

2 Samuel 1:11–12 REB

87.3 The people ask, 'Why should we fast if the Lord never notices? Why should we go without food if he pays no attention?' The Lord says to them, 'The truth is that at the same time as you fast, you pursue your own interests and oppress your workers. Your fasting makes you violent, and you quarrel and fight. Do you think this kind of fasting will make me listen to your prayers?... The kind of

fasting I want is this: remove the chains of oppression and the yoke of injustice, and let the oppressed go free.'

Isaiah 58:3–4, 6 GNB

87.4 Yet even now, says the Lord, return to me with all your heart, with fasting, with weeping, and with mourning; rend your hearts and not your clothing.

Joel 2:12–13 NRSV

87.5 He [Jesus] fasted for forty days and forty nights, after which he was hungry.

Matthew 4:2 NJB

87.6 When you fast, do not put on a sad face as the hypocrites do. They neglect their appearance so that everyone will see that they are fasting. I assure you, they have already been paid in full. When you go without food, wash your face and comb your hair, so that others cannot know that you are fasting – only your Father, who is unseen, will know. And your Father, who sees what you do in private, will reward you.

Matthew 6:16–18 GNB

87.7 Jesus answered, 'Do you expect the guests at a wedding party to be sad as long as the bridegroom is with them? Of course not! But the day will come when the bridegroom will be taken away from them, and then they will fast.'

Matthew 9:15 GNB

87.8 [A Pharisee] I fast twice in the week, I give tithes of all that I possess.

Luke 18:12 KJV

87.9 While they were worshipping the Lord and fasting, the Holy Spirit said, 'Set apart for me Barnabas and Saul for the work to which I have called them.' Then after fasting and praying they laid their hands on them and sent them off.

Acts 13:2–3 NRSV

Fear

88.1 He [Adam] said, I heard thy voice in the garden, and I was afraid, because I was naked; and I hid myself.

Genesis 3:10 KJV

88.2 Moses hid his face; for he was afraid to look upon God.

Exodus 3:6 KJV

88.3 At this the courage of the people melted and flowed away like water.

Joshua 7:5 REB

88.4 Fear and trembling overwhelm me, and shuddering grips me.

Psalm 55:5 NJB

88.5 So do not be afraid of people. Whatever is now covered up will be uncovered, and every secret will be made known.

Matthew 10:26 GNB

88.6 Do not be afraid of those who kill the body but cannot kill the soul; rather be afraid of God, who can destroy both body and soul in hell.

Matthew 10:28 GNB

88.7 He said to them, 'Why are you afraid? Have you still no faith?'

Mark 4:40 NRSV

88.8 People will faint from fear as they wait for what is coming over the whole earth, for the powers in space will be driven from their courses.

Luke 21:26 GNB

88.9 No one talked freely about him, however, for fear of the Jews.

John 7:13 REB

88.10 God's Spirit doesn't make us slaves who are afraid of him. Instead, we become his children and call him our Father.

Romans 8:15 CEV

88.11 I came before you in weakness, in fear, in great trepidation.

1 Corinthians 2:3 REB

88.12 There is no fear in love, but perfect love casts out fear; for fear has to do with punishment, and whoever fears has not reached perfection in love.

1 John 4:18 NRSV

See also **Comfort, when afraid; Courage; Reverence**

Fellowship

89.1 They continued stedfastly in the apostles' doctrine and fellowship, and in breaking of bread, and in prayers.

Acts 2:42 KJV

89.2 All who believed were together and had all things in common.

Acts 2:44 NRSV

89.3 God is faithful, by whom ye were called unto the fellowship of his Son, Jesus Christ our Lord.

1 Corinthians 1:9 KJV

89.4 When we drink from the cup that we ask God to bless, isn't that sharing in the blood of Christ? When we eat the bread that we break, isn't that sharing in the body of Christ? By sharing in the same loaf of bread, we become one body, even though there are many of us.

1 Corinthians 10:16–17 CEV

89.5 The grace of the Lord Jesus Christ, the love of God, and the fellowship of the Holy Spirit be with you all.

2 Corinthians 13:13 GNB

89.6 When James, Cephas, and John, who seemed to be pillars, perceived the grace that was given unto me, they gave to me and Barnabas the right hand of fellowship; that we should go unto the heathen, and they unto the circumcision.

Galatians 2:9 KJV

89.7 I thank my God… for your fellowship in the gospel.

Philippians 1:3, 5 KJV

89.8 Yours was the only church to share with me in the giving and receiving.

Philippians 4:15 REB

89.9 In so far as you share in the sufferings of Christ, be glad, so that you may enjoy a much greater gladness when his glory is revealed.

1 Peter 4:13 NJB

89.10 That which we have seen and heard declare we unto you, that ye also may have fellowship with us: and truly our fellowship is with the Father, and with his Son Jesus Christ.

1 John 1:3 KJV

89.11 If we say that we have fellowship with him while we are walking in darkness, we lie and do not do what is true; but if we walk in the light as he himself is in the light, we have fellowship with one another, and the blood of Jesus his Son cleanses us from all sin.

1 John 1:6–7 NRSV

See also **Communion; Encouragement; Love, of humanity; Unity**

Christian fellowship: secrets of success

accept one another
Romans 15:7 GNB

bear one another's *burdens*
Galatians 6:2 NRSV

be *concerned* for one another
Hebrews 10:24 GNB

confess your sins to one another
James 5:16 GNB

encourage one another
Hebrews 10:25 GNB

have fellowship with one another
1 John 1:7 GNB

honor one another
Romans 12:10 NIV

live in harmony with one another
Romans 15:5 NRSV

love one another
Romans 12:10 GNB

offer hospitality to one another
1 Peter 4:9 NIV

pray for one another
James 5:16 GNB

serve one another
Galatians 5:13 GNB

stir up one another to love and good works
Hebrews 10:24 RSV

be *subject to* one another
Ephesians 5:21 REB

teach and admonish one another
Colossians 3:16 NIV

Food and drink

90.1 God also said, 'Throughout the earth I give you all plants that bear seed, and every tree that bears fruit with seed: they shall be yours for food. All green plants I give for food to the wild animals, to all the birds of the air, and to everything that creeps on the earth, every living creature.'

Genesis 1:29–30 REB

90.2 Every creature that lives and moves will be food for you; I give them all to you, as I have given you every green plant.

Genesis 9:3 REB

90.3 So he afflicted you with hunger and then fed you on manna… to teach you that people cannot live on bread alone, but that they live on every word that comes from the mouth of the Lord.

Deuteronomy 8:3 REB

Manna
The food that was the Israelites' main food during their wanderings in the wilderness was known as *manna*. It was miraculously provided by God. The meaning of the word is, 'What is it?' It looked like coriander seed and tasted like wafer made with honey, but speculation continues on the exact nature of the food.

90.4 Ravens brought him [Elijah] bread and meat twice a day, and he drank water from the brook.

1 Kings 17:6 CEV

90.5 He causeth the grass to grow for the cattle, and herb for the service of man: that he may bring forth food out of the earth; and wine that maketh glad the heart of man, and oil to make his face shine, and bread which strengtheneth man's heart.

Psalm 104:14–15 KJV

90.6 He hath given meat unto them that fear him: he will ever be mindful of his covenant.

Psalm 111:5 KJV

90.7 Everyone depends on you, and when the time is right, you provide them with food. By your own hand you satisfy the desire of all who live.

Psalm 145:15–16 CEV

90.8 Better a dish of herbs when love is there than a fattened ox and hatred to go with it.

Proverbs 15:17 NJB

90.9 Come for water, all who are thirsty; though you have no money, come, buy grain and eat; come, buy wine and milk, not for money, not for a price. Why spend your money for what is not food, your earnings on what fails to satisfy? Listen to me and you will fare well, you will enjoy the fat of the land.

Isaiah 55:1–2 REB

90.10 Give us this day our daily bread.

Matthew 6:11 KJV

90.11 Jesus said: My food is to do what God wants! He is the one who sent me, and I must finish the work that he gave me to do.

John 4:34 CEV

90.12 Jesus replied to them: In all truth I tell you, if you do not eat the flesh of the Son of man and drink his blood, you have no life in you. Anyone who does eat my flesh and drink my blood has eternal life, and I shall raise that person up on the last day. For my flesh is real food and my blood is real drink. Whoever eats my flesh and drinks my blood lives in me and I live in that person.

John 6:53–56 NJB

90.13 As long as we have food and clothing, we shall be content with that.

1 Timothy 6:8 NJB

See also **Communion; Drunkenness**

Fools and folly

91.1 Please, don't pay any attention to Nabal, that good-for-nothing! He is exactly what his name means – a fool!

1 Samuel 25:25 GNB

91.2 The fool hath said in his heart, There is no God.

Psalm 14:1 KJV

91.3 A fool's conduct is right in his own eyes; to listen to advice shows wisdom.

Proverbs 12:15 REB

91.4 As a dog returneth to his vomit, so a fool returneth to his folly.

Proverbs 26:11 KJV

91.5 A fool speaks foolishly and thinks up evil things to do. What he does and what he says are an insult to the Lord, and he never feeds the hungry or gives thirsty people anything to drink.

Isaiah 32:6 GNB

91.6 Everyone who hears these words of mine and does not act on them will be like a foolish man who built his house on sand.

Matthew 7:26 NRSV

91.7 God said unto him, Thou fool, this night thy soul shall be required of thee: then whose shall those things be, which thou hast provided?

Luke 12:20 KJV

91.8 They claim to be wise, but they are fools. They don't worship the glorious and eternal God. Instead, they worship idols that are made to look like humans who cannot live for ever, and like birds, animals, and reptiles.

Romans 1:22–23 CEV

91.9 The message of the cross is sheer folly to those on the way to destruction, but to us, who are on the way to salvation, it is the power of God.

1 Corinthians 1:18 REB

91.10 God hath chosen the foolish things of the world to confound the wise; and God hath chosen the weak things of the world to confound the things which are mighty.

1 Corinthians 1:27 KJV

91.11 The man without the Spirit does not accept the things that come from the Spirit of God, for they are foolishness to him and he cannot understand them, because they are spiritually discerned.

1 Corinthians 2:14 NIV

91.12 For ye suffer fools gladly, seeing ye yourselves are wise.

2 Corinthians 11:19 KJV

Not suffer fools gladly
A person who does *not suffer fools gladly* is impatient and unsympathetic towards foolish people. The expression derives from this verse: the Corinthians thought themselves to be wise and so respected and submitted themselves naïvely to false teachers.

See also **Wisdom**

Forgiveness

92.1 Happy are those whose transgression is forgiven, whose sin is covered. Happy are those to whom the Lord imputes no iniquity, and in whose spirit there is no deceit.

Psalm 32:1–2 NRSV

92.2 Have mercy upon me, O God, according to thy loving kindness: according unto the multitude of thy tender mercies blot out my transgressions. Wash me thoroughly from mine iniquity, and cleanse me from my sin.

Psalm 51:1–2 KJV

92.3 As far as the east is from the west, so far hath he removed our transgressions from us.

Psalm 103:12 KJV

92.4 If you, Lord, should keep account of sins, who could hold his ground? But with you is forgiveness, so that you may be revered.

Psalm 130:3–4 REB

92.5 They shall teach no more every man his neighbour, and every man his brother, saying, Know the Lord: for they shall all know me, from the least of them unto the greatest of them, saith the Lord: for I will forgive their iniquity, and I will remember their sin no more.

Jeremiah 31:34 KJV

92.6 Our God, no one is like you. We are all that is left of your chosen people, and you freely forgive our sin and guilt. You don't stay angry for ever; you're glad to have pity.

Micah 7:18 CEV

92.7 Forgive us our trespasses, as we forgive them that trespass against us.

Matthew 6:12 BCP

92.8 If you forgive others the wrongs they have done to you, your Father in heaven will also forgive you. But if you do not forgive others, then your Father will not forgive the wrongs you have done.

Matthew 6:14–15 GNB

92.9 'I will show you that the Son of Man has the right to forgive sins here on earth.' So Jesus said to the man, 'Get up! Pick up your mat and go on home.'

Matthew 9:6 CEV

92.10 Therefore I tell you, people will be forgiven for every sin and blasphemy, but blasphemy against the Spirit will not be forgiven.

Matthew 12:31 NRSV

92.11 'Repent', said Peter, 'and be baptized, every one of you, in the name of Jesus the Messiah; then your sins will be forgiven and you will receive the gift of the Holy Spirit.'

Acts 2:38 REB

92.12 It is to him that all the prophets bear this witness: that all who believe in Jesus will have their sins forgiven through his name.

Acts 10:43 NJB

92.13 In whom [Jesus Christ] we have redemption through his blood, the forgiveness of sins, according to the riches of his grace.

Ephesians 1:7 KJV

92.14 Be kind and merciful, and forgive others, just as God forgave you because of Christ.

Ephesians 4:32 CEV

92.15 Indeed, under the law almost everything is purified with blood, and without the shedding of blood there is no forgiveness of sins.

Hebrews 9:22 NRSV

92.16 If we confess our sins, he is faithful and just to forgive us our sins, and to cleanse us from all unrighteousness.

1 John 1:9 KJV

See also **Atonement; Guilt; Repentance; Sin**

Freedom

93.1 The Spirit of the Lord God is upon me; because the Lord hath anointed me to preach good tidings unto the meek; he hath sent me to bind up the brokenhearted, to proclaim liberty to the captives, and the opening of the prison to them that are bound.

Isaiah 61:1 KJV

93.2 Then Jesus said to the Jews who had believed in him, 'If you continue in my word, you are truly my disciples; and you will know the truth, and the truth will make you free… Very truly, I tell you, everyone who commits sin is a slave to sin. The slave does not have a permanent place in the household; the son has a place there for ever. So if the Son makes you free, you will be free indeed.'

John 8:31–32, 34–36 NRSV

93.3 Now that you have been set free from sin and have become slaves to God, the benefit you reap leads to holiness, and the result is eternal life.

Romans 6:22 NIV

93.4 In Christ Jesus the life-giving law of the Spirit has set you free from the law of sin and death. What the law could not do, because human weakness robbed it of all potency, God has done: by sending his own Son in the likeness of our sinful nature and to deal with sin, he has passed judgment against sin within that very nature, so that the commandment of the law may find fulfilment in us, whose conduct is no longer controlled by the old nature, but by the Spirit.

Romans 8:2–4 REB

93.5 With the intention that the whole creation itself might be freed from its slavery to corruption and brought into the same glorious freedom as the children of God.

Romans 8:21 NJB

93.6 Be careful, however, not to let your freedom of action make those who are weak in the faith fall into sin.

1 Corinthians 8:9 GNB

93.7 Now the Lord is the Spirit, and where the Spirit of the Lord is, there is freedom. And all of us, with unveiled faces, seeing the glory of the Lord as though reflected in a mirror, are being transformed into the same image from one degree of glory to another; for this comes from the Lord, the Spirit.

2 Corinthians 3:17–18 NRSV

93.8 For freedom Christ has set us free. Stand firm, therefore, and do not submit again to a yoke of slavery.

Galatians 5:1 NRSV

93.9 As for you, my brothers and sisters, you were called to be free. But do not let this freedom become an excuse for letting your physical desires control you. Instead, let love make you serve one another.

Galatians 5:13 GNB

93.10 Since the children share in flesh and blood, he too shared in them, so that by dying he might break the power of him who had death at his command, that is, the devil.

Hebrews 2:14 REB

See also **Choice; Responsibility, human**

Friends and friendship

94.1 The Lord spake unto Moses face to face, as a man speaketh unto his friend.

Exodus 33:11 KJV

94.2 The friendship of the Lord is for those who fear him, and he makes his covenant known to them.
Psalm 25:14 NRSV

94.3 Friends always show their love.
Proverbs 17:17 GNB

94.4 Some friendships do not last, but some friends are more loyal than brothers.
Proverbs 18:24 GNB

94.5 Faithful are the wounds of a friend; but the kisses of an enemy are deceitful.
Proverbs 27:6 KJV

94.6 A faithful friend is the medicine of life; and they that fear the Lord shall find him.
Ecclesiasticus 6:16 KJV

94.7 Forsake not an old friend; for the new is not comparable to him: a new friend is as new wine; when it is old, thou shalt drink it with pleasure.
Ecclesiasticus 9:10 KJV

94.8 The Son of Man came, eating and drinking, and they say, 'Look at him! A glutton and a drinker, a friend of tax-collectors and sinners!' Yet God's wisdom is proved right by its results.
Matthew 11:19 REB

94.9 Jesus said to him [Judas], 'Friend, do what you are here to do.'
Matthew 26:50 NRSV

94.10 The greatest way to show love for friends is to die for them. And you are my friends, if you obey me. Servants don't know what their master is doing, and so I don't speak to you as my servants. I speak to you as my friends, and I have told you everything that my Father has told me.
John 15:13–15 CEV

94.11 In this way the scripture was fulfilled: Abraham put his faith in God, and this was considered as making him upright; and he received the name 'friend of God'.
James 2:23 NJB

See also Loyalty

Fruit

95.1 He will bless the fruit of your womb.
Deuteronomy 7:13 NIV

95.2 [John the Baptist to the Pharisees and Sadducees] Bring forth therefore fruits meet for repentance.
Matthew 3:8 KJV

95.3 You will know them by their fruits.
Matthew 7:16 NRSV

95.4 I am the vine, and you are the branches. Those who remain in me, and I in them, will bear much fruit; for you can do nothing without me... My Father's glory is shown by your bearing much fruit; and in this way you become my disciples.
John 15:5, 8 GNB

95.5 You did not choose me; I chose you and appointed you to go and bear much fruit, the kind of fruit that endures.
John 15:16 GNB

95.6 The harvest of the Spirit is love, joy, peace, patience, kindness, goodness, fidelity, gentleness, and self-control. Against such things there is no law.
Galatians 5:22–23 REB

Fullness

96.1 The earth is the Lord's, and the fulness thereof; the world, and they that dwell therein.
Psalm 24:1 KJV

96.2 The Word was made flesh, and dwelt among us, (and we beheld his glory, the glory as of the only begotten of the Father,) full of grace and truth.
John 1:14 KJV

96.3 From his full store we have all received grace upon grace.
John 1:16 REB

96.4 [The church] which is his body, the fulness of him that filleth all in all.
Ephesians 1:23 KJV

96.5 [Paul's prayer] That you may be filled with all the fullness of God.
Ephesians 3:19 NRSV

96.6 Be not drunk with wine, wherein is excess; but be filled with the Spirit.
Ephesians 5:18 KJV

96.7 For in him [Christ] the whole fullness of deity dwells bodily, and you have come to fullness in him.
Colossians 2:9–10 NRSV

Generosity

97.1 If there be among you a poor man of one of thy brethren within any of thy gates in thy land which the Lord thy God giveth thee, thou shalt not harden thine heart, nor shut thine hand from thy poor brother: but thou shalt open thine hand wide unto him, and shalt surely lend him sufficient for his need, in that which he wanteth.

Deuteronomy 15:7–8 KJV

97.2 The wicked borrow and do not repay; the righteous give generously.

Psalm 37:21 REB

97.3 All goes well for one who lends generously, who is honest in all his dealing.

Psalm 112:5 NJB

97.4 Sometimes you can become rich by being generous or poor by being greedy. Generosity will be rewarded: give a cup of water, and you will receive a cup of water in return.

Proverbs 11:24–25 CEV

97.5 He that hath a bountiful eye shall be blessed; for he giveth of his bread to the poor.

Proverbs 22:9 KJV

97.6 If anyone requires you to go one mile, go two miles with him. Give to anyone who asks you, and if anyone wants to borrow, do not turn away.

Matthew 5:41–42 NJB

97.7 If you give to others, you will be given a full amount in return. It will be packed down, shaken together, and spilling over into your lap. The way you treat others is the way you will be treated.

Luke 6:38 CEV

97.8 How, throughout continual ordeals of hardship, their [the Macedonian churches'] unfailing joy and their intense poverty have overflowed in a wealth of generosity on their part.

2 Corinthians 8:2 NJB

97.9 Remember: anyone who sows sparsely will reap sparsely as well – and anyone who sows generously will reap generously as well.

2 Corinthians 9:6 NJB

97.10 God gives seed to farmers and provides everyone with food. He will increase what you have, so that you can give even more to those in need. You will be blessed in every way, and you will be able to keep on being generous. Then many people will thank God when we deliver your gift… The way in which you have proved yourselves by this service will bring honour and praise to God. You believed the message about Christ, and you obeyed it by sharing generously with God's people and with everyone else.

2 Corinthians 9:10–11, 13 CEV

97.11 Instruct those who are rich in this world's goods… to do good and to be rich in well-doing, to be ready to give generously and to share with others.

1 Timothy 6:17–18 REB

97.12 According to his mercy he saved us, by the washing of regeneration, and renewing of the Holy Ghost; which he shed on us abundantly through Jesus Christ our Saviour.

Titus 3:5–6 KJV

97.13 If any of you lacks wisdom, he should ask God and it will be given him, for God is a generous giver.

James 1:5 REB

See also Giving

Gentiles

98.1 Ask of me, and I shall give thee the heathen for thine inheritance, and the uttermost parts of the earth for thy possession.
Psalm 2:8 KJV

98.2 In that day there shall be a root of Jesse, which shall stand for an ensign of the people; to it shall the Gentiles seek: and his rest shall be glorious.
Isaiah 11:10 KJV

98.3 A light to lighten the Gentiles, and to be the glory of thy people Israel.
Luke 2:32 BCP

98.4 The Lord said to him [Ananias], 'Go, because I have chosen him [Paul] to serve me, to make my name known to Gentiles and kings and to the people of Israel.'
Acts 9:15 GNB

98.5 The believers who had come with Peter, men of Jewish birth, were amazed that the gift of the Holy Spirit should have been poured out even on Gentiles.
Acts 10:45 REB

98.6 They gave praise to God. 'This means', they said, 'that God has granted life-giving repentance to the Gentiles also.'
Acts 11:18 REB

98.7 When Gentiles, who do not possess the law, do instinctively what the law requires, these, though not having the law, are a law to themselves.
Romans 2:14 NRSV

A law unto themselves
To be *a law to* (or: *unto*) *oneself* means that someone does what he or she wants, setting his or her own guidelines as to what is right and wrong, without considering the usual rules or conventions of society or the advice of others. The expression derives from this verse, which shows that the moral nature of Gentiles serves in place of the law of Moses to show God's demands. In this sense, the Gentiles are 'a law unto themselves'.

98.8 There is neither Jew nor Greek, there is neither bond nor free, there is neither male nor female: for ye are all one in Christ Jesus.
Galatians 3:28 KJV

98.9 Don't forget that you are Gentiles. In fact, you used to be called 'uncircumcised' by those who take pride in being circumcised. At that time you did not know about Christ. You were foreigners to the people of Israel, and you had no part in the promises that God had made to them. You were living in this world without hope and without God, and you were far from God. But Christ offered his life's blood as a sacrifice and brought you near God. Christ has made peace between Jews and Gentiles, and he has united us by breaking down the wall of hatred that separated us. Christ gave his own body to destroy the Law of Moses with all its rules and commands. He even brought Jews and Gentiles together as though we were only one person, when he united us in peace. On the cross Christ did away with our hatred for each other. He also made peace between us and God by uniting Jews and Gentiles in one body. Christ came and preached peace to you Gentiles, who were far from God, and peace to us Jews, who were near God. And because of Christ, all of us can come to the Father by the same Spirit. You Gentiles are no longer strangers and foreigners. You are citizens with everyone else who belongs to the family of God.

Ephesians 2:11–19 CEV

98.10 After that I saw that there was a huge number, impossible for anyone to count, of people from every nation, race, tribe and language; they were standing in front of the throne and in front of the Lamb, dressed in white robes and holding palms in their hands.

Revelation 7:9 NJB

See also **Israel**

Gentleness

99.1 Take my yoke upon you, and learn of me; for I am meek and lowly in heart: and ye shall find rest unto your souls.

Matthew 11:29 KJV

99.2 I myself, Paul, appeal to you by the meekness and gentleness of Christ – I who am humble when face to face with you, but bold towards you when I am away!

2 Corinthians 10:1 NRSV

99.3 By contrast, the fruit of the Spirit is… gentleness.

Galatians 5:22–23 NRSV

99.4 If anyone is caught doing something wrong, you, my friends, who live by the Spirit must gently set him right.

Galatians 6:1 REB

99.5 We were gentle among you, like a nurse tenderly caring for her own children.

1 Thessalonians 2:7 NRSV

99.6 The Lord's servant must not be quarrelsome but kindly to everyone, an apt teacher, patient, correcting opponents with gentleness.

2 Timothy 2:24 NRSV

99.7 The wisdom from above is first pure, then peaceable, gentle, willing to yield, full of mercy and good fruits, without a trace of partiality or hypocrisy.

James 3:17 NRSV

99.8 [Paul's instructions to wives] Your beauty should consist of your true inner self, the ageless beauty of a gentle and quiet spirit, which is of the greatest value in God's sight.

1 Peter 3:4 GNB

Gift

100.1 For God so loved the world, that he gave his only begotten Son, that whosoever believeth in him should not perish, but have everlasting life.

John 3:16 KJV

100.2 Peter said to them, 'Each one of you must turn away from your sins and be baptized in the name of Jesus Christ, so that your sins will be forgiven; and you will receive God's gift, the Holy Spirit.'

Acts 2:38 GNB

100.3 God exalted him at his right hand as Leader and Saviour, so that he might give repentance to Israel and forgiveness of sins.

Acts 5:31 NRSV

100.4 For the wages of sin is death; but the gift of God is eternal life through Jesus Christ our Lord.

Romans 6:23 KJV

100.5 We have different gifts, according to the grace given us.

Romans 12:6 NIV

100.6 There are different kinds of spiritual gifts, but they all come from the same Spirit. There are different ways to serve the same Lord, and we can each do different things. Yet the same God works in all of us and helps us in everything we do. The Spirit has given each of us a special way of serving others... But it is the Spirit who does all this and decides which gifts to give to each of us.

1 Corinthians 12:4–7, 11 CEV

100.7 Love should be your guide. Be eager to have the gifts that come from the Holy Spirit, especially the gift of prophecy.

1 Corinthians 14:1 CEV

100.8 Thanks be to God for his gift which is beyond all praise!

2 Corinthians 9:15 REB

100.9 For by grace are ye saved through faith; and that not of yourselves: it is the gift of God.

Ephesians 2:8 KJV

100.10 Do not neglect the spiritual gift that is in you, which was given to you when the prophets spoke and the elders laid their hands on you.

1 Timothy 4:14 GNB

100.11 Every good gift and every perfect gift is from above, and cometh down from the Father of lights, with whom is no variableness, neither shadow of turning.

James 1:17 KJV

See also **Abilities**

Giving

101.1 [Melchizedek] Blessed be Abram of the most high God, possessor of heaven and earth: and blessed be the most high God, which hath delivered thine enemies into thy hand. And he [Abram] gave him tithes of all.

Genesis 14:19–20 KJV

101.2 For all things come of thee, and of thine own have we given thee.

1 Chronicles 29:14 KJV

101.3 Bring the full tithe into the storehouse, so that there may be food in my house, and thus put me to the test, says the Lord of hosts; see if I will not open the windows of heaven for you and pour down for you an overflowing blessing.

Malachi 3:10 NRSV

101.4 So when you give something to a needy person, do not make a big show of it, as the hypocrites do in the houses of worship and on the streets. They do it so that people will praise them... But when you help a needy person, do it in such a way that even your closest friend will not know about it.

Matthew 6:2–3 GNB

101.5 Presently there came a poor widow who dropped in two tiny coins, together worth a penny. He [Jesus] called his disciples to him and said, 'Truly I tell you: this poor widow has given more than all those giving to the treasury; for the others who have given had more than enough, but she, with less than enough, has given all that she had to live on.'

Mark 12:42–44 REB

101.6 If you give to others, you will be given a full amount in return. It will be packed down, shaken together, and spilling over into your lap. The way you treat others is the way you will be treated.

Luke 6:38 CEV

101.7 On the first day of every week, each of you is to put aside and save whatever extra you earn, so that collections need not be taken when I come.

1 Corinthians 16:2 NRSV

101.8 We must tell you, friends, about the grace that God has given to the churches in Macedonia. The troubles they have been through have tried them hard, yet in all this they have been so exuberantly happy that from the depths of their poverty they have shown themselves lavishly open-handed. Going to the limit of their resources, as I can testify, and even beyond that limit, they begged us most insistently, and on their own initiative, to be allowed to share in this generous service to their fellow-Christians. And their giving surpassed our expectations; for first of all they gave themselves to the Lord and, under God, to us.

2 Corinthians 8:1–5 REB

101.9 Each one should give as much as he has decided on his own initiative, not reluctantly or under compulsion, for God loves a cheerful giver.

2 Corinthians 9:7 NJB

See also **Generosity; Money and material goods; Stewardship**

Glory

102.1 Moses prayed, 'Show me your glory.'

Exodus 33:18 REB

102.2 As truly as I live, all the earth shall be filled with the glory of the Lord.

Numbers 14:21 KJV

102.3 She [the wife of Phinehas] named the boy Ichabod, explaining, 'God's glory has left Israel' – referring to the capture of the Covenant Box and the death of her father-in-law and her husband.

1 Samuel 4:21 GNB

102.4 What is a frail mortal, that you should be mindful of him, a human being, that you should take notice of him? Yet you have made him little less than a god, crowning his head with glory and honour.

Psalm 8:4–5 REB

102.5 There in their presence he [Jesus] was transfigured: his face shone like the sun and his clothes became as dazzling as light.

Matthew 17:2 NJB

102.6 Those who are ashamed of me and of my words in this adulterous and sinful generation, of them the Son of Man will also be ashamed when he comes in the glory of his Father with the holy angels.

Mark 8:38 NRSV

102.7 Jesus performed this first miracle in Cana in Galilee; there he revealed his glory, and his disciples believed in him.

John 2:11 GNB

102.8 So now, Father, glorify me in your own presence with the glory that I had in your presence before the world existed.

John 17:5 NRSV

102.9 For all have sinned, and come short of the glory of God.

Romans 3:23 KJV

102.10 I am sure that what we are suffering now cannot compare with the glory that will be shown to us.

Romans 8:18 CEV

102.11 So, whether you eat or drink, or whatever you do, do everything for the glory of God.

1 Corinthians 10:31 NRSV

102.12 A man has no need to cover his head, because he reflects the image and glory of God. But woman reflects the glory of man.

1 Corinthians 11:7 GNB

102.13 We all, with open face beholding as in a glass the glory of the Lord, are changed into the same image from glory to glory, even as by the Spirit of the Lord.

2 Corinthians 3:18 KJV

102.14 The Son is the radiance of God's glory and the exact representation of his being, sustaining all things by his powerful word.

Hebrews 1:3 NIV

God

See also **Trinity**

ALL-KNOWING

103.1 O Lord, you have searched me and known me. You know when I sit down and when I rise up; you discern my thoughts from far away. You search out my path and my lying down, and are acquainted with all my ways. Even before a word is on my tongue, O Lord, you know it completely. You hem me in, behind and before, and lay your hand upon me. Such knowledge is too wonderful for me; it is so high that I cannot attain it.

Psalm 139:1–6 NRSV

103.2 O the depth of the riches both of the wisdom and knowledge of God! how unsearchable are his judgments, and his ways past finding out!

Romans 11:33 KJV

103.3 Nothing in creation can hide from him; everything lies bare and exposed to the eyes of him to whom we must render account.

Hebrews 4:13 REB

ALL-PRESENT

103.4 Where can I go from your spirit? Or where can I flee from your presence? If I ascend to heaven, you are there; if I make my bed in Sheol, you are there. If I take the wings of the morning and settle at the farthest limits of the sea, even there your hand shall lead me, and your right hand shall hold me fast.

Psalm 139:7–10 NRSV

ALMIGHTY

103.5 [Job to the Lord] I know that you can do all things and that no purpose is beyond you.

Job 42:2 REB

103.6 For nothing will be impossible with God.

Luke 1:37 NRSV

103.7 Alleluia: for the Lord God omnipotent reigneth.

Revelation 19:6 KJV

See also **Sovereignty of God**

CREATOR

103.8 In the beginning God created the heaven and the earth.

Genesis 1:1 KJV

103.9 Know ye that the Lord he is God: it is he that hath made us, and not we ourselves; we are his people, and the sheep of his pasture.
Psalm 100:3 KJV

103.10 Hast thou not known? hast thou not heard, that the everlasting God, the Lord, the Creator of the ends of the earth, fainteth not, neither is weary? there is no searching of his understanding.
Isaiah 40:28 KJV

103.11 It was I who made the earth and I created human beings on it, mine were the hands that spread out the heavens and I have given the orders to all their array.
Isaiah 45:12 NJB

103.12 God made the earth by his power, fixed the world in place by his wisdom, and by his knowledge unfurled the skies.
Jeremiah 10:12 REB

See also **Creation**

ETERNAL

103.13 Before you created the hills or brought the world into being, you were eternally God and will be God for ever.
Psalm 90:2 GNB

103.14 Now unto the King eternal, immortal, invisible, the only wise God, be honour and glory for ever and ever. Amen.
1 Timothy 1:17 KJV

FAITHFUL

103.15 Know therefore that the Lord your God is God, the faithful God who maintains covenant loyalty with those who love him and keep his commandments, to a thousand generations.
Deuteronomy 7:9 NRSV

103.16 The steadfast love of the Lord never ceases, his mercies never come to an end; they are new every morning; great is your faithfulness.
Lamentations 3:22–23 NRSV

103.17 It is God himself who called you to share in the life of his Son Jesus Christ our Lord; and God keeps faith.
1 Corinthians 1:9 REB

FATHER

103.18 Take to heart this lesson: that the Lord your God was disciplining you as a father disciplines his son.
Deuteronomy 8:5 REB

103.19 The Lord said to me, 'Your son Solomon will build my temple, and it will honour me. Solomon will be like a son to me, and I will be like a father to him.'
1 Chronicles 28:6 CEV

103.20 A father of the fatherless, and a judge of the widows, is God in his holy habitation.
Psalm 68:5 KJV

103.21 Thou art my father, my God, and the rock of my salvation.
Psalm 89:26 KJV

103.22 For you are our Father. Though Abraham were not to know us nor Israel to acknowledge us, you, Lord, are our Father; our Redeemer from of old is your name.
Isaiah 63:16 REB

103.23 You, Lord, are our Father. We are nothing but clay, but you are the potter who moulded us.
Isaiah 64:8 CEV

103.24 Have we not all one Father? Did not one God create us? Why do we profane the covenant of our fathers by breaking faith with one another?

Malachi 2:10 NIV

103.25 I tell you to love your enemies and pray for anyone who ill-treats you. Then you will be acting like your Father in heaven. He makes the sun rise on both good and bad people.

Matthew 5:44–45 CEV

103.26 Our Father which art in heaven, Hallowed be thy name.

Matthew 6:9 KJV

103.27 You must call no one on earth your father, since you have only one Father, and he is in heaven.

Matthew 23:9 NJB

103.28 On seeing the Lord the disciples were overjoyed. Jesus said again, 'Peace be with you! As the Father sent me, so I send you.'

John 20:20–21 REB

103.29 For us there is one God, the Father, from whom are all things, and we exist for him.

1 Corinthians 8:6 REB

103.30 I will receive you, and will be a Father unto you, and ye shall be my sons and daughters, saith the Lord Almighty.

2 Corinthians 6:17–18 KJV

103.31 There is one Lord, one faith, one baptism, and one God and Father of all, over all, through all and within all.

Ephesians 4:5–6 NJB

See also **Adoption**

GOOD

103.32 Find out for yourself how good the Lord is. Happy are those who find safety with him.

Psalm 34:8 GNB

103.33 O give thanks unto the Lord; for he is good: for his mercy endureth for ever.

Psalm 136:1 KJV

103.34 Jesus said to him, 'Why do you call me good? No one is good but God alone.'

Mark 10:18 NJB

103.35 Or do you despise his wealth of kindness and tolerance and patience, failing to see that God's kindness is meant to lead you to repentance?

Romans 2:4 REB

See also **Providence**

HOLY

103.36 Holy, holy, holy, is the Lord of hosts: the whole earth is full of his glory.

Isaiah 6:3 KJV

103.37 Your eyes are too pure to behold evil, and you cannot look on wrongdoing.

Habakkuk 1:13 NRSV

103.38 Lord, who doesn't honour and praise your name? You alone are holy, and all nations will come and worship you, because you have shown that you judge with fairness.

Revelation 15:4 CEV

INFINITE

103.39 [Solomon's prayer] Even heaven and the highest heaven cannot contain you, much less this house that I have built!

1 Kings 8:27 NRSV

103.40 With whom took he counsel, and who instructed him, and taught him in the path of judgment, and taught him knowledge, and shewed to him the way of understanding? Behold, the nations are as a drop of a bucket, and are counted as the small dust of the balance: behold, he taketh up the isles as a very little thing.

Isaiah 40:14–15 KJV

A drop in the ocean

A drop in the ocean (or: *bucket*) is something very small compared with the much larger thing that is required. For example, a tiny grant of money may be just *a drop in the ocean* when one considers the total amount that is really needed. The origin of the expression shows the insignificance of the earthly nations when compared with the supreme greatness of God.

103.41 For thus saith the high and lofty One that inhabiteth eternity, whose name is Holy; I dwell in the high and holy place, with him also that is of a contrite and humble spirit, to revive the spirit of the humble, and to revive the heart of the contrite ones.

Isaiah 57:15 KJV

103.42 Can anyone hide in some secret place and I not see him? Do I not fill heaven and earth? This is the word of the Lord.

Jeremiah 23:24 REB

JUST

103.43 [Abraham pleading for Sodom] Far be it from you to do such a thing, to slay the righteous with the wicked, so that the righteous fare as the wicked! Far be that from you! Shall not the Judge of all the earth do what is just?

Genesis 18:25 NRSV

103.44 The Lord is your mighty defender, perfect and just in all his ways; Your God is faithful and true; he does what is right and fair.

Deuteronomy 32:4 GNB

103.45 He has fixed a day when the whole world will be judged in uprightness by a man he has appointed. And God has publicly proved this by raising him from the dead.

Acts 17:31 NJB

103.46 If we confess our sins, he is faithful and just to forgive us our sins, and to cleanse us from all unrighteousness.

1 John 1:9 KJV

See also **Justice; Last things, Judgment**

LOVING

103.47 The Lord did not love you and choose you because you outnumbered other peoples; you were the smallest nation on earth. But the Lord loved you and wanted to keep the promise that he made to your ancestors. That is why he saved you by his great might and set you free from slavery to the king of Egypt. Remember that the Lord your God is the only God and that he is faithful. He will keep his covenant and show his constant love to a thousand generations of those who love him and obey his commands.

Deuteronomy 7:7–9 GNB

103.48 For God so loved the world, that he gave his only begotten Son, that whosoever believeth in him should not perish, but have everlasting life.

John 3:16 KJV

103.49 Herein is love, not that we loved God, but that he loved us, and sent his Son to be the propitiation for our sins.

1 John 4:10 KJV

MERCIFUL

103.50 The Lord passed before him, and proclaimed, 'The Lord, the Lord, a God merciful and gracious, slow to anger, and abounding in steadfast love and faithfulness, keeping steadfast love for the thousandth generation, forgiving iniquity and transgression and sin, yet by no means clearing the guilty, but visiting the iniquity of the parents upon the children and the children's children, to the third and the fourth generation.'

Exodus 34:6–7 NRSV

103.51 [The Lord] who crowneth thee with lovingkindness and tender mercies.

Psalm 103:4 KJV

103.52 For the Lord is full of compassion and mercy, longsuffering, and very pitiful, and forgiveth sins, and saveth in time of affliction.

Ecclesiasticus 2:11 KJV

103.53 We will fall into the hands of the Lord, and not into the hands of men: for as his majesty is, so is his mercy.

Ecclesiasticus 2:18 KJV

103.54 Because of his great love for us, God, who is rich in mercy, made us alive with Christ even when we were dead in transgressions – it is by grace you have been saved.

Ephesians 2:4–5 NIV

SELF-EXISTENT

103.55 God said to Moses, 'I am who I am.'

Exodus 3:14 NRSV

103.56 For as the Father has life in himself, so he has granted the Son to have life in himself.

John 5:26 NIV

SPIRITUAL

103.57 The time is coming, indeed it is already here, when true worshippers will worship the Father in spirit and in truth. These are the worshippers the Father wants. God is spirit, and those who worship him must worship in spirit and in truth.

John 4:23–24 REB

TRANSCENDENT

103.58 Can God indeed dwell on earth? Heaven itself, the highest heaven, cannot contain you; how much less this house that I have built!

1 Kings 8:27 REB

103.59 Can you understand the mysteries surrounding God All-Powerful? They are higher than the heavens and deeper than the grave. So what can you do when you know so little, and these mysteries outreach the earth and the sea?

Job 11:7–9 CEV

103.60 Be thou exalted, O God, above the heavens; let thy glory be above all the earth.

Psalm 57:5 KJV

103.61 For thou, Lord, art high above all the earth: thou art exalted far above all gods.

Psalm 97:9 KJV

103.62 High is the Lord above all nations, high his glory above the heavens.

Psalm 113:4 REB

103.63 It is he that sitteth upon the circle of the earth, and the inhabitants thereof are as grasshoppers; that stretcheth out the heavens as a curtain, and spreadeth them out as a tent to dwell in.

Isaiah 40:22 KJV

103.64 The Lord says: 'My thoughts and my ways are not like yours. Just as the heavens are higher than the earth, my thoughts and my ways are higher than yours.'

Isaiah 55:8–9 CEV

103.65 Our holy God lives for ever in the highest heavens, and this is what he says: Though I live high above in the holy place, I am here to help those who are humble and depend only on me.

Isaiah 57:15 CEV

103.66 Since the God who made the world and everything in it is himself Lord of heaven and earth, he does not make his home in shrines made by human hands. Nor is he in need of anything, that he should be served by human hands; on the contrary, it is he who gives everything – including life and breath – to everyone.

Acts 17:24–25 NJB

103.67 His mighty strength was seen at work when he raised Christ from the dead, and enthroned him at his right hand in the heavenly realms, far above all government and authority, all power and dominion, and any title of sovereignty that commands allegiance, not only in this age but also in the age to come.

Ephesians 1:19–21 REB

UNCHANGEABLE

103.68 God is not a human being, that he should lie, or a mortal, that he should change his mind. Has he promised, and will he not do it? Has he spoken, and will he not fulfil it?

Numbers 23:19 NRSV

103.69 For I am the Lord, I change not; therefore ye sons of Jacob are not consumed.

Malachi 3:6 KJV

103.70 Every good gift and every perfect gift is from above, and cometh down from the Father of lights, with whom is no variableness, neither shadow of turning.

James 1:17 KJV

WISE

103.71 O Lord, how manifold are thy works! in wisdom hast thou made them all: the earth is full of thy riches.

Psalm 104:24 KJV

103.72 God is wise and powerful! Praise him for ever and ever.

Daniel 2:20 GNB

103.73 Now unto the King eternal, immortal, invisible, the only wise God, be honour and glory for ever and ever. Amen.

1 Timothy 1:17 KJV

Names, titles and descriptions of God

Ancient of Days
Daniel 7:22

Creator
Isaiah 40:28

Father
Malachi 2:10; Matthew 5:45, 6:9; John 14:6, 20:17; Romans 8:15

Father of lights
James 1:17

God almighty
Genesis 17:1

God most high
Genesis 14:18

God of all flesh
Jeremiah 32:27

God of heaven
Nehemiah 2:4

God of hosts
Psalm 80:7, 14

God of Israel
Joshua 24:2

Holy One
Job 6:10

Holy One of Israel
Isaiah 1:4

I am
Exodus 3:14

Judge
Genesis 18:25

King
Jeremiah 10:7

King of kings
1 Timothy 6:15

Lord (Jehovah)
Exodus 6:3; Malachi 3:6

Lord of hosts
Jeremiah 32:18

Lord of lords
1 Timothy 6:15

Lord will provide (Jehovah jireh)
Genesis 22:14

Saviour
Isaiah 43:3

See also **Creation; Providence; Sovereignty of God**

Godless

104.1 The triumph of a wicked person is short-lived, the glee of one who is godless lasts but a moment!
Job 20:5 REB

104.2 What hope is there for the godless in the hour when God demands their life?
Job 27:8 GNB

104.3 The kings of the earth stand up, and the rulers take counsel together, against the Lord, and against his anointed.
Psalm 2:2 BCP

104.4 Let the arrogant be put to shame, because they have subverted me with guile; as for me, I will meditate on your precepts.
Psalm 119:78 NRSV

104.5 Through his mouth the godless is the ruin of his neighbour, but by knowledge the upright are safeguarded.
Proverbs 11:9 NJB

104.6 Let the wicked forsake his way, and the unrighteous man his thoughts: and let him return unto the Lord, and he will have mercy upon him; and to our God, for he will abundantly pardon.
Isaiah 55:7 KJV

104.7 For the wrath of God is revealed from heaven against all ungodliness and unrighteousness of men, who hold the truth in unrighteousness.
Romans 1:18 KJV

104.8 Christ died for us at a time when we were helpless and sinful.
Romans 5:6 CEV

See also **Unbeliever**

Good

105.1 God saw every thing that he had made, and, behold, it was very good.
Genesis 1:31 KJV

105.2 The song was raised, with trumpets and cymbals and other musical instruments, in praise to the Lord, 'For he is good, for his steadfast love endures for ever.'
2 Chronicles 5:13 NRSV

105.3 Do good in thy good pleasure unto Zion: build thou the walls of Jerusalem.
Psalm 51:18 KJV

105.4 'Why do you call me good?' Jesus asked him. 'No one is good except God alone.'
Mark 10:18 GNB

105.5 Because God was with him he [Jesus] went about doing good and healing all who were oppressed by the devil.
Acts 10:38 REB

105.6 So then, the Law is holy, and what it commands is holy and upright and good.
Romans 7:12 NJB

105.7 I know that my selfish desires won't let me do anything that is good.
Romans 7:18 CEV

105.8 We know that all things work together for good for those who love God, who are called according to his purpose.
Romans 8:28 NRSV

105.9 Be not conformed to this world: but be ye transformed by the renewing of your mind, that ye may prove what is that good, and acceptable, and perfect, will of God.
Romans 12:2 KJV

105.10 Let love be genuine; hate what is evil, hold fast to what is good.
Romans 12:9 NRSV

105.11 Do not let evil defeat you; instead, conquer evil with good.
Romans 12:21 GNB

105.12 The fruit of the Spirit is love, joy, peace, longsuffering, gentleness, goodness, faith.
Galatians 5:22 KJV

105.13 For we are his workmanship, created in Christ Jesus unto good works, which God hath before ordained that we should walk in them.
Ephesians 2:10 KJV

105.14 Everything God created is good. And if you give thanks, you may eat anything.
1 Timothy 4:4 CEV

See also **God, Good; Works, good**

Gospel

106.1 This good news of the kingdom will be proclaimed throughout the world, as a testimony to all the nations; and then the end will come.
Matthew 24:14 NRSV

106.2 Now after that John was put in prison, Jesus came into Galilee, preaching the gospel of the kingdom of God, and saying, The time is fulfilled, and the kingdom of God is at hand: repent ye, and believe the gospel.
Mark 1:14–15 KJV

106.3 He said to them, 'Go out to the whole world; proclaim the gospel to all creation.'
Mark 16:15 NJB

106.4 [Jesus reading the book of Isaiah] 'The Spirit of the Lord is upon me, because he has chosen me to bring good news to the poor. He has sent me to proclaim liberty to the captives and recovery of sight to the blind; to set free the oppressed and announce that the time has come when the Lord will save his people.' Jesus rolled up the scroll, gave it back to the attendant, and sat down. All the people in the synagogue had their eyes fixed on him, as he said to them, 'This passage of scripture has come true today, as you heard it being read.'
Luke 4:18–21 GNB

106.5 I do not count my life of any value to myself, if only I may finish my course and the ministry that I received from the Lord Jesus, to testify to the good news of God's grace.

Acts 20:24 NRSV

106.6 For I am not ashamed of the gospel of Christ: for it is the power of God unto salvation to every one that believeth; to the Jew first, and also to the Greek. For therein is the righteousness of God revealed from faith to faith: as it is written, The just shall live by faith.

Romans 1:16–17 KJV

106.7 Even if I preach the gospel, I can claim no credit for it; I cannot help myself; it would be agony for me not to preach.

1 Corinthians 9:16 REB

106.8 Now, my friends, I must remind you of the gospel that I preached to you; the gospel which you received, on which you have taken your stand.

1 Corinthians 15:1 REB

106.9 I told you the most important part of the message exactly as it was told to me. That part is: Christ died for our sins, as the Scriptures say. He was buried, and three days later he was raised to life, as the Scriptures say. Christ appeared to Peter, then to the twelve.

1 Corinthians 15:3–5 CEV

106.10 Even if our gospel is veiled, it is veiled to those who are perishing. In their case the god of this world has blinded the minds of the unbelievers, to keep them from seeing the light of the gospel of the glory of Christ, who is the image of God.

2 Corinthians 4:3–4 NRSV

106.11 Let me tell you, my brothers and sisters, that the gospel I preach is not of human origin. I did not receive it from any human being, nor did anyone teach it to me. It was Jesus Christ himself who revealed it to me.

Galatians 1:11–12 GNB

106.12 It was because scripture foresaw that God would give saving justice to the gentiles through faith, that it announced the future gospel to Abraham in the words: All nations will be blessed in you.

Galatians 3:8 NJB

106.13 [Paul asks for prayer] That utterance may be given unto me, that I may open my mouth boldly, to make known the mystery of the gospel.

Ephesians 6:19 KJV

106.14 Whatever happens, conduct yourselves in a manner worthy of the gospel of Christ. Then, whether I come and see you or only hear about you in my absence, I will know that you stand firm in one spirit, contending as one man for the faith of the gospel.

Philippians 1:27 NIV

106.15 The glorious gospel of the blessed God, which was committed to my trust.

1 Timothy 1:11 KJV

Gossip

107.1 Thou shalt not go up and down as a talebearer among thy people.

Leviticus 19:16 KJV

107.2 Lord, set a guard on my mouth; keep watch at the door of my lips.

Psalm 141:3 REB

107.3 A gossip tells everything, but a true friend will keep a secret.

Proverbs 11:13 CEV

107.4 Gossip is no good! It causes hard feelings and comes between friends.
Proverbs 16:28 CEV

107.5 There's nothing so delicious as the taste of gossip! It melts in your mouth.
Proverbs 18:8 CEV

107.6 Stay away from gossips – they tell everything.
Proverbs 20:19 CEV

107.7 For lack of wood a fire dies down and for want of a tale-bearer a quarrel subsides.
Proverbs 26:20 REB

107.8 If thou hast heard a word, let it die with thee; and be bold, it will not burst thee.
Ecclesiasticus 19:10 KJV

107.9 I say unto you, That every idle word that men shall speak, they shall give account thereof in the day of judgment. For by thy words thou shalt be justified, and by thy words thou shalt be condemned.
Matthew 12:36–37 KJV

107.10 For we hear that there are some which walk among you disorderly, working not at all, but are busybodies.
2 Thessalonians 3:11 KJV

107.11 Have nothing to do with godless myths and old wives' tales.
1 Timothy 4:7 NJB

107.12 They [young widows] learn how to be idle and go round from house to house; and then, not merely idle, they learn to be gossips and meddlers in other people's affairs and to say what should remain unsaid.
1 Timothy 5:13 NJB

107.13 The older women, similarly, should be reverent in their demeanour, not scandalmongers.
Titus 2:3 REB

107.14 If you do suffer, it must not be for murder, theft, or any other crime, nor should it be for meddling in other people's business.
1 Peter 4:15 REB

See also **Speech**

Grace

108.1 Israel, you are the chosen people of the Lord your God. There are many nations on this earth, but he chose only Israel to be his very own. You were the weakest of all nations, but the Lord chose you because he loves you and because he had made a promise to your ancestors. Then with his mighty arm, he rescued you from the king of Egypt, who had made you his slaves. You know that the Lord your God is the only true God. So love him and obey his commands, and he will faithfully keep his agreement with you and your descendants for a thousand generations.
Deuteronomy 7:6–9 CEV

108.2 The Word was made flesh, and dwelt among us, (and we beheld his glory, the glory as of the only begotten of the Father,) full of grace and truth.
John 1:14 KJV

108.3 From his fullness we have all received, grace upon grace. The law indeed was given through Moses; grace and truth came through Jesus Christ.
John 1:16–17 NRSV

108.4 With great power the apostles gave their testimony to the resurrection of the

Lord Jesus, and great grace was upon them all.

Acts 4:33 NRSV

108.5 Paul and Barnabas… spoke to them and encouraged them to keep on living in the grace of God.

Acts 13:43 GNB

108.6 Being justified freely by his grace through the redemption that is in Christ Jesus.

Romans 3:24 KJV

108.7 By whom [the Lord Jesus Christ] also we have access by faith into this grace wherein we stand, and rejoice in hope of the glory of God.

Romans 5:2 KJV

108.8 Law intruded into this process to multiply law-breaking. But where sin was multiplied, grace immeasurably exceeded it, in order that, as sin established its reign by way of death, so God's grace might establish its reign in righteousness, and result in eternal life through Jesus Christ our Lord. What are we to say, then? Shall we persist in sin, so that there may be all the more grace? Certainly not! We died to sin: how can we live in it any longer?

Romans 5:20–6:2 REB

108.9 God was kind! He made me what I am, and his wonderful kindness wasn't wasted. I worked much harder than any of the other apostles, although it was really God's kindness at work and not me.

1 Corinthians 15:10 CEV

108.10 For ye know the grace of our Lord Jesus Christ, that, though he was rich, yet for your sakes he became poor, that ye through his poverty might be rich.

2 Corinthians 8:9 KJV

108.11 My grace is sufficient for you, for power is made perfect in weakness.

2 Corinthians 12:9 NRSV

108.12 The grace of the Lord Jesus Christ, the love of God, and the fellowship of the Holy Spirit be with you all.

2 Corinthians 13:13 GNB

108.13 Christ is become of no effect unto you, whosoever of you are justified by the law; ye are fallen from grace.

Galatians 5:4 KJV

Fall from grace

The idiomatic expression to *fall from grace*, to lose one's privileged and favored position, has its origin in this verse. The meaning in the biblical text is different, however, from its contemporary meaning. The Galatians were trying to put themselves right with God by relying on their own efforts to keep the law. They were therefore falling away from receiving God's favor only by grace – his love and kindness – and so were rejecting Christ.

108.14 Because of his great love for us, God, who is rich in mercy, made us alive with Christ even when we were dead in transgressions – it is by grace you have been saved.

Ephesians 2:4–5 NIV

108.15 For by grace are ye saved through faith; and that not of yourselves: it is the gift of God.

Ephesians 2:8 KJV

108.16 [Because Jesus can sympathize with our weaknesses] Let us therefore boldly approach the throne of grace, in order that we may receive mercy and find grace to give us timely help.

Hebrews 4:16 REB

108.17 Grow in the grace and knowledge of our Lord and Saviour Jesus Christ. To him be the glory both now and to the day of eternity. Amen.

2 Peter 3:18 NRSV

See also **Election; God, Merciful; Jesus Christ, Love; Love, of God; Mercy**

Grief

109.1 For my life is spent with grief, and my years with sighing: my strength faileth because of mine iniquity, and my bones are consumed.

Psalm 31:10 KJV

109.2 The sacrifices of God are a broken spirit: a broken and a contrite heart, O God, thou wilt not despise.

Psalm 51:17 KJV

109.3 A time to weep, and a time to laugh; a time to mourn, and a time to dance.

Ecclesiastes 3:4 KJV

109.4 I said: 'Woe is me! I am lost, for I am a man of unclean lips, and I live among a people of unclean lips; yet my eyes have seen the King, the Lord of hosts!'

Isaiah 6:5 NRSV

109.5 He is despised and rejected of men; a man of sorrows, and acquainted with grief: and we hid as it were our faces from him; he was despised, and we esteemed him not. Surely he hath borne our griefs, and carried our sorrows: yet we did esteem him stricken, smitten of God, and afflicted.

Isaiah 53:3–4 KJV

109.6 Is there no balm in Gilead; is there no physician there? why then is not the health of the daughter of my people recovered?

Jeremiah 8:22 KJV

109.7 The children of the kingdom shall be cast out into outer darkness: there shall be weeping and gnashing of teeth.

Matthew 8:12 KJV

109.8 He took with him Peter and the two sons of Zebedee. Distress and anguish overwhelmed him, and he said to them, 'My heart is ready to break with grief. Stop here, and stay awake with me.'

Matthew 26:37–38 REB

109.9 He [Jesus] came closer to the city, and when he saw it, he wept over it, saying, 'If you only knew today what is needed for peace! But now you cannot see it!'

Luke 19:41–42 GNB

109.10 When he rose from prayer he went to the disciples and found them sleeping for sheer grief.

Luke 22:45 NJB

109.11 The Lord turned, and looked upon Peter. And Peter remembered the word of the Lord, how he had said unto him, Before the cock crow, thou shalt deny me thrice. And Peter went out, and wept bitterly.

Luke 22:61–62 KJV

109.12 Jesus wept.

John 11:35 KJV

Jesus wept
This verse is the shortest verse in the Bible. Its two words describe Jesus' grief at the death of Lazarus and his sympathy with the tears of others.

109.13 Sorrowful, yet always rejoicing.

2 Corinthians 6:10 NRSV

109.14 Pain borne in God's way brings no regrets but a change of heart leading to salvation; pain borne in the world's way brings death.

2 Corinthians 7:10 REB

See also Comfort, in bereavement and sorrow; Despair; Mourning; Repentance

Guidance

110.1 He leadeth me beside the still waters. He restoreth my soul: he leadeth me in the paths of righteousness for his name's sake.

Psalm 23:2–3 KJV

The Lord is my Shepherd

The hymn *The Lord's my shepherd* is based on Psalm 23. The Psalms have inspired many other hymns including:
Psalm 18:2; 32:7 – *Rock of ages, cleft for me*
Psalm 23 – *The King of love my shepherd is; The Lord's my shepherd*
Psalm 29:2; 96:9; 116:13–14 – *O worship the Lord in the beauty of holiness*
Psalm 34 – *Through all the changing scenes of life*
Psalm 36:5–6; 66:7; 104:1–2 – *Immortal, invisible, God only wise*
Psalm 46 – *A safe stronghold our God is still; A mighty fortress is our God (Ein' feste Burg)*
Psalm 48:14; 78:14; 105:40 – *Guide me, O thou great Jehovah*
Psalm 61:2 – *O safe to the rock that is higher than I*
Psalm 72 – *Hail to the Lord's anointed; Jesus shall reign where'er the sun*
Psalm 87 – *Glorious things of thee are spoken*

Psalm 90 – *Our God, our help in ages past*
Psalm 97:1 – *The Lord is King; lift up thy voice*
Psalm 98 – *Joy to the world! The Lord is come!*
Psalm 100 – *All people that on earth do dwell*
Psalm 103 – *Praise, my soul, the King of heaven; Praise to the Lord, the Almighty, the King of creation*
Psalm 103:1 – *Bless the Lord, O my soul*
Psalm 104 – *O worship the King*
Psalm 126:3 – *Now thank we all our God*
Psalm 136 – *Let us with a gladsome mind*

110.2 Trust in the Lord, and do good; so you will live in the land, and enjoy security. Take delight in the Lord, and he will give you the desires of your heart. Commit your way to the Lord; trust in him, and he will act.

Psalm 37:3–5 NRSV

110.3 The Lord guides people in the way they should go and protects those who please him.

Psalm 37:23 GNB

110.4 Give your food to the hungry and care for the homeless. Then your light will shine in the dark; your darkest hour will be like the noonday sun. The Lord will always guide you and provide good things to eat when you are in the desert. He will make you healthy. You will be like a garden that has plenty of water or like a stream that never runs dry.

Isaiah 58:10–11 CEV

110.5 However, when the Spirit of truth comes, he will guide you into all the truth; for he will not speak on his own authority, but will speak only what he hears; and he will make known to you what is to come.

John 16:13 REB

110.6 Then the apostles and elders, with the whole church, decided to choose delegates from among themselves to send to Antioch with Paul and Barnabas.

Acts 15:22 NJB

110.7 For it has seemed good to the Holy Spirit and to us to impose on you no further burden than these essentials…

Acts 15:28 NRSV

110.8 Be not conformed to this world, but be ye transformed by the renewing of your mind, that ye may prove what is that good, and acceptable, and perfect, will of God.

Romans 12:2 KJV

110.9 If any of you lack wisdom, you should pray to God, who will give it to you; because God gives generously and graciously to all.

James 1:5 GNB

See also Counsel; Decisions; Sovereignty of God; Way; Will of God

Guilt

111.1 They heard the voice of the Lord God walking in the garden in the cool of the day: and Adam and his wife hid themselves from the presence of the Lord God amongst the trees of the garden… And he [Adam] said, I heard thy voice in the garden, and I was afraid, because I was naked; and I hid myself.

Genesis 3:8, 10 KJV

111.2 Thou shalt not take the name of the Lord thy God in vain; for the Lord will not hold him guiltless that taketh his name in vain.

Exodus 20:7 KJV

111.3 Then I acknowledged my sin to you, and I did not hide my iniquity; I said, 'I will confess my transgressions to the Lord', and you forgave the guilt of my sin.

Psalm 32:5 NRSV

111.4 Have mercy upon me, O God, according to thy loving kindness: according unto the multitude of thy tender mercies blot out my transgressions. Wash me thoroughly from mine iniquity, and cleanse me from my sin. For I acknowledge my transgressions: and my sin is ever before me. Against thee, thee only, have I sinned, and done this evil in thy sight: that thou mightest be justified when thou speakest, and be clear when thou judgest.

Psalm 51:1–4 KJV

111.5 The seraph touched my mouth with it [a live coal] and said: 'Now that this has touched your lips, your guilt has departed and your sin is blotted out.'

Isaiah 6:7 NRSV

111.6 Thus condemnation will never come to those who are in Christ Jesus.

Romans 8:1 NJB

111.7 It follows that if anyone eats the Lord's bread or drinks from his cup in a way that dishonours him, he or she is guilty of sin against the Lord's body and blood.

1 Corinthians 11:27 GNB

111.8 For if a man breaks just one commandment and keeps all the others, he is guilty of breaking all of them.

James 2:10 REB

See also Conscience; Conviction of sin; Forgiveness

Hardness

112.1 The Lord said to Moses, 'When you go back to Egypt, see that you perform before Pharaoh all the wonders that I have put in your power; but I will harden his heart, so that he will not let the people go.'
Exodus 4:21 NRSV

112.2 If there be among you a poor man of one of thy brethren within any of thy gates in thy land which the Lord thy God giveth thee, thou shalt not harden thine heart, nor shut thine hand from thy poor brother.
Deuteronomy 15:7 KJV

112.3 Always obey the Lord and you will be happy. If you are stubborn, you will be ruined.
Proverbs 28:14 GNB

112.4 Then the Lord told me to go and speak this message to the people: 'You will listen and listen, but never understand. You will look and look, but never see.' The Lord also said, 'Make these people stubborn! Make them stop up their ears, cover their eyes, and fail to understand. Don't let them turn to me and be healed.'
Isaiah 6:9–10 CEV

112.5 Jesus replied, 'Moses permitted you to divorce your wives because your hearts were hard. But it was not this way from the beginning.'
Matthew 19:8 NIV

112.6 Looking round at them with anger and sorrow at their obstinate stupidity.
Mark 3:5 REB

112.7 [Jesus to the Jews] You refuse to come to me to receive life!
John 5:40 NJB

112.8 'How stubborn you are!' Stephen went on to say. 'How heathen your hearts, how deaf you are to God's message! You are just like your ancestors: you too have always resisted the Holy Spirit!'
Acts 7:51 GNB

112.9 By your hard and impenitent heart you are storing up wrath for yourself on the day of wrath, when God's righteous judgement will be revealed.
Romans 2:5 NRSV

112.10 Their [the Israelites'] minds were hardened. Indeed, to this very day, when they hear the reading of the old covenant, that same veil is still there, since only in Christ is it set aside.
2 Corinthians 3:14 NRSV

112.11 Their [the Gentiles'] minds are closed, they are alienated from the life that is in God, because ignorance prevails among them and their hearts have grown hard as stone.
Ephesians 4:18 REB

112.12 To day if ye will hear his voice, harden not your hearts, as in the provocation.
Hebrews 3:15 KJV

See also Falling away; Heart; Rejection; Unbelief

Hatred

113.1 Do I not hate those who hate you, O Lord? And do I not loathe those who rise up against you? I hate them with perfect hatred; I count them my enemies.
Psalm 139:21–22 NRSV

113.2 There are seven things that the Lord hates and cannot tolerate: a proud look, a lying tongue, hands that kill innocent people, a mind that thinks up wicked plans, feet that hurry off to do evil, a witness who tells one lie after another, and someone who stirs up trouble among friends.

Proverbs 6:16–19 GNB

113.3 Better is a dinner of herbs where love is, than a stalled ox and hatred therewith.

Proverbs 15:17 KJV

113.4 Hate evil and love good, and establish justice in the gate; it may be that the Lord, the God of hosts, will be gracious to the remnant of Joseph.

Amos 5:15 NRSV

113.5 You will then be handed over for punishment and execution; all nations will hate you for your allegiance to me.

Matthew 24:9 REB

113.6 People who do evil hate the light and won't come to the light, because it clearly shows what they have done.

John 3:20 CEV

113.7 The world cannot hate you, but it does hate me, because I give evidence that its ways are evil.

John 7:7 NJB

113.8 If the world hates you, just remember that it has hated me first. If you belonged to the world, then the world would love you as its own. But I chose you from this world, and you do not belong to it; that is why the world hates you.

John 15:18–19 GNB

Healing

114.1 He [Elijah] stretched himself upon the child three times, and cried unto the Lord, and said, O Lord my God, I pray

thee, let this child's soul come into him again. And the Lord heard the voice of Elijah; and the soul of the child came into him again, and he revived.

1 Kings 17:21–22 KJV

114.2 So he [Naaman] went down and immersed himself seven times in the Jordan, according to the word of the man of God; his flesh was restored like the flesh of a young boy, and he was clean.

2 Kings 5:14 NRSV

114.3 [The Lord's promise to Solomon] If my people who are called by my name humble themselves, pray, seek my face, and turn from their wicked ways, then I will hear from heaven, and will forgive their sin and heal their land.

2 Chronicles 7:14 NRSV

114.4 Bless the Lord, O my soul, and forget not all his benefits: who forgiveth all thine iniquities; who healeth all thy diseases.

Psalm 103:2–3 KJV

114.5 He sent his word to heal them and snatch them out of the pit of death.

Psalm 107:20 REB

114.6 Jesus went all over Galilee, teaching in the synagogues, preaching the Good News about the Kingdom, and healing people who had all kinds of disease and sickness.

Matthew 4:23 GNB

114.7 Jesus called together his twelve disciples. He gave them the power to force out evil spirits and to heal every kind of disease and sickness.

Matthew 10:1 CEV

114.8 Then Peter said, Silver and gold have I none; but such as I have give I thee: In the name of Jesus Christ of

Nazareth rise up and walk. And he took him by the right hand, and lifted him up: and immediately his feet and ankle bones received strength.

Acts 3:6–7 KJV

114.9 To another the gifts of healing by the same Spirit…

1 Corinthians 12:9 KJV

114.10 Is any sick among you? let him call for the elders of the church; and let them pray over him, anointing him with oil in the name of the Lord: and the prayer of faith shall save the sick, and the Lord shall raise him up; and if he have committed sins, they shall be forgiven him. Confess your faults one to another, and pray one for another, that ye may be healed. The effectual fervent prayer of a righteous man availeth much.

James 5:14–16 KJV

See also Comfort, in suffering; Health and wholeness; Illness, Help in; Suffering

Health and wholeness

115.1 Ye shall walk in all the ways which the Lord your God hath commanded you, that ye may live, and that it may be well with you, and that ye may prolong your days in the land which ye shall possess.

Deuteronomy 5:33 KJV

115.2 God be merciful unto us, and bless us; and cause his face to shine upon us; that thy way may be known upon earth, thy saving health among all nations.

Psalm 67:1–2 KJV

115.3 The righteous flourish like a palm tree, they grow tall as a cedar on Lebanon; planted in the house of the Lord, and flourishing in the courts of our God, they still bear fruit in old age; they are luxuriant, wide-spreading trees.

Psalm 92:12–14 REB

115.4 Don't ever think that you are wise enough, but respect the Lord and stay away from evil. This will make you healthy, and you will feel strong.

Proverbs 3:7–8 CEV

115.5 My son, attend to my words, pay heed to my sayings; do not let them slip from your sight, keep them fixed in your mind; for they are life to those who find them, and health to their whole being.

Proverbs 4:20–22 REB

115.6 Thoughtless words can wound like a sword, but the tongue of the wise brings healing.

Proverbs 12:18 NJB

115.7 A merry heart doeth good like a medicine: but a broken spirit drieth the bones.

Proverbs 17:22 KJV

115.8 Happy the righteous! All goes well with them; they enjoy the fruit of their actions.

Isaiah 3:10 REB

115.9 Now I shall bring healing and care for her; I shall cure Judah and Israel, and let them see lasting peace and security.

Jeremiah 33:6 REB

115.10 Jesus turned him about, and when he saw her, he said, Daughter, be of good comfort; thy faith hath made thee whole. And the woman was made whole from that hour.

Matthew 9:22 KJV

115.11 If you have light for your whole body with no trace of darkness, it will all be full of light, as when the light of a lamp shines on you.

Luke 11:36 REB

115.12 I pray that God, who gives peace, will make you completely holy. And may your spirit, soul, and body be kept healthy and faultless until our Lord Jesus Christ returns.

1 Thessalonians 5:23 CEV

115.13 My dear friend, I hope everything is going happily with you and that you are as well physically as you are spiritually.

3 John v. 2 NJB

See also **Healing; Illness**

Heart

116.1 Thou shalt love the Lord thy God with all thine heart, and with all thy soul, and with all thy might.

Deuteronomy 6:5 KJV

116.2 [Samuel to Saul] Now your kingdom will not continue; the Lord has sought out a man after his own heart... because you have not kept what the Lord commanded you.

1 Samuel 13:14 NRSV

A man after his own heart
A person who is *after someone's own heart* is one who is exactly the kind that someone likes most, because they share the same ideals. The source of this phrase is this verse; God was seeking the kind of man he wanted – one who would closely follow his ways.

116.3 The Lord said unto Samuel, Look not on his countenance, or on the height of his stature; because I have refused him: for the Lord seeth not as man seeth; for man looketh on the outward appearance, but the Lord looketh on the heart.

1 Samuel 16:7 KJV

116.4 God, create a pure heart for me, and give me a new and steadfast spirit.

Psalm 51:10 REB

116.5 Above all else, guard your heart, for it is the wellspring of life.

Proverbs 4:23 NIV

116.6 The heart is deceitful above all things, and desperately wicked: who can know it? I the Lord search the heart.

Jeremiah 17:9–10 KJV

116.7 A new heart I will give you, and a new spirit I will put within you; and I will remove from your body the heart of stone and give you a heart of flesh.

Ezekiel 36:26 NRSV

116.8 Blessed are the pure in heart: for they shall see God.

Matthew 5:8 KJV

116.9 Your heart will always be where your treasure is.

Matthew 6:21 CEV

116.10 He went on to say, 'It is what comes out of a person that makes him unclean. For from the inside, from a person's heart, come the evil ideas which lead him to do immoral things, to rob, kill, commit adultery, be greedy, and do all sorts of evil things; deceit, indecency, jealousy, slander, pride, and folly.'

Mark 7:20–22 GNB

116.11 Let anyone who believes in me come and drink! As scripture says, 'From his heart shall flow streams of living water.' He was speaking of the Spirit which those who believed in him were to receive.
John 7:38–39 NJB

116.12 Thanks be to God that you, having once been slaves of sin, have become obedient from the heart to the form of teaching to which you were entrusted.
Romans 6:17 NRSV

116.13 God who searches our inmost being knows what the Spirit means, because he pleads for God's people as God himself wills.
Romans 8:27 REB

116.14 That if thou shalt confess with thy mouth the Lord Jesus, and shalt believe in thine heart that God hath raised him from the dead, thou shalt be saved.
Romans 10:9 KJV

116.15 Let the peace of God rule in your hearts, to the which also ye are called in one body; and be ye thankful.
Colossians 3:15 KJV

116.16 Now that by your obedience to the truth you have purified yourselves and have come to have a sincere love for your fellow-believers, love one another earnestly with all your heart.
1 Peter 1:22 GNB

116.17 By this we will know that we are from the truth and will reassure our hearts before him whenever our hearts condemn us; for God is greater than our hearts, and he knows everything. Beloved, if our hearts do not condemn us, we have boldness before God.
1 John 3:19–21 NRSV

See also **Hardness; Mind; Soul; Spirit**

Help

117.1 Then Samuel took a stone and set it up between Mizpah and Jeshanah, and named it Ebenezer; for he said, 'Thus far the Lord has helped us.'
1 Samuel 7:12 NRSV

117.2 God is our refuge and strength, a very present help in trouble.
Psalm 46:1 KJV

117.3 I will lift up mine eyes unto the hills, from whence cometh my help. My help cometh from the Lord, which made heaven and earth. He will not suffer thy foot to be moved: he that keepeth thee will not slumber. Behold, he that keepeth Israel shall neither slumber nor sleep. The Lord is thy keeper: the Lord is thy shade upon thy right hand. The sun shall not smite thee by day, nor the moon by night. The Lord shall preserve thee from all evil: he shall preserve thy soul. The Lord shall preserve thy going out and thy coming in from this time forth, and even for evermore.
Psalm 121:1–8 KJV

117.4 The woman came closer. Then she knelt down and begged, 'Please help me, Lord!'
Matthew 15:25 CEV

117.5 Apollos then decided to go to Achaia, so the believers in Ephesus helped him by writing to the believers in Achaia, urging them to welcome him. When he arrived, he was a great help to those who through God's grace had become believers.
Acts 18:27 GNB

117.6 By every means I have shown you that we must exert ourselves in this way to support the weak, remembering the words

of the Lord Jesus, who himself said,
'There is more happiness in giving than
in receiving.'
Acts 20:35 NJB

117.7 In the same way the Spirit comes
to the aid of our weakness. We do not
even know how we ought to pray, but
through our inarticulate groans the Spirit
himself is pleading for us.
Romans 8:26 REB

117.8 First, God chose some people to be
apostles and prophets and teachers for the
church. But he also chose some to perform
miracles or heal the sick or help others.
1 Corinthians 12:28 CEV

117.9 As you also join in helping us by
your prayers, so that many will give thanks
on our behalf for the blessing granted to us
through the prayers of many.
2 Corinthians 1:11 NRSV

117.10 Help to carry one another's
burdens, and in this way you will obey
the law of Christ.
Galatians 6:2 GNB

117.11 He hath said, I will never leave
thee, nor forsake thee. So that we may
boldly say, The Lord is my helper, and I
will not fear what man shall do unto me.
Hebrews 13:5–6 KJV

See also Comfort; Kindness; Service

Holiness

118.1 He said, Draw not nigh hither:
put off thy shoes from off thy feet, for
the place whereon thou standest is holy
ground.
Exodus 3:5 KJV

118.2 Remember the sabbath day, to
keep it holy.
Exodus 20:8 KJV

118.3 For I am the Lord your God;
sanctify yourselves therefore, and be holy,
for I am holy.
Leviticus 11:44 NRSV

118.4 Holy, holy, holy is the Lord of
Hosts: the whole earth is full of his glory.
Isaiah 6:3 REB

118.5 Now you have been set free from
sin, and you are God's slaves. This will
make you holy and will lead you to
eternal life.
Romans 6:22 CEV

118.6 Since we have these promises, dear
friends, let us purify ourselves from everything that contaminates body and spirit,
perfecting holiness out of reverence for God.
2 Corinthians 7:1 NIV

118.7 God did not call us to live in
immorality, but in holiness.
1 Thessalonians 4:7 GNB

118.8 Such a high priest is indeed suited
to our need: he is holy, innocent,
undefiled, set apart from sinners, and
raised high above the heavens.
Hebrews 7:26 REB

118.9 Our human fathers were training us
for a short life and according to their own
lights; but he does it all for our own good,
so that we may share his own holiness.
Hebrews 12:10 NJB

118.10 Pursue peace with everyone, and
the holiness without which no one will see
the Lord.
Hebrews 12:14 NRSV

118.11 You are a chosen race, a royal priesthood, a holy nation, God's own people, in order that you may proclaim the mighty acts of him who called you out of darkness into his marvellous light.

1 Peter 2:9 NRSV

See also **God, Holy; Jesus Christ, Holiness; Sanctification**

Holy Spirit

119.1 The Spirit of God moved upon the face of the waters.

Genesis 1:2 KJV

119.2 I have filled him [Bezalel] with divine spirit, with ability, intelligence, and knowledge in every kind of craft.

Exodus 31:3 NRSV

119.3 The spirit of the Lord came upon him [Othniel], and he became Israel's leader. Othniel went to war, and the Lord gave him victory over the king of Mesopotamia.

Judges 3:10 GNB

119.4 Cast me not away from thy presence; and take not thy holy spirit from me.

Psalm 51:11 KJV

119.5 The spirit of the Lord shall rest upon him, the spirit of wisdom and understanding, the spirit of counsel and might, the spirit of knowledge and of the fear of the Lord.

Isaiah 11:2 KJV

119.6 I will put my spirit in you and I will see to it that you follow my laws and keep all the commands I have given you.

Ezekiel 36:27 GNB

119.7 After this I shall pour out my spirit on all mankind; your sons and daughters will prophesy, your old men will dream dreams and your young men see visions.

Joel 2:28 REB

119.8 This is the word of the Lord unto Zerubbabel, saying, Not by might, nor by power, but by my spirit, saith the Lord of hosts.

Zechariah 4:6 KJV

119.9 [John the Baptist] I baptise you in water for repentance, but the one who comes after me is more powerful than I, and I am not fit to carry his sandals; he will baptise you with the Holy Spirit and fire.

Matthew 3:11 NJB

119.10 So Jesus was baptized. And as soon as he came out of the water, the sky opened, and he saw the Spirit of God coming down on him like a dove.

Matthew 3:16 CEV

119.11 Therefore I tell you, people will be forgiven for every sin and blasphemy, but blasphemy against the Spirit will not be forgiven.

Matthew 12:31 NRSV

119.12 The angel answered, 'The Holy Spirit will come on you, and God's power will rest upon you. For this reason the holy child will be called the Son of God.'

Luke 1:35 GNB

119.13 If ye then, being evil, know how to give good gifts unto your children: how much more shall your heavenly Father give the Holy Spirit to them that ask him?

Luke 11:13 KJV

119.14 Jesus answered, Verily, verily, I say unto thee, Except a man be born of water and of the Spirit, he cannot enter into the kingdom of God. That which is born of the flesh is flesh; and that which is born of the Spirit is spirit.

John 3:5–6 KJV

119.15 Let the one who believes in me drink. As the scripture has said, 'Out of the believer's heart shall flow rivers of living water.' Now he said this about the Spirit, which believers in him were to receive; for as yet there was no Spirit, because Jesus was not yet glorified.

John 7:38–39 NRSV

119.16 I will pray the Father, and he shall give you another Comforter, that he may abide with you for ever; even the Spirit of truth; whom the world cannot receive, because it seeth him not, neither knoweth him: but ye know him: for he dwelleth with you, and shall be in you.

John 14:16–17 KJV

119.17 But the Advocate, the Holy Spirit, whom the Father will send in my name, will teach you everything, and remind you of all that I have said to you.

John 14:26 NRSV

119.18 The Helper will come – the Spirit, who reveals the truth about God and who comes from the Father. I will send him to you from the Father, and he will speak about me.

John 15:26 GNB

119.19 I tell you that I am going to do what is best for you. That is why I am going away. The Holy Spirit cannot come to help you until I leave. But after I am gone, I will send the Spirit to you. The Spirit will come and show the people of this world the truth about sin and God's justice and the judgment. The Spirit will show them that they are wrong about sin, because they didn't have faith in me. They are wrong about God's justice, because I am going to the Father, and you won't see

me again. And they are wrong about the judgment, because God has already judged the ruler of this world… The Spirit shows what is true and will come and guide you into the full truth. The Spirit doesn't speak on his own. He will tell you only what he has heard from me, and he will let you know what is going to happen. The Spirit will bring glory to me by taking my message and telling it to you.

John 16:7–11, 13–14 CEV

119.20 You will receive power when the Holy Spirit comes upon you; and you will bear witness for me in Jerusalem, and throughout all Judaea and Samaria, and even in the farthest corners of the earth.

Acts 1:8 REB

119.21 When the day of Pentecost had come, they were all together in one place. And suddenly from heaven there came a sound like the rush of a violent wind, and it filled the entire house where they were sitting. Divided tongues, as of fire, appeared among them, and a tongue rested on each of them. All of them were filled with the Holy Spirit and began to speak in other languages, as the Spirit gave them ability.

Acts 2:1–4 NRSV

119.22 Peter said to them, 'Repent, and be baptized every one of you in the name of Jesus Christ so that your sins may be forgiven; and you will receive the gift of the Holy Spirit.'

Acts 2:38 NRSV

119.23 Then Peter, filled with the Holy Spirit, addressed them, 'Rulers of the people, and elders…'

Acts 4:8 NJB

119.24 Peter said to him, 'Ananias, why did you let Satan take control of you and make you lie to the Holy Spirit by keeping part of the money you received for the

property?… You have not lied to human beings – you have lied to God!'
Acts 5:3–4 GNB

119.25 'How stubborn you are!' Stephen went on to say. 'How heathen your hearts, how deaf you are to God's message! You are just like your ancestors: you too have always resisted the Holy Spirit!'
Acts 7:51 GNB

119.26 While they were worshipping the Lord and going without eating, the Holy Spirit told them, 'Appoint Barnabas and Saul to do the work for which I have chosen them.'
Acts 13:2 CEV

119.27 It is the decision of the Holy Spirit, and our decision, to lay no further burden upon you beyond these essentials…
Acts 15:28 REB

119.28 The love of God is shed abroad in our hearts by the Holy Ghost which is given unto us.
Romans 5:5 KJV

119.29 Those who are living by their natural inclinations have their minds on the things human nature desires; those who live in the Spirit have their minds on spiritual things. And human nature has nothing to look forward to but death, while the Spirit looks forward to life and peace.
Romans 8:5–6 NJB

119.30 You are no longer ruled by your desires, but by God's Spirit, who lives in you. People who don't have the Spirit of Christ in them don't belong to him… God's Spirit now lives in you, and he will raise you to life by his Spirit. My dear friends, we must not live to satisfy our desires. If you do, you will die. But you will live, if by the help of God's Spirit you

say 'No' to your desires. Only those people who are led by God's Spirit are his children. God's Spirit doesn't make us slaves who are afraid of him. Instead, we become his children and call him our Father. God's Spirit makes us sure that we are his children.
Romans 8:9, 11–16 CEV

119.31 Likewise the Spirit helps us in our weakness; for we do not know how to pray as we ought, but that very Spirit intercedes with sighs too deep for words. And God, who searches the heart, knows what is the mind of the Spirit, because the Spirit intercedes for the saints according to the will of God.
Romans 8:26–27 NRSV

119.32 Never give up. Eagerly follow the Holy Spirit and serve the Lord.
Romans 12:11 CEV

119.33 My speech and my proclamation were not with plausible words of wisdom, but with a demonstration of the Spirit and of power.
1 Corinthians 2:4 NRSV

119.34 For the Spirit explores everything, even the depths of God's own nature.
1 Corinthians 2:10 REB

119.35 The particular manifestation of the Spirit granted to each one is to be used for the general good.
1 Corinthians 12:7 NJB

119.36 Now the Lord is the Spirit, and where the Spirit of the Lord is, there is freedom. And all of us, with unveiled faces, seeing the glory of the Lord as though reflected in a mirror, are being transformed into the same image from one degree of glory to another; for this comes from the Lord, the Spirit.
2 Corinthians 3:17–18 NRSV

119.37 By contrast, the fruit of the Spirit is love, joy, peace, patience, kindness, generosity, faithfulness, gentleness, and self-control. There is no law against such things.
Galatians 5:22–23 NRSV

119.38 Grieve not the holy Spirit of God, whereby ye are sealed unto the day of redemption.
Ephesians 4:30 KJV

119.39 Be filled with the Spirit; Speaking to yourselves in psalms and hymns and spiritual songs, singing and making melody in your heart to the Lord; Giving thanks always for all things unto God and the Father in the name of our Lord Jesus Christ; Submitting yourselves one to another in the fear of God.
Ephesians 5:18–21 KJV

119.40 Take the helmet of salvation, and the sword of the Spirit, which is the word of God.
Ephesians 6:17 KJV

119.41 Quench not the Spirit.
1 Thessalonians 5:19 KJV

119.42 For no prophetic message ever came just from human will, but people were under the control of the Holy Spirit as they spoke the message that came from God.
2 Peter 1:21 GNB

See also Trinity

Homes

120.1 These words, which I command thee this day, shall be in thine heart: and thou shalt teach them diligently unto thy children, and shalt talk of them when thou sittest in thine house, and when thou walkest by the way, and when thou liest down, and when thou risest up.
Deuteronomy 6:6–7 KJV

120.2 Naomi said to her daughters-in-law, 'Go back, both of you, home to your own mothers. May the Lord keep faith with you… and may he grant each of you the security of a home with a new husband.'
Ruth 1:8–9 REB

120.3 He lets the barren woman be seated at home, the happy mother of sons.
Psalm 113:9 NJB

120.4 The curse of the Lord is in the house of the wicked: but he blesseth the habitation of the just.
Proverbs 3:33 KJV

120.5 He that troubleth his own house shall inherit the wind.
Proverbs 11:29 KJV

120.6 Better a dish of herbs when love is there than a fattened ox and hatred to go with it.
Proverbs 15:17 NJB

120.7 Better to live on a corner of the housetop than share the house with a nagging wife.
Proverbs 25:24 REB

120.8 Like a bird that strays from its nest, so is anyone who strays away from home.
Proverbs 27:8 NJB

120.9 My people will live in a peaceful home, in peaceful houses, tranquil dwellings.
Isaiah 32:18 NJB

120.10 Jesus replied, 'Foxes have their holes and birds their roosts; but the Son of Man has nowhere to lay his head.'
Matthew 8:20 REB

120.11 When you go to a town or a village, find someone worthy enough to have you as their guest and stay with them until you leave. When you go to a home, give it your blessing of peace. If the home is deserving, let your blessing remain with them. But if the home isn't deserving, take back your blessing of peace. If someone won't welcome you or listen to your message, leave their home or town.
Matthew 10:11–14 CEV

120.12 Jesus said, 'Truly I tell you: there is no one who has given up home, brothers or sisters, mother, father or children, or land, for my sake and for the gospel, who will not receive in this age a hundred times as much.'
Mark 10:29–30 REB

120.13 The Lord and his disciples were travelling along and came to a village. When they got there, a woman named Martha welcomed him into her home.
Luke 10:38 CEV

120.14 When Jesus saw his mother and his favourite disciple with her, he said to his mother, 'This man is now your son.' Then he said to the disciple, 'She is now your mother.' From then on, that disciple took her into his own home.
John 19:26–27 CEV

120.15 One and all they kept up their daily attendance at the temple, and, breaking bread in their homes, they shared their meals with unaffected joy.
Acts 2:46 REB

120.16 Every day they spent time in the temple and in one home after another. They never stopped teaching and telling the good news that Jesus is the Messiah.
Acts 5:42 CEV

See also **Family**

Homosexuality

121.1 No man is to have sexual relations with another man; God hates that.
Leviticus 18:22 GNB

121.2 If a man has sexual relations with another man, they have done a disgusting thing, and both shall be put to death. They are responsible for their own death.
Leviticus 20:13 GNB

121.3 Therefore God gave them over in the sinful desires of their hearts to sexual impurity for the degrading of their bodies with one another.
Romans 1:24 NIV

121.4 As a result God has given them up to shameful passions. Among them women have exchanged natural intercourse for unnatural, and men too, giving up natural relations with women, burn with lust for one another; males behave indecently with males, and are paid in their own persons the fitting wage of such perversion.
Romans 1:26–27 REB

121.5 Don't you know that evil people won't have a share in the blessings of God's kingdom? Don't fool yourselves! No one who is immoral or worships idols or is unfaithful in marriage or is a pervert or behaves like a homosexual will share in God's kingdom.
1 Corinthians 6:9–10 CEV

See also **Sex, Misuse of**

Honesty

122.1 A false balance is abomination to the Lord: but a just weight is his delight.
Proverbs 11:1 KJV

122.2 The seed in good soil represents those who bring a good and honest heart to the hearing of the word, hold it fast, and by their perseverance yield a harvest.

Luke 8:15 REB

122.3 We have renounced the shameful things that one hides; we refuse to practise cunning or to falsify God's word; but by the open statement of the truth we commend ourselves to the conscience of everyone in the sight of God.

2 Corinthians 4:2 NRSV

122.4 Our purpose is to do what is right, not only in the sight of the Lord, but also in the sight of man.

2 Corinthians 8:21 GNB

122.5 Let him that stole steal no more: but rather let him labour, working with his hands the thing which is good, that he may have to give to him that needeth.

Ephesians 4:28 KJV

122.6 We were not lazy when we were with you. We did not accept anyone's support without paying for it. Instead, we worked and toiled.

2 Thessalonians 3:7–8 GNB

See also **Dishonesty**; **Lying**; **Truth**

Hope

123.1 Why art thou cast down, O my soul? and why art thou disquieted in me? hope thou in God: for I shall yet praise him for the help of his countenance.

Psalm 42:5 KJV

123.2 Abraham believed and hoped, even when there was no reason for hoping, and so became 'the father of many nations.'

Romans 4:18 GNB

123.3 We... rejoice in hope of the glory of God... hope maketh not ashamed; because the love of God is shed abroad in our hearts by the Holy Ghost which is given unto us.

Romans 5:2, 5 KJV

123.4 Not only the creation, but we ourselves, who have the first fruits of the Spirit, groan inwardly while we wait for adoption, the redemption of our bodies. For in hope we were saved. Now hope that is seen is not hope. For who hopes for what is seen? But if we hope for what we do not see, we wait for it with patience.

Romans 8:23–25 NRSV

123.5 I pray that God, who gives hope, will bless you with complete happiness and peace because of your faith. And may the power of the Holy Spirit fill you with hope.

Romans 15:13 CEV

123.6 There are three things that last for ever: faith, hope, and love; and the greatest of the three is love.

1 Corinthians 13:13 REB

123.7 You [Gentiles] were at that time without Christ, being aliens from the commonwealth of Israel, and strangers to the covenants of promise, having no hope and without God in the world.

Ephesians 2:12 NRSV

123.8 It was God's purpose to reveal to them how rich is the glory of this mystery among the gentiles; it is Christ among you, your hope of glory.

Colossians 1:27 NJB

123.9 We who have taken refuge might be strongly encouraged to seize the hope set before us. We have this hope, a sure and steadfast anchor of the soul, a hope that enters the inner shrine behind the curtain.

Hebrews 6:18–19 NRSV

123.10 Keep alert and set your hope completely on the blessing which will be given you when Jesus Christ is revealed.

1 Peter 1:13 GNB

Hospitality

124.1 I was an hungred, and ye gave me meat: I was thirsty, and ye gave me drink: I was a stranger, and ye took me in.

Matthew 25:35 KJV

124.2 She [Lydia] was baptized, and her household with her, and then she urged us, 'Now that you have accepted me as a believer in the Lord, come and stay at my house.' And she insisted on our going.

Acts 16:15 REB

124.3 Take care of God's needy people and welcome strangers into your home.

Romans 12:13 CEV

124.4 A bishop then must be blameless, the husband of one wife, vigilant, sober, of good behaviour, given to hospitality…

1 Timothy 3:2 KJV

124.5 [A widow]is well known for her good deeds, such as bringing up children, showing hospitality, washing the feet of the saints, helping those in trouble and devoting herself to all kinds of good deeds.

1 Timothy 5:10 NIV

124.6 Do not neglect to show hospitality; by doing this, some have entertained angels unawares.

Hebrews 13:2 REB

124.7 Be hospitable to one another without complaining.

1 Peter 4:9 NRSV

Human beings

125.1 God said, Let us make man in our image, after our likeness: and let them have dominion over the fish of the sea, and over the fowl of the air, and over the cattle, and over all the earth, and over every creeping thing that creepeth upon the earth. So God created man in his own image, in the image of God created he him; male and female created he them.

Genesis 1:26–27 KJV

125.2 The Lord God formed man of the dust of the ground, and breathed into his nostrils the breath of life; and man became a living soul.

Genesis 2:7 KJV

125.3 The Lord saw how great man's wickedness on the earth had become, and that every inclination of the thoughts of his heart was only evil all the time.

Genesis 6:5 NIV

125.4 In his hand is the soul of every living thing and the breath of every human being!

Job 12:10 NJB

125.5 What is man, that thou art mindful of him? and the son of man, that thou visitest him? For thou hast made him a little lower than the angels, and hast crowned him with glory and honour. Thou madest him to have dominion over the works of thy hands; thou hast put all things under his feet: all sheep and oxen, yea, and the beasts of the field; the fowl of the air, and the fish of the sea, and whatsoever passeth through the paths of the seas.

Psalm 8:4–8 KJV

125.6 The Lord looks out from heaven; he sees the whole race of mortals, he surveys from his dwelling-place all the inhabitants of the earth. It is he who fashions the hearts of them all, who discerns everything they do.

Psalm 33:13–15 REB

125.7 As for mortals, their days are like grass; they flourish like a flower of the field; for the wind passes over it, and it is gone, and its place knows it no more.

Psalm 103:15–16 NRSV

125.8 All go unto one place; all are of the dust, and all turn to dust again.

Ecclesiastes 3:20 KJV

125.9 Lo, this only have I found, that God hath made man upright; but they have sought out many inventions.

Ecclesiastes 7:29 KJV

125.10 Yet, Lord, you are our Father; we are the clay, you the potter, and all of us are your handiwork.

Isaiah 64:8 REB

125.11 He [Jesus] knew them all, and had no need of evidence from others about anyone, for he himself could tell what was in people.

John 2:24–25 REB

125.12 Who knows what a human being is but the human spirit within him?

1 Corinthians 2:11 REB

See also **Adam; Jesus Christ, Jesus, the man; Responsibility, human**

MALE AND FEMALE

125.13 The Lord God said, It is not good that the man should be alone; I will make him an help meet for him… And the Lord God caused a deep sleep to fall upon Adam, and he slept: and he took one of his ribs, and closed up the flesh instead thereof; and the rib, which the Lord God had taken from man, made he a woman, and brought her unto the man. And Adam said, This is now bone of my bones, and flesh of my flesh: she shall be called Woman, because she was taken out of Man.

Genesis 2:18, 21–23 KJV

125.14 Unto the woman he said, I will greatly multiply thy sorrow and thy conception; in sorrow thou shalt bring forth children; and thy desire shall be to thy husband, and he shall rule over thee.

Genesis 3:16 KJV

125.15 Unto Adam he said, Because thou hast hearkened unto the voice of thy wife, and hast eaten of the tree, of which I commanded thee, saying, Thou shalt not eat of it: cursed is the ground for thy sake; in sorrow shalt thou eat of it all the days of thy life.

Genesis 3:17 KJV

125.16 Adam called his wife's name Eve; because she was the mother of all living.

Genesis 3:20 KJV

125.17 On the day when God created human beings he made them in his own likeness. He created them male and female, and on the day when he created them, he blessed them and called them man.

Genesis 5:1–2 REB

125.18 Three times a year all your males must come into the presence of the Lord your God in the place which he will choose: at the pilgrim-feasts of Unleavened Bread, of Weeks, and of Booths.

Deuteronomy 16:16 REB

125.19 As a man is, so is his strength.

Judges 8:21 NJB

125.20 How then can a mere mortal be justified in God's sight, or one born of woman be regarded as virtuous? If the circling moon is found wanting, and the stars are not innocent in his eyes, much more so man, who is but a maggot, mortal man, who is a worm.

Job 25:4–6 REB

125.21 They [Jesus' parents] took him up to Jerusalem to present him to the Lord – observing what is written in the Law of the Lord: Every first-born male must be consecrated to the Lord.

Luke 2:22 NJB

125.22 I would have you know, that the head of every man is Christ; and the head of the woman is the man; and the head of Christ is God.

1 Corinthians 11:3 KJV

125.23 It was the woman who was made from a man, and not the man who was made from a woman.

1 Corinthians 11:8 CEV

125.24 As in all the churches of the saints, women should be silent in the churches. For they are not permitted to speak, but should be subordinate, as the law also says.

1 Corinthians 14:33–34 NRSV

125.25 There is neither Jew nor Greek, there is neither bond nor free, there is neither male nor female: for ye are all one in Christ Jesus.

Galatians 3:28 KJV

125.26 Let a woman learn in silence with full submission. I permit no woman to teach or to have authority over a man; she is to keep silent… the woman was deceived and became a transgressor. Yet she will be saved through childbearing, provided they continue in faith and love and holiness, with modesty.

1 Timothy 2:11–12, 14–15 NRSV

See also **Family, Husbands and wives; Marriage**

Humility

126.1 This is the one to whom I will look, to the humble and contrite in spirit, who trembles at my word.

Isaiah 66:2 NRSV

126.2 Blessed are the poor in spirit: for theirs is the kingdom of heaven.

Matthew 5:3 KJV

126.3 Whosoever therefore shall humble himself as this little child, the same is greatest in the kingdom of heaven.

Matthew 18:4 KJV

126.4 Among you this is not to happen. No; anyone who wants to become great among you must be your servant.

Mark 10:43 NJB

126.5 Jesus knew that he had come from God and would go back to God. He also knew that the Father had given him complete power. So during the meal Jesus got up, removed his outer garment, and wrapped a towel around his waist. He put some water into a large bowl. Then he began washing his disciples' feet and drying them with the towel he was wearing… [Then Jesus said] 'And if your Lord and teacher has washed your feet, you should do the same for each other.

John 13:3–5, 14 CEV

126.6 Don't do anything from selfish ambition or from a cheap desire to boast, but be humble towards one another, always considering others better than yourselves... The attitude you should have is the one that Christ Jesus had: He always had the nature of God, but he did not think that by force he should try to remain equal with God. Instead of this, of his own free will he gave up all he had, and took the nature of a servant. He became like a human being and appeared in human likeness. He was humble and walked the path of obedience all the way to death – his death on the cross. For this reason God raised him to the highest place above and gave him the name that is greater than any other name. And so, in honour of the name of Jesus all beings in heaven, on earth, and in the world below will fall on their knees, and all will openly proclaim that Jesus Christ is Lord, to the glory of God the Father.

Philippians 2:3, 5–11 GNB

126.7 In the same way, you who are younger must accept the authority of the elders. And all of you must clothe yourselves with humility in your dealings with one another, for 'God opposes the proud, but gives grace to the humble.' Humble yourselves therefore under the mighty hand of God, so that he may exalt you in due time.

1 Peter 5:5–6 NRSV

See also **Jesus Christ, Humility; Pride**

Hypocrisy

127.1 So when you give something to a needy person, do not make a big show of it, as the hypocrites do in the houses of worship and on the streets. They do it so that people will praise them. I assure you, they have already been paid in full... When you pray, do not be like the hypocrites! They love to stand up and pray in the houses of worship and on the street corners, so that everyone will see them. I assure you, they have already been paid in full... And when you fast, do not put on a sad face as the hypocrites do. They neglect their appearance so that everyone will see that they are fasting. I assure you, they have already been paid in full.

Matthew 6:2, 5, 16 GNB

127.2 You hypocrite! First take the plank out of your own eye, and then you will see clearly to take the speck out of your brother's.

Matthew 7:5 REB

127.3 [Jesus to the Pharisees and scribes] You hypocrites! Isaiah prophesied rightly about you when he said: 'This people honours me with their lips, but their hearts are far from me; in vain do they worship me, teaching human precepts as doctrines.'

Matthew 15:7–9 NRSV

127.4 Why do you call me, 'Lord, Lord,' and yet don't do what I tell you?

Luke 6:46 GNB

127.5 They [people in the last days] will hold to the outward form of our religion, but reject its real power. Keep away from such people.

2 Timothy 3:5 GNB

See also **Pharisees; Scribes; Self-righteousness**

Idolatry

128.1 Thou shalt have no other gods before me. Thou shalt not make unto thee any graven image, or any likeness of any thing that is in heaven above, or that is in the earth beneath, or that is in the water under the earth: thou shalt not bow down thyself to them, nor serve them.
Exodus 20:3–5 KJV

128.2 He [Aaron] took the gold from them, formed it in a mould, and cast an image of a calf.
Exodus 32:4 NRSV

128.3 Their idols are silver and gold, made by human hands. They have mouths, but cannot speak, eyes, but cannot see; they have ears, but cannot hear, nostrils, but cannot smell; with their hands they cannot feel, with their feet they cannot walk, and no sound comes from their throats.
Psalm 115:4–7 REB

128.4 When self-indulgence is at work the results are obvious:… the worship of false gods.
Galatians 5:19–20 NJB

128.5 Everyone is talking about how you welcomed us and how you turned away from idols to serve the true and living God.
1 Thessalonians 1:9 CEV

128.6 Little children, keep yourselves from idols.
1 John 5:21 KJV

Illness

129.1 In the thirty-ninth year of his reign Asa was afflicted with a disease in his feet. Though his disease was severe, even in his illness he did not seek help from the Lord, but only from the physicians.
2 Chronicles 16:12 NIV

129.2 When the Adversary left the Lord's presence, he afflicted Job with running sores from the soles of his feet to the crown of his head.
Job 2:7 REB

129.3 Because of your anger, I am in great pain; my whole body is diseased because of my sins.
Psalm 38:3 GNB

129.4 He had cured many, so that all who had diseases pressed upon him to touch him.
Mark 3:10 NRSV

129.5 The sisters sent this message to Jesus, 'Lord, the man you love is ill.'
John 11:3 NJB

See also **Suffering**

HELP IN

129.6 The Lord will help them when they are sick and will restore them to health.
Psalm 41:3 GNB

129.7 Surely he hath borne our griefs, and carried our sorrows: yet we did esteem him stricken, smitten of God, and afflicted.
Isaiah 53:4 KJV

129.8 There was a leper who came to him and knelt before him, saying, 'Lord, if you choose, you can make me clean.' He stretched out his hand and touched him, saying, 'I do choose. Be made clean!' Immediately his leprosy was cleansed.
Matthew 8:2–3 NRSV

129.9 Is any sick among you? let him call for the elders of the church; and let them pray over him, anointing him with oil in the name of the Lord: and the prayer of faith shall save the sick, and the Lord shall raise him up; and if he have committed sins, they shall be forgiven him. Confess your faults one to another, and pray one for another, that ye may be healed. The effectual fervent prayer of a righteous man availeth much.

James 5:14–16 KJV

See also **Comfort; Healing; Health and wholeness; Restoration**

Immigrants

130.1 You shall not wrong or oppress a resident alien, for you were aliens in the land of Egypt.

Exodus 22:21 NRSV

130.2 Do not ill-treat foreigners who are living in your land. Treat them as you would a fellow-Israelite, and love them as you love yourselves.

Leviticus 19:33–34 GNB

130.3 He secures justice for the fatherless and the widow, and he shows love towards the alien who lives among you, giving him food and clothing. You too must show love towards the alien, for you once lived as aliens in Egypt.

Deuteronomy 10:18–19 REB

130.4 The Lord watches over the strangers; he upholds the orphan and the widow.

Psalm 146:9 NRSV

130.5 I was an hungred, and ye gave me meat: I was thirsty, and ye gave me drink: I was a stranger, and ye took me in.

Matthew 25:35 KJV

130.6 Be sure to welcome strangers into your home. By doing this, some people have welcomed angels as guests, without even knowing it.

Hebrews 13:2 CEV

See also **Race**

Inheritance

131.1 Then shall the King say unto them on his right hand, Come, ye blessed of my Father, inherit the kingdom prepared for you from the foundation of the world.

Matthew 25:34 KJV

131.2 Now I commend you to God and to the word of his grace that has power to build you up and to give you your inheritance among all the sanctified.

Acts 20:32 NJB

131.3 [Children of God are] heirs, heirs of God and fellow-heirs with Christ; but we must share his sufferings if we are also to share his glory.

Romans 8:17 REB

131.4 Do you not know that the wicked will not inherit the kingdom of God? Do not be deceived: Neither the sexually immoral nor idolaters nor adulterers nor male prostitutes nor homosexual offenders nor thieves nor the greedy nor drunkards nor slanderers nor swindlers will inherit the kingdom of God.

1 Corinthians 6:9–10 NIV

131.5 What I am saying, brothers and sisters, is this: flesh and blood cannot inherit the kingdom of God, nor does the perishable inherit the imperishable.

1 Corinthians 15:50 NRSV

131.6 So then, you are no longer a slave but a son or daughter. And since that is what you are, God will give you all that he has for his heirs.

Galatians 4:7 GNB

131.7 In whom also we have obtained an inheritance, being predestinated according to the purpose of him who worketh all things after the counsel of his own will.

Ephesians 1:11 KJV

131.8 In Christ you also – once you had heard the message of the truth, the good news of your salvation, and had believed it – in him you were stamped with the seal of the promised Holy Spirit; and that Spirit is a pledge of the inheritance which will be ours when God has redeemed what is his own, to his glory and praise.

Ephesians 1:13–14 REB

131.9 [Paul's prayer] That… you may know what is the hope to which he has called you, what are the riches of his glorious inheritance among the saints.

Ephesians 1:18 NRSV

131.10 So that, having been justified by his grace, we might become heirs according to the hope of eternal life.

Titus 3:7 NRSV

131.11 [God] hath in these last days spoken unto us by his Son, whom he hath appointed heir of all things, by whom also he made the worlds.

Hebrews 1:2 KJV

131.12 Lest there be any fornicator, or profane person, as Esau, who for one morsel of meat sold his birthright. For ye know how that afterward, when he would have inherited the blessing, he was rejected: for he found no place of repentance, though he sought it carefully with tears.

Hebrews 12:16–17 KJV

A mess of pottage

The saying *Esau sold his birthright for a mess of pottage* is an inaccurate rendering of the original. The misquotation derives from the story of Esau giving up his birthright (the right of the firstborn son to inherit his father's estate) to his brother Jacob for a meal (Genesis 25:30–34 and Hebrews 12:16–17). The actual expression does not, however, appear in the Bible text.

131.13 Because of his great mercy he gave us new life… we look forward to possessing the rich blessings that God keeps for his people. He keeps them for you in heaven, where they cannot decay or spoil or fade away.

1 Peter 1:3–4 GNB

131.14 [Husband and wife] Heirs together of the grace of life.

1 Peter 3:7 KJV

Injustice

132.1 Do not spread false rumours, and do not help a guilty person by giving false evidence.

Exodus 23:1 GNB

132.2 You are not to pervert justice, either by favouring the poor or by subservience to the great. You are to administer justice to your fellow-countryman with strict fairness.

Leviticus 19:15 REB

132.3 Do not cheat anyone by using false measures of length, weight, or quantity.

Leviticus 19:35 GNB

132.4 Now, let the fear of the Lord be upon you; take care what you do, for there is no perversion of justice with the Lord our God, or partiality, or taking of bribes.

2 Chronicles 19:7 NRSV

132.5 How long will you keep judging unfairly and favouring evil people?

Psalm 82:2 CEV

132.6 The Lord hates people who use dishonest weights and measures.

Proverbs 20:10 GNB

132.7 Woe unto him that buildeth his house by unrighteousness, and his chambers by wrong; that useth his neighbour's service without wages, and giveth him not for his work.

Jeremiah 22:13 KJV

132.8 The Lord within it is righteous; he does no wrong. Every morning he renders his judgement, each dawn without fail; but the unjust knows no shame.

Zephaniah 3:5 NRSV

See also **Cruelty; Justice; Oppression**

Israel

133.1 He said, Thy name shall be called no more Jacob, but Israel: for as a prince hast thou power with God and with men, and hast prevailed.

Genesis 32:28 KJV

133.2 Thou, Bethlehem Ephratah, though thou be little among the thousands of Judah, yet out of thee shall he come forth unto me that is to be ruler in Israel; whose goings forth have been from of old, from everlasting.

Micah 5:2 KJV

133.3 Jesus said to them, 'You can be sure that when the Son of Man sits on his glorious throne in the New Age, then you twelve followers of mine will also sit on thrones, to rule the twelve tribes of Israel.'

Matthew 19:28 GNB

133.4 Pilate had an inscription written and fastened to the cross; it read, 'Jesus of Nazareth, King of the Jews.'

John 19:19 REB

133.5 For a person is not a Jew who is one outwardly, nor is true circumcision something external and physical. Rather, a person is a Jew who is one inwardly, and real circumcision is a matter of the heart – it is spiritual and not literal. Such a person receives praise not from others but from God.

Romans 2:28–29 NRSV

133.6 It cannot be that God's word has proved false. Not all the offspring of Israel are truly Israel, nor does being Abraham's descendants make them all his true children; but, in the words of scripture, 'It is through the line of Isaac's descendants that your name will be traced.'

Romans 9:6–7 REB

133.7 I do not want you to be ignorant of this mystery, brothers, so that you may not be conceited: Israel has experienced a hardening in part until the full number of the Gentiles has come in. And so all Israel will be saved, as it is written: 'The deliverer will come from Zion; he will turn godlessness away from Jacob.'

Romans 11:25–26 NIV

133.8 It is not being circumcised or uncircumcised that matters; but what matters is a new creation. Peace and mercy to all who follow this as their rule and to the Israel of God.

Galatians 6:15–16 NJB

133.9 We are the ones who are truly circumcised, because we worship by the power of God's Spirit and take pride in Christ Jesus. We don't boast about what we have done.

Philippians 3:3 CEV

See also **Gentiles**

Jealousy

134.1 Thou shalt not bow down thyself to them, nor serve them: for I the Lord thy God am a jealous God, visiting the iniquity of the fathers upon the children unto the third and fourth generation of them that hate me.
Exodus 20:5 KJV

134.2 You shall worship no other god, because the Lord, whose name is Jealous, is a jealous God.
Exodus 34:14 NRSV

134.3 Anger is cruel and destructive, but it is nothing compared to jealousy.
Proverbs 27:4 GNB

134.4 For the ear of jealousy heareth all things: and the noise of murmurings is not hid.
Wisdom of Solomon 1:10 KJV

134.5 The elder son had been out in the field. But when he came near the house, he heard the music and dancing… The elder brother got so angry that he would not even go into the house. His father came out and begged him to go in. But he said to his father, 'For years I have worked for you like a slave and have always obeyed you. But you have never even given me a little goat, so that I could give a dinner for my friends. This other son of yours wasted your money on prostitutes. And now that he has come home, you ordered the best calf to be killed for a feast.'
Luke 15:25, 28–30 CEV

134.6 Love is patient and kind; it is not jealous or conceited or proud.
1 Corinthians 13:4 GNB

134.7 Anyone can see the behaviour that belongs to the unspiritual nature:… jealousies.
Galatians 5:19–21 REB

134.8 If at heart you have the bitterness of jealousy, or selfish ambition, do not be boastful or hide the truth… Wherever there are jealousy and ambition, there are also disharmony and wickedness of every kind.
James 3:14, 16 NJB

134.9 Do you suppose that it is for nothing that the scripture says, 'God yearns jealously for the spirit that he has made to dwell in us'?
James 4:5 NRSV

See also **Bitterness; Envy**

Jesus Christ

See also **Trinity**

ASCENSION

135.1 Was it not necessary that the Messiah should suffer these things and then enter into his glory?
Luke 24:26 NRSV

135.2 While he blessed them, he was parted from them, and carried up into heaven.
Luke 24:51 KJV

135.3 Jesus was talking about the Holy Spirit, who would be given to everyone that had faith in him. The Spirit had not yet been given to anyone, since Jesus had not yet been given his full glory.
John 7:39 CEV

135.4 'Do not cling to me,' said Jesus, 'for I have not yet ascended to the Father. But go to my brothers, and tell them that I am ascending to my Father and your Father, to my God and your God.'

John 20:17 REB

135.5 After saying this, he was taken up to heaven as they watched him, and a cloud hid him from their sight.

Acts 1:9 GNB

135.6 Being therefore exalted at the right hand of God, and having received from the Father the promise of the Holy Spirit, he has poured out this that you both see and hear.

Acts 2:33 NRSV

135.7 He [God] raised him [Christ] from the dead, and set him at his own right hand in the heavenly places, far above all principality, and power, and might, and dominion, and every name that is named, not only in this world, but also in that which is to come: and hath put all things under his feet, and gave him to be the head over all things to the church, which is his body, the fulness of him that filleth all in all.

Ephesians 1:20–23 KJV

135.8 Therefore God also highly exalted him and gave him the name that is above every name.

Philippians 2:9 NRSV

Authority

135.9 Unlike their scribes he [Jesus] taught with a note of authority.

Matthew 7:29 REB

135.10 'So that you may know that the Son of Man has authority on earth to forgive sins' – he then said to the paralytic

– 'Stand up, take your bed and go to your home.'

Matthew 9:6 NRSV

135.11 Jesus drew near and said to them, 'I have been given all authority in heaven and on earth.'

Matthew 28:18 GNB

135.12 They were all amazed and kept saying to one another, 'What kind of utterance is this? For with authority and power he commands the unclean spirits, and out they come!'

Luke 4:36 NRSV

135.13 He [the Father] has given his Son the right to judge everyone, because he is the Son of Man.

John 5:27 CEV

135.14 No-one takes it [my life] from me, but I lay it down of my own accord. I have authority to lay it down and authority to take it up again. This command I received from my Father.

John 10:18 NIV

Death

135.15 [God to the serpent] I will put enmity between thee and the woman, and between thy seed and her seed; it shall bruise thy head, and thou shalt bruise his heel.

Genesis 3:15 KJV

135.16 He is despised and rejected of men; a man of sorrows, and acquainted with grief: and we hid as it were our faces from him; he was despised, and we esteemed him not. Surely he hath borne our griefs, and carried our sorrows: yet we did esteem him stricken, smitten of God, and afflicted. But he was wounded for our transgressions, he was bruised for our iniquities: the chastisement of our peace was upon him; and with his stripes we are healed. All we like sheep have gone astray; we have turned every one to his own way; and the Lord hath laid on him the iniquity of us all. He was oppressed, and he was afflicted, yet he opened not his mouth: he is brought as a lamb to the slaughter, and as a sheep before her shearers is dumb, so he openeth not his mouth. He was taken from prison and from judgment: and who shall declare his generation? for he was cut off out of the land of the living: for the transgression of my people was he stricken. And he made his grave with the wicked, and with the rich in his death; because he had done no violence, neither was any deceit in his mouth.

Isaiah 53:3–9 KJV

Like a lamb to the slaughter

The expression *like a lamb to the slaughter* means quietly and without complaining. It is often used to refer to someone who is unwittingly about to go into a dangerous or difficult situation, or to be the helpless victim of punishment. Sometimes the word *lamb* is replaced by *sheep*. The basis of the expression is Isaiah 53:7, which describes the sacrifice of the suffering servant, and Acts 8:32, where the prophecy is applied to Jesus Christ.

135.17 From that time forth began Jesus to shew unto his disciples, how that he must go unto Jerusalem, and suffer many things of the elders and chief priests and scribes, and be killed, and be raised again the third day.

Matthew 16:21 KJV

135.18 I am the good shepherd; the good shepherd lays down his life for the sheep.

John 10:11 REB

135.19 This man, handed over to you according to the definite plan and foreknowledge of God, you crucified and killed by the hands of those outside the law.

Acts 2:23 NRSV

135.20 You killed the author of life, but God raised him from the dead.

Acts 3:15 NIV

135.21 [Jesus] was delivered for our offences, and was raised again for our justification.

Romans 4:25 KJV

135.22 For while we were still weak, at the right time Christ died for the ungodly. Indeed, rarely will anyone die for a righteous person – though perhaps for a good person someone might actually dare to die. But God proves his love for us in that while we were still sinners Christ died for us.

Romans 5:6–8 NRSV

135.23 The message of the cross is folly for those who are on the way to ruin, but for those of us who are on the road to salvation it is the power of God.

1 Corinthians 1:18 NJB

135.24 We preach Christ crucified, unto the Jews a stumblingblock, and unto the Greeks foolishness; but unto them which are called, both Jews and Greeks, Christ the power of God, and the wisdom of God.

1 Corinthians 1:23–24 KJV

135.25 First and foremost, I handed on to you the tradition I had received: that Christ died for our sins, in accordance with the scriptures.

1 Corinthians 15:3 REB

135.26 I have been put to death with Christ on his cross, so that it is no longer I who live, but it is Christ who lives in me. This life that I live now, I live by faith in the Son of God, who loved me and gave his life for me.

Galatians 2:19–20 GNB

135.27 I will never boast about anything except the cross of our Lord Jesus Christ. Because of his cross, the world is dead as far as I am concerned, and I am dead as far as the world is concerned.

Galatians 6:14 CEV

135.28 He disarmed the rulers and authorities and made a public example of them, triumphing over them in it.

Colossians 2:15 NRSV

135.29 Since, therefore, the children share flesh and blood, he himself likewise shared the same things, so that through death he might destroy the one who has the power of death, that is, the devil, and free those who all their lives were held in slavery by the fear of death.

Hebrews 2:14–15 NRSV

See also **Atonement; Blood; Reconciliation; Redemption**

ETERNAL SON OF GOD

135.30 The Lord created me the first of his works long ago, before all else that he made. I was formed in earliest times, at the beginning, before earth itself.

Proverbs 8:22–23 REB

135.31 In the beginning was the Word, and the Word was with God, and the Word was God. The same was in the beginning with God.

John 1:1–2 KJV

135.32 Jesus said unto them, Verily, verily, I say unto you, Before Abraham was, I am.

John 8:58 KJV

135.33 He is the image of the invisible God, the firstborn of all creation; for in him all things in heaven and on earth were created, things visible and invisible, whether thrones or dominions or rulers or powers – all things have been created through him and for him. He himself is before all things, and in him all things hold together. He is the head of the body, the church; he is the beginning, the firstborn from the dead, so that he might come to have first place in everything. For in him all the fullness of God was pleased to dwell.

Colossians 1:15–19 NRSV

135.34 His Son, whom he appointed heir of all things, and through whom he made the universe. The Son is the radiance of God's glory and the exact representation of his being, sustaining all things by his powerful word. After he had provided purification for sins, he sat down at the right hand of the Majesty in heaven. So he became as much superior to the angels as the name he has inherited is superior to theirs. For to which of the angels did God ever say, 'You are my Son; today I have become your Father'? Or again, 'I will be his Father, and he will be my Son'? And again, when God brings his firstborn into the world, he says, 'Let all God's angels worship him.' In speaking of the angels he says, 'He makes his angels winds, his servants flames of fire.' But about the Son he says, 'Your throne, O God, will last for ever and ever, and righteousness will be the sceptre of your kingdom.'

Hebrews 1:2–8 NIV

135.35 Jesus Christ is the same yesterday, today, and for ever.

Hebrews 13:8 GNB

135.36 'I am the Alpha and the Omega', says the Lord God, who is and who was and who is to come, the Almighty.

Revelation 1:8 NRSV

> **The alpha and omega**
> The *alpha and omega* is the start and end of something, including its most significant aspects. The expression denotes the first and last letters of the Greek alphabet and derives from Revelation 1:8, referring to the eternity of God.

HOLINESS

135.37 Which one of you can prove that I am guilty of sin?

John 8:46 GNB

135.38 Ours is not a high priest unable to sympathize with our weaknesses, but one who has been tested in every way as we are, only without sinning.

Hebrews 4:15 REB

135.39 For it was fitting that we should have such a high priest, holy, blameless, undefiled, separated from sinners, and exalted above the heavens.

Hebrews 7:26 NRSV

135.40 He had done nothing wrong, and had spoken no deceit.

1 Peter 2:22 NJB

HUMILITY

135.41 Rejoice greatly, O Daughter of Zion! Shout, Daughter of Jerusalem! See, your king comes to you, righteous and having salvation, gentle and riding on a donkey, on a colt, the foal of a donkey.

Zechariah 9:9 NIV

135.42 For ye know the grace of our Lord Jesus Christ, that, though he was rich, yet for your sakes he became poor, that ye through his poverty might be rich.

2 Corinthians 8:9 KJV

135.43 Who, though he was in the form of God, did not regard equality with God as something to be exploited, but emptied himself, taking the form of a slave, being born in human likeness. And being found in human form, he humbled himself and became obedient to the point of death – even death on a cross.

Philippians 2:6–8 NRSV

JESUS AS KING

135.44 The Lord said unto my Lord, Sit thou at my right hand, until I make thine enemies thy footstool.

Psalm 110:1 KJV

135.45 The days are surely coming, says the Lord, when I will raise up for David a righteous Branch, and he shall reign as king and deal wisely, and shall execute justice and righteousness in the land.

Jeremiah 23:5 NRSV

135.46 In my vision at night I looked, and there before me was one like a son of man, coming with the clouds of heaven. He approached the Ancient of Days and was led into his presence. He was given authority, glory and sovereign power; all peoples, nations and men of every language worshipped him. His dominion is an everlasting dominion that will not pass away, and his kingdom is one that will never be destroyed.

Daniel 7:13–14 NIV

135.47 Rejoice, rejoice, people of Zion! Shout for joy, you people of Jerusalem! Look, your king is coming to you! He comes triumphant and victorious, but humble and riding on a donkey – on a colt, the foal of a donkey.

Zechariah 9:9 GNB

135.48 Jesus replied, 'My kingdom does not belong to this world. If it did, my followers would be fighting to save me from the clutches of the Jews. My kingdom belongs elsewhere.'

John 18:36 REB

135.49 Pilate wrote out a notice and had it fixed to the cross; it ran: 'Jesus the Nazarene, King of the Jews'… The Jewish chief priests said to Pilate, 'You should not write "King of the Jews", but that the man said, "I am King of the Jews".'

John 19:19, 21 NJB

135.50 About the Son he says, 'Your throne, O God, will last for ever and ever, and righteousness will be the sceptre of your kingdom.'

Hebrews 1:8 NIV

135.51 Then I heard a loud voice in heaven, proclaiming, 'Now have come the salvation and the power and the kingdom of our God and the authority of his Messiah, for the accuser of our comrades has been thrown down, who accuses them day and night before our God.'

Revelation 12:10 NRSV

JESUS, THE MAN

135.52 Therefore the Lord himself shall give you a sign; Behold, a virgin shall conceive, and bear a son, and shall call his name Immanuel.

Isaiah 7:14 KJV

135.53 For unto us a child is born, unto us a son is given: and the government shall be upon his shoulder: and his name shall be called Wonderful, Counsellor, The mighty God, The everlasting Father, The Prince of Peace.

Isaiah 9:6 KJV

135.54 She [Mary] brought forth her firstborn son, and wrapped him in swaddling clothes, and laid him in a manger; because there was no room for them in the inn.

Luke 2:7 KJV

135.55 The Word was made flesh, and dwelt among us, (and we beheld his glory, the glory as of the only begotten of the Father,) full of grace and truth.

John 1:14 KJV

135.56 For God so loved the world, that he gave his only begotten Son, that whosoever believeth in him should not perish, but have everlasting life. For God sent not his Son into the world to condemn the world; but that the world through him might be saved.

John 3:16–17 KJV

135.57 When the fullness of time had come, God sent his Son, born of a woman, born under the law, in order to redeem those who were under the law.

Galatians 4:4 NRSV

135.58 Take heart among yourselves what you find in Christ Jesus: 'He was in the form of God; yet he laid no claim to equality with God, but made himself nothing, assuming the form of a slave. Bearing the human likeness, sharing the human lot, he humbled himself, and was obedient, even to the point of death, death on a cross!'

Philippians 2:5–8 REB

135.59 For there is one God, and one mediator between God and men, the man Christ Jesus.

1 Timothy 2:5 KJV

135.60 Without any doubt, the mystery of our religion is great: He was revealed in flesh, vindicated in spirit, seen by angels, proclaimed among Gentiles, believed in throughout the world, taken up in glory.

1 Timothy 3:16 NRSV

135.61 We see Jesus, who was made a little lower than the angels for the suffering of death, crowned with glory and honour.

Hebrews 2:9 KJV

135.62 Since the children, as he calls them, are people of flesh and blood, Jesus himself became like them and shared their human nature. He did this so that through his death he might destroy the Devil, who has the power over death.

Hebrews 2:14 GNB

135.63 For the high priest we have is not incapable of feeling our weaknesses with us, but has been put to the test in exactly the same way as ourselves, apart from sin.

Hebrews 4:15 NJB

135.64 The way to recognize the Spirit of God is this: every spirit which acknowledges that Jesus Christ has come in the flesh is from God.

1 John 4:2 REB

JESUS, THE ONE TO BE WORSHIPPED

135.65 When they were come into the house, they saw the young child with Mary his mother, and fell down, and worshipped him: and when they had opened their treasures, they presented unto him gifts; gold, and frankincense, and myrrh.

Matthew 2:11 KJV

135.66 Simon Peter answered and said, Thou art the Christ, the Son of the living God.

Matthew 16:16 KJV

135.67 When Simon Peter saw it, he fell down at Jesus' knees, saying, Depart from me; for I am a sinful man, O Lord.

Luke 5:8 KJV

135.68 Thomas said, 'My Lord and my God!'

John 20:28 REB

135.69 The Lamb who was killed is worthy to receive power, wealth, wisdom, and strength, honour, glory, and praise!

Revelation 5:12 GNB

JESUS AS PRIEST

135.70 For there is one God, and one mediator between God and men, the man Christ Jesus.

1 Timothy 2:5 KJV

135.71 Since, then, we have a great high priest who has passed through the heavens, Jesus, the Son of God, let us hold fast to our confession. For we do not have a high priest who is unable to sympathize with our weaknesses, but we have one who in every respect has been tested as we are, yet without sin.

Hebrews 4:14–15 NRSV

135.72 So also Christ glorified not himself to be made an high priest; but he that said unto him, Thou art my Son, to day have I begotten thee. As he saith also in another place, Thou art a priest for ever after the order of Melchisedec.

Hebrews 5:5–6 KJV

135.73 He holds his priesthood permanently, because he continues for ever. Consequently he is able for all time to save those who approach God through him, since he always lives to make intercession for them. For it was fitting that we should have such a high priest, holy, blameless, undefiled, separated from sinners, and exalted above the heavens.

Hebrews 7:24–26 NRSV

135.74 For this reason he is the mediator of a new covenant, so that those who are called may receive the promised eternal inheritance, because a death has occurred that redeems them from the transgressions under the first covenant.

Hebrews 9:15 NRSV

135.75 The priests do their work each day, and they keep on offering sacrifices that can never take away sins. But Christ offered himself as a sacrifice that is good for ever. Now he is sitting at God's right side.

Hebrews 10:11–12 CEV

JESUS AS PROPHET

135.76 Instead he [the Lord your God] will choose one of your own people to be a prophet just like me, and you must do what that prophet says.

Deuteronomy 18:15 CEV

135.77 The crowds replied, 'This is the prophet Jesus, from Nazareth in Galilee.'

Matthew 21:11 REB

135.78 Fear seized all of them; and they glorified God, saying, 'A great prophet has risen among us!' and 'God has looked favourably on his people!'

Luke 7:16 NRSV

135.79 This man [Jesus of Nazareth] was a prophet and was considered by God and by all the people to be powerful in everything he said and did.

Luke 24:19 GNB

LOVE

135.80 When he saw the crowds, he had compassion for them, because they were harassed and helpless, like sheep without a shepherd.

Matthew 9:36 NRSV

135.81 It was now the day before the Passover Festival. Jesus knew that the hour had come for him to leave this world and go to the Father. He had always loved those in the world who were his own, and he loved them to the very end.

John 13:1 GNB

135.82 As the Father hath loved me, so have I loved you: continue ye in my love.

John 15:9 KJV

135.83 For I am convinced that there is nothing in death or life, in the realm of spirits or superhuman powers, in the world as it is or the world as it shall be, in the forces of the universe, in heights or depths – nothing in all creation that can separate us from the love of God in Christ Jesus our Lord.

Romans 8:38–39 REB

135.84 [Paul's prayer] That Christ may dwell in your hearts through faith, as you are being rooted and grounded in love. I pray that you may have the power to comprehend, with all the saints, what is the breadth and length and height and depth, and to know the love of Christ that surpasses knowledge.

Ephesians 3:17–19 NRSV

135.85 He loves us and has washed away our sins with his blood.

Revelation 1:5 NJB

OBEDIENCE

135.86 I delight to do your will, O my God; your law is within my heart.
Psalm 40:8 NRSV

135.87 He went away again the second time, and prayed, saying, O my Father, if this cup may not pass away from me, except I drink it, thy will be done.
Matthew 26:42 KJV

135.88 'My food,' Jesus said to them, 'is to obey the will of the one who sent me and to finish the work he gave me to do.'
John 4:34 GNB

135.89 The one who sent me is with me. I always do what pleases him, and he will never leave me.
John 8:29 CEV

135.90 Sharing the human lot, he humbled himself, and was obedient, even to the point of death, death on a cross!
Philippians 2:8 REB

135.91 Even though he was God's Son, he learnt through his sufferings to be obedient.
Hebrews 5:8 GNB

RESURRECTION

135.92 For you will not abandon me to Sheol or suffer your faithful servant to see the pit.
Psalm 16:10 REB

135.93 Yet it pleased the Lord to bruise him; he hath put him to grief: when thou shalt make his soul an offering for sin, he shall see his seed, he shall prolong his days, and the pleasure of the Lord shall prosper in his hand. He shall see of the travail of his soul, and shall be satisfied: by his knowledge shall my righteous servant justify many; for he shall bear their iniquities. Therefore will I divide him a portion with the great, and he shall divide the spoil with the strong; because he hath poured out his soul unto death: and he was numbered with the transgressors; and he bare the sin of many, and made intercession for the transgressors.
Isaiah 53:10–12 KJV

135.94 From that time forth began Jesus to shew unto his disciples, how that he must go unto Jerusalem, and suffer many things of the elders and chief priests and scribes, and be killed, and be raised again the third day.
Matthew 16:21 KJV

135.95 He is not here: for he is risen, as he said. Come, see the place where the Lord lay.
Matthew 28:6 KJV

135.96 God raised this man Jesus to life, and of that we are all witnesses.
Acts 2:32 NJB

135.97 He has fixed a day on which he will have the world judged in righteousness by a man whom he has appointed, and of this he has given assurance to all by raising him from the dead.
Acts 17:31 NRSV

135.98 [Jesus] was delivered for our offences, and was raised again for our justification.
Romans 4:25 KJV

135.99 By our baptism, then, we were buried with him and shared his death, in order that, just as Christ was raised from death by the glorious power of the Father, so also we might live a new life. For since we have become one with him in dying as he did, in the same way we shall be one with him by being raised to life as he was.

Romans 6:4–5 GNB

135.100 We know that Christ, being raised from the dead, will never die again; death no longer has dominion over him. The death he died, he died to sin, once for all; but the life he lives, he lives to God. So you also must consider yourselves dead to sin and alive to God in Christ Jesus.

Romans 6:9–11 NRSV

135.101 That he was buried; that he was raised to life on the third day, in accordance with the scriptures; and that he appeared to Cephas, and afterwards to the Twelve.

1 Corinthians 15:4 REB

135.102 If we preach that Christ was raised from death, how can some of you say that the dead will not be raised to life? If they won't be raised to life, Christ himself wasn't raised to life. And if Christ wasn't raised to life, our message is worthless, and so is your faith. If the dead won't be raised to life, we have told lies about God by saying that he raised Christ to life, when he really did not. So if the dead won't be raised to life, Christ wasn't raised to life. Unless Christ was raised to life, your faith is useless, and you are still living in your sins. And those people who died after putting their faith in him are completely lost. If our hope in Christ is good only for this life, we are worse off than anyone else. But Christ has been raised to life! And he makes us certain that others will also be raised to life. Just as we will die because of Adam, we will be raised to life because of Christ.

1 Corinthians 15:12–21 CEV

135.103 If ye then be risen with Christ, seek those things which are above, where Christ sitteth on the right hand of God.

Colossians 3:1 KJV

135.104 When I saw him, I fell at his feet as though I were dead. But he laid his right hand on me and said, 'Do not be afraid. I am the first and the last, and I am the living One; I was dead and now I am alive for evermore, and I hold the keys of death and Hades.'

Revelation 1:17–18 REB

See also **Eternal life**; **Last things**, **Resurrection**

SEVEN WORDS FROM THE CROSS

135.105 About three Jesus cried aloud, 'Eli, Eli, lema sabachthani?' which means, 'My God, my God, why have you forsaken me?'

Matthew 27:46 REB

135.106 Then said Jesus, Father, forgive them; for they know not what they do.

Luke 23:34 KJV

135.107 Jesus said unto him, Verily I say unto thee, To day shalt thou be with me in paradise.

Luke 23:43 KJV

135.108 When Jesus had cried with a loud voice, he said, Father, into thy hands I commend my spirit: and having said thus, he gave up the ghost.

Luke 23:46 KJV

135.109 When Jesus saw his mother and the disciple whom he loved standing beside her, he said to his mother, 'Woman, here is your son.' Then he said to the disciple, 'Here is your mother.'

John 19:26–27 NRSV

135.110 After this, Jesus knew that everything had now been completed and, so that the scripture should be completely fulfilled, he said: I am thirsty.

John 19:28 NJB

135.111 Jesus drank the wine and said, 'It is finished!' Then he bowed his head and died.

John 19:30 GNB

Titles and portraits of Jesus

Alpha and Omega
Revelation 1:8

Bread of life
John 6:35

Christ
Matthew 16:16

Door
John 10:9

Immanuel
Isaiah 7:14; Matthew 1:23

Everlasting Father
Isaiah 9:6

Firstborn Son
Colossians 1:18

Good shepherd
John 10:11

Holy One of God
Mark 1:24

Jesus
Matthew 1:21

King of kings
Revelation 17:14

Lamb of God
John 1:29

Light of the world
John 8:12

Lord
Luke 1:43

Lord of lords
Revelation 17:14

Messiah
John 1:41

Mighty God
Isaiah 9:6

Prince of peace
Isaiah 9:6

Resurrection and the life
John 11:25

Saviour
Titus 2:13

Second Adam
1 Corinthians 15:45

Son of God
Matthew 26:63

Son of man
Matthew 8:20

Vine
John 15:5

Way, the truth and the life
John 14:6

Wonderful Counsellor
Isaiah 9:6

Word
John 1:1

Journeys

136.1 Then Jacob went on his journey, and came into the land of the people of the east.

Genesis 29:1 KJV

136.2 These are the stages in the journey of the Israelites, when they were led by Moses and Aaron in their tribal hosts out of Egypt...

Numbers 33:1 REB

136.3 He himself [Elijah] went a day's journey into the wilderness, and came and sat down under a juniper tree: and he requested for himself that he might die.

1 Kings 19:4 KJV

136.4 The king... asked me, 'How long will the journey last, and when will you return?'

Nehemiah 2:6 REB

136.5 Come on, we'll make love as much as we like, till morning... For my husband is not at home, he has gone on a very long journey, taking his moneybags with him; he will not be back till the moon is full.

Proverbs 7:18–20 NJB

136.6 After this he [Jesus] went journeying from town to town and village to village, proclaiming the good news of the kingdom of God.

Luke 8:1 REB

136.7 Calling the Twelve together he… sent them out to proclaim the kingdom of God and to heal the sick. 'Take nothing for the journey,' he told them, 'neither stick nor pack, neither bread nor money; nor are you to have a second coat.'… So they set out and travelled from village to village, and everywhere they announced the good news and healed the sick.

Luke 9:1–3, 6 REB

136.8 Jesus also told them another story: Once a man had two sons. The younger son said to his father, 'Give me my share of the property.' So the father divided his property between his two sons. Not long after that, the younger son packed up everything he owned and left for a foreign country, where he wasted all his money in wild living.

Luke 15:11–13 CEV

136.9 Jesus, therefore, being wearied with his journey, sat thus on the well.

John 4:6 KJV

136.10 When they came up from the water the Spirit snatched Philip away; the eunuch did not see him again, but went on his way rejoicing. Philip appeared at Azotus, and toured the country, preaching in all the towns till he reached Caesarea.

Acts 8:39–40 REB

136.11 While he was travelling to Damascus and approaching the city,

suddenly a light from heaven shone all round him.

Acts 9:3 NJB

A Damascus road experience
To have a *Damascus road experience* is to have a sudden conversion in one's beliefs. Hence someone's conversion is sometimes referred to as his or her *road to Damascus*. The expressions allude to the experience of Saul of Tarsus, who, while on his way to the city of Damascus to persecute Christianity there, encountered Jesus Christ. Suddenly a light shone around him (hence our phrase *see the light*); he fell to the ground, and he heard Christ speak to him (Acts 9:1–9). So he became a disciple and an apostle of Jesus Christ.

136.12 For years I have wanted to visit you. So I plan to stop off on my way to Spain. Then after a short, but refreshing, stay with you, I hope you will quickly send me on.

Romans 15:23–24 CEV

136.13 Continually travelling, I have been in danger from rivers, in danger from brigands, in danger from my own people and in danger from the gentiles, in danger in the towns and in danger in the open country, in danger at sea and in danger from people masquerading as brothers.

2 Corinthians 11:26 NJB

Joy

137.1 'Go now,' he [Nehemiah] continued… 'the day is holy to our Lord. Let there be no sadness, for joy in the Lord is your strength.'

Nehemiah 8:10 REB

137.2 Thou wilt shew me the path of life: in thy presence is fulness of joy; at thy right hand there are pleasures for evermore.

Psalm 16:11 KJV

137.3 This is the day that the Lord has made; let us rejoice and be glad in it.

Psalm 118:24 NRSV

137.4 I rejoice in your promise like one who finds a vast treasure.

Psalm 119:162 NJB

137.5 The Lord has done great things for us, and we are filled with joy.

Psalm 126:3 NIV

137.6 They that sow in tears shall reap in joy. He that goeth forth and weepeth, bearing precious seed, shall doubtless come again with rejoicing, bringing his sheaves with him.

Psalm 126:5–6 KJV

137.7 With joy you will all draw water from the wells of deliverance.

Isaiah 12:3 REB

137.8 The ransomed of the Lord shall return, and come to Zion with singing; everlasting joy shall be upon their heads; they shall obtain joy and gladness, and sorrow and sighing shall flee away.

Isaiah 35:10 NRSV

137.9 The seeds that fell on rocky ground stand for those who receive the message gladly as soon as they hear it. But it does not sink deep into them, and they don't last long. So when trouble or persecution comes because of the message, they give up at once.

Matthew 13:20–21 GNB

137.10 Just so, I tell you, there will be more joy in heaven over one sinner who repents than over ninety-nine righteous persons who need no repentance.

Luke 15:7 NRSV

137.11 These things have I spoken unto you, that my joy might remain in you, and that your joy might be full.

John 15:11 KJV

137.12 Ask and you will receive, that your joy may be complete.

John 16:24 REB

137.13 The Lord's followers in Antioch were very happy and were filled with the Holy Spirit.

Acts 13:52 CEV

137.14 Our Lord Jesus Christ: by whom also we have access by faith into this grace wherein we stand, and rejoice in hope of the glory of God.

Romans 5:1–2 KJV

137.15 May the God of hope fill you with all joy and peace in believing, so that you may abound in hope by the power of the Holy Spirit.

Romans 15:13 NRSV

137.16 I will boast all the more gladly of my weaknesses, so that the power of Christ may dwell in me.

2 Corinthians 12:9 NRSV

137.17 The fruit of the Spirit is… joy…

Galatians 5:22 KJV

137.18 Rejoice in the Lord alway: and again I say, Rejoice.

Philippians 4:4 KJV

137.19 Instruct those who are rich in this world's goods not to be proud, and to fix their hopes not on so uncertain a thing as money, but on God, who richly provides all things for us to enjoy.

1 Timothy 6:17 REB

137.20 Looking unto Jesus the author and finisher of our faith; who for the joy that was set before him endured the cross, despising the shame, and is set down at the right hand of the throne of God.

Hebrews 12:2 KJV

137.21 You love him, although you have not seen him, and you believe in him, although you do not now see him. So you rejoice with a great and glorious joy which words cannot express.

1 Peter 1:8 GNB

137.22 I have no greater joy than this, to hear that my children are walking in the truth.

3 John v. 4 NRSV

See also Celebration; Contentment; Laughter; Thankfulness and thanksgiving

Justice

138.1 Do not take advantage of anyone or rob him. Do not hold back the wages of someone you have hired, not even for one night.

Leviticus 19:13 GNB

138.2 Justice, and justice alone, must be your aim, so that you may live and occupy the land which the Lord your God is giving you.

Deuteronomy 16:20 REB

138.3 Give the king your justice, O God, and your righteousness to a king's son. May he judge your people with righteousness, and your poor with justice.

Psalm 72:1–2 NRSV

138.4 Doing what is right and fair pleases the Lord more than an offering.

Proverbs 21:3 CEV

138.5 Seek justice, encourage the oppressed. Defend the cause of the fatherless, plead the case of the widow.

Isaiah 1:17 NIV

138.6 We growl, all of us, like bears, like doves we make no sound but moaning, waiting for the fair judgement that never comes, for salvation, but that is far away.

Isaiah 59:11 NJB

138.7 Justice is driven away, and right cannot come near. Truth stumbles in the public square, and honesty finds no place there.

Isaiah 59:14 GNB

138.8 The Lord says, 'I love justice and I hate oppression and crime. I will faithfully reward my people and make an eternal covenant with them.'

Isaiah 61:8 GNB

138.9 Let justice roll down like waters, and righteousness like an ever-flowing stream.

Amos 5:24 NRSV

138.10 He hath shewed thee, O man, what is good; and what doth the Lord require of thee, but to do justly, and to love mercy, and to walk humbly with thy God?

Micah 6:8 KJV

138.11 Slave owners, be fair and honest with your slaves. Don't forget that you have a Master in heaven.

Colossians 4:1 CEV

See also God, Just; Injustice; Poverty; Righteousness

Justification

139.1 He [Abraham] believed in the Lord; and he counted it to him for righteousness.
Genesis 15:6 KJV

139.2 Then Job answered: 'Indeed I know that this is so; but how can a mortal be just before God?'
Job 9:1–2 NRSV

139.3 Happy is he whose offence is forgiven, whose sin is blotted out! Happy is he to whom the Lord imputes no fault, in whose spirit there is no deceit.
Psalm 32:1–2 REB

139.4 He is near that justifieth me; who will contend with me? let us stand together: who is mine adversary? let him come near to me. Behold, the Lord God will help me; who is he that shall condemn me?
Isaiah 50:8–9 KJV

139.5 I will greatly rejoice in the Lord, my whole being shall exult in my God;
for he has clothed me with the garments of salvation, he has covered me with the robe of righteousness.
Isaiah 61:10 NRSV

139.6 'The tax collector stood at a distance and would not even raise his face to heaven, but beat on his breast and said, "God, have pity on me, a sinner!" I tell you,' said Jesus, 'the tax collector, and not the Pharisee, was in the right with God when he went home. For all who make themselves great will be humbled, and all who humble themselves will be made great.'
Luke 18:13–14 GNB

139.7 Being justified freely by his grace through the redemption that is in Christ Jesus.
Romans 3:24 KJV

139.8 To one who without works trusts him who justifies the ungodly, such faith is reckoned as righteousness.
Romans 4:5 NRSV

139.9 Therefore being justified by faith, we have peace with God through our Lord Jesus Christ.
Romans 5:1 KJV

139.10 How much more can we be sure, therefore, that, now that we have been justified by his death, we shall be saved through him from the retribution of God.
Romans 5:9 NJB

139.11 Adam disobeyed God and caused many others to be sinners. But Jesus obeyed him and will make many people acceptable to God.
Romans 5:19 CEV

139.12 Those whom he predestined he also called; and those whom he called he also justified; and those whom he justified he also glorified… Who will bring any charge against God's elect? It is God who justifies. Who is to condemn? It is Christ Jesus, who died, yes, who was raised, who is at the right hand of God, who indeed intercedes for us.
Romans 8:30, 33–34 NRSV

139.13 For he hath made him to be sin for us, who knew no sin; that we might be made the righteousness of God in him.
2 Corinthians 5:21 KJV

See also Atonement; Faith; Redemption; Righteousness

Kindness

140.1 If you give food to the hungry and satisfy those who are in need, then the darkness around you will turn to the brightness of noon.

Isaiah 58:10 GNB

140.2 When the Son of Man comes in his glory with all his angels, he will sit on his royal throne. The people of all nations will be brought before him, and he will separate them, as shepherds separate their sheep from their goats. He will place the sheep on his right and the goats on his left. Then the king will say to those on his right, 'My father has blessed you! Come and receive the kingdom that was prepared for you before the world was created. When I was hungry, you gave me something to eat, and when I was thirsty, you gave me something to drink. When I was a stranger, you welcomed me, and when I was naked, you gave me clothes to wear. When I was sick, you took care of me, and when I was in jail, you visited me.'... The king will answer, 'Whenever you did it for any of my people, no matter how unimportant they seemed, you did it for me.'

Matthew 25:31–36, 40 CEV

140.3 A man was going down from Jerusalem to Jericho, and fell into the hands of robbers, who stripped him, beat him, and went away, leaving him half dead... a Samaritan while travelling came near him; and when he saw him, he was moved with pity. He went to him and bandaged his wounds, having poured oil and wine on them. Then he put him on his own animal, brought him to an inn, and took care of him. The next day he took out two denarii, gave them to the innkeeper, and said, 'Take care of him; and when I come back, I will repay you whatever more you spend.'

Luke 10:30, 33–35 NRSV

The good Samaritan

A *good Samaritan* is someone who helps others who are in need. The expression alludes to the parable Jesus told of the Samaritan who rescued and helped the injured man who had been attacked and robbed.
A priest and a Levite went by, *passed by on the other side,* without taking any action. It was a Samaritan – and the story is all the more pointed because Jews regarded Samaritans with contempt – who helped the man and looked after him personally and generously. It is the good Samaritan's kind and selfless actions to the person in distress that are remembered in the expression which has become part of the language.

140.4 I have shewed you all things, how that so labouring ye ought to support the weak, and to remember the words of the Lord Jesus, how he said, It is more blessed to give than to receive.

Acts 20:35 KJV

140.5 The fruit of the Spirit is love... gentleness, goodness, faith...

Galatians 5:22 KJV

140.6 Be kind to one another, tender-hearted, forgiving one another, as God in Christ has forgiven you.

Ephesians 4:32 NRSV

140.7 We ought to see how each of us may best arouse others to love and active goodness.

Hebrews 10:24 REB

See also **Caring; Help; Love, of humanity; Service**

Kingdom, kingdom of God

141.1 Blessed are the poor in spirit: for theirs is the kingdom of heaven.
Matthew 5:3 KJV

141.2 Thy kingdom come. Thy will be done, in earth as it is in heaven.
Matthew 6:10 BCP

141.3 Seek ye first the kingdom of God, and his righteousness; and all these things shall be added unto you.
Matthew 6:33 KJV

141.4 Not everyone who says to me, 'Lord, Lord' will enter the kingdom of Heaven, but only those who do the will of my heavenly Father.
Matthew 7:21 REB

141.5 Then shall the King say unto them on his right hand, Come, ye blessed of my Father, inherit the kingdom prepared for you from the foundation of the world.
Matthew 25:34 KJV

141.6 The time is fulfilled, and the kingdom of God has come near; repent, and believe in the good news.
Mark 1:15 NRSV

141.7 Verily I say unto you, Whosoever shall not receive the kingdom of God as a little child, he shall not enter therein.
Mark 10:15 KJV

141.8 When he was demanded of the Pharisees, when the kingdom of God should come, he answered them and said, The kingdom of God cometh not with observation: neither shall they say, Lo here! or, lo there! for, behold, the kingdom of God is within you.
Luke 17:20–21 KJV

141.9 Jesus answered and said unto him [Nicodemus], Verily, verily, I say unto thee, Except a man be born again, he cannot see the kingdom of God.
John 3:3 KJV

141.10 [Paul and Barnabas] strengthened the souls of the disciples and encouraged them to continue in the faith, saying, 'It is through many persecutions that we must enter the kingdom of God.'
Acts 14:22 NRSV

141.11 God's kingdom isn't about eating and drinking. It is about pleasing God, about living in peace, and about true happiness. All this comes from the Holy Spirit.
Romans 14:17 CEV

141.12 For the kingdom of God consists not in spoken words but in power.
1 Corinthians 4:20 NJB

141.13 Do you not know that the wicked will not inherit the kingdom of God? Do not be deceived.
1 Corinthians 6:9 NIV

141.14 Then the end will come; Christ will overcome all spiritual rulers, authorities, and powers, and will hand over the Kingdom to God the Father.
1 Corinthians 15:24 GNB

141.15 He [God the Father] has rescued us from the power of darkness and transferred us into the kingdom of his beloved Son, in whom we have redemption, the forgiveness of sins.
Colossians 1:13 NRSV

141.16 The kingdom we are given is unshakeable; let us therefore give thanks to God for it, and so worship God as he would be worshipped, with reverence and awe.

Hebrews 12:28 REB

141.17 The kingdom of the world has become the kingdom of our Lord and of his Messiah, and he will reign for ever and ever.

Revelation 11:15 NRSV

See also Jesus Christ, Jesus as king

Knowledge

142.1 Out of the ground made the Lord God to grow every tree that is pleasant to the sight, and good for food; the tree of life also in the midst of the garden, and the tree of knowledge of good and evil.

Genesis 2:9 KJV

142.2 For I know that my redeemer liveth, and that he shall stand at the latter day upon the earth.

Job 19:25 KJV

142.3 Be still, and know that I am God! I am exalted among the nations, I am exalted in the earth.

Psalm 46:10 NRSV

142.4 I am your servant; give me understanding, so that I may know your teachings.

Psalm 119:125 GNB

142.5 You have looked deep into my heart, Lord, and you know all about me. You know when I am resting or when I am working, and from heaven you discover my thoughts. You notice everything I do and everywhere I go. Before I even speak a word, you know what I will say, and with

your powerful arm you protect me from every side. I can't understand all this! Such wonderful knowledge is far above me.

Psalm 139:1–6 CEV

142.6 They shall not hurt nor destroy in all my holy mountain: for the earth shall be full of the knowledge of the Lord, as the waters cover the sea.

Isaiah 11:9 KJV

142.7 Let us know, let us press on to know the Lord; his appearing is as sure as the dawn; he will come to us like the showers, like the spring rains that water the earth.

Hosea 6:3 NRSV

142.8 Everything is entrusted to me by my Father; and no one knows the Son but the Father, and no one knows the Father but the Son and those to whom the Son chooses to reveal him.

Matthew 11:27 REB

142.9 I am the good shepherd. As the Father knows me and I know the Father, in the same way I know my sheep and they know me. And I am willing to die for them.

John 10:14–15 GNB

142.10 Eternal life is this: to know you, the only true God, and Jesus Christ whom you have sent.

John 17:3 NJB

142.11 Knowledge… puffs a person up with pride; but love builds up.

1 Corinthians 8:1 GNB

142.12 I may have the gift of prophecy and the knowledge of every hidden truth; I may have faith enough to move mountains; but if I have no love, I am nothing… At present we see only puzzling reflections in a mirror, but one day we shall see face to face. My knowledge now is partial; then it will be whole, like God's knowledge of me.

1 Corinthians 13:2, 12 REB

142.13 [Paul's prayer] To know the love of Christ that surpasses knowledge, so that you may be filled with all the fullness of God.

Ephesians 3:19 NRSV

142.14 That I may know him, and the power of his resurrection, and the fellowship of his sufferings, being made conformable unto his death.

Philippians 3:10 KJV

142.15 For this reason we have always prayed for you, ever since we heard about you. We ask God to fill you with the knowledge of his will, with all the wisdom and understanding that his Spirit gives. Then you will be able to live as the Lord wants and will always do what pleases him. Your lives will produce all kinds of good deeds, and you will grow in your knowledge of God.

Colossians 1:9–10 GNB

142.16 I am not ashamed of it, because I know whom I have trusted, and am confident of his power to keep safe what he has put into my charge until the great day.

2 Timothy 1:12 REB

142.17 Hereby do we know that we know him, if we keep his commandments.

1 John 2:3 KJV

See also **Discernment; Understanding; Wisdom**

Land

143.1 For six years you shall sow your land and gather in its yield; but the seventh year you shall let it rest and lie fallow, so that the poor of your people may eat; and what they leave the wild animals may eat.

Exodus 23:10–11 NRSV

143.2 Ye shall hallow the fiftieth year, and proclaim liberty throughout all the land unto all the inhabitants thereof: it shall be a jubilee unto you; and ye shall return every man unto his possession, and ye shall return every man unto his family. A jubilee shall that fiftieth year be unto you: ye shall not sow, neither reap that which groweth of itself in it, nor gather the grapes in it of thy vine undressed.

Leviticus 25:10–11 KJV

143.3 Your land must not be sold on a permanent basis, because you do not own it; it belongs to God, and you are like foreigners who are allowed to make use of it.

Leviticus 25:23 GNB

143.4 He brought us into this place and gave us this land, a land flowing with milk and honey. So now I bring the first of the fruit of the ground that you, O Lord, have given me.

Deuteronomy 26:9–10 NRSV

A land flowing with milk and honey
The expression *a land flowing with milk and honey* is used to refer to a place or state that promises to provide plentiful resources, great happiness and security, and abundant fulfilment of all one's hopes. The phrase has a similar meaning to the expression *the promised land*, originally the land of Canaan promised by God to the Israelites.

143.5 The following blessings will all come and light on you, because you obey the Lord your God. A blessing on you in the town; a blessing on you in the country. A blessing on the fruit of your body, the fruit of your land and cattle, the offspring of your herds and lambing flocks.

Deuteronomy 28:2–4 REB

143.6 [The Lord's promise to Solomon] If my own people will humbly pray and turn back to me and stop sinning, then I will answer them from heaven. I will forgive them and make their land fertile once again.

2 Chronicles 7:14 CEV

143.7 To the Lord belong the earth and everything in it, the world and all its inhabitants.

Psalm 24:1 REB

143.8 There was not a needy person among them, for as many as owned lands or houses sold them and brought the proceeds of what was sold. They laid it at the apostles' feet, and it was distributed to each as any had need.

Acts 4:34–35 NRSV

See also **Creation; Earth, the; World, Created universe**

Last things

EVENTS BEFORE THE SECOND COMING

144.1 Ye shall hear of wars and rumours of wars: see that ye be not troubled: for all these things must come to pass, but the end is not yet.

Matthew 24:6 KJV

144.2 You will be arrested, punished, and even killed. Because of me, you will be hated by people of all nations. Many will give up and will betray and hate each other. Many false prophets will come and fool a lot of people. Evil will spread and cause many people to stop loving others. But if you keep on being faithful right to the end, you will be saved. When the good news about the kingdom has been preached all over the world and told to all nations, the end will come.

Matthew 24:9–14 CEV

144.3 For at that time there will be great suffering, such as has not been from the beginning of the world until now, no, and never will be. And if those days had not been cut short, no one would be saved; but for the sake of the elect those days will be cut short.

Matthew 24:21–22 NRSV

144.4 As soon as that time of distress has passed, the sun will be darkened, the moon will not give her light; the stars will fall from the sky, the celestial powers will be shaken.

Matthew 24:29 REB

144.5 Let no one deceive you in any way; for that day will not come unless the rebellion comes first and the lawless one is revealed, the one destined for destruction. He opposes and exalts himself above every so-called god or object of worship, so that he takes his seat in the temple of God, declaring himself to be God.

2 Thessalonians 2:3–4 NRSV

144.6 Then the lawless one will be revealed, whom the Lord Jesus will overthrow with the breath of his mouth and destroy by the splendour of his coming.

2 Thessalonians 2:8 NIV

144.7 He seized the dragon, that ancient serpent – that is, the Devil, or Satan – and chained him up for a thousand years. The

angel threw him into the abyss, locked it, and sealed it, so that he could not deceive the nations any more until the thousand years were over. After that he must be let loose for a little while.

Revelation 20:2–3 GNB

144.8 After the thousand years are over, Satan will be let loose from his prison, and he will go out to deceive the nations scattered over the whole world, that is, Gog and Magog. Satan will bring them all together for battle, as many as the grains of sand on the seashore.

Revelation 20:7–8 GNB

HEAVEN

144.9 Whom have I in heaven but thee? and there is none upon earth that I desire beside thee.

Psalm 73:25 KJV

144.10 Thus saith the Lord, The heaven is my throne, and the earth is my footstool: where is the house that ye build unto me? and where is the place of my rest?

Isaiah 66:1 KJV

144.11 Our Father, which art in heaven, hallowed be thy name. Thy kingdom come. Thy will be done, in earth as it is in heaven.

Matthew 6:9–10 BCP

144.12 In my Father's house are many mansions: if it were not so, I would have told you. I go to prepare a place for you. And if I go and prepare a place for you, I will come again, and receive you unto myself; that where I am, there ye may be also.

John 14:2–3 KJV

144.13 Father, I desire that those also, whom you have given me, may be with me where I am, to see my glory, which you have given me because you loved me before the foundation of the world.

John 17:24 NRSV

144.14 Suddenly there was a noise from heaven like the sound of a mighty wind! It filled the house where they were meeting.

Acts 2:2 CEV

144.15 As it is written, Eye hath not seen, nor ear heard, neither have entered into the heart of man, the things which God hath prepared for them that love him.

1 Corinthians 2:9 KJV

144.16 We, however, are citizens of heaven, and we eagerly wait for our Saviour, the Lord Jesus Christ, to come from heaven.

Philippians 3:20 GNB

144.17 It is not as though Christ had entered a man-made sanctuary which was merely a model of the real one; he entered heaven itself, so that he now appears in the presence of God on our behalf.

Hebrews 9:24 NJB

144.18 After that I looked and saw a vast throng, which no one could count, from all races and tribes, nations and languages, standing before the throne and the Lamb. They were robed in white and had palm branches in their hands.

Revelation 7:9 REB

144.19 For this reason they are before the throne of God, and worship him day and night within his temple, and the one who is seated on the throne will shelter them.

Revelation 7:15 NRSV

144.20 Then I saw thrones, and those who sat on them were given the power to judge. I also saw the souls of those who had been executed because they had

proclaimed the truth that Jesus revealed and the word of God.

Revelation 20:4 GNB

144.21 I heard a great voice out of heaven saying, Behold, the tabernacle of God is with men, and he will dwell with them, and they shall be his people, and God himself shall be with them, and be their God.

Revelation 21:3 KJV

144.22 Nothing accursed will be found there any more. But the throne of God and of the Lamb will be in it, and his servants will worship him; they will see his face, and his name will be on their foreheads. And there will be no more night; they need no light of lamp or sun, for the Lord God will be their light, and they will reign for ever and ever.

Revelation 22:3–5 NRSV

See also **Reward**

HELL

144.23 Enter through the narrow gate; for the gate is wide and the road is easy that leads to destruction, and there are many who take it.

Matthew 7:13 NRSV

144.24 The children of the kingdom shall be cast out into outer darkness: there shall be weeping and gnashing of teeth.

Matthew 8:12 KJV

144.25 Do not be afraid of those who kill the body but cannot kill the soul; rather be afraid of God, who can destroy both body and soul in hell.

Matthew 10:28 GNB

144.26 Then shall he say also unto them on the left hand, Depart from me, ye

cursed, into everlasting fire, prepared
for the devil and his angels... And these
shall go away into everlasting punishment:
but the righteous into life eternal.

Matthew 25:41, 46 KJV

144.27 Beside all this, between us and
you [heaven and hell] there is a great
gulf fixed: so that they which would pass
from hence to you cannot; neither can
they pass to us, that would come from
thence.

Luke 16:26 KJV

144.28 They will suffer the punishment of
eternal destruction, separated from the
presence of the Lord and from his glorious
might.

2 Thessalonians 1:9 GNB

144.29 Whoever worships the beast and
its image and receives the mark on their
forehead or on their hand will themselves
drink God's wine, the wine of his fury,
which he has poured at full strength into
the cup of his anger! All who do this will
be tormented in fire and sulphur before
the holy angels and the Lamb. The smoke
of the fire that torments them goes up for
ever and ever. There is no relief day or
night for those who worship the beast and
its image, for anyone who has the mark of
its name.

Revelation 14:9–11 GNB

144.30 Then the Devil, who deceived
them, was thrown into the lake of fire and
sulphur, where the beast and the false
prophet had already been thrown; and
they will be tormented day and night for
ever and ever.

Revelation 20:10 GNB

144.31 Whosoever was not found written
in the book of life was cast into the lake
of fire.

Revelation 20:15 KJV

144.32 The legacy for cowards, for those
who break their word, or worship
obscenities, for murderers and the sexually
immoral, and for sorcerers, worshippers of
false gods or any other sort of liars, is the
second death in the burning lake of
sulphur.

Revelation 21:8 NJB

See also Punishment

JUDGMENT

144.33 For those who declare publicly
that they belong to me, I will do the same
before my Father in heaven. But if anyone
rejects me publicly, I will reject him before
my Father in heaven.

Matthew 10:32–33 GNB

144.34 When the Son of man shall come
in his glory, and all the holy angels with
him, then shall he sit upon the throne of
his glory: and before him shall be gathered
all nations: and he shall separate them one
from another, as a shepherd divideth his
sheep from the goats: and he shall set the
sheep on his right hand, but the goats on
the left.

Matthew 25:31–33 KJV

144.35 He [God] has fixed a day on
which he will have the world judged in
righteousness by a man whom he has
appointed, and of this he has given
assurance to all by raising him from
the dead.

Acts 17:31 NRSV

144.36 So you should not pass judgement
on anyone before the right time comes.
Final judgement must wait until the Lord
comes; he will bring to light the dark
secrets and expose the hidden purposes of
people's minds. And then all will receive
from God the praise they deserve.

1 Corinthians 4:5 GNB

144.37 It is God's people who are to judge the world; surely you know that. And if the world is subject to your judgement, are you not competent to deal with these trifling cases? Are you not aware that we are to judge angels, not to mention day to day affairs?

1 Corinthians 6:2–3 REB

144.38 For all of us must appear before the judgement seat of Christ, so that each may receive recompense for what has been done in the body, whether good or evil.

2 Corinthians 5:10 NRSV

144.39 It is appointed unto men once to die, but after this the judgment.

Hebrews 9:27 KJV

144.40 The angels who did not keep their own position, but left their proper dwelling, he has kept in eternal chains in deepest darkness for the judgement of the great day.

Jude v. 6 NRSV

144.41 [They] said to the mountains and rocks, Fall on us, and hide us from the face of him that sitteth on the throne, and from the wrath of the Lamb: for the great day of his wrath is come; and who shall be able to stand?

Revelation 6:16–17 KJV

144.42 I saw a great white throne, and him that sat on it, from whose face the earth and the heaven fled away; and there was found no place for them. And I saw the dead, small and great, stand before God; and the books were opened: and another book was opened, which is the book of life: and the dead were judged out of those things which were written in the books, according to their works. And the sea gave up the dead which were in it; and death and hell delivered up the dead which were in them: and they were judged every man according to their works. And

death and hell were cast into the lake of fire. This is the second death. And whosoever was not found written in the book of life was cast into the lake of fire.

Revelation 20:11–15 KJV

See also **God, Just**

RENEWAL OF ALL THINGS

144.43 Jesus said to them, 'You can be sure that when the Son of Man sits on his glorious throne in the New Age, then you twelve followers of mine will also sit on thrones, to rule the twelve tribes of Israel.'

Matthew 19:28 GNB

144.44 [Jesus Christ] whom the heaven must receive until the times of restitution of all things, which God hath spoken by the mouth of all his holy prophets since the world began.

Acts 3:21 KJV

144.45 The creation itself will be set free from its bondage to decay and will obtain the freedom of the glory of the children of God.

Romans 8:21 NRSV

144.46 The day of the Lord's return will surprise us like a thief. The heavens will disappear with a loud noise, and the heat will melt the whole universe. Then the earth and everything on it will be seen for what they are. Everything will be destroyed. So you should serve and honour God by the way you live. You should look forward to the day when God judges everyone, and you should try to make it come soon. On that day the heavens will be destroyed by fire, and everything else will melt in the heat. But God has promised us a new heaven and a new earth, where justice will rule. We are really looking forward to that!

2 Peter 3:10–13 CEV

144.47 I saw a new heaven and a new earth: for the first heaven and the first earth were passed away; and there was no more sea. And I John saw the holy city, new Jerusalem, coming down from God out of heaven, prepared as a bride adorned for her husband. And I heard a great voice out of heaven saying, Behold, the tabernacle of God is with men, and he will dwell with them, and they shall be his people, and God himself shall be with them, and be their God. And God shall wipe away all tears from their eyes; and there shall be no more death, neither sorrow, nor crying, neither shall there be any more pain: for the former things are passed away. And he that sat upon the throne said, Behold, I make all things new. And he said unto me, Write: for these words are true and faithful.

Revelation 21:1–5 KJV

See also **Renewal**

RESURRECTION

144.48 As they go out they will see the corpses of those who rebelled against me, where the devouring worm never dies and the fire is not quenched. All mankind will view them with horror.

Isaiah 66:24 REB

144.49 Many of those who sleep in the dust of the earth shall awake, some to everlasting life, and some to shame and everlasting contempt. Those who are wise shall shine like the brightness of the sky, and those who lead many to righteousness, like the stars for ever and ever.

Daniel 12:2–3 NRSV

144.50 'I am the God of Abraham, the God of Isaac and the God of Jacob.' He is God, not of the dead, but of the living.

Matthew 22:32 NJB

144.51 Do not be surprised at this; the time is coming when all the dead will hear his voice and come out of their graves: those who have done good will rise and live, and those who have done evil will rise and be condemned.

John 5:28–29 GNB

144.52 Martha saith unto him, I know that he shall rise again in the resurrection at the last day. Jesus said unto her, I am the resurrection, and the life: he that believeth in me, though he were dead, yet shall he live.

John 11:24–25 KJV

144.53 So it is with the resurrection of the dead. What is sown is perishable, what is raised is imperishable. It is sown in dishonour, it is raised in glory. It is sown in weakness, it is raised in power. It is sown a physical body, it is raised a spiritual body. If there is a physical body, there is also a spiritual body.

1 Corinthians 15:42–44 NRSV

144.54 In a moment, in the twinkling of an eye, at the last trump: for the trumpet shall sound, and the dead shall be raised incorruptible, and we shall be changed.

1 Corinthians 15:52 KJV

144.55 The Lord Jesus Christ... will transfigure our humble bodies, and give them a form like that of his own glorious body, by that power which enables him to make all things subject to himself.

Philippians 3:20–21 REB

144.56 For the Lord himself shall descend from heaven with a shout, with the voice of the archangel, and with the trump of God: and the dead in Christ shall rise first.

1 Thessalonians 4:16 KJV

144.57 Then the Devil, who deceived them, was thrown into the lake of fire and sulphur, where the beast and the false prophet had already been thrown; and they will be tormented day and night for ever and ever.

Revelation 20:10 GNB

See also **Eternal life; Jesus Christ, Resurrection; Life**

SECOND COMING OF JESUS

144.58 In my vision at night I looked, and there before me was one like a son of man, coming with the clouds of heaven. He approached the Ancient of Days and was led into his presence.

Daniel 7:13 NIV

144.59 Immediately after the suffering of those days the sun will be darkened, and the moon will not give its light; the stars will fall from heaven, and the powers of heaven will be shaken. Then the sign of the Son of Man will appear in heaven, and then all the tribes of the earth will mourn, and they will see the Son of Man coming on the clouds of heaven with power and great glory… But about that day and hour no one knows, neither the angels of heaven, nor the Son, but only the Father.

Matthew 24:29–30, 36 NRSV

144.60 If I go and prepare a place for you, I will come again, and receive you unto myself; that where I am, there ye may be also.

John 14:3 KJV

144.61 Men of Galilee, why stand there looking up into the sky? This Jesus who has been taken from you up to heaven will come in the same way as you have seen him go.

Acts 1:11 REB

144.62 For if we believe that Jesus died and rose again, even so them also which sleep in Jesus will God bring with him. For this we say unto you by the word of the Lord, that we which are alive and remain unto the coming of the Lord shall not prevent them which are asleep. For the Lord himself shall descend from heaven with a shout, with the voice of the archangel, and with the trump of God: and the dead in Christ shall rise first: then we which are alive and remain shall be caught up together with them in the clouds, to meet the Lord in the air: and so shall we ever be with the Lord.

1 Thessalonians 4:14–17 KJV

144.63 For you are well aware in any case that the Day of the Lord is going to come like a thief in the night.

1 Thessalonians 5:2 NJB

A thief in the night
If something happens like *a thief in the night,* it comes unexpectedly. The expression derives from this verse. The day of the Lord – Jesus Christ's second coming – will take place at a sudden, unforeseen time.

144.64 He will do this when the Lord Jesus appears from heaven with his mighty angels… when he comes on that Day to receive glory from all his people and honour from all who believe.

2 Thessalonians 1:7, 10 GNB

144.65 In the same manner Christ also was offered in sacrifice once to take away the sins of many. He will appear a second time, not to deal with sin, but to save those who are waiting for him.

Hebrews 9:28 GNB

144.66 Look! He is coming with the clouds; every eye will see him, even those who pierced him; and on his account all the tribes of the earth will wail. So it is to be. Amen.

Revelation 1:7 NRSV

STATE BETWEEN DEATH AND RESURRECTION

144.67 The wicked shall be turned into hell, and all the nations that forget God.

Psalm 9:17 KJV

144.68 There was a certain rich man, which was clothed in purple and fine linen, and fared sumptuously every day: and there was a certain beggar named Lazarus, which was laid at his gate, full of sores, and desiring to be fed with the crumbs which fell from the rich man's table: moreover the dogs came and licked his sores. And it came to pass, that the beggar died, and was carried by the angels into Abraham's bosom: the rich man also died, and was buried; and in hell he lift up his eyes, being in torments, and seeth Abraham afar off, and Lazarus in his bosom. And he cried and said, Father Abraham, have mercy on me, and send Lazarus, that he may dip the tip of his finger in water, and cool my tongue; for I am tormented in this flame. But Abraham said… between us and you there is a great gulf fixed: so that they which would pass from hence to you cannot; neither can they pass to us, that would come from thence.

Luke 16:19–26 KJV

144.69 Jesus said unto him, Verily I say unto thee, To day shalt thou be with me in paradise.

Luke 23:43 KJV

144.70 Whosoever liveth and believeth in me shall never die. Believest thou this?

John 11:26 KJV

144.71 Yes, we do have confidence, and we would rather be away from the body and at home with the Lord.

2 Corinthians 5:8 NRSV

144.72 I am pulled in two directions. I want very much to leave this life and be with Christ, which is a far better thing.

Philippians 1:23 GNB

144.73 For if we believe that Jesus died and rose again, even so them also which sleep in Jesus will God bring with him.

1 Thessalonians 4:14 KJV

144.74 To the assembly of the firstborn who are enrolled in heaven, and to God the judge of all, and to the spirits of the righteous made perfect.

Hebrews 12:23 NRSV

144.75 Each of them was given a white robe, and they were told to be patient a little longer, until the roll was completed of their fellow-servants and brothers who were still to be killed as they had been.

Revelation 6:11 NJB

144.76 I heard a voice from heaven saying, 'Write this: Blessed are the dead who from now on die in the Lord.' 'Yes,' says the Spirit, 'they will rest from their labours, for their deeds follow them.'

Revelation 14:13 NRSV

Laughter

145.1 Sarah said, God hath made me to laugh, so that all that hear will laugh with me.

Genesis 21:6 KJV

145.2 Be sure, God will not spurn the blameless man, nor will he clasp the hand of the wrongdoer. He will yet fill your mouth with laughter, and shouts of joy will be on your lips.

Job 8:20–21 REB

145.3 He who sits enthroned in the heavens laughs, the Lord derides them [the nations].

Psalm 2:4 REB

145.4 The righteous will look on, awestruck, then laugh at his plight: 'This is the man', they say, 'who would not make God his refuge, but trusted in his great wealth and took refuge in his riches.'

Psalm 52:6–7 REB

145.5 When the Lord brought us back to Jerusalem, it was like a dream! How we laughed, how we sang for joy!

Psalm 126:1–2 GNB

145.6 Even in laughter the heart finds sadness, and joy makes way for sorrow.

Proverbs 14:13 NJB

145.7 She [the capable woman] is clothed in strength and dignity, she can laugh at the day to come.

Proverbs 31:25 NJB

145.8 A time to weep, and a time to laugh; a time to mourn, and a time to dance.

Ecclesiastes 3:4 KJV

145.9 Choose sorrow over laughter because a sad face may hide a happy heart. A sensible person mourns, but fools always laugh… Foolish laughter is stupid. It sounds like thorns crackling in a fire.

Ecclesiastes 7:3–4, 6 CEV

145.10 A feast is made for laughter, and wine maketh merry: but money answereth all things.

Ecclesiastes 10:19 KJV

145.11 Blessed are you who are weeping now: you shall laugh… Alas for you who are laughing now: you shall mourn and weep.

Luke 6:21, 25 NJB

145.12 [Sinners] be sorrowful, mourn, and weep. Turn your laughter into mourning and your gaiety into gloom.

James 4:9 REB

See also Joy

Law

146.1 The law of the Lord is perfect, converting the soul: the testimony of the Lord is sure, making wise the simple.

Psalm 19:7 KJV

146.2 Open thou mine eyes, that I may behold wondrous things out of thy law.

Psalm 119:18 KJV

146.3 Do not think that I have come to do away with the Law of Moses and the teachings of the prophets. I have not come to do away with them, but to make their teachings come true.

Matthew 5:17 GNB

146.4 Now all the words of the law are addressed, as we know, to those who are under the law, so that no one may have anything to say in self-defence, and the whole world may be exposed to God's judgement. For no human being can be justified in the sight of God by keeping the law: law brings only the consciousness of sin.

Romans 3:19–20 REB

146.5 Do we then make void the law through faith? God forbid: yea, we establish the law.

Romans 3:31 KJV

146.6 For sin shall not have dominion over you: for ye are not under the law, but under grace.

Romans 6:14 KJV

146.7 What then should we say? That the law is sin? By no means! Yet, if it had not been for the law, I would not have known sin. I would not have known what it is to covet if the law had not said, 'You shall not covet.'

Romans 7:7 NRSV

146.8 So then, the Law itself is holy, and the commandment is holy, right, and good.

Romans 7:12 GNB

146.9 In my inmost self I delight in the law of God, but I perceive in my outward actions a different law, fighting against the law that my mind approves, and making me a prisoner under the law of sin which controls my conduct.

Romans 7:22–23 REB

146.10 The Holy Spirit will give you life that comes from Christ Jesus and will set you free from sin and death. The Law of Moses cannot do this, because our selfish desires make the Law weak. But God set you free when he sent his own Son to be like us sinners and to be a sacrifice for our sin. God used Christ's body to condemn sin. He did this, so that we would do what the Law commands by obeying the Spirit instead of our own desires.

Romans 8:2–4 CEV

146.11 Love can cause no harm to your neighbour, and so love is the fulfilment of the Law.

Romans 13:10 NJB

146.12 Yet we know that a person is put right with God only through faith in Jesus Christ, never by doing what the Law requires... For no one is put right with God by doing what the Law requires.

Galatians 2:16 GNB

146.13 So the Law was in charge of us until Christ came, in order that we might then be put right with God through faith.

Galatians 3:24 GNB

146.14 When the fullness of time had come, God sent his Son, born of a woman, born under the law, in order to redeem those who were under the law, so that we might receive adoption as children.

Galatians 4:4–5 NRSV

146.15 This is the covenant that I will make with the house of Israel after those days, says the Lord: I will put my laws in their minds, and write them on their hearts, and I will be their God, and they shall be my people.

Hebrews 8:10 NRSV

146.16 The law contains but a shadow of the good things to come, not the true picture. With the same sacrifices offered year after year for all time, it can never bring the worshippers to perfection.

Hebrews 10:1 REB

146.17 Those who look into the perfect law, the law of liberty, and persevere, being not hearers who forget but doers who act – they will be blessed in their doing.

James 1:25 NRSV

146.18 If ye fulfil the royal law according to the scripture, Thou shalt love thy neighbour as thyself, ye do well.

James 2:8 KJV

See also Bible; Will of God

Laying on of hands

147.1 Israel stretched out his right hand and laid it on the head of Ephraim, who was the younger, and his left hand on the head of Manasseh, crossing his hands, for Manasseh was the firstborn.

Genesis 48:14 NRSV

147.2 He [Aaron] shall put both his hands on the goat's head and confess over it all the evils, sins, and rebellions of the people of Israel, and so transfer them to the goat's head. Then the goat is to be driven off into the desert by someone appointed to do it.

Leviticus 16:21 GNB

147.3 Joshua the son of Nun was full of the spirit of wisdom; for Moses had laid his hands upon him: and the children of Israel harkened unto him, and did as the Lord commanded Moses.

Deuteronomy 34:9 KJV

147.4 He [Jesus] could work no miracle there, except that he cured a few sick people by laying his hands on them.

Mark 6:5 NJB

147.5 He took them up in his arms, put his hands upon them, and blessed them.

Mark 10:16 KJV

147.6 The group presented them to the apostles, who prayed and placed their hands on them.

Acts 6:6 GNB

147.7 While they were offering worship to the Lord and fasting, the Holy Spirit said, 'Set Barnabas and Saul apart for me, to do the work to which I have called them.' Then, after further fasting and prayer, they laid their hands on them and sent them on their way.

Acts 13:2–3 REB

147.8 When Paul had laid his hands on them, the Holy Spirit came upon them, and they spoke in tongues and prophesied.

Acts 19:6 NRSV

147.9 Use the gift you were given when the prophets spoke and the group of church leaders blessed you by placing their hands on you.

1 Timothy 4:14 CEV

147.10 Be in no hurry to lay hands on anyone in dedication to the Lord's service.

1 Timothy 5:22 GNB

147.11 Let us go forward, then, to mature teaching and leave behind us the first lessons of the Christian message. We should not lay again the foundation of turning away from useless works and believing in God; of the teaching about baptisms and the laying on of hands; of the resurrection of the dead and the eternal judgement.

Hebrews 6:1–2 GNB

Laziness

148.1 Go to the ant, thou sluggard; consider her ways, and be wise.

Proverbs 6:6 KJV

148.2 How long wilt thou sleep, O sluggard? when wilt thou arise out of thy sleep?

Proverbs 6:9 KJV

148.3 If you are lazy, you will meet difficulty everywhere, but if you are honest, you will have no trouble.

Proverbs 15:19 GNB

148.4 Our brothers and sisters, we command you in the name of our Lord

Jesus Christ to keep away from all believers who are living a lazy life and who do not follow the instructions that we gave them. You yourselves know very well that you should do just what we did. We were not lazy when we were with you. We did not accept anyone's support without paying for it. Instead, we worked and toiled; we kept working day and night so as not to be an expense to any of you.

2 Thessalonians 3:6–8 GNB

148.5 While we were with you, we used to say to you, 'Whoever refuses to work is not allowed to eat.' We say this because we hear that there are some people among you who live lazy lives and who do nothing except meddle in other people's business. In the name of the Lord Jesus Christ we command these people and warn them to lead orderly lives and work to earn their own living.

2 Thessalonians 3:10–12 GNB

148.6 Besides, they [young widows] will become lazy and get into the habit of going from house to house. Next, they will start gossiping and become busybodies, talking about things that are none of their business.

1 Timothy 5:13 CEV

148.7 We do not want you to become lazy, but to be like those who believe and are patient, and so receive what God has promised.

Hebrews 6:12 GNB

See also **Work**

Leadership

149.1 Let them sit as judges for the people at all times; let them bring every important case to you, but decide every minor case themselves. So it will be easier

for you, and they will bear the burden with you. If you do this, and God so commands you, then you will be able to endure, and all these people will go to their home in peace.

Exodus 18:22–23 NRSV

149.2 The Lord said to Moses, 'Choose a leader from each tribe and send them into Canaan to explore the land I am giving you.'

Numbers 13:1–2 CEV

149.3 [Samuel to Saul] Now your line will not endure; the Lord will seek out a man after his own heart, and appoint him prince over his people, because you have not kept the Lord's command.

1 Samuel 13:14 REB

149.4 People of Jerusalem, run through your streets! Look around! See for yourselves! Search the market places! Can you find one person who does what is right and tries to be faithful to God? If you can, the Lord will forgive Jerusalem.

Jeremiah 5:1 GNB

149.5 Anyone who wants to become great among you must be your servant.

Mark 10:43 NJB

149.6 If it [a man's gift] is leadership, let him govern diligently.

Romans 12:8 NIV

149.7 Besides other things, I am under daily pressure because of my anxiety for all the churches.

2 Corinthians 11:28 NRSV

149.8 Now we ask you, brothers, to respect those who work hard among you, who are over you in the Lord and who admonish you. Hold them in the highest regard in love because of their work.

1 Thessalonians 5:12–13 NIV

149.9 Here is a saying you may trust: 'To aspire to leadership is an honourable ambition.'

1 Timothy 3:1 REB

149.10 What you have heard from me through many witnesses entrust to faithful people who will be able to teach others as well.

2 Timothy 2:2 NRSV

149.11 Do not lord it over the group which is in your charge, but be an example for the flock.

1 Peter 5:3 NJB

See also **Deacons; Elders; Pastor; Service**

Life

150.1 The Lord God formed man of the dust of the ground, and breathed into his nostrils the breath of life; and man became a living soul… And out of the ground made the Lord God to grow every tree that is pleasant to the sight, and good for food; the tree of life also in the midst of the garden, and the tree of knowledge of good and evil.

Genesis 2:7, 9 KJV

150.2 Honour thy father and thy mother: that thy days may be long upon the land which the Lord thy God giveth thee.

Exodus 20:12 KJV

150.3 He made you go hungry, and then he gave you manna to eat, food that you and your ancestors had never eaten before. He did this to teach you that human beings must not depend on bread alone to sustain them, but on everything that the Lord says.

Deuteronomy 8:3 GNB

150.4 I call heaven and earth to witness against you today that I have set before you life and death, blessings and curses. Choose life so that you and your descendants may live.

Deuteronomy 30:19 NRSV

150.5 For I know that my redeemer liveth, and that he shall stand at the latter day upon the earth.

Job 19:25 KJV

150.6 Because thy lovingkindness is better than life, my lips shall praise thee.

Psalm 63:3 KJV

150.7 I shall satisfy him with long life and show him my salvation.

Psalm 91:16 REB

150.8 By finding me [wisdom], you find life, and the Lord will be pleased with you.

Proverbs 8:35 CEV

150.9 Incline your ear, and come unto me: hear, and your soul shall live; and I will make an everlasting covenant with you, even the sure mercies of David.

Isaiah 55:3 KJV

150.10 He said to me, 'O man, can these bones live?' I answered, 'Only you, Lord God, know that.'

Ezekiel 37:3 REB

150.11 God says to them [the people of Israel], 'You are not my people,' but the day is coming when he will say to them, 'You are the children of the living God!'

Hosea 1:10 GNB

150.12 Therefore I say unto you, Take no thought for your life, what ye shall eat, or what ye shall drink; nor yet for your body, what ye shall put on. Is not the life more than meat, and the body than raiment?

Matthew 6:25 KJV

150.13 The gate to life is narrow and the way that leads to it is hard, and there are few people who find it.
Matthew 7:14 GNB

150.14 For what will it profit them if they gain the whole world but forfeit their life?
Matthew 16:26 NRSV

150.15 'I am the God worshipped by Abraham, Isaac, and Jacob.' He isn't the God of the dead, but of the living.
Matthew 22:32 CEV

150.16 These shall go away into everlasting punishment: but the righteous into life eternal.
Matthew 25:46 KJV

150.17 Very truly, I tell you, anyone who hears my word and believes him who sent me has eternal life, and does not come under judgement, but has passed from death to life.
John 5:24 NRSV

150.18 Jesus said unto them, I am the bread of life: he that cometh to me shall never hunger; and he that believeth on me shall never thirst.
John 6:35 KJV

150.19 Then Simon Peter answered him, Lord, to whom shall we go? thou hast the words of eternal life.
John 6:68 KJV

150.20 The thief comes only in order to steal, kill, and destroy. I have come in order that you might have life – life in all its fullness.
John 10:10 GNB

150.21 I give unto them [my sheep] eternal life; and they shall never perish, neither shall any man pluck them out of my hand.
John 10:28 KJV

150.22 Jesus said unto her, I am the resurrection, and the life: he that believeth in me, though he were dead, yet shall he live.
John 11:25 KJV

150.23 Jesus saith unto him, I am the way, the truth, and the life: no man cometh unto the Father, but by me.
John 14:6 KJV

150.24 Because I live, you also will live.
John 14:19 GNB

150.25 Those written here have been recorded in order that you may believe that Jesus is the Christ, the Son of God, and that through this faith you may have life by his name.
John 20:31 REB

150.26 For 'In him we live and move and have our being'; even as some of your own poets have said, 'For we too are his offspring.'
Acts 17:28 NRSV

150.27 For the wages of sin is death; but the gift of God is eternal life through Jesus Christ our Lord.
Romans 6:23 KJV

150.28 If our minds are ruled by our desires, we will die. But if our minds are ruled by the Spirit, we will have life and peace.
Romans 8:6 CEV

150.29 For if you live according to your human nature, you are going to die; but if by the Spirit you put to death your sinful actions, you will live.
Romans 8:13 GNB

150.30 Always carrying in the body the death of Jesus, so that the life of Jesus may also be made visible in our bodies.

2 Corinthians 4:10 NRSV

150.31 I have been crucified with Christ and yet I am alive; yet it is no longer I, but Christ living in me. The life that I am now living, subject to the limitation of human nature, I am living in faith, faith in the Son of God who loved me and gave himself for me.

Galatians 2:20 NJB

150.32 [God] made us alive with Christ even when we were dead in transgressions – it is by grace you have been saved.

Ephesians 2:5 NIV

150.33 For me to live is Christ, and to die is gain.

Philippians 1:21 KJV

150.34 When Christ, who is our life, shall appear, then shall ye also appear with him in glory.

Colossians 3:4 KJV

150.35 Our love for each other proves that we have gone from death to life. But if you don't love each other, you are still under the power of death.

1 John 3:14 CEV

150.36 He that hath the Son hath life; and he that hath not the Son of God hath not life.

1 John 5:12 KJV

See also Adam; Death; Eternal life; Last things

Light

151.1 God said, Let there be light: and there was light.

Genesis 1:3 KJV

151.2 The Lord is my light and my salvation; whom shall I fear? the Lord is the strength of my life; of whom shall I be afraid?

Psalm 27:1 KJV

151.3 Your word is a lamp to my feet and a light to my path.

Psalm 119:105 NRSV

151.4 The entrance of thy words giveth light; it giveth understanding unto the simple.

Psalm 119:130 KJV

151.5 The people that walked in darkness have seen a great light: they that dwell in the land of the shadow of death, upon them hath the light shined.

Isaiah 9:2 KJV

151.6 I will also make you a light to the nations – so that all the world may be saved.

Isaiah 49:6 GNB

151.7 Arise, shine; for thy light is come, and the glory of the Lord is risen upon thee.

Isaiah 60:1 KJV

151.8 Ye are the light of the world. A city that is set on an hill cannot be hid. Neither do men light a candle, and put it under a bushel, but on a candlestick; and it giveth light unto all that are in the house. Let your light so shine before men, that they may see your good works, and glorify your Father which is in heaven.

Matthew 5:14–16 KJV

151.9 In him [the Word] was life; and the life was the light of men. And the light shineth in darkness; and the darkness comprehended it not.

John 1:4–5 KJV

151.10 He [John the Baptist] came as a witness to testify to the light, so that all might believe through him. He himself was not the light, but he came to testify to the light. The true light, which enlightens everyone, was coming into the world.

John 1:7–9 NRSV

151.11 This is the judgement: the light has come into the world, but people preferred darkness to light because their deeds were evil. Wrongdoers hate the light and avoid it, for fear their misdeeds should be exposed. Those who live by the truth come to the light so that it may be clearly seen that God is in all they do.

John 3:19–21 REB

151.12 Jesus spoke to the Pharisees again. 'I am the light of the world,' he said. 'Whoever follows me will have the light of life and will never walk in darkness.'

John 8:12 GNB

151.13 [The Lord Jesus Christ to Paul] I will rescue you from your people and from the Gentiles – to whom I am sending you to open their eyes so that they may turn from darkness to light and from the power of Satan to God, so that they may receive forgiveness of sins and a place among those who are sanctified by faith in me.

Acts 26:17–18 NRSV

151.14 The Scriptures say, 'God commanded light to shine in the dark.' Now God is shining in our hearts to let you know that his glory is seen in Jesus Christ.

2 Corinthians 4:6 CEV

151.15 Be ye not unequally yoked together with unbelievers: for what fellowship hath righteousness with unrighteousness? and what communion hath light with darkness?

2 Corinthians 6:14 KJV

151.16 Though you once were darkness, now as Christians you are light. Prove yourselves at home in the light, for where light is, there is a harvest of goodness, righteousness, and truth.

Ephesians 5:8–9 REB

151.17 Everything exposed by light becomes visible, for it is light that makes everything visible. This is why it is said: 'Wake up, O sleeper, rise from the dead, and Christ will shine on you.'

Ephesians 5:13–14 NIV

151.18 Do everything without complaining or arguing, so that you may be innocent and pure as God's perfect children, who live in a world of corrupt and sinful people. You must shine among them like stars lighting up the sky.

Philippians 2:15 GNB

151.19 He [God] alone is immortal; he lives in the light that no one can approach. No one has ever seen him; no one can ever see him. To him be honour and eternal dominion! Amen.

1 Timothy 6:16 GNB

151.20 You are a chosen race, a royal priesthood, a dedicated nation, a people claimed by God for his own, to proclaim the glorious deeds of him who has called you out of darkness into his marvellous light.

1 Peter 2:9 REB

151.21 This is the message we have heard from him and proclaim to you, that God is light and in him there is no darkness at all.

1 John 1:5 NRSV

151.22 If we say that we have fellowship with him while we are walking in darkness, we lie and do not do what is true; but if we walk in the light as he himself is in the light, we have fellowship with one another, and the blood of Jesus his Son cleanses us from all sin.

1 John 1:6–7 NRSV

151.23 Never again will night appear, and no one who lives there will ever need a lamp or the sun. The Lord God will be their light, and they will rule for ever.

Revelation 22:5 CEV

See also Darkness

Listening

152.1 Then the Lord came, and standing there called, 'Samuel, Samuel!' as before. Samuel answered, 'Speak, your servant is listening.'

1 Samuel 3:10 REB

152.2 They [the heathen] have ears, but they hear not.

Psalm 115:6 KJV

152.3 The wise ear listens to get knowledge.

Proverbs 18:15 REB

152.4 Keep thy foot when thou goest to the house of God, and be more ready to hear, than to give the sacrifice of fools.

Ecclesiastes 5:1 KJV

152.5 The Lord God gives me the right words to encourage the weary. Each morning he awakens me eager to learn his teaching; he made me willing to listen and not rebel or run away.

Isaiah 50:4–5 CEV

152.6 Come to me and listen to my words, hear me and you will have life.

Isaiah 55:3 REB

152.7 Don't listen to the lies of these false prophets, you people of Judah!

Jeremiah 23:16 CEV

152.8 Anyone who has ears should listen!

Matthew 11:15 NJB

152.9 A cloud came, covering them in shadow; and from the cloud there came a voice, 'This is my Son, the Beloved. Listen to him.'

Mark 9:7 NJB

152.10 Remember this, my dear brothers: everyone should be quick to listen but slow to speak.

James 1:19 NJB

152.11 You must do what the Word tells you and not just listen to it and deceive yourselves. Anyone who listens to the Word and takes no action is like someone who looks at his own features in a mirror and, once he has seen what he looks like, goes off and immediately forgets it.

James 1:22–24 NJB

152.12 We belong to God, and everyone who knows God will listen to us. But the people who don't know God won't listen to us.

1 John 4:6 CEV

152.13 Behold, I stand at the door, and knock: if any man hear my voice, and open the door, I will come in to him, and will sup with him, and he with me.

Revelation 3:20 KJV

Loneliness

153.1 He [Elijah] said, I have been very jealous for the Lord God of hosts: for the children of Israel have forsaken thy covenant, thrown down thine altars, and slain thy prophets with the sword; and I, even I only, am left; and they seek my life, to take it away.

1 Kings 19:10 KJV

153.2 He has put my family far from me, and my acquaintances are wholly estranged from me. My relatives and my close friends have failed me.

Job 19:13–14 NRSV

A Job's comforter

A *Job's comforter* is someone who, while perhaps intending to sympathize with a person who is unhappy, in reality makes that person even more unhappy by telling him or her of the hopelessness of the situation. The expression derives from the three 'friends' of Job, who offered him miserable comfort in his affliction: 'Miserable comforters are ye all,' said Job. Nevertheless, even in this affliction Job showed the very great patience which has become proverbially linked with his name.

The expression *to escape by the skin of one's teeth*, to escape something narrowly, also has its origin in the book of Job (Job 19:20).

153.3 He said to them, 'My heart is ready to break with grief. Stop here, and stay awake with me.'

Matthew 26:38 REB

153.4 All Jesus' disciples left him and ran away.

Matthew 26:56 CEV

153.5 About three o'clock Jesus cried with a loud voice, 'Eli, Eli lema sabachthani?' that is, 'My God, my God, why have you forsaken me?'

Matthew 27:46 NRSV

153.6 You know that everyone in the province of Asia... has deserted me.

2 Timothy 1:15 GNB

See also **Comfort, when lonely**

Love

OF GOD

154.1 It was not because you were more numerous than any other nation that the Lord cared for you and chose you, for you were the smallest of all nations; it was because the Lord loved you and stood by his oath to your forefathers,
that he brought you out with his strong hand and redeemed you from the place of slavery, from the power of Pharaoh king of Egypt.

Deuteronomy 7:7–8 REB

154.2 He found him in a desert land, and in the waste howling wilderness; he led him about, he instructed him, he kept him as the apple of his eye. As an eagle stirreth up her nest, fluttereth over her young, spreadeth abroad her wings, taketh them, beareth them on her wings: so the Lord alone did lead him, and there was no strange god with him.

Deuteronomy 32:10–12 KJV

The apple of his eye

The apple of one's eye is a person that one treasures as precious. The phrase comes from this verse, describing God's tender love for his people. The apple was originally a metaphor for the pupil of the eye, since an apple and a pupil are both round. The phrase was applied to someone who was as valuable to a person as his or her own eyes.

154.3 For God so loved the world, that he gave his only begotten Son, that whosoever believeth in him should not perish, but have everlasting life.

John 3:16 KJV

154.4 Hope maketh not ashamed; because the love of God is shed abroad in our hearts by the Holy Ghost which is given unto us.

Romans 5:5 KJV

154.5 God has shown us how much he loves us – it was while we were still sinners that Christ died for us!

Romans 5:8 GNB

154.6 Can anything separate us from the love of Christ? Can trouble, suffering, and hard times, or hunger and nakedness, or danger and death? It is exactly as the Scriptures say, 'For you we face death all day long. We are like sheep on their way to be butchered.' In everything we have won more than a victory because of Christ who loves us. I am sure that nothing can separate us from God's love – not life or death, not angels or spirits, not the present or the future, and not powers above or powers below. Nothing in all creation can separate us from God's love for us in Christ Jesus our Lord!

Romans 8:35–39 CEV

154.7 I have been crucified with Christ; and it is no longer I who live, but it is Christ who lives in me. And the life I now live in the flesh I live by faith in the Son of God, who loved me and gave himself for me.

Galatians 2:19–20 NRSV

154.8 Because of his great love for us, God, who is rich in mercy, made us alive with Christ.

Ephesians 2:4–5 NIV

154.9 He that love God; for God is lov manifested the love because that God s Son into the world, through him. Herei loved God, but that he loved us, and sent his Son to be the propitiation for our sins.

1 John 4:8–10 KJV

See also Faithfulness; God, Loving; Grace; Jesus Christ, Love; Mercy

OF HUMANITY

154.10 Honour thy father and thy mother.

Exodus 20:12 KJV

154.11 You shall not take vengeance or bear a grudge against any of your people, but you shall love your neighbour as yourself: I am the Lord.

Leviticus 19:18 NRSV

154.12 Treat them [foreigners] as you would a fellow-Israelite, and love them as you love yourselves.

Leviticus 19:34 GNB

154.13 I say unto you, Love your enemies, bless them that curse you, do good to them that hate you… For if ye love them which love you, what reward have ye? do not even the publicans the same?

Matthew 5:44, 46 KJV

154.14 Always treat others as you would like them to treat you: that is the law and the prophets.

Matthew 7:12 REB

154.15 See that you don't despise any of these little ones. Their angels in heaven, I tell you, are always in the presence of my Father in heaven.

Matthew 18:10 GNB

A new commandment I give unto
[y]at ye love one another; as I have
[love]d you, that ye also love one another.
[B]y this shall all men know that ye are
my disciples, if ye have love one to
another.

John 13:34–35 KJV

154.17 No one can have greater love
than to lay down his life for his friends.

John 15:13 NJB

154.18 What if I could speak all
languages of humans and of angels? If I
did not love others, I would be nothing
more than a noisy gong or a clanging
cymbal. What if I could prophesy and
understand all secrets and all knowledge?
And what if I had faith that moved
mountains? I would be nothing unless I
loved others. What if I gave away all that I
owned and let myself be burnt alive? I
would gain nothing, unless I loved others.
Love is kind and patient, never jealous,
boastful, proud, or rude. Love isn't selfish
or quick-tempered. It doesn't keep a
record of wrongs that others do. Love
rejoices in the truth, but not in evil. Love
is always supportive, loyal, hopeful, and
trusting... For now there are faith, hope,
and love. But of these three, the greatest is
love.

1 Corinthians 13:1–7, 13 CEV

154.19 The fruit of the Spirit is love...

Galatians 5:22 NRSV

154.20 Husbands, love your wives, as
Christ loved the church and gave himself
up for it.

Ephesians 5:25 REB

154.21 And above all things have fervent
charity among yourselves: for charity shall
cover the multitude of sins.

1 Peter 4:8 KJV

Cover a multitude of sins
If something *covers a multitude
of sins*, it deliberately hides many
different things, especially faults and
weaknesses. The phrase has its origin
in this verse: charity (love) in the
Christian community forgives again
and again.

154.22 Beloved, let us love one another:
for love is of God; and every one that
loveth is born of God, and knoweth
God... Beloved, if God so loved us, we
ought also to love one another... If we
love one another, God dwelleth in us, and
his love is perfected in us.

1 John 4:7, 11–12 KJV

154.23 It follows that when we love God
and obey his commands we love his
children too.

1 John 5:2 REB

See also **Fellowship; Kindness; Neighbor**

OF HUMANITY FOR GOD

154.24 Thou shalt love the Lord thy God
with all thine heart, and with all thy soul,
and with all thy might.

Deuteronomy 6:5 KJV

154.25 So now, O Israel, what does the
Lord your God require of you? Only to
fear the Lord your God, to walk in all his
ways, to love him, to serve the Lord your
God with all your heart and with all your
soul.

Deuteronomy 10:12 NRSV

154.26 I love the Lord, for he has heard
me and listened to my prayer.

Psalm 116:1 REB

154.27 If ye love me, keep my commandments.

John 14:15 KJV

154.28 He that hath my commandments, and keepeth them, he it is that loveth me: and he that loveth me shall be loved of my Father, and I will love him, and will manifest myself to him.

John 14:21 KJV

154.29 We know that all things work together for good for those who love God, who are called according to his purpose.

Romans 8:28 NRSV

154.30 As it is written, Eye hath not seen, nor ear heard, neither have entered into the heart of man, the things which God hath prepared for them that love him.

1 Corinthians 2:9 KJV

154.31 I pray that God will put a curse on everyone who doesn't love the Lord. And may the Lord come soon.

1 Corinthians 16:22 CEV

154.32 You love him, although you have not seen him, and you believe in him, although you do not now see him. So you rejoice with a great and glorious joy which words cannot express.

1 Peter 1:8 GNB

154.33 Those who say, 'I love God', and hate their brothers or sisters, are liars; for those who do not love a brother or sister whom they have seen, cannot love God whom they have not seen. The commandment we have from him is this: those who love God must love their brothers and sisters also.

1 John 4:20–21 NRSV

See also Christian life, Longing for God; Worship

Loyalty

155.1 Ruth said, 'Do not press me to leave you and to stop going with you, for wherever you go, I shall go, wherever you live, I shall live. Your people will be my people, and your God will be my God.'

Ruth 1:16 NJB

155.2 [David to Jonathan] My lord, keep faith with me; for you and I have entered into a solemn compact before the Lord.

1 Samuel 20:8 REB

155.3 Ahimelech replied to the king, 'Of all those in your service, who is more loyal than David?'

1 Samuel 22:14 NJB

155.4 [David's prayer] Shape the purpose of your people's heart and direct their hearts to you, and give an undivided heart to Solomon my son to keep your commandments, your decrees and your statutes, to put them all into effect and to build the palace for which I have made provision.

1 Chronicles 29:18–19 NJB

155.5 They [Israel] were not loyal to him in their hearts, nor were they faithful to his covenant.

Psalm 78:37 REB

155.6 Let faithful love and constancy never leave you: tie them round your neck, write them on the tablet of your heart. Thus you will find favour and success in the sight of God and of people.

Proverbs 3:3–4 NJB

155.7 Guilt is wiped out by loyalty and faith, and the fear of the Lord makes mortals turn from evil.

Proverbs 16:6 REB

155.8 A friend shows his friendship at all times, and a brother is born to share troubles.
Proverbs 17:17 REB

155.9 Some companions are good only for idle talk, but there is a friend who sticks closer than a brother.
Proverbs 18:24 REB

155.10 What matters most is loyalty.
Proverbs 19:22 CEV

155.11 You cannot be the slave of two masters! You will like one more than the other or be more loyal to one than the other. You cannot serve both God and money.
Matthew 6:24 CEV

155.12 I will not leave you comfortless: I will come to you.
John 14:18 KJV

See also **Faithfulness; Friends and friendship**

Lying

156.1 Thou shalt not bear false witness against thy neighbour.
Exodus 20:16 KJV

156.2 God is not a human being, that he should lie, or a mortal, that he should change his mind. Has he promised, and will he not do it? Has he spoken, and will he not fulfil it?
Numbers 23:19 NRSV

156.3 Save me, Lord, from liars and deceivers.
Psalm 120:2 GNB

156.4 They all deceive their neighbours, and no one speaks the truth; they have taught their tongues to speak lies; they commit iniquity and are too weary to repent.
Jeremiah 9:5 NRSV

156.5 Your father is the devil, and you do exactly what he wants. He has always been a murderer and a liar. There is nothing truthful about him. He speaks on his own, and everything he says is a lie. Not only is he a liar himself, but he is also the father of all lies.
John 8:44 CEV

156.6 Peter said to him, 'Ananias, why did you let Satan take control of you and make you lie to the Holy Spirit by keeping part of the money you received for the property? Before you sold the property, it belonged to you; and after you sold it, the money was yours. Why, then, did you decide to do such a thing? You have not lied to human beings – you have lied to God!'
Acts 5:3–4 GNB

156.7 Do not lie to one another, seeing that you have stripped off the old self with its practices.
Colossians 3:9 NRSV

156.8 Those who say that they know him, but do not obey his commands, are liars and there is no truth in them.
1 John 2:4 GNB

156.9 Anyone who denies that Jesus is the Christ is nothing but a liar. He is the antichrist, for he denies both the Father and the Son.
1 John 2:22 REB

See also **Dishonesty; Honesty**

Marriage

157.1 The Lord God said, It is not good that the man should be alone; I will make him an help meet for him.
Genesis 2:18 KJV

157.2 Therefore shall a man leave his father and his mother, and shall cleave unto his wife: and they shall be one flesh.
Genesis 2:24 KJV

157.3 What therefore God hath joined together, let not man put asunder.
Matthew 19:6 KJV

157.4 In the resurrection men and women do not marry; they are like angels in heaven.
Matthew 22:30 REB

157.5 A wife is bound as long as her husband lives. But if the husband dies, she is free to marry anyone she wishes, only in the Lord.
1 Corinthians 7:39 NRSV

157.6 A bishop then must be blameless, the husband of one wife.
1 Timothy 3:2 KJV

157.7 God's Spirit clearly says that in the last days many people will turn from their faith. They will be fooled by evil spirits and by teachings that come from demons. They will also be fooled by the false claims of liars whose consciences have lost all feeling. These liars will forbid people to marry or to eat certain foods. But God created these foods to be eaten with thankful hearts by his followers who know the truth.
1 Timothy 4:1–3 CEV

157.8 Marriage must be honoured by all, and marriages must be kept undefiled.
Hebrews 13:4 NJB

See also **Family, Husbands and wives; Human beings, Male and female; Sex**

ADULTERY

157.9 Thou shalt not commit adultery.
Exodus 20:14 KJV

157.10 The adulterer has no sense; he works his own destruction.
Proverbs 6:32 NJB

157.11 You have heard that it was said, 'Do not commit adultery.' But now I tell you: anyone who looks at a woman and wants to possess her is guilty of committing adultery with her in his heart.
Matthew 5:27–28 GNB

DIVORCE

157.12 Did not one God make her? Both flesh and spirit are his. And what does the one God desire? Godly offspring. So look to yourselves, and do not let anyone be faithless to the wife of his youth. For I hate divorce, says the Lord, the God of Israel… So take heed to yourselves and do not be faithless.
Malachi 2:15–16 NRSV

157.13 It was also said, 'Anyone who divorces his wife must give her a written notice of divorce.' But now I tell you: if a man divorces his wife, for any cause other than her unfaithfulness, then he is guilty of making her commit adultery if she marries again; and the man who marries her commits adultery also.
Matthew 5:31–32 GNB

157.14 'Why then,' they asked, 'did Moses command that a man give his wife a certificate of divorce and send her away?' Jesus replied, 'Moses permitted you to divorce your wives because your hearts were hard. But it was not this way from the beginning. I tell you that anyone who divorces his wife, except for marital unfaithfulness, and marries another woman commits adultery.'

Matthew 19:7–9 NIV

157.15 For married people I have a command which is not my own but the Lord's: a wife must not leave her husband; but if she does, she must remain single or else be reconciled to her husband; and a husband must not divorce his wife.

1 Corinthians 7:10–11 GNB

Meditation

158.1 This book of the law shall not depart out of your mouth; you shall meditate on it day and night, so that you may be careful to act in accordance with all that is written in it. For then you shall make your way prosperous, and then you shall be successful.

Joshua 1:8 NRSV

158.2 His delight is in the law of the Lord; it is his meditation day and night. He is like a tree planted beside water channels; it yields its fruit in season and its foliage never fades. So he too prospers in all he does.

Psalm 1:2–3 REB

158.3 Each of you had better tremble and turn from your sins. Silently search your heart as you lie in bed.

Psalm 4:4 CEV

158.4 Let the words of my mouth, and the meditation of my heart, be acceptable in thy sight, O Lord, my strength, and my redeemer.

Psalm 19:14 KJV

158.5 Be still before the Lord and wait patiently for him; do not fret when men succeed in their ways, when they carry out their wicked schemes.

Psalm 37:7 NIV

158.6 I shall meditate on your precepts and keep your paths before my eyes.

Psalm 119:15 REB

158.7 I remember the days gone by; I think about all that you have done, I bring to mind all your deeds.

Psalm 143:5 GNB

158.8 Mary kept all these things, and pondered them in her heart.

Luke 2:19 KJV

158.9 All of us, with unveiled faces, seeing the glory of the Lord as though reflected in a mirror, are being transformed into the same image from one degree of glory to another; for this comes from the Lord, the Spirit.

2 Corinthians 3:18 NRSV

See also **Mind; Thought**

Mercy

159.1 Then he passed in front of Moses and called out, 'I am the Lord God. I am merciful and very patient with my people. I show great love, and I can be trusted. I keep my promises to my people for ever, but I also punish anyone who sins. When people sin, I punish them and their children, and also their grandchildren and great-grandchildren.'

Exodus 34:6–7 CEV

159.2 With faithfulness and love he leads all who keep his covenant and obey his commands.

Psalm 25:10 GNB

159.3 Have mercy upon me, O God, according to thy loving kindness: according unto the multitude of thy tender mercies blot out my transgressions.

Psalm 51:1 KJV

159.4 Yet I shall not deprive him of my love, nor swerve from my faithfulness.

Psalm 89:33 REB

159.5 O give thanks to the Lord, for he is good, for his steadfast love endures for ever.

Psalm 136:1 NRSV

159.6 The steadfast love of the Lord never ceases, his mercies never come to an end; they are new every morning; great is your faithfulness.

Lamentations 3:22–23 NRSV

159.7 Listen, my God, listen to us; open your eyes and look at our plight and at the city that bears your name. Relying not on our upright deeds but on your great mercy, we pour out our plea to you.

Daniel 9:18 NJB

159.8 For I desire steadfast love and not sacrifice, the knowledge of God rather than burnt-offerings.

Hosea 6:6 NRSV

159.9 He hath shewed thee, O man, what is good; and what doth the Lord require of thee, but to do justly, and to love mercy, and to walk humbly with thy God?

Micah 6:8 KJV

159.10 Blessed are the merciful: for they shall obtain mercy.

Matthew 5:7 KJV

159.11 Be merciful just as your Father is merciful.

Luke 6:36 GNB

159.12 The tax collector stood off at a distance and did not think he was good enough even to look up towards heaven. He was so sorry for what he had done that he pounded his chest and prayed, 'God, have pity on me! I am such a sinner!'

Luke 18:13 CEV

159.13 I beseech you therefore, brethren, by the mercies of God, that ye present your bodies a living sacrifice, holy, acceptable unto God, which is your reasonable service.

Romans 12:1 KJV

159.14 You are the people of God; he loved you and chose you for his own. So then, you must clothe yourselves with compassion, kindness, humility, gentleness, and patience.

Colossians 3:12 GNB

See also **Caring; Faithfulness; God, Merciful; Grace; Love, of God**

Mind

160.1 Those of steadfast mind you keep in peace – in peace because they trust in you.

Isaiah 26:3 NRSV

160.2 Jesus said unto him, Thou shalt love the Lord thy God with all thy heart, and with all thy soul, and with all thy mind.

Matthew 22:37 KJV

160.3 According to his usual habit Paul went to the synagogue. There during three Sabbaths he held discussions with the people, quoting and explaining the Scriptures and proving from them that the Messiah had to suffer and rise from death... Some of them were convinced and joined Paul and Silas.

Acts 17:2–4 GNB

160.4 Knowing God, they have refused to honour him as God, or to render him thanks. Hence all their thinking has ended in futility, and their misguided minds are plunged in darkness.

Romans 1:21 REB

160.5 For those who live according to the flesh set their minds on the things of the flesh, but those who live according to the Spirit set their minds on the things of the Spirit. To set the mind on the flesh is death, but to set the mind on the Spirit is life and peace.

Romans 8:5–6 NRSV

160.6 O the depth of the riches both of the wisdom and knowledge of God! how unsearchable are his judgments, and his ways past finding out! For who hath known the mind of the Lord? or who hath been his counsellor?

Romans 11:33–34 KJV

160.7 Be not conformed to this world; but be ye transformed by the renewing of your mind, that ye may prove what is that good, and acceptable, and perfect, will of God.

Romans 12:2 KJV

160.8 'For who has known the mind of the Lord that he may instruct him?' But we have the mind of Christ.

1 Corinthians 2:16 NIV

160.9 Make your own the mind of Christ Jesus.

Philippians 2:5 NJB

160.10 The peace of God, which surpasses all understanding, will guard your hearts and your minds in Christ Jesus.

Philippians 4:7 NRSV

160.11 Fix your thoughts on that higher realm, not on this earthly life.

Colossians 3:2 REB

See also **Heart; Meditation; Spirit; Thought; Understanding**

Miracles

161.1 Then Moses stretched out his hand over the sea. The Lord drove the sea back by a strong east wind all night, and turned the sea into dry land; and the waters were divided.

Exodus 14:21 NRSV

161.2 Israel saw that great work which the Lord did upon the Egyptians: and the people feared the Lord, and believed the Lord, and his servant Moses.

Exodus 14:31 KJV

161.3 [Elijah's prayer] 'Answer me, O Lord, answer me, so that this people may know that you, O Lord, are God, and that you have turned their hearts back.' Then the fire of the Lord fell and consumed the burnt-offering, the wood, the stones, and the dust, and even licked up the water that was in the trench.

1 Kings 18:37–38 NRSV

161.4 Praise the Lord, the God of Israel! He alone does these wonderful things.

Psalm 72:18 GNB

Miracles of Jesus

	Matthew	Mark	Luke	John
HEALING OF PHYSICAL AND MENTAL DISORDERS				
Leper	8:2–4	1:40–42	5:12–14	
Centurion's servant	8:5–13		7:1–10	
Peter's mother-in-law	8:14–15	1:30–31	4:38–39	
Many demon-possessed	8:16–17	1:32–34	4:40–41	
Two Gadarenes	8:28–34	5:1–20	8:27–39	
Paralyzed man	9:2–8	2:3–12	5:18–25	
Woman with a hemorrhage	9:20–22	5:25–34	8:43–48	
Two blind men	9:27–31			
Man dumb and possessed	9:32–33			
Man with a withered hand	12:10–13	3:1–5	6:6–10	
Man blind, dumb and possessed	12:22		11:14	
Canaanite woman's daughter	15:21–28	7:25–30		
Boy with epilepsy	17:14–18	9:17–29	9:38–43	
Bartimaeus, and another blind man	20:29–34	10:46–52	18:35–43	
Man possessed, synagogue		1:23–26	4:33–35	
Deaf and dumb man		7:32–37		
Blind man at Bethsaida		8:22–26		
Woman bent double			13:11–13	
Man with dropsy			14:1–4	
Ten lepers			17:11–19	
Malchus' ear			22:50–51	
Official's son at Capernaum				4:46–54
Sick man, Pool of Bethesda				5:2–9
Man born blind				9:1–41
COMMAND OVER THE FORCES OF NATURE				
Calming of the storm	8:23–27	4:37–41	8:22–25	
Walking on the water	14:25–27	6:48–51		6:19–21
5,000 people fed	14:15–21	6:35–44	9:12–17	6:5–13
4,000 people fed	15:32–38	8:1–9		
Coin in the fish's mouth	17:24–27			
Fig tree withered	21:18–22	11:12–14, 20–23		
Catch of fish			5:1–11	
Water turned into wine				2:1–11
Another catch of fish				21:4–11
BRINGING THE DEAD BACK TO LIFE				
Jairus' daughter	9:18–19, 23–26	5:22–24, 35–43	8:41–42, 49–56	
Widow's son at Nain			7:11–15	
Lazarus				11:1–44

161.5 Impostors will come claiming to be messiahs or prophets, and they will produce great signs and wonders to mislead, if possible, even God's chosen.

Matthew 24:24 REB

161.6 For nothing is impossible to God.

Luke 1:37 NJB

161.7 Jesus performed this first miracle in Cana in Galilee; there he revealed his glory, and his disciples believed in him.

John 2:11 GNB

161.8 I am telling you the truth: those who believe in me will do what I do – yes, they will do even greater things, because I am going to the Father.

John 14:12 GNB

161.9 Show your mighty power, as we heal people and perform miracles and wonders in the name of your holy Servant Jesus.

Acts 4:30 CEV

161.10 Peter put all of them outside, and then he knelt down and prayed. He turned to the body and said, 'Tabitha, get up.' Then she opened her eyes, and seeing Peter, she sat up.

Acts 9:40 NRSV

161.11 To another the working of miracles.

1 Corinthians 12:10 KJV

161.12 The things that mark an apostle – signs, wonders and miracles – were done among you with great perseverance.

2 Corinthians 12:12 NIV

161.13 God added his testimony by signs and wonders and various miracles, and by gifts of the Holy Spirit, distributed according to his will.

Hebrews 2:4 NRSV

Money and material goods

162.1 If you love money and wealth, you will never be satisfied with what you have. This doesn't make sense either.

Ecclesiastes 5:10 CEV

162.2 Do not store up for yourselves treasure on earth, where moth and rust destroy, and thieves break in and steal.

Matthew 6:19 REB

162.3 No one can serve two masters; for a slave will either hate the one and love the other, or be devoted to the one and despise the other. You cannot serve God and wealth.

Matthew 6:24 NRSV

162.4 [The Pharisees] 'Tell us, then, what you think. Is it lawful to pay taxes to the emperor, or not?' But Jesus, aware of their malice, said, 'Why are you putting me to the test, you hypocrites? Show me the coin used for the tax.' And they brought him a denarius. Then he said to them, 'Whose head is this, and whose title?' They answered, 'The emperor's.' Then he said to them, 'Give therefore to the emperor the things that are the emperor's, and to God the things that are God's.'

Matthew 22:17–21 NRSV

162.5 [A church leader] must not love money.

1 Timothy 3:3 GNB

162.6 Godliness with contentment is great gain. For we brought nothing into this world, and it is certain we can carry nothing out.

1 Timothy 6:6–7 KJV

162.7 For the love of money is the root of all evil.

1 Timothy 6:10 KJV

Money is the root of all evil
The saying *money is the root of all evil* is a misquotation of the biblical text of this verse. It is not money itself, but the love of money that is condemned by Paul in this letter.

162.8 Do not live for money; be content with what you have, for God has said, 'I will never leave you or desert you.'

Hebrews 13:5 REB

See also **Giving**; **Riches**

Motives

163.1 The Lord was pleased with Abel and his offering, but not with Cain and his offering.

Genesis 4:4–5 CEV

163.2 Solomon my son, know thou the God of thy father, and serve him with a perfect heart and with a willing mind: for the Lord searcheth all hearts, and understandeth all the imaginations of the thoughts.

1 Chronicles 28:9 KJV

163.3 A mortal's whole conduct may seem right to him, but the Lord weighs up his motives.

Proverbs 16:2 REB

163.4 Counsel in another's heart is like deep water, but a discerning person will draw it up.

Proverbs 20:5 REB

163.5 We may think we are doing the right thing, but the Lord always knows what is in our hearts.

Proverbs 21:2 CEV

163.6 The heart is deceitful above all things, and desperately wicked: who can know it? I the Lord search the heart, I try the reins, even to give every man according to his ways, and according to the fruit of his doings.

Jeremiah 17:9–10 KJV

163.7 I will take away your stubborn heart and give you a new heart and a desire to be faithful.

Ezekiel 36:26 CEV

163.8 Be careful not to parade your uprightness in public to attract attention; otherwise you will lose all reward from your Father in heaven.

Matthew 6:1 NJB

163.9 Then Judas Iscariot – one of his disciples, the man who was to betray him – said, 'Why was this ointment not sold for three hundred denarii and the money given to the poor?' He said this, not because he cared about the poor, but because he was a thief; he was in charge of the common fund and used to help himself to the contents.

John 12:4–6 NJB

163.10 Do not judge anything before the due time, until the Lord comes; he will bring to light everything that is hidden in darkness and reveal the designs of all hearts. Then everyone will receive from God the appropriate commendation.

1 Corinthians 4:5 NJB

163.11 What does it matter? Only that in both ways, whether with false motives or true, Christ is proclaimed, and for that I am happy.

Philippians 1:18 NJB

163.12 The appeal we make does not spring from delusion or sordid motive or from any attempt to deceive; but God has approved us as fit to be entrusted with the gospel.

1 Thessalonians 2:3–4 REB

163.13 Yet even when you do pray, your prayers are not answered, because you pray just for selfish reasons.

James 4:3 CEV

See also **Right and wrong**

Mourning

164.1 At that time David and all the men with him took hold of their clothes and tore them. They mourned and wept, and they fasted till evening because Saul and Jonathan his son and the army of the Lord and the house of Israel had fallen in battle.

2 Samuel 1:11–12 REB

164.2 [God] giveth rain upon the earth, and sendeth waters upon the fields: to set up on high those that be low; that those which mourn may be exalted to safety.

Job 5:10–11 KJV

164.3 Lord, be thou my helper. Thou hast turned for me my mourning into dancing: thou hast put off my sackcloth, and girded me with gladness.

Psalm 30:10–11 KJV

164.4 I truly prayed for them, as I would for a friend or a relative. I was in sorrow and mourned, as I would for my mother.

Psalm 35:13–14 CEV

164.5 For everything its season, and for every activity under heaven its time… a time for mourning and a time for dancing.

Ecclesiastes 3:1, 4 REB

164.6 Better go to the house of mourning than to the house of feasting; for to this end everyone comes, let the living take this to heart… The heart of the wise is in the house of mourning, the heart of fools in the house of gaiety.

Ecclesiastes 7:2, 4 NJB

164.7 The Lord will be your everlasting light and your days of mourning will be ended.

Isaiah 60:20 REB

164.8 The Spirit of the Lord God is upon me; because the Lord hath anointed me… to comfort all that mourn; to appoint unto them that mourn in Zion, to give unto them beauty for ashes, the oil of joy for mourning, the garment of praise for the spirit of heaviness.

Isaiah 61:1–3 KJV

164.9 I shall change their mourning into gladness, comfort them, give them joy after their troubles.

Jeremiah 31:13 NJB

164.10 Blessed are they that mourn: for they shall be comforted.

Matthew 5:4 KJV

164.11 Alas for you who are laughing now: you shall mourn and weep.

Luke 6:25 NJB

164.12 Jesus wept.

John 11:35 KJV

164.13 [Sinners] be sorrowful, mourn, and weep. Turn your laughter into mourning and your gaiety into gloom.

James 4:9 REB

See also **Comfort, in bereavement and sorrow; Grief**

Murder

165.1 Cain said to his brother Abel, 'Let us go out into the country.' Once there, Cain attacked and murdered his brother. The Lord asked Cain, 'Where is your brother Abel?' 'I do not know,' Cain answered. 'Am I my brother's keeper?' The Lord said, 'What have you done? Your brother's blood is crying out to me from the ground.'

Genesis 4:8–10 REB

My brother's keeper

The phrase to be *one's brother's keeper* is used in contemporary English to mean that one accepts responsibility for another's behavior or well-being. The phrase derives from Cain's reply, 'Am I my brother's keeper?' to God after Cain had killed his brother Abel.

165.2 I created humans to be like me, and I will punish any animal or person that takes a human life. If an animal kills someone, that animal must die. And if a person takes the life of another, that person must be put to death.

Genesis 9:5–6 CEV

165.3 Do not commit murder.

Exodus 20:13 GNB

165.4 Now this is the case of a homicide who might flee there [to special cities] and live, that is someone who has killed another person unintentionally when the two had not been at enmity before: Suppose someone goes into the forest with another to cut wood, and when one of them swings the axe to cut down a tree, the head slips from the handle and strikes the other person who then dies; the killer may flee to one of these cities and live. But if the distance is too great, the avenger of

blood in hot anger might pursue and overtake and put the killer to death, although a death sentence was not deserved, since the two had not been at enmity before.

Deuteronomy 19:4–6 NRSV

165.5 When one person has a feud with another, and lies in wait for him, attacks him, and strikes him a fatal blow, and then takes sanctuary in one of these cities, the elders of his own town must send to fetch him and hand him over to the next-of-kin to be put to death.

Deuteronomy 19:11–12 REB

165.6 You have heard that people were told in the past, 'Do not commit murder; anyone who does will be brought to trial.' But now I tell you: whoever is angry with his brother will be brought to trial.

Matthew 5:21–22 GNB

165.7 All who hate others are murderers, and you know that murderers have not got eternal life in them.

1 John 3:15 GNB

165.8 As for the cowardly, the faithless, the polluted, the murderers, the fornicators, the sorcerers, the idolaters, and all liars, their place will be in the lake that burns with fire and sulphur, which is the second death.

Revelation 21:8 NRSV

Music

166.1 I shall sing, I shall sing to the Lord, making music to the Lord, the God of Israel.

Judges 5:3 REB

166.2 Some of the people of Israel were playing music on small harps and other stringed instruments, and on tambourines, castanets, and cymbals. David and the others were happy, and they danced for the Lord with all their might.

2 Samuel 6:5 CEV

166.3 These are the men whom David appointed to take charge of the music in the house of the Lord when the Ark should be deposited there. They performed their musical duties at the front of the Tent of Meeting before Solomon built the house of the Lord in Jerusalem.

1 Chronicles 6:31–32 REB

166.4 David... assigned special duties to the sons of Asaph... leaders in inspired prophecy to the accompaniment of lyres, lutes, and cymbals.

1 Chronicles 25:1 REB

166.5 Praise the Lord with harp: sing unto him with the psaltery and an instrument of ten strings. Sing unto him a new song; play skilfully with a loud noise.

Psalm 33:2–3 KJV

166.6 We have seen crowds marching to your place of worship, our God and King. The singers come first, and then the musicians, surrounded by young women playing tambourines.

Psalm 68:24–25 CEV

166.7 Sing out in praise of God our refuge, acclaim the God of Jacob. Raise a melody; beat the drum, play the tuneful lyre and harp.

Psalm 81:1–2 REB

166.8 Praise him with the sound of the trumpet: praise him with the psaltery and harp. Praise him with the timbrel and dance: praise him with stringed instruments and organs. Praise him upon the loud cymbals: praise him upon the high sounding cymbals.

Psalm 150:3–5 KJV

166.9 The Lord is at hand to save me; so let the music of our praises resound all our life long in the house of the Lord.

Isaiah 38:20 REB

166.10 The elders have deserted the gateway; the young have given up their music. Joy has vanished from our hearts; our dancing has turned to mourning.

Lamentations 5:14–15 NJB

166.11 Spare me the din of your chanting, let me hear none of your strumming on lyres, but let justice flow like water, and uprightness like a never-failing stream!

Amos 5:23–24 NJB

166.12 Judith said, Begin unto my God with timbrels, sing unto my Lord with cymbals: tune unto him a new psalm: exalt him, and call upon his name.

Judith 16:2 KJV

166.13 When you meet together, sing psalms, hymns, and spiritual songs, as you praise the Lord with all your heart.

Ephesians 5:19 CEV

166.14 With gratitude in your hearts sing psalms and hymns and inspired songs to God.

Colossians 3:16 NJB

See also **Praise**; **Worship**

Name

167.1 He [Abram]… pitched his tent, with Bethel on the west and Ai on the east; and there he built an altar to the Lord and invoked the name of the Lord.
Genesis 12:8 NRSV

167.2 Moses answered, 'I will tell the people of Israel that the God their ancestors worshipped has sent me to them. But what should I say, if they ask me your name?' God said to Moses: I am the eternal God. So tell them that the Lord, whose name is 'I Am', has sent you. This is my name for ever, and it is the name that people must use from now on.
Exodus 3:13–15 CEV

167.3 Thou shalt not take the name of the Lord thy God in vain; for the Lord will not hold him guiltless that taketh his name in vain.
Exodus 20:7 KJV

167.4 The name of the Lord is a tower of strength, where the righteous may run for refuge.
Proverbs 18:10 REB

167.5 Our Father, which art in heaven, hallowed be thy name.
Matthew 6:9 BCP

167.6 For where two or three are gathered together in my name, there am I in the midst of them.
Matthew 18:20 KJV

167.7 Go, then, to all peoples everywhere and make them my disciples: baptize them in the name of the Father, the Son, and the Holy Spirit.
Matthew 28:19 GNB

167.8 Repentance and remission of sins should be preached in his name among all nations, beginning at Jerusalem.
Luke 24:47 KJV

167.9 Anything you ask in my name I will do, so that the Father may be glorified in the Son.
John 14:13 REB

167.10 The Paraclete, the Holy Spirit, whom the Father will send in my name, will teach you everything and remind you of all I have said to you.
John 14:26 NJB

167.11 Then Peter said, Silver and gold have I none; but such as I have give I thee: In the name of Jesus Christ of Nazareth rise up and walk.
Acts 3:6 KJV

167.12 Only Jesus has the power to save! His name is the only one in all the world that can save anyone.
Acts 4:12 CEV

167.13 All were awestruck, while the name of the Lord Jesus gained in honour.
Acts 19:17 REB

167.14 Therefore God also highly exalted him and gave him the name that is above every name, so that at the name of Jesus every knee should bend, in heaven and on earth and under the earth.
Philippians 2:9–10 NRSV

167.15 Whatsoever ye do in word or deed, do all in the name of the Lord Jesus, giving thanks to God and the Father by him.
Colossians 3:17 KJV

Neighbor

168.1 Thou shalt not bear false witness against thy neighbour. Thou shalt not covet thy neighbour's house, thou shalt not covet thy neighbour's wife, nor his manservant, nor his maidservant, nor his ox, nor his ass, nor any thing that is thy neighbour's.

Exodus 20:16–17 KJV

168.2 Never seek revenge or cherish a grudge towards your kinsfolk; you must love your neighbour as yourself. I am the Lord.

Leviticus 19:18 REB

168.3 The man wanted to show that he knew what he was talking about. So he asked Jesus, 'Who are my neighbours?' Jesus replied: As a man was going down from Jerusalem to Jericho, robbers attacked him and grabbed everything he had. They beat him up and ran off, leaving him half dead. A priest happened to be going down the same road. But when he saw the man, he walked by on the other side. Later a temple helper came to the same place. But when he saw the man who had been beaten up, he also went by on the other side. A man from Samaria then came travelling along that road. When he saw the man, he felt sorry for him and went over to him. He treated his wounds with olive oil and wine and bandaged them. Then he put him on his own donkey and took him to an inn, where he took care of him. The next morning he gave the innkeeper two silver coins and said, 'Please take care of the man. If you spend more than this on him, I will pay you when I return.' Then Jesus asked, 'Which one of these three people was a real neighbour to the man who was beaten up by robbers?' The teacher answered, 'The one who showed pity.' Jesus said, 'Go and do the same!'

Luke 10:29–37 CEV

168.4 For the whole Law is summed up in one commandment: 'Love your neighbour as you love yourself.'

Galatians 5:14 GNB

See also **Love, of humanity**

New birth

169.1 Create in me a clean heart, O God; and renew a right spirit within me.

Psalm 51:10 KJV

169.2 I will sprinkle clean water upon you, and you shall be clean from all your uncleannesses, and from all your idols I will cleanse you. A new heart I will give you, and a new spirit I will put within you; and I will remove from your body the heart of stone and give you a heart of flesh. I will put my spirit within you, and make you follow my statutes and be careful to observe my ordinances.

Ezekiel 36:25–27 NRSV

169.3 Jesus answered and said unto him, Verily, verily, I say unto thee, Except a man be born again, he cannot see the kingdom of God. Nicodemus saith unto him, How can a man be born when he is old? can he enter the second time into his mother's womb, and be born? Jesus answered, Verily, verily, I say unto thee, Except a man be born of water, and of the Spirit, he cannot enter into the kingdom of God. That which is born of the flesh is flesh; and that which is born of the Spirit is spirit. Marvel not that I said unto thee, Ye must be born again. The wind bloweth where it listeth, and thou hearest the sound thereof, but canst not tell whence it cometh, and whither it goeth: so is every one that is born of the Spirit.

John 3:3–8 KJV

Born again

Born again in contemporary English is sometimes used to describe an enthusiastic conversion to a particular cause, or even as a synonym for 'renewed; fresh or new'. The origin of the expression is Jesus' explanation to Nicodemus that unless he was reborn spiritually – was radically changed by the Spirit of God in his inner being – he could not see the kingdom of God.

169.4 Therefore if any man be in Christ, he is a new creature: old things are passed away; behold, all things are become new.

2 Corinthians 5:17 KJV

169.5 As for you, you were dead in your transgressions and sins, in which you used to live when you followed the ways of this world and of the ruler of the kingdom of the air, the spirit who is now at work in those who are disobedient. All of us also lived among them at one time, gratifying the cravings of our sinful nature and following its desires and thoughts. Like the rest, we were by nature objects of wrath. But because of his great love for us, God, who is rich in mercy, made us alive with Christ even when we were dead in transgressions – it is by grace you have been saved.

Ephesians 2:1–5 NIV

169.6 [God our Saviour] saved us, not because of any works of righteousness that we had done, but according to his mercy, through the water of rebirth and renewal by the Holy Spirit.

Titus 3:5 NRSV

169.7 For through the living and eternal word of God you have been born again as the children of a parent who is immortal, not mortal.

1 Peter 1:23 GNB

169.8 None of those who are children of God continue to sin, for God's very nature is in them; and because God is their Father, they cannot continue to sin.

1 John 3:9 GNB

See also **Birth; Conversion; Eternal life**

Obedience

170.1 All nations on earth will wish to be blessed as your descendants are blessed, because you have been obedient to me.
Genesis 22:18 REB

170.2 My servant Caleb, because he has a different spirit and has followed me wholeheartedly, I will bring into the land into which he went, and his descendants shall possess it.
Numbers 14:24 NRSV

170.3 All these blessings shall come upon you and overtake you, if you obey the Lord your God…
Deuteronomy 28:2 NRSV

170.4 Samuel said, Hath the Lord as great delight in burnt offerings and sacrifices, as in obeying the voice of the Lord? Behold, to obey is better than sacrifice, and to hearken than the fat of rams.
1 Samuel 15:22 KJV

170.5 Not everyone who calls me their Lord will get into the kingdom of heaven. Only the ones who obey my Father in heaven will get in.
Matthew 7:21 CEV

170.6 If ye love me, keep my commandments.
John 14:15 KJV

170.7 'We gave you strict orders not to teach in this name, yet here you have filled Jerusalem with your teaching and you are determined to bring this man's blood on us.' But Peter and the apostles answered, 'We must obey God rather than any human authority.'
Acts 5:28–29 NRSV

170.8 We are witnesses to this, we and the Holy Spirit whom God has given to those who obey him.
Acts 5:32 NJB

170.9 You used to be slaves of sin. But I thank God that with all your heart you obeyed the teaching you received from me.
Romans 6:17 CEV

170.10 Being found in human form, he humbled himself and became obedient to the point of death – even death on a cross.
Philippians 2:7–8 NRSV

170.11 Even though he was God's Son, he learnt through his sufferings to be obedient.
Hebrews 5:8 GNB

170.12 Be ye doers of the word, and not hearers only, deceiving your own selves.
James 1:22 KJV

170.13 Be obedient to God, and do not allow your lives to be shaped by those desires you had when you were still ignorant. Instead, be holy in all that you do, just as God who called you is holy.
1 Peter 1:14–15 GNB

170.14 We receive from him whatever we ask, because we obey his commandments and do what pleases him.
1 John 3:22 NRSV

170.15 It follows that when we love God and obey his commands we love his children too.
1 John 5:2 REB

See also Blessing; Disobedience; Jesus Christ, Obedience; Respect; Reward; Submission

Occult

171.1 Do not practise divination or sorcery.
Leviticus 19:26 NIV

171.2 Do not go for advice to people who consult the spirits of the dead. If you do, you will be ritually unclean. I am the Lord your God.
Leviticus 19:31 GNB

171.3 Any man or woman who consults the spirits of the dead shall be stoned to death; any person who does this is responsible for his own death.
Leviticus 20:27 GNB

171.4 Let no-one be found among you who sacrifices his son or daughter in the fire, who practises divination or sorcery, interprets omens, engages in witchcraft, or casts spells, or who is a medium or spiritist or who consults the dead. Anyone who does these things is detestable to the Lord.
Deuteronomy 18:10–12 NIV

171.5 Saul died because he was unfaithful and disobeyed the Lord. He even asked advice from a woman who talked to spirits of the dead, instead of asking the Lord. So the Lord had Saul killed and gave his kingdom to David, the son of Jesse.
1 Chronicles 10:13–14 CEV

171.6 Now if people say to you, 'Consult the ghosts and the familiar spirits that chirp and mutter; should not a people consult their gods, the dead on behalf of the living, for teaching and for instruction?' surely, those who speak like this will have no dawn!
Isaiah 8:19–20 NRSV

171.7 Let your astrologers, your star-gazers who foretell your future month by month, persist, and save you! But they are like stubble and fire burns them up; they cannot snatch themselves from the flame. It is not a glowing coal to warm them, not a fire for them to sit by!
Isaiah 47:13–14 REB

171.8 Now for some time a man named Simon had practised sorcery in the city and amazed all the people of Samaria. He boasted that he was someone great.
Acts 8:9 NIV

171.9 Some who had been practising witchcraft even brought their books and burnt them in public.
Acts 19:19 CEV

171.10 Now the works of the flesh are… witchcraft…
Galatians 5:19–20 KJV

See also Demons; Devil

Old age

172.1 Show respect for old people and honour them. Reverently obey me; I am the Lord.
Leviticus 19:32 GNB

172.2 Is wisdom with the aged, and understanding in length of days?
Job 12:12 NRSV

172.3 My times are in thy hand.
Psalm 31:15 KJV

172.4 Do not cast me off when old age comes or forsake me as my strength fails.
Psalm 71:9 REB

172.5 The days of our years are threescore years and ten; and if by reason of strength they be fourscore years, yet is their strength labour and sorrow; for it is soon cut off, and we fly away… So teach us to number our days, that we may apply our hearts unto wisdom.
Psalm 90:10, 12 KJV

> **Threescore years and ten**
> *Threescore years and ten* is seventy years, the period of time that people may be expected to live, or *fourscore*, eighty years, if given the strength. The fine-sounding biblical *threescore years and ten* and *fourscore* still linger on in the English language. It is interesting to note, however, that the original Hebrew had just simply 'seventy' and 'eighty'.

172.6 They [the righteous] are like trees planted in the house of the Lord, that flourish in the Temple of our God, that still bear fruit in old age and are always green and strong.
Psalm 92:13–14 GNB

172.7 Children's children are a crown to the aged, and parents are the pride of their children.
Proverbs 17:6 NIV

172.8 There was a very old prophet, a widow named Anna, daughter of Phanuel of the tribe of Asher. She had been married for only seven years and was now 84 years old. She never left the Temple; day and night she worshipped God, fasting and praying.
Luke 2:36–37 GNB

172.9 For in this tent we groan, longing to be clothed with our heavenly dwelling.
2 Corinthians 5:2 NRSV

172.10 For me to live is Christ, and to die is gain.
Philippians 1:21 KJV

172.11 Instruct the older men to be sober, sensible, and self-controlled; to be sound in their faith, love, and endurance. In the same way instruct the older women to behave as women should who live a holy life. They must not be slanderers or slaves to wine. They must teach what is good.
Titus 2:2–3 GNB

See also **Time**; **Youth**

Oppression

173.1 You shall not wrong or oppress a resident alien, for you were aliens in the land of Egypt.
Exodus 22:21 NRSV

173.2 You shall not withhold the wages of poor and needy labourers, whether other Israelites or aliens who reside in your land in one of your towns.
Deuteronomy 24:14 NRSV

173.3 May the Lord be a tower of strength for the oppressed.
Psalm 9:9 REB

173.4 The Lord judges in favour of the oppressed and gives them their rights.
Psalm 103:6 GNB

173.5 If you ill-treat the poor, you insult your Creator; if you are kind to them, you show him respect.
Proverbs 14:31 CEV

173.6 My eyes are weary with looking upwards. O Lord, I am oppressed; be my security!
Isaiah 38:14 NRSV

73.7 He was oppressed, and he was afflicted, yet he opened not his mouth.
Isaiah 53:7 KJV

173.8 Do not oppress widows, orphans, foreigners who live among you, or anyone else in need. And do not plan ways of harming one another.
Zechariah 7:10 GNB

173.9 Save the oppressed from the hand of the oppressor, and do not be mean-spirited in your judgements.
Ecclesiasticus 4:9 NJB

173.10 You have humiliated the poor man. Moreover, are not the rich your oppressors? Is it not they who drag you into court?
James 2:6 REB

See also **Cruelty; Injustice**

Parables of Jesus

	Matthew	Mark	Luke
Lamp under a bushel	5:14–16	4:21–22	8:16; 11:33
Houses on rock and on sand	7:24–27		6:47–49
New cloth on an old garment	9:16	2:21	5:36
New wine in old wineskins	9:17	2:22	5:37–39
Sower and soils	13:3–8	4:3–8	8:5–8
Mustard seed	13:31–32	4:30–32	13:18–19
Tares	13:24–30		
Leaven (yeast)	13:33		13:20–21
Hidden treasure	13:44		
Pearl of great value	13:45–46		
Drag-net	13:47–50		
Lost sheep	18:12–14		15:4–7
Two debtors (unforgiving servant)	18:23–35		
Workers in the vineyard	20:1–16		
Two sons	21:28–31		
Wicked tenants	21:33–43	12:1–9	20:9–16
Invitation to the wedding feast; man without a wedding-garment	22:2–14		
Fig tree as herald of summer	24:32–33	13:28–29	21:29–31
Ten 'bridesmaids'	25:1–13		
Talents (Matthew); Pounds (Luke)	25:14–30		19:12–27
Sheep and goats	25:31–46		
Seedtime to harvest		4:26–29	
Creditor and the debtors			7:41–43
Good Samaritan			10:30–37
Friend in need			11:5–10
Rich fool			12:16–21
Alert servants			12:35–40
Faithful steward			12:42–48
Fig-tree without figs			13:6–9
Places of honor at the wedding feast			14:7–14
Great banquet and the reluctant guests			14:16–24
Counting the cost			14:28–33
Lost coin			15:8–10
The prodigal son			15:11–32
Dishonest steward			16:1–8
Rich man and Lazarus			16:19–31
The master and his servant			17:7–10
The persistent widow and the unrighteous judge			18:2–8
The Pharisee and the tax-collector			18:10–14

Passover

174.1 Tell the people of Israel that on the tenth day of this month the head of each family must choose a lamb or a young goat for his family to eat… it must be a one-year-old male that has nothing wrong with it. And it must be large enough for everyone to have some of the meat. Each family must take care of its animal until the evening of the fourteenth day of the month, when the animals are to be killed. Some of the blood must be put on the two doorposts and above the door of each house where the animals are to be eaten. That night the animals are to be roasted and eaten, together with bitter herbs and thin bread made without yeast… When you eat the meal, be dressed and ready to travel. Have your sandals on, carry your walking stick in your hand, and eat quickly. This is the Passover Festival in honour of me, your Lord. That same night I will pass through Egypt and kill the firstborn son in every family and the firstborn male of all animals. I am the Lord, and I will punish the gods of Egypt. The blood on the houses will show me where you live, and when I see the blood, I will pass over you. Then you won't be bothered by the terrible disasters I will bring on Egypt.

Exodus 12:3, 5–8, 11–13 CEV

174.2 You are to observe this as a statute for you and your children for all time.

Exodus 12:24 REB

174.3 Now every year his parents went to Jerusalem for the festival of the Passover.

Luke 2:41 NRSV

174.4 They went off and found everything just as Jesus had told them, and they prepared the Passover meal.

Luke 22:13 GNB

174.5 You must remove the old yeast of sin so that you will be entirely pure. Then you will be like a new batch of dough without any yeast, as indeed I know you actually are. For our Passover Festival is ready, now that Christ, our Passover lamb, has been sacrificed.

1 Corinthians 5:7 GNB

See also **Communion; Sacrifice**

Pastor

175.1 The gifts he gave were that some would be apostles, some prophets, some evangelists, some pastors and teachers, to equip the saints for the work of ministry, for building up the body of Christ.

Ephesians 4:11–12 NRSV

175.2 You know that we treated each one of you just as a father treats his own children. We encouraged you, we comforted you, and we kept urging you to live the kind of life that pleases God.

1 Thessalonians 2:11–12 GNB

175.3 You must keep your head whatever happens; put up with hardship, work to spread the gospel, discharge all the duties of your calling.

2 Timothy 4:5 REB

See also **Elders; Leadership; Shepherd; Teachers and teaching**

Patience

176.1 Be still before the Lord and wait patiently for him; do not fret when men succeed in their ways, when they carry out their wicked schemes.

Psalm 37:7 NIV

176.2 If you stay calm, you are wise, but if you have a hot temper, you only show how stupid you are.

Proverbs 14:29 GNB

176.3 They that wait upon the Lord shall renew their strength; they shall mount up with wings as eagles; they shall run, and not be weary; and they shall walk, and not faint.

Isaiah 40:31 KJV

176.4 Or do you despise the riches of his kindness and forbearance and patience? Do you not realize that God's kindness is meant to lead you to repentance?

Romans 2:4 NRSV

176.5 Let your hope make you glad. Be patient in time of trouble and never stop praying.

Romans 12:12 CEV

176.6 Love is patient and kind…
There is nothing love cannot face;
there is no limit to its faith, its hope,
its endurance.

1 Corinthians 13:4, 7 REB

176.7 The Spirit produces… patience…

Galatians 5:22 GNB

176.8 We urge you, brothers, warn those who are idle, encourage the timid, help the weak, be patient with everyone.

1 Thessalonians 5:14 NIV

176.9 Be patient, therefore, beloved, until the coming of the Lord. The farmer waits for the precious crop from the earth, being patient with it until it receives the early and the late rains. You also must be patient. Strengthen your hearts, for the coming of the Lord is near.

James 5:7–8 NRSV

176.10 [To the church in Ephesus] I know what you have done; I know how hard you have worked and how patient you have been. I know that you cannot tolerate evil people and that you have tested those who say they are apostles but are not, and have found out that they are liars.

Revelation 2:2 GNB

See also **Endurance; Waiting**

Peace

177.1 The Lord lift up his countenance upon thee, and give thee peace.

Numbers 6:26 KJV

177.2 His name shall be called Wonderful, Counsellor, The mighty God, The everlasting Father, The Prince of Peace. Of the increase of his government and peace there shall be no end.

Isaiah 9:6–7 KJV

177.3 The Lord gives perfect peace to those whose faith is firm.

Isaiah 26:3 CEV

177.4 There is no peace for the wicked, says the Lord.

Isaiah 48:22 REB

No peace for the wicked
There is no peace for the wicked is often used ironically as a mild comment when one is under pressure or has to do something that one does not want to do. The expression comes originally from the prophet Isaiah: anxiety and fear are experienced by those who do evil.

177.5 When Jesus had been baptized, just as he came up from the water, suddenly the heavens were opened to him and he saw the Spirit of God descending like a dove and alighting on him.

Matthew 3:16 NRSV

177.6 Blessed are the peacemakers: for they shall be called the children of God.

Matthew 5:9 KJV

177.7 Do not think that I have come to bring peace to the world. No, I did not come to bring peace, but a sword.

Matthew 10:34 GNB

177.8 He woke up and rebuked the wind, and said to the sea, 'Peace! Be still!' Then the wind ceased, and there was a dead calm.

Mark 4:39 NRSV

177.9 Glory to God in highest heaven, and on earth peace to all in whom he delights.

Luke 2:14 REB

177.10 [Simeon's 'Nunc Dimittis'] Lord, now lettest thou thy servant depart in peace, according to thy word.

Luke 2:29 BCP

177.11 Whenever you go into a house, first say, 'Peace be with this house.' If a peace-loving person lives there, let your greeting of peace remain on him; if not, take back your greeting of peace.

Luke 10:5–6 GNB

177.12 I give you peace, the kind of peace that only I can give. It isn't like the peace that this world can give. So don't be worried or afraid.

John 14:27 CEV

177.13 These things I have spoken unto you, that in me ye might have peace. In the world ye shall have tribulation: but be of good cheer; I have overcome the world.

John 16:33 KJV

177.14 Jesus came and stood among them. He said to them, 'Peace be with you.'

John 20:19 NJB

177.15 Therefore being justified by faith, we have peace with God through our Lord Jesus Christ.

Romans 5:1 KJV

177.16 To set the mind on the flesh is death, but to set the mind on the Spirit is life and peace.

Romans 8:6 NRSV

177.17 If possible, so far as it lies with you, live at peace with all.

Romans 12:18 REB

177.18 God does not want us to be in disorder but in harmony and peace.

1 Corinthians 14:33 GNB

177.19 The fruit of the Spirit is... peace...

Galatians 5:22 KJV

177.20 For he is our peace; in his flesh he has made both groups into one and has broken down the dividing wall, that is, the hostility between us.

Ephesians 2:14 NRSV

177.21 Your feet shod with the preparation of the gospel of peace.

Ephesians 6:15 KJV

177.22 Then the peace of God, which is beyond all understanding, will guard your hearts and your thoughts in Christ Jesus.

Philippians 4:7 REB

177.23 Let the peace of God rule in your hearts, to the which also ye are called in one body; and be ye thankful.

Colossians 3:15 KJV

177.24 May the Lord of peace himself give you peace at all times and in every way.

2 Thessalonians 3:16 NJB

See also **Quiet**; **Reconciliation**

Perfection

(Completeness, Maturity)

178.1 [David's song of victory] The way of God is blameless; the Lord's word has stood the test; he is the shield of all who take refuge in him.

2 Samuel 22:31 REB

178.2 The law of the Lord is perfect, converting the soul.

Psalm 19:7 KJV

178.3 Be ye therefore perfect, even as your Father which is in heaven is perfect.

Matthew 5:48 KJV

178.4 Jesus said unto him [the rich young man], If thou wilt be perfect, go and sell that thou hast, and give to the poor, and thou shalt have treasure in heaven: and come and follow me.

Matthew 19:21 KJV

178.5 Be not conformed to this world, but be ye transformed by the renewing of your mind, that ye may prove what is that good, and acceptable, and perfect, will of God.

Romans 12:2 KJV

178.6 For our knowledge and our prophecy alike are partial, and the partial vanishes when wholeness comes.

1 Corinthians 13:9–10 REB

178.7 The gifts he gave were that some would be apostles, some prophets, some evangelists, some pastors and teachers, to equip the saints for the work of ministry, for building up the body of Christ, until all of us come to the unity of the faith and of the knowledge of the Son of God, to maturity, to the measure of the full stature of Christ.

Ephesians 4:11–13 NRSV

178.8 Not that I have already obtained all this, or have already been made perfect, but I press on to take hold of that for which Christ Jesus took told of me.

Philippians 3:12 NIV

178.9 All of us who are spiritually mature should have this same attitude. But if some of you have a different attitude, God will make this clear to you.

Philippians 3:15 GNB

178.10 It is he whom we proclaim, warning everyone and teaching everyone in all wisdom, so that we may present everyone mature in Christ.

Colossians 1:28 NRSV

178.11 [The purpose of Scripture] That the man of God may be capable and equipped for good work of every kind.

2 Timothy 3:17 REB

178.12 Even though he was God's Son, he learnt through his sufferings to be obedient. When he was made perfect, he became the source of eternal salvation for all those who obey him.

Hebrews 5:8–9 GNB

178.13 For when for the time ye ought to be teachers, ye have need that one teach you again which be the first principles of the oracles of God; and are become such as have need of milk, and not of strong meat. For every one that useth milk is unskilful in the word of righteousness: for he is a babe. But strong meat belongeth to them that are of full age, even those who by reason of use have their senses exercised to discern both good and evil.

Hebrews 5:12–14 KJV

Strong meat

If something is *strong meat,* it is thought not to be suitable for people who are easily distressed or upset. The expression comes from this verse. The Hebrews needed someone to teach them again the 'milk' of the elementary truths of God's word. They were not yet ready for the 'solid food' of more advanced teaching.

178.14 For by a single offering he has perfected for all time those who are sanctified.

Hebrews 10:14 NRSV

Persecution

179.1 Happy are those who are persecuted because they do what God requires; the Kingdom of heaven belongs to them! Happy are you when people insult you and persecute you and tell all kinds of evil lies against you because you are my followers. Be happy and glad, for a great reward is kept for you in heaven. This is how the prophets who lived before you were persecuted.

Matthew 5:10–12 GNB

179.2 I say unto you, Love your enemies, bless them that curse you, do good to them that hate you, and pray for them which despitefully use you, and persecute you.

Matthew 5:44 KJV

179.3 Such a person has no root, but endures only for a while, and when trouble or persecution arises on account of the word, that person immediately falls away.

Matthew 13:21 NRSV

179.4 Before all this happens they will seize you and persecute you. You will be handed over to synagogues and put in prison; you will be haled before kings and governors for your allegiance to me.

Luke 21:12 REB

179.5 Remember what I told you: 'Slaves are not greater than their master.' If people persecuted me, they will persecute you too; if they obeyed my teaching, they will obey yours too.

John 15:20 GNB

179.6 That day a bitter persecution started against the church in Jerusalem, and everyone except the apostles scattered to the country districts of Judaea and Samaria.

Acts 8:1 NJB

179.7 He fell to the ground and heard a voice saying to him, 'Saul, Saul, why do you persecute me?'

Acts 9:4 NRSV

179.8 Who shall separate us from the love of Christ? Shall tribulation, or distress, or persecution, or famine, or nakedness, or peril, or sword?… Nay, in all these things we are more than conquerors through him that loved us.

Romans 8:35, 37 KJV

179.9 Bless those who persecute you; bless and do not curse.

Romans 12:14 NIV

179.10 Persecution will indeed come to everyone who wants to live a godly life as a follower of Christ Jesus.

2 Timothy 3:12 REB

See also **Comfort, in suffering; Cruelty; Suffering**

Pharisees

180.1 Then the Pharisees went out, and held a council against him, how they might destroy him.

Matthew 12:14 KJV

180.2 The Pharisees went off and made a plan to trap Jesus with questions.

Matthew 22:15 GNB

180.3 Woe unto you, scribes and Pharisees, hypocrites! for ye shut up the kingdom of heaven against men: for ye neither go in yourselves, neither suffer ye them that are entering to go in.

Matthew 23:13 KJV

180.4 One day when Jesus was teaching, some Pharisees and teachers of the Law were sitting there who had come from every town in Galilee and Judea and from Jerusalem.

Luke 5:17 GNB

180.5 The Pharisees, some of whom were scribes, complained to his disciples: 'Why', they said, 'do you eat and drink with tax-collectors and sinners?' Jesus answered them: 'It is not the healthy that need a doctor, but the sick; I have not come to call the virtuous but sinners to repentance.'

Luke 5:30–32 REB

180.6 When the Pharisee saw this, he said to himself, 'If this man really were a prophet, he would know who this woman is who is touching him; he would know what kind of sinful life she lives!'

Luke 7:39 GNB

180.7 The Pharisee was amazed to see that he did not first wash before dinner. Then the Lord said to him, 'Now you Pharisees clean the outside of the cup and of the dish, but inside you are full of greed and wickedness.'

Luke 11:38–39 NRSV

180.8 Jesus told a story to some people who thought they were better than others and who looked down on everyone else: Two men went into the temple to pray. One was a Pharisee and the other a tax collector. The Pharisee stood over by himself and prayed, 'God, I thank you that I am not greedy, dishonest, and unfaithful in marriage like other people. And I am really glad that I am not like that tax collector over there. I go without eating for two days a week, and I give you one tenth of all I earn.'

Luke 18:9–12 CEV

180.9 Even then, many of the Jewish authorities believed in Jesus; but because of the Pharisees they did not talk about it openly, so as not to be expelled from the synagogue.

John 12:42 GNB

180.10 When Paul noticed that some were Sadducees and others were Pharisees, he called out in the council, 'Brothers, I am a Pharisee, a son of Pharisees. I am on trial concerning the hope of the resurrection of the dead.'

Acts 23:6 NRSV

See also **Hypocrisy; Scribes**

Poverty

181.1 You must not deprive the poor man of justice in his lawsuit.

Exodus 23:6 REB

181.2 If there is among you anyone in need, a member of your community in any of your towns within the land that the Lord your God is giving you, do not be hard-hearted or tight-fisted towards your needy neighbour.

Deuteronomy 15:7 NRSV

181.3 He raises the poor from the dust, he lifts the needy from the dunghill to give them a place with princes, to assign them a seat of honour.

1 Samuel 2:8 NJB

181.4 If you oppress poor people, you insult the God who made them; but kindness shown to the poor is an act of worship.

Proverbs 14:31 GNB

181.5 When you give to the poor, it is like lending to the Lord, and the Lord will pay you back.

Proverbs 19:17 GNB

181.6 Blessed are the poor in spirit: for theirs is the kingdom of heaven.

Matthew 5:3 KJV

181.7 You will always have the poor with you, but you won't always have me.

Matthew 26:11 CEV

181.8 Then he called his disciples and said to them, 'Truly I tell you, this poor widow has put in more than all those who are contributing to the treasury. For all of them have contributed out of their abundance; but she out of her poverty has put in everything she had, all she had to live on.'

Mark 12:43–44 NRSV

181.9 The Spirit of the Lord is upon me, because he hath anointed me to preach the gospel to the poor.

Luke 4:18 KJV

181.10 When you give a party, ask the poor, the crippled, the lame, and the blind.

Luke 14:13 REB

181.11 For ye know the grace of our Lord Jesus Christ, that, though he was rich, yet for your sakes he became poor, that ye through his poverty might be rich.

2 Corinthians 8:9 KJV

181.12 Has not God chosen the poor in the world to be rich in faith and to be heirs of the kingdom that he has promised to those who love him? But you have dishonoured the poor.

James 2:5–6 NRSV

See also Debt; Justice; Riches

Power

182.1 They that wait upon the Lord shall renew their strength; they shall mount up with wings as eagles; they shall run, and not be weary; and they shall walk, and not faint.

Isaiah 40:31 KJV

182.2 For thine is the kingdom, and the power, and the glory, for ever. Amen.

Matthew 6:13 KJV

182.3 Jesus answered them, 'You are wrong, because you know neither the scriptures nor the power of God.'

Matthew 22:29 NRSV

182.4 Then will appear in heaven the sign that heralds the Son of Man. All the peoples of the world will make lamentation, and they will see the Son of Man coming on the clouds of heaven with power and great glory.

Matthew 24:30 REB

182.5 At that moment Jesus felt power go out from him. He turned to the crowd and asked, 'Who touched my clothes?'

Mark 5:30 CEV

182.6 Jesus returned in the power of the Spirit into Galilee.

Luke 4:14 KJV

182.7 When the Holy Spirit comes upon you, you will be filled with power, and you will be witnesses for me in Jerusalem, in all Judea and Samaria, and to the ends of the earth.

Acts 1:8 GNB

182.8 For I am not ashamed of the gospel of Christ: for it is the power of God unto salvation to every one that believeth; to the Jew first, and also to the Greek.

Romans 1:16 KJV

182.9 May the God of hope fill you with all joy and peace in believing, so that you may abound in hope by the power of the Holy Spirit.

Romans 15:13 NRSV

182.10 We preach Christ crucified, unto the Jews a stumblingblock, and unto the Greeks foolishness; but unto them which are called, both Jews and Greeks, Christ the power of God, and the wisdom of God.

1 Corinthians 1:23–24 KJV

182.11 We have this treasure in earthen vessels, that the excellency of the power may be of God, and not of us.

2 Corinthians 4:7 KJV

182.12 He said to me, 'My grace is sufficient for you, for power is made perfect in weakness.' So, I will boast all the more gladly of my weaknesses, so that the power of Christ may dwell in me.

2 Corinthians 12:9 NRSV

182.13 How very great is his power at work in us who believe. This power working in us is the same as the mighty strength which he used when he raised Christ from death and seated him at his right side in the heavenly world.

Ephesians 1:19–20 GNB

182.14 Finally, my brethren, be strong in the Lord, and in the power of his might. Put on the whole armour of God, that ye may be able to stand against the wiles of the devil.

Ephesians 6:10–11 KJV

182.15 My one desire is to know Christ and the power of his resurrection, and to share his sufferings in growing conformity with his death.

Philippians 3:10 REB

182.16 I have the strength to face all conditions by the power that Christ gives me.

Philippians 4:13 GNB

182.17 When we told you the good news, it was with the power and assurance that come from the Holy Spirit, and not simply with words.

1 Thessalonians 1:5 CEV

182.18 They [people in the last days] will hold to the outward form of our religion, but reject its real power. Keep away from such people.

2 Timothy 3:5 GNB

182.19 You, who are being protected by the power of God through faith for a salvation ready to be revealed in the last time.

1 Peter 1:4–5 NRSV

See also Authority; Tiredness; Weakness

Praise

183.1 I will bless the Lord at all times; his praise shall continually be in my mouth… O magnify the Lord with me, and let us exalt his name together.

Psalm 34:1, 3 NRSV

183.2 Whoso offereth praise glorifieth me: and to him that ordereth his conversation aright will I shew the salvation of God.

Psalm 50:23 KJV

183.3 Make a joyful noise unto the Lord, all ye lands. Serve the Lord with gladness: come before his presence with singing. Know ye that the Lord he is God: it is he that hath made us, and not we ourselves; we are his people, and the sheep of his pasture. Enter into his gates with thanksgiving, and into his courts with praise: be thankful unto him, and bless his name.

Psalm 100:1–4 KJV

183.4 This people I have formed for myself, and they will proclaim my praises.

Isaiah 43:21 REB

183.5 He hath sent me… to appoint unto them that mourn in Zion, to give unto them beauty for ashes, the oil of joy for mourning, the garment of praise for the spirit of heaviness; that they might be called trees of righteousness, the planting of the Lord, that he might be glorified.

Isaiah 61:1, 3 KJV

183.6 Let us now praise famous men, and our fathers that begat us.

Ecclesiasticus 44:1 KJV

183.7 Day after day they met as a group in the Temple, and they had their meals together in their homes, eating with glad and humble hearts, praising God, and enjoying the good will of all the people. And every day the Lord added to their group those who were being saved.

Acts 2:46–47 GNB

183.8 Speaking to yourselves in psalms and hymns and spiritual songs, singing and making melody in your heart to the Lord.

Ephesians 5:19 KJV

183.9 Let us, then, always offer praise to God as our sacrifice through Jesus, which is the offering presented by lips that confess him as Lord.

Hebrews 13:15 GNB

183.10 Worthy is the Lamb that was sacrificed to receive power, riches, wisdom, strength, honour, glory and blessing.

Revelation 5:12 NJB

See also Celebration; Music; Prayer; Thankfulness and thanksgiving; Worship

Prayer

ANSWERS TO PRAYER

184.1 This poor man cried, and the Lord heard him, and saved him out of all his troubles.

Psalm 34:6 KJV

184.2 When he had entered the house, his disciples asked him privately, 'Why could we not cast it out?' He said to them, 'This kind can come out only through prayer.'

Mark 9:28–29 NRSV

184.3 You co-operate by praying for us. Then, with so many people praying for our deliverance, there will be many to give thanks on our behalf for God's gracious favour towards us.

2 Corinthians 1:11 REB

184.4 Three times I prayed to the Lord about this and asked him to take it away. But his answer was: 'My grace is all you need, for my power is greatest when you are weak.'

2 Corinthians 12:8–9 GNB

184.5 Now unto him that is able to do exceeding abundantly above all that we ask or think, according to the power that worketh in us, unto him be glory in the church by Christ Jesus throughout all ages, world without end. Amen.

Ephesians 3:20–21 KJV

184.6 Do not worry about anything, but in everything by prayer and supplication with thanksgiving let your requests be made known to God. And the peace of God, which surpasses all understanding, will guard your hearts and your minds in Christ Jesus.

Philippians 4:6–7 NRSV

184.7 So whenever we are in need, we should come bravely before the throne of our merciful God. There we will be treated with undeserved kindness, and we will find help.

Hebrews 4:16 CEV

184.8 When you do pray and do not receive, it is because you prayed wrongly, wanting to indulge your passions.

James 4:3 NJB

184.9 The effectual fervent prayer of a righteous man availeth much.

James 5:16 KJV

ENCOURAGEMENTS TO PRAY

184.10 [David's thanksgiving] Seek the Lord and his strength, seek his face continually.

1 Chronicles 16:11 KJV

184.11 The Lord watches over the righteous and listens to their cries.

Psalm 34:15 GNB

184.12 Trust in God at all times, my people. Tell him all your troubles, for he is our refuge.

Psalm 62:8 GNB

184.13 Before they call I will answer, while they are yet speaking I will hear.

Isaiah 65:24 NRSV

184.14 When you pray, go to your room, close the door, and pray to your Father, who is unseen. And your Father, who sees what you do in private, will reward you.

Matthew 6:6 GNB

184.15 He told them a parable to show that they should keep on praying and never lose heart.

Luke 18:1 REB

184.16 Pray without ceasing.

1 Thessalonians 5:17 KJV

184.17 Behold, I stand at the door, and knock: if any man hear my voice, and open the door, I will come in to him, and will sup with him, and he with me.

Revelation 3:20 KJV

HINDRANCES TO PRAYER

184.18 I told you what the Lord had said, but you paid no attention. You disobeyed him… Then you came back to the place of worship at Kadesh-Barnea and wept, but the Lord would not listen to your prayers.

Deuteronomy 1:43, 45 CEV

184.19 If I had cherished evil thoughts, the Lord would not have listened.

Psalm 66:18 REB

184.20 You will ask for my help, but I won't listen; you will search, but you won't find me. No, you would not learn, and you refused to respect the Lord. You rejected my advice and paid no attention when I warned you.

Proverbs 1:28–30 CEV

184.21 If you won't help the poor, don't expect to be heard when you cry out for help.

Proverbs 21:13 CEV

184.22 When ye spread forth your hands, I will hide mine eyes from you: yea, when ye make many prayers, I will not hear: your hands are full of blood. Wash you, make you clean; put away the evil of your doings from before mine eyes; cease to do evil; learn to do well; seek judgment, relieve the oppressed, judge the fatherless, plead for the widow.

Isaiah 1:15–17 KJV

184.23 Your iniquities have separated between you and your God, and your sins have hid his face from you, that he will not hear.

Isaiah 59:2 KJV

184.24 Then they will call to the Lord, but he will not answer. When that time comes he will hide his face from them, so wicked are their deeds.

Micah 3:4 REB

184.25 They were adamant in their refusal to accept the law and the teaching which the Lord of Hosts had sent by his spirit through the prophets of old; and in great anger the Lord of Hosts said: As they did not listen when I called, so I would not listen when they called.

Zechariah 7:12–13 REB

184.26 When you pray, do not be like the hypocrites; they love to say their prayers standing up in synagogues and at street corners for everyone to see them. Truly I tell you: they have their reward already. But when you pray, go into a room by yourself, shut the door, and pray to your Father who is in secret; and your Father who sees what is done in secret will reward you. In your prayers do not go babbling on like the heathen, who imagine that the more they say the more likely they are to be heard. Do not imitate them, for your Father knows what your needs are before you ask him.

Matthew 6:5–8 REB

184.27 Now it is impossible to please God without faith, since anyone who comes to him must believe that he exists and rewards those who seek him.

Hebrews 11:6 NJB

184.28 When you ask for something, you must have faith and not doubt.

James 1:6 CEV

184.29 When you do pray and do not receive, it is because you prayed wrongly, wanting to indulge your passions.

James 4:3 NJB

184.30 We are certain that God will hear our prayers when we ask for what pleases him.

1 John 5:14 CEV

Prayers of the Bible

Abraham's prayer for Sodom
Genesis 18:22–33

Isaac's blessing
Genesis 27:28–29

Jacob's desperate prayer at Penuel
Genesis 32:9–12

Jacob blesses his sons
Genesis 48:15–16, 20; 49:1–27

Moses' song of thanksgiving for deliverance from Egypt
Exodus 15:1–18

Moses' plea for Israel when they had worshipped the golden calf
Exodus 32:31–32; Deuteronomy 9:15–21

Moses asks to see God's glory
Exodus 33:18–23

Aaron's blessing
Numbers 6:22–27

Moses' song: God and his people
Deuteronomy 32:1–43

Moses blesses the people of Israel
Deuteronomy 33

Deborah's song of thanksgiving for victory
Judges 5

Gideon's prayer for signs
Judges 6:17–18, 36–40

Hannah's prayer for a son
1 Samuel 1:9–18

Hannah's thanksgiving
1 Samuel 2:1–10

Samuel's prayer for the nation
1 Samuel 7:7–11

David's prayer following God's promise of a lasting succession
2 Samuel 7:22–29; 1 Chronicles 17:16–27

David's song of thanksgiving for deliverance
2 Samuel 22; Psalm 18:

Solomon's prayer for wisdom
1 Kings 3:7–9; 2 Chronicles 1:7–10

Solomon's prayer at the dedication of the temple
1 Kings 8; 2 Chronicles 6

Elijah's prayer on Mt Carmel
1 Kings 18:36–39

Elijah and the 'still, small voice'
1 Kings 19:4–18

Hezekiah's prayer at the time of Sennacherib's siege
2 Kings 19:15–19; Isaiah 37:16–20

Thanksgiving as the ark is brought to Jerusalem
1 Chronicles 16:8–36

David's prayer for Solomon
1 Chronicles 29:10–19

Ezra's confession of the nation's sin
Ezra 9:6–15

Nehemiah's prayer for his people
Nehemiah 1:5–11

The public confession led by Ezra
Nehemiah 9:5–37

Job seeks the reason for his suffering
Job 10

Job pleads his case
Job 13–14

Job's confession
Job 42:1–6

The Psalms include a large number of prayers: some are listed here, under themes:

Evening prayer, 4

Morning prayer, 5

The shepherd psalm, 23

Praise and worship, 24; 67; 92; 95–98; 100; 113; 145; 148; 150

Guidance, 25

Trust, 37; 62

Deliverance, 40; 116

Longing for God, 27; 42; 63; 84

Forgiveness, 51; 130

Thanksgiving, 65; 111; 136

Help in trouble, 69; 86; 88; 102; 140; 143

God's constant love and care, 89; 103; 107; 146

God's majesty and glory, 8; 29; 93; 104

God's knowledge and presence, 139

God's word, 19; 119

God's protection, 46; 91; 125

Prayers of Isaiah
Isaiah 25; 33:2–24; 63–64

Hezekiah's prayer in his illness
Isaiah 38:10–20

Jeremiah's prayers
Jeremiah 11:20; 14:2–9, 19–22; 20:7–18; 32:17–25

The king's dream: Daniel's prayer
Daniel 2:20–23

Nebuchadnezzar praises God
Daniel 4:34–35

Daniel's prayer at the end of the exile
Daniel 9:4–19

Jonah's prayer
Jonah 2:2–9

Habakkuk questions God
Habakkuk 1:2–17

Habakkuk's prayer
Habakkuk 3:2–19

PRAYERS OF JESUS

The Lord's Prayer
Matthew 6:9–13; Luke 11:2–4

In the Garden of Gethsemane
Matthew 26:36–44; Mark 14:32–39; Luke 22:40–46

From the cross
Matthew 27:46; Mark 15:34; Luke 23:34, 46

At the raising of Lazarus
John 11:41–42

Facing death
John 12:27–28

For his followers
John 17

Mary's thanksgiving ('Magnificat')
Luke 1:46–55

Zechariah's prayer ('Benedictus')
Luke 1:68–79

Simeon's prayer ('Nunc Dimittis')
Luke 2:29–35

Prayers of the Pharisee and the tax-collector
Luke 18:10–14

The church's prayer in the face of threats
Acts 4:24–30

Stephen's prayer at his death
Acts 7:59–60

PRAYERS OF PAUL

For the Christians at Rome
Romans 1:8–10

For Israel
Romans 10:1

For the church at Corinth
1 Corinthians 1:4–9; 2 Corinthians 13:7–9

Thanksgiving for God's comfort in trouble
2 Corinthians 1:3–4

Thanksgiving for spiritual riches in Christ
Ephesians 1:3–14

For the Ephesian Christians
Ephesians 1:16–23; 3:14–19

For the Philippian Christians
Philippians 1:3–11

For the church at Colossae
Colossians 1:3–14

For the Thessalonian Christians
1 Thessalonians 1:2–3; 2:13; 3:9–13; 5:23; 2 Thessalonians 1:3; 2:13, 16–17; 3:16, 18

For Timothy
2 Timothy 1:3–4

For Philemon
Philemon 4–6

DOXOLOGIES, PRAISE TO GOD, AND BENEDICTIONS
Romans 16:25–27; Ephesians 3:20–21; Philippians 4:20; 1 Thessalonians 3:11–13; Hebrews 13:20–21, 1 Peter 5:10–11; 2 Peter 3:18; Jude vv. 24–25

HOW TO PRAY

184.31 When you pray, do not use a lot of meaningless words, as the pagans do, who think that their gods will hear them because their prayers are long. Do not be like them. Your Father already knows what you need before you ask him. This, then, is how you should pray...

Matthew 6:7–9 GNB

184.32 Our Father, which art in heaven, hallowed be thy name. Thy kingdom come. Thy will be done, in earth as it is in heaven. Give us this day our daily bread. And forgive us our trespasses, as we forgive them that trespass against us. And lead us not into temptation; but deliver us from evil.

Matthew 6:9–13 BCP

184.33 For thine is the kingdom, and the power, and the glory, for ever. Amen.

Matthew 6:13 KJV

184.34 Stay awake, and pray that you may be spared the test. The spirit is willing, but the flesh is weak.

Matthew 26:41 REB

184.35 Likewise the Spirit helps us in our weakness; for we do not know how to pray as we ought, but that very Spirit intercedes with sighs too deep for words.

Romans 8:26 NRSV

184.36 Praying always with all prayer and supplication in the Spirit, and watching thereunto with all perseverance and supplication for all saints; and for me, that utterance may be given unto me, that I may open my mouth boldly, to make known the mystery of the gospel.

Ephesians 6:18–19 KJV

184.37 I exhort, therefore, that, first of all, supplications, prayers, intercessions, and giving of thanks, be made for all men; for kings, and for all that are in authority; that we may lead a quiet and peaceable life in all godliness and honesty.

1 Timothy 2:1–2 KJV

184.38 If any of you is lacking in wisdom, ask God, who gives to all generously and ungrudgingly, and it will be given you. But ask in faith, never doubting, for the one who doubts is like a wave of the sea, driven and tossed by the wind.

James 1:5–6 NRSV

PROMISES IN PRAYER

184.39 [The Lord's promise to Solomon] If my people, which are called by my name, shall humble themselves, and pray, and seek my face, and turn from their wicked ways; then will I hear from heaven, and will forgive their sin, and will heal their land.

2 Chronicles 7:14 KJV

184.40 Delight in the Lord, and he will grant you your heart's desire.

Psalm 37:4 REB

184.41 If my thoughts had been sinful, he would have refused to hear me.

Psalm 66:18 CEV

184.42 Ask, and it will be given to you; search, and you will find; knock, and the door will be opened for you. For everyone who asks receives, and everyone who searches finds, and for everyone who knocks, the door will be opened.

Matthew 7:7–8 NRSV

184.43 I tell you more: whenever two of you on earth agree about anything you pray for, it will be done for you by my Father in heaven. For where two or three come together in my name, I am there with them.

Matthew 18:19–20 GNB

184.44 If you have faith, everything you ask for in prayer, you will receive.
Matthew 21:22 NJB

184.45 Whatever you ask in my name I will do, so that the Father may be glorified in the Son.
John 14:13 NJB

184.46 Abide in me as I abide in you. Just as the branch cannot bear fruit by itself unless it abides in the vine, neither can you unless you abide in me… If you abide in me, and my words abide in you, ask for whatever you wish, and it will be done for you.
John 15:4, 7 NRSV

184.47 When that day comes you will ask me nothing more. In very truth I tell you, if you ask the Father for anything in my name, he will give it you. So far you have asked nothing in my name. Ask and you will receive, that your joy may be complete.
John 16:23–24 REB

184.48 Whatsoever we ask, we receive of him, because we keep his commandments, and do those things that are pleasing in his sight.
1 John 3:22 KJV

184.49 We are certain that God will hear our prayers when we ask for what pleases him.
1 John 5:14 CEV

See also Access; Praise; Worship

Preaching

185.1 How beautiful upon the mountains are the feet of him that bringeth good tidings, that publisheth peace; that bringeth good tidings of good, that publisheth salvation; that saith unto Zion, Thy God reigneth!
Isaiah 52:7 KJV

185.2 The Spirit of the Lord God is upon me; because the Lord hath anointed me to preach good tidings unto the meek…
Isaiah 61:1 KJV

185.3 Repentance and remission of sins should be preached in his name among all nations, beginning at Jerusalem.
Luke 24:47 KJV

185.4 I [Paul] have disclosed to you the whole purpose of God.
Acts 20:27 REB

185.5 How are they to call on one in whom they have not believed? And how are they to believe in one of whom they have never heard? And how are they to hear without someone to proclaim him? And how are they to proclaim him unless they are sent? As it is written, 'How beautiful are the feet of those who bring good news!'
Romans 10:14–15 NRSV

185.6 For after that in the wisdom of God the world by wisdom knew not God, it pleased God by the foolishness of preaching to save them that believe… But we preach Christ crucified, unto the Jews a stumblingblock, and unto the Greeks foolishness; but unto them which are called, both Jews and Greeks, Christ the power of God, and the wisdom of God.
1 Corinthians 1:21, 23–24 KJV

185.7 In fact, preaching the gospel gives me nothing to boast of, for I am under compulsion and I should be in trouble if I failed to do it.
1 Corinthians 9:16 NJB

185.8 For we brought the Good News to you, not with words only, but also with power and the Holy Spirit, and with complete conviction of its truth.

1 Thessalonians 1:5 GNB

185.9 Until I arrive, be sure to keep on reading the Scriptures in worship, and don't stop preaching and teaching.

1 Timothy 4:13 CEV

185.10 Church leaders who do their job well deserve to be paid twice as much, especially if they work hard at preaching and teaching.

1 Timothy 5:17 CEV

185.11 Do your best to present yourself to God as one approved by him, a worker who has no need to be ashamed, rightly explaining the word of truth.

2 Timothy 2:15 NRSV

185.12 Preach the word; be instant in season, out of season; reprove, rebuke, exhort with all longsuffering and doctrine.

2 Timothy 4:2 KJV

See also **Teachers and teaching; Witness**

Pride

186.1 Do not say to yourself, 'My power and the might of my own hand have gained me this wealth.'

Deuteronomy 8:17 NRSV

186.2 Pride goeth before destruction, and an haughty spirit before a fall.

Proverbs 16:18 KJV

Pride goes before a fall

The English proverb *pride goes before a fall* means that a person who behaves in an overconfident and vain manner is soon likely to suffer misfortune. The expression is a rendering of this verse.

186.3 Whoever exalts himself will be humbled; and whoever humbles himself will be exalted.

Matthew 23:12 REB

186.4 It is what comes out of a person that defiles. For it is from within, from the human heart, that evil intentions come: fornication, theft, murder, adultery, avarice, wickedness, deceit, licentiousness, envy, slander, pride, folly.

Mark 7:20–22 NRSV

186.5 He hath shewed strength with his arm, he hath scattered the proud in the imaginations of their hearts.

Luke 1:51 BCP

186.6 For by the grace given to me I say to everyone among you not to think of yourself more highly than you ought to think, but to think with sober judgement, each according to the measure of faith that God has assigned.

Romans 12:3 NRSV

186.7 Do not be proud, but be willing to associate with people of low position. Do not be conceited.

Romans 12:16 NIV

186.8 As scripture says: 'If anyone wants to boast, let him boast of the Lord.'

1 Corinthians 1:31 NJB

186.9 Even if you think you can stand up to temptation, be careful not to fall.

1 Corinthians 10:12 CEV

186.10 Love is kind and patient, never jealous, boastful, proud, or rude.

1 Corinthians 13:4–5 CEV

186.11 To keep me from being unduly elated by the magnificence of such revelations, I was given a thorn in my flesh, a messenger of Satan sent to buffet me; this was to save me from being unduly elated.

2 Corinthians 12:7 REB

See also **Conceit; Dignity; Humility; Self-righteousness**

Priest

187.1 You will be to me a kingdom of priests, my holy nation.

Exodus 19:6 REB

187.2 Then bring near to you your brother Aaron, and his sons with him, from among the Israelites, to serve me as priests.

Exodus 28:1 NRSV

187.3 Whenever cattle or sheep are sacrificed, the priests are to be given the shoulder, the jaw, and the stomach.

Deuteronomy 18:3 GNB

187.4 Then the priests, the sons of Levi, shall come forward, for the Lord your God has chosen them to minister to him and to pronounce blessings in the name of the Lord, and by their decision all cases of dispute and assault shall be settled.

Deuteronomy 21:5 NRSV

187.5 They shall teach Jacob thy judgments, and Israel thy law: they shall put incense before thee, and whole burnt sacrifice upon thine altar.

Deuteronomy 33:10 KJV

187.6 Then they led Jesus away to the high priest's house, where the chief priests, elders, and scribes were all assembling.

Mark 14:53 REB

187.7 So Judas went off and spoke with the chief priests and the officers of the temple guard about how he could betray Jesus to them.

Luke 22:4 GNB

187.8 The word of the Lord continued to spread: the number of disciples in Jerusalem was greatly increased, and a large group of priests made their submission to the faith.

Acts 6:7 NJB

187.9 Every high priest chosen from among mortals is put in charge of things pertaining to God on their behalf, to offer gifts and sacrifices for sins. He is able to deal gently with the ignorant and wayward, since he himself is subject to weakness; and because of this he must offer sacrifice for his own sins as well as for those of the people. And one does not presume to take this honour, but takes it only when called by God, just as Aaron was.

Hebrews 5:1–4 NRSV

187.10 Since all priests must offer gifts and sacrifices, Christ also needed to have something to offer.

Hebrews 8:3 CEV

187.11 The priests do their work each day, and they keep on offering sacrifices that can never take away sins. But Christ offered himself as a sacrifice that is good for ever. Now he is sitting at God's right side.

Hebrews 10:11–12 CEV

187.12 Like living stones, let yourselves be built into a spiritual house, to be a holy priesthood, to offer spiritual sacrifices acceptable to God through Jesus Christ… you are a chosen race, a royal priesthood, a holy nation, God's own people.

1 Peter 2:5, 9 NRSV

See also **Jesus Christ, Jesus as priest**

Privilege

188.1 When I consider thy heavens, the work of thy fingers, the moon and the stars, which thou hast ordained; what is man, that thou art mindful of him? and the son of man, that thou visitest him? For thou hast made him a little lower than the angels, and hast crowned him with glory and honour. Thou madest him to have dominion over the works of thy hands; thou hast put all things under his feet.

Psalm 8:3–6 KJV

188.2 The disciples came, and said unto him, Why speakest thou unto them in parables? He answered and said unto them, Because it is given unto you to know the mysteries of the kingdom of heaven, but to them it is not given.

Matthew 13:10–11 KJV

188.3 When he was alone with his disciples he turned to them and said, 'Happy the eyes that see what you are seeing! I tell you, many prophets and kings wished to see what you now see, yet never saw it; to hear what you hear, yet never heard it.'

Luke 10:23–24 REB

188.4 Where someone has been given much, much will be expected of him; and the more he has had entrusted to him the more will be demanded of him.

Luke 12:48 REB

188.5 Eternal life is this: to know you, the only true God, and Jesus Christ whom you have sent.

John 17:3 NJB

188.6 Through him [Jesus Christ our Lord] I received the privilege of an apostolic commission to bring people of all nations to faith and obedience in his name.

Romans 1:5 REB

188.7 Therefore being justified by faith, we have peace with God through our Lord Jesus Christ: by whom also we have access by faith into this grace wherein we stand, and rejoice in hope of the glory of God. And not only so, but we glory in tribulations also: knowing that tribulation worketh patience; and patience, experience; and experience, hope: and hope maketh not ashamed; because the love of God is shed abroad in our hearts by the Holy Ghost which is given unto us.

Romans 5:1–5 KJV

188.8 There is great grief and unceasing sorrow in my heart. I would even pray to be an outcast myself, cut off from Christ, if it would help my brothers, my kinsfolk by natural descent. They are descendants of Israel, chosen to be God's sons; theirs is the glory of the divine presence, theirs the covenants, the law, the temple worship, and the promises. The patriarchs are theirs, and from them by natural descent came the Messiah.

Romans 9:2–5 REB

188.9 For, as I can testify, they [the Macedonian churches] voluntarily gave according to their means, and even beyond their means, begging us earnestly for the privilege of sharing in this ministry to the saints.

2 Corinthians 8:3–4 NRSV

188.10 God sent his Son, born of a woman, born a subject of the Law, to redeem the subjects of the Law, so that we could receive adoption as sons. As you are sons, God has sent into our hearts the Spirit of his Son crying, 'Abba, Father'; and so you are no longer a slave, but a son; and if a son, then an heir, by God's own act.

Galatians 4:4–7 NJB

188.11 Blessed be God the Father of our Lord Jesus Christ, who has blessed us with all the spiritual blessings of heaven in

Christ. Thus he chose us in Christ before the world was made to be holy and faultless before him in love, marking us out for himself beforehand, to be adopted sons, through Jesus Christ. Such was his purpose and good pleasure.

Ephesians 1:3–5 NJB

188.12 In him [Christ Jesus our Lord] we are bold enough to approach God in complete confidence, through our faith in him.

Ephesians 3:12 NJB

188.13 It is he who has rescued us from the ruling force of darkness and transferred us to the kingdom of the Son that he loves, and in him we enjoy our freedom, the forgiveness of sin.

Colossians 1:13–14 NJB

188.14 So now, my friends, the blood of Jesus makes us free to enter the sanctuary with confidence by the new and living way which he has opened for us through the curtain, the way of his flesh. We have a great priest set over the household of God.

Hebrews 10:19–21 REB

188.15 You are God's chosen and special people. You are a group of royal priests and a holy nation. God has brought you out of darkness into his marvellous light. Now you must tell all the wonderful things that he has done. The Scriptures say, 'Once you were nobody. Now you are God's people. At one time no one had pity on you. Now God has treated you with kindness.'

1 Peter 2:9–10 CEV

188.16 Since everything is coming to an end like this, what holy and saintly lives you should be living while you wait for the Day of God to come, and try to hasten its coming.

2 Peter 3:11–12 NJB

188.17 You must see what great love the Father has lavished on us by letting us be called God's children – which is what we are!

1 John 3:1 NJB

See also **Responsibility, human**

Promise

189.1 Behold, I send the promise of my Father upon you: but tarry ye in the city of Jerusalem, until ye be endued with power from on high.

Luke 24:49 KJV

189.2 It is not the natural children who are God's children, but it is the children of the promise who are regarded as Abraham's offspring.

Romans 9:8 NIV

189.3 For in him [Jesus Christ] every one of God's promises is a 'Yes'.

2 Corinthians 1:20 NRSV

189.4 You were at that time separate from Christ, excluded from the community of Israel, strangers to God's covenants and the promise that goes with them. Yours was a world without hope and without God.

Ephesians 2:12 REB

189.5 Jesus has been given priestly work which is superior to theirs, just as the covenant which he arranged between God and his people is a better one, because it is based on promises of better things.

Hebrews 8:6 GNB

189.6 Let us hold fast the profession of our faith without wavering; (for he is faithful that promised).

Hebrews 10:23 KJV

189.7 Blessed is anyone who endures temptation. Such a one has stood the test and will receive the crown of life that the Lord has promised to those who love him.

James 1:12 NRSV

189.8 Through these he has given us his very great and precious promises, so that through them you may participate in the divine nature and escape the corruption in the world caused by evil desires.

2 Peter 1:4 NIV

189.9 The Lord isn't slow about keeping his promises, as some people think he is. In fact, God is patient, because he wants everyone to turn from sin and no one to be lost... But God has promised us a new heaven and a new earth, where justice will rule.

2 Peter 3:9, 13 CEV

Prophets and prophecy

190.1 When a word spoken by a prophet in the name of the Lord is not fulfilled and does not come true, it is not a word spoken by the Lord. The prophet has spoken presumptuously; have no fear of him.

Deuteronomy 18:22 REB

190.2 From the day that your ancestors came out of the land of Egypt until this day, I have persistently sent all my servants the prophets to them, day after day; yet they did not listen to me, or pay attention, but they stiffened their necks.

Jeremiah 7:25–26 NRSV

190.3 Many will say to me in that day, Lord, Lord, have we not prophesied in thy name? and in thy name have cast out devils? and in thy name done many wonderful works? And then will I profess unto them, I never knew you: depart from me, ye that work iniquity.

Matthew 7:22–23 KJV

190.4 And they were offended in him. But Jesus said unto them, A prophet is not without honour, save in his own country, and in his own house.

Matthew 13:57 KJV

A prophet is without honor
The saying *a prophet is without honor in his own country* is based on this statement by Jesus after he was rejected in his home town of Nazareth. In contemporary usage, the expression is applied to anyone who is generally recognized as great, except by his own family, compatriots, etc.

190.5 For false Messiahs and false prophets will appear; they will perform great miracles and wonders in order to deceive even God's chosen people, if possible.

Matthew 24:24 GNB

190.6 On my servants and on my handmaidens I will pour out in those days of my Spirit; and they shall prophesy.

Acts 2:18 KJV

190.7 During this time some prophets from Jerusalem came to Antioch. One of them was Agabus. Then with the help of the Spirit, he told that there would be a terrible famine everywhere in the world. And it happened when Claudius was Emperor.

Acts 11:27–28 CEV

190.8 Those whom God has appointed in the Church are, first apostles, secondly prophets...

1 Corinthians 12:28 NJB

190.9 Love never ends. But as for prophecies, they will come to an end.
1 Corinthians 13:8 NRSV

190.10 Make love your aim; then be eager for the gifts of the Spirit, above all for prophecy.
1 Corinthians 14:1 REB

190.11 You can all prophesy, but one at a time, then all will learn something and all receive encouragement. The prophetic spirit is to be under the prophets' control.
1 Corinthians 14:31–32 NJB

190.12 You, too, are built upon the foundation laid by the apostles and prophets, the cornerstone being Christ Jesus himself.
Ephesians 2:20 GNB

190.13 Despise not prophesyings. Prove all things; hold fast that which is good.
1 Thessalonians 5:20–21 KJV

190.14 The prophets did not think these things up on their own, but they were guided by the Spirit of God.
2 Peter 1:21 CEV

See also **Jesus Christ, Jesus as prophet**

Propitiation

191.1 Yet it pleased the Lord to bruise him; he hath put him to grief: when thou shalt make his soul an offering for sin, he shall see his seed, he shall prolong his days, and the pleasure of the Lord shall prosper in his hand.
Isaiah 53:10 KJV

191.2 The tax-collector, standing far off, would not even look up to heaven, but was beating his breast and saying, 'God, be merciful to me, a sinner!'
Luke 18:13 NRSV

191.3 [Christ Jesus] Whom God hath set forth to be a propitiation through faith in his blood, to declare his righteousness for the remission of sins that are past, through the forbearance of God.
Romans 3:25 KJV

191.4 By becoming a curse for us Christ has redeemed us from the curse that the Law brings; for the scripture says, 'Anyone who is hanged on a tree is under God's curse.'
Galatians 3:13 GNB

191.5 For this reason he had to be made like his brothers in every way, in order that he might become a merciful and faithful high priest in service to God, and that he might make atonement for the sins of the people.
Hebrews 2:17 NIV

191.6 Over it the cherubims of glory shadowing the mercy seat; of which we cannot now speak particularly.
Hebrews 9:5 KJV

191.7 He is the propitiation for our sins: and not for ours only, but also for the sins of the whole world.
1 John 2:2 KJV

191.8 Herein is love, not that we loved God, but that he loved us, and sent his Son to be the propitiation for our sins.
1 John 4:10 KJV

See also **Anger, Divine; Atonement; Reconciliation**

Providence

192.1 As long as the earth lasts, seedtime and harvest, cold and heat, summer and winter, day and night, they will never cease.
Genesis 8:22 REB

192.2 So Abraham called that place 'The Lord will provide'; as it is said to this day, 'On the mount of the Lord it shall be provided.'
Genesis 22:14 NRSV

192.3 For all things come of thee, and of thine own have we given thee.
1 Chronicles 29:14 KJV

192.4 Ezra said: 'You are the Lord, you alone; you have made heaven, the heaven of heavens, with all their host, the earth and all that is on it, the seas and all that is in them. To all of them you give life, and the host of heaven worships you.'
Nehemiah 9:6 NRSV

192.5 He does whatever he wishes in heaven and on earth, in the seas and in the depths below. He brings storm clouds from the ends of the earth; he makes lightning for the storms, and he brings out the wind from his storeroom.
Psalm 135:6–7 GNB

192.6 We humans make plans, but the Lord has the final word.
Proverbs 16:1 CEV

192.7 The lots may be cast into the lap, but the issue depends wholly on the Lord.
Proverbs 16:33 REB

192.8 For only a penny you can buy two sparrows, yet not one sparrow falls to the ground without your Father's consent. As for you, even the hairs of your head have all been counted. So do not be afraid; you are worth much more than many sparrows!
Matthew 10:29–31 GNB

192.9 It is in him that we live, and move, and exist.
Acts 17:28 NJB

192.10 [God] who worketh all things after the counsel of his own will.
Ephesians 1:11 KJV

192.11 Christ existed before all things, and in union with him all things have their proper place.
Colossians 1:17 GNB

192.12 [God] Upholding all things by the word of his power.
Hebrews 1:3 KJV

See also Creation; God, Good; Sovereignty of God

Punishment

193.1 Whoever hits someone and kills him is to be put to death.
Exodus 21:12 GNB

193.2 Be sure your sin will find you out.
Numbers 32:23 KJV

193.3 If I say to the wicked, 'O wicked ones, you shall surely die', and you do not speak to warn the wicked to turn from their ways, the wicked shall die in their iniquity, but their blood I will require at your hand.
Ezekiel 33:8 NRSV

193.4 These shall go away into everlasting punishment: but the righteous into life eternal.
Matthew 25:46 KJV

193.5 No one who believes in him will be judged; but whoever does not believe is judged already, because that person does not believe in the Name of God's only Son.
John 3:18 NJB

193.6 The retribution of his wrath awaits those who are governed by selfish ambition, who refuse obedience to truth and take evil for their guide. There will be affliction and distress for every human being who is a wrong-doer, for the Jew first and for the Greek also.
Romans 2:8–9 REB

193.7 For the wages of sin is death; but the gift of God is eternal life through Jesus Christ our Lord.
Romans 6:23 KJV

193.8 They [those in authority] are God's servants working for your own good. But if you do evil, then be afraid of them, because their power to punish is real.
Romans 13:4 GNB

193.9 They [those who do not obey the Good News about the Lord Jesus] will suffer the punishment of eternal destruction, separated from the presence of the Lord and from his glorious might.
2 Thessalonians 1:9 GNB

193.10 What, then, of those who despise the Son of God? who treat as a cheap thing the blood of God's covenant which purified them from sin? who insult the Spirit of grace? Just think how much worse is the punishment they will deserve!
Hebrews 10:29 GNB

See also **Anger, Divine; Discipline; Disobedience; Last things, Hell**

Purity

194.1 The statutes of the Lord are right, rejoicing the heart: the commandment of the Lord is pure, enlightening the eyes.
Psalm 19:8 KJV

194.2 Your eyes are too pure to behold evil, and you cannot look on wrongdoing.
Habakkuk 1:13 NRSV

194.3 Blessed are the pure in heart: for they shall see God.
Matthew 5:8 KJV

194.4 Take no part in the sins of others; keep yourself pure.
1 Timothy 5:22 GNB

194.5 To the pure all things are pure; but nothing is pure to tainted disbelievers, tainted both in reason and in conscience.
Titus 1:15 REB

194.6 The wisdom from above is first pure…
James 3:17 NRSV

194.7 Come near to God, and he will come near to you. Clean up your lives, you sinners. Purify your hearts, you people who can't make up your mind.
James 4:8 CEV

194.8 Now that by your obedience to the truth you have purified yourselves and have come to have a sincere love for your fellow-believers, love one another earnestly with all your heart.
1 Peter 1:22 GNB

Quiet

195.1 He said, Go forth, and stand upon the mount before the Lord. And, behold, the Lord passed by, and a great and strong wind rent the mountains, and brake in pieces the rocks before the Lord; but the Lord was not in the wind: and after the wind an earthquake; but the Lord was not in the earthquake: and after the earthquake a fire; but the Lord was not in the fire: and after the fire a still small voice. And it was so, when Elijah heard it, that he wrapped his face in his mantle, and went out, and stood in the entering in of the cave. And, behold, there came a voice unto him, and said, What doest thou here, Elijah?

1 Kings 19:11–13 KJV

The still small voice

A still small voice is sometimes used in modern English to stand for the 'voice' of one's conscience, one's inner sense of right and wrong, an expression of a calm and sensible viewpoint. The phrase comes from the quiet gentle means with which God spoke to Elijah after he had fled to Horeb.

195.2 Be still and acknowledge that I am God, supreme over nations, supreme over the world.

Psalm 46:10 NJB

195.3 They cried to the Lord in their trouble, and he brought them out of their distress. The storm sank to a murmur and the waves of the sea were stilled. They rejoiced because it was calm, and he guided them to the harbour they were making for.

Psalm 107:28–30 REB

195.4 Better is a dry morsel, and quietness therewith, than an house full of sacrifices with strife.

Proverbs 17:1 KJV

195.5 Better is an handful with quietness, than both the hands full with travail and vexation of spirit.

Ecclesiastes 4:6 KJV

195.6 A wise man speaking quietly is more to be heeded than a commander shouting orders among fools.

Ecclesiastes 9:17 REB

195.7 For thus saith the Lord God, the Holy One of Israel; In returning and rest shall ye be saved; in quietness and in confidence shall be your strength.

Isaiah 30:15 KJV

195.8 The work of righteousness shall be peace; and the effect of righteousness quietness and assurance for ever.

Isaiah 32:17 KJV

195.9 It is good that a man should both hope and quietly wait for the salvation of the Lord.

Lamentations 3:26 KJV

195.10 Times are so evil that anyone with good sense will keep quiet.

Amos 5:13 CEV

195.11 The Lord your God is with you, he is mighty to save. He will take great delight in you, he will quiet you with his love, he will rejoice over you with singing.

Zephaniah 3:17 NIV

195.12 Pray for kings and others in power, so that we may live quiet and peaceful lives as we worship and honour God.

1 Timothy 2:2 CEV

195.13 Your beauty should lie, not in outward adornment... but in the inmost self, with its imperishable quality of a gentle, quiet spirit, which is of high value in the sight of God.

1 Peter 3:3–4 REB

See also Peace; Rest; Silence

Race

(Ethnic)

196.1 So God created man in his own image, in the image of God created he him; male and female created he them. And God blessed them, and God said unto them, Be fruitful, and multiply, and replenish the earth, and subdue it.
Genesis 1:27–28 KJV

196.2 Peter began to speak: 'I now realize that it is true that God treats everyone on the same basis. Those who worship him and do what is right are acceptable to him.'
Acts 10:34–35 GNB

196.3 From one ancestor he made all nations to inhabit the whole earth, and he allotted the times of their existence and the boundaries of the places where they would live.
Acts 17:26 NRSV

196.4 There is neither Jew nor Greek, there is neither bond nor free, there is neither male nor female: for ye are all one in Christ Jesus.
Galatians 3:28 KJV

196.5 After that I looked and saw a vast throng, which no one could count, from all races and tribes, nations and languages, standing before the throne and the Lamb.
Revelation 7:9 REB

See also **Immigrants**

Rebellion

197.1 You must not act in defiance of the Lord.
Numbers 14:9 REB

197.2 I [Moses] know how stubborn and rebellious you and the rest of the Israelites are. You have rebelled against the Lord while I have been alive, and it will only get worse after I am gone.
Deuteronomy 31:27 CEV

197.3 If you will revere the Lord and give true and loyal service, if you do not rebel against his commands, and if you and the king who reigns over you are faithful to the Lord your God, well and good; but if you do not obey the Lord, and if you rebel against his commands, then his hand will be against you and against your king.
1 Samuel 12:14–15 REB

197.4 For rebellion is as the sin of witchcraft, and stubbornness is as iniquity and idolatry.
1 Samuel 15:23 KJV

197.5 Let us rejoice in him, who rules for ever by his power; his eyes keep watch on the nations to forestall rebellion against him.
Psalm 66:6–7 NJB

197.6 God gives the lonely a home to live in, leads prisoners out into prosperity, but rebels must live in the bare wastelands.
Psalm 68:6 NJB

197.7 The wicked person thinks of nothing but rebellion, but a cruel messenger will be sent to such a one.
Proverbs 17:11 NJB

197.8 If ye be willing and obedient, ye shall eat the good of the land: but if ye refuse and rebel, ye shall be devoured with the sword: for the mouth of the Lord hath spoken it.
Isaiah 1:19–20 KJV

197.9 Woe betide the rebellious children! says the Lord, who make plans, but not of my devising, who weave schemes, but not inspired by me, so piling sin on sin.

Isaiah 30:1 REB

197.10 They will see the corpses of those who rebelled against me; for their worm will never die nor their fire be put out, and they will be held in horror by all humanity.

Isaiah 66:24 NJB

197.11 This people has a rebellious and defiant heart; they have rebelled and gone their own way.

Jeremiah 5:23 REB

197.12 [Jeremiah to Hananiah] These are the words of the Lord: I shall remove you from the face of the earth; within a year you will die, because you have preached rebellion against the Lord.

Jeremiah 28:16 REB

197.13 I will separate the sinful rebels from the rest of you, and even though I will bring them from the nations where they live in exile, they won't be allowed to return to Israel. Then you will know that I am the Lord.

Ezekiel 20:38 CEV

197.14 Let no one deceive you in any way. That day [of the Lord] cannot come before the final rebellion against God, when wickedness will be revealed in human form, the man doomed to destruction.

2 Thessalonians 2:3 REB

See also Rejection; Unbelief; World, Humanity in rebellion against God

Reconciliation

198.1 He shall judge between the nations, and shall arbitrate for many peoples; they shall beat their swords into ploughshares, and their spears into pruning-hooks; nation shall not lift up sword against nation, neither shall they learn war any more.

Isaiah 2:4 NRSV

198.2 If you are bringing your offering to the altar and there remember that your brother has something against you, leave your offering there before the altar, go and be reconciled with your brother first, and then come back and present your offering.

Matthew 5:23–24 NJB

198.3 For if, when we were God's enemies, we were reconciled to him through the death of his Son, how much more, now that we have been reconciled, shall we be saved by his life! But that is not all: we also exult in God through our Lord Jesus, through whom we have now been granted reconciliation.

Romans 5:10–11 REB

198.4 God has done it all! He sent Christ to make peace between himself and us, and he has given us the work of making peace between himself and others. What we mean is that God was in Christ, offering peace and forgiveness to the people of this world. And he has given us the work of sharing his message about peace. We were sent to speak for Christ, and God is begging you to listen to our message. We speak for Christ and sincerely ask you to make peace with God.

2 Corinthians 5:18–20 CEV

198.5 That he [Christ] might reconcile both [Jew and Gentile] unto God in one body by the cross, having slain the enmity thereby.

Ephesians 2:16 KJV

198.6 Through him [Christ] God was pleased to reconcile to himself all things, whether on earth or in heaven, by making peace through the blood of his cross.

Colossians 1:20 NRSV

198.7 Now, by means of the physical death of his Son, God has made you his friends, in order to bring you, holy, pure, and faultless, into his presence.

Colossians 1:22 GNB

See also Atonement; Jesus Christ, Death; Peace; Propitiation

Redemption

199.1 Say therefore to the Israelites, 'I am the Lord, and I will free you from the burdens of the Egyptians and deliver you from slavery to them. I will redeem you with an outstretched arm and with mighty acts of judgement.'

Exodus 6:6 NRSV

199.2 For I know that my redeemer liveth, and that he shall stand at the latter day upon the earth.

Job 19:25 KJV

199.3 The ransomed of the Lord shall return, and come to Zion with singing; everlasting joy shall be upon their heads; they shall obtain joy and gladness, and sorrow and sighing shall flee away.

Isaiah 35:10 NRSV

199.4 Now thus saith the Lord that created thee, O Jacob, and he that formed thee, O Israel, Fear not: for I have redeemed thee, I have called thee by thy name; thou art mine.

Isaiah 43:1 KJV

199.5 For even the Son of Man did not come to be served; he came to serve and to give his life to redeem many people.

Mark 10:45 GNB

199.6 Being justified freely by his grace through the redemption that is in Christ Jesus.

Romans 3:24 KJV

199.7 Not only the creation, but we ourselves, who have the first fruits of the Spirit, groan inwardly while we wait for adoption, the redemption of our bodies.

Romans 8:23 NRSV

199.8 By God's act you are in Christ Jesus; God has made him our wisdom, and in him we have our righteousness, our holiness, our liberation.

1 Corinthians 1:30 REB

199.9 You are not your own property, then; you have been bought at a price. So use your body for the glory of God.

1 Corinthians 6:20 NJB

199.10 By becoming a curse for us Christ has redeemed us from the curse that the Law brings; for the scripture says, 'Anyone who is hanged on a tree is under God's curse.'

Galatians 3:13 GNB

199.11 When the fulness of the time was come, God sent forth his Son, made of a woman, made under the law, to redeem them that were under the law, that we might receive the adoption of sons.

Galatians 4:4–5 KJV

199.12 For by the blood of Christ we are set free, that is, our sins are forgiven. How great is the grace of God, which he gave to us in such large measure!

Ephesians 1:7 GNB

199.13 [God's dear Son] who forgives our sins and sets us free.

Colossians 1:14 CEV

199.14 Christ Jesus, who offered himself as a ransom for all.

1 Timothy 2:5–6 NJB

199.15 [Jesus Christ] who gave himself for us that he might redeem us from all iniquity and purify for himself a people of his own who are zealous for good deeds.

Titus 2:14 NRSV

199.16 The blood of his sacrifice is his own blood, not the blood of goats and calves; and thus he has entered the sanctuary once for all and secured an eternal liberation.

Hebrews 9:12 REB

199.17 You know that you were ransomed from the futile ways inherited from your ancestors, not with perishable things like silver or gold, but with the precious blood of Christ, like that of a lamb without defect or blemish.

1 Peter 1:18–19 NRSV

See also **Atonement; Justification**

Rejection

200.1 For rebellion is no less a sin than divination, and stubbornness is like iniquity and idolatry. Because you have rejected the word of the Lord, he has also rejected you from being king.

1 Samuel 15:23 NRSV

200.2 The stone which the builders rejected has become the main corner-stone.

Psalm 118:22 REB

200.3 The Lord God hath opened mine ear, and I was not rebellious, neither turned away back. I gave my back to the smiters, and my cheeks to them that plucked off the hair: I hid not my face from shame and spitting.

Isaiah 50:5–6 KJV

200.4 He is despised and rejected of men; a man of sorrows, and acquainted with grief: and we hid as it were our faces

from him; he was despised, and we esteemed him not.

Isaiah 53:3 KJV

200.5 You stubborn people have rebelled and turned your backs on me.

Jeremiah 5:23 CEV

200.6 If anyone will not receive you or listen to what you say, then as you leave that house or that town shake the dust of it off your feet.

Matthew 10:14 REB

200.7 Jesus continued, 'You have a clever way of rejecting God's law in order to uphold your own teaching.'

Mark 7:9 GNB

200.8 He came unto his own, and his own received him not.

John 1:11 KJV

200.9 There is a judge for anyone who rejects me and does not accept my words; the word I have spoken will be his judge on the last day.

John 12:48 REB

200.10 Come to him, a living stone, though rejected by mortals yet chosen and precious in God's sight.

1 Peter 2:4 NRSV

See also **Falling away; Hardness; Rebellion; Unbelief**

Remembering

201.1 Remember the Sabbath day and keep it holy.

Exodus 20:8 NJB

201.2 Remember the whole way by which the Lord your God has led you these forty years in the wilderness to humble and test you, and to discover whether or not it was in your heart to keep his commandments.

Deuteronomy 8:2 REB

201.3 He is ever mindful of his covenant, the promise he ordained for a thousand generations.

1 Chronicles 16:15 REB

201.4 Let all the ends of the earth remember and turn again to the Lord.

Psalm 22:27 REB

201.5 Remember the marvels he has done, his wonders, the judgements he has spoken.

Psalm 105:5 NJB

201.6 The righteous shall be in everlasting remembrance.

Psalm 112:6 KJV

201.7 My son, do not forget my teaching, but treasure my commandments in your heart.

Proverbs 3:1 REB

201.8 Remember now thy Creator in the days of thy youth.

Ecclesiastes 12:1 KJV

201.9 Remember the former things of old: for I am God, and there is none else.

Isaiah 46:9 KJV

201.10 The people of Zion said, 'The Lord has turned away and forgotten us.' The Lord answered, 'Could a mother forget a child who nurses at her breast? Could she fail to love an infant who came from her own body? Even if a mother could forget, I will never forget you. A picture of your city is drawn on my hand. You are always in my thoughts!'

Isaiah 49:14–16 CEV

201.11 Then he took bread, and when he had given thanks, he broke it and gave it to them, saying, 'This is my body given for you; do this in remembrance of me.'

Luke 22:19 NJB

201.12 He said to Jesus, 'Remember me when you come into power!'

Luke 23:42 CEV

201.13 The Comforter, which is the Holy Ghost, whom the Father will send in my name, he shall teach you all things, and bring all things to your remembrance, whatsoever I have said unto you.

John 14:26 KJV

201.14 They [James, Peter, and John] only asked us to remember the poor, and that was something I had always been eager to do.

Galatians 2:10 CEV

201.15 Remember that Jesus Christ of the seed of David was raised from the dead according to my gospel.

2 Timothy 2:8 KJV

201.16 Anyone who looks steadily at the perfect law of freedom and keeps to it – not listening and forgetting, but putting it into practice – will be blessed in every undertaking.

James 1:25 NJB

201.17 My dear friends, remember the warning you were given by the apostles of our Lord Jesus Christ…

Jude v. 17 CEV

Renewal

202.1 King Josiah called together the older leaders of Judah and Jerusalem. Then he went to the Lord's temple, together

229

with the people of Judah and Jerusalem, the priests, and the prophets. Finally, when everybody was there, he read aloud The Book of God's Law that had been found in the temple. After Josiah had finished reading, he stood by one of the columns. He asked the people to promise in the Lord's name to obey the Lord faithfully and to follow his commands. The people agreed to do everything written in the book.

2 Kings 23:1–3 CEV

202.2 While Ezra was praying and making confession, prostrate in tears before the house of God, there gathered round him a vast throng of Israelites, men, women, and children, and there was widespread lamentation among the crowd. Shecaniah... said to Ezra, 'We have broken faith with our God in taking foreign wives from the peoples of the land. But in spite of this, there is still hope for Israel. Let us now pledge ourselves to our God to get rid of all such wives with their children... and let the law take its course. Rise up, the matter is in your hands; and we are with you.'

Ezra 10:1–4 REB

202.3 Create in me a clean heart, O God; and renew a right spirit within me.

Psalm 51:10 KJV

202.4 Send out your breath and life begins; you renew the face of the earth.

Psalm 104:30 NJB

202.5 They that wait upon the Lord shall renew their strength; they shall mount up with wings as eagles; they shall run, and not be weary; and they shall walk, and not faint.

Isaiah 40:31 KJV

202.6 Lord, turn us back to you, and we shall come back; renew our days as in times long past.

Lamentations 5:21 REB

202.7 O Lord, I have heard of your renown, and I stand in awe, O Lord, of your work. In our own time revive it; in our own time make it known; in wrath may you remember mercy.

Habakkuk 3:2 NRSV

202.8 Do not model your behaviour on the contemporary world, but let the renewing of your minds transform you, so that you may discern for yourselves what is the will of God.

Romans 12:2 NJB

202.9 Though our outward man perish, yet the inward man is renewed day by day.

2 Corinthians 4:16 KJV

202.10 Renouncing your former way of life, you must lay aside the old human nature which... is in process of decay: you must be renewed in mind and spirit, and put on the new nature created in God's likeness, which shows itself in the upright and devout life called for by the truth.

Ephesians 4:22–24 REB

202.11 You have stripped off your old behaviour with your old self, and you have put on a new self which will progress towards true knowledge the more it is renewed in the image of its Creator.

Colossians 3:9–10 NJB

202.12 It was not because of any upright actions we had done ourselves; it was for no reason except his own faithful love that he saved us, by means of the cleansing water of rebirth and renewal in the Holy Spirit.

Titus 3:5 NJB

202.13 For it is impossible for those who were once enlightened... If they shall fall away, to renew them again unto repentance.

Hebrews 6:4, 6 KJV

See also Last things, Renewal of all things; Restoration; Revival

Repentance

203.1 [The Lord's promise to Solomon] If my people who are called by my name humble themselves, pray, seek my face, and turn from their wicked ways, then I will hear from heaven, and will forgive their sin and heal their land.

2 Chronicles 7:14 NRSV

203.2 Let the wicked forsake his way, and the unrighteous man his thoughts: and let him return unto the Lord, and he will have mercy upon him; and to our God, for he will abundantly pardon.

Isaiah 55:7 KJV

203.3 Therefore, O house of Israel, I will judge you, each one according to his ways, declares the Sovereign Lord. Repent! Turn away from all your offences; then sin will not be your downfall.

Ezekiel 18:30 NIV

203.4 Yet even now, says the Lord, return to me with all your heart, with fasting, with weeping, and with mourning; rend your hearts and not your clothing. Return to the Lord, your God, for he is gracious and merciful, slow to anger, and abounding in steadfast love, and relents from punishing.

Joel 2:12–13 NRSV

203.5 Do something to show that you have really given up your sins.

Matthew 3:8 CEV

203.6 'The right time has come,' he said, 'and the kingdom of God is near! Turn away from your sins and believe the Good News!'

Mark 1:15 GNB

203.7 I have not come to call the virtuous but sinners to repentance.

Luke 5:32 REB

203.8 Unless you repent you will all perish as they did.

Luke 13:3 NJB

203.9 Just so, I tell you, there will be more joy in heaven over one sinner who repents than over ninety-nine righteous people who need no repentance.

Luke 15:7 NRSV

203.10 When he [the prodigal son] came to himself, he said, How many hired servants of my father's have bread enough and to spare, and I perish with hunger! I will arise and go to my father, and will say unto him, Father, I have sinned against heaven, and before thee.

Luke 15:17–18 KJV

The prodigal son
A *prodigal* or a *prodigal son* is a reformed spendthrift – for example someone who leaves his family early and spends all his money carelessly but later returns home sorry for his actions. The expression alludes to this parable of Jesus. When the son returned, he was welcomed home by his father, who celebrated his homecoming by holding a feast. They *killed the fatted calf* in his honor – they gave him the best possible food and treatment.

203.11 Repentance and remission of sins should be preached in his name among all nations, beginning at Jerusalem.

Luke 24:47 KJV

203.12 Repent ye therefore, and be converted, that your sins may be blotted out, when the times of refreshing shall come from the presence of the Lord.

Acts 3:19 KJV

203.13 They praised God, saying, 'Then God has given even to the Gentiles the repentance that leads to life.'
Acts 11:18 NRSV

203.14 God has overlooked the times when people did not know him, but now he commands all of them everywhere to turn away from their evil ways.
Acts 17:30 GNB

203.15 To Jews and Gentiles alike I gave solemn warning that they should turn from their sins to God and believe in our Lord Jesus.
Acts 20:21 GNB

203.16 Or do you despise the riches of his kindness and forbearance and patience? Do you not realize that God's kindness is meant to lead you to repentance?
Romans 2:4 NRSV

203.17 Pain borne in God's way brings no regrets but a change of heart leading to salvation; pain borne in the world's way brings death.
2 Corinthians 7:10 REB

203.18 The Lord isn't slow about keeping his promises, as some people think he is. In fact, God is patient, because he wants everyone to turn from sin and no one to be lost.
2 Peter 3:9 CEV

203.19 Remember therefore from whence thou art fallen, and repent, and do the first works; or else I will come unto thee quickly, and will remove thy candlestick out of his place, except thou repent.
Revelation 2:5 KJV

See also **Confession, of sin; Conversion; Faith; Falling away; Forgiveness; Grief; Sin**

Respect

204.1 'Come no nearer,' he said. 'Take off your sandals, for the place where you are standing is holy ground.'
Exodus 3:5 NJB

204.2 Respect your father and your mother, and you will live a long time in the land I am giving you.
Exodus 20:12 CEV

204.3 Ye shall keep my sabbaths, and reverence my sanctuary: I am the Lord.
Leviticus 19:30 KJV

204.4 Rise in the presence of grey hairs, give honour to the aged, and fear your God. I am the Lord.
Leviticus 19:32 REB

204.5 Ascribe to the Lord the glory due to his name; in holy attire worship the Lord.
Psalm 29:2 REB

204.6 A gracious woman will be respected, but a man must work hard to get rich.
Proverbs 11:16 CEV

204.7 See that you never despise any of these little ones, for I tell you that their angels in heaven are continually in the presence of my Father in heaven.
Matthew 18:10 NJB

204.8 The owner then said to himself, 'What am I going to do? I know what. I'll send my son, the one I love so much. They will surely respect him!' When the tenants saw the owner's son, they said to one another, 'Some day he will own the vineyard. Let's kill him! Then we can have it all for ourselves.' So they threw him out of the vineyard and killed him.
Luke 20:13–15 CEV

204.9 Then Peter opened his mouth, and said, Of a truth I perceive that God is no respecter of persons: but in every nation he that feareth him, and worketh righteousness, is accepted with him.

Acts 10:34–35 KJV

No respecter of persons

The expression *no respecter of persons* describes an attitude that treats all the people involved in the same way, regardless of their wealth, fame, class, etc.: 'The epidemic was no respecter of persons – young and old, rich and poor – thousands died as the plague swept across the country.' This verse is the origin of the phrase: God 'had no favorites' between one nation and another. He accepted all, Jews and Gentiles, who feared him and acted in the right way.

204.10 Esteem others more highly than yourself.

Romans 12:10 REB

204.11 Pay to each one what is due to each: taxes to the one to whom tax is due, tolls to the one to whom tolls are due, respect to the one to whom respect is due, honour to the one to whom honour is due.

Romans 13:7 NJB

204.12 Each husband should love his wife as much as he loves himself, and each wife should respect her husband.

Ephesians 5:33 CEV

204.13 We appeal to you, my brothers, to be considerate to those who work so hard among you as your leaders in the Lord and those who admonish you. Have the greatest respect and affection for them because of their work.

1 Thessalonians 5:12–13 NJB

204.14 Deacons with a good record of service are entitled to high standing and the right to be heard on matters of the Christian faith.

1 Timothy 3:13 REB

204.15 Obey your leaders and submit to their authority.

Hebrews 13:17 REB

204.16 Have respect for everyone and love for your fellow-believers; fear God and honour the emperor.

1 Peter 2:17 NJB

See also **Obedience; Reverence**

Responsibility, human

205.1 Let us hear the conclusion of the whole matter: Fear God, and keep his commandments: for this is the whole duty of man.

Ecclesiastes 12:13 KJV

205.2 He hath shewed thee, O man, what is good; and what doth the Lord require of thee, but to do justly, and to love mercy, and to walk humbly with thy God?

Micah 6:8 KJV

205.3 Jesus said unto him, Thou shalt love the Lord thy God with all thy heart, and with all thy soul, and with all thy mind. This is the first and great commandment. And the second is like unto it, Thou shalt love thy neighbour as thyself.

Matthew 22:37–39 KJV

205.4 When Pilate saw that he could prevail nothing, but that rather a tumult was made, he took water, and washed his hands before the multitude, saying, I am innocent of the blood of this just person: see ye to it.

Matthew 27:24 KJV

Wash one's hands of

The expression *to wash one's hands of something* means to say or show that one no longer wants to be responsible for or involved in an action. This idiomatic phrase has its origins in this verse: Pilate washed his hands, symbolizing his dissociation from the desire of the people to crucify Jesus. He refused to assume responsibility for Jesus' death.

205.5 For in this city, in fact, both Herod and Pontius Pilate, with the Gentiles and the peoples of Israel, gathered together against your holy servant Jesus, whom you anointed, to do whatever your hand and your plan had predestined to take place.

Acts 4:27–28 NRSV

205.6 When the Gentiles heard this, they were overjoyed and thankfully acclaimed the word of the Lord, and those who were marked out for eternal life became believers.

Acts 13:48 REB

205.7 None of us lives for himself only, none of us dies for himself only. If we live, it is for the Lord that we live, and if we die, it is for the Lord that we die. So whether we live or die, we belong to the Lord.

Romans 14:7–8 GNB

205.8 When you eat or drink or do anything else, always do it to honour God.

1 Corinthians 10:31 CEV

205.9 Work out your own salvation with fear and trembling; for it is God who is at work in you, enabling you both to will and to work for his good pleasure.

Philippians 2:12–13 NRSV

205.10 Wherefore the rather, brethren, give diligence to make your calling and election sure: for if ye do these things, ye shall never fall.

2 Peter 1:10 KJV

See also **Decisions; Human beings; Privilege; Service; Sovereignty of God**

Rest

206.1 For thus saith the Lord God, the Holy One of Israel; In returning and rest shall ye be saved; in quietness and in confidence shall be your strength.

Isaiah 30:15 KJV

206.2 Come to me, all you that are weary and are carrying heavy burdens, and I will give you rest. Take my yoke upon you, and learn from me; for I am gentle and humble in heart, and you will find rest for your souls. For my yoke is easy, and my burden is light.

Matthew 11:28–30 NRSV

206.3 He said to them, 'Come with me, by yourselves, to some remote place and rest a little.' With many coming and going they had no time even to eat.

Mark 6:31 REB

206.4 Now, God has offered us the promise that we may receive that rest he spoke about. Let us take care, then, that none of you will be found to have failed to receive that promised rest... We who believe, then, do receive that rest which God promised. It is just as he said: 'I was angry and made a solemn promise: "They will never enter the land where I would have given them rest!"' He said this even though his work had been finished from the time he created the world. For somewhere in the Scriptures this is said about the seventh day: 'God rested on the seventh day from all his work.' This same matter is spoken of again: 'They will never enter that land where I would have given them rest.' Those who first heard the Good News did not receive that rest, because they did not believe. There are, then, others who are allowed to receive it. This is shown by the fact that God sets another day, which is called 'Today'. Many years later he spoke of it through David in the scripture already quoted: 'If you hear God's voice today, do not be stubborn.' If Joshua had given the people the rest that God had promised, God would not have spoken later about another day. As it is, however, there still remains for God's people a rest like God's resting on the seventh day. For those who receive that rest which God promised will rest from their own work, just as God rested from his. Let us, then, do our best to receive that rest, so that no one of us will fail as they did because of their lack of faith.

Hebrews 4:1, 3–11 GNB

See also Sabbath

Restitution

207.1 If you steal an ox and slaughter or sell it, you must replace it with five oxen; if you steal a sheep and slaughter it or sell it, you must replace it with four sheep. But if you cannot afford to replace the animals, you must be sold as a slave to pay for what you have stolen. If you steal an ox, donkey, or sheep, and are caught with it still alive, you must pay the owner double.

Exodus 22:1–2 CEV

207.2 When any person commits an offence by inadvertently defaulting in dues

sacred to the Lord, he must bring to the Lord as his reparation-offering a ram... he must make good his default in sacred dues, adding one fifth of the value. He must give it to the priest, who is to offer expiation for his sin with the ram of the reparation-offering, and it will be forgiven him.

Leviticus 5:15–16 REB

207.3 Anyone who strikes down an animal will make restitution for it: a life for a life.

Leviticus 24:18 NJB

207.4 The Lord told Moses to say to the Israelites: 'When anyone, man or woman, wrongs another and thereby breaks faith with the Lord, that person has incurred guilt which demands reparation. He must confess the sin he has committed, make restitution in full with the addition of one fifth, and give it to the one to whom compensation is due.'

Numbers 5:5–7 REB

207.5 That is how the Philistines sent gifts to the Lord to make up for taking the sacred chest. They sent five gold sores, one each for their towns... They also sent one gold rat for each walled town and for every village that the five Philistine rulers controlled.

1 Samuel 6:17–18 CEV

207.6 David was very angry, and burst out, 'As the Lord lives, the man who did this deserves to die! He shall pay for the lamb four times over, because he has done this and shown no pity.'

2 Samuel 12:5–6 REB

207.7 Ben-Hadad said, 'I shall restore the towns which my father took from your father.'

1 Kings 20:34 NJB

207.8 Restore, I pray you, to them, even this day, their lands, their vineyards, their oliveyards, and their houses, also the hundredth part of the money, and of the corn, the wine, and the oil, that ye exact of them. Then said they, We will restore them, and will require nothing of them.

Nehemiah 5:11–12 KJV

207.9 People attach but little blame to a thief who steals only to satisfy his hunger; yet even he, if caught, will have to repay sevenfold and hand over all his family resources.

Proverbs 6:30–31 NJB

207.10 If the wicked restore the pledge, give again that he had robbed, walk in the statutes of life, without committing iniquity; he shall surely live, he shall not die.

Ezekiel 33:15 KJV

207.11 Zacchaeus stood his ground and said to the Lord, 'Look, sir, I am going to give half my property to the poor, and if I have cheated anybody I will pay him back four times the amount.'

Luke 19:8 NJB

See also **Stealing**

Restoration

208.1 If you and your children turn back to him and obey him heart and soul in all that I command you this day, then the Lord your God will restore your fortunes. In compassion for you he will gather you again from all the peoples to which he has dispersed you.

Deuteronomy 30:2–3 REB

208.2 If only deliverance for Israel might come from Zion! When the Lord restores his people's fortunes, let Jacob rejoice, let Israel be glad.

Psalm 14:7 REB

208.3 The Lord is my shepherd; I shall not want. He maketh me to lie down in green pastures: he leadeth me beside the still waters. He restoreth my soul.

Psalm 23:1–3 KJV

208.4 Restore to me the joy of your deliverance and grant me a willing spirit to uphold me.

Psalm 51:12 REB

208.5 God, restore us, and make your face shine on us, that we may be saved.

Psalm 80:3 REB

208.6 Restore our fortunes, Lord, as streams return in the Negeb.

Psalm 126:4 REB

208.7 Buildings long in ruins will be restored by your own kindred and you will build on ancient foundations; you will be called the rebuilder of broken walls, the restorer of houses in ruins.

Isaiah 58:12 REB

208.8 They will rebuild the ancient ruins, they will raise what has long lain waste, they will restore the ruined cities, all that has lain waste for ages past.

Isaiah 61:4 NJB

208.9 For I shall restore you to health and heal your wounds.

Jeremiah 30:17 NJB

208.10 I will restore to you the years that the locust hath eaten.

Joel 2:25 KJV

208.11 He touched their eyes, and said, 'As you have believed, so let it be'; and their sight was restored.

Matthew 9:29–30 REB

208.12 He saith unto the man, Stretch forth thine hand. And he stretched it out:

and his hand was restored whole as the other.
Mark 3:5 KJV

208.13 Then he will send you the Christ he has predestined, that is Jesus, whom heaven must keep till the universal restoration which God proclaimed, speaking through his holy prophets.
Acts 3:20–21 NJB

208.14 Brethren, if a man be overtaken in a fault, ye which are spiritual, restore such an one in the spirit of meekness; considering thyself, lest thou also be tempted.
Galatians 6:1 KJV

208.15 Perhaps Onesimus was taken from you for a little while so that you could have him back for good, but not as a slave. Onesimus is much more than a slave. To me he is a dear friend, but to you he is even more, both as a person and as a follower of the Lord... welcome Onesimus as you would welcome me. If he has cheated you or owes you anything, charge it to my account.
Philemon vv. 15–18 CEV

See also **Illness, Help in; Renewal**

Retaliation

209.1 You shall not take vengeance or bear a grudge against any of your people, but you shall love your neighbour as yourself: I am the Lord.
Leviticus 19:18 NRSV

209.2 Vengeance is mine, and recompense, for the time when their foot shall slip; because the day of their calamity is at hand, their doom comes swiftly.
Deuteronomy 32:35 NRSV

209.3 Do not think to repay evil for evil; wait for the Lord to deliver you.
Proverbs 20:22 REB

209.4 You have heard that it was said, 'An eye for an eye, and a tooth for a tooth.' But now I tell you: do not take revenge on someone who wrongs you. If anyone slaps you on the right cheek, let him slap your left cheek too. And if someone takes you to court to sue you for your shirt, let him have your coat as well. And if one of the occupation troops forces you to carry his pack one kilometre, carry it two kilometres. When someone asks you for something, give it to him; when someone wants to borrow something, lend it to him.
Matthew 5:38–42 GNB

209.5 Dear friends, don't try to get even. Let God take revenge. In the Scriptures the Lord says, 'I am the one to take revenge and pay them back.' The Scriptures also say, 'If your enemies are hungry, give them something to eat. And if they are thirsty, give them something to drink. This will be the same as piling burning coals on their heads.' Don't let evil defeat you, but defeat evil with good.
Romans 12:19–21 CEV

Revelation

210.1 The heavens declare the glory of God; and the firmament sheweth his handywork. Day unto day uttereth speech, and night unto night sheweth knowledge.
Psalm 19:1–2 KJV

210.2 For my thoughts are not your thoughts, neither are your ways my ways, saith the Lord. For as the heavens are higher than the earth, so are my ways higher than your ways, and my thoughts than your thoughts. For as the rain cometh down, and the snow from heaven, and returneth not thither, but watereth the earth, and maketh it bring forth and bud, that it may give seed to the sower, and bread to the eater: so shall my word be that goeth forth out of my mouth: it shall not return unto me void, but it shall accomplish that which I please, and it shall prosper in the thing whereto I sent it.

Isaiah 55:8–11 KJV

210.3 All things have been handed over to me by my Father; and no one knows the Son except the Father, and no one knows the Father except the Son and anyone to whom the Son chooses to reveal him.

Matthew 11:27 NRSV

210.4 Simon Peter answered and said, Thou art the Christ, the Son of the living God. And Jesus answered and said unto him, Blessed art thou, Simon Bar-jona: for flesh and blood hath not revealed it unto thee, but my Father which is in heaven.

Matthew 16:16–17 KJV

210.5 He has not left you without some clue to his nature, in the benefits he bestows: he sends you rain from heaven and the crops in their seasons, and gives you food in plenty and keeps you in good heart.

Acts 14:17 REB

210.6 For what can be known about God is plain to them, because God has shown it to them. Ever since the creation of the world his eternal power and divine nature, invisible though they are, have been understood and seen through the things he has made. So they are without excuse.

Romans 1:19–20 NRSV

210.7 As it is written, Eye hath not seen, nor ear heard, neither have entered into the heart of man, the things which God hath prepared for them that love him. But

God hath revealed them unto us by his Spirit.

1 Corinthians 2:9–10 KJV

210.8 Let me tell you, my brothers and sisters, that the gospel I preach is not of human origin. I did not receive it from any human being, nor did anyone teach it to me. It was Jesus Christ himself who revealed it to me.

Galatians 1:11–12 GNB

210.9 All scripture is inspired by God and is useful for teaching, for reproof, for correction…

2 Timothy 3:16 NRSV

210.10 God, who at sundry times and in divers manners spake in time past unto the fathers by the prophets, hath in these last days spoken unto us by his Son, whom he hath appointed heir of all things, by whom also he made the worlds.

Hebrews 1:1–2 KJV

See also Bible; Creation; Will of God

Reverence

211.1 That you and your children and your children's children may fear the Lord your God all the days of your life, and keep all his decrees and his commandments that I am commanding you, so that your days may be long.

Deuteronomy 6:2 NRSV

211.2 The fear of the Lord is clean, enduring for ever: the judgments of the Lord are true and righteous altogether.

Psalm 19:9 KJV

211.3 For as the heaven is high above the earth, so great is his mercy toward them that fear him.

Psalm 103:11 KJV

211.4 The fear of the Lord is the beginning of wisdom: a good understanding have all they that do his commandments: his praise endureth for ever.
Psalm 111:10 KJV

211.5 To honour the Lord is to hate evil; I hate pride and arrogance, evil ways and false words.
Proverbs 8:13 GNB

211.6 Let us hear the conclusion of the whole matter: Fear God, and keep his commandments: for this is the whole duty of man.
Ecclesiastes 12:13 KJV

211.7 The spirit of the Lord shall rest upon him, the spirit of wisdom and understanding, the spirit of counsel and might, the spirit of knowledge and of the fear of the Lord.
Isaiah 11:2 KJV

211.8 They were filled with great awe and said to one another, 'Who then is this, that even the wind and the sea obey him?'
Mark 4:41 NRSV

211.9 So it was that the church throughout Judea, Galilee, and Samaria had a time of peace. Through the help of the Holy Spirit it was strengthened and grew in numbers, as it lived in reverence for the Lord.
Acts 9:31 GNB

211.10 There is no fear of God before their eyes.
Romans 3:18 KJV

211.11 We know what it means to respect the Lord, and we encourage everyone to turn to him. God himself knows what we are like, and I hope you also know what kind of people we are.
2 Corinthians 5:11 CEV

211.12 Since we have these promises, dear friends, let us purify ourselves from everything that contaminates body and spirit, perfecting holiness out of reverence for God.
2 Corinthians 7:1 NIV

211.13 You must work out your own salvation in fear and trembling; for it is God who works in you, inspiring both the will and the deed, for his own chosen purpose.
Philippians 2:12–13 REB

211.14 Therefore, since we are receiving a kingdom that cannot be shaken, let us give thanks, by which we offer to God an acceptable worship with reverence and awe.
Hebrews 12:28 NRSV

211.15 In your hearts sanctify Christ as Lord. Always be ready to make your defence to anyone who demands from you an account of the hope that is in you; yet do it with gentleness and reverence.
1 Peter 3:15 NRSV

See also **Respect; Worship**

Revival

212.1 [The Lord's promise to Solomon] If my people who are called by my name humble themselves, pray, seek my face, and turn from their wicked ways, then I will hear from heaven, and will forgive their sin and heal their land.
2 Chronicles 7:14 NRSV

212.2 Wilt thou not revive us again: that thy people may rejoice in thee?
Psalm 85:6 KJV

212.3 Oh, that you would rend the heavens and come down, that the mountains would tremble before you! As when fire sets twigs ablaze and causes water to boil, come down to make your name known to your enemies and cause the nations to quake before you!

Isaiah 64:1–2 NIV

212.4 He said to me, 'O man, can these bones live?' I answered, 'Only you, Lord God, know that.' He said, 'Prophesy over these bones; say: Dry bones, hear the word of the Lord. The Lord God says to these bones: I am going to put breath into you, and you will live.'

Ezekiel 37:3–5 REB

The valley of dry bones
Ezekiel's vision of the valley of dry bones is a remarkable story. Israel was in a state of despair in exile, having been punished by God for sin. Yet the vision of the prophet showed a message of restoration, a promise of new life given by God's Spirit. God would revive his people.

212.5 Afterwards I will pour out my Spirit on everyone: your sons and daughters will proclaim my message; your old people will have dreams, and your young people will see visions.

Joel 2:28 GNB

212.6 O Lord, revive thy work in the midst of the years, in the midst of the years make known; in wrath remember mercy.

Habakkuk 3:2 KJV

212.7 Repent ye therefore, and be converted, that your sins may be blotted out, when the times of refreshing shall come from the presence of the Lord.

Acts 3:19 KJV

212.8 When they had prayed, the place in which they were gathered together was shaken; and they were all filled with the Holy Spirit and spoke the word of God with boldness.

Acts 4:31 NRSV

212.9 The word of God continued to spread; the number of the disciples increased greatly in Jerusalem, and a great many of the priests became obedient to the faith.

Acts 6:7 NRSV

See also **Renewal; Restoration**

Reward

213.1 After these things the word of the Lord came unto Abram in a vision, saying, Fear not, Abram: I am thy shield, and thy exceeding great reward.

Genesis 15:1 KJV

213.2 Moreover by them [the judgments of the Lord] is thy servant warned: and in keeping of them there is great reward.

Psalm 19:11 KJV

213.3 Ye that fear the Lord, believe him; and your reward shall not fail.

Ecclesiasticus 2:8 KJV

213.4 Happy are you when people insult you and persecute you and tell all kinds of evil lies against you because you are my followers. Be happy and glad, for a great reward is kept for you in heaven.

Matthew 5:11–12 GNB

213.5 Then Peter spoke up. 'Look,' he said, 'we have left everything and followed you. What will we have?' Jesus said to them, 'You can be sure that when the Son of Man sits on his glorious throne in the New Age, then you twelve followers of mine will also sit on thrones, to rule the twelve tribes of Israel. And everyone who has left houses or brothers or sisters or father or mother or children or fields for my sake, will receive a hundred times more and will be given eternal life.'

Matthew 19:27–29 GNB

213.6 These shall go away into everlasting punishment: but the righteous into life eternal.

Matthew 25:46 KJV

213.7 Love your enemies and do good to them; lend and expect nothing back. You will then have a great reward, and you will be children of the Most High God. For he is good to the ungrateful and the wicked.

Luke 6:35 GNB

213.8 The work of each builder will become visible, for the Day will disclose it, because it will be revealed with fire, and the fire will test what sort of work each has done. If what has been built on the foundation survives, the builder will receive a reward.

1 Corinthians 3:13–14 NRSV

213.9 For scripture says, 'You shall not muzzle an ox while it is treading out the grain'; besides, 'The worker earns his pay.'

1 Timothy 5:18 REB

213.10 Without faith it is impossible to please him: for he that cometh to God must believe that he is, and that he is a rewarder of them that diligently seek him.

Hebrews 11:6 KJV

See also Last things, Heaven; Obedience

Riches

214.1 Do not say to yourself, 'My power and the might of my own hand have gained me this wealth.' But remember the Lord your God, for it is he who gives you power to get wealth, so that he may confirm his covenant that he swore to your ancestors, as he is doing today.

Deuteronomy 8:17–18 NRSV

214.2 It made me jealous to see proud and evil people and to watch them prosper.

Psalm 73:3 CEV

214.3 Woe to them that are at ease in Zion, and trust in the mountain of Samaria.

Amos 6:1 KJV

214.4 He hath filled the hungry with good things, and the rich he hath sent empty away.

Luke 1:53 BCP

214.5 There was a certain rich man, which was clothed in purple and fine linen, and fared sumptuously every day: and there was a certain beggar named Lazarus, which was laid at his gate, full of sores, and desiring to be fed with the crumbs which fell from the rich man's table: moreover the dogs came and licked his sores. And it came to pass, that the beggar died, and was carried by the angels into Abraham's bosom: the rich man also died, and was buried; and in hell he lift up his eyes, being in torments, and seeth Abraham afar off, and Lazarus in his bosom. And he cried and said, Father Abraham, have mercy on me, and send Lazarus, that he may dip the tip of his finger in water, and cool my tongue; for I am tormented in this flame. But Abraham said, Son, remember that thou in thy lifetime receivedst thy good things, and likewise Lazarus evil things: but now he is comforted, and thou art tormented. And beside all this, between us and you there is a great gulf fixed: so that they which would pass from hence to you cannot; neither can they pass to us, that would come from thence. Then he said, I pray thee therefore, father, that thou wouldest send him to my father's house: for I have five brethren; that he may testify unto them, lest they also come into this place of torment.

Luke 16:19–28 KJV

214.6 On hearing this Jesus said [to the rich young ruler], 'There is still one thing you lack: sell everything you have and give to the poor, and you will have treasure in heaven; then come and follow me.' When he heard this his heart sank, for he was a very rich man. When Jesus saw it he said, 'How hard it is for the wealthy to enter the kingdom of God! It is easier for a camel to go through the eye of a needle than for a rich man to enter the kingdom of God.'

Luke 18:22–25 REB

214.7 The unsearchable riches of Christ.

Ephesians 3:8 KJV

214.8 Instruct those who are rich in this world's goods that they should not be proud and should set their hopes not on money, which is untrustworthy, but on God who gives us richly all that we need for our happiness.

1 Timothy 6:17 NJB

214.9 Come now, you rich people, weep and wail for the miseries that are coming to you. Your riches have rotted, and your clothes are moth-eaten. Your gold and silver have rusted, and their rust will be evidence against you, and it will eat your flesh like fire. You have laid up treasure for the last days. Listen! The wages of the labourers who mowed your fields, which you kept back by fraud, cry out, and the cries of the harvesters have reached the ears of the Lord of hosts. You have lived on the earth in luxury and in pleasure; you have fattened your hearts on a day of slaughter.

James 5:1–5 NRSV

214.10 If we have all we need and see one of our own people in need, we must have pity on that person, or else we cannot say we love God.

1 John 3:17 CEV

See also **Ambition, Negative; Desire, wrong; Money and material goods; Poverty**

Right and wrong

215.1 [The Lord to Cain] If you had done the right thing, you would be smiling. But you did the wrong thing, and now sin is waiting to attack you like a lion. Sin wants to destroy you, but don't let it!

Genesis 4:7 CEV

215.2 In those days there was no king in Israel and everyone did what was right in his own eyes.

Judges 17:6 REB

215.3 I [Samuel] shall show you what is right and good: to revere the Lord and worship him faithfully with all your heart; for consider what great things he has done for you. But if you persist in wickedness, both you and your king will be swept away.

1 Samuel 12:23–25 REB

215.4 [Solomon's prayer] Grant your servant, therefore, a heart with skill to listen, so that he may govern your people justly and distinguish good from evil. Otherwise who is equal to the task of governing this great people of yours?

1 Kings 3:9 REB

215.5 He [Josiah] did what was right in the eyes of the Lord, following in the footsteps of his forefather David and deviating neither to the right nor to the left.

2 Kings 22:2 REB

215.6 He [Ahaziah] did what was wrong in the eyes of the Lord like the house of Ahab, for they had been his counsellors after his father's death, to his undoing.

2 Chronicles 22:4 REB

215.7 You have been upright in all that has happened to us, for you acted faithfully, while we did wrong.

Nehemiah 9:33 NJB

215.8 Wash and be clean; put away your evil deeds far from my sight; cease to do evil, learn to do good. Pursue justice, guide the oppressed; uphold the rights of the fatherless, and plead the widow's cause.

Isaiah 1:16 REB

215.9 Woe to those who call what is bad, good, and what is good, bad, who substitute darkness for light and light for darkness, who substitute bitter for sweet and sweet for bitter.

Isaiah 5:20 NJB

215.10 Behold, a virgin shall conceive, and bear a son, and shall call his name Immanuel. Butter and honey shall he eat, that he may know to refuse the evil, and choose the good. For before the child shall know to refuse the evil, and choose the good, the land that thou abhorrest shall be forsaken of both her kings.

Isaiah 7:14–16 KJV

215.11 Peter began: 'I now understand how true it is that God has no favourites, but that in every nation those who are god-fearing and do what is right are acceptable to him.'

Acts 10:34–35 REB

215.12 What credit is there in enduring the beating you deserve when you have done wrong? On the other hand, when you have behaved well and endured

suffering for it, that is a sign of grace in the sight of God.

1 Peter 2:20 REB

215.13 Whoever acts uprightly is upright, just as he is upright. Whoever lives sinfully belongs to the devil, since the devil has been a sinner from the beginning.

1 John 3:7–8 NJB

215.14 Evil people will keep on being evil, and everyone who is dirty-minded will still be dirty-minded. But good people will keep on doing right, and God's people will always be holy.

Revelation 22:11 CEV

See also **Motives**; **Righteousness**

Righteousness

216.1 Noah was a righteous man, blameless among the people of his time, and he walked with God.

Genesis 6:9 NIV

216.2 He [Abraham] believed in the Lord; and he counted it to him for righteousness.

Genesis 15:6 KJV

216.3 Righteousness exalteth a nation: but sin is a reproach to any people.

Proverbs 14:34 KJV

216.4 The effect of righteousness will be peace, and the result of righteousness, quietness and trust for ever.

Isaiah 32:17 NRSV

216.5 All our righteousnesses are as filthy rags; and we all do fade as a leaf; and our iniquities, like the wind, have taken us away.

Isaiah 64:6 KJV

216.6 Let justice flow on like a river and righteousness like a never-failing torrent.

Amos 5:24 REB

216.7 Blessed are they which do hunger and thirst after righteousness: for they shall be filled.

Matthew 5:6 KJV

216.8 For I tell you, unless your righteousness exceeds that of the scribes and Pharisees, you will never enter the kingdom of heaven.

Matthew 5:20 NRSV

216.9 Seek ye first the kingdom of God, and his righteousness; and all these things shall be added unto you.

Matthew 6:33 KJV

216.10 For he has fixed a day in which he will judge the whole world with justice by means of a man he has chosen. He has given proof of this to everyone by raising that man from death!

Acts 17:31 GNB

216.11 For therein [in the gospel] is the righteousness of God revealed from faith to faith: as it is written, The just shall live by faith.

Romans 1:17 KJV

216.12 As it is written, There is none righteous, no, not one.

Romans 3:10 KJV

216.13 Now the righteousness of God without the law is manifested, being witnessed by the law and the prophets; even the righteousness of God which is by faith of Jesus Christ unto all and upon all them that believe: for there is no difference: for all have sinned, and come short of the glory of God; being justified freely by his grace through the redemption that is in Christ Jesus: whom God hath set forth to be a propitiation through faith in his blood, to declare his righteousness for the remission of sins that are past, through the forbearance of God; to declare, I say, at this time his righteousness: that he might be just, and the justifier of him which believeth in Jesus.

Romans 3:21–26 KJV

216.14 If, because of the one man's trespass, death exercised dominion through that one, much more surely will those who receive the abundance of grace and the free gift of righteousness exercise dominion in life through the one man, Jesus Christ. Therefore just as one man's trespass led to condemnation for all, so one man's act of righteousness leads to justification and life for all. For just as by the one man's disobedience the many were made sinners, so by the one man's obedience the many will be made righteous. But law came in, with the result that the trespass multiplied; but where sin increased, grace abounded all the more, so that, just as sin exercised dominion in death, so grace might also exercise dominion through justification leading to eternal life through Jesus Christ our Lord.

Romans 5:17–21 NRSV

216.15 By God's act you are in Christ Jesus; God has made him our wisdom, and in him we have our righteousness, our holiness, our liberation. Therefore, in the words of scripture, 'If anyone must boast, let him boast of the Lord.'

1 Corinthians 1:30 REB

216.16 For our sake he made the sinless one a victim for sin, so that in him we might become the uprightness of God.

2 Corinthians 5:21 NJB

216.17 Stand therefore, having your loins girt about with truth, and having on the breastplate of righteousness.

Ephesians 6:14 KJV

216.18 All I want is Christ and to know that I belong to him. I could not make myself acceptable to God by obeying the Law of Moses. God accepted me simply because of my faith in Christ.

Philippians 3:8–9 CEV

216.19 A harvest of righteousness is sown in peace for those who make peace.

James 3:18 NRSV

216.20 For Christ died for sins once and for all, a good man on behalf of sinners, in order to lead you to God. He was put to death physically, but made alive spiritually.

1 Peter 3:18 GNB

See also Faith; Justice; Justification; Right and wrong; Self-righteousness

Ritual

217.1 Samuel then said: 'Does the Lord desire whole-offerings and sacrifices as he desires obedience? To obey is better than sacrifice, and to listen to him better than the fat of rams.'

1 Samuel 15:22 REB

217.2 The Lord said, Forasmuch as this people draw near me with their mouth, and with their lips do honour me, but have removed their heart far from me, and their fear toward me is taught by the precept of men.

Isaiah 29:13 KJV

217.3 Even though you offer me your burnt-offerings and grain-offerings, I will not accept them; and the offerings of well-being of your fatted animals I will not look upon… But let justice roll down like waters, and righteousness like an ever-flowing stream.

Amos 5:22, 24 NRSV

217.4 'What a weariness this is,' you say, and you sniff at me, says the Lord of hosts. You bring what has been taken by violence or is lame or sick, and this you bring as your offering! Shall I accept that from your hand? says the Lord.

Malachi 1:13 NRSV

217.5 Woe unto you, scribes and Pharisees, hypocrites! for ye make clean the outside of the cup and of the platter, but within they are full of extortion and excess. Thou blind Pharisee, cleanse first that which is within the cup and platter, that the outside of them may be clean also. Woe unto you, scribes and Pharisees, hypocrites! for ye are like unto whited sepulchres, which indeed appear beautiful outward, but are within full of dead men's bones, and of all uncleanness. Even so ye also outwardly appear righteous unto men, but within ye are full of hypocrisy and iniquity.

Matthew 23:25–28 KJV

217.6 To be a real Jew you must obey the Law. True circumcision is something that happens deep in your heart, not something done to your body.

Romans 2:29 CEV

217.7 They [people in the last days] will hold to the outward form of our religion, but reject its real power. Keep away from such people.

2 Timothy 3:5 GNB

Rulers

218.1 Don't speak evil of me or of the ruler of your people.

Exodus 22:28 CEV

218.2 When thou sittest to eat with a ruler, consider diligently what is before thee: and put a knife to thy throat, if thou be a man given to appetite.

Proverbs 23:1–2 KJV

218.3 A country in revolt throws up many leaders: with one person wise and experienced, you have stability.

Proverbs 28:2 NJB

218.4 Many seek audience of a ruler, but it is the Lord who decides each case.

Proverbs 29:26 REB

218.5 Thou, Bethlehem Ephratah, though thou be little among the thousands of Judah, yet out of thee shall he come forth unto me that is to be ruler in Israel.

Micah 5:2 KJV

218.6 You know that among the gentiles the rulers lord it over them, and great men make their authority felt. Among you this is not to happen.

Matthew 20:25–26 NJB

218.7 Behold, there cometh one of the rulers of the synagogue, Jairus by name; and when he saw him, he fell at his feet.

Mark 5:22 KJV

218.8 One of the rulers put this question to him, 'Good Master, what shall I do to inherit eternal life?'

Luke 18:18 NJB

218.9 The kings of earth prepare for war, and the rulers join together against the Lord and his Messiah.

Acts 4:26 CEV

218.10 Let every soul be subject unto the higher powers. For there is no power but of God: the powers that be are ordained of God. Whosoever therefore resisteth the power, resisteth the ordinance of God: and they that resist shall receive to themselves damnation. For rulers are not a terror to good works, but to the evil. Wilt thou then not be afraid of the power? do that which is good, and thou shalt have praise of the same.

Romans 13:1–3 KJV

The powers that be

The expression *the powers that be* refers to the controlling authority or the governing body; in other words, the Establishment. The phrase comes from this verse, which teaches subjection to the governing authorities because they are instituted by God.

218.11 We are not fighting against humans. We are fighting against forces and authorities and against rulers of darkness and powers in the spiritual world.

Ephesians 6:12 CEV

218.12 I urge then, first of all that petitions, prayers, intercessions and thanksgiving should be offered for everyone, for kings and others in authority, so that we may be able to live peaceful and quiet lives with all devotion and propriety.

1 Timothy 2:1–2 NJB

218.13 God, the blessed and only Ruler of all, the King of kings and the Lord of lords.

1 Timothy 6:15 NJB

218.14 Remind your people to obey the rulers and authorities and not to be rebellious.

Titus 3:1 CEV

See also **State, responsibility to**

Sabbath

219.1 Remember the sabbath day, to keep it holy. Six days shalt thou labour, and do all thy work: but the seventh day is the sabbath of the Lord thy God: in it thou shalt not do any work, thou, nor thy son, nor thy daughter, thy manservant, nor thy maidservant, nor thy cattle, nor thy stranger that is within thy gates: for in six days the Lord made heaven and earth, the sea, and all that in them is, and rested the seventh day: wherefore the Lord blessed the sabbath day, and hallowed it.

Exodus 20:8–11 KJV

219.2 At that time I saw people in Judah pressing juice from grapes on the Sabbath. Others were loading corn, wine, grapes, figs, and other things on their donkeys and taking them into Jerusalem; I warned them not to sell anything on the Sabbath. Some people from the city of Tyre were living in Jerusalem, and they brought fish and all kinds of goods into the city to sell to our people on the Sabbath. I reprimanded the Jewish leaders and said, 'Look at the evil you're doing! You're making the Sabbath unholy. This is exactly why God punished your ancestors when he brought destruction on this city. And yet you insist on bringing more of God's anger down on Israel by profaning the Sabbath.'

Nehemiah 13:15–18 GNB

219.3 The Lord says, 'If you treat the Sabbath as sacred and do not pursue your own interests on that day; if you value my holy day and honour it by not travelling, working, or talking idly on that day, then you will find the joy that comes from serving me. I will make you honoured all over the world, and you will enjoy the land I gave to your ancestor, Jacob.'

Isaiah 58:13–14 GNB

219.4 Jesus answered, 'What if one of you has a sheep and it falls into a deep hole on the Sabbath? Will you not take hold of it and lift it out? And a human being is worth much more than a sheep! So then, our Law does allow us to help someone on the Sabbath.'

Matthew 12:11–12 GNB

219.5 The sabbath was made for humankind, and not humankind for the sabbath; so the Son of Man is lord even of the sabbath.

Mark 2:27–28 NRSV

219.6 On the first day of the week we met for the breaking of bread. Paul was due to leave the next day, and he preached a sermon that went on till the middle of the night.

Acts 20:7 NJB

219.7 On the first day of every week, each of you is to put aside and save whatever extra you earn, so that collections need not be taken when I come.

1 Corinthians 16:2 NRSV

See also Rest

Sacrifice

220.1 Noah built an altar where he could offer sacrifices to the Lord. Then he offered on the altar one of each kind of animal and bird that could be used for a sacrifice.

Genesis 8:20 CEV

220.2 Your lamb shall be without blemish, a year-old male; you may take it from the sheep or from the goats. You shall keep it until the fourteenth day of this month; then the whole assembled congregation of Israel shall slaughter it at twilight. They shall take some of the blood and put it on the two doorposts and the lintel of the houses in which they eat it.

Exodus 12:5–7 NRSV

220.3 He shall put his hand upon the head of the burnt offering; and it shall be accepted for him to make atonement for him.

Leviticus 1:4 KJV

220.4 Samuel said, 'Has the Lord as great delight in burnt-offerings and sacrifices, as in obedience to the voice of the Lord? Surely, to obey is better than sacrifice, and to heed than the fat of rams.'

1 Samuel 15:22 NRSV

220.5 For thou desirest not sacrifice; else would I give it: thou delightest not in burnt offering. The sacrifices of God are a broken spirit: a broken and a contrite heart, O God, thou wilt not despise.

Psalm 51:16–17 KJV

220.6 The Lord says, 'I hate your religious festivals; I cannot stand them! When you bring me burnt offerings and grain offerings, I will not accept them; I will not accept the animals you have fattened to bring me as offerings. Stop your noisy songs; I do not want to listen to your harps. Instead, let justice flow like a stream, and righteousness like a river that never goes dry.'

Amos 5:21–24 GNB

220.7 Go and learn what this text means, 'I require mercy, not sacrifice.' I did not come to call the virtuous, but sinners.

Matthew 9:13 REB

220.8 I beseech you therefore, brethren, by the mercies of God, that ye present your bodies a living sacrifice, holy, acceptable unto God, which is your reasonable service.

Romans 12:1 KJV

220.9 Every priest stands day after day at his service, offering again and again the same sacrifices that can never take away sins. But when Christ had offered for all time a single sacrifice for sins, 'he sat down at the right hand of God'.

Hebrews 10:11–12 NRSV

220.10 Let us, then, always offer praise to God as our sacrifice through Jesus, which is the offering presented by lips that confess him as Lord. Do not forget to do good and to help one another, because these are the sacrifices that please God.

Hebrews 13:15–16 GNB

See also **Blood; Passover**

Salvation and Savior

221.1 The Lord is my light and my salvation; whom shall I fear? the Lord is the strength of my life; of whom shall I be afraid?

Psalm 27:1 KJV

221.2 Then everyone who calls on the name of the Lord shall be saved; for in Mount Zion and in Jerusalem there shall be those who escape, as the Lord has said, and among the survivors shall be those whom the Lord calls.

Joel 2:32 NRSV

221.3 She [Mary] will bear a son; and you [Joseph] shall give him the name Jesus, for he will save his people from their sins.

Matthew 1:21 REB

221.4 'Who, then, can be saved?' they [the disciples] asked. Jesus looked straight at them and answered, 'This is impossible for human beings, but for God everything is possible.'

Matthew 19:25–26 GNB

221.5 If you keep on being faithful right to the end, you will be saved.

Matthew 24:13 CEV

221.6 For unto you is born this day in the city of David a Saviour, which is Christ the Lord.

Luke 2:11 KJV

221.7 Someone said to him, 'Sir, will there be only a few saved?' He said to them, 'Try your hardest to enter by the narrow door, because, I tell you, many will try to enter and will not succeed.'

Luke 13:23–24 NJB

221.8 For the Son of man is come to seek and to save that which was lost.

Luke 19:10 KJV

221.9 For God sent not his Son into the world to condemn the world; but that the world through him might be saved.

John 3:17 KJV

221.10 There is salvation in no one else, for there is no other name under heaven given among mortals by which we must be saved.

Acts 4:12 NRSV

221.11 'Sirs, what must I do to be saved?' They answered, 'Put your trust in the Lord Jesus, and you will be saved, you and your household.'

Acts 16:30–31 REB

221.12 The message about the cross doesn't make any sense to lost people. But for those of us who are being saved, it is God's power at work.

1 Corinthians 1:18 CEV

221.13 For he says, 'At an acceptable time I have listened to you, and on a day of salvation I have helped you.' See, now is

the acceptable time; see, now is the day of salvation!

2 Corinthians 6:2 NRSV

221.14 For by grace are ye saved through faith; and that not of yourselves: it is the gift of God.

Ephesians 2:8 KJV

221.15 You must work out your own salvation in fear and trembling; for it is God who works in you, inspiring both the will and the deed, for his own chosen purpose.

Philippians 2:12–13 REB

221.16 God our Saviour, who wants everyone to be saved and to come to know the truth.

1 Timothy 2:3–4 GNB

221.17 Ever since you were a child, you have known the Holy Scriptures, which are able to give you the wisdom that leads to salvation through faith in Christ Jesus.

2 Timothy 3:15 GNB

221.18 How shall we escape, if we neglect so great salvation?

Hebrews 2:3 KJV

221.19 [We] who are being protected by the power of God through faith for a salvation ready to be revealed in the last time.

1 Peter 1:5 NRSV

221.20 We have seen and do testify that the Father sent the Son to be the Saviour of the world.

1 John 4:14 KJV

221.21 Salvation belongs to our God who is seated on the throne, and to the Lamb!

Revelation 7:10 NRSV

See also Atonement; Christian life, Coming to faith; Sin

Sanctification

222.1 Sanctify them through thy truth: thy word is truth.

John 17:17 KJV

222.2 For just as you once presented your members as slaves to impurity and to greater and greater iniquity, so now present your members as slaves to righteousness for sanctification.

Romans 6:19 NRSV

222.3 For I delight in the law of God in my inmost self, but I see in my members another law at war with the law of my mind, making me captive to the law of sin that dwells in my members.

Romans 7:22–23 NRSV

222.4 I beseech you therefore, brethren, by the mercies of God, that ye present your bodies a living sacrifice, holy, acceptable unto God, which is your reasonable service. And be not conformed to this world, but be ye transformed by the renewing of your mind, that ye may prove what is that good, and acceptable, and perfect, will of God.

Romans 12:1–2 KJV

222.5 It is by him that you exist in Christ Jesus, who for us was made wisdom from God, and saving justice and holiness and redemption.

1 Corinthians 1:30 NJB

222.6 God wants you to be holy, so don't be immoral in matters of sex.

1 Thessalonians 4:3 CEV

222.7 The very God of peace sanctify you wholly; and I pray God your whole spirit and soul and body be preserved blameless unto the coming of our Lord Jesus Christ.

1 Thessalonians 5:23 KJV

222.8 Elect according to the foreknowledge of God the Father, through sanctification of the Spirit, unto obedience and sprinkling of the blood of Jesus Christ.

1 Peter 1:2 KJV

See also **Christian life, Character of the Christian; Holiness**

Scribes

223.1 All the people gathered together into the square before the Water Gate. They told the scribe Ezra to bring the book of the law of Moses, which the Lord had given to Israel.

Nehemiah 8:1 NRSV

223.2 I tell you, unless you show yourselves far better than the scribes and Pharisees, you can never enter the kingdom of Heaven.

Matthew 5:20 REB

223.3 He [Jesus] taught them with authority, unlike their own scribes.

Matthew 7:29 NJB

223.4 A scribe came up and said to him, 'Teacher, I will follow you wherever you go.'

Matthew 8:19 REB

223.5 When the chief priests and the scribes saw the amazing things that he did, and heard the children crying out in the temple, 'Hosanna to the Son of David', they became angry.

Matthew 21:15 NRSV

223.6 The Pharisees and the teachers of the Law are experts in the Law of Moses. So obey everything they teach you, but don't do as they do. After all, they say one thing and do something else. They pile heavy burdens on people's shoulders and won't lift a finger to help. Everything they do is just to show off in front of others. They even make a big show of wearing Scripture verses on their foreheads and arms, and they wear big tassels for everyone to see. They love the best seats at banquets and the front seats in the meeting places. And when they are in the market, they like to have people greet them as their teachers.

Matthew 23:2–7 CEV

223.7 Immediately, while he was still speaking, Judas, one of the twelve, arrived; and with him there was a crowd with swords and clubs, from the chief priests, the scribes, and the elders.

Mark 14:43 NRSV

See also Hypocrisy; Pharisees

Seeking God

224.1 [David to Solomon] If you search for him, he will let you find him, but if you forsake him, he will cast you off for ever.

1 Chronicles 28:9 REB

224.2 Let all who seek you be jubilant and rejoice in you.

Psalm 40:16 REB

224.3 As the hart panteth after the water brooks, so panteth my soul after thee, O God.

Psalm 42:1 KJV

224.4 God looked down from heaven upon the children of men, to see if there were any that did understand, that did seek God.

Psalm 53:2 KJV

224.5 Look to the Lord and be strong; at all times seek his presence.

Psalm 105:4 REB

224.6 With all my heart I seek you, do not let me stray from your commandments.

Psalm 119:10 NJB

224.7 I love those who love me; whoever searches eagerly for me finds me.

Proverbs 8:17 NJB

224.8 Seek ye the Lord while he may be found, call ye upon him while he is near.

Isaiah 55:6 KJV

224.9 When you seek me, you will find me; if you search wholeheartedly, I shall let you find me, says the Lord.

Jeremiah 29:13–14 REB

224.10 The Lord is good unto them that wait for him, to the soul that seeketh him.

Lamentations 3:25 KJV

224.11 Let us strive to know the Lord, whose coming is as sure as the sunrise. He will come to us like the rain, like spring rains that water the earth.

Hosea 6:3 REB

224.12 Ask, and it will be given to you; search, and you will find; knock, and the door will be opened to you. Everyone who asks receives; everyone who searches finds; everyone who knocks will have the door opened.

Matthew 7:7–8 NJB

224.13 They were to seek God in the hope that, groping after him, they might find him; though indeed he is not far from each one of us.

Acts 17:27 REB

224.14 Now it is impossible to please God without faith, since anyone who comes to him must believe that he exists and rewards those who seek him.

Hebrews 11:6 NJB

See also **Ambition, Godly; Christian life, Longing for God**

Self-control

225.1 Be ye not as the horse, or as the mule, which have no understanding: whose mouth must be held in with bit and bridle.

Psalm 32:9 KJV

225.2 Set a watch, O Lord, before my mouth; keep the door of my lips.

Psalm 141:3 KJV

225.3 He that keepeth his mouth keepeth his life: but he that openeth wide his lips shall have destruction.

Proverbs 13:3 KJV

225.4 Controlling your temper is better than being a hero who captures a city.

Proverbs 16:32 CEV

225.5 An open town, and without defences: such is anyone who lacks self-control.

Proverbs 25:28 NJB

225.6 The stupid give free rein to their anger; the wise wait for it to cool.

Proverbs 29:11 REB

225.7 I do not spare my body, but bring it under strict control, for fear that after preaching to others I should find myself disqualified.

1 Corinthians 9:27 REB

225.8 The harvest of the Spirit is… self-control.

Galatians 5:22 REB

225.9 God did not give us a spirit of timidity, but the Spirit of power and love and self-control.

2 Timothy 1:7 NJB

225.10 Tell the young men to have self-control in everything.

Titus 2:6 CEV

225.11 If you think you are being religious, but can't control your tongue, you are fooling yourself, and everything you do is useless.

James 1:26 CEV

225.12 Your minds, then, must be sober and ready for action… Do not allow yourselves to be shaped by the passions of your old ignorance.

1 Peter 1:13–14 NJB

225.13 The end of all things is upon us; therefore to help you pray you must lead self-controlled and sober lives.

1 Peter 4:7 REB

225.14 You should make every effort to add virtue to your faith, knowledge to virtue, self-control to knowledge, fortitude to self-control…

2 Peter 1:5–6 REB

See also **Dignity; Discipline; Temperance**

Self-denial

226.1 A poor widow came and put in two small copper coins, which are worth a penny. Then he called his disciples and said to them, 'Truly I tell you, this poor widow has put in more than all those who are contributing to the treasury. For all of them contributed out of their abundance; but she out of her poverty has put in everything she had, all she had to live on.'

Mark 12:42–44 NRSV

226.2 To everybody he said, 'Anyone who wants to be a follower of mine must renounce self; day after day he must take up his cross, and follow me. Whoever wants to save his life will lose it, but whoever loses his life for my sake will save it.'

Luke 9:23–24 REB

226.3 He must increase, but I must decrease.

John 3:30 KJV

226.4 Those who love their own life will lose it; those who hate their own life in this world will keep it for life eternal.

John 12:25 GNB

226.5 The fruit of the Spirit is… longsuffering, gentleness, goodness, faith, meekness, temperance…

Galatians 5:22–23 KJV

See also Disciples; Discipline; Service

Self-examination

227.1 I thought on my ways, and turned my feet unto thy testimonies.

Psalm 119:59 KJV

227.2 Now these are the words of the Lord of Hosts: Consider your way of life.

Haggai 1:5 REB

227.3 Examine yourselves, and only then eat of the bread and drink of the cup. For all who eat and drink without discerning the body, eat and drink judgement against

themselves. For this reason many of you are weak and ill, and some have died.

1 Corinthians 11:28–30 NRSV

227.4 Put yourselves to the test to make sure you are in the faith. Examine yourselves. Do you not recognise yourselves as people in whom Jesus Christ is present? – unless, that is, you fail the test.

2 Corinthians 13:5 NJB

227.5 If someone thinks he or she is somebody when really they are nobody, they are only deceiving themselves. You should each judge your own conduct. If it is good, then you can be proud of what you yourself have done, without having to compare it with what someone else has done.

Galatians 6:3–4 GNB

See also Discernment; Examination

Selfishness

228.1 Whoever holds back his grain is cursed by the people, but one who sells it earns their blessing.

Proverbs 11:26 REB

228.2 He that is first in his own cause seemeth just; but his neighbour cometh and searcheth him.

Proverbs 18:17 KJV

228.3 For men to search their own glory is not glory.

Proverbs 25:27 KJV

228.4 You stupid leaders are a pack of hungry and greedy dogs that never get enough. You are shepherds who ill-treat your own sheep for selfish gain.

Isaiah 56:11 CEV

228.5 You seek great things for yourself; leave off seeking them. I am about to bring disaster on all mankind.

Jeremiah 45:5 REB

228.6 For whosoever will save his life shall lose it; but whosoever shall lose his life for my sake and the gospel's, the same shall save it.

Mark 8:35 KJV

228.7 He will show how angry and furious he can be with every selfish person who rejects the truth and wants to do evil.

Romans 2:8 CEV

228.8 Nobody should be looking for selfish advantage, but everybody for someone else's.

1 Corinthians 10:24 NJB

228.9 Christ… died so we would no longer live for ourselves, but for the one who died and was raised to life for us.

2 Corinthians 5:15 CEV

228.10 Look to each other's interests and not merely to your own.

Philippians 2:4 REB

228.11 For all seek their own, not the things which are Jesus Christ's.

Philippians 2:21 KJV

228.12 You may be quite sure that in the last days there will be some difficult times. People will be self-centred…

2 Timothy 3:1–2 NJB

228.13 If anyone is well-off in worldly possessions and sees his brother in need but closes his heart to him, how can the love of God be remaining in him?

1 John 3:17 NJB

See also **Desire, wrong; Unselfishness**

Self-righteousness

229.1 After the Lord your God has driven them out for you, do not say to yourselves that he brought you in to possess this land because you deserved it. No, the Lord is going to drive these people out for you because they are wicked.

Deuteronomy 9:4 GNB

229.2 All one's ways may be pure in one's own eyes, but the Lord weighs the spirit.

Proverbs 16:2 NRSV

229.3 Which say, Stand by thyself, come not near to me; for I am holier than thou. These are a smoke in my nose, a fire that burneth all the day.

Isaiah 65:5 KJV

Holier than thou
People who are *holier than thou* behave towards others in a way that shows they think they are better, especially more moral or virtuous, than others. The origin of this phrase lies in this verse. Isaiah was prophesying against the self-righteousness of some who smugly claimed to be superior to others.

229.4 Be careful not to parade your religion before others; if you do, no reward awaits you with your Father in heaven.

Matthew 6:1 REB

229.5 Outside you look good, but inside you are evil and only pretend to be good.

Matthew 23:28 CEV

229.6 He also told this parable to some who trusted in themselves that they were righteous and regarded others with contempt: 'Two men went up to the temple to pray, one a Pharisee and the other a tax-collector. The Pharisee, standing by himself, was praying thus, "God, I thank you that I am not like other people: thieves, rogues, adulterers, or even like this tax-collector. I fast twice a week; I give a tenth of all my income." But the tax-collector, standing far off, would not even look up to heaven, but was beating his breast and saying, "God, be merciful to me, a sinner!" I tell you, this man went down to his home justified rather than the other; for all who exalt themselves will be humbled, but all who humble themselves will be exalted.'

Luke 18:9–14 NRSV

See also **Hypocrisy; Pride; Righteousness**

Service

230.1 [God to Moses] He said, 'I will be with you; and this shall be the sign for you that it is I who sent you: when you have brought the people out of Egypt, you shall worship God on this mountain.'

Exodus 3:12 NRSV

230.2 It is written, Thou shalt worship the Lord thy God, and him only shalt thou serve.

Matthew 4:10 KJV

230.3 No pupil ranks above his teacher, no servant above his master.

Matthew 10:24 REB

230.4 If you want to be great, you must be the servant of all the others. And if you want to be first, you must be everyone's slave. The Son of Man did not come to be a slave master, but a slave who will give his life to rescue many people.

Mark 10:43–45 CEV

230.5 Whoever wants to serve me must follow me, so that my servant will be with

me where I am. And my Father will honour anyone who serves me.

John 12:26 GNB

230.6 After he had washed their feet, had put on his robe, and had returned to the table, he said to them, 'Do you know what I have done to you? You call me Teacher and Lord – and you are right, for that is what I am. So if I, your Lord and Teacher, have washed your feet, you also ought to wash one another's feet.'

John 13:12–14 NRSV

230.7 If it [a man's gift] is serving, let him serve.

Romans 12:7 NIV

230.8 As we have therefore opportunity, let us do good unto all men, especially unto them who are of the household of faith.

Galatians 6:10 KJV

230.9 Whatever your task, put yourselves into it, as done for the Lord and not for your masters.

Colossians 3:23 NRSV

230.10 Whoever serves must do so with the strength that God supplies, so that God may be glorified in all things through Jesus Christ.

1 Peter 4:11 NRSV

See also **Deacons; Help; Kindness; Leadership; Responsibility, human; Self-denial; Works, good; Worship**

Sex

GIFT OF

231.1 So God created man in his own image, in the image of God created he him; male and female created he them.

And God blessed them, and God said unto them, Be fruitful, and multiply, and replenish the earth, and subdue it.

Genesis 1:27–28 KJV

231.2 Therefore shall a man leave his father and his mother, and shall cleave unto his wife: and they shall be one flesh. And they were both naked, the man and his wife, and were not ashamed.

Genesis 2:24–25 KJV

231.3 A man should fulfil his duty as a husband, and a woman should fulfil her duty as a wife, and each should satisfy the other's needs. A wife is not the master of her own body, but her husband is; in the same way a husband is not the master of his own body, but his wife is. Do not deny yourselves to each other, unless you first agree to do so for a while in order to spend your time in prayer; but then resume normal marital relations. In this way you will be kept from giving in to Satan's temptation because of your lack of self-control.

1 Corinthians 7:3–5 GNB

See also **Marriage**

MISUSE OF

231.4 Now Joseph was handsome and good-looking. And after a time his master's wife cast her eyes on Joseph and said, 'Lie with me.' But he refused and said to his master's wife, '… How then could I do this great wickedness, and sin against God?'

Genesis 39:6–9 NRSV

231.5 Do you not know that the wicked will not inherit the kingdom of God? Do not be deceived: Neither the sexually immoral nor idolaters nor adulterers nor

male prostitutes nor homosexual offenders… will inherit the kingdom of God.

1 Corinthians 6:9–10 NIV

231.6 You know that your bodies are parts of the body of Christ. Shall I take a part of Christ's body and make it part of the body of a prostitute? Impossible! Or perhaps you don't know that the man who joins his body to a prostitute becomes physically one with her? The scripture says quite plainly, 'The two will become one body.' But he who joins himself to the Lord becomes spiritually one with him. Avoid immorality. Any other sin a man commits does not affect his body; but the man who is guilty of sexual immorality sins against his own body. Don't you know that your body is the temple of the Holy Spirit, who lives in you and who was given to you by God? You do not belong to yourselves but to God.

1 Corinthians 6:15–19 GNB

231.7 Now the works of the flesh are manifest, Adultery, fornication, uncleanness, lasciviousness…

Galatians 5:19 KJV

231.8 Since you are God's people, it is not right that any matters of sexual immorality or indecency or greed should even be mentioned among you.

Ephesians 5:3 GNB

See also **Homosexuality**

Shame

232.1 They were both naked, the man and his wife, and were not ashamed… And he [Adam] said, I heard thy voice in the garden, and I was afraid, because I was naked; and I hid myself.

Genesis 2:25, 3:10 KJV

232.2 They who look to him are radiant with joy; they will never be put out of countenance.
Psalm 34:5 REB

232.3 Those who are ashamed of me and of my words in this adulterous and sinful generation, of them the Son of Man will also be ashamed when he comes in the glory of his Father with the holy angels.
Mark 8:38 NRSV

232.4 For I am not ashamed of the gospel of Christ: for it is the power of God unto salvation to every one that believeth; to the Jew first, and also to the Greek.
Romans 1:16 KJV

232.5 I am not ashamed! I know the one I have faith in, and I am sure that he can guard until the last day what he has trusted me with.
2 Timothy 1:12 CEV

232.6 Instead, it was a better country they longed for, the heavenly country. And so God is not ashamed for them to call him their God, because he has prepared a city for them.
Hebrews 11:16 GNB

232.7 Looking unto Jesus the author and finisher of our faith; who for the joy that was set before him endured the cross, despising the shame, and is set down at the right hand of the throne of God.
Hebrews 12:2 KJV

232.8 However, if you suffer because you are a Christian, don't be ashamed of it, but thank God that you bear Christ's name.
1 Peter 4:16 GNB

232.9 Now, little children, abide in him, so that when he is revealed we may have

confidence and not be put to shame before him at his coming.
1 John 2:28 NRSV

Shepherd

233.1 The Lord is my shepherd; I shall not want.
Psalm 23:1 KJV

233.2 He shall feed his flock like a shepherd: he shall gather the lambs with his arm, and carry them in his bosom, and shall gently lead those that are with young.
Isaiah 40:11 KJV

233.3 My people have been lost sheep; their shepherds have led them astray and caused them to roam on the mountains. They wandered over mountain and hill and forgot their own resting place.
Jeremiah 50:6 NIV

233.4 The word of the Lord came to me: 'Mortal, prophesy against the shepherds of Israel: prophesy, and say to them – to the shepherds: Thus says the Lord God: Ah, you shepherds of Israel who have been feeding yourselves! Should not shepherds feed the sheep?'
Ezekiel 34:1–2 NRSV

233.5 I shall set over them one shepherd to take care of them, my servant David; he will care for them and be their shepherd.
Ezekiel 34:23 REB

233.6 Then Jesus said to them, 'You will all fall away from me tonight, for the scripture says: I shall strike the shepherd and the sheep of the flock will be scattered.'
Matthew 26:31 NJB

233.7 The shepherds returned, glorifying and praising God for all the things that they had heard and seen, as it was told unto them.
Luke 2:20 KJV

233.8 I am the good shepherd, who is willing to die for the sheep.
John 10:11 GNB

233.9 Now the God of peace, that brought again from the dead our Lord Jesus, that great shepherd of the sheep, through the blood of the everlasting covenant...
Hebrews 13:20 KJV

233.10 You had wandered away like sheep. Now you have returned to the one who is your shepherd and protector.
1 Peter 2:25 CEV

233.11 When Christ the Chief Shepherd returns, you will be given a crown that will never lose its glory.
1 Peter 5:4 CEV

See also **Pastor**

Silence

234.1 He will guard the footsteps of his loyal servants, while the wicked will be silenced in darkness.
1 Samuel 2:9 REB

234.2 They sat there on the ground beside him for seven days and seven nights. To Job they spoke never a word, for they saw how much he was suffering.
Job 2:13 NJB

234.3 Unto thee will I cry, O Lord my rock; be not silent to me: lest, if thou be silent to me, I become like them that go down into the pit.
Psalm 28:1 KJV

234.4 When you did all this, I didn't say a word, and you thought, 'God is just like us!' But now I will accuse you.
Psalm 50:21 CEV

234.5 Even fools seem clever when they are quiet.
Proverbs 17:28 CEV

234.6 To every thing there is a season, and a time to every purpose under the heaven... a time to keep silence, and a time to speak.
Ecclesiastes 3:1, 7 KJV

234.7 Ill-treated and afflicted, he never opened his mouth, like a lamb led to the slaughter-house, like a sheep dumb before its shearers he never opened his mouth.
Isaiah 53:7 NJB

234.8 The Lord is in his holy temple; let all the earth be silent in his presence.
Habakkuk 2:20 REB

234.9 Hold thy peace at the presence of the Lord God: for the day of the Lord is at hand.
Zephaniah 1:7 KJV

234.10 Everyone, be silent! The Lord is present and moving about in his holy place.
Zechariah 2:13 CEV

234.11 He answered, 'I tell you, if my disciples are silent the stones will shout aloud.'
Luke 19:40 REB

234.12 Herod asked him a lot of questions, but Jesus did not answer.
Luke 23:9 CEV

234.13 The Lamb then broke the seventh seal, and there was silence in heaven for about half an hour.

Revelation 8:1 NJB

See also Quiet

Simplicity

235.1 The law of the Lord is perfect and revives the soul. The Lord's instruction never fails; it makes the simple wise.

Psalm 19:7 REB

235.2 The Lord preserveth the simple: I was brought low, and he helped me.

Psalm 116:6 KJV

235.3 As your word unfolds it gives light, and even the simple understand.

Psalm 119:130 NJB

235.4 How long will you simple fools be content with your simplicity? If only you would respond to my reproof, I would fill you with my spirit and make my precepts known to you.

Proverbs 1:22–23 REB

235.5 I am sending you out like sheep among wolves; so be cunning as snakes and yet innocent as doves.

Matthew 10:16 NJB

235.6 At that time Jesus exclaimed, 'I bless you, Father, Lord of heaven and of earth, for hiding these things from the learned and the clever and revealing them to little children.'

Matthew 11:25 NJB

235.7 Then he said, 'In truth I tell you, unless you change and become like little children you will never enter the kingdom of Heaven.'

Matthew 18:3 NJB

235.8 Your obedience has become known to everyone, and I am very pleased with you for it; but I should want you to be learned only in what is good, and unsophisticated about all that is evil.

Romans 16:19 NJB

235.9 God says in the Scriptures, 'I will destroy the wisdom of all who claim to be wise. I will confuse those who think they know so much.' What happened to those wise people? What happened to those experts in the Scriptures? What happened to the ones who think they have all the answers? Didn't God show that the wisdom of this world is foolish? God was wise and decided not to let the people of this world use their wisdom to learn about him. Instead, God chose to save only those who believe the foolish message we preach.

1 Corinthians 1:19–21 CEV

235.10 For our rejoicing is this, the testimony of our conscience, that in simplicity and godly sincerity, not with fleshly wisdom, but by the grace of God, we have had our conversation in the world, and more abundantly to you-ward.

2 Corinthians 1:12 KJV

235.11 I fear, lest by any means, as the serpent beguiled Eve through his subtilty, so your minds should be corrupted from the simplicity that is in Christ.

2 Corinthians 11:3 KJV

Sin

236.1 But the goat chosen by lot as the scapegoat shall be presented alive before the Lord to be used for making atonement by sending it into the desert as a scapegoat.

Leviticus 16:10 NIV

The scapegoat

Someone who is made to take the blame for the actions of other people is called a *scapegoat*. The English word was coined from the words *escape* and *goat*. A scapegoat was originally the goat that symbolically carried all the sins of Israel and was sent off into the wilderness.

236.2 Be sure your sin will find you out.

Numbers 32:23 KJV

236.3 Against thee, thee only, have I sinned, and done this evil in thy sight: that thou mightest be justified when thou speakest, and be clear when thou judgest. Behold, I was shapen in iniquity; and in sin did my mother conceive me.

Psalm 51:4–5 KJV

236.4 'Come now, let us reason together,' says the Lord. 'Though your sins are like scarlet, they shall be as white as snow; though they are red as crimson, they shall be like wool.'

Isaiah 1:18 NIV

236.5 All we like sheep have gone astray; we have turned every one to his own way; and the Lord hath laid on him the iniquity of us all.

Isaiah 53:6 KJV

236.6 Your iniquities have separated between you and your God, and your sins have hid his face from you, that he will not hear.

Isaiah 59:2 KJV

236.7 Your eyes are too pure to behold evil, and you cannot look on wrongdoing.

Habakkuk 1:13 NRSV

236.8 [An angel of the Lord to Joseph] You are to give him the name Jesus, because he will save his people from their sins.

Matthew 1:21 NIV

236.9 The next day he [John the Baptist] saw Jesus coming towards him. 'There is the Lamb of God,' he said, 'who takes away the sin of the world.'

John 1:29 REB

236.10 Jesus said to them, 'I am telling you the truth: everyone who sins is a slave of sin.'

John 8:34 GNB

236.11 For all have sinned, and come short of the glory of God.

Romans 3:23 KJV

236.12 As by one man sin entered into the world, and death by sin... so death passed upon all men, for that all have sinned.

Romans 5:12 KJV

236.13 What shall we say then? Shall we continue in sin, that grace may abound? God forbid. How shall we, that are dead to sin, live any longer therein?

Romans 6:1–2 KJV

236.14 For the wages of sin is death; but the gift of God is eternal life through Jesus Christ our Lord.

Romans 6:23 KJV

236.15 Christ never sinned! But God treated him as a sinner, so that Christ could make us acceptable to God.

2 Corinthians 5:21 CEV

236.16 As for you, you were dead in your transgressions and sins, in which you used to live when you followed the ways of this world and of the ruler of the kingdom of the air, the spirit who is now at work in those who are disobedient. All of us also lived among them at one time, gratifying the cravings of our sinful nature and following its desires and thoughts. Like the rest, we were by nature objects of wrath.

Ephesians 2:1–3 NIV

236.17 This is a faithful saying, and worthy of all acceptation, that Christ Jesus came into the world to save sinners; of whom I am chief.

1 Timothy 1:15 KJV

236.18 Indeed, under the law almost everything is purified with blood, and without the shedding of blood there is no forgiveness of sins.

Hebrews 9:22 NRSV

236.19 He was bearing our sins in his own body on the cross, so that we might die to our sins and live for uprightness.

1 Peter 2:24 NJB

236.20 If we live in the light as he himself is in the light, then we share a common life, and the blood of Jesus his Son cleanses us from all sin. If we claim to be sinless, we are self-deceived and the truth is not in us. If we confess our sins, he is just and may be trusted to forgive our sins and cleanse us from every kind of wrongdoing.

1 John 1:7–9 REB

236.21 Everyone who commits sin is guilty of lawlessness; sin is lawlessness. You know that he was revealed to take away sins, and in him there is no sin.

1 John 3:4–5 NRSV

236.22 None of those who are children of God continue to sin, for God's very nature is in them; and because God is their Father, they cannot continue to sin.

1 John 3:9 GNB

See also **Confession, of sin; Conviction of sin; Forgiveness; Repentance; Salvation and Savior; Unbeliever**

Avoidance of

236.23 Depart from evil, and do good; and dwell for evermore.

Psalm 37:27 KJV

236.24 Thy word have I hid in mine heart, that I might not sin against thee.

Psalm 119:11 KJV

236.25 By mercy and truth iniquity is purged: and by the fear of the Lord men depart from evil.

Proverbs 16:6 KJV

236.26 Snares and pitfalls lie in the path of the crooked; the cautious person will steer clear of them.

Proverbs 22:5 REB

236.27 This is how you should pray… do not put us to the test, but save us from the evil one.

Matthew 6:9, 13 REB

236.28 You must regard yourselves as dead to sin and alive to God, in union with Christ Jesus. Therefore sin must no longer reign in your mortal body, exacting obedience to the body's desires. You must no longer put any part of it at sin's disposal, as an implement for doing wrong. Put yourselves instead at the disposal of God; think of yourselves as raised from death to life, and yield your bodies to God as implements for doing right. Sin shall no longer be your master, for you are no longer under law, but under grace.

Romans 6:11–14 REB

236.29 Keep away from sexual immorality… Do you not realise that your body is the temple of the Holy Spirit, who is in you and whom you received from God? You are not your own property, then; you have been bought at a price. So use your body for the glory of God.

1 Corinthians 6:18–20 NJB

236.30 Make no mistake: 'Bad company ruins good character.'

1 Corinthians 15:33 REB

236.31 You must kill everything in you that is earthly: sexual vice, impurity, uncontrolled passion, evil desires and especially greed.

Colossians 3:5 NJB

236.32 Abstain from all appearance of evil.

1 Thessalonians 5:22 KJV

236.33 Exhort one another daily, while it is called To day; lest any of you be hardened through the deceitfulness of sin.

Hebrews 3:13 KJV

236.34 He who called you is holy; like him, be holy in all your conduct. Does not scripture say, 'You shall be holy, for I am holy'?

1 Peter 1:15–16 REB

236.35 Dear friends, you are foreigners and strangers on this earth. So I beg you not to surrender to those desires that fight against you.

1 Peter 2:11 CEV

236.36 Take care not to let these unprincipled people seduce you with their errors; do not lose your own safe foothold. But grow in grace and in the knowledge of our Lord and Saviour Jesus Christ.

2 Peter 3:17–18 REB

236.37 Never follow a bad example, but keep following the good one.

3 John v. 11 NJB

Sinful nature

237.1 All of them are corrupt; no one does right.

Psalm 14:3 CEV

237.2 From my birth I have been evil, sinful from the time my mother conceived me.

Psalm 51:5 REB

237.3 You have done wrong and lied from the day you were born.

Psalm 58:3 CEV

237.4 No one on earth is sufficiently upright to do good without ever sinning.

Ecclesiastes 7:20 NJB

237.5 They kept on asking Jesus about the woman. Finally, he stood up and said, 'If any of you have never sinned, then go ahead and throw the first stone at her!'

John 8:7 CEV

237.6 For all have sinned, and come short of the glory of God.

Romans 3:23 KJV

237.7 It was through one man that sin entered the world, and through sin death, and thus death pervaded the whole human race, inasmuch as all have sinned. For sin was already in the world before there was law.

Romans 5:12–13 REB

237.8 For I know that in me (that is, in my flesh,) dwelleth no good thing: for to will is present with me; but how to perform that which is good I find not. For the good that I would I do not: but the evil which I would not, that I do. Now if I do that I would not, it is no more I that do it, but sin that dwelleth in me. I find then a law, that, when I would do good, evil is present with me.

Romans 7:18–21 KJV

237.9 What the law could not do, because human weakness robbed it of all potency, God has done: by sending his own Son in the likeness of our sinful nature and to deal with sin, he has passed judgement against sin within that very nature, so that the commandment of the law may find fulfilment in us, whose conduct is no longer controlled by the old nature, but by the Spirit.

Romans 8:3–4 REB

237.10 Those who live according to the sinful nature have their minds set on what that nature desires; but those who live in accordance with the Spirit have their minds set on what the Spirit desires. The mind of sinful man is death, but the mind controlled by the Spirit is life and peace, because the sinful mind is hostile to God. It does not submit to God's law, nor can it do so. Those controlled by the sinful nature cannot please God. You, however, are controlled not by the sinful nature but by the Spirit, if the Spirit of God lives in you. And if anyone does not have the Spirit of Christ, he does not belong to Christ. But if Christ is in you, your body is dead because of sin, yet your spirit is alive because of righteousness. And if the Spirit of him who raised Jesus from the dead is living in you, he who raised Christ from the dead will also give life to your mortal bodies through his Spirit, who lives in you. Therefore, brothers, we have an obligation – but it is not to the sinful nature, to live according to it. For if you live according to the sinful nature, you will die; but if by the Spirit you put to death the misdeeds of the body, you will live.

Romans 8:5–13 NIV

237.11 Be guided by the Spirit and you will not gratify the desires of your unspiritual nature. That nature sets its desires against the Spirit, while the Spirit fights against it. They are in conflict with one another so that you cannot do what you want.

Galatians 5:16–17 REB

237.12 We were ruled by our physical desires, and did what instinct and evil imagination suggested. In our natural condition we lay under the condemnation of God like the rest of mankind. But God is rich in mercy, and because of his great love for us, he brought us to life with Christ when we were dead because of our sins; it is by grace you are saved.

Ephesians 2:3–5 REB

237.13 Everyone who knows what is the right thing to do and does not do it commits a sin.

James 4:17 NJB

237.14 If we say, 'We have no sin,' we are deceiving ourselves, and truth has no place in us… If we say, 'We have never sinned,' we make him a liar, and his word has no place in us.

1 John 1:8, 10 NJB

See also **Adam; Fall, the; Sin**

Sleep

238.1 I sleep and wake up refreshed because you, Lord, protect me.

Psalm 3:5 CEV

238.2 I will both lay me down in peace, and sleep: for thou, Lord, only makest me dwell in safety.

Psalm 4:8 KJV

238.3 Look now, Lord my God, and answer me. Give light to my eyes lest I sleep the sleep of death.

Psalm 13:3 REB

238.4 My help comes only from the Lord, maker of heaven and earth. He will not let your foot stumble; he who guards you will not sleep. The guardian of Israel never slumbers, never sleeps.

Psalm 121:2–4 REB

238.5 In vain you get up earlier, and put off going to bed, sweating to make a living, since it is he who provides for his beloved as they sleep.

Psalm 127:2 NJB

238.6 I will give myself no rest, nor allow myself sleep, until I find a sanctuary for the Lord, a dwelling for the Mighty One of Jacob.

Psalm 132:4–5 REB

238.7 How long wilt thou sleep, O sluggard? when wilt thou arise out of thy sleep? Yet a little sleep, a little slumber, a little folding of the hands to sleep: so shall thy poverty come as one that travelleth, and thy want as an armed man.

Proverbs 6:9–11 KJV

238.8 If you sleep all the time, you will starve; if you get up and work, you will have enough food.

Proverbs 20:13 CEV

238.9 The labourer's sleep is sweet, whether he has eaten little or much, but the surfeit of the rich will not let him sleep at all.

Ecclesiastes 5:11 NJB

238.10 Stay awake, because you do not know when the master of the house is coming, evening, midnight, cockcrow or dawn; if he comes unexpectedly, he must not find you asleep. And what I am saying to you I say to all: Stay awake!

Mark 13:35–37 NJB

238.11 Why sleep ye? rise and pray, lest ye enter into temptation.

Luke 22:46 KJV

238.12 Now it is high time to awake out of sleep: for now is our salvation nearer than when we believed. The night is far spent, the day is at hand: let us therefore cast off the works of darkness, and let us put on the armour of light.

Romans 13:11–12 KJV

238.13 We do not belong to night and darkness, and we must not sleep like the rest, but keep awake and sober. Sleepers sleep at night... but we, who belong to the daylight, must keep sober.

1 Thessalonians 5:5–8 REB

Soul

239.1 He restoreth my soul: he leadeth me in the paths of righteousness for his name's sake.

Psalm 23:3 KJV

239.2 My soul thirsteth for God, for the living God: when shall I come and appear before God?... Why art thou cast down, O my soul? and why art thou disquieted in me? hope thou in God: for I shall yet praise him for the help of his countenance. O my God, my soul is cast down within me: therefore will I remember thee from the land of Jordan.

Psalm 42:2, 5–6 KJV

239.3 Bless the Lord, O my soul: and all that is within me, bless his holy name. Bless the Lord, O my soul, and forget not all his benefits.

Psalm 103:1–2 KJV

239.4 [The Lord] Every living soul belongs to me; parent and child alike are mine. It is the person who sins that will die.
Ezekiel 18:4 REB

239.5 Do not be afraid of those who kill the body but cannot kill the soul; rather be afraid of God, who can destroy both body and soul in hell.
Matthew 10:28 GNB

239.6 Take my yoke upon you, and learn from me; for I am gentle and humble in heart, and you will find rest for your souls.
Matthew 11:29 NRSV

239.7 Then he saith unto them, My soul is exceeding sorrowful, even unto death: tarry ye here, and watch with me.
Matthew 26:38 KJV

239.8 [Mary's Magnificat] My soul doth magnify the Lord...
Luke 1:46 BCP

See also **Heart; Spirit**

Sovereignty of God

240.1 Know therefore this day, and consider it in thine heart, that the Lord he is God in heaven above, and upon the earth beneath: there is none else.
Deuteronomy 4:39 KJV

240.2 The Lord said to Satan, 'Very well, all that he has is in your power; only do not stretch out your hand against him!'
Job 1:12 NRSV

240.3 People may plan all kinds of things, but the Lord's will is going to be done.
Proverbs 19:21 GNB

240.4 The Son of Man will die in the way that has been decided for him, but it will be terrible for the one who betrays him!
Luke 22:22 CEV

240.5 The wind bloweth where it listeth, and thou hearest the sound thereof, but canst not tell whence it cometh, and whither it goeth: so is every one that is born of the Spirit.
John 3:8 KJV

240.6 All that the Father giveth me shall come to me; and him that cometh to me I will in no wise cast out.
John 6:37 KJV

240.7 This man, handed over to you according to the definite plan and foreknowledge of God, you crucified and killed by the hands of those outside the law.
Acts 2:23 NRSV

240.8 In everything, as we know, he co-operates for good with those who love God and are called according to his purpose.
Romans 8:28 REB

240.9 At work in all these [gifts] is one and the same Spirit, distributing them at will to each individual.
1 Corinthians 12:11 NJB

240.10 [God] who worketh all things after the counsel of his own will.
Ephesians 1:11 KJV

240.11 Keep on working with fear and trembling to complete your salvation, because God is always at work in you to make you willing and able to obey his own purpose.
Philippians 2:12–13 GNB

See also **Election; God, Almighty; Guidance; Providence; Responsibility, human**

Speech

241.1 The Gileadites captured the fords of the Jordan leading to Ephraim, and whenever a survivor of Ephraim said, 'Let me cross over,' the men of Gilead asked him, 'Are you an Ephraimite?' If he replied, 'No,' they said, 'All right, say "Shibboleth".' If he said, 'Sibboleth', because he could not pronounce the word correctly, they seized him and killed him at the fords of the Jordan. Forty-two thousand Ephraimites were killed at that time.

Judges 12:5–6 NIV

The first shibboleth

A *shibboleth* is a use of language, or a saying or custom, especially one that distinguishes members of a certain group. The origin of the word lies in Judges 12:4–6: anyone who gave the incorrect pronunciation of *shibboleth* to the Gileadites in charge of the ford was killed.

241.2 Lord, set a guard on my mouth; keep watch at the door of my lips.

Psalm 141:3 REB

241.3 A word fitly spoken is like apples of gold in pictures of silver.

Proverbs 25:11 KJV

241.4 Many have fallen by the edge of the sword: but not so many as have fallen by the tongue.

Ecclesiasticus 28:18 KJV

241.5 Let thy speech be short, comprehending much in few words; be as one that knoweth and yet holdeth his tongue.

Ecclesiasticus 32:8 KJV

241.6 You can be sure that on Judgement Day everyone will have to give account of every useless word he has ever spoken.

Matthew 12:36 GNB

241.7 Speaking the truth in love, we must grow up in every way into him who is the head, into Christ.

Ephesians 4:15 NRSV

241.8 Stop all your dirty talk. Say the right thing at the right time and help others by what you say.

Ephesians 4:29 CEV

241.9 Let your speech be alway with grace, seasoned with salt, that ye may know how ye ought to answer every man.

Colossians 4:6 KJV

241.10 The tongue is like a fire. It is a world of wrong, occupying its place in our bodies and spreading evil through our whole being. It sets on fire the entire course of our existence with the fire that comes to it from hell itself… But no one has ever been able to tame the tongue. It is evil and uncontrollable, full of deadly poison. We use it to give thanks to our Lord and Father and also to curse other people, who are created in the likeness of God. Words of thanksgiving and cursing pour out from the same mouth. My brothers and sisters, this should not happen!

James 3:6, 8–10 GNB

241.11 For who among you delights in life, longs for time to enjoy prosperity? Guard your tongue from evil, your lips from any breath of deceit.

1 Peter 3:10 NJB

241.12 Always be ready to make your defence to anyone who demands from you an account of the hope that is in you; yet do it with gentleness and reverence.

1 Peter 3:15–16 NRSV

See also **Gossip**

Spirit

242.1 While they were crossing, Elijah said to Elisha, 'Tell me what I can do for you before I am taken from you.' Elisha said, 'Let me inherit a double share of your spirit.'

2 Kings 2:9 REB

242.2 Create in me a clean heart, O God; and renew a right spirit within me.

Psalm 51:10 KJV

242.3 You may think everything you do is right, but the Lord judges your motives.

Proverbs 16:2 GNB

242.4 Blessed are the poor in spirit: for theirs is the kingdom of heaven.

Matthew 5:3 KJV

242.5 Keep watch and pray that you will not fall into temptation. The spirit is willing, but the flesh is weak.

Matthew 26:41 GNB

242.6 Jesus again cried aloud and breathed his last.

Matthew 27:50 REB

242.7 The hour is coming, and is now here, when the true worshippers will worship the Father in spirit and truth, for the Father seeks such as these to worship him. God is spirit, and those who worship him must worship in spirit and truth.

John 4:23–24 NRSV

242.8 For what you received was not the spirit of slavery to bring you back into fear; you received the Spirit of adoption, enabling us to cry out, 'Abba, Father!' The Spirit himself joins with our spirit to bear witness that we are children of God.

Romans 8:15–16 NJB

242.9 For what human being knows what is truly human except the human spirit that is within? So also no one comprehends what is truly God's except the Spirit of God.

1 Corinthians 2:11 NRSV

242.10 The spiritual man makes judgments about all things, but he himself is not subject to any man's judgment.

1 Corinthians 2:15 NIV

242.11 For if I pray in an unknown tongue, my spirit prayeth, but my understanding is unfruitful. What is it then? I will pray with the spirit, and I will pray with the understanding also: I will sing with the spirit, and I will sing with the understanding also.

1 Corinthians 14:14–15 KJV

242.12 Forasmuch as ye are manifestly declared to be the epistle of Christ ministered by us, written not with ink, but with the Spirit of the living God; not in tables of stone, but in fleshy tables of the heart. And such trust have we through Christ to God-ward: not that we are sufficient of ourselves to think any thing as of ourselves; but our sufficiency is of God; who also hath made us able ministers of the new testament; not of the letter, but of the spirit: for the letter killeth, but the spirit giveth life.

2 Corinthians 3:3–6 KJV

The letter of the law
The *letter of the law* is a literal understanding of the law as it is expressed. This phrase is often used in contrast with the *spirit of the law*, the law's general purpose or effect. Both expressions derive from these verses.

See also **God, Spirit; Heart; Holy Spirit; Mind; Soul**

State, responsibility to

243.1 Then saith he unto them, Render therefore unto Caesar the things which are Caesar's; and unto God the things that are God's.

Matthew 22:21 KJV

243.2 'We gave you strict orders not to teach in this name, yet here you have filled Jerusalem with your teaching and you are determined to bring this man's blood on us.' But Peter and the apostles answered, 'We must obey God rather than any human authority.'

Acts 5:28–29 NRSV

243.3 Everyone must obey the state authorities, because no authority exists without God's permission, and the existing authorities have been put there by God. Whoever opposes the existing authority opposes what God has ordered; and anyone who does so will bring judgement on himself. For rulers are not to be feared by those who do good, but by those who do evil. Would you like to be unafraid of those in authority? Then do what is good, and they will praise you, because they are God's servants working for your own good. But if you do evil, then be afraid of them, because their power to punish is real. They are God's servants and carry out God's punishment on those who do evil. For this reason you must obey the authorities – not just because of God's punishment, but also as a matter of conscience. That is also why you pay taxes, because the authorities are working for God when they fulfil their duties. Pay, then, what you owe them; pay them your personal and property taxes, and show respect and honour for them all.

Romans 13:1–7 GNB

243.4 [An encouragement to pray] for kings, and for all that are in authority; that we may lead a quiet and peaceable life in all godliness and honesty.

1 Timothy 2:2 KJV

243.5 As servants of God, live as free people, yet do not use your freedom as a pretext for evil. Honour everyone. Love the family of believers. Fear God. Honour the emperor.

1 Peter 2:16–17 NRSV

See also **Rulers**

Stealing

244.1 Thou shalt not steal.

Exodus 20:15 KJV

244.2 When someone steals an ox or a sheep, and slaughters it or sells it, the thief shall pay five oxen for an ox, and four sheep for a sheep. The thief shall make restitution, but if unable to do so, shall be sold for the theft.

Exodus 22:1 NRSV

244.3 [Jesus] said unto them, It is written, My house shall be called the house of prayer; but ye have made it a den of thieves.

Matthew 21:13 KJV

244.4 Out of your heart come evil thoughts… stealing…

Mark 7:21 CEV

244.5 He [Judas] said this, not because he cared about the poor, but because he was a thief. He carried the money bag and would help himself from it.

John 12:6 GNB

Judas

A *Judas* is a traitor, a person who betrays a friend. The word comes from the name of Christ's betrayer, Judas Iscariot.

244.6 Neither... thieves nor the greedy nor... swindlers will inherit the kingdom of God.

1 Corinthians 6:9–10 NIV

244.7 The thief must give up stealing, and work hard with his hands to earn an honest living, so that he may have something to share with the needy.

Ephesians 4:28 REB

244.8 Tell slaves to be submissive to their masters and to give satisfaction in every respect; they are not to answer back, not to pilfer.

Titus 2:9–10 NRSV

244.9 You deserve to suffer if you are a murderer, a thief, a criminal, or a busybody.

1 Peter 4:15 CEV

Stewardship

245.1 It is like a man going abroad, who called his servants and entrusted his capital to them; to one he gave five bags of gold, to another two, to another one, each according to his ability.

Matthew 25:14–15 REB

245.2 Then Jesus said to the disciples, 'There was a rich man who had a manager, and charges were brought to him that this man was squandering his property. So he summoned him and said to him, "What is this that I hear about you?

Give me an account of your management, because you cannot be my manager any longer." Then the manager said to himself, "What will I do, now that my master is taking the position away from me?"'

Luke 16:1–3 NRSV

245.3 We are to be regarded as Christ's subordinates and as stewards of the secrets of God. Now stewards are required to show themselves trustworthy.

1 Corinthians 4:1–2 REB

245.4 I have no right to boast just because I preach the gospel. After all, I am under orders to do so. And how terrible it would be for me if I did not preach the gospel! If I did my work as a matter of free choice, then I could expect to be paid; but I do it as a matter of duty, because God has entrusted me with this task.

1 Corinthians 9:16–17 GNB

245.5 You have surely heard the way in which God entrusted me with the grace he gave me for your sake.

Ephesians 3:2 NJB

245.6 I am not ashamed, for I know the one in whom I have put my trust, and I am sure that he is able to guard until that day what I have entrusted to him... Guard the good treasure entrusted to you, with the help of the Holy Spirit living in us.

2 Timothy 1:12, 14 NRSV

245.7 As every man hath received the gift, even so minister the same one to another, as good stewards of the manifold grace of God.

1 Peter 4:10 KJV

See also Giving; Time

Stress

246.1 I am worn out and weak, moaning and in distress.

Psalm 38:8 CEV

246.2 When I was burdened with worries, you comforted me and made me feel secure.

Psalm 94:19 CEV

246.3 Worry makes a heart heavy.

Proverbs 12:25 NJB

246.4 With all my wisdom I tried to understand everything that happens here on earth. And God has made this so hard for us humans to do… The more you know, the more it hurts; the more you understand, the more you suffer.

Ecclesiastes 1:13, 18 CEV

246.5 From the fish's belly Jonah offered this prayer to the Lord his God: 'In my distress I called to the Lord, and he answered me; from deep within Sheol I cried for help, and you heard my voice.'

Jonah 2:1–2 REB

246.6 Come to me, all who are weary and whose load is heavy; I will give you rest.

Matthew 11:28 REB

246.7 The seed sown among thistles represents the person who hears the word, but worldly cares and the false glamour of wealth choke it, and it proves barren.

Matthew 13:22 REB

246.8 They came to a plot of land called Gethsemane, and he said to his disciples, 'Stay here while I pray.' Then he took Peter and James and John with him. And he began to feel terror and anguish. And he said to them, 'My soul is sorrowful to the point of death. Wait here, and stay awake.' And going on a little further he threw himself on the ground and prayed that, if it were possible, this hour might pass him by. '*Abba,* Father!' he said, 'For you everything is possible. Take this cup away from me. But let it be as you, not I, would have it.'

Mark 14:32–36 NJB

246.9 In his anguish he prayed even more earnestly, and his sweat fell to the ground like great drops of blood.

Luke 22:44 NJB

246.10 I have told you all this so that you may find peace in me. In the world you will have hardship, but be courageous: I have conquered the world.

John 16:33 NJB

246.11 We even exult in our present sufferings, because we know that suffering is a source of endurance, endurance of approval, and approval of hope.

Romans 5:3–4 REB

246.12 For we would not, brethren, have you ignorant of our trouble which came to us in Asia, that we were pressed out of measure, above strength, insomuch that we despaired even of life.

2 Corinthians 1:8 KJV

246.13 Do not be anxious, but in everything make your requests known to God in prayer and petition with thanksgiving. Then the peace of God, which is beyond all understanding, will guard your hearts and your thoughts in Christ Jesus.

Philippians 4:6–7 REB

See also Comfort, when anxious

Submission

247.1 Everyone must obey the state authorities, because no authority exists without God's permission, and the existing authorities have been put there by God.

Romans 13:1 GNB

247.2 Be subject to one another out of reverence for Christ. Wives, be subject to your husbands as though to the Lord… as the church is subject to Christ, so must women be subject to their husbands in everything.

Ephesians 5:21–22, 24 REB

247.3 Children, you belong to the Lord, and you do the right thing when you obey your parents. The first commandment with a promise says, 'Obey your father and your mother, and you will have a long and happy life.'

Ephesians 6:1–2 CEV

247.4 Slaves, obey your human masters with fear and trembling; and do it with a sincere heart, as though you were serving Christ.

Ephesians 6:5 GNB

247.5 Obey your leaders and submit to them, for they are keeping watch over your souls and will give an account. Let them do this with joy and not with sighing – for that would be harmful to you.

Hebrews 13:17 NRSV

247.6 Surrender to God! Resist the devil, and he will run from you.

James 4:7 CEV

See also **Accepting the will of God; Disobedience; Obedience**

Suffering

248.1 Yet man is born unto trouble, as the sparks fly upward.

Job 5:7 KJV

The patience of Job
The Old Testament figure of Job was a man of upright character who lost his wealth, his ten children, and his health. Satan brought these disasters on him, with God's permission. The book of Job tells how he kept his faith in God in the midst of all his afflictions. Thus to have *the patience of Job* means to endure difficulties, misfortunes or laborious tasks with supreme patience, courage and tolerance.

248.2 Such a person has no root, but endures only for a while, and when trouble or persecution arises on account of the word, that person immediately falls away.

Matthew 13:21 NRSV

248.3 Then you will be arrested and handed over to be punished and be put to death. All nations will hate you because of me.

Matthew 24:9 GNB

248.4 For then shall be great tribulation, such as was not since the beginning of the world to this time, no, nor ever shall be.

Matthew 24:21 KJV

248.5 Was not the Messiah bound to suffer in this way before entering upon his glory?

Luke 24:26 REB

248.6 They [Paul and Barnabas] strengthened the souls of the disciples and encouraged them to continue in the faith, saying, 'It is through many persecutions that we must enter the kingdom of God.'

Acts 14:22 NRSV

248.7 There will be anguish and distress for everyone who does evil, the Jew first and also the Greek.

Romans 2:9 NRSV

248.8 I am sure that what we are suffering now cannot compare with the glory that will be shown to us. In fact, all creation is eagerly waiting for God to show who his children are. Meanwhile, creation is confused, but not because it wants to be confused. God made it this way in the hope that creation would be set free from decay and would share in the glorious freedom of his children.

Romans 8:18–21 CEV

248.9 If one member suffers, all suffer together with it; if one member is honoured, all rejoice together with it.

1 Corinthians 12:26 NRSV

248.10 We are often troubled, but not crushed; sometimes in doubt, but never in despair; there are many enemies, but we are never without a friend; and though badly hurt at times, we are not destroyed.

2 Corinthians 4:8–9 GNB

248.11 It is now my joy to suffer for you; for the sake of Christ's body, the church, I am completing what still remains for Christ to suffer in my own person.

Colossians 1:24 REB

248.12 Stand up to him [the devil], strong in faith and in the knowledge that it is the same kind of suffering that the community of your brothers throughout the world is undergoing.

1 Peter 5:9 NJB

See also **Comfort, in suffering; Persecution**

PURPOSES OF

248.13 He delivereth the poor in his affliction, and openeth their ears in oppression.

Job 36:15 KJV

248.14 It is good for me that I have been afflicted; that I might learn thy statutes.

Psalm 119:71 KJV

248.15 As Jesus was walking along, he saw a man who had been born blind. His disciples asked him, 'Teacher, whose sin caused him to be born blind? Was it his own or his parents' sin?' Jesus answered, 'His blindness has nothing to do with his sins or his parents' sins. He is blind so that God's power might be seen at work in him.'

John 9:1–3 GNB

248.16 We glory in tribulations also: knowing that tribulation worketh patience.

Romans 5:3 KJV

248.17 [God] comforts us in all our troubles, so that we can comfort those in any trouble with the comfort we ourselves have received from God.

2 Corinthians 1:4 NIV

248.18 Therefore, to keep me from being too elated, a thorn was given to me in the flesh, a messenger of Satan to torment me, to keep me from being too elated.

2 Corinthians 12:7 NRSV

248.19 For they [our human parents] disciplined us for a short time as seemed best to them, but he disciplines us for our good, in order that we may share his holiness.

Hebrews 12:10 NRSV

248.20 On that day you will be glad, even if you have to go through many hard trials for a while. Your faith will be like gold that has been tested in a fire. And these trials will prove that your faith is worth much more than gold that can be destroyed. They will show that you will be given praise and honour and glory when Jesus Christ returns.

1 Peter 1:6–7 CEV

See also **Comfort, in suffering; Healing**

Sympathy

249.1 To him that is afflicted pity should be shewed from his friend.

Job 6:14 KJV

249.2 All Job's brothers and sisters and former friends came to visit him and feasted with him in his house. They expressed their sympathy and comforted him for all the troubles the Lord had brought on him.

Job 42:11 GNB

249.3 Insults have broken my heart, and I am in despair. I had hoped for sympathy, but there was none; for comfort, but I found none.

Psalm 69:20 GNB

249.4 In all their affliction he was afflicted, and the angel of his presence saved them: in his love and in his pity he redeemed them; and he bare them, and carried them all the days of old.

Isaiah 63:9 KJV

249.5 When he saw the crowds he felt sorry for them because they were harassed and dejected, like sheep without a shepherd.

Matthew 9:36 NJB

249.6 Jesus went forth, and saw a great multitude, and was moved with compassion toward them, and he healed their sick.

Matthew 14:14 KJV

249.7 Jesus felt sorry for them and touched their eyes. Straight away they could see, and they became his followers.

Matthew 20:34 CEV

249.8 When the Lord saw her his heart went out to her, and he said, 'Do not weep.'

Luke 7:13 REB

249.9 Rejoice with them that do rejoice, and weep with them that weep.

Romans 12:15 KJV

249.10 He consoles us in all our troubles, so that we in turn may be able to console others in any trouble of theirs and to share with them the consolation we ourselves receive from God.

2 Corinthians 1:4 REB

249.11 So if in Christ there is anything that will move you, any incentive in love, any fellowship in the Spirit, any warmth or sympathy... make my joy complete by being of a single mind, one in love, one in heart and one in mind.

Philippians 2:1–2 NJB

249.12 For we have not an high priest which cannot be touched with the feeling of our infirmities; but was in all points tempted like as we are, yet without sin.

Hebrews 4:15 KJV

249.13 Remember the Lord's people who are in jail and be concerned for them. Don't forget those who are suffering, but imagine that you are there with them.

Hebrews 13:3 CEV

249.14 Finally: you should all agree among yourselves and be sympathetic; love the brothers, have compassion and be self-effacing.

1 Peter 3:8 NJB

See also **Comfort, in bereavement and sorrow; Compassion**

Teachers and teaching

250.1 Teach them [the words the Lord commands] to your children. Repeat them when you are at home and when you are away, when you are resting and when you are working.

Deuteronomy 6:7 GNB

250.2 Teach me, Lord, the way of your statutes, and in keeping them I shall find my reward.

Psalm 119:33 REB

250.3 Go ye therefore, and teach all nations... teaching them to observe all things whatsoever I have commanded you.

Matthew 28:19–20 KJV

250.4 Jesus answered, 'What I teach is not my own teaching, but it comes from God, who sent me.'

John 7:16 GNB

250.5 The Holy Spirit will come and help you, because the Father will send the Spirit to take my place. The Spirit will teach you everything and will remind you of what I said while I was with you.

John 14:26 CEV

250.6 They continued stedfastly in the apostles' doctrine and fellowship, and in breaking of bread, and in prayers.

Acts 2:42 KJV

250.7 I did not shrink from doing anything helpful, proclaiming the message to you and teaching you publicly and from house to house.

Acts 20:20 NRSV

250.8 All of you are Christ's body, and each one is a part of it. In the church God has put all in place: in the first place apostles, in the second place prophets, and in the third place teachers.

1 Corinthians 12:27–28 GNB

250.9 Let the word of Christ dwell in you richly in all wisdom; teaching and admonishing one another in psalms and hymns and spiritual songs, singing with grace in your hearts to the Lord.

Colossians 3:16 KJV

250.10 Remember that from early childhood you have been familiar with the sacred writings which have power to make you wise and lead you to salvation through faith in Christ Jesus. All inspired scripture has its use for teaching the truth and refuting error, or for reformation of manners and discipline in right living.

2 Timothy 3:15–16 REB

See also Family, Children and the whole family; Pastor; Preaching

Teachers, false

251.1 Prophets or interpreters of dreams may promise a miracle or a wonder, in order to lead you to worship and serve gods that you have not worshipped before. Even if what they promise comes true, do not pay any attention to them. The Lord your God is using them to test you, to see if you love the Lord with all your heart.

Deuteronomy 13:1–3 GNB

251.2 Watch out for false prophets! They dress up like sheep, but inside they are wolves who have come to attack you. You can tell what they are by what they do.

Matthew 7:15–16 CEV

251.3 In vain they do worship me, teaching for doctrines the commandments of men.

Matthew 15:9 KJV

251.4 Jesus answered them, 'Beware that no one leads you astray. For many will come in my name, saying, "I am the Messiah!" and they will lead many astray.'

Matthew 24:4–5 NRSV

251.5 I urge you, brothers and sisters, to keep an eye on those who cause dissensions and offences, in opposition to the teaching that you have learned; avoid them.

Romans 16:17 NRSV

251.6 I am astonished to find you turning away so quickly from him who called you by grace, and following a different gospel. Not that it is in fact another gospel; only there are some who unsettle your minds by trying to distort the gospel of Christ. But should anyone, even I myself or an angel from heaven, preach a gospel other than the gospel I preached to you, let him be banned!

Galatians 1:6–8 REB

251.7 The Spirit has explicitly said that during the last times some will desert the faith and pay attention to deceitful spirits and doctrines that come from devils.

1 Timothy 4:1 NJB

251.8 Such people claim to know God, but their actions prove that they really don't. They are disgusting. They won't obey God, and they are too worthless to do anything good.

Titus 1:16 CEV

251.9 False prophets also arose among the people, just as there will be false teachers among you, who will secretly bring in destructive opinions. They will even deny the Master who bought them – bringing swift destruction on themselves.

2 Peter 2:1 NRSV

251.10 Beloved, believe not every spirit, but try the spirits whether they are of God: because many false prophets are gone out into the world. Hereby know ye the Spirit of God: every spirit that confesseth that Jesus Christ is come in the flesh is of God.

1 John 4:1–2 KJV

251.11 Beloved, while eagerly preparing to write to you about the salvation we share, I find it necessary to write and appeal to you to contend for the faith that was once for all entrusted to the saints. For certain intruders have stolen in among you, people who long ago were designated for this condemnation as ungodly, who pervert the grace of our God into licentiousness and deny our only Master and Lord, Jesus Christ.

Jude vv. 3–4 NRSV

Temperance

252.1 Let us then pursue what makes for peace and for mutual edification… it is good not to eat meat or drink wine or do anything that makes your brother or sister stumble.

Romans 14:19, 21 NRSV

252.2 The Spirit produces… self-control.

Galatians 5:22–23 GNB

252.3 People sleep during the night, and some even get drunk. But we belong to the day. So we must stay sober.

1 Thessalonians 5:7–8 CEV

252.4 Deacons likewise must be serious, not double-tongued, not indulging in much wine… Women likewise must be… temperate, faithful in all things.

1 Timothy 3:8, 11 NRSV

252.5 Drink no longer water, but use a little wine for thy stomach's sake and thine often infirmities.

1 Timothy 5:23 KJV

See also **Drunkenness; Self-control**

The spirit is willing

The saying *the spirit is willing but the flesh is weak* is used to show that someone lacks the ability, energy, or willpower to put his or her good intentions into practice. The expression is often used as an explanation of someone's failure to do something. The phrase derives from this warning by Jesus to his disciples to remain alert and not to yield to temptation.

Temptation

253.1 Remember the whole way by which the Lord your God has led you these forty years in the wilderness to humble and test you, and to discover whether or not it was in your heart to keep his commandments.

Deuteronomy 8:2 REB

253.2 The Lord said to Satan, 'Very well, all that he has is in your power; only do not stretch out your hand against him!'

Job 1:12 NRSV

253.3 Can a man take fire in his bosom, and his clothes not be burned?

Proverbs 6:27 KJV

253.4 Then the Spirit led Jesus into the desert to be tempted by the Devil.

Matthew 4:1 GNB

253.5 Lead us not into temptation; but deliver us from evil.

Matthew 6:13 BCP

253.6 Keep watch and pray that you will not fall into temptation. The spirit is willing, but the flesh is weak.

Matthew 26:41 GNB

253.7 He said to his disciples, 'There are bound to be causes of stumbling; but woe betide the person through whom they come.'

Luke 17:1 REB

253.8 I am afraid that as the serpent deceived Eve by its cunning, your thoughts will be led astray from a sincere and pure devotion to Christ.

2 Corinthians 11:3 NRSV

253.9 Brethren, if a man be overtaken in a fault, ye which are spiritual, restore such an one in the spirit of meekness; considering thyself, lest thou also be tempted.

Galatians 6:1 KJV

253.10 It was faith that made Abraham offer his son Isaac as a sacrifice when God put Abraham to the test. Abraham was the one to whom God had made the promise, yet he was ready to offer his only son as a sacrifice.

Hebrews 11:17 GNB

253.11 No one, when tempted, should say, 'I am being tempted by God'; for God cannot be tempted by evil and he himself tempts no one. But one is tempted by one's own desire, being lured and enticed by it.

James 1:13–14 NRSV

Help in

253.12 Keep back thy servant also from presumptuous sins; let them not have dominion over me: then shall I be upright, and I shall be innocent from the great transgression.
Psalm 19:13 KJV

253.13 Lord, set a guard on my mouth; keep watch at the door of my lips.
Psalm 141:3 REB

253.14 Do not follow the path of the wicked, do not walk the way that the evil go.
Proverbs 4:14 NJB

253.15 The Lord said, Simon, Simon, behold, Satan hath desired to have you, that he may sift you as wheat: but I have prayed for thee, that thy faith fail not: and when thou art converted, strengthen thy brethren.
Luke 22:31–32 KJV

253.16 How shall we, that are dead to sin, live any longer therein?
Romans 6:2 KJV

253.17 No testing has overtaken you that is not common to everyone. God is faithful, and he will not let you be tested beyond your strength, but with the testing he will also provide the way out so that you may be able to endure it.
1 Corinthians 10:13 NRSV

253.18 Put on the whole armour of God, that ye may be able to stand against the wiles of the devil.
Ephesians 6:11 KJV

253.19 Because he himself suffered when he was tempted, he is able to help those who are being tempted.
Hebrews 2:18 NIV

253.20 Ours is not a high priest unable to sympathize with our weaknesses, but one who has been tested in every way as we are, only without sinning.
Hebrews 4:15 REB

253.21 My brethren, count it all joy when ye fall into divers temptations; knowing this, that the trying of your faith worketh patience.
James 1:2–3 KJV

253.22 In this you rejoice, even if now for a little while you have had to suffer various trials, so that the genuineness of your faith – being more precious than gold that, though perishable, is tested by fire – may be found to result in praise and glory and honour when Jesus Christ is revealed.
1 Peter 1:6–7 NRSV

253.23 Dear friends, don't be surprised or shocked that you are going through testing that is like walking through fire. Be glad for the chance to suffer as Christ suffered. It will prepare you for even greater happiness when he makes his glorious return.
1 Peter 4:12–13 CEV

253.24 Discipline yourselves; keep alert. Like a roaring lion your adversary the devil prowls around, looking for someone to devour. Resist him, steadfast in your faith, for you know that your brothers and sisters throughout the world are undergoing the same kinds of suffering.
1 Peter 5:8–9 NRSV

See also **Victory**

Thankfulness and thanksgiving

254.1 Offer unto God thanksgiving; and pay thy vows unto the most High.
Psalm 50:14 KJV

254.2 It is good to give thanks to the Lord, for his love endures for ever.
Psalm 136:1 REB

254.3 He prostrated himself at Jesus' feet and thanked him. And he was a Samaritan. Then Jesus asked, 'Were not ten made clean? But the other nine, where are they? Was none of them found to return and give praise to God except this foreigner?'
Luke 17:16–18 NRSV

254.4 Thank God, then, for giving us the victory through Jesus Christ our Lord.
1 Corinthians 15:57 NJB

254.5 Thanks be unto God for his unspeakable gift.
2 Corinthians 9:15 KJV

254.6 I have not stopped giving thanks to God for you. I remember you in my prayers.
Ephesians 1:16 GNB

254.7 Nor is it fitting for you to use language which is obscene, profane, or vulgar. Rather you should give thanks to God.
Ephesians 5:4 GNB

254.8 Speaking to yourselves in psalms and hymns and spiritual songs, singing and making melody in your heart to the Lord; giving thanks always for all things unto God and the Father in the name of our Lord Jesus Christ.
Ephesians 5:19–20 KJV

254.9 Don't worry about anything, but pray about everything. With thankful hearts offer up your prayers and requests to God.
Philippians 4:6 CEV

254.10 In every thing give thanks: for this is the will of God in Christ Jesus concerning you.
1 Thessalonians 5:18 KJV

See also Joy; Praise; Worship

Thought

255.1 We ponder your steadfast love, O God, in the midst of your temple.
Psalm 48:9 NRSV

255.2 How mysterious, God, are your thoughts to me, how vast in number they are! Were I to try counting them, they would be more than the grains of sand; to finish the count, my years must equal yours.
Psalm 139:17–18 REB

255.3 Search me, O God, and know my heart: try me, and know my thoughts: and see if there be any wicked way in me, and lead me in the way everlasting.
Psalm 139:23–24 KJV

255.4 For my thoughts are not your thoughts, neither are your ways my ways, saith the Lord. For as the heavens are higher than the earth, so are my ways higher than your ways, and my thoughts than your thoughts.
Isaiah 55:8–9 KJV

255.5 What think ye of Christ? whose son is he?
Matthew 22:42 KJV

255.6 You are the only one who knows what is in your own mind, and God's Spirit is the only one who knows what is in God's mind.

1 Corinthians 2:11 CEV

255.7 Brothers and sisters, do not be children in your thinking; rather, be infants in evil, but in thinking be adults.

1 Corinthians 14:20 NRSV

255.8 We destroy false arguments; we pull down every proud obstacle that is raised against the knowledge of God; we take every thought captive and make it obey Christ.

2 Corinthians 10:4–5 GNB

255.9 Finally, brethren, whatsoever things are true, whatsoever things are honest, whatsoever things are just, whatsoever things are pure, whatsoever things are lovely, whatsoever things are of good report; if there be any virtue, and if there be any praise, think on these things.

Philippians 4:8 KJV

See also **Meditation; Mind; Understanding**

Time

256.1 God said, Let there be lights in the firmament of the heaven to divide the day from the night; and let them be for signs, and for seasons, and for days, and years.

Genesis 1:14 KJV

256.2 Remember the sabbath day, to keep it holy.

Exodus 20:8 KJV

256.3 For everything there is a season, and a time for every matter under heaven: a time to be born, and a time to die.

Ecclesiastes 3:1–2 NRSV

A time and a place for everything

The expression *there's a time and a place for everything* means that there are certain circumstances when a particular action is appropriate. It is often used with the implication that a particular action may not be done at any time or in any place. The origin of the expression lies in the Preacher's statement of the varying seasons of human existence.

Other expressions from the book of Ecclesiastes that have become part of the language are *nothing new under the sun*, applied to something that looks original and novel but in fact is not, and *a fly in the ointment*, used to refer to a person or thing that spoils a situation which is perfect in every other way. The source of this expression shows that as dead flies give even sweet-smelling perfume a bad odor, so a little folly spoils the virtues of wisdom and honor.

256.4 Envy and wrath shorten the life, and carefulness bringeth age before the time.

Ecclesiasticus 30:24 KJV

256.5 And about the eleventh hour he went out, and found others standing idle, and saith unto them, Why stand ye here all the day idle?

Matthew 20:6 KJV

At the eleventh hour

At the eleventh hour means at the last possible moment; nearly, but just not, too late for something to happen. The expression refers to the time of the hiring of the final workers in Jesus' parable about the laborers in the vineyard (Matthew 20:1–16).

256.6 The time has arrived; the kingdom of God is upon you. Repent, and believe the gospel.
Mark 1:15 REB

256.7 Jesus answered, 'For me the right time has not come yet, but for you any time is the right time.'
John 7:6 NJB

256.8 Jesus answered, 'Aren't there twelve hours in each day? If you walk during the day, you will have light from the sun, and you won't stumble.'
John 11:9 CEV

256.9 He answered, 'It is not for you to know about dates or times which the Father has set within his own control.'
Acts 1:7 REB

256.10 [Jesus Christ] Whom the heaven must receive until the times of restitution of all things, which God hath spoken by the mouth of all his holy prophets since the world began.
Acts 3:21 KJV

256.11 Hear what God says: 'When the time came for me to show you favour I heard you; when the day arrived for me to save you, I helped you.' Listen! This is the hour to receive God's favour; today is the day to be saved!
2 Corinthians 6:2 GNB

256.12 When the right time finally came, God sent his own Son. He came as the son of a human mother and lived under the Jewish Law, to redeem those who were under the Law, so that we might become God's sons and daughters.
Galatians 4:4 GNB

256.13 Redeeming the time, because the days are evil.
Ephesians 5:16 KJV

256.14 When you are with unbelievers, always make good use of the time.
Colossians 4:5 CEV

256.15 Do not ignore this one fact, beloved, that with the Lord one day is like a thousand years, and a thousand years are like one day.
2 Peter 3:8 NRSV

See also **Old age**; **Stewardship**; **Youth**

Tiredness

257.1 Of making many books there is no end; and much study is a weariness of the flesh.
Ecclesiastes 12:12 KJV

257.2 Hast thou not known? hast thou not heard, that the everlasting God, the Lord, the Creator of the ends of the earth, fainteth not, neither is weary? there is no searching of his understanding. He giveth power to the faint; and to them that have no might he increaseth strength. Even youths shall faint and be weary, and the young men shall utterly fall: but they that wait upon the Lord shall renew their strength; they shall mount up with wings as eagles; they shall run, and not be weary; and they shall walk, and not faint.
Isaiah 40:28–31 KJV

257.3 The Lord God hath given me the tongue of the learned, that I should know how to speak a word in season to him that is weary: he wakeneth morning by morning, he wakeneth mine ear to hear as the learned.
Isaiah 50:4 KJV

257.4 Come to me, all you that are weary and are carrying heavy burdens, and I will give you rest.
Matthew 11:28 NRSV

257.5 Jesus, tired out by the journey, sat down by the well.

John 4:6 GNB

257.6 We never give up. Our bodies are gradually dying, but we ourselves are being made stronger each day.

2 Corinthians 4:16 CEV

257.7 Let us never tire of doing good, for if we do not slacken our efforts we shall in due time reap our harvest.

Galatians 6:9 REB

257.8 Think of him [Jesus] who submitted to such opposition from sinners: that will help you not to lose heart and grow faint.

Hebrews 12:3 REB

See also **Power**

Tongues, gift of

SPEAKING IN TONGUES

258.1 The Holy Spirit took control of everyone, and they began speaking whatever languages the Spirit let them speak.

Acts 2:4 CEV

258.2 When Paul had laid his hands on them, the Holy Spirit came upon them, and they spoke in tongues and prophesied.

Acts 19:6 NRSV

258.3 All of you are Christ's body, and each one is a part of it. In the church God has put all in place: in the first place apostles, in the second place prophets, and in the third place teachers; then those

who perform miracles, followed by those who... speak in strange tongues... Not everyone has the power... to speak in strange tongues... Set your hearts, then, on the more important gifts.

1 Corinthians 12:27–31 GNB

258.4 Though I speak with the tongues of men and of angels, and have not charity, I am become as sounding brass, or a tinkling cymbal... whether there be tongues, they shall cease.

1 Corinthians 13:1, 8 KJV

258.5 For those who speak in a tongue do not speak to other people but to God; for nobody understands them, since they are speaking mysteries in the Spirit... Those who speak in a tongue build up themselves, but those who prophesy build up the church.

1 Corinthians 14:2, 4 NRSV

258.6 One who speaks in a tongue should pray for the power to interpret. For if I pray in a tongue, my spirit prays but my mind is unproductive.

1 Corinthians 14:13–14 NRSV

258.7 I thank God that I speak in tongues more than all of you. But in the church I would rather speak five intelligible words to instruct others than ten thousand words in a tongue.

1 Corinthians 14:18–19 NIV

258.8 We read in the law: 'I will speak to this people through strange tongues, and by the lips of foreigners; and even so they will not heed me, says the Lord.' Clearly then these 'strange tongues' are not intended as a sign for believers, but for unbelievers, whereas prophecy is designed not for unbelievers but for believers.

1 Corinthians 14:21–22 REB

INTERPRETATION

258.9 Yet another has the gift of tongues of various kinds, and another the ability to interpret them.

1 Corinthians 12:10 REB

258.10 One who prophesies is greater than one who speaks in tongues, unless someone interprets, so that the church may be built up.

1 Corinthians 14:5 NRSV

258.11 If anyone speaks in a tongue, two – or at the most three – should speak, one at a time, and someone must interpret. If there is no interpreter, the speaker should keep quiet in the church and speak to himself and God.

1 Corinthians 14:27–28 NIV

Trinity

259.1 Hear, O Israel: The Lord our God is one Lord.

Deuteronomy 6:4 KJV

259.2 When Jesus had been baptized, just as he came up from the water, suddenly the heavens were opened to him and he saw the Spirit of God descending like a dove and alighting on him. And a voice from heaven said, 'This is my Son, the Beloved, with whom I am well pleased.'

Matthew 3:16–17 NRSV

259.3 Go ye therefore, and teach all nations, baptizing them in the name of the Father, and of the Son, and of the Holy Ghost.

Matthew 28:19 KJV

259.4 Now there are varieties of gifts, but the same Spirit; and there are varieties of

services, but the same Lord; and there are varieties of activities, but it is the same God who activates all of them in everyone.

1 Corinthians 12:4–6 NRSV

259.5 The grace of the Lord Jesus Christ, the love of God, and the fellowship of the Holy Spirit be with you all.

2 Corinthians 13:13 GNB

259.6 There is one body and one Spirit, just as there is one hope held out in God's call to you; one Lord, one faith, one baptism; one God and Father of all, who is over all and through all and in all.

Ephesians 4:4–6 REB

259.7 Elect according to the foreknowledge of God the Father, through sanctification of the Spirit, unto obedience and sprinkling of the blood of Jesus Christ: Grace unto you, and peace, be multiplied.

1 Peter 1:2 KJV

See also God; Jesus Christ; Holy Spirit

Truth

260.1 You, Lord, are the true God, you are the living God and the eternal king.

Jeremiah 10:10 GNB

260.2 Truth abides and remains strong for ever.

1 Esdras 4:38 REB

260.3 The Word was made flesh, and dwelt among us.

John 1:14 KJV

260.4 Everyone who lives by the truth will come to the light, because they want others to know that God is really the one doing what they do.

John 3:21 CEV

260.5 Then Jesus said to the Jews who had believed in him, 'If you continue in my word, you are truly my disciples; and you will know the truth, and the truth will make you free.'
John 8:31–32 NRSV

260.6 Jesus saith unto him, I am the way, the truth, and the life: no man cometh unto the Father, but by me.
John 14:6 KJV

260.7 When the Spirit of truth comes, he will guide you into all the truth; for he will not speak on his own, but will speak whatever he hears, and he will declare to you the things that are to come.
John 16:13 NRSV

260.8 Sanctify them through thy truth: thy word is truth.
John 17:17 KJV

260.9 Pilate said, 'What is truth?'
John 18:38 REB

260.10 Speaking the truth in love, we must grow up in every way into him who is the head, into Christ.
Ephesians 4:15 NRSV

260.11 Stand therefore, having your loins girt about with truth.
Ephesians 6:14 KJV

260.12 God's household, which is the church of the living God, the pillar and support of the truth.
1 Timothy 3:15 GNB

260.13 Do your best to present yourself to God as one approved by him, a worker who has no need to be ashamed, rightly explaining the word of truth.
2 Timothy 2:15 NRSV

See also **Honesty**

Unbelief

261.1 They [the children of Israel] spoke against God, saying, 'Can God spread a table in the wilderness?'... In spite of all this they still sinned; they did not believe in his wonders.

Psalm 78:19, 32 NRSV

261.2 He did not work many miracles there because of their lack of faith.

Matthew 13:58 NJB

261.3 'O unbelieving and perverse generation,' Jesus replied, 'how long shall I stay with you? How long shall I put up with you?'

Matthew 17:17 NIV

261.4 He was amazed at their lack of faith.

Mark 6:6 NJB

261.5 'If it is possible!' said Jesus. 'Everything is possible to one who believes.' At once the boy's father cried: 'I believe; help my unbelief.'

Mark 9:23–24 REB

261.6 Later he appeared to the eleven themselves as they were sitting at the table; and he upbraided them for their lack of faith and stubbornness, because they had not believed those who saw him after he had risen.

Mark 16:14 NRSV

261.7 The seeds that fell along the path stand for those who hear; but the Devil comes and takes the message away from their hearts in order to keep them from believing and being saved.

Luke 8:12 GNB

261.8 He [the Holy Spirit] will prove the world wrong... about sin, because they refuse to believe in me.

John 16:8–9 REB

261.9 He [Thomas] said to them, 'Unless I see the mark of the nails in his hands, and put my finger in the mark of the nails and my hand in his side, I will not believe.'... Then he said to Thomas, 'Put your finger here and see my hands. Reach out your hand and put it in my side. Do not doubt but believe.'

John 20:25, 27 NRSV

261.10 See to it, brothers, that none of you has a sinful, unbelieving heart that turns away from the living God.

Hebrews 3:12 NIV

See also **Doubt; Faith; Falling away; Hardness; Rebellion; Rejection**

Unbeliever

262.1 Those who believe in him are not condemned; but those who do not believe are condemned already, because they have not believed in the name of the only Son of God. And this is the judgement, that the light has come into the world, and people loved darkness rather than light because their deeds were evil.

John 3:18–19 NRSV

262.2 I told you that you will die in your sins. And you will die in your sins if you do not believe that 'I Am Who I Am'.

John 8:24 GNB

262.3 Knowing God, they have refused to honour him as God, or to render him thanks. Hence all their thinking has ended in futility, and their misguided minds are plunged in darkness.

Romans 1:21 REB

262.4 The man without the Spirit does not accept the things that come from the Spirit of God, for they are foolishness to him and he cannot understand them, because they are spiritually discerned.

1 Corinthians 2:14 NIV

262.5 The god who rules this world has blinded the minds of unbelievers. They cannot see the light, which is the good news about our glorious Christ, who shows what God is like.

2 Corinthians 4:4 CEV

262.6 Be ye not unequally yoked together with unbelievers: for what fellowship hath righteousness with unrighteousness? and what communion hath light with darkness?

2 Corinthians 6:14 KJV

262.7 As for you, you were dead in your transgressions and sins, in which you used to live when you followed the ways of this world and of the ruler of the kingdom of the air, the spirit who is now at work in those who are disobedient. All of us also lived among them at one time, gratifying the cravings of our sinful nature and following its desires and thoughts. Like the rest, we were by nature objects of wrath.

Ephesians 2:1–3 NIV

262.8 Remember that you were at that time without Christ, being aliens from the commonwealth of Israel, and strangers to the covenants of promise, having no hope and without God in the world.

Ephesians 2:12 NRSV

262.9 He that hath the Son hath life; and he that hath not the Son of God hath not life.

1 John 5:12 KJV

See also **Godless; Sin**

Understanding

263.1 Do not be like a horse or a mule, without understanding, whose temper must be curbed with bit and bridle.

Psalm 32:9 NRSV

263.2 Beg for knowledge; plead for insight. Look for it as hard as you would for silver or some hidden treasure. If you do, you will know what it means to fear the Lord and you will succeed in learning about God. It is the Lord who gives wisdom; from him come knowledge and understanding.

Proverbs 2:3–6 GNB

263.3 Trust in the Lord with all thine heart; and lean not unto thine own understanding.

Proverbs 3:5 KJV

263.4 The fear of the Lord is the beginning of wisdom, and knowledge of the Holy One is understanding.

Proverbs 9:10 NIV

263.5 The Lord says, 'My people are stupid; they don't know me. They are like foolish children; they have no understanding. They are experts at doing what is evil, but failures at doing what is good.'

Jeremiah 4:22 GNB

263.6 I shall light a candle of understanding in thine heart, which shall not be put out.

2 Esdras 14:25 KJV

263.7 When anyone hears the word of the kingdom and does not understand it, the evil one comes and snatches away what is sown in the heart... As for what was sown on good soil, this is the one who hears the word and understands it, who indeed bears fruit and yields, in one case a hundredfold, in another sixty, and in another thirty.

Matthew 13:19, 23 NRSV

263.8 When Philip ran up he heard him reading from the prophet Isaiah and asked, 'Do you understand what you are reading?' He said, 'How can I without someone to guide me?' and invited Philip to get in and sit beside him.

Acts 8:30–31 REB

263.9 Don't be stupid. Instead, find out what the Lord wants you to do.

Ephesians 5:17 CEV

263.10 The peace of God which is beyond our understanding will guard your hearts and your thoughts in Christ Jesus.

Philippians 4:7 NJB

263.11 By faith we understand that the worlds were prepared by the word of God, so that what is seen was made from things that are not visible.

Hebrews 11:3 NRSV

See also **Knowledge; Mind; Thought; Wisdom**

Unity

264.1 Behold, how good and how pleasant it is for brethren to dwell together in unity!

Psalm 133:1 KJV

264.2 Though one might prevail against another, two will withstand one. A threefold cord is not quickly broken.

Ecclesiastes 4:12 NRSV

264.3 Can two walk together, except they be agreed?

Amos 3:3 KJV

264.4 Again I tell you: if two of you agree on earth about any request you have to make, that request will be granted by my heavenly Father. For where two or three meet together in my name, I am there among them.

Matthew 18:19–20 REB

264.5 [Jesus' prayer] That they all may be one; as thou, Father, art in me, and I in thee, that they also may be one in us: that the world may believe that thou hast sent me.

John 17:21 KJV

264.6 The whole group of believers was united, heart and soul; no one claimed private ownership of any possessions, as everything they owned was held in common.

Acts 4:32 NJB

264.7 Making every effort to maintain the unity of the Spirit in the bond of peace. There is one body and one Spirit, just as you were called to the one hope of your calling, one Lord, one faith, one baptism, one God and Father of all, who is above all and through all and in all.

Ephesians 4:3–6 NRSV

264.8 Make my joy complete: be of the same mind, having the same love, being in full accord and of one mind.

Philippians 2:2 NRSV

See also **Fellowship**

Unselfishness

265.1 A generous person enjoys prosperity, and one who refreshes others will be refreshed.

Proverbs 11:25 REB

265.2 You must love your neighbour as yourself.
Mark 12:31 NJB

265.3 I seek to do not my own will but the will of him who sent me.
John 5:30 NJB

265.4 Greater love hath no man than this, that a man lay down his life for his friends.
John 15:13 KJV

265.5 If our faith is strong, we should be patient with the Lord's followers whose faith is weak. We should try to please them instead of ourselves. We should think of their good and try to help them by doing what pleases them. Even Christ did not try to please himself.
Romans 15:1–3 CEV

265.6 So though I was not a slave to any human being, I put myself in slavery to all people, to win as many as I could.
1 Corinthians 9:19 NJB

265.7 You should each look after the interests of others, not your own.
1 Corinthians 10:24 REB

265.8 For my part I always try to be considerate to everyone, not seeking my own good but the good of the many, so that they may be saved.
1 Corinthians 10:33 REB

265.9 Love isn't selfish.
1 Corinthians 13:5 CEV

265.10 Not that we are sufficient of ourselves to think any thing as of ourselves; but our sufficiency is of God.
2 Corinthians 3:5 KJV

265.11 You know the generosity of our Lord Jesus Christ: he was rich, yet for your sake he became poor, so that through his poverty you might become rich.
2 Corinthians 8:9 REB

265.12 I will very gladly spend and be spent for you.
2 Corinthians 12:15 KJV

265.13 This is the proof of love, that he laid down his life for us, and we too ought to lay down our lives for our brothers.
1 John 3:16 NJB

See also **Selfishness**

Victory

266.1 Have no fear, for I am with you; be not afraid, for I am your God. I shall strengthen you and give you help and uphold you with my victorious right hand.

Isaiah 41:10 REB

266.2 These things I have spoken unto you, that in me ye might have peace. In the world ye shall have tribulation: but be of good cheer; I have overcome the world.

John 16:33 KJV

266.3 What then are we to say about these things? If God is for us, who is against us?... No, in all these things we are more than conquerors through him who loved us.

Romans 8:31, 37 NRSV

266.4 Then God, who gives peace, will soon crush Satan under your feet.

Romans 16:20 CEV

266.5 Thanks be to God! He gives us victory through our Lord Jesus Christ.

1 Corinthians 15:57 REB

266.6 The weapons with which we do battle are not those of human nature, but they have the power, in God's cause, to demolish fortresses.

2 Corinthians 10:4 NJB

266.7 He said to me, 'My grace is sufficient for you, for power is made perfect in weakness.' So, I will boast all the more gladly of my weaknesses, so that the power of Christ may dwell in me.

2 Corinthians 12:9 NRSV

266.8 There [on the cross] Christ defeated all powers and forces. He let the whole world see them being led away as prisoners when he celebrated his victory.

Colossians 2:15 CEV

266.9 Greater is he that is in you, than he that is in the world.

1 John 4:4 KJV

266.10 Every child of God is able to defeat the world. And we win the victory over the world by means of our faith.

1 John 5:4 GNB

266.11 They have conquered him by the blood of the Lamb and by the word of their testimony, for they did not cling to life even in the face of death.

Revelation 12:11 NRSV

See also **Assurance; Devil; Endurance; Temptation, Help in**

Visions

267.1 As the sun was going down, Abram fell into a trance and great and fearful darkness came over him.

Genesis 15:12 REB

267.2 If there be a prophet among you, I the Lord will make myself known unto him in a vision, and will speak unto him in a dream.

Numbers 12:6 KJV

267.3 The boy Samuel was in the Lord's service under Eli. In those days the word of the Lord was rarely heard, and there was no outpouring of vision.

1 Samuel 3:1 REB

267.4 In dreams, in visions of the night, when deepest slumber falls on mortals, while they lie asleep in bed God imparts his message.

Job 33:15–16 REB

267.5 Where there is no vision, the people perish.
Proverbs 29:18 KJV

267.6 In the year that King Uzziah died I saw also the Lord sitting upon a throne, high and lifted up, and his train filled the temple. Above it stood the seraphims: each one had six wings; with twain he covered his face, and with twain he covered his feet, and with twain he did fly. And one cried unto another, and said, Holy, holy, holy, is the Lord of hosts: the whole earth is full of his glory. And the posts of the door moved at the voice of him that cried, and the house was filled with smoke.
Isaiah 6:1–4 KJV

267.7 Is it not a false vision that you prophets have seen? Is not your divination a lie? You call it the word of the Lord, but it is not I who have spoken.
Ezekiel 13:7 REB

267.8 The Lord's hand was upon me, and he carried me out by his spirit and set me down in a plain that was full of bones.
Ezekiel 37:1 REB

267.9 As I, Daniel, gazed at the vision and tried to understand it, I saw someone standing in front of me... as he approached, I was seized with terror and fell prostrate on the ground. 'Son of man,' he said to me, 'understand this: the vision shows the time of the End.'
Daniel 8:15, 17 NJB

267.10 After this I shall pour out my spirit on all mankind; your sons and daughters will prophesy, your old men will dream dreams and your young men see visions.
Joel 2:28 REB

267.11 For the vision is for its appointed time, it hastens towards its end and it will not lie; although it may take some time, wait for it, for come it certainly will before too long.
Habakkuk 2:3 NJB

267.12 The Lord spoke to me in a vision during the night: in a valley among myrtle trees, I saw someone on a red horse...
Zechariah 1:7–8 CEV

267.13 The crowd was waiting for Zechariah and kept wondering why he was staying so long in the temple. When he did come out, he could not speak, and they knew he had seen a vision.
Luke 1:21–22 CEV

267.14 When they [certain women] found not his body, they came, saying, that they had also seen a vision of angels, which said that he was alive.
Luke 24:23 KJV

267.15 He [Peter] fell sound asleep and had a vision. He saw heaven open, and something came down like a huge sheet held up by its four corners. In it were all kinds of animals, snakes, and birds.
Acts 10:10–12 CEV

267.16 During the night a vision came to Paul: a Macedonian stood there appealing to him, 'Cross over to Macedonia and help us.'
Acts 16:9 REB

267.17 So, King Agrippa, I did not disobey the heavenly vision. I preached first to the inhabitants of Damascus, and then to Jerusalem and all the country of Judaea.
Acts 26:19–20 REB

See also Dreams

Vow

268.1 Then Jacob made a vow to the Lord: 'If you will be with me and protect me on the journey I am making and give me food and clothing, and if I return safely to my father's home, then you will be my God. This memorial stone which I have set up will be the place where you are worshipped, and I will give you a tenth of everything you give me.'
Genesis 28:20–22 GNB

268.2 If you make a vow to the Lord your God, do not postpone fulfilling it; for the Lord your God will surely require it of you, and you would incur guilt. But if you refrain from vowing, you will not incur guilt. Whatever your lips utter you must diligently perform, just as you have freely vowed to the Lord your God with your own mouth.
Deuteronomy 23:21–23 NRSV

268.3 My praise shall be of thee in the great congregation: I will pay my vows before them that fear him.
Psalm 22:25 KJV

268.4 Offer unto God thanksgiving; and pay thy vows unto the most High.
Psalm 50:14 KJV

268.5 It is dangerous to dedicate a gift rashly, to make a vow and then have second thoughts.
Proverbs 20:25 REB

268.6 Celebrate your festivals, O Judah, fulfil your vows, for never again shall the wicked invade you; they are utterly cut off.
Nahum 1:15 NRSV

See also Blasphemy

Waiting

269.1 At the end of forty days Noah opened the window he had made in the ark and released a raven, which flew back and forth as it waited for the waters to dry up on earth. He then released a dove... But the dove, finding nowhere to perch, returned to him in the ark... After waiting seven more days, he again released the dove from the ark. In the evening, the dove came back to him and there in its beak was a freshly-picked olive leaf! So Noah realised that the waters were receding from the earth. After waiting seven more days, he released the dove, and now it returned to him no more.

Genesis 8:6–12 NJB

269.2 [Samuel to Saul] Go down to Gilgal ahead of me, and I shall come to you... Wait seven days until I join you; then I shall tell you what to do.

1 Samuel 10:8 REB

269.3 Wait on the Lord: be of good courage, and he shall strengthen thine heart: wait, I say, on the Lord.

Psalm 27:14 KJV

269.4 We have waited eagerly for the Lord; he is our help and our shield.

Psalm 33:20 REB

269.5 Rest in the Lord, and wait patiently for him.

Psalm 37:7 KJV

269.6 Patiently I waited for the Lord; he bent down to me and listened to my cry.

Psalm 40:1 REB

269.7 With all my heart, I am waiting, Lord, for you! I trust your promises. I wait for you more eagerly than a soldier on guard duty waits for the dawn.

Psalm 130:5–6 CEV

269.8 Do not think to repay evil for evil; wait for the Lord to deliver you.

Proverbs 20:22 REB

269.9 Therefore will the Lord wait, that he may be gracious unto you, and therefore will he be exalted, that he may have mercy upon you: for the Lord is a God of judgment: blessed are all they that wait for him.

Isaiah 30:18 KJV

269.10 They that wait upon the Lord shall renew their strength; they shall mount up with wings as eagles; they shall run, and not be weary; and they shall walk, and not faint.

Isaiah 40:31 KJV

269.11 It is good to wait in patience for deliverance by the Lord.

Lamentations 3:26 REB

269.12 Turn back by God's help; maintain loyalty and justice and wait continually for your God.

Hosea 12:6 REB

269.13 Jonah then left through the east gate of the city and made a shelter to protect himself from the sun. He sat under the shelter, waiting to see what would happen to Nineveh.

Jonah 4:5 CEV

269.14 Joseph [of Arimathea] was a highly respected member of the Jewish council, and he was also waiting for God's kingdom to come.

Mark 15:43 CEV

269.15 Behold, there was a man in Jerusalem, whose name was Simeon; and the same man was just and devout, waiting for the consolation of Israel: and the Holy Ghost was upon him.

Luke 2:25 KJV

269.16 Having this hope for what we cannot yet see, we are able to wait for it with persevering confidence.

Romans 8:25 NJB

269.17 For it is by the Spirit and through faith that we hope to attain that righteousness which we eagerly await.

Galatians 5:5 REB

269.18 You must be patient, my friends, until the Lord comes. Consider: the farmer looking for the precious crop from his land can only wait in patience until the early and late rains have fallen. You too must be patient and stout-hearted, for the coming of the Lord is near.

James 5:7–8 REB

See also **Endurance; Patience**

War

270.1 The Lord is a man of war.

Exodus 15:3 KJV

270.2 When you go out to war against your enemies, and see horses and chariots, an army larger than your own, you shall not be afraid of them; for the Lord your God is with you, who brought you up from the land of Egypt.

Deuteronomy 20:1 NRSV

270.3 [Jehoshaphat's prayer] Judge them, God our God, for we have not the strength to face this great host which is invading our land; we do not know what we ought to do, but our eyes look to you.

2 Chronicles 20:12 REB

270.4 Though an host should encamp against me, my heart shall not fear: though war should rise against me, in this will I be confident. One thing have I desired of the Lord, that will I seek after; that I may dwell in the house of the Lord all the days of my life.

Psalm 27:3–4 KJV

270.5 A king does not win because of his powerful army; a soldier does not triumph because of his strength.

Psalm 33:16 GNB

270.6 The Lord said, 'Assyria! I use Assyria like a club to punish those with whom I am angry. I sent Assyria to attack a godless nation, people who have made me angry.'

Isaiah 10:5–6 GNB

270.7 You will soon hear about wars and threats of wars, but don't be afraid. These things will have to happen first, but that isn't the end. Nations and kingdoms will go to war against each other. People will starve to death, and in some places there will be earthquakes.

Matthew 24:6–7 CEV

270.8 Who will separate us from the love of Christ? Will hardship, or distress, or persecution, or famine, or nakedness, or peril, or sword? As it is written, 'For your sake we are being killed all day long; we are accounted as sheep to be slaughtered.' No, in all these things we are more than conquerors through him who loved us.

Romans 8:35–37 NRSV

270.9 [Those in authority] are God's servants working for your own good. But if you do evil, then be afraid of them, because their power to punish is real. They are God's servants and carry out God's punishment on those who do evil.

Romans 13:4 GNB

Warfare, spiritual

271.1 Not by might, nor by power, but by my spirit, saith the Lord of hosts.

Zechariah 4:6 KJV

271.2 The seventy returned with joy, saying, 'Lord, in your name even the demons submit to us!' He said to them, 'I watched Satan fall from heaven like a flash of lightning. See, I have given you authority to tread on snakes and scorpions, and over all the power of the enemy; and nothing will hurt you. Nevertheless, do not rejoice at this, that the spirits submit to you, but rejoice that your names are written in heaven.'

Luke 10:17–20 NRSV

271.3 For although we are human, it is not by human methods that we do battle. The weapons with which we do battle are not those of human nature, but they have the power, in God's cause, to demolish fortresses. It is ideas that we demolish, every presumptuous notion that is set up against the knowledge of God, and we bring every thought into captivity and obedience to Christ.

2 Corinthians 10:3–5 NJB

271.4 That [unspiritual] nature sets its desires against the Spirit, while the Spirit fights against it. They are in conflict with one another so that you cannot do what you want.

Galatians 5:17 REB

271.5 Put on the whole armour of God, that ye may be able to stand against the wiles of the devil. For we wrestle not against flesh and blood, but against principalities, against powers, against the rulers of the darkness of this world, against spiritual wickedness in high places.

Ephesians 6:11–12 KJV

271.6 Therefore take up the whole armour of God, so that you may be able to withstand on that evil day, and having done everything, to stand firm. Stand therefore, and fasten the belt of truth around your waist, and put on the breastplate of righteousness. As shoes for your feet put on whatever will make you ready to proclaim the gospel of peace. With all of these, take the shield of faith, with which you will be able to quench all the flaming arrows of the evil one. Take the helmet of salvation, and the sword of the Spirit, which is the word of God. Pray in the Spirit at all times in every prayer and supplication. To that end keep alert and always persevere in supplication for all the saints.

Ephesians 6:13–18 NRSV

271.7 He [Christ] disarmed the rulers and authorities and made a public example of them, triumphing over them in it.

Colossians 2:15 NRSV

271.8 Fight the good fight of the faith. Take hold of the eternal life to which you were called when you made your good confession in the presence of many witnesses.

1 Timothy 6:12 NIV

271.9 What causes fighting and quarrels among you? Is not their origin the appetites that war in your bodies?

James 4:1 REB

271.10 Submit yourselves therefore to God. Resist the devil, and he will flee from you. Draw near to God, and he will draw near to you.

James 4:7–8 NRSV

271.11 Dear friends, I appeal to you, as aliens in a foreign land, to avoid bodily desires which make war on the soul.

1 Peter 2:11 REB

271.12 Like a roaring lion your adversary the devil prowls around, looking for someone to devour. Resist him, steadfast in your faith, for you know that your brothers and sisters throughout the world are undergoing the same kinds of suffering.

1 Peter 5:8–9 NRSV

271.13 Now have come the salvation and the power and the kingdom of our God and the authority of his Messiah, for the accuser of our comrades has been thrown down, who accuses them day and night before our God. But they have conquered him by the blood of the Lamb and by the word of their testimony, for they did not cling to life even in the face of death.

Revelation 12:10–11 NRSV

See also **Christian life, Continuing in the faith; Endurance**

Water

272.1 They shall not hurt nor destroy in all my holy mountain: for the earth shall be full of the knowledge of the Lord, as the waters cover the sea.

Isaiah 11:9 KJV

272.2 With great joy, you people will get water from the well of victory.

Isaiah 12:3 CEV

272.3 Ho, every one that thirsteth, come ye to the waters, and he that hath no money; come ye, buy, and eat.

Isaiah 55:1 KJV

272.4 The Lord, the fountain of living waters.

Jeremiah 17:13 KJV

272.5 I will sprinkle clean water upon you, and you shall be clean from all your uncleannesses, and from all your idols I will cleanse you.

Ezekiel 36:25 NRSV

272.6 [John the Baptist] I baptize you with water, for repentance; but the one who comes after me is mightier than I am, whose sandals I am not worthy to remove. He will baptize you with the Holy Spirit and with fire.

Matthew 3:11 REB

272.7 Jesus answered, Verily, verily, I say unto thee, Except a man be born of water, and of the Spirit, he cannot enter into the kingdom of God.

John 3:5 KJV

272.8 Whoever drinks the water I shall give will never again be thirsty. The water that I shall give will be a spring of water within him, welling up and bringing eternal life.

John 4:14 REB

272.9 Jesus said unto them, I am the bread of life: he that cometh to me shall never hunger; and he that believeth on me shall never thirst.

John 6:35 KJV

272.10 On the last day of the festival, the great day, while Jesus was standing there, he cried out, 'Let anyone who is thirsty come to me, and let the one who believes in me drink. As the scripture has said, "Out of the believer's heart shall flow rivers of living water."' Now he said this about the Spirit, which believers in him were to receive; for as yet there was no Spirit, because Jesus was not yet glorified.

John 7:37–39 NRSV

272.11 Christ loved the church and gave his life for it. He did this to dedicate the church to God by his word, after making it clean by washing it in water.

Ephesians 5:25–26 GNB

272.12 It was not because of any upright actions we had done ourselves; it was for no reason except his own faithful love that he [God] saved us, by means of the cleansing water of rebirth and renewal in the Holy Spirit.

Titus 3:5 NJB

272.13 Let us draw near with a true heart in full assurance of faith, having our hearts sprinkled from an evil conscience, and our bodies washed with pure water.

Hebrews 10:22 KJV

Way

273.1 [David's song of victory] This God – how perfect are his deeds, how dependable his words! He is like a shield for all who seek his protection.

2 Samuel 22:31 GNB

273.2 For the Lord knoweth the way of the righteous: but the way of the ungodly shall perish.

Psalm 1:6 KJV

273.3 Good and upright is the Lord; therefore he instructs sinners in the way. He leads the humble in what is right, and teaches the humble his way.

Psalm 25:8–9 NRSV

273.4 There is a way which seemeth right unto a man, but the end thereof are the ways of death.

Proverbs 14:12 KJV

273.5 Though the Lord give you the bread of adversity, and the water of affliction, yet shall not thy teachers be removed into a corner any more, but thine eyes shall see thy teachers: And thine ears shall hear a word behind thee, saying, This is the way, walk ye in it, when ye turn to the right hand, and when ye turn to the left.

Isaiah 30:20–21 KJV

273.6 Why sayest thou, O Jacob, and speakest, O Israel, My way is hid from the Lord, and my judgment is passed over from my God? Hast thou not known? hast thou not heard, that the everlasting God, the Lord, the Creator of the ends of the earth, fainteth not, neither is weary?

Isaiah 40:27–28 KJV

273.7 Say to them, As I live, says the Lord God, I have no pleasure in the death of the wicked, but that the wicked turn from their ways and live; turn back, turn back from your evil ways; for why will you die, O house of Israel?… Yet your people say, 'The way of the Lord is not just', when it is their own way that is not just.

Ezekiel 33:11, 17 NRSV

273.8 Enter by the narrow gate. Wide is the gate and broad the road that leads to destruction, and many enter that way; narrow is the gate and constricted the road that leads to life, and those who find them are few.

Matthew 7:13–14 REB

273.9 Jesus saith unto him, I am the way, the truth, and the life: no man cometh unto the Father, but by me.

John 14:6 KJV

273.10 [Paul] I do admit this to you: I worship the God of our ancestors by following that Way which they [the Jews] say is false.

Acts 24:14 GNB

273.11 Therefore, my friends, since we have confidence to enter the sanctuary by the blood of Jesus, by the new and living way that he opened for us through the curtain (that is, through his flesh).

Hebrews 10:19–20 NRSV

***See also* Counsel; Guidance**

Weakness

274.1 Strengthen ye the weak hands, and confirm the feeble knees.

Isaiah 35:3 KJV

274.2 Thou, O king, sawest, and behold a great image. This great image, whose brightness was excellent, stood before thee; and the form thereof was terrible. This image's head was of fine gold, his breast and his arms of silver, his belly and his thighs of brass, his legs of iron, his feet part of iron and part of clay. Thou sawest till that a stone was cut out without hands, which smote the image upon his feet that were of iron and clay, and brake them to pieces.

Daniel 2:31–34 KJV

Feet of clay

Someone is said to have *feet of clay* when, although being a person who is respected, he or she has a fundamental and usually hidden weakness. The expression comes from Daniel 2:33, where the statue seen in Nebuchadnezzar's dream is described: it had a head made of gold, a chest and arms of silver, a belly and thighs of bronze, legs of iron and feet of iron and clay. The feet, according to Daniel's explanation, were struck by a stone which broke them to pieces and so smashed the rest of the statue. Thus *feet of clay* in modern usage means a vulnerable or weak point.

274.3 As my senses failed I remembered the Lord, and my prayer reached you in your holy temple.

Jonah 2:7 REB

274.4 Watch and pray, that ye enter not into temptation: the spirit indeed is willing, but the flesh is weak.

Matthew 26:41 KJV

274.5 In all this I have given you an example that by such work we must support the weak, remembering the words of the Lord Jesus, for he himself said, 'It is more blessed to give than to receive.'

Acts 20:35 NRSV

274.6 In the same way the Spirit comes to the aid of our weakness. We do not even know how we ought to pray, but through our inarticulate groans the Spirit himself is pleading for us.

Romans 8:26 REB

274.7 Welcome those who are weak in faith, but do not argue with them about their personal opinions.

Romans 14:1 GNB

274.8 If our faith is strong, we should be patient with the Lord's followers whose faith is weak. We should try to please them instead of ourselves.

Romans 15:1 CEV

274.9 God hath chosen the foolish things of the world to confound the wise; and God hath chosen the weak things of the world to confound the things which are mighty.

1 Corinthians 1:27 KJV

274.10 Be careful, however, not to let your freedom of action make those who are weak in the faith fall into sin.

1 Corinthians 8:9 GNB

274.11 To the weak became I as weak, that I might gain the weak: I am made all things to all men, that I might by all means save some.

1 Corinthians 9:22 KJV

All things to all men

People who are *all things to all men* try to please everyone, modifying their behavior to adapt to those whom they are with. The expression has its source in this verse. Paul was willing to be completely versatile to fit in with different groups of people in an attempt to bring about their salvation.

274.12 It is sown in dishonour; it is raised in glory: it is sown in weakness; it is raised in power.

1 Corinthians 15:43 KJV

274.13 His answer was: 'My grace is all you need, for my power is greatest when you are weak.' I am most happy, then, to be proud of my weaknesses, in order to feel the protection of Christ's power over me. I am content with weaknesses, insults, hardships, persecutions, and difficulties for Christ's sake. For when I am weak, then I am strong.

2 Corinthians 12:9–10 GNB

274.14 True, he died on the cross in weakness, but he lives by the power of God; so you will find that we who share his weakness shall live with him by the power of God.

2 Corinthians 13:4 REB

See also **Power**

Widows

275.1 He secures justice for the fatherless and the widow, and he shows love towards the alien who lives among you, giving him food and clothing.

Deuteronomy 10:18 REB

275.2 The Levites, because they have no allotment or inheritance with you, as well as the... widows in your towns, may come and eat their fill so that the Lord your God may bless you in all the work that you undertake.

Deuteronomy 14:29 NRSV

275.3 The Lord preserveth the strangers; he relieveth the fatherless and widow: but the way of the wicked he turneth upside down.

Psalm 146:9 KJV

275.4 Seek justice, encourage the oppressed. Defend the cause of the fatherless, plead the case of the widow.

Isaiah 1:17 NIV

275.5 Jesus was sitting in the temple near the offering box and watching people put in their gifts. He noticed that many rich people were giving a lot of money. Finally, a poor widow came up and put in two coins that were worth only a few pennies. Jesus told his disciples to gather around him. Then he said: I tell you that this poor widow has put in more than all the others. Everyone else gave what they didn't need. But she is very poor and gave everything she had. Now she doesn't have a penny to live on.

Mark 12:41–44 CEV

The widow's mite

A *widow's mite* is a small gift of money that is more than the giver can afford. The phrase alludes to the offering (in this contemporary translation rendered as 'two coins that were worth only a few pennies') by the widow whose commitment to God was total: she gave all she had to live on.

275.6 There was a very old prophet, a widow named Anna, daughter of Phanuel of the tribe of Asher. She had been married for only seven years and was now 84 years old. She never left the Temple; day and night she worshipped God, fasting and praying.

Luke 2:36–37 GNB

275.7 Now during those days, when the disciples were increasing in number, the Hellenists complained against the Hebrews because their widows were being neglected in the daily distribution of food.

Acts 6:1 NRSV

275.8 A wife is bound to her husband as long as he lives. But if the husband dies, she is free to marry whom she will, provided the marriage is within the Lord's fellowship.

1 Corinthians 7:39 REB

275.9 A widow who is all alone, with no one to take care of her, has placed her hope in God and continues to pray and ask him for his help night and day.

1 Timothy 5:5 GNB

275.10 [A widow]… well known for her good deeds, such as bringing up children, showing hospitality, washing the feet of the saints, helping those in trouble and devoting herself to all kinds of good deeds.

1 Timothy 5:10 NIV

275.11 They [young widows] also learn to waste their time in going round from house to house; but even worse, they learn to be gossips and busybodies, talking of things they should not. So I would prefer that the younger widows get married, have children, and take care of their homes, so as to give our enemies no chance of speaking evil of us.

1 Timothy 5:13–14 GNB

275.12 Religion that is pure and undefiled before God, the Father, is this: to care for orphans and widows in their distress, and to keep oneself unstained by the world.

James 1:27 NRSV

Will of God

276.1 I delight to do thy will, O my God: yea, thy law is within my heart.

Psalm 40:8 KJV

276.2 Yet it pleased the Lord to bruise him; he hath put him to grief: when thou shalt make his soul an offering for sin, he shall see his seed, he shall prolong his days, and the pleasure of the Lord shall prosper in his hand.

Isaiah 53:10 KJV

276.3 Jesus said: My food is to do the will of the one who sent me, and to complete his work.

John 4:34 NJB

276.4 Be not conformed to this world, but be ye transformed by the renewing of your mind, that ye may prove what is that good, and acceptable, and perfect, will of God.

Romans 12:2 KJV

276.5 He made known to us the mystery of his will according to his good pleasure, which he purposed in Christ, to be put into effect when the times will have reached their fulfilment – to bring all things in heaven and on earth together under one head, even Christ.

Ephesians 1:9–10 NIV

276.6 Do not be foolish, but understand what the will of the Lord is.

Ephesians 5:17 REB

276.7 For this is the will of God, your sanctification: that you abstain from fornication.

1 Thessalonians 4:3 NRSV

276.8 Rejoice evermore. Pray without ceasing. In every thing give thanks: for this is the will of God in Christ Jesus concerning you.

1 Thessalonians 5:16–18 KJV

276.9 The world passeth away, and the lust thereof: but he that doeth the will of God abideth for ever.

1 John 2:17 KJV

276.10 What he commands is that we believe in his Son Jesus Christ and love one another, just as Christ commanded us.

1 John 3:23 GNB

See also **Accepting the will of God; Bible; Guidance; Law; Revelation**

Wisdom

277.1 God gave Solomon very great wisdom, discernment, and breadth of understanding as vast as the sand on the seashore, so that Solomon's wisdom surpassed the wisdom of all the people of the east, and all the wisdom of Egypt.

1 Kings 4:29–30 NRSV

277.2 The fear of the Lord is the beginning of wisdom: a good understanding have all they that do his commandments: his praise endureth for ever.

Psalm 111:10 KJV

> **The fear of the Lord**
> 'The fear of the Lord is the beginning of knowledge.' This is the general motto of the Wisdom writings. The fundamental principle of this wise way to live is a relationship of reverence and submission to the Lord.

277.3 Happy are those who find wisdom, and those who get understanding... She

[wisdom] is more precious than jewels, and nothing you desire can compare with her. Long life is in her right hand; in her left hand are riches and honour. Her ways are ways of pleasantness, and all her paths are peace. She is a tree of life to those who lay hold of her.

Proverbs 3:13, 15–18 NRSV

277.4 The spirit of the Lord shall rest upon him, the spirit of wisdom and understanding, the spirit of counsel and might, the spirit of knowledge and of the fear of the Lord.

Isaiah 11:2 KJV

277.5 The true beginning of wisdom is the desire to learn.

Wisdom of Solomon 6:17 REB

277.6 The basis of wisdom is to fear the Lord.

Ecclesiasticus 1:14 NJB

277.7 Learn where is wisdom, where is strength, where is understanding; that thou mayest know also where is length of days, and life, where is the light of the eyes, and peace.

Baruch 3:14 KJV

277.8 So then, anyone who hears these words of mine and obeys them is like a wise man who built his house on rock.

Matthew 7:24 GNB

277.9 Behold, I send you forth as sheep in the midst of wolves: be ye therefore wise as serpents, and harmless as doves.

Matthew 10:16 KJV

277.10 The Son of man came, eating and drinking, and they say, 'Look, a glutton and a drunkard, a friend of tax collectors and sinners.' Yet wisdom is justified by her deeds.

Matthew 11:19 NJB

277.11 Jesus became wise, and he grew strong. God was pleased with him and so were the people.

Luke 2:52 CEV

277.12 The lord commended the unjust steward, because he had done wisely: for the children of this world are in their generation wiser than the children of light.

Luke 16:8 KJV

277.13 So then, brothers and sisters, choose seven men among you who are known to be full of the Holy Spirit and wisdom, and we will put them in charge of this matter.

Acts 6:3 GNB

277.14 O the depth of the riches both of the wisdom and knowledge of God! how unsearchable are his judgments, and his ways past finding out!

Romans 11:33 KJV

277.15 For after that in the wisdom of God the world by wisdom knew not God, it pleased God by the foolishness of preaching to save them that believe.

1 Corinthians 1:21 KJV

277.16 He is the source of your life in Christ Jesus, who became for us wisdom from God.

1 Corinthians 1:30 NRSV

277.17 Yet I do proclaim a message of wisdom to those who are spiritually mature. But it is not the wisdom that belongs to this world or to the powers that rule this world – powers that are losing their power. The wisdom I proclaim is God's hidden wisdom, which he had already chosen for our glory even before the world was made.

1 Corinthians 2:6–7 GNB

277.18 To one is given through the Spirit the utterance of wisdom.

1 Corinthians 12:8 NRSV

277.19 [Paul's prayer] That the God of our Lord Jesus Christ, the Father of glory, may give unto you the spirit of wisdom and revelation in the knowledge of him.

Ephesians 1:17 KJV

277.20 [Christ] in whom are hid all the treasures of wisdom and knowledge.

Colossians 2:3 KJV

277.21 If any of you lacks wisdom, he should ask God and it will be given him, for God is a generous giver who neither grudges nor reproaches anyone.

James 1:5 REB

277.22 The wisdom from above is in the first place pure; and then peace-loving, considerate, and open-minded; it is straightforward and sincere, rich in compassion and in deeds of kindness that are its fruit.

James 3:17 REB

See also **Discernment**; **Fools and folly**; **God, Wise**; **Knowledge**; **Understanding**

Witness

278.1 Declare among the nations, 'The Lord is King.'

Psalm 96:10 REB

278.2 Then I heard the voice of the Lord saying, 'Whom shall I send, and who will go for us?' And I said, 'Here am I; send me!'

Isaiah 6:8 NRSV

278.3 [Jesus to Simon Peter and Andrew] He saith unto them, Follow me, and I will make you fishers of men.

Matthew 4:19 KJV

278.4 Then he said to his disciples, 'The harvest is rich but the labourers are few, so ask the Lord of the harvest to send out labourers to his harvest.'

Matthew 9:37 NJB

278.5 Go therefore and make disciples of all nations, baptizing them in the name of the Father and of the Son and of the Holy Spirit, and teaching them to obey everything that I have commanded you. And remember, I am with you always, to the end of the age.

Matthew 28:19–20 NRSV

278.6 Before the end comes, the good news must be preached to all nations.

Mark 13:10 CEV

278.7 Go and preach the good news to everyone in the world. Anyone who believes me and is baptized will be saved. But anyone who refuses to believe me will be condemned.

Mark 16:15–16 CEV

278.8 [Jesus] said unto them, Thus it is written, and thus it behoved Christ to suffer, and to rise from the dead the third day: and that repentance and remission of sins should be preached in his name among all nations, beginning at Jerusalem. And ye are witnesses of these things.

Luke 24:46–48 KJV

278.9 When the advocate has come, whom I shall send you from the Father – the Spirit of truth that issues from the Father – he will bear witness to me. And you also are my witnesses, because you have been with me from the first.

John 15:26–27 REB

278.10 As you sent me into the world, I have sent them into the world... I pray not only for these but also for those who through their teaching will come to believe in me. May they all be one... so that the world may believe it was you who sent me.

John 17:18, 20–21 NJB

278.11 When the Holy Spirit comes upon you, you will be filled with power, and you will be witnesses for me in Jerusalem, in all Judea and Samaria, and to the ends of the earth.

Acts 1:8 GNB

278.12 [Peter and John] For we cannot stop speaking of what we ourselves have seen and heard.

Acts 4:20 GNB

278.13 For this is what the Lord commanded us to do when he said: I have made you a light to the nations, so that my salvation may reach the remotest parts of the earth.

Acts 13:47 NJB

278.14 We were sent to speak for Christ, and God is begging you to listen to our message. We speak for Christ and sincerely ask you to make peace with God.

2 Corinthians 5:20 CEV

278.15 [Paul asks for prayer] That utterance may be given unto me, that I may open my mouth boldly, to make known the mystery of the gospel.

Ephesians 6:19 KJV

See also **Evangelists; Preaching**

Work

279.1 The Lord God took the man, and put him into the garden of Eden to dress it and to keep it.

Genesis 2:15 KJV

279.2 In the sweat of thy face shalt thou eat bread, till thou return unto the ground.

Genesis 3:19 KJV

279.3 You have six days to labour and do all your work; but the seventh day is a sabbath of the Lord your God; that day you must not do any work.

Exodus 20:9–10 REB

279.4 Then people go out to do their work and keep working until evening.

Psalm 104:23 GNB

279.5 Except the Lord build the house, they labour in vain that build it: except the Lord keep the city, the watchman waketh but in vain.

Psalm 127:1 KJV

279.6 Commit to the Lord all that you do, and your plans will be successful.

Proverbs 16:3 REB

279.7 Whatsoever thy hand findeth to do, do it with thy might; for there is no work, nor device, nor knowledge, nor wisdom, in the grave, whither thou goest.

Ecclesiastes 9:10 KJV

279.8 The Kingdom of heaven is like this. Once there was a man who went out early in the morning to hire some men to work in his vineyard.

Matthew 20:1 GNB

279.9 The labourer is worthy of his hire.

Luke 10:7 KJV

279.10 Slaves, obey your human masters with fear and trembling; and do it with a sincere heart, as though you were serving Christ. Do this not only when they are watching you, because you want to gain their approval; but with all your heart do what God wants, as slaves of Christ. Do your work as slaves cheerfully, as though you served the Lord, and not merely human beings. Remember that the Lord will reward everyone, whether slave or free, for the good work they do. Masters, behave in the same way towards your slaves and stop using threats. Remember that you and your slaves belong to the same Master in heaven, who judges everyone by the same standard.

Ephesians 6:5–9 GNB

279.11 Whatsoever ye do in word or deed, do all in the name of the Lord Jesus, giving thanks to God and the Father by him.

Colossians 3:17 KJV

279.12 Whoever does not provide for relatives, and especially for family members, has denied the faith and is worse than an unbeliever.

1 Timothy 5:8 NRSV

279.13 The scripture says, 'You shall not muzzle an ox while it is treading out the grain', and, 'The labourer deserves to be paid.'

1 Timothy 5:18 NRSV

***See also* Laziness**

Works, good

280.1 Can the Ethiopian change his skin, or the leopard his spots? then may ye also do good, that are accustomed to do evil.

Jeremiah 13:23 KJV

280.2 Champion the widow, defend the cause of the fatherless, give to the poor, protect the orphan, provide clothing for those who have none.

2 Esdras 2:20 REB

280.3 Let your light so shine before men, that they may see your good works, and glorify your Father which is in heaven.

Matthew 5:16 KJV

280.4 Why do you call me, 'Lord, Lord,' and yet don't do what I tell you?

Luke 6:46 GNB

280.5 Then they said to him, 'What must we do to perform the works of God?' Jesus answered them, 'This is the work of God, that you believe in him whom he has sent.'

John 6:28–29 NRSV

280.6 I preached first to the inhabitants of Damascus, and then to Jerusalem and all the country of Judaea, and to the Gentiles, calling on them to repent and turn to God, and to prove their repentance by their deeds.

Acts 26:20 REB

280.7 So, my dear brothers, keep firm and immovable, always abounding in energy for the Lord's work, being sure that in the Lord none of your labours is wasted.

1 Corinthians 15:58 NJB

280.8 For by grace are ye saved through faith; and that not of yourselves: it is the gift of God: not of works, lest any man should boast. For we are his workmanship, created in Christ Jesus unto good works, which God hath before ordained that we should walk in them.

Ephesians 2:8–10 KJV

280.9 [The purpose of scripture] That everyone who belongs to God may be proficient, equipped for every good work.

2 Timothy 3:17 NRSV

280.10 We should keep on encouraging each other to be thoughtful and to do helpful things.

Hebrews 10:24 CEV

280.11 Be ye doers of the word, and not hearers only, deceiving your own selves.

James 1:22 KJV

280.12 What good is it, my friends, for someone to say he has faith when his actions do nothing to show it? Can that faith save him?… So with faith; if it does not lead to action, it is by itself a lifeless thing. But someone may say: 'One chooses faith, another action.' To which I reply: 'Show me this faith you speak of with no actions to prove it, while I by my actions will prove to you my faith.'

James 2:14, 17–18 REB

280.13 You see, then, that it is by people's actions that they are put right with God, and not by their faith alone.

James 2:24 GNB

280.14 For just as the body without the spirit is dead, so faith without works is also dead.

James 2:26 NRSV

See also **Service**

World

CREATED UNIVERSE

281.1 The earth is the Lord's, and the fulness thereof; the world, and they that dwell therein.

Psalm 24:1 KJV

281.2 The God who made the world and everything in it, he who is Lord of heaven and earth, does not live in shrines made by human hands.

Acts 17:24 NRSV

281.3 [The Son] He is the one through whom God created the universe.

Hebrews 1:2 GNB

See also Creation; Earth, the; Land

HUMANITY

281.4 For God so loved the world, that he gave his only begotten Son, that whosoever believeth in him should not perish, but have everlasting life. For God sent not his Son into the world to condemn the world; but that the world through him might be saved.

John 3:16–17 KJV

HUMANITY IN REBELLION AGAINST GOD

281.5 If the world hates you, just remember that it has hated me first. If you belonged to the world, then the world would love you as its own. But I chose you from this world, and you do not belong to it; that is why the world hates you.

John 15:18–19 GNB

281.6 Now I am no longer in the world, but they are in the world, and I am

coming to you. Holy Father, protect them in your name that you have given me, so that they may be one, as we are one.

John 17:11 NRSV

281.7 They are not of the world, even as I am not of the world.

John 17:16 KJV

281.8 Love not the world, neither the things that are in the world. If any man love the world, the love of the Father is not in him. For all that is in the world, the lust of the flesh, and the lust of the eyes, and the pride of life, is not of the Father, but is of the world. And the world passeth away, and the lust thereof: but he that doeth the will of God abideth for ever.

1 John 2:15–17 KJV

See also Rebellion; Sin

Worry

282.1 Fret not thyself because of evildoers, neither be thou envious against the workers of iniquity.

Psalm 37:1 KJV

282.2 Don't let it bother you when all goes well for those who do sinful things.

Psalm 37:7 CEV

282.3 When anxious thoughts filled my heart, your comfort brought me joy.

Psalm 94:19 REB

282.4 Worry makes a heart heavy, a kindly word makes it glad.

Proverbs 12:25 NJB

282.5 Rid yourself of all worry and pain, because the wonderful moments of youth quickly disappear.

Ecclesiastes 11:10 CEV

282.6 I am telling you not to worry about your life and what you are to eat, nor about your body and what you are to wear... Can any of you, however much you worry, add one single cubit to your span of life?

Matthew 6:25, 27 NJB

282.7 So do not worry; do not say, 'What are we to eat? What are we to drink? What are we to wear?' It is the gentiles who set their hearts on all these things. Your heavenly Father knows you need them all. Set your hearts on his kingdom first, and on God's saving justice, and all these other things will be given you as well. So do not worry about tomorrow.

Matthew 6:31–34 NJB

282.8 The Lord answered, 'Martha, Martha, you are fretting and fussing about so many things; only one thing is necessary. Mary has chosen what is best; it shall not be taken away from her.'

Luke 10:41–42 REB

282.9 When you are brought to trial in the Jewish meeting places or before rulers or officials, don't worry about how you will defend yourselves or what you will say. At that time the Holy Spirit will tell you what to say.

Luke 12:11–12 CEV

282.10 Jesus said to his disciples, 'Don't be worried! Have faith in God and have faith in me.'

John 14:1 CEV

282.11 I give you peace, the kind of peace that only I can give. It isn't like the peace that this world can give. So don't be worried or afraid.

John 14:27 CEV

282.12 Never worry about anything; but tell God all your desires of every kind in prayer and petition shot through with gratitude.

Philippians 4:6 NJB

282.13 He cares for you, so cast all your anxiety on him.

1 Peter 5:7 REB

See also **Comfort, when anxious; Providence**

Worship

283.1 Thou shalt have no other gods before me. Thou shalt not make unto thee any graven image, or any likeness of any thing that is in heaven above, or that is in the earth beneath, or that is in the water under the earth.

Exodus 20:3–4 KJV

283.2 Give unto the Lord the glory due unto his name: bring an offering, and come before him: worship the Lord in the beauty of holiness.

1 Chronicles 16:29 KJV

283.3 O come, let us worship, and fall down, and kneel before the Lord our Maker.

Psalm 95:6 BCP

283.4 This people worship me with empty words and pay me lip-service while their hearts are far from me, and their religion is but a human precept, learnt by rote.

Isaiah 29:13 REB

283.5 When they were come into the house, they saw the young child with Mary his mother, and fell down, and worshipped him: and when they had opened their treasures, they presented unto him gifts; gold, and frankincense, and myrrh.

Matthew 2:11 KJV

283.6 It is written, Thou shalt worship the Lord thy God, and him only shalt thou serve.

Matthew 4:10 KJV

283.7 The hour is coming, and is now here, when the true worshippers will worship the Father in spirit and truth, for the Father seeks such as these to worship him. God is spirit, and those who worship him must worship in spirit and truth.

John 4:23–24 NRSV

283.8 Day after day they met as a group in the Temple, and they had their meals together in their homes, eating with glad and humble hearts, praising God, and enjoying the good will of all the people. And every day the Lord added to their group those who were being saved.

Acts 2:46–47 GNB

283.9 I beseech you therefore, brethren, by the mercies of God, that ye present your bodies a living sacrifice, holy, acceptable unto God, which is your reasonable service.

Romans 12:1 KJV

283.10 At the name of Jesus every knee should bow – in heaven, on earth, and in the depths.

Philippians 2:10 REB

283.11 Lead a life worthy of the Lord, a life acceptable to him in all its aspects, bearing fruit in every kind of good work and growing in knowledge of God.

Colossians 1:10 NJB

283.12 Let the word of Christ dwell in you richly in all wisdom; teaching and admonishing one another in psalms and hymns and spiritual songs, singing with grace in your hearts to the Lord. And whatsoever ye do in word or deed, do all in the name of the Lord Jesus, giving thanks to God and the Father by him.

Colossians 3:16–17 KJV

283.13 Thou art worthy, O Lord, to receive glory and honour and power: for thou hast created all things, and for thy pleasure they are and were created.

Revelation 4:11 KJV

See also **Celebration; Christian life, Longing for God; Jesus Christ, Jesus, the one to be worshipped; Love, of humanity for God; Music; Praise; Reverence; Service; Thankfulness and thanksgiving**

Youth

284.1 Honour thy father and thy mother: that thy days may be long upon the land which the Lord thy God giveth thee.

Exodus 20:12 KJV

284.2 Would you like to enjoy life? Do you want long life and happiness? Then hold back from speaking evil and from telling lies. Turn away from evil and do good; strive for peace with all your heart.

Psalm 34:12–14 GNB

284.3 How can young people keep their way pure? By guarding it according to your word.

Psalm 119:9 NRSV

284.4 Foolish children bring grief to their fathers and bitter regrets to their mothers.

Proverbs 17:25 GNB

284.5 Remember now thy Creator in the days of thy youth, while the evil days come not, nor the years draw nigh, when thou shalt say, I have no pleasure in them.

Ecclesiastes 12:1 KJV

284.6 Even the youths shall faint and be weary, and the young men shall utterly fall: but they that wait upon the Lord shall renew their strength.

Isaiah 40:30–31 KJV

284.7 When we are young, it is good to struggle hard.

Lamentations 3:27 CEV

284.8 Jesus said unto him [the rich young man], If thou wilt be perfect, go and sell that thou hast, and give to the poor, and thou shalt have treasure in heaven: and come and follow me.

Matthew 19:21 KJV

284.9 He said, A certain man had two sons: and the younger of them said to his father, Father, give me the portion of goods that falleth to me. And he divided unto them his living. And not many days after the younger son gathered all together, and took his journey into a far country, and there wasted his substance with riotous living. And when he had spent all, there arose a mighty famine in that land; and he began to be in want. And he went and joined himself to a citizen of that country; and he sent him into his fields to feed swine. And he would fain have filled his belly with the husks that the swine did eat: and no man gave unto him. And when he came to himself, he said, How many hired servants of my father's have bread enough and to spare, and I perish with hunger! I will arise and go to my father, and will say unto him, Father, I have sinned against heaven, and before thee, and am no more worthy to be called thy son: make me as one of thy hired servants. And he arose, and came to his father. But when he was yet a great way off, his father saw him, and had compassion, and ran, and fell on his neck, and kissed him. And the son said unto him, Father, I have sinned against heaven, and in thy sight, and am no more worthy to be called thy son. But the father said to his servants, Bring forth the best robe, and put it on him; and put a ring on his hand, and shoes on his feet: and bring hither the fatted calf, and kill it; and let us eat, and be merry: for this my son was dead, and is alive again; he was lost, and is found. And they began to be merry.

Luke 15:11–24 KJV

284.10 Let no one underrate you because you are young, but be to believers an example in speech and behaviour, in love, fidelity, and purity.

1 Timothy 4:12 REB

284.11 Avoid the passions of youth, and strive for righteousness, faith, love, and peace, together with those who with a pure heart call out to the Lord for help.

2 Timothy 2:22 GNB

284.12 I write to you, young people, because you are strong and the word of God abides in you, and you have overcome the evil one.

1 John 2:14 NRSV

See also **Family, Children and the whole family; Old age; Time**

Zeal

285.1 Zeal for your house has consumed me; the insults aimed at you have landed on me.

Psalm 69:9 REB

285.2 For I can testify about them [the Israelites] that they are zealous for God, but their zeal is not based on knowledge. Since they did not know the righteousness that comes from God and sought to establish their own, they did not submit to God's righteousness.

Romans 10:2–3 NIV

285.3 In service of the Lord, work not halfheartedly but with conscientiousness and an eager spirit.

Romans 12:11 NJB

285.4 For necessity is laid upon me; yea, woe is unto me, if I preach not the gospel!

1 Corinthians 9:16 KJV

285.5 Therefore, my beloved, be steadfast, immoveable, always excelling in the work of the Lord, because you know that in the Lord your labour is not in vain.

1 Corinthians 15:58 NRSV

285.6 So let us not become tired of doing good; for if we do not give up, the time will come when we will reap the harvest. So then, as often as we have the chance, we should do good to everyone, and especially to those who belong to our family in the faith.

Galatians 6:9–10 GNB

285.7 As to zeal, a persecutor of the church; as to righteousness under the law, blameless. Yet whatever gains I had, these I have come to regard as loss because of Christ.

Philippians 3:6–7 NRSV

285.8 I press towards the finishing line, to win the heavenly prize to which God has called me in Christ Jesus.

Philippians 3:14 REB

285.9 [Jesus Christ] who gave himself for us that he might redeem us from all iniquity and purify for himself a people of his own who are zealous for good deeds.

Titus 2:14 NRSV

285.10 Now that by your obedience to the truth you have purified yourselves and have come to have a sincere love for your fellow-believers, love one another earnestly with all your heart.

1 Peter 1:22 GNB

285.11 Beloved, while eagerly preparing to write to you about the salvation we share, I find it necessary to write and appeal to you to contend for the faith that was once for all entrusted to the saints.

Jude v. 3 NRSV

285.12 Be earnest, therefore, and repent.

Revelation 3:19 NRSV

Laodicean

Laodicean is used to describe someone who is lukewarm and indifferent, especially in religious or political matters. The application of this word comes from the criticism expressed by Jesus Christ of the church at Laodicea (Revelation 3:14–22). The believers there were neither cold nor hot, but showed a tepid, half-hearted commitment, and so were urged to repent.

See also **Endurance**

APPENDIX

The appendix is in two sections: Special Occasions, e.g., Birthday, Holiday, Wedding, listed in alphabetical order, and Special Holidays and Festivals, e.g., Christmas, Easter, Pentecost, listed in time order beginning at Advent.

Under each heading is given a set of key Bible passages followed by additional Bible references (for the full text of these you may want to consult a Bible) and also cross-references to themes in the main text.

SPECIAL OCCASIONS

Anniversary

The Lord your God has blessed you in everything you have undertaken. He has watched over your journey through this great wilderness; these forty years the Lord your God has been with you, and you have gone short of nothing.

Deuteronomy 2:7 REB

Nehemiah, who was the governor, and Ezra the priest and scribe, and the Levites who taught the people said to all the people, 'This day is holy to the Lord your God; do not mourn or weep.' For all the people wept when they heard the words of the law. Then he said to them, 'Go your way, eat the fat and drink sweet wine and send portions of them to those for whom nothing is prepared, for this day is holy to our Lord; and do not be grieved, for the joy of the Lord is your strength.'

Nehemiah 8:9–10 NRSV

I will extol you, my God and King, and bless your name for ever and ever. Every day I will bless you, and praise your name for ever and ever. Great is the Lord, and greatly to be praised; his greatness is unsearchable. One generation shall laud your works to another, and shall declare your mighty acts. On the glorious splendour of your majesty, and on your wondrous works, I will meditate. The might of your awesome deeds shall be proclaimed, and I will declare your greatness. They shall celebrate the fame of your abundant goodness, and shall sing aloud of your righteousness.

Psalm 145:1–7 NRSV

See also **Deuteronomy 8:1–18; 1 Kings 8:62–66; Psalms 98; 100:1–5**

See also in the main text **Marriage; Thankfulness and thanksgiving**

Baptism

Jesus, when he was baptized, went up straightway out of the water: and, lo, the heavens were opened unto him, and he saw the Spirit of God descending like a dove, and lighting upon him. And lo a voice from heaven, saying, This is my beloved Son, in whom I am well pleased.

Matthew 3:16–17 KJV

Have you forgotten that when we were baptized into union with Christ Jesus we were baptized into his death? By that baptism into his death we were buried with him, in order that, as Christ was raised from the dead by the glorious power of the Father, so also we might set out on a new life.

Romans 6:3–4 REB

For in the one Spirit we were all baptized into one body – Jews or Greeks, slaves or free – and we were all made to drink of one Spirit. Indeed, the body does not consist of one member but of many.

1 Corinthians 12:13–14 NRSV

There is one Lord, one faith, one baptism.

Ephesians 4:5 NJB

See also Ezekiel 36:25–28; Mark 1:1–11; Acts 2:38–41; 16:25–34
See also in the main text **Baptism**

Birth

Make a joyful noise unto the Lord, all ye lands. Serve the Lord with gladness: come before his presence with singing. Know ye that the Lord he is God: it is he that hath made us, and not we ourselves; we are his people, and the sheep of his pasture. Enter into his gates with thanksgiving, and into his courts with praise: be thankful unto him, and bless his name. For the Lord is good; his mercy is everlasting; and his truth endureth to all generations.

Psalm 100:1–5 KJV

They brought babies for him to touch, and when the disciples saw them they rebuked them. But Jesus called for the children and said, 'Let the children come to me; do not try to stop them; for the kingdom of God belongs to such as these. Truly I tell you: whoever does not accept the kingdom of God like a child will never enter it.'

Luke 18:15–17 REB

When a woman is in labour, she has pain, because her hour has come. But when her child is born, she no longer remembers the anguish because of the joy of having brought a human being into the world.

John 16:21 NRSV

See also Psalms 22:9–10; 127; 139:13–18; Jeremiah 1:5
See also in the main text **Birth**

Birthday

On the third day, which was Pharaoh's birthday, he made a feast for all his servants.

Genesis 40:20 NRSV

All our days pass under your wrath, our lives are over like a sigh. The span of our life is seventy years – eighty for those who are strong – but their whole extent is anxiety and trouble, they are over in a moment and we are gone... Teach us to count up the days that are ours, and we shall come to the heart of wisdom.

Psalm 90:9–10, 12 NJB

Listen to me, O house of Jacob, all the remnant of the house of Israel, who have been borne by me from your birth, carried from the womb; even to your old age I am he, even when you turn grey I will carry you. I have made, and I will bear; I will carry and will save.

Isaiah 46:3–4 NRSV

Are not two sparrows sold for a farthing? and one of them shall not fall on the ground without your Father. But the very hairs of your head are all numbered. Fear ye not therefore, ye are of more value than many sparrows.

Matthew 10:29–31 KJV

Come now, you who say, 'Today or tomorrow we will go to such and such a town and spend a year there, doing business and making money.' Yet you do not even know what tomorrow will bring. What is your life? For you are a mist that appears for a little while and then vanishes. Instead you ought to say, 'If the Lord wishes, we will live and do this or that.'

James 4:13–15 NRSV

Blessed be the God and Father of our Lord Jesus Christ! By his great mercy he has given us a new birth into a living hope through the resurrection of Jesus Christ from the dead, and into an inheritance that is imperishable, undefiled, and unfading, kept in heaven for you, who are being protected by the power of God through faith for a salvation ready to be revealed in the last time. In this you rejoice, even if now for a little while you have had to suffer various trials, so that the genuineness of your faith – being more precious than gold that, though perishable, is tested by fire – may be found to result in praise and glory and honour when Jesus Christ is revealed. Although you have not seen him, you love him; and even though you do not see him now, you believe in him and rejoice with an indescribable and glorious joy, for you are receiving the outcome of your faith, the salvation of your souls.

1 Peter 1:3–9 NRSV

In accordance with his promise, we wait for new heavens and a new earth, where righteousness is at home. Therefore, beloved, while you are waiting for these things, strive to be found by him at peace, without spot or blemish.

2 Peter 3:13–14 NRSV

See what love the Father has given us, that we should be called children of God; and that is what we are. The reason the world does not know us is that it did not know him. Beloved, we are God's children now; what we will be has not yet been revealed. What we do know is this: when he is revealed, we will be like him, for we will see him as he is. And all who have this hope in him purify themselves, just as he is pure.

1 John 3:1–3 NRSV

See also Job 14:1–6; Psalms 8; 139; Proverbs 3:1–10; Romans 8:28–39; 1 Corinthians 1:3–9; Philippians 1:6; 3:4–14

See also in the main text Assurance; Celebration; Thankfulness and thanksgiving

Funeral

The eternal God is thy refuge, and underneath are the everlasting arms.

Deuteronomy 33:27 KJV

He [Job] said, 'Naked I came from my mother's womb, and naked shall I return there; the Lord gave, and the Lord has taken away; blessed be the name of the Lord.'

Job 1:21 NRSV

The Lord is my shepherd, I shall not want. He makes me lie down in green pastures; he leads me beside still waters; he restores my soul. He leads me in right paths for his name's sake. Even though I walk through the darkest valley, I fear no evil; for you are with me; your rod and your staff – they comfort me. You prepare a table before me in the presence of my enemies; you anoint my head with oil; my cup overflows. Surely goodness and mercy shall follow me all the days of my life, and I shall dwell in the house of the Lord my whole life long.

Psalm 23:1–6 NRSV

Precious in the sight of the Lord is the death of his faithful ones.

Psalm 116:15 NRSV

Eye hath not seen, nor ear heard, neither have entered into the heart of man, the things which God hath prepared for them that love him.

1 Corinthians 2:9 KJV

We believe that Jesus died and rose again; so too will God bring those who died as Christians to be with Jesus… Thus we shall always be with the Lord. Console one another, then, with these words.

1 Thessalonians 4:14, 17–18 REB

We brought nothing into this world, and it is certain we can carry nothing out.

1 Timothy 6:7 KJV

See also **Lamentations 3:22–23; Matthew 5:4; John 3:16; 11:1–44; 14:1–6; Romans 8:38–39**
See also in the main text **Comfort, in bereavement and sorrow**

Holiday

For six days you may do your work, but on the seventh day abstain from work, so that your ox and your donkey may rest, and your home-born slave and the alien may refresh themselves.

Exodus 23:12 REB

Come unto me, all ye that labour and are heavy laden, and I will give you rest. Take my yoke upon you, and learn of me; for I am meek and lowly in heart: and ye shall find rest unto your souls. For my yoke is easy, and my burden is light.

Matthew 11:28–30 KJV

He said to them, 'Come away to a deserted place all by yourselves and rest a while.' For many were coming and going, and they had no leisure even to eat.

Mark 6:31 NRSV

See also **Leviticus 25:10–12; Jeremiah 17:21–27; Hebrews 4:9–11**
See also in the main text **Rest**

Retreat

One thing I asked of the Lord, that will I seek after: to live in the house of the Lord all the days of my life, to behold the beauty of the Lord, and to inquire in his temple.

Psalm 27:4 NRSV

Be still, and know that I am God: I will be exalted among the heathen, I will be exalted in the earth.

Psalm 46:10 KJV

After he had dismissed the crowds, he went up the mountain by himself to pray. When evening came, he was there alone.

Matthew 14:23 NRSV

The apostles rejoined Jesus and told him all they had done and taught. And he said to them, 'Come away to some lonely place all by yourselves and rest for a while'; for there were so many coming and going that there was no time for them even to eat. So they went off in the boat to a lonely place where they could be by themselves.

Mark 6:30–32 NJB

See also **Psalms 42; 92; Matthew 6:5–6; Mark 1:35; Luke 6:12; 2 Corinthians 4:16–18; Ephesians 2:1–10; 3:8**
See also in the main text **Christian life, Longing for God; Quiet; Rest; Seeking God**

Wedding

The Lord God said, It is not good that the man should be alone; I will make him an help meet for him… Adam said, This is now bone of my bones, and flesh of my flesh: she shall be called Woman, because she was taken out of Man. Therefore shall a man leave his father and his mother, and shall cleave unto his wife: and they shall be one flesh.

Genesis 2:18, 23–24 KJV

He who finds a wife finds a good thing, and obtains favour from the Lord.

Proverbs 18:22 NRSV

'What God has joined together, let no one separate.'

Matthew 19:6 NRSV

I may speak in tongues of men or of angels, but if I have no love, I am a sounding gong or a clanging cymbal… Love is patient and kind. Love envies no one, is never boastful, never conceited, never rude; love is never selfish, never quick to take offence. Love keeps no score of wrongs, takes no pleasure in the sins of others, but delights in the truth. There is nothing love cannot face; there is no limit to its faith, its hope, its endurance. Love will never come to an end… There are three things that last for ever: faith, hope, and love; and the greatest of the three is love.

1 Corinthians 13:1, 4–8, 13 REB

See also Proverbs 5:18–19; Song of Solomon 8:6–7; Ephesians 5:21–33; 1 Peter 3:7

See also in the main text Celebration; Marriage

Special Holidays and Festivals

Advent

You, O Bethlehem of Ephrathah, who are one of the little clans of Judah, from you shall come forth for me one who is to rule in Israel, whose origin is from of old, from ancient days… And he shall stand and feed his flock in the strength of the Lord, in the majesty of the name of the Lord his God. And they shall live secure, for now he shall be great to the ends of the earth; and he shall be the one of peace.

Micah 5:2, 4–5 NRSV

I am about to send my messenger to clear a path before me. Suddenly the Lord whom you seek will come to his temple; the messenger of the covenant in whom you delight is here, here already, says the Lord of Hosts.

Malachi 3:1 REB

This was the witness of John… he said, 'I am, as Isaiah prophesied: A voice of one that cries in the desert: Prepare a way for the Lord. Make his paths straight!… I baptise with water; but standing among you – unknown to you – is the one who is coming after me; and I am not fit to undo the strap of his sandal.'

John 1:19, 23, 26–27 NJB

See also Isaiah 7:10–17; Luke 1:26–38, 67–79

Christmas

The people that walked in darkness have seen a great light: they that dwell in the land of the shadow of death, upon them hath the light shined… For unto us a child is born, unto us a son is given: and the government shall be upon his shoulder: and his name shall be called Wonderful, Counsellor, The mighty God, the everlasting Father, The Prince of Peace. Of the increase of his government and peace there shall be no end, upon the throne of David, and upon his kingdom, to order it, and to establish it with judgment and with justice from henceforth even for ever. The zeal of the Lord of hosts will perform this.

Isaiah 9:2, 6–7 KJV

In that region there were shepherds living in the fields, keeping watch over their flock by night. Then an angel of the Lord stood before them, and the glory of the Lord shone around them, and they were terrified. But the angel said to them, 'Do not be afraid; for see – I am bringing you good news of great joy for all the people: to you is born this day in the city of David a Saviour, who is the Messiah, the Lord. This will be a sign for you: you will find a child wrapped in bands of cloth and lying in a manger.' And suddenly there was with the angel a multitude of the heavenly host, praising God and saying,

'Glory to God in the highest heaven, and on earth peace among those whom he favours!' When the angels had left them and gone into heaven, the shepherds said to one another, 'Let us go now to Bethlehem and see this thing that has taken place, which the Lord has made known to us.'

Luke 2:8–15 NRSV

For God so loved the world, that he gave his only begotten Son, that whosoever believeth in him should not perish, but have everlasting life. For God sent not his Son into the world to condemn the world; but that the world through him might be saved.

John 3:16–17 KJV

For the grace of God has dawned upon the world with healing for all mankind.

Titus 2:11 REB

See also Matthew 2:1–18; Luke 2:1–7, 25–32; John 1:1–18; Galatians 4:4–5; 1 Timothy 3:16; Hebrews 1:1–3

See also in the main text Jesus Christ, Jesus, the man

New Year

The Lord says, 'I will teach you the way you should go; I will instruct you and advise you.'

Psalm 32:8 GNB

I am the Lord: that is my name: and my glory will I not give to another, neither my praise to graven images. Behold, the former things are come to pass, and new things do I declare: before they spring forth I tell you of them. Sing unto the Lord a new song, and his praise from the end of the earth.

Isaiah 42:8–10 KJV

For surely I know the plans I have for you, says the Lord, plans for your welfare and not for harm, to give you a future with hope.

Jeremiah 29:11 NRSV

I pray that the God of our Lord Jesus Christ, the Father of glory, may give you a spirit of wisdom and revelation as you come to know him, so that, with the eyes of your heart enlightened, you may know what is the hope to which he has called you, what are the riches of his glorious inheritance among the saints, and what is the immeasurable greatness of his power for us who believe, according to the working of his great power.

Ephesians 1:17–19 NRSV

See also Proverbs 3:5–8; 16:1–3; Isaiah 26:3–4; 43:18–19; Ephesians 3:14–21; Revelation 21:5

See also in the main text Time

Lent

The sacrifices of God are a broken spirit: a broken and a contrite heart, O God, thou wilt not despise.

Psalm 51:17 KJV

Jesus was led up by the Spirit into the wilderness to be tempted by the devil. He fasted for forty days and forty nights, and afterwards he was famished.

Matthew 4:1–2 NRSV

He died for all so that those who live should cease to live for themselves, and should live for him who for their sake died and was raised to life.

2 Corinthians 5:15 REB

Since all the children share the same human nature, he too shared equally in it, so that by his death he could set aside him who held the power of death, namely the devil, and set free all those who had been held in slavery all their lives by the fear of death. For it was not the angels that he took to himself; he took to himself the line of Abraham. It was essential that he should in this way be made completely like his brothers so that he could become a compassionate and trustworthy high priest for their relationship to God, able to expiate the sins of the people. For the suffering he himself passed through while being put to the test enables him to help others when they are being put to the test.

Hebrews 2:14–18 NJB

See also Daniel 9:4–19; Matthew 17:1–13; Luke 4:1–13; John 12:20–32; Hebrews 4:12–16

See also in the main text Confession, of sin; Fasting; Jesus Christ, Death; Self-denial

Mother's Day

Her children rise up and call her happy; her husband too, and he praises her: 'Many women have done excellently, but you surpass them all.'

Proverbs 31:28–29 NRSV

Now there stood by the cross of Jesus his mother… When Jesus therefore saw his mother, and the disciple standing by, whom he loved, he saith unto his mother, Woman, behold thy son! Then saith he to the disciple, Behold thy mother! And from that hour that disciple took her unto his own home.

John 19:25–27 KJV

[Paul to Timothy] I am reminded of the sincerity of your faith, a faith which was alive in Lois your grandmother and Eunice your mother before you, and which, I am confident, now lives in you.

2 Timothy 1:5 REB

See also 1 Samuel 1:20–28; Mark 10:13–16; Luke 2:41–51

See also in the main text Family

Holy Week including Good Friday

Hosanna to the Son of David: Blessed is he that cometh in the name of the Lord; Hosanna in the highest.

Matthew 21:9 KJV

'My Father,' he said, 'if this cup cannot pass by, but I must drink it, your will be done!'

Matthew 26:42 NJB

For the tradition which I handed on to you came to me from the Lord himself: that on the night of his arrest the Lord Jesus took bread, and after giving thanks to God broke it and said: 'This is my body, which is for you; do this in memory of me.' In the same way, he took the cup after supper, and said: 'This cup is the new covenant sealed by my blood. Whenever you drink it, do this in memory of me.' For every time you eat this bread and drink the cup, you proclaim the death of the Lord, until he comes.

1 Corinthians 11:23–26 REB

Let the same mind be in you that was in Christ Jesus, who, though he was in the form of God, did not regard equality with God as something to be exploited, but emptied himself, taking the form of a slave, being born in human likeness. And being found in human form, he humbled himself and became obedient to the point of death – even death on a cross.

Philippians 2:5–8 NRSV

For to this you have been called, because Christ also suffered for you, leaving you an example, so that you should follow in his steps. 'He committed no sin, and no deceit was found in his mouth.' When he was abused, he did not return abuse; when he suffered, he did not threaten; but he entrusted himself to the one who judges justly. He himself bore our sins in his body on the cross, so that, free from sins, we might live for righteousness; by his wounds you have been healed. For you were going astray like sheep, but now you have returned to the shepherd and guardian of your souls.

1 Peter 2:21–25 NRSV

See also Exodus 12:1–14; Psalm 22:1–31; Isaiah 52:13–53:12; Zechariah 9:9–12; Matthew 26:6–13, 47–68; 27:11–31; Mark 14:12–25; Luke 19:29–46; 22:40–46; John 19:28–42; Romans 5:8; Hebrews 10:19–25

See also in the main text Communion; Jesus Christ, Death; Jesus Christ, Seven words from the Cross; Salvation; Savior

Easter

Just as Jonah was in the sea monster's belly for three days and three nights, so the Son of Man will be three days and three nights in the bowels of the earth.

Matthew 12:40 REB

On the first day of the week, at early dawn, they came to the tomb, taking the spices that they had prepared. They found the stone rolled away from the tomb, but when they went in, they did not find the body.

Luke 24:1–3 NRSV

I am the resurrection, and the life: he that believeth in me, though he were dead, yet shall he live. And whosoever liveth and believeth in me shall never die.

John 11:25–26 KJV

The message of the cross is folly for those who are on the way to ruin, but for those of us who are on the road to salvation it is the power of God.

1 Corinthians 1:18 NJB

See also Psalm 22; Matthew 28:1–10; 1 Corinthians 15:12–28; Revelation 1:10–18

See also in the main text Eternal life; Jesus Christ, Resurrection; Last things, Resurrection

Ascension Day

He led them out as far as Bethany, and, lifting up his hands, he blessed them. While he was blessing them, he withdrew from them and was carried up into heaven.

Luke 24:50–51 NRSV

'I came from the Father and have come into the world and now I am leaving the world to go to the Father.'

John 16:28 NJB

Since therefore we have a great high priest who has passed through the heavens, Jesus the Son of God, let us hold fast to the faith we profess.

Hebrews 4:14 REB

Jesus Christ, who has gone into heaven and is at the right hand of God, with angels, authorities, and powers made subject to him.

1 Peter 3:21–22 NRSV

See also Matthew 28:16–20; Acts 1:1–11; Ephesians 1:20–23; 4:7–13; Hebrews 12:1–2

See also in the main text Jesus Christ, Ascension

Pentecost

'You will receive power when the Holy Spirit comes upon you; and you will bear witness for me in Jerusalem, and throughout all Judaea and Samaria, and even in the farthest corners of the earth.'

Acts 1:8 REB

When the day of Pentecost had come, they were all together in one place. And suddenly from heaven there came a sound like the rush of a violent wind, and it filled the entire house where they were sitting. Divided tongues, as of fire, appeared among them, and a tongue rested on each of them. All of them were filled with the Holy Spirit and began to speak in other languages, as the Spirit gave them ability.

Acts 2:1–4 NRSV

As they prayed, the house where they were assembled rocked. From this time they were all filled with the Holy Spirit and began to proclaim the word of God fearlessly… The apostles continued to testify to the resurrection of the Lord Jesus with great power, and they were all accorded great respect.

Acts 4:31, 33 NJB

'The God of our ancestors raised up Jesus, whom you had killed by hanging him on a tree. God exalted him at his right hand as Leader and Saviour, so that he might give repentance to Israel and forgiveness of sins. And we are witnesses to these things, and so is the Holy Spirit whom God has given to those who obey him.'

Acts 5:30–32 NRSV

God has poured out his love into our hearts by means of the Holy Spirit, who is God's gift to us.

Romans 5:5 GNB

Now we have received, not the spirit of the world, but the spirit which is of God; that we might know the things that are freely given to us of God. Which things also we speak, not in the words which man's wisdom teacheth, but which the Holy Ghost teacheth; comparing spiritual things with spiritual. But the natural man receiveth not the things of the Spirit of God: for they are foolishness unto him: neither can he know them, because they are spiritually discerned.

1 Corinthians 2:12–14 KJV

See also Isaiah 61:1–3; John 7:37–39; 14:15–26; Acts 2:5–42; Romans 8:1–17; Galatians 5:22–23; Ephesians 3:16–21
See also in the main text Holy Spirit

Harvest

While the earth remaineth, seedtime and harvest, and cold and heat, and summer and winter, and day and night shall not cease.

Genesis 8:22 KJV

Let the peoples praise you, O God; let all the peoples praise you. The earth has

yielded its increase; God, our God, has blessed us. May God continue to bless us; let all the ends of the earth revere him.

Psalm 67:5–7 NRSV

Then he said to his disciples, 'The crop is heavy, but the labourers too few; you must ask the owner to send labourers to bring in the harvest.'

Matthew 9:37–38 REB

Then another angel came out from the temple and cried out in a loud voice to the one who was sitting on the cloud, 'Use your sickle and reap the harvest, because the time has come; the earth is ripe for the harvest!' Then the one who sat on the cloud swung his sickle on the earth, and the earth's harvest was reaped.

Revelation 14:15–16 GNB

See also Exodus 23:16; Deuteronomy 26:1–11; 28:1–14; Psalms 65; 126:5–6; Matthew 13:24–30; John 4:35–38
See also in the main text Celebration; Thankfulness and thanksgiving

Memorial Day

In days to come the mountain of the Lord's house shall be established as the highest of the mountains, and shall be raised above the hills; all the nations shall stream to it. Many peoples shall come and say, 'Come, let us go up to the mountain of the Lord, to the house of the God of Jacob; that he may teach us his ways and that we may walk in his paths.' For out of Zion shall go forth instruction, and the word of the Lord from Jerusalem. He shall judge between the nations, and shall arbitrate for many peoples; they shall beat their swords into ploughshares, and their spears into pruning-hooks; nation shall not lift up sword against nation, neither shall they learn war any more.

Isaiah 2:2–4 NRSV

I saw a new heaven and a new earth: for the first heaven and the first earth were passed away; and there was no more sea. And I John saw the holy city, new Jerusalem, coming down from God out of heaven, prepared as a bride adorned for her husband. And I heard a great voice out of heaven saying, Behold, the tabernacle of God is with men, and he will dwell with them, and they shall be his people, and God himself shall be with them, and be their God. And God shall wipe away all tears from their eyes; and there shall be no more death, neither sorrow, nor crying, neither shall there be any more pain: for the former things are passed away. And he that sat upon the throne said, Behold, I make all things new.

Revelation 21:1–5 KJV

See also **Psalms 46; 78; Isaiah 10:33 – 11:9; 61:1–11; Ezekiel 37:1–14; Ecclesiasticus 44:1–15; Matthew 5:1–12; Romans 8:31–39**

See also in the main text **Remembering**

INDEX OF THEMES

References are to page numbers

A

Abilities   10

Accepting the will of God   10

Access   11

Adam   12

Adoption   12

Adultery *see* Marriage

Advice *see* Counsel

Age *see* Old age

Ambition, Godly   13

Ambition, Negative   14

Angels   15

Anger, Divine   16

Anger, Human   17

Animals   17

Antichrist   19

Anxiety *see* Worry

Apostles   19

Arrogance *see* Conceit; Pride

Ascension *see* Jesus Christ, Ascension

Assurance   20

Atonement   21

Authority   22

B

Backsliding *see* Falling away

Baptism   24

Beauty   24

Belief *see* Faith

Bereavement *see* Comfort, in bereavement and sorrow

Bible   25

Birth   26

Bishops *see* Elders

Bitterness   28

Blasphemy   28

Blessing   29

Blindness   30

Blood   31

Boasting *see* Conceit

Body   32

Boldness *see* Confidence

Borrowing *see* Debt

Bribe   32

C

Caring   33

Celebration   33

Celibacy   34

Character   34

Children *see* Family

Choice   35

Christian life, Calling of the Christian   36

Christian life, Character of the Christian   37

Christian life, Coming to faith   38

Christian life, Continuing in the faith   39

Christian life, Longing for God   40

Christlikeness   41

Church   42

Circumcision   43

Comfort, when afraid   43

Comfort, when anxious   44

Comfort, in bereavement and sorrow   45

Comfort, in despair   46

Comfort, when lonely   46

Comfort, in suffering   46

Commitment *see* Covenant; Disciples; Obedience

Communion   48

Compassion *see* Mercy; Sympathy

Conceit   49

Confession   49

Confession, of sin   50

Confidence   50

Conscience   51

Contentment   52

Conversion   52

Conviction of sin   53

Counsel   53

Courage   54

Covenant   55

Covetousness *see* Desire, wrong

Creation   55

Cross *see* Jesus Christ, Death

Cruelty   57

D

Darkness   58

Deacons   59

Death   59

Debt   61

Decisions   62

Dedication *see* Obedience; Vow

Deliverance *see* Redemption; Salvation and Savior

Demons   63

Depression   64

Desire *see* Christian life, Longing for God

Desire, wrong   64

Despair   65

Devil   66

Dignity   68

Diligence *see* Work

Discernment   68

Disciples   69

Discipline   69

Discouragement   70

Dishonesty   71

Disobedience   72

Divorce *see* Marriage

Doubt   72

Dreams   73

Drink *see* Drunkenness; Food and drink

Drunkenness   74

E

Earth, the   76

Eden, Garden of   77

Education *see* Teachers and teaching

Elders   77

Election   78

Encouragement   79

Endurance   80

Enemy   81

Enjoyment *see* Joy

Envy   81

Eternal life   81

Eucharist *see* Communion

Evangelism *see* Witness

Evangelists   82

Evil   83

Examination   84

F

Failure   85

Faith   86

Faithfulness   88

Fall, the   89

Falling away   90

False teachers *see* Teachers, false

Family, Husbands and wives   90

Family, Children and the whole family   91

Fasting   93

Father *see* Family; God, Father

Fear   94

Fear of God *see* Reverence

Fellowship   94

Food and drink   95

Fools and folly   97

Forgiveness   97

Freedom   99

Friends and friendship   99

Fruit   100

Fullness   101

G

Generosity   102

Gentiles   103

Gentleness   104

Gift   104

Giving   105

Glory   106

God, All-knowing   107

God, All-present   107

God, Almighty   107

God, Anger of *see* Anger, Divine

God, Creator   107

God, Eternal   108

God, Faithful   108

God, Father   108

God, Glorious *see* Glory

God, Good   109

God, Gracious *see* God, Merciful

God, Holy   109

God, Infinite   109

God, Just   110

God, Loving   110

God, Merciful   111

God, Powerful *see* God, Almighty

God, Presence of *see* God, All-present

God, Self-existent   111

God, Spiritual   111

God, Transcendent   111

God, Unchangeable   112

God, Wise   112

Godless   113

Good   113

Gospel   114

Gossip   115

Grace   116

Gratitude *see* Thankfulness and thanksgiving

Greed *see* Desire, wrong

Grief   118

Growth, spiritual *see* Christian life, Character of the Christian

Guidance   119

Guilt   120

H

Happiness *see* Joy

Hardness   121

Hatred   121

Healing   122

Health and wholeness   123

Heart   124

Heaven *see* Last things, Heaven

Hell *see* Last things, Hell

Help   125

Helplessness *see* Weakness

High priest *see* Priest

Holiness   126

Holy Spirit   127

Homes   130

Homosexuality   131

Honesty   131

Hope   132

Hospitality   133

Human beings   133

Human beings, Male and female   134

Humility   135

Husband *see* Marriage

Hypocrisy   136

I

Idolatry   137

Illness   137

Illness, Help in   137

Immigrants   138

Incarnation *see* Jesus Christ, Jesus, the man

Inheritance   138

Injustice   139

Israel   140

J

Jealousy   142

Jesus Christ, Ascension   142

Jesus Christ, Authority   143

Jesus Christ, Death   143

Jesus Christ, Eternal Son of God   145

Jesus Christ, Holiness   146

Jesus Christ, Humility   146

Jesus Christ, Jesus as king   146

Jesus Christ, Jesus, the man   147

Jesus Christ, Jesus, the one to be worshipped   148

Jesus Christ, Jesus as priest   148

Jesus Christ, Jesus as prophet   149

Jesus Christ, Love   149

Jesus Christ, Obedience   150

Jesus Christ, Resurrection   150

Jesus Christ, Second coming *see* Last things

Jesus Christ, Seven words from the cross   151

Journeys   152

Joy   153

Judgment *see* Last things

Justice   155

Justification   156

K

Kindness   157

Kingdom, kingdom of God   158

Knowledge   159

L

Land   161

Last Supper *see* Communion

Last things, Events before the second coming   161

Last things, Heaven   162

Last things, Hell   163

Last things, Judgment   164

Last things, Renewal of all things   165

Last things, Resurrection   166

Last things, Second coming of Jesus   167

Last things, State between death and resurrection   168

Laughter   168

Law   169

Laying on of hands   171

Laziness   171

Leadership   172

Lending *see* Debt

Life   173

Light   175

Listening   177

Loneliness   177

Longing for God *see* Christian life, Longing for God

Love, of God   178

Love, of humanity   179

Love, of humanity for God   180

Loyalty   181

Lying   182

M

Man *see* Human beings; Jesus Christ, Jesus the man

Marriage   183

Marriage, Adultery   183

Marriage, Divorce   183

Maturity *see* Christian life, Character of the Christian; Perfection

Meditation   184

Mercy   184

Mind   185

Ministry *see* Service

Miracles   186

Mission *see* Witness

Money and material goods   188

Morality *see* Right and wrong

Mother *see* Family

Motives   189

Mourning   190

Murder   191

Music   191

N

Name   193

Neighbor   194

New birth   194

O

Obedience   196

Occult   197

Old age   197

Oppression   198

P

Parables *see* Parables of Jesus   200

Parent *see* Family

Passover   201

Pastor   201

Patience   201

Peace   202

Perfection (Completeness, Maturity)   204

Persecution   205

Perseverance *see* Christian life, Continuing in
    the faith

Pharisees   206

Possessions *see* Money and material goods

Poverty   207

Power   207

Praise   209

Prayer, Answers to prayer   209

Prayer, Encouragements to pray   210

Prayer, Hindrances to prayer   211

Prayer, How to pray   214

Prayer, Promises in prayer   214

Preaching   215

Pride   216

Priest   217

Privilege   218

Promise   219

Prophets and prophecy   220

Propitiation   221

Providence   222

Punishment   222

Purity   223

Q

Quiet   224

R

Race (Ethnic)   225

Rebellion   225

Reconciliation   226

Redemption   227

Regeneration *see* New birth

Rejection   228

Remembering   228

Renewal   229

Repentance   231

Resentment *see* Bitterness

Respect   232

Responsibility, human   233

Rest   234

Restitution   235

Restoration   236

Resurrection *see* Jesus Christ; Last things

Retaliation   237

Revelation   237

Reverence   238

Revival   239

Reward   240

Riches   241

Right and wrong   242

Righteousness   243

Ritual   245

Rulers   245

S

Sabbath   247

Sacrifice   247

Sadness see Grief

Salvation and Savior   248

Sanctification   250

Satan see Devil

Scribes   250

Scripture see Bible

Second coming see Last things

Seeking God   251

Self-control   252

Self-denial   252

Self-examination   253

Selfishness   253

Self-righteousness   254

Service   255

Sex, Gift of   255

Sex, Misuse of   256

Shame   256

Shepherd   257

Silence   258

Simplicity   259

Sin   259

Sin, Avoidance of   261

Sinful nature   262

Skill see Abilities

Sleep   263

Son of God see Jesus Christ

Sorrow see Comfort, in bereavement and sorrow; Grief

Soul   264

Sovereignty of God   265

Speech   266

Spirit   267

Spiritual growth see Christian life, Character of the Christian

Spiritual warfare see Warfare, spiritual

State, responsibility to   268

Stealing   268

Stewardship   269

Strength see Power; Weakness

Stress   270

Stubbornness see Hardness

Submission   271

Suffering   271

Suffering, Purposes of   272

Sunday see Sabbath

Swearing see Blasphemy

Sympathy   273

T

Talents see Gift

Teachers and teaching   275

Teachers, false   275

Temperance   276

Temptation   277

Temptation, Help in   278

Tests of faith see Temptation

Thankfulness and thanksgiving   279

Thought   279

Time   280

Tiredness   281

Tithing see Giving

Tongues, gift of, Speaking in tongues   282

Tongues, gift of, Interpretation   283

Travel see Journeys

Trinity   283

Trouble see Suffering

Trust *see* Faith

Truth   283

U

Unbelief   285

Unbeliever   285

Understanding   286

Unity   287

Unselfishness   287

Usury *see* Debt

V

Vengeance *see* Retaliation

Victory   289

Visions   289

Vow   291

W

Waiting   292

War   293

Warfare, spiritual   294

Water   295

Way   296

Weakness   297

Wholeness *see* Health and wholeness

Widows   298

Wife *see* Family; Husbands and wives; Marriage

Will of God   299

Wisdom   300

Witness   301

Word of God *see* Bible; Jesus Christ

Work   303

Works, good   303

World, Created universe   305

World, Humanity   305

World, Humanity in rebellion against God   305

Worry   305

Worship   306

Wrong *see* Right and wrong

Y

Youth   308

Z

Zeal   310

INDEX OF BIBLE REFERENCES

References are to paragraph numbers

A

Acts 1:7   Time 256.9

Acts 1:8   Christian life 31.3

Acts 1:8   Holy Spirit 119.20

Acts 1:8   Power 182.7

Acts 1:8   Witness 278.11

Acts 1:9   Jesus Christ 135.5

Acts 1:11   Last things 144.61

Acts 1:21–22   Apostles 11.2

Acts 2:1–4   Holy Spirit 119.21

Acts 2:2   Last things 144.14

Acts 2:4   Abilities 1.8

Acts 2:4   Tongues, gift of 258.1

Acts 2:18   Prophets and prophecy 190.6

Acts 2:23   Jesus Christ 135.19

Acts 2:23   Sovereignty of God 240.7

Acts 2:32   Jesus Christ 135.96

Acts 2:33   Jesus Christ 135.6

Acts 2:37   Conviction of sin 43.5

Acts 2:37–38   Christian life 31.24

Acts 2:38   Forgiveness 92.11

Acts 2:38   Gift 100.2

Acts 2:38   Holy Spirit 119.22

Acts 2:38, 41   Baptism 15.4

Acts 2:40   Encouragement 73.1

Acts 2:42   Christian life 31.33

Acts 2:42   Church 33.3

Acts 2:42   Communion 36.2

Acts 2:42   Fellowship 89.1

Acts 2:42   Teachers and teaching 250.6

Acts 2:44   Fellowship 89.2

Acts 2:46   Homes 120.15

Acts 2:46–47   Praise 183.7

Acts 2:46–47   Worship 283.8

Acts 3:6   Name 167.11

Acts 3:6–7   Healing 114.8

Acts 3:15   Jesus Christ 135.20

Acts 3:19   Repentance 203.12

Acts 3:19   Revival 212.7

Acts 3:20–21   Restoration 208.13

Acts 3:21   Last things 144.44

Acts 3:21   Time 256.10

Acts 4:8   Holy Spirit 119.23

Acts 4:12   Name 167.12

Acts 4:12   Salvation and Savior 221.10

Acts 4:13   Confidence 39.5

Acts 4:20   Witness 278.12

Acts 4:26   Rulers 218.9

Acts 4:27–28   Responsibility, human 205.5

Acts 4:29   Courage 45.7

Acts 4:30   Miracles 161.9

Acts 4:31   Revival 212.8

Acts 4:32   Unity 264.6

Acts 4:33   Grace 108.4

Acts 4:34–35   Land 143.8

Acts 4:36   Encouragement 73.2

Acts 5:3–4   Holy Spirit 119.24

Acts 5:3–4   Lying 156.6

Acts 5:28–29   Obedience 170.7

Acts 5:28–29   State, responsibility to 243.2

Acts 5:31   Gift 100.3

Acts 5:32   Obedience 170.8

Acts 5:42   Homes 120.16

Acts 6:1   Widows 275.7

Acts 6:1–4   Deacons 50.1

Acts 6:3   Wisdom 277.13

Acts 6:5   Faith 82.15

Acts 6:6   Laying on of hands 147.6

Acts 6:7   Priest 187.8

Acts 6:7   Revival 212.9

Acts 7:51   Hardness 112.8

Acts 7:51   Holy Spirit 119.25

Acts 7:53   Angels 7.8

Acts 8:1   Persecution 179.6

Acts 8:1–2, 4–5, 12   Evangelists 78.1

Acts 8:9   Occult 171.8

Acts 8:23   Bitterness 19.10

Acts 8:30–31   Understanding 263.8

Acts 8:35   Evangelists 78.2

Acts 8:36, 38   Baptism 15.5

Acts 8:39–40   Journeys 136.10

Acts 9:3   Journeys 136.11

Acts 9:4   Persecution 179.7

Acts 9:15   Gentiles 98.4

Acts 9:31   Church 33.4

Acts 9:31   Reverence 211.9

Acts 9:40   Miracles 161.10

Acts 10:10–12   Visions 267.15

Acts 10:34–35   Race 196.2

Acts 10:34–35   Respect 204.9

Acts 10:34–35   Right and wrong 215.11

Acts 10:38   Good 105.5

Acts 10:43   Forgiveness 92.12

Acts 10:45   Gentiles 98.5

Acts 11:18   Gentiles 98.6

Acts 11:18   Repentance 203.13

Acts 11:23   Encouragement 73.3

Acts 11:27–28   Prophets and prophecy 190.7

Acts 11:29–30   Elders 71.2

Acts 13:2   Holy Spirit 119.26

Acts 13:2–3   Fasting 87.9

Acts 13:2–3   Laying on of hands 147.7

Acts 13:43   Grace 108.5

Acts 13:47   Witness 278.13

Acts 13:48   Election 72.7

Acts 13:48   Responsibility, human 205.6

Acts 13:52   Joy 137.13

Acts 14:14   Apostles 11.3

Acts 14:15   Conversion 42.5

Acts 14:17   Revelation 210.5

Acts 14:22   Christian life 31.34

Acts 14:22   Encouragement 73.4

Acts 14:22   Kingdom, kingdom of God 141.10

Acts 14:22   Suffering 248.6

Acts 14:23   Church 33.5

Acts 14:23   Elders 71.3

Acts 15:19   Discouragement 63.11

Acts 15:22   Guidance 110.6

Acts 15:28   Guidance 110.7

Acts 15:28   Holy Spirit 119.27

Acts 15:32   Encouragement 73.5

Acts 16:9   Dreams 67.9

Acts 16:9   Visions 267.16

Acts 16:15   Hospitality 124.2

Acts 16:30–31   Christian life 31.25

Acts 16:30–31   Salvation and Savior 221.11

Acts 16:31   Faith 82.16

Acts 16:33   Baptism 15.6

Acts 17:2–4   Mind 160.3

Acts 17:11   Bible 17.5

Acts 17:11   Character 29.6

Acts 17:11   Examination 80.2

Acts 17:24   World 281.2

Acts 17:24–25   God 103.66

Acts 17:26   Decisions 53.11

Acts 17:26   Race 196.3

Acts 17:27   Seeking God 224.13

Acts 17:28   Life 150.26

Acts 17:28   Providence 192.9

Acts 17:30   Repentance 203.14

Acts 17:30–31   Christian life 31.26

Acts 17:31   God 103.45

Acts 17:31   Jesus Christ 135.97

Acts 17:31   Last things 144.35

Acts 17:31   Righteousness 216.10

Acts 18:27   Help 117.5

Acts 19:4–5   Baptism 15.7

Acts 19:6   Laying on of hands 147.8

Acts 19:6   Tongues, gift of 258.2

Acts 20:7   Sabbath 219.6

Acts 19:17   Name 167.13

Acts 19:19   Occult 171.9

Acts 20:20   Teachers and teaching 250.7

Acts 20:21   Repentance 203.15

Acts 20:24   Gospel 106.5

Acts 20:26–27   Counsel 44.8

Acts 20:27   Preaching 185.4

Acts 20:28   Church 33.6

Acts 20:28   Elders 71.4

Acts 20:32   Inheritance 131.2

Acts 20:35   Help 117.6

Acts 20:35   Kindness 140.4

Acts 20:35   Weakness 274.5

Acts 21:8   Evangelists 78.3

Acts 23:6   Pharisees 180.10

Acts 24:14   Way 273.10

Acts 24:16   Conscience 40.2

Acts 26:17–18   Blindness 22.12

Acts 26:17–18   Light 151.13

Acts 26:18   Conversion 42.6

Acts 26:18   Devil 58.6

Acts 26:19–20   Visions 267.17

Acts 26:20   Works, good 280.6

Amos 3:3   Unity 264.3

Amos 3:6   Evil 79.3

Amos 5:13   Quiet 195.10

Amos 5:15   Hatred 113.4

Amos 5:21–24   Sacrifice 220.6

Amos 5:22, 24   Ritual 217.3

Amos 5:23–24   Music 166.11

Amos 5:24   Justice 138.9

Amos 5:24   Righteousness 216.6

Amos 6:1   Riches 214.3

B

Baruch 3:14   Wisdom 277.7

C

1 Chronicles 6:31–32   Music 166.3

1 Chronicles 10:13–14   Occult 171.5

1 Chronicles 16:11   Prayer 184.10

1 Chronicles 16:15   Remembering 201.3

1 Chronicles 16:29   Beauty 16.2

1 Chronicles 16:29   Worship 283.2

1 Chronicles 22:15–16   Abilities 1.4

1 Chronicles 25:1   Music 166.4

1 Chronicles 26:6   Abilities 1.5

1 Chronicles 28:6   God 103.19

1 Chronicles 28:9   Motives 163.2

1 Chronicles 28:9   Seeking God 224.1

1 Chronicles 28:20   Discouragement 63.5

1 Chronicles 28:20–21   Abilities 1.6

1 Chronicles 29:14   Giving 101.2

1 Chronicles 29:14   Providence 192.3

1 Chronicles 29:18–19   Loyalty 155.4

2 Chronicles 5:13   Good 105.2

2 Chronicles 7:14   Healing 114.3

2 Chronicles 7:14   Land 143.6

2 Chronicles 7:14   Prayer 184.39

2 Chronicles 7:14   Repentance 203.1

2 Chronicles 7:14   Revival 212.1

2 Chronicles 16:12   Illness 129.1

2 Chronicles 19:7   Injustice 132.4

2 Chronicles 20:12   War 270.3

2 Chronicles 20:15   Discouragement 63.6

2 Chronicles 22:4   Right and wrong 215.6

2 Chronicles 32:7–8   Courage 45.2

Colossians 1:9–10   Knowledge 142.15

Colossians 1:10   Worship 283.11

Colossians 1:11   Endurance 74.6

Colossians 1:13   Kingdom, kingdom of God 141.15

Colossians 1:13–14   Darkness 49.13

Colossians 1:13–14   Privilege 188.13

Colossians 1:14   Redemption 199.13

Colossians 1:15–16   Creation 47.12

Colossians 1:15–19   Jesus Christ 135.33

Colossians 1:17   Providence 192.11

Colossians 1:18   Body 24.6

Colossians 1:20   Blood 23.6

Colossians 1:20   Reconciliation 198.6

Colossians 1:22   Reconciliation 198.7

Colossians 1:24   Suffering 248.11

Colossians 1:27   Hope 123.8

Colossians 1:28   Christian life 31.36

Colossians 1:28   Perfection 178.10

Colossians 1:28–29   Ambition 6.7

Colossians 2:3   Wisdom 277.20

Colossians 2:9–10   Fullness 96.7

Colossians 2:15   Demons 54.10

Colossians 2:15   Jesus Christ 135.28

Colossians 2:15   Victory 266.8

Colossians 2:15   Warfare, spiritual 271.7

Colossians 3:1   Jesus Christ 135.103

Colossians 3:2   Ambition 6.22

Colossians 3:2   Mind 160.11

Colossians 3:4   Life 150.34

Colossians 3:5   Death 51.21

Colossians 3:5   Sin 236.31

Colossians 3:8   Cruelty 48.11

Colossians 3:9   Lying 156.7

Colossians 3:9–10   Renewal 202.11

Colossians 3:12   Election 72.11

Colossians 3:12   Mercy 159.14

Colossians 3:13   Christlikeness 32.10

Colossians 3:15   Heart 116.15

Colossians 3:15   Peace 177.23

Colossians 3:16   Bible 17.8

Colossians 3:16   Music 166.14

Colossians 3:16   Teachers and teaching 250.9

Colossians 3:16–17   Worship 283.12

Colossians 3:17   Name 167.15

Colossians 3:17   Work 279.11

Colossians 3:20   Family 86.24

Colossians 3:21   Discouragement 63.14

Colossians 3:23   Service 230.9

Colossians 4:1   Justice 138.11

Colossians 4:5   Time 256.14

Colossians 4:6   Speech 241.9

1 Corinthians 1:9   Christian life 31.5

1 Corinthians 1:9   Fellowship 89.3

1 Corinthians 1:9   God 103.17

1 Corinthians 1:18   Fools and folly 91.9

1 Corinthians 1:18   Jesus Christ 135.23

1 Corinthians 1:18   Salvation and Savior 221.12

1 Corinthians 1:19–21   Simplicity 235.9

1 Corinthians 1:21   Wisdom 277.15

1 Corinthians 1:21, 23–24   Preaching 185.6

1 Corinthians 1:23–24   Jesus Christ 135.24

1 Corinthians 1:23–24   Power 182.10

1 Corinthians 1:27   Fools and folly 91.10

1 Corinthians 1:27   Weakness 274.9

1 Corinthians 1:27–29   Choice 30.12

1 Corinthians 1:30   Redemption 199.8

1 Corinthians 1:30   Righteousness 216.15

1 Corinthians 1:30   Sanctification 222.5

1 Corinthians 1:30   Wisdom 277.16

1 Corinthians 1:31   Pride 186.8

1 Corinthians 2:3   Fear 88.11

1 Corinthians 2:4   Holy Spirit 119.33

1 Corinthians 2:6–7   Wisdom 277.17

1 Corinthians 2:9   Last things 144.15

1 Corinthians 2:9   Love 154.30

1 Corinthians 2:9–10   Revelation 210.7

1 Corinthians 2:10   Holy Spirit 119.34

1 Corinthians 2:11   Human beings 125.12

1 Corinthians 2:11   Spirit 242.9

1 Corinthians 2:11   Thought 255.6

1 Corinthians 2:14   Discernment 60.3

1 Corinthians 2:14   Fools and folly 91.11

1 Corinthians 2:14   Unbeliever 262.4

1 Corinthians 2:15   Spirit 242.10

1 Corinthians 2:16   Mind 160.8

1 Corinthians 3:13–14   Reward 213.8

1 Corinthians 4:1–2   Stewardship 245.3

1 Corinthians 4:5   Last things 144.36

1 Corinthians 4:5   Motives 163.10

1 Corinthians 4:20   Kingdom, kingdom of God 141.12

1 Corinthians 5:7   Passover 174.5

1 Corinthians 6:2–3   Last things 144.37

1 Corinthians 6:3   Angels 7.9

1 Corinthians 6:9   Kingdom, kingdom of God 141.13

1 Corinthians 6:9–10   Homosexuality 121.5

1 Corinthians 6:9–10   Inheritance 131.4

1 Corinthians 6:9–10   Sex 231.5

1 Corinthians 6:9–10   Stealing 244.6

1 Corinthians 6:15–19   Sex 231.6

1 Corinthians 6:18–20   Sin 236.29

1 Corinthians 6:19–20   Body 24.3

1 Corinthians 6:20   Redemption 199.9

1 Corinthians 7:3–5   Sex 231.3

1 Corinthians 7:7   Celibacy 28.2

1 Corinthians 7:10–11   Marriage 157.15

1 Corinthians 7:14   Family 86.5

1 Corinthians 7:19   Circumcision 34.4

1 Corinthians 7:32   Celibacy 28.3

1 Corinthians 7:39   Marriage 157.5

1 Corinthians 7:39   Widows 275.8

1 Corinthians 8:1   Knowledge 142.11

1 Corinthians 8:1–2   Conceit 37.8

1 Corinthians 8:6   God 103.29

1 Corinthians 8:7   Conscience 40.5

1 Corinthians 8:9   Freedom 93.6

1 Corinthians 8:9   Weakness 274.10

1 Corinthians 9:1–2   Apostles 11.4

1 Corinthians 9:16   Gospel 106.7

1 Corinthians 9:16   Preaching 185.7

1 Corinthians 9:16   Zeal 285.4

1 Corinthians 9:16–17   Stewardship 245.4

1 Corinthians 9:19   Unselfishness 265.6

1 Corinthians 9:22   Weakness 274.11

1 Corinthians 9:27   Self-control 225.7

1 Corinthians 10:10   Contentment 41.5

1 Corinthians 10:12   Conceit 37.9

1 Corinthians 10:12   Pride 186.9

1 Corinthians 10:13   Comfort 35.49

1 Corinthians 10:13   Endurance 74.4

1 Corinthians 10:13   Faithfulness 83.7

1 Corinthians 10:13   Temptation 253.17

1 Corinthians 10:16–17   Communion 36.3

1 Corinthians 10:16–17   Fellowship 89.4

1 Corinthians 10:24   Selfishness 228.8

1 Corinthians 10:24   Unselfishness 265.7

1 Corinthians 10:31   Glory 102.11

1 Corinthians 10:31   Responsibility, human 205.8

1 Corinthians 10:33   Unselfishness 265.8

1 Corinthians 11:1   Christlikeness 32.5

1 Corinthians 11:3   Family 86.6

1 Corinthians 11:3   Human beings 125.22

1 Corinthians 11:7   Glory 102.12

1 Corinthians 11:8   Human beings 125.23

1 Corinthians 11:23–30   Communion 36.4

1 Corinthians 11:27   Guilt 111.7

1 Corinthians 11:28–30   Self-examination 227.3

1 Corinthians 12:4–6   Trinity 259.4

1 Corinthians 12:4–7, 11   Gift 100.6

1 Corinthians 12:7   Holy Spirit 119.35

1 Corinthians 12:8   Wisdom 277.18

1 Corinthians 12:9   Healing 114.9

1 Corinthians 12:10   Discernment 60.4

1 Corinthians 12:10   Miracles 161.11

1 Corinthians 12:10   Tongues, gift of 258.9

1 Corinthians 12:11   Sovereignty of God 240.9

1 Corinthians 12:13   Baptism 15.9

1 Corinthians 12:26   Suffering 248.9

1 Corinthians 12:27   Body 24.4

1 Corinthians 12:27–28   Apostles 11.5

1 Corinthians 12:27–28   Teachers and teaching 250.8

1 Corinthians 12:27–31   Tongues, gift of 258.3

1 Corinthians 12:28   Help 117.8

1 Corinthians 12:28   Prophets and prophecy 190.8

1 Corinthians 13:1–7, 13   Love 154.18

1 Corinthians 13:1, 8   Tongues, gift of 258.4

1 Corinthians 13:2, 12   Knowledge 142.12

1 Corinthians 13:4   Jealousy 134.6

1 Corinthians 13:4–5   Pride 186.10

1 Corinthians 13:4, 7   Patience 176.6

1 Corinthians 13:5   Anger 8.15

1 Corinthians 13:5   Unselfishness 265.9

1 Corinthians 13:8   Failure 81.12

1 Corinthians 13:8   Prophets and prophecy 190.9

1 Corinthians 13:9–10   Perfection 178.6

1 Corinthians 13:13   Faith 82.21

1 Corinthians 13:13   Hope 123.6

1 Corinthians 14:1   Gift 100.7

1 Corinthians 14:1   Prophets and prophecy 190.10

1 Corinthians 14:2, 4   Tongues, gift of 258.5

1 Corinthians 14:5   Tongues, gift of 258.10

1 Corinthians 14:12   Ambition 6.5

1 Corinthians 14:13–14   Tongues, gift of 258.6

1 Corinthians 14:14–15   Spirit 242.11

1 Corinthians 14:18–19   Tongues, gift of 258.7

1 Corinthians 14:20   Thought 255.7

1 Corinthians 14:21–22   Tongues, gift of 258.8

1 Corinthians 14:27–28   Tongues, gift of 258.11

1 Corinthians 14:29   Discernment 60.5

1 Corinthians 14:31–32   Prophets and prophecy 190.11

1 Corinthians 14:33   Peace 177.18

1 Corinthians 14:33–34   Human beings 125.24

1 Corinthians 15:1   Gospel 106.8

1 Corinthians 15:3   Jesus Christ 135.25

1 Corinthians 15:3–5   Gospel 106.9

1 Corinthians 15:4   Jesus Christ 135.101

1 Corinthians 15:10   Grace 108.9

1 Corinthians 15:12–21   Jesus Christ 135.102

1 Corinthians 15:20   Comfort 35.24

1 Corinthians 15:22   Adam 4.5

1 Corinthians 15:22   Death 51.14

1 Corinthians 15:24   Kingdom, kingdom of God 141.14

1 Corinthians 15:26   Death 51.15

1 Corinthians 15:33   Character 29.8

1 Corinthians 15:33   Sin 236.30

1 Corinthians 15:42–44   Last things 144.53

1 Corinthians 15:43   Weakness 274.12

1 Corinthians 15:44   Body 24.5

1 Corinthians 15:45   Adam 4.6

1 Corinthians 15:50   Inheritance 131.5

1 Corinthians 15:51–54   Eternal life 77.12

1 Corinthians 15:52   Last things 144.54

1 Corinthians 15:53   Comfort 35.25

1 Corinthians 15:54–55   Death 51.16

1 Corinthians 15:57   Thankfulness and thanksgiving 254.4

1 Corinthians 15:57   Victory 266.5

1 Corinthians 15:58   Works, good 280.7

1 Corinthians 15:58   Zeal 285.5

1 Corinthians 16:2   Giving 101.7

1 Corinthians 16:2   Sabbath 219.7

1 Corinthians 16:22   Love 154.31

2 Corinthians 1:3–4   Comfort 35.50

2 Corinthians 1:4   Suffering 248.17

2 Corinthians 1:4   Sympathy 249.10

2 Corinthians 1:8   Despair 57.15

2 Corinthians 1:8   Stress 246.12

2 Corinthians 1:11   Help 117.9

2 Corinthians 1:11   Prayer 184.3

2 Corinthians 1:12   Simplicity 235.10

2 Corinthians 1:20   Promise 189.3

2 Corinthians 2:11   Devil 58.7

2 Corinthians 3:3–6   Spirit 242.12

2 Corinthians 3:5   Unselfishness 265.10

2 Corinthians 3:14   Hardness 112.10

2 Corinthians 3:17–18   Freedom 93.7

2 Corinthians 3:17–18   Holy Spirit 119.36

2 Corinthians 3:18   Christlikeness 32.6

2 Corinthians 3:18   Glory 102.13

2 Corinthians 3:18   Meditation 158.9

2 Corinthians 4:2   Honesty 122.3

2 Corinthians 4:3–4   Blindness 22.13

2 Corinthians 4:3–4   Gospel 106.10

2 Corinthians 4:4   Devil 58.8

2 Corinthians 4:4   Unbeliever 262.5

2 Corinthians 4:6   Light 151.14

2 Corinthians 4:7   Power 182.11

2 Corinthians 4:8   Comfort 35.33

2 Corinthians 4:8–10   Despair 57.16

2 Corinthians 4:8–9   Suffering 248.10

2 Corinthians 4:10   Life 150.30

2 Corinthians 4:16   Renewal 202.9

2 Corinthians 4:16   Tiredness 257.6

2 Corinthians 4:16–18   Comfort 35.51

2 Corinthians 5:2   Old age 172.9

2 Corinthians 5:7   Faith 82.22

2 Corinthians 5:8   Death 51.17

2 Corinthians 5:8   Last things 144.71

2 Corinthians 5:10   Last things 144.38

2 Corinthians 5:11   Reverence 211.11

2 Corinthians 5:14   Atonement 13.6

2 Corinthians 5:15   Selfishness 228.9

2 Corinthians 5:17   Creation 47.10

2 Corinthians 5:17   New birth 169.4

2 Corinthians 5:18–20   Reconciliation 198.4

2 Corinthians 5:20   Witness 278.14

2 Corinthians 5:20–21   Christian life 31.28

2 Corinthians 5:21   Atonement 13.7

2 Corinthians 5:21   Justification 139.13

2 Corinthians 5:21   Righteousness 216.16

2 Corinthians 5:21   Sin 236.15

2 Corinthians 6:2   Salvation and Savior 221.13

2 Corinthians 6:2   Time 256.11

2 Corinthians 6:10   Grief 109.13

2 Corinthians 6:14   Light 151.15

2 Corinthians 6:14   Unbeliever 262.6

2 Corinthians 6:17–18   God 103.30

2 Corinthians 6:18   Adoption 5.6

2 Corinthians 7:1   Holiness 118.6

2 Corinthians 7:1   Reverence 211.12

2 Corinthians 7:10   Grief 109.14

2 Corinthians 7:10   Repentance 203.17

2 Corinthians 8:1–5   Giving 101.8

2 Corinthians 8:2   Generosity 97.8

2 Corinthians 8:3–4   Privilege 188.9

2 Corinthians 8:9   Grace 108.10

2 Corinthians 8:9   Jesus Christ 135.42

2 Corinthians 8:9   Poverty 181.11

2 Corinthians 8:9   Unselfishness 265.11

2 Corinthians 8:21   Honesty 122.4

2 Corinthians 9:6   Generosity 97.9

2 Corinthians 9:7   Giving 101.9

2 Corinthians 9:10–11, 13   Generosity 97.10

2 Corinthians 9:15   Gift 100.8

2 Corinthians 9:15   Thankfulness and thanksgiving 254.5

2 Corinthians 10:1   Gentleness 99.2

2 Corinthians 10:3–5   Warfare, spiritual 271.3

2 Corinthians 10:4   Victory 266.6

2 Corinthians 10:4–5   Thought 255.8

2 Corinthians 10:18   Conceit 37.10

2 Corinthians 11:3   Simplicity 235.11

2 Corinthians 11:3   Temptation 253.8

2 Corinthians 11:14   Devil 58.9

2 Corinthians 11:19   Fools and folly 91.12

2 Corinthians 11:26   Journeys 136.13

2 Corinthians 11:28   Leadership 149.7

2 Corinthians 12:7   Pride 186.11

2 Corinthians 12:7   Suffering 248.18

2 Corinthians 12:8–9   Prayer 184.4

2 Corinthians 12:9   Accepting the will of God 2.8

2 Corinthians 12:9   Comfort 35.52

2 Corinthians 12:9   Grace 108.11

2 Corinthians 12:9   Joy 137.16

2 Corinthians 12:9   Power 182.12

2 Corinthians 12:9   Victory 266.7

2 Corinthians 12:9–10   Weakness 274.13

2 Corinthians 12:12   Miracles 161.12

2 Corinthians 12:15   Unselfishness 265.12

2 Corinthians 13:4   Weakness 274.14

2 Corinthians 13:5   Self-examination 227.4

2 Corinthians 13:5–7   Failure 81.13

2 Corinthians 13:13   Fellowship 89.5

2 Corinthians 13:13   Grace 108.12

2 Corinthians 13:13   Trinity 259.5

D

Daniel 1:8   Decisions 53.8

Daniel 2:20   God 103.72

Daniel 2:27–28   Dreams 67.6

Daniel 2:31–34   Weakness 274.2

Daniel 3:28   Angels 7.2

Daniel 5:27   Failure 81.5

Daniel 7:8   Antichrist 10.1

Daniel 7:13   Last things 144.58

Daniel 7:13–14   Jesus Christ 135.46

Daniel 7:25   Antichrist 10.2

Daniel 8:15, 17   Visions 267.9

Daniel 9:18   Mercy 159.7

Daniel 10:18–19   Dignity 59.7

Daniel 12:1   Angels 7.3

Daniel 12:2–3   Last things 144.49

Deuteronomy 1:21   Discouragement 63.2

Deuteronomy 1:43, 45   Prayer 184.18

Deuteronomy 4:39   Sovereignty of God 240.1

Deuteronomy 5:33   Health and wholeness 115.1

Deuteronomy 6:2   Reverence 211.1

Deuteronomy 6:4   Trinity 259.1

Deuteronomy 6:5   Heart 116.1

Deuteronomy 6:5   Love 154.24

Deuteronomy 6:6–7   Homes 120.1

Deuteronomy 6:7   Family 86.10

Deuteronomy 6:7   Teachers and teaching 250.1

Deuteronomy 7:6   Choice 30.1

Deuteronomy 7:6–9   Grace 108.1

Deuteronomy 7:7–8   Love 154.1

Deuteronomy 7:7–9   God 103.47

Deuteronomy 7:9   Faithfulness 83.1

Deuteronomy 7:9   God 103.15

Deuteronomy 7:13   Fruit 95.1

Deuteronomy 8:2   Remembering 201.2

Deuteronomy 8:2   Temptation 253.1

Deuteronomy 8:3   Food and drink 90.3

Deuteronomy 8:3   Life 150.3

Deuteronomy 8:5   God 103.18

Deuteronomy 8:17   Pride 186.1

Deuteronomy 8:17–18   Riches 214.1

Deuteronomy 9:4   Self-righteousness 229.1

Deuteronomy 10:12   Love 154.25

Deuteronomy 10:18   Widows 275.1

Deuteronomy 10:18–19   Immigrants 130.3

Deuteronomy 13:1–3   Teachers, false 251.1

Deuteronomy 13:1–5   Dreams 67.3

Deuteronomy 14:4–8   Animals 9.4

Deuteronomy 14:29   Widows 275.2

Deuteronomy 15:1–6   Debt 52.1

Deuteronomy 15:7   Hardness 112.2

Deuteronomy 15:7   Poverty 181.2

Deuteronomy 15:7–8   Generosity 97.1

Deuteronomy 16:9–10, 13–15   Celebration 27.2

Deuteronomy 16:16   Human beings 125.18

Deuteronomy 16:19   Blindness 22.2

Deuteronomy 16:20   Justice 138.2

Deuteronomy 18:3   Priest 187.3

Deuteronomy 18:10–12   Occult 171.4

Deuteronomy 18:15   Jesus Christ 135.76

Deuteronomy 18:22   Prophets and prophecy 190.1

Deuteronomy 19:4–6   Murder 165.4

Deuteronomy 19:11–12   Murder 165.5

Deuteronomy 20:1   War 270.2

Deuteronomy 21:5   Priest 187.4

Deuteronomy 23:10–12   Love 154.2

Deuteronomy 23:21–23   Vow 268.2

Deuteronomy 24:14   Oppression 173.2

Deuteronomy 25:16   Dishonesty 64.2

Deuteronomy 26:9–10   Land 143.4

Deuteronomy 27:18   Blindness 22.3

Deuteronomy 28:2   Blessing 21.4

Deuteronomy 28:2   Obedience 170.3

Deuteronomy 28:2–4   Land 143.5

Deuteronomy 28:15   Disobedience 65.1

Deuteronomy 30:2–3   Restoration 208.1

Deuteronomy 30:19   Choice 30.2

Deuteronomy 30:19   Decisions 53.1

Deuteronomy 30:19   Life 150.4

Deuteronomy 31:8   Discouragement 63.3

Deuteronomy 31:27   Rebellion 197.2

Deuteronomy 32:4   God 103.44

Deuteronomy 32:35   Retaliation 209.2

Deuteronomy 33:10   Priest 187.5

Deuteronomy 33:27   Comfort 35.41

Deuteronomy 34:9   Laying on of hands 147.3

E

Ecclesiastes 1:13, 18   Stress 246.4

Ecclesiastes 2:17, 20–21   Despair 57.11

Ecclesiastes 3:1–2   Birth 18.6

Ecclesiastes 3:1–2   Time 256.3

Ecclesiastes 3:1, 4   Mourning 164.5

Ecclesiastes 3:1, 7   Silence 234.6

Ecclesiastes 3:4   Grief 109.3

Ecclesiastes 3:4   Laughter 145.8

Ecclesiastes 3:11   Beauty 16.9

Ecclesiastes 3:20   Human beings 125.8

Ecclesiastes 4:4   Envy 76.3

Ecclesiastes 4:6   Quiet 195.5

Ecclesiastes 4:12   Unity 264.2

Ecclesiastes 5:1   Listening 152.4

Ecclesiastes 5:10   Money and material goods 162.1

Ecclesiastes 5:10–11   Ambition 6.13

Ecclesiastes 5:11   Sleep 238.9

Ecclesiastes 7:2, 4   Mourning 164.6

Ecclesiastes 7:3–4, 6   Laughter 145.9

Ecclesiastes 7:20   Sinful nature 237.4

Ecclesiastes 7:29   Human beings 125.9

Ecclesiastes 9:10   Work 279.7

Ecclesiastes 9:17   Quiet 195.6

Ecclesiastes 10:6   Dignity 59.6

Ecclesiastes 10:19   Laughter 145.10

Ecclesiastes 11:10   Worry 282.5

Ecclesiastes 12:1   Remembering 201.8

Ecclesiastes 12:1   Youth 284.5

Ecclesiastes 12:12   Tiredness 257.1

Ecclesiastes 12:13   Responsibility, human 205.1

Ecclesiastes 12:13   Reverence 211.6

Ecclesiasticus 1:14   Wisdom 277.6

Ecclesiasticus 2:8   Reward 213.3

Ecclesiasticus 2:11   God 103.52

Ecclesiasticus 2:18   God 103.53

Ecclesiasticus 4:9   Oppression 173.9

Ecclesiasticus 5:1   Confidence 39.4

Ecclesiasticus 6:16   Friends and friendship 94.6

Ecclesiasticus 7:11   Bitterness 19.8

Ecclesiasticus 9:10   Friends and friendship 94.7

Ecclesiasticus 19:10   Gossip 107.8

Ecclesiasticus 28:18   Speech 241.4

Ecclesiasticus 30:24   Time 256.4

Ecclesiasticus 32:8   Speech 241.5

Ecclesiasticus 44:1   Praise 183.6

Ephesians 1:3   Blessing 21.8

Ephesians 1:3–5   Privilege 188.11

Ephesians 1:4–5   Election 72.10

Ephesians 1:5   Adoption 5.8

Ephesians 1:7   Blood 23.5

Ephesians 1:7   Forgiveness 92.13

Ephesians 1:7   Redemption 199.12

Ephesians 1:9–10   Will of God 276.5

Ephesians 1:11   Inheritance 131.7

Ephesians 1:11   Providence 192.10

Ephesians 1:11   Sovereignty of God 240.10

Ephesians 1:13–14   Inheritance 131.8

Ephesians 1:16   Thankfulness and thanksgiving 254.6

Ephesians 1:17   Wisdom 277.19

Ephesians 1:18   Inheritance 131.9

Ephesians 1:19–20   Power 182.13

Ephesians 1:19–21   God 103.67

Ephesians 1:20–23   Jesus Christ 135.7

Ephesians 1:23   Fullness 96.4

Ephesians 2:1   Death 51.18

Ephesians 2:1–3   Sin 236.16

Ephesians 2:1–3   Unbeliever 262.7

Ephesians 2:1–5   New birth 169.5

Ephesians 2:1–2   Devil 58.10

Ephesians 2:2   Disobedience 65.4

Ephesians 2:3   Anger 8.8

Ephesians 2:3–5   Sinful nature 237.12

Ephesians 2:4–5   God 103.54

Ephesians 2:4–5   Grace 108.14

Ephesians 2:4–5   Love 154.8

Ephesians 2:5   Life 150.32

Ephesians 2:8   Faith 82.24

Ephesians 2:8   Gift 100.9

Ephesians 2:8   Grace 108.15

Ephesians 2:8   Salvation and Savior 221.14

Ephesians 2:8–10   Works, good 280.8

Ephesians 2:10   Creation 47.11

Ephesians 2:10   Good 105.13

Ephesians 2:11–19   Gentiles 98.9

Ephesians 2:12   Covenant 46.5

Ephesians 2:12   Hope 123.7

Ephesians 2:12   Promise 189.4

Ephesians 2:12   Unbeliever 262.8

Ephesians 2:13, 18   Access 3.5

Ephesians 2:14   Peace 177.20

Ephesians 2:16   Reconciliation 198.5

Ephesians 2:19–20   Apostles 11.6

Ephesians 2:20   Prophets and prophecy 190.12

Ephesians 3:2   Stewardship 245.5

Ephesians 3:8   Riches 214.7

Ephesians 3:9–10   Angels 7.10

Ephesians 3:12   Access 3.6

Ephesians 3:12   Privilege 188.12

Ephesians 3:12–13   Discouragement 63.13

Ephesians 3:17–19   Jesus Christ 135.84

Ephesians 3:19   Fullness 96.5

Ephesians 3:19   Knowledge 142.13

Ephesians 3:20–21   Prayer 184.5

Ephesians 4:1   Christian life 31.6

Ephesians 4:3–6   Unity 264.7

Ephesians 4:4–5   Baptism 15.10

Ephesians 4:4–6   Trinity 259.6

Ephesians 4:5–6   God 103.31

Ephesians 4:11   Evangelists 78.4

Ephesians 4:11–12   Pastor 175.1

Ephesians 4:11–13   Perfection 178.7

Ephesians 4:15   Speech 241.7

Ephesians 4:15   Truth 260.10

Ephesians 4:18   Hardness 112.11

Ephesians 4:22–24   Renewal 202.10

Ephesians 4:26–27, 31   Anger 8.17

Ephesians 4:28   Dishonesty 64.14

Ephesians 4:28   Honesty 122.5

Ephesians 4:28   Stealing 244.7

Ephesians 4:29   Speech 241.8

Ephesians 4:30   Holy Spirit 119.38

Ephesians 4:31   Bitterness 19.11

Ephesians 4:31   Cruelty 48.10

Ephesians 4:32   Forgiveness 92.14

Ephesians 4:32   Kindness 140.6

Ephesians 5:2   Atonement 13.8

Ephesians 5:3   Sex 231.8

Ephesians 5:4   Thankfulness and thanksgiving 254.7

Ephesians 5:5   Desire, wrong 56.6

Ephesians 5:8–9   Light 151.16

Ephesians 5:11   Darkness 49.12

Ephesians 5:13–14   Light 151.17

Ephesians 5:16   Time 256.13

Ephesians 5:17   Understanding 263.9

Ephesians 5:17   Will of God 276.6

Ephesians 5:18   Drunkenness 68.7

Ephesians 5:18   Fullness 96.6

Ephesians 5:18–21   Holy Spirit 119.39

Ephesians 5:19   Music 166.13

Ephesians 5:19   Praise 183.8

Ephesians 5:19–20   Thankfulness and thanksgiving 254.8

Ephesians 5:21–22, 24   Submission 247.2

Ephesians 5:21–25, 28   Family 86.7

Ephesians 5:23, 25–27   Church 33.7

Ephesians 5:25   Love 154.20

Ephesians 5:25–26   Water 272.11

Ephesians 5:33   Respect 204.12

Ephesians 6:1–2   Family 86.22

Ephesians 6:1–2   Submission 247.3

Ephesians 6:4   Family 86.23

Ephesians 6:5   Submission 247.4

Ephesians 6:5–9   Work 279.10

Ephesians 6:10–11   Power 182.14

Ephesians 6:11   Devil 58.11

Ephesians 6:11   Temptation 253.18

Ephesians 6:11–12   Warfare, spiritual 271.5

Ephesians 6:11, 18   Endurance 74.5

Ephesians 6:12   Demons 54.9

Ephesians 6:12   Rulers 218.11

Ephesians 6:13–18   Warfare, spiritual 271.6

Ephesians 6:14   Righteousness 216.17

Ephesians 6:14   Truth 260.11

Ephesians 6:15   Peace 177.21

Ephesians 6:16   Faith 82.25

Ephesians 6:17   Bible 17.7

Ephesians 6:17   Holy Spirit 119.40

Ephesians 6:18–19   Prayer 184.36

Ephesians 6:19   Gospel 106.13

Ephesians 6:19   Witness 278.15

1 Esdras 4:38   Truth 260.2

2 Esdras 2:20   Works, good 280.2

2 Esdras 14:25   Understanding 263.6

Esther 1:10–11   Beauty 16.3

Exodus 2:24–25   Comfort 35.40

Exodus 3:5   Holiness 118.1

Exodus 3:5   Respect 204.1

Exodus 3:6   Fear 88.2

Exodus 3:12   Service 230.1

Exodus 3:13–15   Name 167.2

Exodus 3:14   God 103.55

Exodus 3:16   Elders 71.1

Exodus 4:10–12   Accepting the will of God 2.1

Exodus 4:11   Blindness 22.1

Exodus 4:21   Hardness 112.1

Exodus 6:6   Redemption 199.1

Exodus 6:9   Despair 57.1

Exodus 12:3, 5–8, 11–13   Passover 174.1

Exodus 12:5–7   Sacrifice 220.2

Exodus 12:24   Passover 174.2

Exodus 14:21   Miracles 161.1

Exodus 14:31   Miracles 161.2

Exodus 15:3   War 270.1

Exodus 18:21   Bribe 25.1

Exodus 18:22–23   Leadership 149.1

Exodus 19:6   Priest 187.1

Exodus 20:3–4   Worship 283.1

Exodus 20:3–5   Idolatry 128.1

Exodus 20:5   Jealousy 134.1

Exodus 20:7   Blasphemy 20.1

Exodus 20:7   Guilt 111.2

Exodus 20:7   Name 167.3

Exodus 20:8   Holiness 118.2

Exodus 20:8   Remembering 201.1

Exodus 20:8   Time 256.2

Exodus 20:8–11   Sabbath 219.1

Exodus 20:9–10   Work 279.3

Exodus 20:11   Earth, the 69.3

Exodus 20:12   Family 86.9

Exodus 20:12   Life 150.2

Exodus 20:12   Love 154.10

Exodus 20:12   Respect 204.2

Exodus 20:12   Youth 284.1

Exodus 20:13   Murder 165.3

Exodus 20:14   Marriage 157.9

Exodus 20:15   Stealing 244.1

Exodus 20:16   Lying 156.1

Exodus 20:16–17   Neighbor 168.1

Exodus 20:17   Desire, wrong 56.1

Exodus 21:12   Punishment 193.1

Exodus 22:1   Stealing 244.2

Exodus 22:1–2   Restitution 207.1

Exodus 22:21   Immigrants 130.1

Exodus 22:21   Oppression 173.1

Exodus 22:28   Rulers 218.1

Exodus 23:1   Injustice 132.1

Exodus 23:4–5   Enemy 75.1

Exodus 23:6   Poverty 181.1

Exodus 23:8   Bribe 25.2

Exodus 23:10–11   Land 143.1

Exodus 24:8   Covenant 46.2

Exodus 28:1   Priest 187.2

Exodus 28:2   Dignity 59.2

Exodus 28:3   Abilities 1.1

Exodus 31:3   Holy Spirit 119.2

Exodus 32:4   Idolatry 128.2

Exodus 33:11   Friends and friendship 94.1

Exodus 33:18   Christian life 31.43

Exodus 33:18   Glory 102.1

Exodus 34:6–7   God 103.50

Exodus 34:6–7   Mercy 159.1

Exodus 34:14   Jealousy 134.2

Exodus 36:1   Abilities 1.2

Ezekiel 13:7   Visions 267.7

Ezekiel 18:4   Soul 239.4

Ezekiel 18:5, 7–8   Debt 52.7

Ezekiel 18:30   Repentance 203.3

Ezekiel 18:32   Death 51.7

Ezekiel 20:27   Blasphemy 20.3

Ezekiel 20:38   Rebellion 197.13

Ezekiel 28:17   Beauty 16.11

Ezekiel 33:8   Punishment 193.3

Ezekiel 33:11, 17   Way 273.7

Ezekiel 33:15   Restitution 207.10

Ezekiel 34:1–2   Shepherd 233.4

Ezekiel 34:23   Shepherd 233.5

Ezekiel 36:25   Water 272.5

Ezekiel 36:25–27   New birth 169.2

Ezekiel 36:26   Heart 116.7

Ezekiel 36:26   Motives 163.7

Ezekiel 36:27   Holy Spirit 119.6

Ezekiel 37:1   Visions 267.8

Ezekiel 37:3   Life 150.10

Ezekiel 37:3–5   Revival 212.4

Ezra 4:4   Discouragement 63.7

Ezra 6:16   Celebration 27.4

Ezra 10:1–4   Renewal 202.2

G

Galatians 1:6–8   Teachers, false 251.6

Galatians 1:11–12   Gospel 106.11

Galatians 1:11–12   Revelation 210.8

Galatians 2:9   Fellowship 89.6

Galatians 2:10   Remembering 201.14

Galatians 2:16   Law 146.12

Galatians 2:19–20   Jesus Christ 135.26

Galatians 2:19–20   Love 154.7

Galatians 2:20   Faith 82.23

Galatians 2:20   Life 150.31

Galatians 3:8   Gospel 106.12

Galatians 3:13   Propitiation 191.4

Galatians 3:13   Redemption 199.10

Galatians 3:24   Law 146.13

Galatians 3:28   Gentiles 98.8

Galatians 3:28   Human beings 125.25

Galatians 3:28   Race 196.4

Galatians 4:4   Jesus Christ 135.57

Galatians 4:4   Time 256.12

Galatians 4:4–5   Law 146.14

Galatians 4:4–5   Redemption 199.11

Galatians 4:4–6   Adoption 5.7

Galatians 4:4–7   Privilege 188.10

Galatians 4:7   Inheritance 131.6

Galatians 4:14   Caring 26.5

Galatians 4:19   Christlikeness 32.7

Galatians 5:1   Freedom 93.8

Galatians 5:4   Grace 108.13

Galatians 5:5   Waiting 269.17

Galatians 5:6   Circumcision 34.5

Galatians 5:13   Freedom 93.9

Galatians 5:14   Neighbor 168.4

Galatians 5:16–17   Sinful nature 237.11

Galatians 5:17   Warfare, spiritual 271.4

Galatians 5:19   Sex 231.7

Galatians 5:19–20   Anger 8.16

Galatians 5:19–20   Idolatry 128.4

Galatians 5:19–20   Occult 171.10

Galatians 5:19, 21   Drunkenness 68.6

Galatians 5:19, 21   Envy 76.5

Galatians 5:19–21   Jealousy 134.7

Galatians 5:22   Faithfulness 83.8

Galatians 5:22   Good 105.12

Galatians 5:22   Joy 137.17

Galatians 5:22   Kindness 140.5

Galatians 5:22   Love 154.19

Galatians 5:22   Patience 176.7

Galatians 5:22   Peace 177.19

Galatians 5:22   Self-control 225.8

Galatians 5:22–23   Christian life 31.15

Galatians 5:22–23   Fruit 95.6

Galatians 5:22–23   Gentleness 99.3

Galatians 5:22–23   Holy Spirit 119.37

Galatians 5:22–23   Self-denial 226.5

Galatians 5:22–23   Temperance 252.2

Galatians 5:26   Conceit 37.11

Galatians 6:1   Gentleness 99.4

Galatians 6:1   Restoration 208.14

Galatians 6:1   Temptation 253.9

Galatians 6:2   Comfort 35.15

Galatians 6:2   Help 117.10

Galatians 6:3   Conceit 37.12

Galatians 6:3–4   Self-examination 227.5

Galatians 6:9   Tiredness 257.7

Galatians 6:9–10   Zeal 285.6

Galatians 6:10   Service 230.8

Galatians 6:14   Jesus Christ 135.27

Galatians 6:15–16   Israel 133.8

Genesis 1:1   Creation 47.1

Genesis 1:1   God 103.8

Genesis 1:1–2   Earth, the 69.1

Genesis 1:1–5   Darkness 49.1

Genesis 1:2   Holy Spirit 119.1

Genesis 1:3   Light 151.1

Genesis 1:14   Time 256.1

Genesis 1:24–25   Animals 9.1

Genesis 1:26–27   Human beings 125.1

Genesis 1:27   Adam 4.1

Genesis 1:27   Creation 47.2

Genesis 1:27   Dignity 59.1

Genesis 1:27–28   Race 196.1

Genesis 1:27–28   Sex 231.1

Genesis 1:29–30   Food and drink 90.1

Genesis 1:31   Good 105.1

Genesis 2:7   Birth 18.1

Genesis 2:7   Human beings 125.2

Genesis 2:7, 18   Adam 4.2

Genesis 2:7, 9   Life 150.1

Genesis 2:8–9, 15–17   Eden, Garden of 70.1

Genesis 2:9   Knowledge 142.1

Genesis 2:15   Caring 26.1

Genesis 2:15   Work 279.1

Genesis 2:17   Death 51.1

Genesis 2:18   Marriage 157.1

Genesis 2:18, 21–23   Human beings 125.13

Genesis 2:19–20   Animals 9.2

Genesis 2:24   Family 86.1

Genesis 2:24   Marriage 157.2

Genesis 2:24–25   Sex 231.2

Genesis 2:25   Shame 232.1

Genesis 3:1   Devil 58.1

Genesis 3:1, 4, 6–8   Fall, the 84.1

Genesis 3:5   Evil 79.1

Genesis 3:8, 10   Guilt 111.1

Genesis 3:10   Fear 88.1

Genesis 3:10   Shame 232.1

Genesis 3:15   Jesus Christ 135.15

Genesis 3:16   Birth 18.2

Genesis 3:16   Human beings 125.14

Genesis 3:16–17, 19   Fall, the 84.2

Genesis 3:17   Human beings 125.15

Genesis 3:19   Death 51.2

Genesis 3:19   Work 279.2

Genesis 3:20   Human beings 125.16

Genesis 3:23–24   Eden, Garden of 70.2

Genesis 4:4–5   Motives 163.1

Genesis 4:7   Right and wrong 215.1

Genesis 4:8–10   Murder 165.1

Genesis 5:1–2   Human beings 125.17

Genesis 6:5   Human beings 125.3

Genesis 6:9   Righteousness 216.1

Genesis 7:8–9   Animals 9.3

Genesis 8:6–12   Waiting 269.1

Genesis 8:20   Sacrifice 220.1

Genesis 8:22   Earth, the 69.2

Genesis 8:22   Providence 192.1

Genesis 9:3   Food and drink 90.2

Genesis 9:5–6   Murder 165.2

Genesis 11:4   Ambition 6.9

Genesis 12:1–3   Blessing 21.1

Genesis 12:8   Name 167.1

Genesis 14:19–20   Giving 101.1

Genesis 15:1   Comfort 35.1

Genesis 15:1   Reward 213.1

Genesis 15:6   Faith 82.1

Genesis 15:6   Justification 139.1

Genesis 15:6   Righteousness 216.2

Genesis 15:12   Visions 267.1

Genesis 17:7–8, 10   Covenant 46.1

Genesis 17:9–13   Circumcision 34.1

Genesis 18:12–14   Doubt 66.1

Genesis 18:25   God 103.43

Genesis 21:6   Laughter 145.1

Genesis 22:14   Providence 192.2

Genesis 22:18   Obedience 170.1

Genesis 27:34   Bitterness 19.1

Genesis 28:12   Dreams 67.1

Genesis 28:20–22   Vow 268.1

Genesis 29:1   Journeys 136.1

Genesis 32:26   Blessing 21.2

Genesis 32:28   Israel 133.1

Genesis 37:5   Dreams 67.2

Genesis 39:6–9   Sex 231.4

Genesis 48:14   Laying on of hands 147.1

H

Habakkuk 1:13   Evil 79.4

Habakkuk 1:13   God 103.37

Habakkuk 1:13   Purity 194.2

Habakkuk 1:13   Sin 236.7

Habakkuk 2:3   Visions 267.11

Habakkuk 2:4   Faith 82.5

Habakkuk 2:6–7   Debt 52.8

Habakkuk 2:20   Silence 234.8

Habakkuk 3:2   Anger 8.3

Habakkuk 3:2   Renewal 202.7

Habakkuk 3:2   Revival 212.6

Habakkuk 3:17–18   Comfort 35.46

Haggai 1:5   Self-examination 227.2

Hebrews 1:1–2   Revelation 210.10

Hebrews 1:2   Inheritance 131.11

Hebrews 1:2   World 281.3

Hebrews 1:2–8   Jesus Christ 135.34

Hebrews 1:3   Atonement 13.9

Hebrews 1:3   Glory 102.14

Hebrews 1:3   Providence 192.12

Hebrews 1:8   Jesus Christ 135.50

Hebrews 1:14   Angels 7.11

Hebrews 2:3   Salvation and Savior 221.18

Hebrews 2:4   Miracles 161.13

Hebrews 2:9   Jesus Christ 135.61

Hebrews 2:14   Death 51.25

Hebrews 2:14   Devil 58.12

Hebrews 2:14   Freedom 93.10

Hebrews 2:14   Jesus Christ 135.62

Hebrews 2:14–15   Comfort 35.11

Hebrews 2:14–15   Jesus Christ 135.29

Hebrews 2:17   Faithfulness 83.11

Hebrews 2:17   Propitiation 191.5

Hebrews 2:18   Temptation 253.19

Hebrews 3:1   Apostles 11.7

Hebrews 3:12   Unbelief 261.10

Hebrews 3:13   Encouragement 73.10

Hebrews 3:13   Sin 236.33

Hebrews 3:15   Hardness 112.12

Hebrews 4:1, 3–11   Rest 206.4

Hebrews 4:12   Bible 17.12

Hebrews 4:12   Discernment 60.7

Hebrews 4:13   God 103.3

Hebrews 4:14–15   Jesus Christ 135.71

Hebrews 4:15   Jesus Christ 135.38

Hebrews 4:15   Jesus Christ 135.63

Hebrews 4:15   Sympathy 249.12

Hebrews 4:15   Temptation 253.20

Hebrews 4:15–16   Confidence 39.6

Hebrews 4:15–16   Failure 81.14

Hebrews 4:16   Comfort 35.53

Hebrews 4:16   Grace 108.16

Hebrews 4:16   Prayer 184.7

Hebrews 5:1–4   Priest 187.9

Hebrews 5:5–6   Jesus Christ 135.72

Hebrews 5:8   Jesus Christ 135.91

Hebrews 5:8   Obedience 170.11

Hebrews 5:8–9   Perfection 178.12

Hebrews 5:12–14   Perfection 178.13

Hebrews 5:14   Discernment 60.8

Hebrews 6:1–2   Laying on of hands 147.11

Hebrews 6:4, 6   Renewal 202.13

Hebrews 6:4–6   Falling away 85.9

Hebrews 6:12   Laziness 148.7

Hebrews 6:18–19   Hope 123.9

Hebrews 7:22   Covenant 46.6

Hebrews 7:24–26   Jesus Christ 135.73

Hebrews 7:26   Holiness 118.8

Hebrews 7:26   Jesus Christ 135.39

Hebrews 8:3   Priest 187.10

Hebrews 8:6   Promise 189.5

Hebrews 8:10   Covenant 46.7

Hebrews 8:10   Law 146.15

Hebrews 9:5   Propitiation 191.6

Hebrews 9:12   Redemption 199.16

Hebrews 9:15   Covenant 46.8

Hebrews 9:15   Jesus Christ 135.74

Hebrews 9:22   Blood 23.7

Hebrews 9:22   Forgiveness 92.15

Hebrews 9:22   Sin 236.18

Hebrews 9:24   Last things 144.17

Hebrews 9:27   Death 51.26

Hebrews 9:27   Last things 144.39

Hebrews 9:28   Last things 144.65

Hebrews 10:1   Law 146.16

Hebrews 10:11–12   Jesus Christ 135.75

Hebrews 10:11–12   Priest 187.11

Hebrews 10:11–12   Sacrifice 220.9

Hebrews 10:14   Perfection 178.14

Hebrews 10:19   Blood 23.8

Hebrews 10:19   Confidence 39.7

Hebrews 10:19–20   Way 273.11

Hebrews 10:19–21   Privilege 188.14

Hebrews 10:19–22   Access 3.7

Hebrews 10:22   Assurance 12.9

Hebrews 10:22   Conscience 40.7

Hebrews 10:22   Water 272.13

Hebrews 10:23   Christian life 31.37

Hebrews 10:23   Promise 189.6

Hebrews 10:24   Kindness 140.7

Hebrews 10:24   Works, good 280.10

Hebrews 10:24–25   Encouragement 73.11

Hebrews 10:25   Church 33.8

Hebrews 10:26   Falling away 85.10

Hebrews 10:29   Punishment 193.10

Hebrews 11:1   Faith 82.26

Hebrews 11:3   Creation 47.13

Hebrews 11:3   Faith 82.27

Hebrews 11:3   Understanding 263.11

Hebrews 11:6   Faith 82.28

Hebrews 11:6   Prayer 184.27

Hebrews 11:6   Reward 213.10

Hebrews 11:6   Seeking God 224.14

Hebrews 11:16   Shame 232.6

Hebrews 11:17   Temptation 253.10

Hebrews 11:24–25   Choice 30.13

Hebrews 11:36–37   Cruelty 48.12

Hebrews 12:1–2   Christian life 31.38

Hebrews 12:2   Comfort 35.54

Hebrews 12:2   Endurance 74.9

Hebrews 12:2   Joy 137.20

Hebrews 12:2   Shame 232.7

Hebrews 12:3   Tiredness 257.8

Hebrews 12:5–7   Adoption 5.9

Hebrews 12:7–11   Discipline 62.4

Hebrews 12:10   Holiness 118.9

Hebrews 12:10   Suffering 248.19

Hebrews 12:14   Holiness 118.10

Hebrews 12:15   Bitterness 19.13

Hebrews 12:16–17   Inheritance 131.12

Hebrews 12:23   Last things 144.74

Hebrews 12:28   Kingdom, kingdom of God 141.16

Hebrews 12:28   Reverence 211.14

Hebrews 13:2   Hospitality 124.6

Hebrews 13:2   Immigrants 130.6

Hebrews 13:3   Sympathy 249.13

Hebrews 13:4   Marriage 157.8

Hebrews 13:5   Contentment 41.8

Hebrews 13:5   Money and material goods 162.8

Hebrews 13:5–6   Help 117.11

Hebrews 13:6   Confidence 39.8

Hebrews 13:7   Elders 71.9

Hebrews 13:8   Jesus Christ 135.35

Hebrews 13:15   Praise 183.9

Hebrews 13:15–16   Sacrifice 220.10

Hebrews 13:17   Elders 71.10

Hebrews 13:17   Respect 204.15

Hebrews 13:17   Submission 247.5

Hebrews 13:20   Blood 23.9

Hebrews 13:20   Covenant 46.9

Hebrews 13:20   Shepherd 233.9

Hosea 1:10   Life 150.11

Hosea 6:3   Knowledge 142.7

Hosea 6:3   Seeking God 224.11

Hosea 6:6   Mercy 159.8

Hosea 8:7–8   Evil 79.2

Hosea 12:6   Waiting 269.12

I

Isaiah 1:15–17   Prayer 184.22

Isaiah 1:16   Right and wrong 215.8

Isaiah 1:17   Justice 138.5

Isaiah 1:17   Widows 275.4

Isaiah 1:18   Sin 236.4

Isaiah 1:19–20   Rebellion 197.8

Isaiah 2:4   Reconciliation 198.1

Isaiah 3:10   Health and wholeness 115.8

Isaiah 5:11   Drunkenness 68.2

Isaiah 5:20   Darkness 49.6

Isaiah 5:20   Right and wrong 215.9

Isaiah 5:21   Conceit 37.5

Isaiah 5:24–25   Anger 8.2

Isaiah 6:1–4   Visions 267.6

Isaiah 6:3   God 103.36

Isaiah 6:3   Holiness 118.4

Isaiah 6:5   Conviction of sin 43.2

Isaiah 6:5   Grief 109.4

Isaiah 6:7   Guilt 111.5

Isaiah 6:8   Witness 278.2

Isaiah 6:9–10   Hardness 112.4

Isaiah 7:14   Jesus Christ 135.52

Isaiah 7:14–15   Choice 30.10

Isaiah 7:14–16   Right and wrong 215.10

Isaiah 8:19–20   Occult 171.6

Isaiah 8:22–23   Despair 57.12

Isaiah 9:2   Darkness 49.7

Isaiah 9:2   Light 151.5

Isaiah 9:6   Birth 18.7

Isaiah 9:6   Counsel 44.6

Isaiah 9:6   Jesus Christ 135.53

Isaiah 9:6–7   Peace 177.2

Isaiah 10:1–2   Cruelty 48.6

Isaiah 10:5–6   War 270.6

Isaiah 11:2   Discernment 60.2

Isaiah 11:2   Holy Spirit 119.5

Isaiah 11:2   Reverence 211.7

Isaiah 11:2   Wisdom 277.4

Isaiah 11:6–9   Animals 9.10

Isaiah 11:9   Earth, the 69.10

Isaiah 11:9   Knowledge 142.6

Isaiah 11:9   Water 272.1

Isaiah 11:10   Gentiles 98.2

Isaiah 12:3   Joy 137.7

Isaiah 12:3   Water 272.2

Isaiah 13:9   Cruelty 48.7

Isaiah 14:12–14   Ambition 6.14

Isaiah 22:13   Drunkenness 68.3

Isaiah 25:1   Counsel 44.7

Isaiah 26:3   Mind 160.1

Isaiah 26:3   Peace 177.3

Isaiah 28:7   Drunkenness 68.4

Isaiah 29:13   Ritual 217.2

Isaiah 29:13   Worship 283.4

Isaiah 29:18   Blindness 22.5

Isaiah 30:1   Rebellion 197.9

Isaiah 30:15   Quiet 195.7

Isaiah 30:15   Rest 206.1

Isaiah 30:18   Waiting 269.9

Isaiah 30:20–21   Way 273.5

Isaiah 32:6   Fools and folly 91.5

Isaiah 32:17   Quiet 195.8

Isaiah 32:17   Righteousness 216.4

Isaiah 32:18   Homes 120.9

Isaiah 35:3   Weakness 274.1

Isaiah 35:5   Blindness 22.6

Isaiah 35:10   Joy 137.8

Isaiah 35:10   Redemption 199.3

Isaiah 38:14   Oppression 173.6

Isaiah 38:20   Music 166.9

Isaiah 40:1–2   Comfort 35.44

Isaiah 40:11   Shepherd 233.2

Isaiah 40:14–15   God 103.40

Isaiah 40:22   God 103.63

Isaiah 40:26, 28   Creation 47.6

Isaiah 40:27–28   Doubt 66.3

Isaiah 40:27–28   Way 273.6

Isaiah 40:28   God 103.10

Isaiah 40:28–31   Tiredness 257.2

Isaiah 40:30–31   Youth 284.6

Isaiah 40:31   Patience 176.3

Isaiah 40:31   Power 182.1

Isaiah 40:31   Renewal 202.5

Isaiah 40:31   Waiting 269.10

Isaiah 41:10   Comfort 35.36

Isaiah 41:10   Victory 266.1

Isaiah 42:3   Comfort 35.31

Isaiah 42:3–4   Discouragement 63.10

Isaiah 42:6–7   Blindness 22.7

Isaiah 43:1   Christian life 31.1

Isaiah 43:1   Redemption 199.4

Isaiah 43:1–2   Comfort 35.6

Isaiah 43:21   Praise 183.4

Isaiah 44:18   Blindness 22.8

Isaiah 45:12   God 103.11

Isaiah 46:9   Remembering 201.9

Isaiah 47:13–14   Occult 171.7

Isaiah 48:22   Peace 177.4

Isaiah 49:6   Light 151.6

Isaiah 49:14–16   Comfort 35.37

Isaiah 49:14–16   Remembering 201.10

Isaiah 49:15   Caring 26.3

Isaiah 50:4   Tiredness 257.3

Isaiah 50:4–5   Listening 152.5

Isaiah 50:5–6   Rejection 200.3

Isaiah 50:8–9   Justification 139.4

Isaiah 52:5   Blasphemy 20.2

Isaiah 52:7   Preaching 185.1

Isaiah 53:3   Rejection 200.4

Isaiah 53:3–4   Grief 109.5

Isaiah 53:3–9   Jesus Christ 135.16

Isaiah 53:4   Comfort 35.45

Isaiah 53:4   Illness 129.7

Isaiah 53:4–6, 10–12   Atonement 13.2

Isaiah 53:6   Sin 236.5

Isaiah 53:7   Oppression 173.7

Isaiah 53:7   Silence 234.7

Isaiah 53:10   Propitiation 191.1

Isaiah 53:10   Will of God 276.2

Isaiah 53:10–12   Jesus Christ 135.93

Isaiah 55:1   Water 272.3

Isaiah 55:1–2   Food and drink 90.9

Isaiah 55:3   Life 150.9

Isaiah 55:3   Listening 152.6

Isaiah 55:6   Seeking God 224.8

Isaiah 55:6–7   Christian life 31.17

Isaiah 55:7   Godless 104.6

Isaiah 55:7   Repentance 203.2

Isaiah 55:8–9   God 103.64

Isaiah 55:8–9   Thought 255.4

Isaiah 55:8–11   Revelation 210.2

Isaiah 55:10–11   Bible 17.1

Isaiah 56:11   Selfishness 228.4

Isaiah 57:15   God 103.41

Isaiah 57:15   God 103.65

Isaiah 58:3–4, 6   Fasting 87.3

Isaiah 58:10   Kindness 140.1

Isaiah 58:10–11   Contentment 41.2

Isaiah 58:10–11   Guidance 110.4

Isaiah 58:12   Restoration 208.7

Isaiah 58:13–14   Sabbath 219.3

Isaiah 59:2   Prayer 184.23

Isaiah 59:2   Sin 236.6

Isaiah 59:11   Justice 138.6

Isaiah 59:14   Justice 138.7

Isaiah 60:1   Light 151.7

Isaiah 60:1–2   Darkness 49.8

Isaiah 60:20   Mourning 164.7

Isaiah 61:1   Freedom 93.1

Isaiah 61:1   Preaching 185.2

Isaiah 61:1, 3   Praise 183.5

Isaiah 61:1–3   Mourning 164.8

Isaiah 61:4   Restoration 208.8

Isaiah 61:8   Justice 138.8

Isaiah 61:10   Justification 139.5

Isaiah 63:9   Sympathy 249.4

Isaiah 63:16   God 103.22

Isaiah 64:1–2   Revival 212.3

Isaiah 64:6   Righteousness 216.5

Isaiah 64:8   God 103.23

Isaiah 64:8   Human beings 125.10

Isaiah 65:5   Self-righteousness 229.3

Isaiah 65:17   Earth, the 69.11

Isaiah 65:24   Prayer 184.13

Isaiah 66:1   Earth, the 69.12

Isaiah 66:1   Last things 144.10

Isaiah 66:2   Humility 126.1

Isaiah 66:24   Last things 144.48

Isaiah 66:24   Rebellion 197.10

J

James 1:2–3   Temptation 253.21

James 1:5   Generosity 97.13

James 1:5   Guidance 110.9

James 1:5   Wisdom 277.21

James 1:5–6   Prayer 184.38

James 1:6   Doubt 66.9

James 1:6   Prayer 184.28

James 1:12   Endurance 74.10

James 1:12   Promise 189.7

James 1:13–14   Temptation 253.11

James 1:15   Death 51.27

James 1:17   Gift 100.11

James 1:17   God 103.70

James 1:19   Listening 152.10

James 1:19–20   Anger 8.18

James 1:22   Obedience 170.12

James 1:22   Works, good 280.11

James 1:22–24   Listening 152.11

James 1:25   Law 146.17

James 1:25   Remembering 201.16

James 1:26   Self-control 225.11

James 1:27   Widows 275.12

James 2:5–6   Poverty 181.12

James 2:6   Oppression 173.10

James 2:7   Blasphemy 20.7

James 2:8   Law 146.18

James 2:10   Guilt 111.8

James 2:14   Faith 82.29

James 2:14, 17–18   Works, good 280.12

James 2:19   Demons 54.11

James 2:22, 26   Faith 82.30

James 2:23   Friends and friendship 94.11

James 2:24   Works, good 280.13

James 2:26   Works, good 280.14

James 3:2   Failure 81.15

James 3:6, 8–10   Speech 241.10

James 3:14   Bitterness 19.14

James 3:14, 16   Jealousy 134.8

James 3:17   Gentleness 99.7

James 3:17   Purity 194.6

James 3:17   Wisdom 277.22

James 3:18   Righteousness 216.19

James 4:1   Warfare, spiritual 271.9

James 4:2   Desire, wrong 56.8

James 4:3   Motives 163.13

James 4:3   Prayer 184.8

James 4:3   Prayer 184.29

James 4:4   Choice 30.14

James 4:5   Jealousy 134.9

James 4:7   Submission 247.6

James 4:7–8   Warfare, spiritual 271.10

James 4:8   Access 3.8

James 4:8   Purity 194.7

James 4:9   Laughter 145.12

James 4:9   Mourning 164.13

James 4:17   Sinful nature 237.13

James 5:1–5   Riches 214.9

James 5:7–8   Patience 176.9

James 5:7–8   Waiting 269.18

James 5:14   Elders 71.11

James 5:14–16   Healing 114.10

James 5:14–16   Illness 129.9

James 5:16   Confession 38.10

James 5:16   Prayer 184.9

Jeremiah 1:4–5   Birth 18.8

Jeremiah 4:22   Understanding 263.5

Jeremiah 5:1   Leadership 149.4

Jeremiah 5:23   Rebellion 197.11

Jeremiah 5:23   Rejection 200.5

Jeremiah 6:13   Desire, wrong 56.4

Jeremiah 7:24   Falling away 85.2

Jeremiah 7:24–28   Disobedience 65.2

Jeremiah 7:25–26   Prophets and prophecy 190.2

Jeremiah 8:20   Despair 57.13

Jeremiah 8:22   Grief 109.6

Jeremiah 9:5   Lying 156.4

Jeremiah 9:25–26   Circumcision 34.2

Jeremiah 10:10   Truth 260.1

Jeremiah 10:12   God 103.12

Jeremiah 13:23   Works, good 280.1

Jeremiah 14:7   Falling away 85.3

Jeremiah 17:9–10   Heart 116.6

Jeremiah 17:9–10   Motives 163.6

Jeremiah 17:11   Dishonesty 64.11

Jeremiah 17:13   Water 272.4

Jeremiah 22:13   Injustice 132.7

Jeremiah 23:5   Jesus Christ 135.45

Jeremiah 23:16   Listening 152.7

Jeremiah 23:24   God 103.42

Jeremiah 23:32   Dreams 67.5

Jeremiah 28:16   Rebellion 197.12

Jeremiah 29:13–14   Seeking God 224.9

Jeremiah 30:17   Restoration 208.9

Jeremiah 31:13   Mourning 164.9

Jeremiah 31:34   Forgiveness 92.5

Jeremiah 33:6   Health and wholeness 115.9

Jeremiah 45:5   Ambition 6.15

Jeremiah 45:5   Selfishness 228.5

Jeremiah 50:6   Shepherd 233.3

Job 1:12   Sovereignty of God 240.2

Job 1:12   Temptation 253.2

Job 1:21   Comfort 35.18

Job 2:7   Devil 58.2

Job 2:7   Illness 129.2

Job 2:13   Silence 234.2

Job 3:2–3   Depression 55.1

Job 4:3–6   Discouragement 63.8

Job 5:7   Suffering 248.1

Job 5:10–11   Mourning 164.2

Job 6:14   Despair 57.2

Job 6:14   Sympathy 249.1

Job 8:20–21   Laughter 145.2

Job 9:1–2   Justification 139.2

Job 10:1   Bitterness 19.3

Job 10:1   Despair 57.3

Job 11:7–9   God 103.59

Job 12:10   Human beings 125.4

Job 12:12   Old age 172.2

Job 12:22   Darkness 49.2

Job 13:15   Accepting the will of God 2.2

Job 13:15   Comfort 35.42

Job 19:13–14   Loneliness 153.2

Job 19:25   Knowledge 142.2

Job 19:25   Life 150.5

Job 19:25   Redemption 199.2

Job 20:5   Godless 104.1

Job 25:4–6   Human beings 125.20

Job 27:8   Godless 104.2

Job 30:15   Dignity 59.4

Job 30:20–21   Cruelty 48.1

Job 33:15–16   Visions 267.4

Job 34:4   Choice 30.5

Job 36:15   Suffering 248.13

Job 38:39–40   Animals 9.5

Job 39:1–5   Animals 9.5

Job 39:9–10, 19   Animals 9.6

Job 40:15–16, 25   Animals 9.7

Job 42:2   God 103.5

Job 42:11   Sympathy 249.2

Joel 2:12–13   Fasting 87.4

Joel 2:12–13   Repentance 203.4

Joel 2:25   Restoration 208.10

Joel 2:28   Dreams 67.7

Joel 2:28   Holy Spirit 119.7

Joel 2:28   Revival 212.5

Joel 2:28   Visions 267.10

Joel 2:32   Salvation and Savior 221.2

Joel 3:14   Decisions 53.9

1 John 1:3   Fellowship 89.10

1 John 1:5   Darkness 49.15

1 John 1:5   Light 151.21

1 John 1:6–7   Fellowship 89.11

1 John 1:6–7   Light 151.22

1 John 1:7   Blood 23.11

1 John 1:7, 9   Assurance 12.10

1 John 1:7–9   Sin 236.20

1 John 1:8, 10   Sinful nature 237.14

1 John 1:9   Confession 38.11

1 John 1:9   Forgiveness 92.16

1 John 1:9   God 103.46

1 John 2:2   Atonement 13.12

1 John 2:2   Propitiation 191.7

1 John 2:3   Knowledge 142.17

1 John 2:4   Lying 156.8

1 John 2:9–11   Darkness 49.16

1 John 2:13   Evil 79.14

1 John 2:14   Youth 284.12

1 John 2:15–16   Desire, wrong 56.9

1 John 2:15–17   World 281.8

1 John 2:16   Ambition 6.23

1 John 2:17   Will of God 276.9

1 John 2:18   Antichrist 10.6

1 John 2:22   Antichrist 10.7

1 John 2:22   Lying 156.9

1 John 2:28   Confidence 39.9

1 John 2:28   Shame 232.9

1 John 3:1   Christian life 31.11

1 John 3:1   Privilege 188.17

1 John 3:1–2   Adoption 5.10

1 John 3:2   Christlikeness 32.12

1 John 3:4–5   Sin 236.21

1 John 3:7–8   Right and wrong 215.13

1 John 3:8   Devil 58.14

1 John 3:9   New birth 169.8

1 John 3:9   Sin 236.22

1 John 3:14   Life 150.35

1 John 3:15   Murder 165.7

1 John 3:16   Christlikeness 32.13

1 John 3:16   Unselfishness 265.13

1 John 3:17   Riches 214.10

1 John 3:17   Selfishness 228.13

1 John 3:19–21   Heart 116.17

1 John 3:20–21   Conscience 40.8

1 John 3:21   Confidence 39.10

1 John 3:22   Obedience 170.14

1 John 3:22   Prayer 184.48

1 John 3:23   Will of God 276.10

1 John 4:1   Examination 80.5

1 John 4:1–2   Teachers, false 251.10

1 John 4:2   Jesus Christ 135.64

1 John 4:3   Antichrist 10.8

1 John 4:4   Victory 266.9

1 John 4:6   Listening 152.12

1 John 4:7   Birth 18.13

1 John 4:7, 11–12   Love 154.22

1 John 4:8–10   Love 154.9

1 John 4:10   God 103.49

1 John 4:10   Propitiation 191.8

1 John 4:13   Assurance 12.11

1 John 4:14   Salvation and Savior 221.20

1 John 4:15   Confession 38.4

1 John 4:17   Confidence 39.11

1 John 4:18   Fear 88.12

1 John 4:20–21   Love 154.33

1 John 5:1   Birth 18.14

1 John 5:1   Faith 82.31

1 John 5:2   Love 154.23

1 John 5:2   Obedience 170.15

1 John 5:4   Faith 82.32

1 John 5:4   Victory 266.10

1 John 5:11–12   Eternal life 77.14

1 John 5:12   Assurance 12.12

1 John 5:12   Life 150.36

1 John 5:12   Unbeliever 262.9

1 John 5:14   Confidence 39.12

1 John 5:14   Prayer 184.30

1 John 5:14   Prayer 184.49

1 John 5:19   Devil 58.15

1 John 5:21   Idolatry 128.6

2 John v. 7   Antichrist 10.9

3 John v. 2   Health and wholeness 115.13

3 John v. 4   Joy 137.22

3 John v. 11   Sin 236.37

John 1:1–2   Jesus Christ 135.31

John 1:4–5   Light 151.9

John 1:5   Darkness 49.9

John 1:7–9   Light 151.10

John 1:11   Rejection 200.8

John 1:12   Adoption 5.4

John 1:12   Authority 14.9

John 1:12   Christian life 31.20

John 1:12   Faith 82.9

John 1:12–13   Birth 18.10

John 1:14   Fullness 96.2

John 1:14   Grace 108.2

John 1:14   Jesus Christ 135.55

John 1:14   Truth 260.3

John 1:16   Fullness 96.3

John 1:16–17   Grace 108.3

John 1:29   Sin 236.9

John 2:11   Glory 102.7

John 2:11   Miracles 161.7

John 2:24–25   Human beings 125.11

John 3:3   Kingdom, kingdom of God 141.9

John 3:3–8   Birth 18.11

John 3:3–8   New birth 169.3

John 3:5   Water 272.7

John 3:5–6   Holy Spirit 119.14

John 3:8   Sovereignty of God 240.5

John 3:16   Christian life 31.21

John 3:16   Eternal life 77.3

John 3:16   Faith 82.10

John 3:16   Gift 100.1

John 3:16   God 103.48

John 3:16   Love 154.3

John 3:16–17   Jesus Christ 135.56

John 3:16–17   World 281.4

John 3:17   Salvation and Savior 221.9

John 3:18   Faith 82.11

John 3:18   Punishment 193.5

John 3:18–19   Unbeliever 262.1

John 3:19   Evil 79.8

John 3:19–21   Light 151.11

John 3:20   Hatred 113.6

John 3:21   Truth 260.4

John 3:30   Self-denial 226.3

John 3:36   Anger 8.6

John 3:36   Eternal life 77.4

John 4:6   Journeys 136.9

John 4:6   Tiredness 257.5

John 4:14   Water 272.8

John 4:23–24   God 103.57

John 4:23–24   Spirit 242.7

John 4:23–24   Worship 283.7

John 4:34   Food and drink 90.11

John 4:34   Jesus Christ 135.88

John 4:34   Will of God 276.3

John 5:24   Life 150.17

John 5:26   God 103.56

John 5:26–27   Authority 14.10

John 5:27   Jesus Christ 135.13

John 5:28–29   Last things 144.51

John 5:30   Unselfishness 265.3

John 5:39–40   Bible 17.3

John 5:39–40   Eternal life 77.5

John 5:40   Hardness 112.7

John 6:27   Ambition 6.20

John 6:28–29   Works, good 280.5

John 6:29   Faith 82.12

John 6:35   Contentment 41.4

John 6:35   Life 150.18

John 6:35   Water 272.9

John 6:37   Assurance 12.1

John 6:37   Christian life 31.22

John 6:37   Election 72.3

John 6:37   Sovereignty of God 240.6

John 6:44   Election 72.4

John 6:53–56   Food and drink 90.12

John 6:68   Life 150.19

John 6:68–69   Eternal life 77.6

John 7:6   Time 256.7

John 7:7   Hatred 113.7

John 7:13   Fear 88.9

John 7:16   Teachers and teaching 250.4

John 7:37–39   Water 272.10

John 7:38–39   Heart 116.11

John 7:38–39   Holy Spirit 119.15

John 7:39   Jesus Christ 135.3

John 8:7   Sinful nature 237.5

John 8:12   Light 151.12

John 8:24   Unbeliever 262.2

John 8:29   Jesus Christ 135.89

John 8:31   Disciples 61.4

John 8:31, 51   Christian life 31.30

John 8:31–32   Truth 260.5

John 8:31–32, 34–36   Freedom 93.2

John 8:34   Sin 236.10

John 8:44   Devil 58.5

John 8:44   Lying 156.5

John 8:46   Jesus Christ 135.37

John 8:51   Death 51.9

John 8:58   Jesus Christ 135.32

John 9:1–3   Suffering 248.15

John 9:39–41   Blindness 22.11

John 10:10   Life 150.20

John 10:11   Jesus Christ 135.18

John 10:11   Shepherd 233.8

John 10:14–15   Knowledge 142.9

John 10:18   Authority 14.11

John 10:18   Jesus Christ 135.14

John 10:27–28   Eternal life 77.7

John 10:28   Assurance 12.2

John 10:28   Life 150.21

John 11:3   Illness 129.5

John 11:9   Time 256.8

John 11:24–25   Last things 144.52

John 11:25   Life 150.22

John 11:25–26   Comfort 35.21

John 11:26   Last things 144.70

John 11:35   Grief 109.12

John 11:35   Mourning 164.12

John 12:4–6   Motives 163.9

John 12:6   Stealing 244.5

John 12:21   Christian life 31.49

John 12:25   Eternal life 77.8

John 12:25   Self-denial 226.4

John 12:26   Service 230.5

John 12:35   Darkness 49.10

John 12:42   Pharisees 180.9

John 12:48   Rejection 200.9

John 13:1   Jesus Christ 135.81

John 13:3–5, 14   Humility 126.5

John 13:12–14   Service 230.6

John 13:34–35   Love 154.16

John 13:35   Disciples 61.5

John 14:1   Faith 82.13

John 14:1   Worry 282.10

John 14:2–3   Last things 144.12

John 14:3   Comfort 35.22

John 14:3   Last things 144.60

John 14:6   Access 3.2

John 14:6   Christian life 31.23

John 14:6   Life 150.23

John 14:6   Truth 260.6

John 14:6   Way 273.9

John 14:12   Miracles 161.8

John 14:13   Name 167.9

John 14:13   Prayer 184.45

John 14:15   Love 154.27

John 14:15   Obedience 170.6

John 14:16–17   Holy Spirit 119.16

John 14:18   Comfort 35.38

John 14:18   Loyalty 155.12

John 14:19   Life 150.24

John 14:21   Love 154.28

John 14:26   Bible 17.4

John 14:26   Holy Spirit 119.17

John 14:26   Name 167.10

John 14:26   Remembering 201.13

John 14:26   Teachers and teaching 250.5

John 14:27   Comfort 35.10

John 14:27   Peace 177.12

John 14:27   Worry 282.11

John 15:4, 7   Prayer 184.46

John 15:5, 8   Fruit 95.4

John 15:5, 9   Christian life 31.31

John 15:6   Falling away 85.6

John 15:8   Disciples 61.6

John 15:9   Jesus Christ 135.82

John 15:11   Joy 137.11

John 15:13   Love 154.17

John 15:13   Unselfishness 265.4

John 15:13–15   Friends and friendship 94.10

John 15:16   Choice 30.11

John 15:16   Election 72.5

John 15:16   Fruit 95.5

John 15:18–19   Hatred 113.8

John 15:18–19   World 281.5

John 15:20   Persecution 179.5

John 15:26   Holy Spirit 119.18

John 15:26–27   Witness 278.9

John 16:1   Falling away 85.7

John 16:7–11, 13–14   Holy Spirit 119.19

John 16:8–9   Conviction of sin 43.4

John 16:8–9   Unbelief 261.8

John 16:13   Guidance 110.5

John 16:13   Truth 260.7

John 16:21   Birth 18.12

John 16:23–24   Prayer 184.47

John 16:24   Joy 137.12

John 16:33   Courage 45.6

John 16:33   Peace 177.13

John 16:33   Stress 246.10

John 16:33   Victory 266.2

John 17:2   Authority 14.12

John 17:3   Eternal life 77.9

John 17:3   Knowledge 142.10

John 17:3   Privilege 188.5

John 17:5   Glory 102.8

John 17:6   Election 72.6

John 17:11   Christian life 31.32

John 17:11   World 281.6

John 17:16   World 281.7

John 17:17   Sanctification 222.1

John 17:17   Truth 260.8

John 17:18, 20–21   Witness 278.10

John 17:21   Unity 264.5

John 17:24   Access 3.3

John 17:24   Last things 144.13

John 18:36   Jesus Christ 135.48

John 18:38   Truth 260.9

John 19:19   Israel 133.4

John 19:19, 21   Jesus Christ 135.49

John 19:26–27   Homes 120.14

John 19:26–27   Jesus Christ 135.109

John 19:28   Jesus Christ 135.110

John 19:30   Jesus Christ 135.111

John 20:17   Jesus Christ 135.4

John 20:19   Peace 177.14

John 20:20–21   God 103.28

John 20:25   Doubt 66.8

John 20:25, 27   Unbelief 261.9

John 20:28   Jesus Christ 135.68

John 20:31   Faith 82.14

John 20:31   Life 150.25

Jonah 2:1–2   Stress 246.5

Jonah 2:7   Despair 57.14

Jonah 2:7   Weakness 274.3

Jonah 4:5   Waiting 269.13

Joshua 1:6–9   Courage 45.1

Joshua 1:8   Meditation 158.1

Joshua 1:9   Discouragement 63.4

Joshua 7:5   Fear 88.3

Joshua 21:45   Failure 81.1

Joshua 24:15   Choice 30.3

Joshua 24:15   Family 86.11

Jude v. 1   Christian life 31.12

Jude v. 3   Zeal 285.11

Jude vv. 3–4   Teachers, false 251.11

Jude v. 6   Last things 144.40

Jude v. 17   Remembering 201.17

Jude vv. 21, 24   Christian life 31.41

Judges 3:10   Holy Spirit 119.3

Judges 5:3   Music 166.1

Judges 8:21   Human beings 125.19

Judges 12:5–6   Speech 241.1

Judges 17:6   Right and wrong 215.2

Judith 16:2   Music 166.12

K

1 Kings 2:1–2   Death 51.3

1 Kings 3:9   Discernment 60.1

1 Kings 3:9   Right and wrong 215.4

1 Kings 4:29–30   Wisdom 277.1

1 Kings 5:6   Abilities 1.3

1 Kings 8:27   God 103.39

1 Kings 8:27   God 103.58

1 Kings 17:6   Food and drink 90.4

1 Kings 17:21–22   Healing 114.1

1 Kings 18:21   Choice 30.4

1 Kings 18:37–38   Miracles 161.3

1 Kings 19:4   Journeys 136.3

1 Kings 19:10   Loneliness 153.1

1 Kings 19:11–13   Quiet 195.1

1 Kings 20:34   Restitution 207.7

2 Kings 2:9   Spirit 242.1

2 Kings 5:14   Healing 114.2

2 Kings 22:2   Right and wrong 215.5

2 Kings 23:1–3   Renewal 202.1

2 Kings 23:21–23   Celebration 27.3

L

Lamentations 3:15   Bitterness 19.7

Lamentations 3:17, 19–24   Depression 55.7

Lamentations 3:21–23   Comfort 35.32

Lamentations 3:21–23   Failure 81.4

Lamentations 3:22–23   Faithfulness 83.3

Lamentations 3:22–23   God 103.16

Lamentations 3:22–23   Mercy 159.6

Lamentations 3:25   Seeking God 224.10

Lamentations 3:26   Quiet 195.9

Lamentations 3:26   Waiting 269.11

Lamentations 3:27   Youth 284.7

Lamentations 5:14–15   Music 166.10

Lamentations 5:21   Renewal 202.6

Leviticus 1:4   Atonement 13.1

Leviticus 1:4   Sacrifice 220.3

Leviticus 5:5   Confession 38.5

Leviticus 5:15–16   Restitution 207.2

Leviticus 11:44   Holiness 118.3

Leviticus 16:10   Sin 236.1

Leviticus 16:21   Laying on of hands 147.2

Leviticus 17:11   Blood 23.1

Leviticus 18:22   Homosexuality 121.1

Leviticus 19:11   Dishonesty 64.1

Leviticus 19:13   Justice 138.1

Leviticus 19:15   Injustice 132.2

Leviticus 19:16   Gossip 107.1

Leviticus 19:18   Love 154.11

Leviticus 19:18   Neighbour 168.2

Leviticus 19:18   Retaliation 209.1

Leviticus 19:26   Occult 171.1

Leviticus 19:30   Respect 204.3

Leviticus 19:31   Occult 171.2

Leviticus 19:32   Old age 172.1

Leviticus 19:32   Respect 204.4

Leviticus 19:33–34   Immigrants 130.2

Leviticus 19:34   Love 154.12

Leviticus 19:35   Injustice 132.3

Leviticus 20:13   Homosexuality 121.2

Leviticus 20:27   Occult 171.3

Leviticus 23:1   Celebration 27.1

Leviticus 23:27   Fasting 87.1

Leviticus 24:18   Restitution 207.3

Leviticus 25:10–11   Land 143.2

Leviticus 25:23   Land 143.3

Leviticus 26:13   Dignity 59.3

Luke 1:21–22   Visions 267.13

Luke 1:26   Angels 7.6

Luke 1:35   Holy Spirit 119.12

Luke 1:37   God 103.6

Luke 1:37   Miracles 161.6

Luke 1:46   Soul 239.8

Luke 1:51   Pride 186.5

Luke 1:53   Riches 214.4

Luke 2:6–7   Birth 18.9

Luke 2:7   Jesus Christ 135.54

Luke 2:10   Comfort 35.8

Luke 2:11   Salvation and Savior 221.6

Luke 2:14   Peace 177.9

Luke 2:19   Meditation 158.8

Luke 2:20   Shepherd 233.7

Luke 2:22   Human beings 125.21

Luke 2:25   Waiting 269.15

Luke 2:29   Peace 177.10

Luke 2:32   Gentiles 98.3

Luke 2:36–37   Old age 172.8

Luke 2:36–37   Widows 275.6

Luke 2:41   Passover 174.3

Luke 2:51–52   Family 86.21

Luke 2:52   Wisdom 277.11

Luke 3:14   Contentment 41.3

Luke 4:14   Power 182.6

Luke 4:18   Poverty 181.9

Luke 4:18–21   Gospel 106.4

Luke 4:36   Jesus Christ 135.12

Luke 5:8   Conviction of sin 43.3

Luke 5:8   Jesus Christ 135.67

Luke 5:17   Pharisees 180.4

Luke 5:30–32   Pharisees 180.5

Luke 5:32   Repentance 203.7

Luke 6:21, 25   Laughter 145.11

Luke 6:25   Mourning 164.11

Luke 6:35   Reward 213.7

Luke 6:36   Mercy 159.11

Luke 6:38   Generosity 97.7

Luke 6:38   Giving 101.6

Luke 6:46   Hypocrisy 127.4

Luke 6:46   Works, good 280.4

Luke 7:13   Sympathy 249.8

Luke 7:16   Jesus Christ 135.78

Luke 7:39   Pharisees 180.6

Luke 8:1   Journeys 136.6

Luke 8:12   Unbelief 261.7

Luke 8:15   Honesty 122.2

Luke 8:27   Demons 54.6

Luke 9:1   Demons 54.7

Luke 9:1–3, 6   Journeys 136.7

Luke 9:23–24   Self-denial 226.2

Luke 10:5–6   Peace 177.11

Luke 10:7   Work 279.9

Luke 10:17–20   Warfare, spiritual 271.2

Luke 10:23–24   Privilege 188.3

Luke 10:29–37   Neighbor 168.3

Luke 10:30, 33–35   Kindness 140.3

Luke 10:38   Homes 120.13

Luke 10:41–42   Worry 282.8

Luke 11:13   Holy Spirit 119.13

Luke 11:14   Demons 54.8

Luke 11:36   Health and wholeness 115.11

Luke 11:38–39   Pharisees 180.7

Luke 12:5   Authority 14.8

Luke 12:11–12   Worry 282.9

Luke 12:15   Desire, wrong 56.5

Luke 12:20   Fools and folly 91.7

Luke 12:32   Comfort 35.9

Luke 12:33–34   Failure 81.9

Luke 12:48   Privilege 188.4

Luke 13:3   Repentance 203.8

Luke 13:23–24   Salvation and Savior 221.7

Luke 13:24   Ambition 6.3

Luke 14:12–13   Caring 26.4

Luke 14:13   Poverty 181.10

Luke 14:25–27   Christian life 31.19

Luke 14:26–27, 33   Disciples 61.3

Luke 15:7   Joy 137.10

Luke 15:7   Repentance 203.9

Luke 15:10   Angels 7.7

Luke 15:10   Celebration 27.7

Luke 15:11–13   Journeys 136.8

Luke 15:11–24   Youth 284.9

Luke 15:17–18   Repentance 203.10

Luke 15:25, 28–30   Jealousy 134.5

Luke 16:1–3   Stewardship 245.2

Luke 16:8   Dishonesty 64.12

Luke 16:8   Wisdom 277.12

Luke 16:10   Dishonesty 64.13

Luke 16:10   Faithfulness 83.6

Luke 16:19–26   Last things 144.68

Luke 16:19–28   Riches 214.5

Luke 16:26   Last things 144.27

Luke 17:1   Temptation 253.7

Luke 17:16–18   Thankfulness and thanksgiving 254.3

Luke 17:20–21   Kingdom, kingdom of God 141.8

Luke 18:1   Prayer 184.15

Luke 18:9–12   Pharisees 180.8

Luke 18:9–14   Self-righteousness 229.6

Luke 18:12   Fasting 87.8

Luke 18:13   Mercy 159.12

Luke 18:13   Propitiation 191.2

Luke 18:13–14   Justification 139.6

Luke 18:18   Eternal life 77.2

Luke 18:18   Rulers 218.8

Luke 18:22–25   Riches 214.6

Luke 19:8   Restitution 207.11

Luke 19:10   Salvation and Savior 221.8

Luke 19:40   Silence 234.11

Luke 19:41–42   Grief 109.9

Luke 20:13–15   Respect 204.8

Luke 21:12   Persecution 179.4

Luke 21:26   Fear 88.8

Luke 22:4   Priest 187.7

Luke 22:13   Passover 174.4

Luke 22:19   Remembering 201.11

Luke 22:22   Sovereignty of God 240.4

Luke 22:31–32   Failure 81.10

Luke 22:31–32   Temptation 253.15

Luke 22:32   Conversion 42.4

Luke 22:44   Stress 246.9

Luke 22:45   Grief 109.10

Luke 22:46   Sleep 238.11

Luke 22:61–62   Failure 81.11

Luke 22:61–62   Grief 109.11

Luke 22:63–65   Cruelty 48.8

Luke 23:9   Silence 234.12

Luke 23:34   Jesus Christ 135.106

Luke 23:42   Remembering 201.12

Luke 23:43   Jesus Christ 135.107

Luke 23:43   Last things 144.69

Luke 23:46   Jesus Christ 135.108

Luke 24:19   Jesus Christ 135.79

Luke 24:23   Visions 267.14

Luke 24:26   Jesus Christ 135.1

Luke 24:26   Suffering 248.5

Luke 24:46–48   Witness 278.8

Luke 24:47   Name 167.8

Luke 24:47   Preaching 185.3

Luke 24:47   Repentance 203.11

Luke 24:49   Promise 189.1

Luke 24:51   Jesus Christ 135.2

M

2 Maccabees 7:9   Death 51.8

Malachi 1:13   Ritual 217.4

Malachi 2:7   Authority 14.1

Malachi 2:10   God 103.24

Malachi 2:15–16   Marriage 157.12

Malachi 3:6   God 103.69

Malachi 3:7   Falling away 85.4

Malachi 3:10   Blessing 21.5

Malachi 3:10   Giving 101.3

Mark 1:14–15   Gospel 106.2

Mark 1:15   Kingdom, kingdom of God 141.6

Mark 1:15   Repentance 203.6

Mark 1:15   Time 256.6

Mark 1:27   Authority 14.7

Mark 2:27–28   Sabbath 219.5

Mark 3:5   Anger 8.5

Mark 3:5   Hardness 112.6

Mark 3:5   Restoration 208.12

Mark 3:10   Illness 129.4

Mark 3:11   Demons 54.4

Mark 3:22   Demons 54.5

Mark 4:4–5   Failure 81.7

Mark 4:12   Conversion 42.3

Mark 4:39   Peace 177.8

Mark 4:40   Fear 88.7

Mark 4:41   Reverence 211.8

Mark 5:22   Rulers 218.7

Mark 5:30   Power 182.5

Mark 6:5   Laying on of hands 147.4

Mark 6:6   Unbelief 261.4

Mark 6:31   Rest 206.3

Mark 7:9   Rejection 200.7

Mark 7:11–12   Family 86.19

Mark 7:20–22   Heart 116.10

Mark 7:20–22   Pride 186.4

Mark 7:21   Evil 79.7

Mark 7:21   Stealing 244.4

Mark 8:35   Selfishness 228.6

Mark 8:38   Glory 102.6

Mark 8:38   Shame 232.3

Mark 9:7   Listening 152.9

Mark 9:23–24   Faith 82.7

Mark 9:23–24   Unbelief 261.5

Mark 9:28–29   Prayer 184.2

Mark 10:13–16   Family 86.20

Mark 10:15   Kingdom, kingdom of God 141.7

Mark 10:16   Blessing 21.6

Mark 10:16   Laying on of hands 147.5

Mark 10:18   God 103.34

Mark 10:18   Good 105.4

Mark 10:29–30   Homes 120.12

Mark 10:36–37   Ambition 6.18

Mark 10:43   Humility 126.4

Mark 10:43   Leadership 149.5

Mark 10:43–44   Ambition 6.19

Mark 10:43–45   Service 230.4

Mark 10:45   Atonement 13.3

Mark 10:45   Redemption 199.5

Mark 11:22, 24   Faith 82.8

Mark 12:31   Unselfishness 265.2

Mark 12:41–44   Widows 275.5

Mark 12:42–44   Giving 101.5

Mark 12:42–44   Self-denial 226.1

Mark 12:43–44   Poverty 181.8

Mark 13:10   Witness 278.6

Mark 13:35–37   Sleep 238.10

Mark 14:32–36   Stress 246.8

Mark 14:37   Failure 81.8

Mark 14:43   Scribes 223.7

Mark 14:53   Priest 187.6

Mark 15:43   Waiting 269.14

Mark 16:14   Unbelief 261.6

Mark 16:15   Creation 47.7

Mark 16:15   Gospel 106.3

Mark 16:15–16   Witness 278.7

Matthew 1:20   Dreams 67.8

Matthew 1:21   Salvation and Savior 221.3

Matthew 1:21   Sin 236.8

Matthew 2:11   Jesus Christ 135.65

Matthew 2:11   Worship 283.5

Matthew 3:7   Anger 8.4

Matthew 3:8   Fruit 95.2

Matthew 3:8   Repentance 203.5

Matthew 3:11   Baptism 15.1

Matthew 3:11   Holy Spirit 119.9

Matthew 3:11   Water 272.6

Matthew 3:16   Baptism 15.2

Matthew 3:16   Holy Spirit 119.10

Matthew 3:16   Peace 177.5

Matthew 3:16–17   Trinity 259.2

Matthew 4:1   Devil 58.3

Matthew 4:1   Temptation 253.4

Matthew 4:2   Fasting 87.5

Matthew 4:4   Bible 17.2

Matthew 4:10   Service 230.2

Matthew 4:10   Worship 283.6

Matthew 4:19   Witness 278.3

Matthew 4:23   Healing 114.6

Matthew 5:1–11   Christian life 31.14

Matthew 5:3   Humility 126.2

Matthew 5:3   Kingdom, kingdom of God 141.1

Matthew 5:3   Poverty 181.6

Matthew 5:3   Spirit 242.4

Matthew 5:4   Comfort 35.20

Matthew 5:4   Mourning 164.10

Matthew 5:6   Ambition 6.2

Matthew 5:6   Righteousness 216.7

Matthew 5:7   Mercy 159.10

Matthew 5:8   Heart 116.8

Matthew 5:8   Purity 194.3

Matthew 5:9   Peace 177.6

Matthew 5:10–12   Persecution 179.1

Matthew 5:11–12   Reward 213.4

Matthew 5:13–16   Christian life 31.2

Matthew 5:14–16   Light 151.8

Matthew 5:16   Character 29.4

Matthew 5:16   Works, good 280.3

Matthew 5:17   Law 146.3

Matthew 5:20   Righteousness 216.8

Matthew 5:20   Scribes 223.2

Matthew 5:21–22   Anger 8.14

Matthew 5:21–22   Murder 165.6

Matthew 5:23–24   Reconciliation 198.2

Matthew 5:25–26   Debt 52.9

Matthew 5:27–28   Marriage 157.11

Matthew 5:31–32   Marriage 157.13

Matthew 5:38–42   Retaliation 209.4

Matthew 5:41–42   Generosity 97.6

Matthew 5:43–44   Enemy 75.5

Matthew 5:44   Bitterness 19.9

Matthew 5:44   Persecution 179.2

Matthew 5:44–45   Adoption 5.1

Matthew 5:44–45   God 103.25

Matthew 5:44, 46   Love 154.13

Matthew 5:48   Character 29.5

Matthew 5:48   Perfection 178.3

Matthew 6:1   Motives 163.8

Matthew 6:1   Self-righteousness 229.4

Matthew 6:2–3   Giving 101.4

Matthew 6:2, 5, 16   Hypocrisy 127.1

Matthew 6:5–8   Prayer 184.26

Matthew 6:6   Prayer 184.14

Matthew 6:7–9   Prayer 184.31

Matthew 6:9   Adoption 5.2

Matthew 6:9   God 103.26

Matthew 6:9   Name 167.5

Matthew 6:9, 13   Sin 236.27

Matthew 6:9–10   Last things 144.11

Matthew 6:9–13   Prayer 184.32

Matthew 6:10   Accepting the will of God 2.5

Matthew 6:10   Earth, the 69.13

Matthew 6:10   Kingdom, kingdom of God 141.2

Matthew 6:11   Food and drink 90.10

Matthew 6:12   Debt 52.10

Matthew 6:12   Forgiveness 92.7

Matthew 6:13   Power 182.2

Matthew 6:13   Prayer 184.33

Matthew 6:13   Temptation 253.5

Matthew 6:14–15   Forgiveness 92.8

Matthew 6:16–18   Fasting 87.6

Matthew 6:19   Money and material goods 162.2

Matthew 6:21   Heart 116.9

Matthew 6:24   Decisions 53.10

Matthew 6:24   Loyalty 155.11

Matthew 6:24   Money and material goods 162.3

Matthew 6:25   Life 150.12

Matthew 6:25, 27   Worry 282.6

Matthew 6:25–33   Comfort 35.12

Matthew 6:31–33   Adoption 5.3

Matthew 6:31–34   Worry 282.7

Matthew 6:33   Kingdom, kingdom of God 141.3

Matthew 6:33   Righteousness 216.9

Matthew 6:34   Evil 79.5

Matthew 7:5   Hypocrisy 127.2

Matthew 7:7–8   Prayer 184.42

Matthew 7:7–8   Seeking God 224.12

Matthew 7:12   Love 154.14

Matthew 7:13   Last things 144.23

Matthew 7:13–14   Way 273.8

Matthew 7:14   Life 150.13

Matthew 7:15–16   Teachers, false 251.2

Matthew 7:16   Fruit 95.3

Matthew 7:21   Kingdom, kingdom of God 141.4

Matthew 7:21   Obedience 170.5

Matthew 7:22–23   Prophets and prophecy 190.3

Matthew 7:24   Wisdom 277.8

Matthew 7:26   Fools and folly 91.6

Matthew 7:29   Authority 14.2

Matthew 7:29   Jesus Christ 135.9

Matthew 7:29   Scribes 223.3

Matthew 8:2–3   Illness 129.8

Matthew 8:8–9   Authority 14.3

Matthew 8:12   Grief 109.7

Matthew 8:12   Last things 144.24

Matthew 8:16   Demons 54.1

Matthew 8:19   Scribes 223.4

Matthew 8:20   Homes 120.10

Matthew 8:26   Faith 82.6

Matthew 8:31   Demons 54.2

Matthew 9:2   Courage 45.4

Matthew 9:6   Authority 14.4

Matthew 9:6   Forgiveness 92.9

Matthew 9:6   Jesus Christ 135.10

Matthew 9:13   Sacrifice 220.7

Matthew 9:15   Fasting 87.7

Matthew 9:22   Courage 45.5

Matthew 9:22   Health and wholeness 115.10

Matthew 9:29–30   Restoration 208.11

Matthew 9:36   Jesus Christ 135.80

Matthew 9:36   Sympathy 249.5

Matthew 9:37   Witness 278.4

Matthew 10:1   Authority 14.5

Matthew 10:1   Disciples 61.1

Matthew 10:1   Healing 114.7

Matthew 10:1–4   Apostles 11.1

Matthew 10:11–14   Homes 120.11

Matthew 10:14   Rejection 200.6

Matthew 10:16   Simplicity 235.5

Matthew 10:16   Wisdom 277.9

Matthew 10:19   Comfort 35.13

Matthew 10:22   Endurance 74.1

Matthew 10:24   Service 230.3

Matthew 10:24–25   Christlikeness 32.2

Matthew 10:26   Fear 88.5

Matthew 10:28   Fear 88.6

Matthew 10:28   Last things 144.25

Matthew 10:28   Soul 239.5

Matthew 10:29–31   Providence 192.8

Matthew 10:32   Confession 38.1

Matthew 10:32–33   Last things 144.33

Matthew 10:34   Peace 177.7

Matthew 10:37   Family 86.18

Matthew 11:2–3   Doubt 66.4

Matthew 11:5   Blindness 22.9

Matthew 11:15   Listening 152.8

Matthew 11:19   Friends and friendship 94.8

Matthew 11:19   Wisdom 277.10

Matthew 11:25   Simplicity 235.6

Matthew 11:27   Election 72.1

Matthew 11:27   Knowledge 142.8

Matthew 11:27   Revelation 210.3

Matthew 11:28 Christian life 31.18

Matthew 11:28 Comfort 35.14

Matthew 11:28 Stress 246.6

Matthew 11:28 Tiredness 257.4

Matthew 11:28–30 Rest 206.2

Matthew 11:29 Gentleness 99.1

Matthew 11:29 Soul 239.6

Matthew 12:11–12 Sabbath 219.4

Matthew 12:14 Pharisees 180.1

Matthew 12:31 Blasphemy 20.4

Matthew 12:31 Forgiveness 92.10

Matthew 12:31 Holy Spirit 119.11

Matthew 12:36 Speech 241.6

Matthew 12:36–37 Gossip 107.9

Matthew 13:10–11 Privilege 188.2

Matthew 13:19 Devil 58.4

Matthew 13:19, 23 Understanding 263.7

Matthew 13:20–21 Joy 137.9

Matthew 13:21 Endurance 74.2

Matthew 13:21 Persecution 179.3

Matthew 13:21 Suffering 248.2

Matthew 13:22 Stress 246.7

Matthew 13:57 Prophets and prophecy 190.4

Matthew 13:58 Unbelief 261.2

Matthew 14:14 Sympathy 249.6

Matthew 14:26–27 Comfort 35.7

Matthew 14:31 Doubt 66.5

Matthew 15:7–9 Hypocrisy 127.3

Matthew 15:9 Teachers, false 251.3

Matthew 15:14 Blindness 22.10

Matthew 15:25 Help 117.4

Matthew 16:16 Jesus Christ 135.66

Matthew 16:16–17 Revelation 210.4

Matthew 16:18 Church 33.1

Matthew 16:21 Jesus Christ 135.17

Matthew 16:21 Jesus Christ 135.94

Matthew 16:26 Ambition 6.17

Matthew 16:26 Life 150.14

Matthew 17:2 Glory 102.5

Matthew 17:17 Unbelief 261.3

Matthew 18:3 Conversion 42.2

Matthew 18:3 Simplicity 235.7

Matthew 18:4 Humility 126.3

Matthew 18:10 Angels 7.4

Matthew 18:10 Love 154.15

Matthew 18:10 Respect 204.7

Matthew 18:15–18 Discipline 62.2

Matthew 18:17 Church 33.2

Matthew 18:19–20 Prayer 184.43

Matthew 18:19–20 Unity 264.4

Matthew 18:20 Name 167.6

Matthew 19:6 Marriage 157.3

Matthew 19:7–9 Marriage 157.14

Matthew 19:8 Hardness 112.5

Matthew 19:10–12 Celibacy 28.1

Matthew 19:21 Perfection 178.4

Matthew 19:21 Youth 284.8

Matthew 19:25–26 Salvation and Savior 221.4

Matthew 19:27–29 Reward 213.5

Matthew 19:28 Israel 133.3

Matthew 19:28 Last things 144.43

Matthew 20:1 Work 279.8

Matthew 20:6 Time 256.5

Matthew 20:25–26 Rulers 218.6

Matthew 20:27–28 Christlikeness 32.3

Matthew 20:34 Sympathy 249.7

Matthew 21:11 Jesus Christ 135.77

Matthew 21:13 Stealing 244.3

Matthew 21:15 Scribes 223.5

Matthew 21:21 Doubt 66.6

Matthew 21:22 Prayer 184.44

Matthew 22:15 Pharisees 180.2

Matthew 22:17–21 Money and material goods 162.4

Matthew 22:21 State, responsibility to 243.1

Matthew 22:29 Power 182.3

Matthew 22:30 Marriage 157.4

Matthew 22:32 Last things 144.50

Matthew 22:32   Life 150.15

Matthew 22:37   Mind 160.2

Matthew 22:37–39   Responsibility, human 205.3

Matthew 22:42   Thought 255.5

Matthew 23:2–7   Scribes 223.6

Matthew 23:9   God 103.27

Matthew 23:12   Pride 186.3

Matthew 23:13   Pharisees 180.3

Matthew 23:25–28   Ritual 217.5

Matthew 23:28   Self-righteousness 229.5

Matthew 24:4–5   Teachers, false 251.4

Matthew 24:5, 24   Antichrist 10.3

Matthew 24:6   Last things 144.1

Matthew 24:6–7   War 270.7

Matthew 24:9   Hatred 113.5

Matthew 24:9   Suffering 248.3

Matthew 24:9–14   Last things 144.2

Matthew 24:13   Salvation and Savior 221.5

Matthew 24:14   Gospel 106.1

Matthew 24:21   Suffering 248.4

Matthew 24:21–22   Last things 144.3

Matthew 24:24   Miracles 161.5

Matthew 24:24   Prophets and prophecy 190.5

Matthew 24:29   Last things 144.4

Matthew 24:29–30, 36   Last things 144.59

Matthew 24:30   Power 182.4

Matthew 24:45   Faithfulness 83.4

Matthew 25:14–15   Stewardship 245.1

Matthew 25:15   Abilities 1.7

Matthew 25:21   Faithfulness 83.5

Matthew 25:24–25   Failure 81.6

Matthew 25:31   Angels 7.5

Matthew 25:31–33   Last things 144.34

Matthew 25:31–36, 40   Kindness 140.2

Matthew 25:34   Election 72.2

Matthew 25:34   Inheritance 131.1

Matthew 25:34   Kingdom, kingdom of God 141.5

Matthew 25:35   Hospitality 124.1

Matthew 25:35   Immigrants 130.5

Matthew 25:41   Demons 54.3

Matthew 25:41, 46   Last things 144.26

Matthew 25:46   Eternal life 77.1

Matthew 25:46   Life 150.16

Matthew 25:46   Punishment 193.4

Matthew 25:46   Reward 213.6

Matthew 26:11   Poverty 181.7

Matthew 26:26   Body 24.1

Matthew 26:26–28   Communion 36.1

Matthew 26:28   Blood 23.2

Matthew 26:28   Covenant 46.4

Matthew 26:31   Falling away 85.5

Matthew 26:31   Shepherd 233.6

Matthew 26:37–38   Grief 109.8

Matthew 26:38   Loneliness 153.3

Matthew 26:38   Soul 239.7

Matthew 26:39   Accepting the will of God 2.6

Matthew 26:41   Prayer 184.34

Matthew 26:41   Spirit 242.5

Matthew 26:41   Temptation 253.6

Matthew 26:41   Weakness 274.4

Matthew 26:42   Jesus Christ 135.87

Matthew 26:50   Friends and friendship 94.9

Matthew 26:56   Loneliness 153.4

Matthew 26:63–65   Blasphemy 20.5

Matthew 27:18   Envy 76.4

Matthew 27:23   Evil 79.6

Matthew 27:24   Responsibility, human 205.4

Matthew 27:46   Jesus Christ 135.105

Matthew 27:46   Loneliness 153.5

Matthew 27:50   Spirit 242.6

Matthew 28:6   Jesus Christ 135.95

Matthew 28:17   Doubt 66.7

Matthew 28:17–18   Authority 14.6

Matthew 28:18   Jesus Christ 135.11

Matthew 28:19   Baptism 15.3

Matthew 28:19   Name 167.7

Matthew 28:19   Trinity 259.3

Matthew 28:19–20   Disciples 61.2

Matthew 28:19–20   Teachers and teaching 250.3

Matthew 28:19–20   Witness 278.5

Micah 3:4   Prayer 184.24

Micah 5:2   Israel 133.2

Micah 5:2   Rulers 218.5

Micah 6:8   Justice 138.10

Micah 6:8   Mercy 159.9

Micah 6:8   Responsibility, human 205.2

Micah 7:3   Bribe 25.5

Micah 7:18   Forgiveness 92.6

N

Nahum 1:15   Vow 268.6

Nehemiah 2:6   Journeys 136.4

Nehemiah 5:2–5   Debt 52.2

Nehemiah 5:11–12   Restitution 207.8

Nehemiah 8:1   Scribes 223.1

Nehemiah 8:9–12   Celebration 27.5

Nehemiah 8:10   Joy 137.1

Nehemiah 9:6   Earth, the 69.4

Nehemiah 9:6   Providence 192.4

Nehemiah 9:33   Right and wrong 215.7

Nehemiah 13:15–18   Sabbath 219.2

Numbers 5:5–7   Restitution 207.4

Numbers 6:24–26   Blessing 21.3

Numbers 6:26   Peace 177.1

Numbers 12:6   Visions 267.2

Numbers 13:1–2   Leadership 149.2

Numbers 14:9   Rebellion 197.1

Numbers 14:21   Glory 102.2

Numbers 14:24   Obedience 170.2

Numbers 21:4   Discouragement 63.1

Numbers 23:19   God 103.68

Numbers 23:19   Lying 156.2

Numbers 32:23   Punishment 193.2

Numbers 32:23   Sin 236.2

Numbers 33:1   Journeys 136.2

O

Obadiah 4   Ambition 6.16

P

1 Peter 1:2   Election 72.13

1 Peter 1:2   Sanctification 222.8

1 Peter 1:2   Trinity 259.7

1 Peter 1:3–4   Inheritance 131.13

1 Peter 1:4–5   Power 182.19

1 Peter 1:5   Christian life 31.39

1 Peter 1:5   Salvation and Savior 221.19

1 Peter 1:6–7   Suffering 248.20

1 Peter 1:6–7   Temptation 253.22

1 Peter 1:8   Joy 137.21

1 Peter 1:8   Love 154.32

1 Peter 1:13   Hope 123.10

1 Peter 1:13–14   Self-control 225.12

1 Peter 1:14–15   Obedience 170.13

1 Peter 1:15   Christian life 31.8

1 Peter 1:15–16   Sin 236.34

1 Peter 1:18–19   Blood 23.10

1 Peter 1:18–19   Redemption 199.17

1 Peter 1:22   Heart 116.16

1 Peter 1:22   Purity 194.8

1 Peter 1:22   Zeal 285.10

1 Peter 1:23   New birth 169.7

1 Peter 2:1   Envy 76.6

1 Peter 2:4   Rejection 200.10

1 Peter 2:5, 9   Priest 187.12

1 Peter 2:7   Christian life 31.51

1 Peter 2:9   Christian life 31.9

1 Peter 2:9   Darkness 49.14

1 Peter 2:9   Election 72.14

1 Peter 2:9   Holiness 118.11

1 Peter 2:9   Light 151.20

1 Peter 2:9–10   Privilege 188.15

1 Peter 2:11   Sin 236.35

1 Peter 2:11   Warfare, spiritual 271.11

1 Peter 2:16–17   State, responsibility to 243.5

1 Peter 2:17   Respect 204.16

1 Peter 2:20   Right and wrong 215.12

1 Peter 2:20–21   Christian life 31.10

1 Peter 2:22   Jesus Christ 135.40

1 Peter 2:24   Atonement 13.10

1 Peter 2:24   Sin 236.19

1 Peter 2:25   Conversion 42.8

1 Peter 2:25   Shepherd 233.10

1 Peter 3:1–7   Family 86.8

1 Peter 3:3–4   Quiet 195.13

1 Peter 3:3–5   Beauty 16.14

1 Peter 3:4   Gentleness 99.8

1 Peter 3:7   Inheritance 131.14

1 Peter 3:8   Sympathy 249.14

1 Peter 3:9   Blessing 21.9

1 Peter 3:10   Speech 241.11

1 Peter 3:15   Reverence 211.15

1 Peter 3:15–16   Speech 241.12

1 Peter 3:18   Access 3.9

1 Peter 3:18   Atonement 13.11

1 Peter 3:18   Christian life 31.29

1 Peter 3:18   Righteousness 216.20

1 Peter 4:7   Self-control 225.13

1 Peter 4:8   Love 154.21

1 Peter 4:9   Hospitality 124.7

1 Peter 4:10   Stewardship 245.7

1 Peter 4:10–11   Abilities 1.12

1 Peter 4:11   Service 230.10

1 Peter 4:12–13   Accepting the will of God 2.9

1 Peter 4:12–13   Comfort 35.55

1 Peter 4:12–13   Temptation 253.23

1 Peter 4:13   Fellowship 89.9

1 Peter 4:15   Gossip 107.14

1 Peter 4:15   Stealing 244.9

1 Peter 4:16   Shame 232.8

1 Peter 5:1–3   Elders 71.12

1 Peter 5:2–3   Caring 26.8

1 Peter 5:3   Leadership 149.11

1 Peter 5:4   Shepherd 233.11

1 Peter 5:5–6   Humility 126.7

1 Peter 5:7   Caring 26.9

1 Peter 5:7   Comfort 35.17

1 Peter 5:7   Worry 282.13

1 Peter 5:8–9   Devil 58.13

1 Peter 5:8–9   Temptation 253.24

1 Peter 5:8–9   Warfare, spiritual 271.12

1 Peter 5:9   Suffering 248.12

2 Peter 1:3–8   Christian life 31.16

2 Peter 1:4   Promise 189.8

2 Peter 1:5–6   Self-control 225.14

2 Peter 1:5–8   Character 29.11

2 Peter 1:10   Christian life 31.40

2 Peter 1:10   Election 72.15

2 Peter 1:10   Responsibility, human 205.10

2 Peter 1:20–21   Bible 17.13

2 Peter 1:21   Holy Spirit 119.42

2 Peter 1:21   Prophets and prophecy 190.14

2 Peter 2:1   Teachers, false 251.9

2 Peter 3:8   Time 256.15

2 Peter 3:9   Repentance 203.18

2 Peter 3:9, 13   Promise 189.9

2 Peter 3:10–13   Last things 144.46

2 Peter 3:11–12   Privilege 188.16

2 Peter 3:13   Earth, the 69.14

2 Peter 3:17–18   Sin 236.36

2 Peter 3:18   Grace 108.17

Philemon vv. 15–18   Restoration 208.15

Philippians 1:5   Fellowship 89.7

Philippians 1:6   Assurance 12.7

Philippians 1:6   Christian life 31.35

Philippians 1:9   Discernment 60.6

Philippians 1:18   Motives 163.11

Philippians 1:21   Death 51.19

Philippians 1:21   Life 150.33

Philippians 1:21   Old age 172.10

Philippians 1:23   Death 51.20

Philippians 1:23   Last things 144.72

Philippians 1:27   Gospel 106.14

Philippians 1:27–28   Courage 45.8

Philippians 2:1–2   Sympathy 249.11

Philippians 2:2   Unity 264.8

Philippians 2:3   Ambition 6.21

Philippians 2:3   Conceit 37.13

Philippians 2:3, 5–11   Humility 126.6

Philippians 2:4   Selfishness 228.10

Philippians 2:5   Christlikeness 32.8

Philippians 2:5   Mind 160.9

Philippians 2:5–8   Jesus Christ 135.58

Philippians 2:6–8   Jesus Christ 135.43

Philippians 2:7–8   Obedience 170.10

Philippians 2:8   Jesus Christ 135.90

Philippians 2:9   Jesus Christ 135.8

Philippians 2:9–10   Name 167.14

Philippians 2:10   Worship 283.10

Philippians 2:11   Confession 38.3

Philippians 2:12–13   Responsibility, human 205.9

Philippians 2:12–13   Reverence 211.13

Philippians 2:12–13   Salvation and Savior 221.15

Philippians 2:12–13   Sovereignty of God 240.11

Philippians 2:15   Light 151.18

Philippians 2:21   Selfishness 228.11

Philippians 3:3   Circumcision 34.6

Philippians 3:3   Israel 133.9

Philippians 3:6–7   Zeal 285.7

Philippians 3:8–14   Ambition 6.6

Philippians 3:8–9   Righteousness 216.18

Philippians 3:10   Knowledge 142.14

Philippians 3:10   Power 182.15

Philippians 3:10–11   Christlikeness 32.9

Philippians 3:12   Perfection 178.8

Philippians 3:14   Zeal 285.8

Philippians 3:15   Perfection 178.9

Philippians 3:20   Last things 144.16

Philippians 3:20–21   Last things 144.55

Philippians 4:4   Joy 137.18

Philippians 4:6   Caring 26.6

Philippians 4:6   Thankfulness and thanksgiving 254.9

Philippians 4:6   Worry 282.12

Philippians 4:6–7   Comfort 35.16

Philippians 4:6–7   Prayer 184.6

Philippians 4:6–7   Stress 246.13

Philippians 4:7   Mind 160.10

Philippians 4:7   Peace 177.22

Philippians 4:7   Understanding 263.10

Philippians 4:8   Beauty 16.13

Philippians 4:8   Thought 255.9

Philippians 4:11–13   Contentment 41.6

Philippians 4:13   Abilities 1.10

Philippians 4:13   Power 182.16

Philippians 4:15   Fellowship 89.8

Prayer of Manasseh 12   Confession 38.9

Proverbs 1:22–23   Simplicity 235.4

Proverbs 1:28–30   Prayer 184.20

Proverbs 2:3–6   Understanding 263.2

Proverbs 3:1   Remembering 201.7

Proverbs 3:3–4   Loyalty 155.6

Proverbs 3:5   Faith 82.4

Proverbs 3:5   Understanding 263.3

Proverbs 3:5–6   Decisions 53.4

Proverbs 3:7   Conceit 37.2

Proverbs 3:7–8   Health and wholeness 115.4

Proverbs 3:11–12   Accepting the will of God 2.4

Proverbs 3:11–12   Discipline 62.1

Proverbs 3:13, 15–18   Wisdom 277.3

Proverbs 3:33   Homes 120.4

Proverbs 4:14   Temptation 253.14

Proverbs 4:19   Darkness 49.5

Proverbs 4:20–22   Health and wholeness 115.5

Proverbs 4:23   Heart 116.5

Proverbs 6:6   Laziness 148.1

Proverbs 6:9   Laziness 148.2

Proverbs 6:9–11   Sleep 238.7

Proverbs 6:16–19   Hatred 113.2

Proverbs 6:25   Beauty 16.7

Proverbs 6:27   Temptation 253.3

Proverbs 6:30–31   Restitution 207.9

Proverbs 6:32   Marriage 157.10

Proverbs 7:18–20   Journeys 136.5

Proverbs 8:13   Reverence 211.5

Proverbs 8:17   Seeking God 224.7

Proverbs 8:22–23   Earth, the 69.9

Proverbs 8:22–23   Jesus Christ 135.30

Proverbs 8:35   Life 150.8

Proverbs 9:10   Understanding 263.4

Proverbs 10:2   Dishonesty 64.5

Proverbs 10:9   Dishonesty 64.6

Proverbs 11:1   Honesty 122.1

Proverbs 11:9   Godless 104.5

Proverbs 11:13   Gossip 107.3

Proverbs 11:16   Respect 204.6

Proverbs 11:17   Cruelty 48.4

Proverbs 11:24–25   Generosity 97.4

Proverbs 11:25   Unselfishness 265.1

Proverbs 11:26   Selfishness 228.1

Proverbs 11:29   Homes 120.5

Proverbs 12:4   Family 86.2

Proverbs 12:10   Cruelty 48.5

Proverbs 12:15   Counsel 44.4

Proverbs 12:15   Fools and folly 91.3

Proverbs 12:18   Health and wholeness 115.6

Proverbs 12:25   Stress 246.3

Proverbs 12:25   Worry 282.4

Proverbs 13:3   Self-control 225.3

Proverbs 13:11   Dishonesty 64.7

Proverbs 13:12   Discouragement 63.9

Proverbs 13:24   Family 86.15

Proverbs 14:2   Dishonesty 64.8

Proverbs 14:10   Bitterness 19.5

Proverbs 14:12   Death 51.6

Proverbs 14:12   Way 273.4

Proverbs 14:13   Laughter 145.6

Proverbs 14:14   Falling away 85.1

Proverbs 14:26   Confidence 39.2

Proverbs 14:29   Anger 8.11

Proverbs 14:29   Patience 176.2

Proverbs 14:31   Oppression 173.5

Proverbs 14:31   Poverty 181.4

Proverbs 14:34   Righteousness 216.3

Proverbs 15:17   Food and drink 90.8

Proverbs 15:17   Hatred 113.3

Proverbs 15:17   Homes 120.6

Proverbs 15:18   Anger 8.12

Proverbs 15:19   Laziness 148.3

Proverbs 15:27   Bribe 25.3

Proverbs 15:27   Desire, wrong 56.3

Proverbs 16:1   Providence 192.6

Proverbs 16:2   Motives 163.3

Proverbs 16:2   Self-righteousness 229.2

Proverbs 16:2   Spirit 242.3

Proverbs 16:3   Work 279.6

Proverbs 16:6   Loyalty 155.7

Proverbs 16:6   Sin 236.25

Proverbs 16:7   Enemy 75.2

Proverbs 16:16   Choice 30.8

Proverbs 16:18   Pride 186.2

Proverbs 16:28   Gossip 107.4

Proverbs 16:32   Anger 8.13

Proverbs 16:32   Self-control 225.4

Proverbs 16:33   Decisions 53.5

Proverbs 16:33   Providence 192.7

Proverbs 17:1   Quiet 195.4

Proverbs 17:6   Family 86.16

Proverbs 17:6   Old age 172.7

Proverbs 17:11   Rebellion 197.7

Proverbs 17:17   Friends and friendship 94.3

Proverbs 17:17   Loyalty 155.8

Proverbs 17:22   Health and wholeness 115.7

Proverbs 17:23   Bribe 25.4

Proverbs 17:25   Bitterness 19.6

Proverbs 17:25   Youth 284.4

Proverbs 17:28   Silence 234.5

Proverbs 18:8   Gossip 107.5

Proverbs 18:10   Comfort 35.5

Proverbs 18:10   Name 167.4

Proverbs 18:14   Depression 55.6

Proverbs 18:14   Despair 57.10

Proverbs 18:15   Decisions 53.6

Proverbs 18:15   Listening 152.3

Proverbs 18:17   Selfishness 228.2

Proverbs 18:22   Family 86.3

Proverbs 18:24   Friends and friendship 94.4

Proverbs 18:24   Loyalty 155.9

Proverbs 19:17   Poverty 181.5

Proverbs 19:20   Counsel 44.5

Proverbs 19:21   Sovereignty of God 240.3

Proverbs 19:22   Loyalty 155.10

Proverbs 20:5   Motives 163.4

Proverbs 20:6   Faithfulness 83.2

Proverbs 20:10   Injustice 132.6

Proverbs 20:13   Sleep 238.8

Proverbs 20:17   Dishonesty 64.9

Proverbs 20:18   Decisions 53.7

Proverbs 20:19   Gossip 107.6

Proverbs 20:22   Retaliation 209.3

Proverbs 20:22   Waiting 269.8

Proverbs 20:23   Dishonesty 64.10

Proverbs 20:25   Vow 268.5

Proverbs 21:2   Motives 163.5

Proverbs 21:3   Justice 138.4

Proverbs 21:13   Prayer 184.21

Proverbs 22:1   Character 29.3

Proverbs 22:1   Choice 30.9

Proverbs 22:5   Sin 236.26

Proverbs 22:6   Family 86.17

Proverbs 22:7   Debt 52.5

Proverbs 22:9   Generosity 97.5

Proverbs 22:26–27   Debt 52.6

Proverbs 23:1–2   Rulers 218.2

Proverbs 23:4–5   Ambition 6.11

Proverbs 23:29–31   Drunkenness 68.1

Proverbs 24:17   Enemy 75.3

Proverbs 25:6–7   Ambition 6.12

Proverbs 25:11   Speech 241.3

Proverbs 25:21–22   Enemy 75.4

Proverbs 25:24   Homes 120.7

Proverbs 25:27   Selfishness 228.3

Proverbs 25:28   Self-control 225.5

Proverbs 26:11   Fools and folly 91.4

Proverbs 26:12   Conceit 37.3

Proverbs 26:20   Gossip 107.7

Proverbs 27:4   Jealousy 134.3

Proverbs 27:6   Friends and friendship 94.5

Proverbs 27:8   Homes 120.8

Proverbs 28:1   Confidence 39.3

Proverbs 28:2   Rulers 218.3

Proverbs 28:11   Conceit 37.4

Proverbs 28:13   Confession 38.7

Proverbs 28:14   Hardness 112.3

Proverbs 29:11   Self-control 225.6

Proverbs 29:18   Visions 267.5

Proverbs 29:26   Rulers 218.4

Proverbs 31:10   Family 86.4

Proverbs 31:25   Dignity 59.5

Proverbs 31:25   Laughter 145.7

Proverbs 31:30   Beauty 16.8

Psalm 1:1   Counsel 44.1

Psalm 1:1–3   Christian life 31.13

Psalm 1:2–3   Meditation 158.2

Psalm 1:6   Way 273.2

Psalm 2:2   Godless 104.3

Psalm 2:4   Laughter 145.3

Psalm 2:8   Gentiles 98.1

Psalm 3:5   Sleep 238.1

Psalm 4:4   Meditation 158.3

Psalm 4:8   Sleep 238.2

Psalm 5:11   Celebration 27.6

Psalm 6:6–7   Depression 55.2

Psalm 8:2   Family 86.13

Psalm 8:3–4   Creation 47.3

Psalm 8:3–6   Privilege 188.1

Psalm 8:4–5   Glory 102.4

Psalm 8:4–8   Human beings 125.5

Psalm 8:6–8   Animals 9.8

Psalm 9:9   Oppression 173.3

Psalm 9:17   Last things 144.67

Psalm 12:1   Failure 81.2

Psalm 13:1–2   Depression 55.3

Psalm 13:3   Sleep 238.3

Psalm 14:1   Fools and folly 91.2

Psalm 14:3   Sinful nature 237.1

Psalm 14:7   Restoration 208.2

Psalm 15:1–2   Character 29.2

Psalm 16:10   Jesus Christ 135.92

Psalm 16:11   Joy 137.2

Psalm 17:15   Christlikeness 32.1

Psalm 18:2   Faith 82.2

Psalm 18:28   Darkness 49.3

Psalm 19:1–2   Revelation 210.1

Psalm 19:7   Law 146.1

Psalm 19:7   Perfection 178.2

Psalm 19:7   Simplicity 235.1

Psalm 19:8   Purity 194.1

Psalm 19:9   Decisions 53.2

Psalm 19:9   Reverence 211.2

Psalm 19:11   Reward 213.2

Psalm 19:13   Temptation 253.12

Psalm 19:14   Meditation 158.4

Psalm 22:1   Despair 57.4

Psalm 22:25   Vow 268.3

Psalm 22:27   Conversion 42.1

Psalm 22:27   Remembering 201.4

Psalm 23:1   Shepherd 233.1

Psalm 23:1–3   Restoration 208.3

Psalm 23:2–3   Guidance 110.1

Psalm 23:3   Soul 239.1

Psalm 23:4–6   Comfort 35.19

Psalm 24:1   Earth, the 69.5

Psalm 24:1   Fullness 96.1

Psalm 24:1   Land 143.7

Psalm 24:1   World 281.1

Psalm 24:3–4   Access 3.1

Psalm 25:8–9   Way 273.3

Psalm 25:9   Decisions 53.3

Psalm 25:10   Mercy 159.2

Psalm 25:14   Covenant 46.3

Psalm 25:14   Friends and friendship 94.2

Psalm 25:16   Comfort 35.34

Psalm 27:1   Comfort 35.2

Psalm 27:1   Light 151.2

Psalm 27:1   Salvation and Savior 221.1

Psalm 27:3–4   Confidence 39.1

Psalm 27:3–4   War 270.4

Psalm 27:4   Ambition 6.1

Psalm 27:4   Beauty 16.4

Psalm 27:4   Christian life 31.44

Psalm 27:14   Courage 45.3

Psalm 27:14   Waiting 269.3

Psalm 28:1   Silence 234.3

Psalm 29:2   Respect 204.5

Psalm 30:10–11   Mourning 164.3

Psalm 31:10   Grief 109.1

Psalm 31:15   Old age 172.3

Psalm 31:22   Doubt 66.2

Psalm 32:1–2   Forgiveness 92.1

Psalm 32:1–2   Justification 139.3

Psalm 32:2–5   Confession 38.6

Psalm 32:4   Depression 55.4

Psalm 32:5   Guilt 111.3

Psalm 32:8–9   Counsel 44.2

Psalm 32:9   Self-control 225.1

Psalm 32:9   Understanding 263.1

Psalm 33:2–3   Music 166.5

Psalm 33:6   Creation 47.4

Psalm 33:10–11   Counsel 44.3

Psalm 33:13–15   Human beings 125.6

Psalm 33:16   War 270.5

Psalm 33:20   Waiting 269.4

Psalm 34:1, 3   Praise 183.1

Psalm 34:4   Comfort 35.3

Psalm 34:5   Shame 232.2

Psalm 34:6   Prayer 184.1

Psalm 34:8   God 103.32

Psalm 34:12–14   Youth 284.2

Psalm 34:15   Prayer 184.11

Psalm 34:18   Comfort 35.27

Psalm 35:13–14   Mourning 164.4

Psalm 36:2   Conceit 37.1

Psalm 37:1   Envy 76.1

Psalm 37:1   Worry 282.1

Psalm 37:1–2   Bitterness 19.4

Psalm 37:3   Contentment 41.1

Psalm 37:3–5   Faith 82.3

Psalm 37:3–5   Guidance 110.2

Psalm 37:4   Prayer 184.40

Psalm 37:7   Meditation 158.5

Psalm 37:7   Patience 176.1

Psalm 37:7   Waiting 269.5

Psalm 37:7   Worry 282.2

Psalm 37:21   Debt 52.3

Psalm 37:21   Generosity 97.2

Psalm 37:23   Guidance 110.3

Psalm 37:27   Sin 236.23

Psalm 38:3   Illness 129.3

Psalm 38:3–8   Despair 57.5

Psalm 38:8   Stress 246.1

Psalm 40:1   Waiting 269.6

Psalm 40:1–2   Comfort 35.28

Psalm 40:8   Jesus Christ 135.86

Psalm 40:8   Will of God 276.1

Psalm 40:12   Despair 57.6

Psalm 40:16   Seeking God 224.2

Psalm 41:3   Illness 129.6

Psalm 42:1   Seeking God 224.3

Psalm 42:1–2   Christian life 31.45

Psalm 42:2, 5–6   Soul 239.2

Psalm 42:3, 7   Depression 55.5

Psalm 42:5   Hope 123.1

Psalm 42:5–6   Comfort 35.29

Psalm 46:1   Help 117.2

Psalm 46:1–2   Comfort 35.4

Psalm 46:1–2   Earth, the 69.6

Psalm 46:10   Knowledge 142.3

Psalm 46:10   Quiet 195.2

Psalm 48:9   Thought 255.1

Psalm 50:2   Beauty 16.5

Psalm 50:8–11   Animals 9.9

Psalm 50:14   Thankfulness and thanksgiving 254.1

Psalm 50:14   Vow 268.4

Psalm 50:21   Silence 234.4

Psalm 50:23   Praise 183.2

Psalm 51:1   Mercy 159.3

Psalm 51:1–2   Forgiveness 92.2

Psalm 51:1–4   Guilt 111.4

Psalm 51:3–4   Conviction of sin 43.1

Psalm 51:4–5   Sin 236.3

Psalm 51:5   Birth 18.3

Psalm 51:5   Sinful nature 237.2

Psalm 51:10   Heart 116.4

Psalm 51:10   New birth 169.1

Psalm 51:10   Renewal 202.3

Psalm 51:10   Spirit 242.2

Psalm 51:11   Holy Spirit 119.4

Psalm 51:11–12   Comfort 35.30

Psalm 51:12   Restoration 208.4

Psalm 51:16–17   Sacrifice 220.5

Psalm 51:17   Grief 109.2

Psalm 51:18   Good 105.3

Psalm 52:6–7   Laughter 145.4

Psalm 53:2   Seeking God 224.4

Psalm 55:5   Fear 88.4

Psalm 57:5   God 103.60

Psalm 58:3   Sinful nature 237.3

Psalm 62:8   Prayer 184.12

Psalm 62:10   Dishonesty 64.4

Psalm 63:1–2   Christian life 31.46

Psalm 63:3   Life 150.6

Psalm 66:6–7   Rebellion 197.5

Psalm 66:18   Prayer 184.19

Psalm 66:18   Prayer 184.41

Psalm 67:1–2   Health and wholeness 115.2

Psalm 68:5   God 103.20

Psalm 68:6   Rebellion 197.6

Psalm 68:24–25   Music 166.6

Psalm 69:9   Zeal 285.1

Psalm 69:20   Sympathy 249.3

Psalm 71:4   Cruelty 48.2

Psalm 71:6   Birth 18.4

Psalm 71:9   Old age 172.4

Psalm 72:1–2   Justice 138.3

Psalm 72:18   Miracles 161.4

Psalm 73:2–3   Envy 76.2

Psalm 73:3   Riches 214.2

Psalm 73:25   Christian life 31.47

Psalm 73:25   Last things 144.9

Psalm 73:26   Comfort 35.43

Psalm 73:26   Failure 81.3

Psalm 74:20   Cruelty 48.3

Psalm 78:19, 32   Unbelief 261.1

Psalm 78:37   Loyalty 155.5

Psalm 80:3   Restoration 208.5

Psalm 81:1–2   Music 166.7

Psalm 82:2   Injustice 132.5

Psalm 84:2   Christian life 31.48

Psalm 85:6   Revival 212.2

Psalm 88:15   Despair 57.7

Psalm 89:26   God 103.21

Psalm 89:33   Mercy 159.4

Psalm 90:2   God 103.13

Psalm 90:10, 12   Old age 172.5

Psalm 91:11   Angels 7.1

Psalm 91:16   Life 150.7

Psalm 92:12–14   Health and wholeness 115.3

Psalm 92:13–14   Old age 172.6

Psalm 94:19   Stress 246.2

Psalm 94:19   Worry 282.3

Psalm 95:6   Creation 47.5

Psalm 95:6   Worship 283.3

Psalm 96:10   Witness 278.1

Psalm 97:9   God 103.61

Psalm 100:1–4   Praise 183.3

Psalm 100:3   God 103.9

Psalm 102:7   Comfort 35.35

Psalm 102:25–27   Earth, the 69.7

Psalm 103:1–2   Soul 239.3

Psalm 103:2–3   Healing 114.4

Psalm 103:4   God 103.51

Psalm 103:6   Oppression 173.4

Psalm 103:8–9   Anger 8.1

Psalm 103:11   Reverence 211.3

Psalm 103:12   Forgiveness 92.3

Psalm 103:15–16   Human beings 125.7

Psalm 104:14–15   Food and drink 90.5

Psalm 104:23   Work 279.4

Psalm 104:24   God 103.71

Psalm 104:30   Renewal 202.4

Psalm 105:4   Seeking God 224.5

Psalm 105:5   Remembering 201.5

Psalm 107:18   Death 51.4

Psalm 107:20   Healing 114.5

Psalm 107:28–30   Quiet 195.3

Psalm 110:1   Jesus Christ 135.44

Psalm 111:5   Food and drink 90.6

Psalm 111:10   Reverence 211.4

Psalm 111:10   Wisdom 277.2

Psalm 112:5   Generosity 97.3

Psalm 112:6   Remembering 201.6

Psalm 113:4   God 103.62

Psalm 113:9   Homes 120.3

Psalm 115:4–7   Idolatry 128.3

Psalm 115:6   Listening 152.2

Psalm 115:16   Earth, the 69.8

Psalm 116:1   Love 154.26

Psalm 116:6   Simplicity 235.2

Psalm 116:12   Debt 52.4

Psalm 116:15   Death 51.5

Psalm 118:22   Rejection 200.2

Psalm 118:24   Joy 137.3

Psalm 119:9   Youth 284.3

Psalm 119:10   Seeking God 224.6

Psalm 119:11   Sin 236.24

Psalm 119:15   Meditation 158.6

Psalm 119:18   Law 146.2

Psalm 119:30   Choice 30.6

Psalm 119:33   Teachers and teaching 250.2

Psalm 119:36–37   Desire, wrong 56.2

Psalm 119:59   Self-examination 227.1

Psalm 119:71   Accepting the will of God 2.3

Psalm 119:71   Suffering 248.14

Psalm 119:78   Godless 104.4

Psalm 119:105   Light 151.3

Psalm 119:125   Knowledge 142.4

Psalm 119:130   Light 151.4

Psalm 119:130   Simplicity 235.3

Psalm 119:162   Joy 137.4

Psalm 119:173   Choice 30.7

Psalm 120:2   Lying 156.3

Psalm 121:1–8   Help 117.3

Psalm 121:2–4   Sleep 238.4

Psalm 121:3   Caring 26.2

Psalm 126:1   Dreams 67.4

Psalm 126:1–2   Laughter 145.5

Psalm 126:3   Joy 137.5

Psalm 126:4   Restoration 208.6

Psalm 126:5–6   Joy 137.6

Psalm 127:1   Work 279.5

Psalm 127:2   Sleep 238.5

Psalm 127:3–5   Family 86.14

Psalm 130:1   Despair 57.8

Psalm 130:3–4   Forgiveness 92.4

Psalm 130:5–6   Waiting 269.7

Psalm 132:4–5   Sleep 238.6

Psalm 133:1   Unity 264.1

Psalm 135:6–7   Providence 192.5

Psalm 136:1   God 103.33

Psalm 136:1   Mercy 159.5

Psalm 136:1   Thankfulness and thanksgiving 254.2

Psalm 139:1–6   God 103.1

Psalm 139:1–6   Knowledge 142.5

Psalm 139:7–10   God 103.4

Psalm 139:11–12   Darkness 49.4

Psalm 139:13–16   Birth 18.5

Psalm 139:17–18   Thought 255.2

Psalm 139:21–22   Hatred 113.1

Psalm 139:23–24   Examination 80.1

Psalm 139:23–24   Thought 255.3

Psalm 141:3   Gossip 107.2

Psalm 141:3   Self-control 225.2

Psalm 141:3   Speech 241.2

Psalm 141:3   Temptation 253.13

Psalm 143:3–4   Despair 57.9

Psalm 143:5   Meditation 158.7

Psalm 145:15–16   Food and drink 90.7

Psalm 146:8   Blindness 22.4

Psalm 146:9   Immigrants 130.4

Psalm 146:9   Widows 275.3

Psalm 149:4   Beauty 16.6

Psalm 150:3–5   Music 166.8

R

Revelation 1:5   Jesus Christ 135.85

Revelation 1:5–6   Blood 23.12

Revelation 1:7   Last things 144.66

Revelation 1:8   Jesus Christ 135.36

Revelation 1:17–18   Jesus Christ 135.104

Revelation 2:2   Apostles 11.8

Revelation 2:2   Patience 176.10

Revelation 2:5   Repentance 203.19

Revelation 2:10   Death 51.28

Revelation 2:10   Faithfulness 83.12

Revelation 3:11   Christian life 31.42

Revelation 3:17   Blindness 22.14

Revelation 3:19   Discipline 62.5

Revelation 3:20   Listening 152.13

Revelation 3:20   Prayer 184.17

Revelation 4:11   Creation 47.14

Revelation 4:11   Worship 283.13

Revelation 5:11–12   Angels 7.12

Revelation 5:12   Jesus Christ 135.69

Revelation 5:12   Praise 183.10

Revelation 6:11   Last things 144.75

Revelation 6:16   Anger 8.10

Revelation 6:16–17   Last things 144.41

Revelation 7:9   Gentiles 98.10

Revelation 7:9   Last things 144.18

Revelation 7:9   Race 196.5

Revelation 7:10   Salvation and Savior 221.21

Revelation 7:15   Last things 144.19

Revelation 8:1   Silence 234.13

Revelation 11:15   Kingdom, kingdom of God 141.17

Revelation 12:9–10   Devil 58.16

Revelation 12:10   Doubt 66.10

Revelation 12:10   Jesus Christ 135.51

Revelation 12:10–11   Warfare, spiritual 271.13

Revelation 12:11   Blood 23.13

Revelation 12:11   Victory 266.11

Revelation 14:9–11   Last things 144.29

Revelation 14:13   Last things 144.76

Revelation 15:4   God 103.38

Revelation 19:6   God 103.7

Revelation 20:2–3   Last things 144.7

Revelation 20:4   Last things 144.20

Revelation 20:7–8   Last things 144.8

Revelation 20:10   Devil 58.17

Revelation 20:10   Last things 144.30

Revelation 20:10   Last things 144.57

Revelation 20:11–15   Last things 144.42

Revelation 20:15   Last things 144.31

Revelation 21:1   Earth, the 69.15

Revelation 21:1–5   Last things 144.47

Revelation 21:3   Covenant 46.10

Revelation 21:3   Last things 144.21

Revelation 21:4   Comfort 35.56

Revelation 21:4   Death 51.29

Revelation 21:8   Last things 144.32

Revelation 21:8   Murder 165.8

Revelation 22:3–5   Last things 144.22

Revelation 22:5   Light 151.23

Revelation 22:11   Right and wrong 215.14

Romans 1:5   Privilege 188.6

Romans 1:16   Power 182.8

Romans 1:16   Shame 232.4

Romans 1:16–17   Gospel 106.6

Romans 1:17   Righteousness 216.11

Romans 1:18   Anger 8.7

Romans 1:18   Godless 104.7

Romans 1:19–20   Revelation 210.6

Romans 1:20   Creation 47.8

Romans 1:21   Mind 160.4

Romans 1:21   Unbeliever 262.3

Romans 1:22–23   Fools and folly 91.8

Romans 1:24   Homosexuality 121.3

Romans 1:26–27   Homosexuality 121.4

Romans 1:28–29   Cruelty 48.9

Romans 2:4   God 103.35

Romans 2:4   Patience 176.4

Romans 2:4   Repentance 203.16

Romans 2:5   Hardness 112.9

Romans 2:7   Eternal life 77.10

Romans 2:8   Selfishness 228.7

Romans 2:8–9   Punishment 193.6

Romans 2:9   Suffering 248.7

Romans 2:14   Gentiles 98.7

Romans 2:14–15   Conscience 40.3

Romans 2:28–29   Circumcision 34.3

Romans 2:28–29   Israel 133.5

Romans 2:29   Ritual 217.6

Romans 3:2   Bible 17.6

Romans 3:10   Righteousness 216.12

Romans 3:18   Reverence 211.10

Romans 3:19–20　　Law 146.4

Romans 3:21–26　　Righteousness 216.13

Romans 3:23　　Glory 102.9

Romans 3:23　　Sin 236.11

Romans 3:23　　Sinful nature 237.6

Romans 3:24　　Grace 108.6

Romans 3:24　　Justification 139.7

Romans 3:24　　Redemption 199.6

Romans 3:24–25　　Atonement 13.4

Romans 3:25　　Blood 23.3

Romans 3:25　　Faith 82.17

Romans 3:25　　Propitiation 191.3

Romans 3:31　　Law 146.5

Romans 4:4　　Debt 52.11

Romans 4:5　　Justification 139.8

Romans 4:18　　Hope 123.2

Romans 4:25　　Jesus Christ 135.21

Romans 4:25　　Jesus Christ 135.98

Romans 5:1　　Faith 82.18

Romans 5:1　　Justification 139.9

Romans 5:1　　Peace 177.15

Romans 5:1–2　　Joy 137.14

Romans 5:1–5　　Assurance 12.3

Romans 5:1–5　　Privilege 188.7

Romans 5:2　　Access 3.4

Romans 5:2　　Grace 108.7

Romans 5:2, 5　　Hope 123.3

Romans 5:3　　Suffering 248.16

Romans 5:3–4　　Stress 246.11

Romans 5:3–5　　Character 29.7

Romans 5:4　　Endurance 74.3

Romans 5:5　　Holy Spirit 119.28

Romans 5:5　　Love 154.4

Romans 5:6　　Godless 104.8

Romans 5:6–8　　Jesus Christ 135.22

Romans 5:8　　Atonement 13.5

Romans 5:8　　Love 154.5

Romans 5:9　　Blood 23.4

Romans 5:9　　Justification 139.10

Romans 5:9–10　　Assurance 12.4

Romans 5:10　　Enemy 75.6

Romans 5:10–11　　Reconciliation 198.3

Romans 5:12　　Adam 4.3

Romans 5:12　　Fall, the 84.3

Romans 5:12　　Sin 236.12

Romans 5:12–13　　Sinful nature 237.7

Romans 5:15–19　　Fall, the 84.4

Romans 5:17–21　　Righteousness 216.14

Romans 5:18–19　　Adam 4.4

Romans 5:19　　Disobedience 65.3

Romans 5:19　　Justification 139.11

Romans 5:20 – 6:2　　Grace 108.8

Romans 6:1–2　　Sin 236.13

Romans 6:2　　Temptation 253.16

Romans 6:3–4　　Baptism 15.8

Romans 6:4–5　　Jesus Christ 135.99

Romans 6:7–8, 11　　Death 51.10

Romans 6:9–11　　Jesus Christ 135.100

Romans 6:11–14　　Sin 236.28

Romans 6:14　　Law 146.6

Romans 6:17　　Heart 116.12

Romans 6:17　　Obedience 170.9

Romans 6:19　　Sanctification 222.2

Romans 6:22　　Freedom 93.3

Romans 6:22　　Holiness 118.5

Romans 6:23　　Death 51.11

Romans 6:23　　Eternal life 77.11

Romans 6:23　　Gift 100.4

Romans 6:23　　Life 150.27

Romans 6:23　　Punishment 193.7

Romans 6:23　　Sin 236.14

Romans 7:7　　Law 146.7

Romans 7:12　　Good 105.6

Romans 7:12　　Law 146.8

Romans 7:18　　Good 105.7

Romans 7:18–21　　Sinful nature 237.8

Romans 7:19　　Evil 79.9

Romans 7:22　　Christian life 31.50

Romans 7:22–23   Law 146.9

Romans 7:22–23   Sanctification 222.3

Romans 8:1   Assurance 12.5

Romans 8:1   Guilt 111.6

Romans 8:2–4   Freedom 93.4

Romans 8:2–4   Law 146.10

Romans 8:3–4   Sinful nature 237.9

Romans 8:5–6   Holy Spirit 119.29

Romans 8:5–6   Mind 160.5

Romans 8:5–13   Sinful nature 237.10

Romans 8:6   Life 150.28

Romans 8:6   Peace 177.16

Romans 8:9, 11–16   Holy Spirit 119.30

Romans 8:10–11   Death 51.12

Romans 8:13   Life 150.29

Romans 8:14–17   Adoption 5.5

Romans 8:15   Fear 88.10

Romans 8:15–16   Spirit 242.8

Romans 8:17   Inheritance 131.3

Romans 8:18   Glory 102.10

Romans 8:18–21   Suffering 248.8

Romans 8:19–23   Creation 47.9

Romans 8:21   Freedom 93.5

Romans 8:21   Last things 144.45

Romans 8:23   Redemption 199.7

Romans 8:23–25   Hope 123.4

Romans 8:25   Waiting 269.16

Romans 8:26   Help 117.7

Romans 8:26   Prayer 184.35

Romans 8:26   Weakness 274.6

Romans 8:26–27   Holy Spirit 119.31

Romans 8:27   Examination 80.3

Romans 8:27   Heart 116.13

Romans 8:28   Good 105.8

Romans 8:28   Love 154.29

Romans 8:28   Sovereignty of God 240.8

Romans 8:28, 30   Christian life 31.4

Romans 8:28, 35–39   Comfort 35.47

Romans 8:29   Christlikeness 32.4

Romans 8:29–30, 33   Election 72.8

Romans 8:30, 33–34   Justification 139.12

Romans 8:31, 37   Victory 266.3

Romans 8:31–35, 37–39   Assurance 12.6

Romans 8:35, 37   Discouragement 63.12

Romans 8:35, 37   Persecution 179.8

Romans 8:35–37   War 270.8

Romans 8:35–39   Love 154.6

Romans 8:38–39   Jesus Christ 135.83

Romans 9:1   Conscience 40.4

Romans 9:2–5   Privilege 188.8

Romans 9:6–7   Israel 133.6

Romans 9:8   Promise 189.2

Romans 9:15–16   Election 72.9

Romans 9:19–21   Accepting the will of God 2.7

Romans 10:2–3   Zeal 285.2

Romans 10:9   Heart 116.14

Romans 10:9–10   Confession 38.2

Romans 10:9–10   Faith 82.19

Romans 10:13   Christian life 31.27

Romans 10:14–15   Preaching 185.5

Romans 10:15   Beauty 16.12

Romans 10:17   Faith 82.20

Romans 11:25–26   Israel 133.7

Romans 11:33   God 103.2

Romans 11:33   Wisdom 277.14

Romans 11:33–34   Mind 160.6

Romans 12:1   Body 24.2

Romans 12:1   Mercy 159.13

Romans 12:1   Sacrifice 220.8

Romans 12:1   Worship 283.9

Romans 12:1–2   Sanctification 222.4

Romans 12:2   Good 105.9

Romans 12:2   Guidance 110.8

Romans 12:2   Mind 160.7

Romans 12:2   Perfection 178.5

Romans 12:2   Renewal 202.8

Romans 12:2   Will of God 276.4

Romans 12:3   Conceit 37.6

Romans 12:3   Pride 186.6

Romans 12:6   Abilities 1.9

Romans 12:6   Gift 100.5

Romans 12:7   Service 230.7

Romans 12:8   Encouragement 73.6

Romans 12:8   Leadership 149.6

Romans 12:9   Evil 79.10

Romans 12:9   Good 105.10

Romans 12:10   Respect 204.10

Romans 12:11   Holy Spirit 119.32

Romans 12:11   Zeal 285.3

Romans 12:12   Comfort 35.48

Romans 12:12   Patience 176.5

Romans 12:13   Hospitality 124.3

Romans 12:14   Blessing 21.7

Romans 12:14   Persecution 179.9

Romans 12:15   Comfort 35.23

Romans 12:15   Sympathy 249.9

Romans 12:16   Conceit 37.7

Romans 12:16   Pride 186.7

Romans 12:17   Debt 52.12

Romans 12:18   Peace 177.17

Romans 12:19–21   Retaliation 209.5

Romans 12:21   Good 105.11

Romans 13:1   Authority 14.13

Romans 13:1   Submission 247.1

Romans 13:1–3   Rulers 218.10

Romans 13:1–7   State, responsibility to 243.3

Romans 13:4   Punishment 193.8

Romans 13:4   War 270.9

Romans 13:7   Respect 204.11

Romans 13:7–8   Debt 52.13

Romans 13:10   Law 146.11

Romans 13:11–12   Sleep 238.12

Romans 13:12   Darkness 49.11

Romans 13:13   Drunkenness 68.5

Romans 14:1   Weakness 274.7

Romans 14:7–8   Responsibility, human 205.7

Romans 14:8–9   Death 51.13

Romans 14:17   Kingdom, kingdom of God 141.11

Romans 14:19, 21   Temperance 252.1

Romans 15:1   Weakness 274.8

Romans 15:1–3   Unselfishness 265.5

Romans 15:13   Hope 123.5

Romans 15:13   Joy 137.15

Romans 15:13   Power 182.9

Romans 15:20   Ambition 6.4

Romans 15:23–24   Journeys 136.12

Romans 16:17   Teachers, false 251.5

Romans 16:19   Simplicity 235.8

Romans 16:20   Victory 266.4

Ruth 1:8–9   Homes 120.2

Ruth 1:16   Loyalty 155.1

Ruth 1:20   Bitterness 19.2

S

1 Samuel 1:11   Family 86.12

1 Samuel 2:8   Poverty 181.3

1 Samuel 2:9   Silence 234.1

1 Samuel 3:1   Visions 267.3

1 Samuel 3:10   Listening 152.1

1 Samuel 4:21   Glory 102.3

1 Samuel 6:17–18   Restitution 207.5

1 Samuel 7:12   Help 117.1

1 Samuel 10:8   Waiting 269.2

1 Samuel 12:14–15   Rebellion 197.3

1 Samuel 12:23–25   Right and wrong 215.3

1 Samuel 13:14   Heart 116.2

1 Samuel 13:14   Leadership 149.3

1 Samuel 15:13   Dishonesty 64.3

1 Samuel 15:22   Obedience 170.4

1 Samuel 15:22   Ritual 217.1

1 Samuel 15:22   Sacrifice 220.4

1 Samuel 15:23   Rebellion 197.4

1 Samuel 15:23   Rejection 200.1

1 Samuel 16:7   Beauty 16.1

1 Samuel 16:7   Character 29.1

1 Samuel 16:7   Heart 116.3

1 Samuel 20:8   Loyalty 155.2

1 Samuel 22:14   Loyalty 155.3

1 Samuel 24:4   Conscience 40.1

1 Samuel 25:25   Fools and folly 91.1

2 Samuel 1:11–12   Fasting 87.2

2 Samuel 1:11–12   Mourning 164.1

2 Samuel 6:5   Music 166.2

2 Samuel 12:5–6   Restitution 207.6

2 Samuel 15:1–4   Ambition 6.10

2 Samuel 22:31   Perfection 178.1

2 Samuel 22:31   Way 273.1

Song of Songs 1:15–16   Beauty 16.10

T

1 Thessalonians 1:5   Power 182.17

1 Thessalonians 1:5   Preaching 185.8

1 Thessalonians 1:6   Christlikeness 32.11

1 Thessalonians 1:9   Conversion 42.7

1 Thessalonians 1:9   Idolatry 128.5

1 Thessalonians 1:10   Anger 8.9

1 Thessalonians 2:3–4   Motives 163.12

1 Thessalonians 2:7   Gentleness 99.5

1 Thessalonians 2:11–12   Encouragement 73.7

1 Thessalonians 2:11–12   Pastor 175.2

1 Thessalonians 2:13   Bible 17.9

1 Thessalonians 4:3   Sanctification 222.6

1 Thessalonians 4:3   Will of God 276.7

1 Thessalonians 4:7   Holiness 118.7

1 Thessalonians 4:13, 16–18   Comfort 35.26

1 Thessalonians 4:14   Last things 144.73

1 Thessalonians 4:14–17   Last things 144.62

1 Thessalonians 4:16   Last things 144.56

1 Thessalonians 4:16–18   Death 51.22

1 Thessalonians 5:2   Last things 144.63

1 Thessalonians 5:5–8   Sleep 238.13

1 Thessalonians 5:7–8   Temperance 252.3

1 Thessalonians 5:12–13   Elders 71.5

1 Thessalonians 5:12–13   Leadership 149.8

1 Thessalonians 5:12–13   Respect 204.13

1 Thessalonians 5:14   Encouragement 73.8

1 Thessalonians 5:14   Patience 176.8

1 Thessalonians 5:15   Evil 79.11

1 Thessalonians 5:16–18   Will of God 276.8

1 Thessalonians 5:17   Prayer 184.16

1 Thessalonians 5:18   Thankfulness and thanksgiving 254.10

1 Thessalonians 5:19   Holy Spirit 119.41

1 Thessalonians 5:20–21   Prophets and prophecy 190.13

1 Thessalonians 5:21   Examination 80.4

1 Thessalonians 5:22   Evil 79.12

1 Thessalonians 5:22   Sin 236.32

1 Thessalonians 5:23   Health and wholeness 115.12

1 Thessalonians 5:23   Sanctification 222.7

2 Thessalonians 1:7, 10   Last things 144.64

2 Thessalonians 1:8   Disobedience 65.5

2 Thessalonians 1:9   Last things 144.28

2 Thessalonians 1:9   Punishment 193.9

2 Thessalonians 2:3   Rebellion 197.14

2 Thessalonians 2:3–4   Antichrist 10.4

2 Thessalonians 2:3–4   Last things 144.5

2 Thessalonians 2:6–10   Antichrist 10.5

2 Thessalonians 2:8   Last things 144.6

2 Thessalonians 2:13   Election 72.12

2 Thessalonians 3:6–8   Laziness 148.4

2 Thessalonians 3:7–8   Honesty 122.6

2 Thessalonians 3:10–12   Laziness 148.5

2 Thessalonians 3:11   Gossip 107.10

2 Thessalonians 3:16   Peace 177.24

1 Timothy 1:11   Gospel 106.15

1 Timothy 1:12   Abilities 1.11

1 Timothy 1:15   Sin 236.17

1 Timothy 1:17   God 103.14

1 Timothy 1:17   God 103.73

1 Timothy 2:1–2   Prayer 184.37

1 Timothy 2:1–2   Rulers 218.12

1 Timothy 2:2   Quiet 195.12

1 Timothy 2:2   State, responsibility to 243.4

1 Timothy 2:3–4   Salvation and Savior 221.16

1 Timothy 2:5   Jesus Christ 135.59

1 Timothy 2:5   Jesus Christ 135.70

1 Timothy 2:5–6   Redemption 199.14

1 Timothy 2:11–12, 14–15   Human beings 125.26

1 Timothy 3:1   Ambition 6.8

1 Timothy 3:1   Leadership 149.9

1 Timothy 3:1–4   Elders 71.6

1 Timothy 3:2   Hospitality 124.4

1 Timothy 3:2   Marriage 157.6

1 Timothy 3:3   Money and material goods 162.5

1 Timothy 3:4   Family 86.25

1 Timothy 3:8   Dignity 59.8

1 Timothy 3:8, 11   Temperance 252.4

1 Timothy 3:8–13   Deacons 50.2

1 Timothy 3:13   Respect 204.14

1 Timothy 3:15   Truth 260.12

1 Timothy 3:16   Jesus Christ 135.60

1 Timothy 4:1   Falling away 85.8

1 Timothy 4:1   Teachers, false 251.7

1 Timothy 4:1–3   Marriage 157.7

1 Timothy 4:4   Good 105.14

1 Timothy 4:7   Gossip 107.11

1 Timothy 4:12   Youth 284.10

1 Timothy 4:13   Preaching 185.9

1 Timothy 4:14   Gift 100.10

1 Timothy 4:14   Laying on of hands 147.9

1 Timothy 5:5   Widows 275.9

1 Timothy 5:8   Family 86.26

1 Timothy 5:8   Work 279.12

1 Timothy 5:10   Hospitality 124.5

1 Timothy 5:10   Widows 275.10

1 Timothy 5:13   Gossip 107.12

1 Timothy 5:13   Laziness 148.6

1 Timothy 5:13–14   Widows 275.11

1 Timothy 5:17   Elders 71.7

1 Timothy 5:17   Preaching 185.10

1 Timothy 5:18   Reward 213.9

1 Timothy 5:18   Work 279.13

1 Timothy 5:22   Laying on of hands 147.10

1 Timothy 5:22   Purity 194.4

1 Timothy 5:23   Temperance 252.5

1 Timothy 6:6–7   Money and material goods 162.6

1 Timothy 6:6–8   Contentment 41.7

1 Timothy 6:8   Food and drink 90.13

1 Timothy 6:9   Desire, wrong 56.7

1 Timothy 6:10   Evil 79.13

1 Timothy 6:10   Money and material goods 162.7

1 Timothy 6:12   Eternal life 77.13

1 Timothy 6:12   Warfare, spiritual 271.8

1 Timothy 6:15   Rulers 218.13

1 Timothy 6:16   Light 151.19

1 Timothy 6:17   Joy 137.19

1 Timothy 6:17   Riches 214.8

1 Timothy 6:17–18   Generosity 97.11

2 Timothy 1:7   Courage 45.9

2 Timothy 1:7   Self-control 225.9

2 Timothy 1:9   Christian life 31.7

2 Timothy 1:10   Death 51.23

2 Timothy 1:12   Assurance 12.8

2 Timothy 1:12   Knowledge 142.16

2 Timothy 1:12   Shame 232.5

2 Timothy 1:12, 14   Stewardship 245.6

2 Timothy 1:15   Loneliness 153.6

2 Timothy 2:2   Faithfulness 83.9

2 Timothy 2:2   Leadership 149.10

2 Timothy 2:3   Endurance 74.7

2 Timothy 2:8   Remembering 201.15

2 Timothy 2:11–12   Death 51.24

2 Timothy 2:12   Endurance 74.8

2 Timothy 2:13   Faithfulness 83.10

2 Timothy 2:15   Bible 17.10

2 Timothy 2:15   Preaching 185.11

2 Timothy 2:15   Truth 260.13

2 Timothy 2:22   Youth 284.11

2 Timothy 2:24   Bitterness 19.12

2 Timothy 2:24   Gentleness 99.6

2 Timothy 3:1–2   Selfishness 228.12

2 Timothy 3:2   Blasphemy 20.6

2 Timothy 3:2   Disobedience 65.6

2 Timothy 3:5   Hypocrisy 127.5

2 Timothy 3:5   Power 182.18

2 Timothy 3:5   Ritual 217.7

2 Timothy 3:12   Persecution 179.10

2 Timothy 3:15   Salvation and Savior 221.17

2 Timothy 3:15–16   Teachers and teaching 250.10

2 Timothy 3:15–17   Bible 17.11

2 Timothy 3:16   Revelation 210.9

2 Timothy 3:17   Perfection 178.11

2 Timothy 3:17   Works, good 280.9

2 Timothy 4:2   Discipline 62.3

2 Timothy 4:2   Encouragement 73.9

2 Timothy 4:2   Preaching 185.12

2 Timothy 4:5   Evangelists 78.5

2 Timothy 4:5   Pastor 175.3

2 Timothy 4:16–17   Comfort 35.39

Titus 1:5   Elders 71.8

Titus 1:7–8   Character 29.9

Titus 1:15   Conscience 40.6

Titus 1:15   Purity 194.5

Titus 1:16   Teachers, false 251.8

Titus 2:2–3   Old age 172.11

Titus 2:3   Gossip 107.13

Titus 2:6   Self-control 225.10

Titus 2:7–8   Character 29.10

Titus 2:9–10   Stealing 244.8

Titus 2:14   Redemption 199.15

Titus 2:14   Zeal 285.9

Titus 3:1   Rulers 218.14

Titus 3:5   New birth 169.6

Titus 3:5   Renewal 202.12

Titus 3:5   Water 272.12

Titus 3:5–6   Generosity 97.12

Titus 3:7   Inheritance 131.10

Titus 3:8   Caring 26.7

Tobit 3:2–3   Confession 38.8

W

Wisdom of Solomon 1:10   Jealousy 134.4

Wisdom of Solomon 6:17   Wisdom 277.5

Z

Zechariah 1:7–8   Visions 267.12

Zechariah 2:13   Silence 234.10

Zechariah 4:6   Holy Spirit 119.8

Zechariah 4:6   Warfare, spiritual 271.1

Zechariah 7:10   Oppression 173.8

Zechariah 7:12–13   Prayer 184.25

Zechariah 9:9   Jesus Christ 135.41

Zechariah 9:9   Jesus Christ 135.47

Zephaniah 1:7   Silence 234.9

Zephaniah 3:5   Injustice 132.8

Zephaniah 3:17   Quiet 195.11

INDEX OF KEY WORDS

References are to paragraph numbers

A

abandon: For how can those who a. their faith
85.9

abandoned: then they a. their faith!   85.9

Abel: The Lord was pleased with A. and his offering
163.1

abide: A. in me as I a. in you.   184.46
If you a.... ask for whatever you wish   184.46

ability: as the Spirit gave them a.   1.8
each in proportion to his a.   1.7
let him do it as of the a. which God giveth   1.12
to all who have a., whom I have endowed with   1.1

abomination: A double standard in weights is an a.
64.10

above: Let your thoughts be on things a.,   6.22

Abraham: A. believed... became 'the father of many
nations   123.2
A. put his faith in God... 'friend of God'   94.11
I am the God of A., the God of Isaac and   144.50
Jesus said... Before A. was, I am.   135.32
when God put A. to the test   253.10

Abraham's: was carried by the angels into A. bosom
144.68

abundantly: Which he shed on us a. through Jesus
Christ   97.12

abyss: The angel threw him into the a., locked it
144.7

acceptable: Jesus... will make many people a. to
God.   139.11

accepted: God a. me simply because of my faith in
Christ.   216.18
it shall be a. for him to make atonement for him.
13.1

access: Jesus Christ: By whom also we have a. by
faith   188.7
through him we... have a. to the Father   3.5
we have a. by faith   3.4
we have a. by faith into this grace wherein we stand,
12.3

acclaimed: thankfully a. the word of the Lord
205.6

accord: being in full a. and of one mind.   264.8

accuser: the a. of our comrades has been thrown
down   271.13
the a. of our comrades has been thrown down
66.10   ·

acknowledges: If anyone a. that Jesus is God's Son,
38.4

actions: Show me this faith you speak of with no a.
280.12
You see, then, that it is by people's a.   280.13

Adam: A. called his wife's name Eve   125.16
As in A. all die, so in Christ   4.5
The first man, A., became a living being   4.6
the last A. became a life-giving spirit.   4.6
Unto A. he said, Because thou hast   125.15

admonish: over you in the Lord and who a. you.
71.5

adopted: to be a. sons, through Jesus Christ.   5.8

adoption: a Spirit of a. enabling us to cry 'Abba!
Father!'   5.5
so that we could receive a. as sons.   188.10
that we might receive a. as children.   5.7
we wait for a. the redemption of our bodies.   199.7

adulterer: The a. has no sense   157.10

adulterers: nor a.... will inherit the kingdom of God.
231.5

adultery: it was said, 'Do not commit a.' But now
157.11
the works of the flesh are manifest, A.   231.7
Thou shalt not commit a.   157.9

advantage: Do not take a. of anyone or rob him.
138.1

adversary: Like a roaring lion your a. the devil prowls
271.12
When the A. left the Lord's presence   58.2

advice: Be sure you have sound a. before making
plans   53.7
Pay attention to a. and accept correction   44.5
Wise people listen to a.   44.4

advocate: But the A., the Holy Spirit   119.17

afflicted: It is good for me that I have been a.
248.14

affliction: He delivereth the poor in his a.   248.13

afraid: Courage! It's me! Don't be a.   35.7
Do not be a. of those who kill the body   88.6
doesn't make us slaves who are a. of him.   88.10
I heard thy voice… and I was a.   88.1
I was a. and thought that he had driven me   66.2
Moses hid his face; for he was a. to look   88.2
So do not be a. of people.   88.5
Thus saith the Lord unto you, Be not a.   63.6
Why are you a.? Have you still no faith?   88.7

age: of full a., even those who by reason of use have
their senses   178.13

aged: Children's children are a crown to the a.
172.7
Is wisdom with the a.   172.2

agree: Again I tell you: if two of you a. on earth
264.4
two of you… a. about anything you pray for
184.43

agreed: Can two walk together, except they be a.?
264.3
The people a. to do everything written   202.1

agreement: Jesus guarantees us a better a. with God.
46.6

aid: the Spirit comes to the a. of our weakness.
117.7

air: meet the Lord in the a.   35.26

alien: he shows love towards the a. who lives among
130.3
You shall not wrong or oppress a resident a.   130.1

aliens: without Christ, being a. from the   262.8

alive: crucified with Christ and yet I am a.   150.31
dead to sin and a. to God in Christ   135.100
God… rich in mercy, made us a. with Christ
169.5
his spirit was made a.   13.11
made us a. with Christ even when we were dead
150.32

all: I am made a. things to a. men   274.11

Alpha: 'I am the A. and the Omega'   135.36

ambassadors: So we are a. for Christ   31.28

ambition: Leave no room for selfish a.   6.21
Thus I make it my a. to proclaim the good news,   6.4

ancient: He approached the A. of Days   144.58

angel: In the sixth month the a. Gabriel   7.6
who hath sent his a., and delivered his servants
7.2

angels: all the holy a. with him,   7.5
A. gave you God's Law,   7.8
Do you not know that we are to judge a.   7.9
For he will charge his a. to guard you   7.1
joy among the a. of God over one sinner   7.7
The a. who did not keep their own position
144.40
the voices of many a.,   7.12
Their a. in heaven,   7.4
What are the a., then?   7.11

anger: Better be slow to a. than a fighter,   8.13
Jesus will save us from God's a.   8.9
let everyone be… slow to a.   8.18
Now the works of the flesh are obvious… a.   8.16
So the a. of the Lord is roused against his people,
8.2
The Lord… slow to a.   8.1

angry: Be ye a., and sin not: 8.17
I tell you: whoever is a. with his brother   165.6
Jesus was a. as he looked round at them,   8.5
The elder brother got so a.   134.5
whoever is a. with his brother   8.14

anguish: he began to feel terror and a.   246.8
In his a. he prayed even more earnestly   246.9

animal: Every a. in the forest belongs to me,   9.9
you put all of it under our power… wild a.,   9.8

animals: God made wild a. in their own species,
9.1
named the tame a. and the birds and the wild a.
9.2
The Lord took some soil and made a. and birds.
9.2
These are the a. you may eat: 9.4

answer: A. me, O Lord, a. me, so that this people
161.3
Herod asked… but Jesus did not a.   234.12
his a. was: 'My grace is all you need   184.4
will call to the Lord, but he will not a.   184.24

antichrist: Any such person is the deceiver and a.
10.9
He is the a., for he denies both the Father   10.7
it is the spirit of A.,   10.8
You were told that an a. was to come.   10.6

antichrists: many a. have already appeared,   10.6

anxiety: He cares for you, so cast all your a. on him. 282.13

anxious: Do not be a., but in everything   246.13
When a. thoughts filled my heart   282.3

apostle: consider the A. and High Priest   11.7
I am an a. to you.   11.4
I am free. I am an a.   11.4

apostles: And God has appointed in the church first a.   11.5
put to the test those who claim to be a.   11.8
the foundation laid by the a. and prophets,   11.6
These are the names of the twelve a.:   11.1
When the a. Barnabas and Paul heard of it,   11.3

appear: He will a. a second time,   144.65

appearance: man looketh on the outward a. but the Lord   116.3
Pay no attention to his outward a.   16.1

appears: when the Lord Jesus a. from heaven 144.64

apple: he kept him as the a. of his eye   154.2

appointed: one must be a. to serve with us as a witness   11.2

approach: we are bold enough to a. God   188.12

arbitrate: He shall judge between the nations, and shall a.   198.1

armor: Put on the whole a. of God   74.5
Therefore take up the whole a. of God   271.6

arms: And he took them up in his a.   86.20
underneath are the everlasting a.   35.41

army: A king does not win because of his powerful a. 270.5

arrogant: Let the a. be put to shame   104.4

ascend: I shall a.... make myself like the Most High!' 6.14

ashamed: For I am not a. of the gospel of Christ 232.4
God is not a. for them to call him their God   232.6
I am not a.! I know the one I have faith in   232.5
if you suffer... don't be a. of it   232.8
They were both naked... and were not a.   232.1
Those who are a. of me and of my words   232.3

ashes: to give unto them beauty for a.   164.8

ask: A., and it will be given to you   184.42
a. God, who gives to all generously   184.38
but the labourers are few, so a. the Lord of the harvest   278.4

Father give the Holy Spirit to them that a. him? 119.13
If any of you lacks wisdom, he should a. God 277.21
If you abide... a. for whatever you wish   184.46
to do... above all that we a. or think   184.5
Whatever you a. in my name I will do   184.45
Whatsoever we a. we receive of him   184.48
When that day comes you will a. me nothing more 184.47
when we a. for what pleases him.   184.30
When you a. for something, you must have faith 184.28

asks: For everyone who a. receives   184.42

asleep: comes unexpectedly, he must not find you a. 238.10
He came back and found them a.   81.8

ass: Who has let the Syrian wild a. range at will 9.5

assemblies: you are to proclaim them as sacred a. 27.1

assurance: sincerity of heart and the full a. of faith, 12.9

astray: All we like sheep have gone a.   236.5
they will lead many a.   251.4
your thoughts will be led a.   253.8

astrologers: Let your a., your star-gazers   171.7

atonement: he might make a. for the sins of the people.   191.5

attack: I sent Assyria to a. a godless nation   270.6

attacks: lies in wait for him, a. him   165.5

attractive: all that is lovable and a., whatever is excellent   16.13

author: Looking unto Jesus the a. and finisher of our 35.54
You killed the a. of life   135.20

authorities: made known to the rulers and a.   7.10
the existing a. have been put there by God.   14.13
the existing a. have been put there by God.   243.3

authority: And hath given him a. to execute judgment also,   14.10
fear him who... has a. to cast into hell.   14.8
For I am a man under a.   14.3
for kings, and for all that are in a.   243.4
For you gave him a. over all humanity,   14.12
He speaks with a.   14.7
He taught... as one having a.   14.2
he taught with a note of a.   135.9

I have a. to lay it down and a. to take it up   14.11

I have been given all a. in heaven and on earth   14.6

I permit no woman to… have a. over a man   125.26

no a. exists without God's permission,   14.13

Son of Man has a. on earth to forgive sins   135.10

the Son of man has a. on earth to forgive sins,   14.4

Then Jesus… gave them a. over unclean spirits,   14.5

We must obey God rather than any human a.   243.2

with a. and power he commands   135.12

await: attain that righteousness which we eagerly a.   269.17

awake: Stay a., because you do not know when   238.10

awe: They were filled with great a.   211.8

B

Baal: if B. is God, worship him!   30.4

babes: Out of the mouth of b. and sucklings   86.13

backs: have rebelled and turned your b. on me.   200.5

they turned their b. and not their faces   85.2

backslider: The b. in heart shall be filled with   85.1

bad: B. company ruins good character.   236.30

Never follow a b. example   236.37

Woe to those who call what is b., good   215.9

balm: Is there no b. in Gilead   109.6

baptism: One Lord, one faith, one b.   15.10

The b. of John was for those who turned from   15.7

we are buried with him by b. into death   15.8

baptize: He will b. you with the Holy Spirit   15.1

he will b. you with the Holy Spirit and fire   119.9

I b. you with water, for repentance;   15.1

baptized: every one of you must be b.   15.4

For in the one Spirit we were all b. into one body   15.9

Jesus, when he was b., went up   15.2

Then he and everyone in his home were b.   15.6

They accepted what he said and were b.   15.4

they were b. in the name of the Lord Jesus.   15.7

were b. into Jesus Christ were b. into his death?   15.8

What is to prevent me from being b.?   15.5

baptizing: b. them in the name of the Father and of the Son   15.3

bare: he b. the sin of many   13.2

barren: ye shall neither be b. nor unfruitful   29.11

battle: Satan will bring them all together for b.   144.8

be: that where I am, there ye may b. also.   144.60

bearing: b. fruit in every kind of good work   283.11

beast: the b. and the false prophet had already   144.30

where the b…. had already been thrown   144.57

Whoever worships the b.   144.29

beasts: Of clean b., and of b. that are not clean,   9.3

beautiful: Be b. in your heart by being gentle and quiet.   16.14

He hath made every thing b. in his time.   16.9

How b. are the feet of them that preach the gospel   16.12

How b. you are, my beloved, how b. you are!   16.10

she was indeed a b. woman.   16.3

beautify: he will b. the meek with salvation.   16.6

beauty: bring Queen Vashti… to display her b.   16.3

Charm can be deceiving, and b. fades away   16.8

Do not covet her b. in your heart   16.7

Out of Zion, the perfection of b., God hath shined.   16.5

This kind of b. will last   16.14

to behold the b. of the Lord   16.4

Worship the Lord in the b. of holiness.   16.2

Your heart has grown proud because of your b.   16.11

beginning: In the b. was the Word   135.31

being: God who searches our inmost b.   116.13

believe: about sin, because they refuse to b. in me.   261.8

b. in thine heart that God hath raised him   82.19

B. on the Lord Jesus, and you will be saved   82.16

b. that he… rewards those who seek him.   184.27

even to them that b. on his name.   82.9

For if we b. that Jesus died and rose again   144.62

my hand in his side, I will not b.   261.9
my hand in his side, I will not b.   66.8
they did not b. in his wonders   261.1
those who do not b. are condemned already   262.1
Unto you therefore which b. he is precious.   31.51
ye b. in God, b. also in me.   82.13
you must b. in the one he has sent.   82.12
you will die in your sins if you do not b.   262.2

believed: because they had not b. those who saw him
      261.6
He b. in the Lord; and he counted it to him   82.1

believer: Become a believer in the Lord J.   31.25

believes: Everyone who b. that Jesus is the Christ
      82.31
Everything is possible to one who b.   261.5

believeth: For with the heart man b. unto
      righteousness   82.19
whosoever b. in him should not perish   82.10
whosoever liveth and b. in me shall never die.
      35.21
Whosoever liveth and b. in me shall never die.
      Believest thou this?   144.70

believing: in order to keep them from b. and being
      saved   261.7

bereft: My soul is b. of peace   55.7

betrays: will be terrible for the one who b. him.
      240.4

beware: B. that no one leads you astray   251.4

birth: From my b. I have been evil   18.3
I am going through the pain of giving b.   32.7
On you I have relied since my b.   18.4
she gave b. to a son, her firstborn.   18.9
when she has given b. to the child she forgets
      18.12

birthright: Esau, who for one morsel of meat sold his
      b.   131.12

bishop: A b. then must be... the husband of one
      wife.   157.6

bitter: b. gall and the chains of sin will be your fate
      19.10
he cried with a great and exceeding b. cry   19.1
no b., noxious weed growing up to contaminate
      19.13

bitterly: the Almighty hath dealt very b. with me.
      19.2

bitterness: A foolish son is... b. to her that bare him.
      19.6
Any b. or bad temper or anger or shouting   19.11

He has given me my fill of b.   19.7
If at heart you have the b. of jealousy   19.14
Laugh no man to scorn in the b. of his soul   19.8
speaking out in the b. of my soul.   19.3
The heart knoweth his own b.   19.5

blameless: soul and body be preserved b.   222.7
The way of God is b.   178.1

blaspheme: Is it not they who b. the excellent name
      20.7

blasphemed: In this also your fathers b. me   20.3

blasphemers: Men shall be... b.   20.6

blasphemy: All manner of sin and b. shall be forgiven
      20.4
b. against the Holy Ghost shall not be forgiven
      20.4
b. against the Spirit will not be forgiven   92.10
b. against the Spirit will not be forgiven.   119.11
High Priest tore his clothes and said, 'B.!'   20.5
You have just heard his b.!   20.5

blemish: Your lamb shall be without b.   220.2

bless: And I will b. them that b. thee   21.1
B. those who persecute you; b. and do not curse.
      21.7
I will not let thee go, except thou b. me.   21.2
The Lord b. thee, and keep thee   21.3

blessed: B. are the poor in spirit: for theirs is
      31.14
For in our union with Christ he has b. us   21.8
He took them up in his arms... and b. them.   21.6
in thee shall all families of the earth be b.   21.1
who has b. us with all the spiritual blessings
      188.11

blessing: giving us every spiritual b.   21.8
pour down for you an overflowing b.   21.5
repay with a b.   21.9
thou shalt be a b.: And I will bless them   21.1

blessings: And the following b. will all come   21.4
the rich b. that God keeps for his people.   131.13

blind: Cursed be he that maketh the b. to wander
      22.3
'Do you mean that we are b.?' 'If you were b.
      22.11
if one b. person leads another   22.10
Teacher, whose sin caused him to be born b.?
      248.15
The b. receive their sight   22.9
the eyes of the b. will see out of... darkness.   22.5
The Lord restores sight to the b.   22.4
Then the eyes of the b. shall be opened   22.6

They are b. leaders of the b.   22.10

To open the b. eyes   22.7

Who gives them sight or makes them b.?   22.1

you are a pitiful wretch, poor, b., and naked.
22.14

blinded: god who rules this world has b. the minds
22.13

blindness: His b. has nothing to do with his sins
248.15

blinds: a bribe b. the eyes of the wise   22.2

blood: a propitiation through faith in his b.   23.3

a propitiation through faith in his b.   191.3

almost everything is purified with b.   23.7

Behold the b. of the covenant   46.2

b. must be put on the two doorposts   174.1

By his b. we are now put right with God   23.4

Christ sacrificed his life's b.   23.5

complete confidence through the b. of Jesus   23.8

For this is my b., the b. of the covenant   36.1

Having made peace through the b. of his cross.
23.6

He... washed away our sins with his b.   135.85

is it not a sharing in the b. of Christ?   36.3

it is the b., which is the life   23.1

making peace through the b. of his cross   198.6

rescued by the precious b. of Christ   23.10

shedding of b. there is no forgiveness of sins
236.18

the b. of Jesus his Son cleanses us   23.11

The life of a creature is in the b.   23.1

They overcame him by the b. of the Lamb   23.13

This is my b. of the covenant   23.2

through faith in his b.,   13.4

through the b. of the everlasting covenant   23.9

washed us from our sins in his own b.   23.12

without the shedding of b. there is no   23.7

you sin against his body and b.   36.4

boast: b.... except the cross of our Lord Jesus C.
135.27

If anyone wants to b., let him b. of the Lord.
186.8

bodies: physical b. will be changed into spiritual b.
24.5

present your b., a living sacrifice   24.2

present your b. a living sacrifice   220.8

So use your b. for God's glory.   24.3

body: a form like that of his own glorious b.
144.55

He is the head of the b., the church.   24.6

He was bearing our sins in his own b.   236.19

isn't that sharing in the b. of Christ?   89.4

life more than meat, and the b. than raiment?
150.12

Now you are the b. of Christ   24.4

So use your b. for the glory of God   199.9

sown a physical b., it is raised a spiritual b.   144.53

Take this and eat; this is my b.   24.1

Take this and eat; this is my b.   36.1

The two will become one b.   231.6

There is one b. and one Spirit,   264.7

This is my b., which is given for you. Eat this   36.4

we who are many are one b.   36.3

your b. is the temple of the Holy Spirit   24.3

your own eyes you saw my b. being formed.   18.5

bold: The righteous are b. as a lion.   39.3

boldly: Let us therefore b. approach the throne
35.53

boldness: enable... to speak your word with all b.
45.7

they were astonished at their b.   39.5

we have b. before God.   39.10

bond: there is neither b. nor free   125.25

bones: Prophesy over these b.; say: Dry b.   212.4

book: not found written in the b. of life   144.31

whosoever was not found written in the b.   144.42

born: A time to be b., and a time to die.   18.6

before you were b. I consecrated you   18.8

Even before I was b., you had written in your book
18.5

every one that loveth is b. of God   18.13

Except a man be b. of water and of the Spirit
272.7

Except a man be b. of water and of the Spirit
119.14

For unto us a child is b.   18.7

For unto you is b. this day in the city of David
221.6

How can a grown man ever be b. a second time?
18.11

Jesus answered... Except a man be b. again   169.3

Jesus replied... you must be b. from above   18.11

Which were b., not of blood   18.10

Whosoever believeth... is b. of God.   18.14

you have been b. again as the children   169.7

borrower: the b. is servant to the lender.   52.5

bother: Don't let it b. you when all goes well
282.2

bought: you have been b. at a price.   199.9

bountiful: He that hath a b. eye shall be blessed
97.5

bow: At the name of Jesus every knee should b.
283.10

the families of the nations b. before him.   42.1

branch: I will raise up for David a righteous B.
135.45

brave: Wait for the Lord; be strong and b.   45.3

bravely: we should come b. before the throne
39.6

bread: b. which strengtheneth man's heart.   90.5
But if you eat the b. and drink the wine   36.4
During supper Jesus took b.   36.1
for we all partake of the one b.   36.3
Give us this day our daily b.   90.10
human beings must not depend on b. alone   150.3
in breaking of b., and in prayers   31.33
in breaking of b., and in prayers.   36.2
people cannot live on b. alone   90.3
Ravens brought him b. and meat twice a day   90.4

break: so that by dying he might b. the power of him
93.10

breath: breathed into his nostrils the b. of life
18.1

breathed: Jesus again cried aloud and b. his last.
242.6

bribe: Do not accept a b., for a b. makes people blind
25.2

bribes: Corrupt judges accept secret b.   25.4
Don't take b. and you will live longer.   25.3
Judges and leaders demand b., and rulers cheat
25.5

bride: prepared as a b. adorned for her husband.
144.47

bring: Christ also suffered... in order to b. you to
God.   3.9

broken: The sacrifices of God are a b. spirit   220.5
The sacrifices of God are a b. spirit: 109.2

brother: The elder b. got so angry   134.5

bruise: b. thy head, and thou shalt b. his heel.
135.15

bucket: the nations are as a drop of a b.   103.40

build: let us b. ourselves a city and a tower   6.9

burden: The b. of it was far too heavy for us
57.15
they will bear the b. with you   149.1

burdens: Carry one another's b.   35.15
They pile heavy b. on people's shoulders   223.6

buried: That he was b.; that he was raised to life
135.101

we are b. with him by baptism into death   15.8

burnt-offerings: Even though you offer me your b.
217.3

busybodies: working not at all, but are b.   107.10

C

Caesar: Render... unto C. the things which are
Caesar's   243.1

Cain: The Lord was pleased... but not with C.
163.1

calf: you ordered the best c. to be killed for a feast.
134.5

call: Before they c. I will answer   184.13
eager to confirm your c. and election   31.40
For whosoever shall c. upon the name of the Lord
31.27
will c. to the Lord, but he will not answer.   184.24

called: c. us with an holy calling   31.7
I have c. thee by thy name   31.1
I have c. thee by thy name; thou art mine.   35.6
just as God who c. you is holy.   31.8
the calling to which you have been c.   31.6
those whom he c. he also justified   31.4
those whom he predestined he also c.   72.8
To those who are c., to those who are dear   31.12
You can rely on God, who has c. you   31.5

calling: brothers, never allow your choice or c.
72.15
discharge all the duties of your c.   175.3
lead a life worthy of the c.   31.6
saved us, and called us with an holy c.   31.7

calls: c. on the name of the Lord shall be saved
221.2

calm: If you stay c., you are wise   176.2
They rejoiced because it was c.   195.3

captives: to proclaim liberty to the c.   93.1

captivity: we bring every thought into c.   271.3

care: Casting all your c. upon him   35.17
Take c. of him; and when I come back   140.3

careful: Be c. for nothing; but in every thing by
prayer   26.6
they which have believed in God might be c.   26.7

cares: person who hears the word, but worldly c.
246.7

careth: he c. for you.   26.9
he c. for you.   35.17

carried: he c. me out by his spirit and set me down
257.8

cast: cometh to me I will in no wise c. out.   240.6
I will in no wise c. out.   31.22

casting: C. all your care upon him; for he   35.17

cease: day and night, they will never c.   192.1

celebrate: Josiah told the people of Judah, 'C.
Passover   27.3

celebrated: The Israelites… joyfully c. the dedication
of   27.4

Cephas: he appeared to C., and afterwards to
135.101

certificate: a man give his wife a c. of divorce
157.14

change: but a c. of heart leading to salvation
203.17
For I am the Lord, I c. not   103.69

changed: c. into the same image from glory to glory
102.13

chanting: Spare me the din of your c.   166.11

character: And endurance builds c., which gives us a
hope   29.7
God's steward… be a man of unimpeachable c.
29.9
Make no mistake: 'Bad company ruins good c.'
29.8

charge: If he has cheated… c. it to my account.
208.15

charity: c. shall cover the multitude of sins
154.21

chasten: As many as I love, I rebuke and c.   62.5

chastened: How good for me to have been c.   2.3

cheat: Do not c. anyone by using false measures
132.3

chest: sent gifts… for taking the sacred c.   207.5

chief: And whosoever will be c. among you   32.3

child: For unto us a c. is born   18.7
For unto us a c. is born   135.53
I shall give the c. to the Lord   86.12
My c., do not regard lightly the discipline   5.9
the Lord… chastises every c. whom he accepts.
5.9

they saw the young c. with Mary his mother
135.65
Train up a c. in the way he should go: 86.17

childbirth: A woman in c. suffers   18.12

children: because you are c. God has sent the Spirit
5.7
C., obey your parents in everything   86.24
C., you belong to the Lord   86.22
Children's c. are a crown to the aged   86.16
Foolish c. bring grief to their fathers   284.4
God is treating you as c.   5.9
he lets us be called his c., as we truly are.   5.10
letting us be called God's c.   188.17
Lo, c. are an heritage of the Lord: 86.14
My dear friends, we are already God's c.   5.10
My dear friends, we are already God's c.   32.12
None of those who are c. of God continue to sin
169.8
Repeat them to your c.   86.10
revealing them to little c.   235.6
Suffer the little c. to come unto me   86.20
the Father… calling us his c.!   31.11
They brought young c. to him   86.20
This also makes your c. holy   86.5
unless you change and become like little c.   235.7
you may become the c. of your Father in heaven.
5.1

choice: I offer you the c. of life or death   53.1
I offer you the c. of life or death   30.2

choose: C. life and you and your descendants
30.2
C. life and you and your descendants will   53.1
c. understanding in preference to silver.   30.8
c. you this day whom ye will serve   30.3
knows how to refuse the bad and c. the good.
30.10
You did not c. me.   30.11
You did not c. me, no, I chose you   72.5

chooses: those to whom the Son c. to reveal him.
72.1
Whoever c. to be the world's friend   30.14

chose: From the beginning of time God c. you
72.12
God c. those who by human standards are fools
30.12
he loved you and c. you for his own.   72.11
I c. you and sent you out   30.11
You did not choose me, no, I c. you;   72.5

chosen: descendants of Israel, c. to be God's sons
188.8
God had already c. us to be his   72.10

good name is rather to be c. than great riches   30.9
he has c. you out of all peoples on earth   30.1
I have c. the path of faithfulness   30.6
Israel, you are the c. people   108.1
Let thine hand help me; for I have c. thy   30.7
those who had been c. for eternal life   72.7
You are a c. race, a royal priesthood   72.14

Christ: appear before the judgment seat of C.   144.38
as your pattern, just as I take C. for mine   32.5
at the right time C. died for the ungodly.   135.22
boast... except the cross of our Lord Jesus C.   135.27
But C. has been raised to life!   135.102
But C. offered himself as a sacrifice   187.11
But we have the mind of C.   160.8
By becoming a curse for us C. has redeemed   191.4
called you to be partners with his Son Jesus C.   31.5
C. died for our sins, in accordance with   135.25
C. died once for our sins.   13.11
C. gave his life for us.   32.13
C. has been raised to life!   35.24
C. himself suffered for you   31.10
C. is the head of the church   33.7
C. Jesus, who became for us wisdom from God.   277.16
C. offered himself as a sacrifice   135.75
C. sacrificed his life's blood   23.5
C. too suffered for our sins once and for all   31.29
dear to God the Father and kept safe for Jesus C.   31.12
For C. died for sins once and for all   216.20
God was in C. offering peace and forgiveness   198.4
grace, which was given us in C. Jesus   31.7
he raised C. from the dead, and enthroned him   103.67
I have been put to death with C. on his cross   135.26
I want very much to... be with C.   144.72
if any man be in C., he is a new creature   169.4
If ye then be risen with C., seek those   135.103
It is not as though C. had entered   144.17
just as C. was raised from death   135.99
Let the word of C. dwell in you richly   17.8
Let this mind be in you, which was also in C.   32.8
My one desire is to know C.   32.9
Now you are the body of C.   24.4
one mediator between God and men... C. Jesus.   135.59
one mediator... the man C. Jesus.   135.70
remains for C. to suffer in my own person.   248.11

separate us from the love of God in C. Jesus   135.83
Simon Peter answered... Thou art the C.   135.66
So also C. glorified not himself   135.72
sprinkling of the blood of Jesus C.   259.7
That C. may dwell in your hearts through faith   135.84
the dead in C. shall rise first.   144.56
Unless C. was raised to life, your faith   135.102
until C. is formed in you.   32.7
until it is finished on the Day of C. Jesus.   31.35
We know that C., being raised from the dead   135.100
We preach C. crucified, unto the Jews   135.24

church: Christ is the head of the c.   33.7
feed the C. of God... bought with the blood   33.6
He is the head of the body, the c.   24.6
so as to present the c. to himself in splendour   33.7
So it was that the c.... had a time of peace.   33.4
tell it to the c.   33.2
upon this rock I will build my c.   33.1

circumcised: All these people are c., but have not kept   34.2
Every male among you shall be c.   34.1
For whether or not a man is c. means nothing   34.4
We are the ones who are truly c.   133.9

circumcision: an external mark in the flesh that makes c.   34.3
For we are the c., which worship God   34.6
his c. is of the heart, spiritual   34.3
True c. is something that happens deep   217.6

citizens: We, however, are c. of heaven   144.16

city: For unto you is born this day in the c. of David   221.6

clay: his feet part of iron and part of c.   274.2
we are the c., you the potter   125.10

clean: Create in me a c. heart, O God   169.1
you shall be c. from all your uncleannesses   169.2

cleanseth: the blood of Jesus Christ his Son c. us   12.10

cleave: shall c. unto his wife: and they shall   86.1

closed: Their minds are c.   112.11

cloud: a c. hid him from their sight.   135.5

clouds: Look! He is coming with the c.   144.66
one like a son of man, coming with the c.   144.58

clue: He has not left you without some c.   210.5

cooperates: In everything, as we know, he c. for good
240.8

cobra: The infant will play over the c. hole,   9.10

collections: so that c. need not be taken when I
come.   101.7

come: C. to me, all who are weary and whose load
31.18
C. to me, all you who labour   35.14
For where two or three c. together in my name
184.43
I will c. again   35.22
I will c. again, and receive you   144.60
I will c. to you.   155.12
Oh, that you would rend the heavens and c. down
212.3
will c. in the same way as you have seen him go
144.61

cometh: him that c. to me   31.22
him that c. to me I will in no wise cast out   12.1
him that c. to me I will in no wise cast out   72.3
no man c. unto the Father, but by me.   3.2

comfort: C. ye, c. ye my people, saith your God
35.44
Praise be to… the God of all c.   35.50
thy rod and thy staff they c. me.   35.19
we can c. those in any trouble with the c.   35.50

comforted: they that mourn: for they shall be c.
35.20

Comforter: he shall give you another C.   119.16

comfortless: I will not leave you c.   35.38

coming: I am c., soon; hold fast to what you have
31.42
Look! He is c. with the clouds   144.66

commandment: This is the first and great c.
205.3

commandments: If ye love me, keep my c.   170.6

commands: he c. is that we believe in his Son
276.10
when we love God and obey his c.   170.15
with authority and power he c.   135.12

commit: C. your way to the Lord; trust in him
110.2

compact: I have entered into a solemn c.   155.2

compassion: clothe yourselves with c., kindness
159.14
For the Lord is full of c.   103.52
Jesus… was moved with c. toward them   249.6
love the brothers, have c. and be self-effacing
249.14

compensation: give it to the one to whom c. is due.
207.4

complaining: I am not c. about having too little
41.6

conceit: The rich man is wise in his own c.   37.4

conceited: Do not be c.   186.7
Don't be c. or make others jealous   37.11

conceits: Be not wise in your own c.   37.7

conceived: sinful from the time my mother c. me.
18.3

conception: I will greatly multiply thy sorrow and thy
c.   18.2

concerned: Remember the Lord's people… be c.
249.13

condemn: not his Son into the world to c. the world
281.4

condemnation: as the result of one misdeed was c.
84.4
C. will never come to those who are in Christ Jesus.
12.5
In our natural condition we lay under the c. of God
8.8
Thus c. will never come to those who   111.6

condemned: those who have done evil will rise and
be c.   144.51

confess: C. them and give them up   38.7
C. your faults one to another   38.10
Every tongue should c. that Jesus Christ is Lord
38.3
I shall c. my offence to the Lord   38.6
if thou shalt c. with thy mouth the Lord Jesus
38.2
If we c. our sins, he who is faithful   38.11
When a person is guilty, he must c. the sin.   38.5

confession: While Ezra was praying and making c.
202.2

confidence: Do not put your c. in your money
39.4
In the fear of the Lord one has strong c.   39.2
makes us free to enter the sanctuary with c.   39.7
we may have c. on the day of judgement   39.11
when he returns we will have c.   39.9

confident: in this will I be c. One thing have I
desired   39.1

conflict: They are in c. with one another   271.4

conquered: They have c. him by the blood of the
Lamb   266.11
they have c. him by the blood of the Lamb and
271.13

conquerors: No, in all these things we are more than c. 35.47

we are more than c. through him who loved us. 266.3

conscience: as my c. testifies... in the Holy Spirit. 40.4

having our hearts sprinkled from an evil c. 40.7

If our c. condemns us 40.8

if our c. does not condemn us, we have courage 40.8

since their c. is weak, it is defiled. 40.5

So I do my best always to have a clear c. 40.2

That person's mind and c. are destroyed. 40.6

to which their own c. also bears witness 40.3

we know that God is greater than our c. 40.8

conscientiousness: In service of the Lord, work... with c. 285.3

consider: C. your way of life. 227.2

considerate: For my part I always try to be c. to everyone 265.8

consoles: He c. us in all our troubles 249.10

constancy: Let faithful love and c. never leave you 155.6

contain: the highest heaven cannot c. you 103.39

content: be c. with what you have 41.8

Be c. with your pay. 41.3

control: If you... can't c. your tongue 225.11

not spare my body, but bring it under strict c. 225.7

controlling: C. your temper is better than being a hero 225.4

converted: that thy faith fail not: and when thou art c. 42.4

Verily I say unto you, Except ye be c. 42.2

when you were c. to God and became servants 42.7

convinced: Some of them were c. and joined Paul and Silas. 160.3

cord: A threefold c. is not quickly broken. 264.2

cornerstone: The stone... has become the main c. 200.2

corpses: they will see the c. of those who rebelled 144.48

correctly: he could not pronounce the word c. 241.1

corrupt: All of them are c.; no one does right. 237.1

counsel: C. in another's heart is like deep water 163.4

The Lord brings the c. of the nations 44.3

who does not take the c. of the wicked 44.1

Counsellor: his name shall be called Wonderful, C., 44.6

Wonderful, C., the mighty God 135.53

counsels: thy c. of old are faithfulness 44.7

countenance: they will never be put out of c. 232.2

country: a blessing on you in the c. 143.5

A prophet is not without honour, save in his own c. 190.4

courage: At this the c. of the people melted 88.3

C.! It's me! Don't be afraid. 35.7

C., my son! Your sins are forgiven. 45.4

my c. fails. 57.6

courageous: Be strong and c. 45.1

Be strong and c. Do not be afraid 45.2

covenant: Behold the blood of the c. 46.2

he is the mediator of a new c. 46.8

his c. is for their instruction. 46.3

I will establish my c. between me and you 46.1

This is my blood of the c. 23.2

This is my blood, which seals God's c. 46.4

This is my c., which you shall keep 34.1

This is the c. that I will make with the house 46.7

through the blood of the everlasting c. 46.9

covenants: Aliens with no part in the c. of the Promise 46.5

strangers to God's c. and the promise 189.4

covet: Thou shalt not c. thy neighbour's house 56.1

created: All things were c. by God's Son 47.12

behold who hath c. these things 47.6

Everything was c. by him 47.12

for thou hast c. all things 47.14

For we are his workmanship, c. in Christ Jesus 47.11

I praise you because of the... way you c. me. 18.5

In the beginning God c. the heaven and the earth 47.1

So God c. man in his own image 47.2

The word of the Lord c. the heavens 47.4

creation: All of creation waits with eager longing for God 47.9

But it is not just c. alone which groans 47.9

Ever since the c. of the world 47.8

If anyone is in Christ, there is a new c. 47.10

Nothing in c. can hide from him   103.3
proclaim the gospel to the whole c.   47.7
The c. itself will be set free   144.45

creator: Lord, the C. of the ends of the earth, fainteth not   103.10
the C. of the ends of the earth   47.6

creature: every wild c. is in my care   9.9
Let the earth produce every kind of living c.   9.1
Look at Behemoth, my c.,   9.7

creatures: the fish in the sea, and all ocean c.   9.8

cried: This poor man c., and the Lord heard him   184.1

cries: The Lord… listens to their c.   184.11

crooked: one whose ways are c. is brought low.   64.6

cross: boast… except the c. of our Lord Jesus Christ   135.27
Having made peace through the blood of his c.   23.6
making peace through the blood of his c.   198.6
The message of the c. is folly for those   135.23
Whoever does not carry the c. and follow me   31.19

crown: let no one rob you of your c.   31.42
receive the c. of life that the Lord has promised   189.7

crowneth: who c. thee with lovingkindness   103.51

crucified: This man… you c. and killed   135.19
We preach Christ c.,   135.24

cruel: he that is c. troubleth his own flesh.   48.4
one who is wicked is c. at heart.   48.5
Others had trial of c. mockings   48.12
save me, Lord God, from vicious and c.   48.2
the day of the Lord cometh, c. both with wrath   48.7
Thou are become c. to me   48.1
You have made c. and unfair laws   48.6
You must no longer say insulting or c.   48.11

cruelty: the earth are full of the habitations of c.   48.3

crush: Then God, who gives peace, will soon c. Satan   266.4

crushed: who can endure if the spirit is c.?   57.10
who can endure if the spirit is c.?   55.6

cry: don't expect to be heard when you c. out for help.   184.21

cup: he took a c., and having offered thanks   36.1
my c. runneth over   35.19
The c. of blessing that we bless   36.3

cure: to c. every disease and every sickness.   14.5

curse: bless them that c. you   19.9
By becoming a c. for us Christ has redeemed   191.4
Christ has redeemed us from the c.   199.10

cursed: c. is the ground for thy sake   84.2
Depart from me, ye c., into everlasting fire   54.3

curtain: way which he has opened for us through the c.   188.14

cymbals: the accompaniment of lyres, lutes, and c.   166.4

D

danced: they d. for the Lord with all their might.   166.2

dancing: our d. has turned to mourning.   166.10

darkness: But anyone who hates his fellow is in d.   49.16
d. covered the deep   49.1
God has brought you out of d. into his   49.14
God is light, and there is no d. in him   49.15
He called the light day, and the d. night.   49.1
He rescued us from the domain of d.   49.13
he separated light from d.   49.1
he that walketh in d. knoweth not whither   49.10
If I say, Surely the d. shall cover me   49.4
into thick d. he brings light.   49.2
light shineth in d.; and the d. comprehended   49.9
shall be cast out into outer d.   144.24
Take no part in the barren deeds of d.   49.12
the d. and the light are both alike to thee   49.4
the d. has made him blind.   49.16
The lifestyle of the wicked is like total d.   49.5
The people that walked in d. have seen a great   49.7
them that sit in d. out of the prison house.   22.7
Though d. covers the earth and dark night   49.8
throw off everything that belongs to the d.   49.11
who substitute d. for light and light for d.   49.6
You, the Lord God… turn d. to light.   49.3

daughter: those who love their son or d. more than me   86.18

daughters: you shall be my sons and d.   5.6

David: D. was very angry, and burst out   207.6

For unto you is born this day in the city of D.
    221.6

day: a thousand years are like one d.   256.15

But about that d. and hour no one knows   144.59

carry it on until it is finished on the D. of Christ
    31.35

Remember the sabbath d., to keep it holy.   256.2

see, now is the d. of salvation!   221.13

the D. of the Lord is going to come like a thief in the
    night.   144.63

This is a special d. for the Lord your God.   27.5

when he comes on that D. to receive glory   144.64

days: all the d. of my life: 35.19

Honour thy father and thy mother: that thy d.
    150.2

sake of the elect those d. will be cut short.   144.3

So teach us to number our d.   172.5

deacons: D. likewise must be serious   50.2

dead: As for you, you were d. in your transgressions
    262.7

Blessed are the d. who from now on die   144.76

d. to sin and alive to God in Christ   135.100

How shall we, that are d. to sin   253.16

if one died for all, then were all d.   13.6

regard yourselves as d. to sin   236.28

the d. in Christ shall rise first   35.26

the d. in Christ shall rise first.   144.56

the d. in Christ shall rise first: 51.22

the d. in Christ shall rise first: 144.62

you must see yourselves as being d. to sin   51.10

you were d. in your transgressions   51.18

you were d. in your transgressions and sins
    236.16

death: Be thou faithful unto d.   51.28

Christ our Saviour defeated d. and brought us
    51.23

D. is swallowed up in victory. O d.   51.16

For I have no pleasure in the d. of anyone   51.7

For the wages of sin is d.   236.14

For the wages of sin is d.   51.11

has passed from d. to life.   150.17

he might break the power of him who had d.
    51.25

I hold the keys of d. and Hades.   135.104

in the Lord's sight is the d. of those who   51.5

put to d. in the body, he was brought to life   31.29

so d. passed upon all men   84.3

the desire conceives… it gives birth to d.   51.27

the end thereof are the ways of d.   51.6

The last enemy that shall be destroyed is d.   51.15

The legacy… is the second d.   144.32

the valley of the shadow of d.   35.19

there shall be no more d.   51.29

was obedient, even to the point of d.   135.90

we were reconciled to him through the d. of his Son
    198.3

Whoever… kills him is to be put to d.   193.1

You must put to d., then, the earthly desires   51.21

death's: even hard at d. door.   51.4

debtor's: he returns the d. pledge   52.7

debtors: Forgive us our debts, as we forgive our d.
    52.10

Will not your d. suddenly start up?   52.8

debts: Forgive us our d., as we forgive our debtors.
    52.10

not be one of those… who go surety for d.   52.6

deceit: He had… spoken no d.   135.40

deceitful: pay attention to d. spirits and doctrines
    251.7

deceitfulness: hardened through the d. of sin
    236.33

deceiver: Any such person is the d. and antichrist.
    10.9

decided: he d. when and where every nation would
    be.   53.11

the whole church, d. to choose delegates   110.6

decision: the Lord is near in the valley of d.   53.9

decisions: All of his d. are correct and fair.   53.2

We make our own d., but the Lord alone   53.5

declare: D. among the nations, 'The Lord is King.'
    278.1

those who d. publicly that they belong to me   38.1

those who d. publicly that they belong to me
    144.33

decrease: He must increase, but I must d.   226.3

deed: Whatsoever ye do in word or d.   279.11

deeds: This God – how perfect are his d.   273.1

to prove their repentance by their d.   280.6

well known for her good d.   275.10

defeat: Every child of God is able to d. the world.
    266.10

defeated: There Christ d. all powers and forces.
    266.8

defence: Always be ready to make your d. to anyone
    241.12

defend: d. the cause of the fatherless   280.2

D. the cause of the fatherless   138.5

defiance: He will hurl d. at the Most High   10.2
You must not act in d. of the Lord.   197.1

delight: For I d. in the law of God   31.50
For I d. in the law of God in my inmost self   222.3
I d. to do your will, O my God   135.86

deluding: he is d. himself.   37.12

demolish: the power, in God's cause, to d. fortresses.
266.6

demon: Jesus forced a d. out of a man   54.8

demons: a man from the town who had d. in him.
54.6
people brought to Jesus many who had d.   54.1
power and authority over all d.   54.7
the chief of the d. who gives him the power   54.5
The d. begged Jesus, 'If you are going to   54.2

demonstration: with a d. of the Spirit and of power.
119.33

denies: he d. both the Father and the Son.   156.9

deny: Before the cock crow, thou shalt d. me thrice.
81.11
Hold a sacred assembly and d. yourselves   87.1

depraved: he has given them up to their own d. ways
48.9

depths: Out of the d. have I cried unto thee, O Lord.
57.8

desert: sending it into the d. as a scapegoat   236.1

deserted: everyone in the province of Asia... has d.
me.   153.6
I defended myself; all d. me.   35.39

deserved: do not say to yourselves... you d. it.
229.1

designs: reveal the d. of all hearts.   163.10

desire: Give me the d. to obey your laws   56.2
he will grant you your heart's d.   184.40
one is tempted by one's own d.   253.11

desires: anyone who d. to be a church official   6.8
I beg you not to surrender to those d.   236.35
not gratify the d. of your unspiritual nature.
237.11
the trap of many foolish and harmful d.   56.7
We were ruled by our physical d.   237.12

desolate: my heart within me is d.   57.9

despair: I am sick of life! And from my deep d.
57.3
Then I turned and gave myself up to d.   57.11

they had reached the depths of d.   57.1
we see no way out but we never d.   35.33

despaired: insomuch that we d. even of life.
246.12

despairs: Devotion is due... to one who d.   57.2

desperate: I suffer your terrors; I am d.   57.7

despise: See that you don't d. any of these little ones.
154.15
See that you never d. any of these little ones   204.7

despised: He is d. and rejected of men; a man of
sorrows   135.16
he was d., and we esteemed him not.   200.4

destroy: They shall not hurt nor d.   272.1

destroyed: On that day the heavens will be d. by fire
144.46

destruction: the one destined for d. He opposes
144.5
the road is easy that leads to d.   144.23

determined: Daniel d. not to become contaminated
53.8

detestable: who does these things is d. to the Lord.
171.4

devil: able to stand against the wiles of the d.
58.11
against the wiles of the d.   253.18
He died to destroy the d.   58.12
Like a roaring lion your adversary the d.   253.24
Like a roaring lion your adversary the d. prowls
271.12
Resist the d., and he will flee from you.   271.10
so that the d. could test him.   58.3
the D., or Satan – and chained him up   144.7
the D.... was thrown into the lake of fire   144.30
Then the D., who deceived them   144.57
Then the D., who deceived them, was thrown
58.17
You are from your father the d.   58.5
your enemy the d. is on the prowl   58.13

devil's: the very purpose of undoing the d. work.
58.14

devils: the d. also believe, and tremble.   54.11

devoting: d. herself to all kinds of good deeds.
275.10

die: even though your bodies must d.   51.12
For as all d. in Adam   51.14
For me to live is Christ, and to d. is gain.   51.19
if we d., we d. for the Lord.   51.13

It is appointed unto men once to d.   51.26
It is appointed unto men once to d.   144.39
said unto the woman, Ye shall not surely d.   84.1
thou eatest thereof thou shalt surely d.   51.1
whoever obeys my teaching will never d.   51.9
Whosoever… believeth in me shall never d.
  144.70

died: Christ d. for our sins, in accordance with
  135.25
Christ d. for the ungodly.   135.22
Christ d. for us while we were still sinners.   13.5
Christ d. once for our sins.   13.11
if one d. for all, then were all dead.   13.6
if we d. with Christ, then we shall live   51.10
The saying is sure: If we have d. with him   51.24
Then he bowed his head and d.   135.111
who have d. for his laws, unto everlasting   51.8

difference: the ability to tell the d. between gifts
  60.4

dignified: Deacons, likewise, must be d.   59.8

dignity: Folly is set in great d.   59.6
sacred vestments to give d. and magnificence.
  59.2
She is clothed in strength and d.   59.5

diligence: give d. to make your calling… sure
  205.10

direct: keep him in mind, and he will d. your path.
  53.4

disarmed: He d. the rulers and authorities   271.7
He d. the rulers and authorities   135.28

discern: able to d. between good and evil   60.1

discerned: they are spiritually d.   60.3

discerner: a d. of the thoughts and intents of the
  heart.   60.7

disciple: carry the cross and follow me cannot be my
  d.   31.19
does not carry the cross… cannot be my d.   61.3
none of you can become my d. if you do not   61.3

disciples: By this shall all men know that ye are my
  d.   61.5
D. are not better than their teacher   32.2
Go therefore and make d. of all nations   278.5
It is enough for d. to be like their teacher   32.2
make them my d.: baptize them in the name   61.2
number of the d. increased greatly   212.9
stand by my teaching, you are truly my d.   31.30
stand by my teaching, you are truly my d.   61.4
When he had called unto him his twelve d.   61.1

ye are my d., if ye have love one to another.
  154.16
you should bear much fruit and be my d.   61.6

discipline: Endure trials for the sake of d.   62.4
I reprove and d. those whom I love   285.12
My child, do not despise the Lord's d.   2.4

disciplined: For they d. us for a short time as seemed
  best   248.19

disciplines: he d. us for our good   248.19

disclosed: I have d. to you the whole purpose of
  God.   185.4
I have d. to you the whole purpose of God.   44.8

discouraged: But now you feel d. when struck by
  trouble.   63.8
Do not be afraid or d.   63.3
do not be afraid or d.   63.2
do not be fearful or d.   63.4
He shall not fail nor be d., till he have   63.10
the soul of the people was much d.   63.1
you should not be d. when I suffer for you.   63.13

discussions: he held d. with the people, quoting
  160.3

disease: Asa was afflicted with a d. in his feet.
  129.1

diseased: my whole body is d. because of my sins.
  129.3

diseases: all who had d. pressed upon him to touch
  him.   129.4

dish: Better a d. of herbs when love is there   120.6

dishonest: anyone who is d. in little matters will be
  d.   64.13
The Lord is disgusted with anyone who… is d.
  64.2
The master applauded the d. steward   64.12

dishonestly: If you try to make a profit d.   56.3

dishonesty: Don't trust in violence or depend on d.
  64.4

dismayed: fear not, nor be d.: for the Lord God
  63.5

disobedience: Just as by one man's d. many were
  made   65.3

disobedient: People will be lovers of themselves… d.
  65.6
who is now at work in those who are d.   65.4

distinguish: trained by practice to d. good from evil.
  60.8

distress: anguish and d. for everyone who does evil
248.7

dark as night for a country in d.?   57.12

I am worn out and weak, moaning and in d.   57.5

I am worn out and weak, moaning and in d.
246.1

In my d. I called to the Lord   246.5

divided: and the waters were d.   161.1

divination: Do not practise d. or sorcery.   171.1

Let no-one be found… who practises d.   171.4

divorce: For I hate d., says the Lord   157.12

Moses permitted you to d. your wives because
157.14

do: Commit to the Lord all that you d.   279.6

leaders will d. anything you tell them   1.6

There is nothing I cannot d.   1.10

Whatsoever thy hand findeth to d.   279.7

doctrine: They continued… in the apostles' d.
33.3

They continued stedfastly in the apostles' d.   31.33

They continued stedfastly in the apostles' d.   250.6

doers: Be ye d. of the word, and not hearers only
280.11

Be ye d. of the word, and not hearers only   170.12

does: He d. whatever he wishes in heaven and on
earth   192.5

dominion: Thou madest him to have d. over the
works   188.1

donkey: riding on a d. – on a colt, the foal of a d.
135.47

door: even hard at death's d.   51.4

Try your hardest to enter by the narrow d.   221.7

double-dealer: the d. scorns him.   64.8

doubt: ask in faith, with never a d. in his mind
66.9

If you have faith and don't d.   66.6

put it in my side. Do not d. but believe.   261.9

doubted: they worshipped him; but some d.   66.7

doubter: the d. is like a wave of the sea tossed
66.9

doubting: But ask in faith, never d.   184.38

dove: he saw the Spirit of God descending like a d.,
15.2

the Spirit of God coming down on him like a d.
119.10

the Spirit of God descending like a d.   177.5

dragon: He seized the d., that ancient serpent
144.7

draw: D. near to God, and he will d. near   271.10

drawn: No one can come to me unless d.   72.4

dream: angel of the Lord appeared to him in a d.
67.8

back to Jerusalem, it was like a d.!   67.4

Joseph had a d.   67.2

These, then, are the d. and the visions   67.6

dreamed: He d., and behold a ladder set up on the
earth   67.1

dreams: But put to death any interpreters of d.
67.3

I am against those… who deal in false d.   67.5

Prophets or interpreters of d. may promise   67.3

your old men shall dream d.   67.7

drink: D. this and remember me.   36.4

Let us eat and d.; for tomorrow we   68.3

my flesh is real food and my blood is real d.   90.12

priest… lose their way through strong d.   68.4

they are set wandering by strong d.   68.4

drinking: You get up early in the morning to start d.
68.2

drinks: Show me someone who d. too much   68.1

drop: the nations are as a d. of a bucket   103.40

drunk: Be not d. with wine, wherein is excess
68.7

you spend long evenings getting d.   68.2

drunkenness: no orgies or d.   68.5

Now the works of the flesh are obvious… d.   68.6

dumb: like a sheep d. before its shearers   234.7

dust: all are of the d., and all turn to d. again.
125.8

for d. thou art, and unto d. shalt thou return   51.2

for d. thou art, and unto d. shalt thou return.   84.2

the nations are… the small d.   103.40

duties: discharge all the d. of your calling.   175.3

duty: for this is the whole d. of man.   205.1

I do it as a matter of d.   245.4

we will appoint them for this d.   50.1

dwell: I may d. in the house of the Lord   6.1

that I may d. in the house of the Lord   31.44

dying: by d. he might break the power of him
51.25

Our bodies are gradually d.   257.6

E

eager: You are, I know, e. for gifts of the Spirit;   6.5

eagerly: Beloved, while e. preparing to write to you
285.11

eagle: As an e. stirreth up her nest, fluttereth
154.2

eagles: they shall mount up with wings as e.
202.5

they shall mount up with wings as e.   182.1

earnest: Be e., therefore, and repent.   285.12

earnestly: love one another e. with all your heart.
285.10

earth: As long as e. lasts, seedtime and harvest
69.2

As long as the e. lasts, seedtime and harvest   192.1

first heaven and the first e. had disappeared   69.15

For in six days the Lord made... the e.   69.3

I am creating new heavens and a new e.   69.11

I go the way of all the e.   51.3

I was there before he began to create the e.   69.9

In the beginning God created... the e.   69.1

It is he that sitteth upon the circle of the e.
103.63

the e. hath he given to the children of men.   69.8

The e. is the Lord's, and the fulness   69.5

The e. is the Lord's, and the fulness thereof   281.1

The e. shall be full of the knowledge   69.10

the e. was without form, and void   69.1

Then I saw a new heaven and a new e.   69.15

Thus saith the Lord... the e. is my footstool   69.12

Thy kingdom come. Thy will be done in e.   69.13

To the Lord belong the e. and everything in it
143.7

we are not afraid though the e. shakes   69.6

we look forward to new heavens and a new e.
69.14

Ye are the salt of the e.   31.2

You alone are the Lord; you created... the e.   69.4

earth's: Long ago you laid e. foundations   69.7

earthly: You must kill everything in you that is e.
236.31

eat: E. this and remember me.   36.4

Eden: God sent him forth from the garden of E.
70.2

put him in the garden of E. to till it   26.1

The Lord God planted a garden eastward in E.
70.1

elated: to save me from being unduly e.   186.11

elder: I, who am an e. myself   71.12

elders: appoint e. in every town, as I directed you.
71.8

delivered their contributions to the e.   71.2

E. who give good service as leaders   71.7

Go and assemble the e. of Israel   71.1

In each church they appointed e.   71.3

let him call for the e. of the church   71.11

They also appointed for them e.   33.5

elect: E. according to the foreknowledge of God
72.13

election: eager to confirm your call and e.   31.40

eleventh: And about the e. hour he went out
256.5

emperor: Fear God. Honour the e.   243.5

encourage: convince, rebuke, and e.,   73.9

If it is encouraging, let him e.   73.6

Instead, let us e. one another   73.11

We urge you, brothers... e. the timid   73.8

encouraged: he rejoiced and e. them all to hold fast
73.3

They e. the followers   73.4

We e. you, we comforted you   73.7

We e. you, we comforted you   175.2

encouragement: Barnabas (which means, 'Son of E.')
73.2

encouraging: If it is e., let him encourage.   73.6

spoke for a long time, e. and strengthening   73.5

Strengthening the disciples and e. them   31.34

We should keep on e. each other   33.8

end: Before the e. comes, the good news must be
preached   278.6

but the e. is not yet.   144.1

faithful right to the e., you will be saved.   221.5

keep on being faithful right to the e.   144.2

endurance: E. produces character, and character
74.3

no limit to its faith, its hope, its e.   176.6

endure: How long must I e. trouble?   55.3

If we e., we will also reign with him   74.8

with all power always to persevere and e.   74.6

you must e. your share of suffering.   74.7

endured: the joy that was set before him e. the cross
74.9

endureth: He that e. to the end shall be saved.
74.1

enemies: I say unto you, Love your e.   19.9

If your e. are hungry, give them bread to eat   75.4

while we were e., we were reconciled to God   75.6

you can make your e. into friends.   75.2

enemy: Do not rejoice at the fall of your e.   75.3

Ye have heard… hate thine e. But I say   75.5

enemy's: Should you come upon your e. ox or donkey   75.1

enjoy: who richly provides all things for us to e. 137.19

enough: food and clothes, that should be e. for us 41.7

enter: Jesus gives us courage to e. the most holy place   3.7

enticed: one's own desire, being lured and e. by it 253.11

entrusted: called his servants and e. his capital to them   245.1

Guard the good treasure e. to you   245.6

heard the way in which God e. me with the grace 245.5

the more he has had e. to him the more   188.4

envious: neither be thou e. against the workers of 19.4

neither be thou e. against the workers of   76.1

envy: he knew that for e. they had delivered him. 76.4

Now the works of the flesh are obvious… e.   76.5

envying: E. the arrogant as I did, and seeing the 76.2

Ephraim: right hand and laid it on the head of E. 147.1

equipped: be capable and e. for good work of every kind.   178.11

erect: I… enabled you to walk e.   59.3

Esau: E. who for one morsel of meat sold his birthright.   131.12

escape: How shall we e. if we neglect so great salvation?   221.18

establish: let us together e. the true good   30.5

esteem: E. others more highly than yourself. 204.10

estranged: my acquaintances are wholly e. from me. 153.2

eternal: but the righteous into life e.   77.1

but the righteous into life e.   144.26

E. life is this: to know you   77.9

Fight the good fight… win the e. life   77.13

God has also said that he gave us e. life   77.14

in well-doing, he will give e. life.   77.10

may not perish but have e. life.   77.3

shall keep it unto life e.   77.8

supposing that in having them you have e. life 77.5

The angels… in e. chains in deepest darkness 144.40

the gift freely given by God is e. life   77.11

the mercy of our Lord Jesus Christ unto e. life 31.41

They follow me, and I give them e. life   77.7

what shall I do to inherit e. life?   77.2

will suffer the punishment of e. destruction 144.28

You have the message of e. life   77.6

Ethiopian: Can the E. change his skin   280.1

eunuch: e. did not see him again, but went on his way   136.10

evangelist: do the work of an e.   78.5

we stayed at the house of Philip the e.   78.3

evangelists: It is he who has given some to be… e. 78.4

Eve: Adam called his wife's name E.   125.16

everlasting: Depart from me, ye cursed, into e. fire 144.26

for that meat which endureth unto e. life,   6.20

He that believeth on the Son hath e. life   77.4

lead me in the way e.   80.1

Many… shall awake, some to e. life   144.49

everyone: Go and preach the good news to e. 278.7

God treats e. on the same basis.   196.2

everything: E. is possible for the person who has faith.   82.7

evil: Abstain from all appearance of e.   79.12

Abstain from all appearance of e.   236.32

but the e. which I would not, that I do   237.8

defeat e. with good.   209.5

Depart from e., and do good   236.23

Do not think to repay e. for e.   209.3

E. people will keep on being e.   215.14

from the heart, that e. intentions emerge   79.7

Hate what is e., hold on to what is good.   79.10

he may know to refuse the e.   215.10

I do the e. that I do not want to do.   79.9

I write… you have conquered the e. one.   79.14

Never pay back e. for e.   52.12

people who do e. things are judged guilty   79.8

put away your e. deeds far from my sight   215.8

See that none of you repays e. for e.   79.11
Shall there be e. in a city   79.3
Sufficient unto the day is the e. thereof.   79.5
the E. One comes and carries off   58.4
the love of money is the root of all e.   79.13
Why, what e. has he done?   79.6
world lies under the power of the e. one.   58.15
ye shall be as gods, knowing good and e.   79.1
Your eyes are too pure to look on e.   79.4

exalt: let us e. his name together.   183.1
Though thou e. thyself as the eagle,   6.16

exalted: Be thou e., O God, above the heavens   103.60
Being therefore e. at the right hand of God   135.6

exalts: Whoever e. himself will be humbled   186.3

examine: e. for ourselves what is right.   30.5
E. yourselves, and only then eat of the bread   227.3
E. yourselves.   227.4

example: Always set a good e. for others.   29.10
be an e. for the flock   149.11

exasperate: Fathers, do not e. your children   63.14

excelling: always e. in the work of the Lord   285.5

exhort: E. one another daily, while it is called Today   73.10

explaining: rightly e. the word of truth.   185.11

eye: An e. for an e., and a tooth for a tooth.   209.4
every e. will see him   144.66
he kept him as the apple of his e.   154.2
In a moment, in the twinkling of an e.   144.54

eyes: he hath shut their e., that they cannot see   22.8
I send you to open their e.   22.12
the e. of him to whom we must render account.   103.3

Ezra: While E. was praying and making confession   202.2

F

fail: his compassions f. not. They are new   81.4
I have prayed… that your faith may not f.   81.10
prayed for thee, that thy faith f. not   253.15
the faithful f. from among the children of men.   81.2
there be prophecies, they shall f.   81.12

failed: As my senses f. I remembered the Lord   274.3
But if Christ isn't living in you, you have f.   81.13
I hope you will discover that we have not f.   81.13
There f. not ought of any good thing   81.1

faileth: Charity never f.:   81.12
My flesh and my heart f.   35.43
My flesh and my heart f.: but God is the   81.3

failures: but to get you to do right, even if we are f.   81.13

faint: help you not to lose heart and grow f.   257.8
they shall walk, and not f.   257.2

fainted: When my soul f. within me   57.14

fair: Slave owners, be f. and honest   138.11

fairness: administer justice with strict f.   132.2

faith: a propitiation through f. in his blood,   191.3
a propitiation through f. in his blood.   82.17
Above all, taking the shield of f.   82.25
And I now live by f. in the Son of God   82.23
But ask in f., never doubting   184.38
By f. we understand that the universe was   82.27
Can f. save you?   82.29
Can't you see? His f. and his actions   82.30
encouraging them to be true to the f.   31.34
Everything is possible for the person who has f.   82.7
f. without actions is dead.   82.30
Fight the good fight of the f.   271.8
For by grace are ye saved through f.   82.24
For by grace are ye saved through f.   221.14
For we walk by f., not by sight.   82.22
Giving all diligence, add to your f. virtue;   29.11
God accepted me simply because of my f. in Christ.   216.18
God keeps f. and will not let you be tested   83.7
He was amazed at their lack of f.   261.4
his f. was made perfect through his actions   82.30
I do have f., but not enough   82.7
If you have f., everything you ask for in prayer   184.44
If you have f. in him, you will have true life   82.14
if you say you have f. but do not have works?   82.29
Jesus answered them, 'Have f. in God   82.8
Jesus the a. and finisher of our f.   35.54
keeps covenant and f. for a thousand generations   83.1
leads to salvation through f. in Christ Jesus.   221.17
miracles there because of their lack of f.   261.2
No one who puts his f. in him comes under   82.11

Now abideth f., hope, charity   82.21
Now f. is the substance of things hoped for   82.26
One Lord, one f., one baptism   15.10
put your f. in Jesus as the Messiah   82.14
So then, f. comes from hearing the message   82.20
take the shield of f.   271.6
The righteous live by their f.   82.5
the victory that conquers the world, our f.   82.32
Therefore, since we have been justified through f. 82.18
They elected Stephen, a man full of f.   82.15
When you ask for something, you must have f. 184.28
Who are kept by the power of God through f. 31.39
Why are ye fearful, O ye of little f.?   82.6
Without f. it is impossible to please him   82.28

faithful: be thou f. unto death, and I will give thee 83.12
Everyone talks about how loyal and f. he is   83.2
f. right to the end, you will be saved   221.5
he is f. and just to forgive us our sins,   12.10
he might become a merciful and f. high priest 83.11
If we are not f., he will still be f.   83.10
If we confess our sins, he is f. and just   103.46
the f. God who maintains covenant loyalty   103.15
thou hast been f. over a few things   83.5
Well done, thou good and f. servant   83.5
Whoever is f. in a very little is f. also   83.6

faithfulness: great is your f.   35.32
The fruit of the Spirit is… f.   83.8
They are new every morning: great is thy f.   83.3

fall: an haughty spirit before a f.   186.2
Jesus said to them, 'You will all f. away   85.5
take care, or you may f.   37.9

fallen: ye are f. from grace   108.13

fallow: seventh year you shall let it rest and lie f. 143.1

false: Do not cheat anyone by using f. measures 132.3
Do not spread f. rumours.   132.1
F. prophets also arose among the people   251.9
many f. prophets are gone out into the world 251.10
there shall arise f. Christs, and f. prophets,   10.3
Thou shalt not bear f. witness   156.1
Watch out for f. prophets!   251.2

familiar: Consult the ghosts and the f. spirits 171.6

family: He has put my f. far from me   153.2
must be able to manage his own f. well   86.25

far: though indeed he is not f. from each one of us 224.13
why art thou so f. from helping me,   57.4

fast: I f. twice in the week   87.8
the day will come when… they will f.   87.7
The people ask, 'Why should we f. if the Lord 87.3
When you f., do not put on a sad face   87.6

fasted: He f. for forty days and forty nights   87.5
mourned and wept, and they f. till evening   87.2

fasting: return to me with all your heart, with f. 87.4
The kind of f. I want is this: 87.3
While they were worshipping the Lord and f.   87.9

Father: A f. of the fatherless… is God   103.20
A f. who spares the rod hates his son   86.15
All that the F. giveth me shall come to me   240.6
All that the F. giveth me shall come to me   31.22
And will be a F. unto you,   103.30
As the F. hath loved me, so have I loved you 135.82
As the F. sent me, so I send you.   103.28
Every good gift… cometh down from the F. 103.70
F. sent the Son to be the Saviour of the world 221.20
For as the F. has life in himself   103.56
For us there is one God, the F.   103.29
for your heavenly F. knoweth   5.3
great is the love which the F. has bestowed   31.11
help his f. or mother… 'This is Corban'   86.19
Honour thy f. and thy mother   284.1
Honour thy f. and thy mother: 86.9
I will be your f.   5.6
no one knows the F. except the Son   210.3
O my F., if this cup may not pass away from me 135.87
one God and F. of all, over all   103.31
Our F., which art in heaven   184.32
Our F., which art in heaven…   5.2
Our F. which art in heaven, Hallowed be thy name. 103.26
pray to your F. who is in secret   184.26
since you have only one F., and he is in heaven. 103.27
the F., and of the Son, and of the Holy Ghost. 259.3
the foreknowledge of God the F.   259.7
Think how much the Father loves us.   5.10
This command I received from my F.   135.14
Those who love their f. or mother more than me 86.18
true worshippers will worship the F.   103.57

what great love the F. has lavished on us   188.17
you will be acting like your F. in heaven.   103.25
you, Lord, are our F.; our Redeemer   103.22
your F. which is in heaven is perfect.   178.3
your God was disciplining you as a f.   103.18

fathers: F., do not provoke your children to anger
86.23

fault: Happy is he to whom the Lord imputes no f.
139.3

fear: F. and trembling overwhelm me   88.4
F. God, and keep his commandments   211.6
F. not, Abram: I am thy shield   35.1
F. not, little flock   35.9
F. not: for, behold, I bring you good   35.8
For God hath not given us the spirit of f.   45.9
I came before you in weakness, in f.   88.11
No one talked… for f. of the Jews.   88.9
People will faint from f. as they wait   88.8
perfect love casts out f.; for f. has to do   88.12
so great is his mercy toward them that f. him.
211.3
spirit of knowledge and of the f. of the Lord.
211.7
The f. of the Lord is clean   211.2
The f. of the Lord is the beginning of wisdom
277.2
The f. of the Lord is the beginning of wisdom
211.4
There is no f. of God before their eyes.   211.10
work out your own salvation in f. and trembling
211.13
your children's children may f. the Lord   211.1

fearlessness: Our f. towards him consists in this
39.12

fed: So he… and then f. you on manna   90.3

feeble: confirm the f. knees.   274.1

feeling: high priest which cannot be touched with
the f.   249.12

feet: hath put all things under his f.   135.7
his f. part of iron and part of clay   274.2
if your Lord and teacher has washed your f.   126.5

fell: some f. by the way side, some f. on stony
ground,   81.7

fellowship: continued… in the apostles' doctrine
and f.   89.1
continued… in the apostles' doctrine and f.   31.33
gave to me and Barnabas the right hand of f.   89.6
If we say that we have f. with him   89.11
that ye also may have f. with us: 89.10

the f. of the Holy Spirit be with you all.   89.5
truly our f. is with the Father   89.10
ye were called unto the f. of his son   89.3
Your f. in the gospel.   89.7

female: male and f. created he them.   125.1
male and f. created he them.   231.1
neither male nor f.: for ye are   196.4

festival: celebrate the F. of Shelters for seven days.
27.2

festivals: The Lord says, 'I hate your religious f.
220.6

fiftieth: hallow the f. year, and proclaim liberty
143.2

fig: Though the f. tree does not blossom   35.46

fight: F. the good f. of the faith   271.8
so you f. to get your way by force.   56.8

fighting: What causes f. and quarrels among you?
271.9

fights: while the Spirit f. against it.   271.4

filled: All of them were f. with the Holy Spirit
119.21
Be f. with the Spirit   119.39
be f. with the Spirit   96.6
Peter, f. with the Holy Spirit, addressed them
119.23

find: By finding me, you f. life   150.8
I shall let you f. me, says the Lord.   224.9

fire: Can a man take f. in his bosom   253.3
he will baptise you with the Holy Spirit and f.
119.9
Then the f. of the Lord fell   161.3
when thou walkest through the f.   35.6
where…the f. is not quenched.   144.48
your faith… is tested by f.   253.22

first: He that is f. in his own cause   228.2
I am the f. and the last, and I am the living
135.104
On the f. day of every week   219.7
On the f. day of the week we met   219.6
whoever wants to be f. must be the slave of all.
6.19

firstborn: Every f. male must be consecrated
125.21
the f. of all creation   135.33

fishers: Follow me, and I will make you f. of men.
278.3

flattering: He sees himself with too f. an eye   37.1

flesh: cleave unto his wife: and they shall be one f.   231.2

He was revealed in f.   135.60

I was given a thorn in my f.   186.11

the spirit is willing, but the f. is weak.   184.34

flock: Fear not, little f.   35.9

Look after the f. of God   26.8

flourish: The righteous f. like a palm tree   115.3

follow: F. me, and I will make you fishers of men.   278.3

left you an example, so that you would f.   31.10

Whoever does not carry the cross and f. me   31.19

followed: Caleb… has f. me wholeheartedly   170.2

f. the ways of this world   262.7

folly: The message of the cross is sheer f.   91.9

food: As long as we have f. and clothing   90.13

Every creature that lives and moves will be f.   90.2

every tree that bears fruit… for f.   90.1

he may bring forth f. out of the earth   90.5

Jesus said: My f. is to do what God wants!   90.11

my flesh is real f. and my blood is real drink   90.12

'My f.,' Jesus said to them, 'is to obey   135.88

Why spend your money for what is not f.   90.9

you provide them with f.   90.7

fool: A f. speaks foolishly and thinks up evil   91.5

f. hath said in his heart, There is no God.   91.2

God said unto him, Thou f.   91.7

He is exactly what his name means – a f.!   91.1

his end shall be a f.   64.11

More to be hoped for from a f. than from him!   37.3

so a f. returneth to his folly.   91.4

fool's: A f. conduct is right in his own eyes   91.3

foolish: F. laughter is stupid.   145.9

God chose… those who believe the f. message   235.9

God hath chosen the f. things of the world   91.10

like a f. man who built his house on sand.   91.6

foolishness: Because of my f., I am covered with sores   57.5

they are f. to him and he cannot understand   91.11

fools: but f. always laugh   145.9

For ye suffer f. gladly   91.12

They claim to be wise, but they are f.   91.8

forehead: receives the mark on their f.   144.29

foreheads: his name will be on their f.   144.22

foreign: left for a f. country, where he wasted   136.8

foreigners: Do not ill-treat f.   130.2

foreknew: For those whom he f. he also predestined   72.8

foreknow: For whom he did f., he also did predestinate   32.4

foreknowledge: according to the definite plan and f. of God   240.7

forget: Even if a mother could f., I will never f. you   201.10

Even if these were to f., I shall not f. you.   26.3

How much longer will you f. me, Lord?   55.3

My son, do not f. my teaching   201.7

they may f., yet will I not f. thee.   35.37

forgetting: not listening and f., but putting it into practice   201.16

forgive: Be kind and merciful, and f. others   92.14

F. us our trespasses, as we f. them that   92.7

he is faithful and just to f. us our sins   92.16

if you do not f. others   92.8

If you f. others   92.8

saith the Lord: for I will f. their iniquity   92.5

Son of man has authority on earth to f. sins,   14.4

the Son of Man has the right to f. sins   92.9

Then said Jesus, Father, f. them   135.106

will f. their sin and heal their land.   203.1

you freely f. our sin and guilt.   92.6

you must f. as the Lord forgave you.   32.10

your Father will not f. the wrongs   92.8

forgiven: believe in Jesus will have their sins f.   92.12

Happy are those whose transgression is f.   92.1

I tell you, people will be f. for every sin   92.10

Repent… then your sins will be f.   92.11

forgiveness: But with you is f., so that you may be revered.   92.4

poured out for many for the f. of sins.   23.2

shedding of blood there is no f. of sins   236.18

shedding of blood there is no f. of sins.   92.15

the f. of sins, according to the riches of   92.13

we enjoy our freedom, the f. of sins.   188.13

formed: The Lord God f. man of the dust of the ground   18.1

the universe was f. by God's command   47.13

fornication: the works of the flesh are manifest… f.   231.7

forsake: he will not fail thee, nor f. thee   63.5

Let the wicked f. his way   31.17

Let the wicked f. his way… the unrighteous man his thoughts   203.2

forsaken: My God, my God, why hast thou f. me?
  57.4

My God, my God, why have you f. me?   153.5

my God, why have you f. me?   135.105

fraud: Bread is sweet when it is got by f.   64.9

free: As for you... you were called to be f.   93.9

For by the blood of Christ we are set f.   199.12

f. those who... were held in slavery   35.11

life-giving law of the Spirit has set you f.   93.4

Now that you have been set f. from sin   93.3

So if the Son makes you f., you will be f.   93.2

who forgives our sins and sets us f.   199.13

freedom: Be careful, however, not to let your f.
  93.6

do not let this f. become an excuse   93.9

For f. Christ has set us free   93.8

in him we enjoy our f., the forgiveness of sins.
  188.13

the same glorious f. as the children of God.   93.5

where the Spirit of the Lord is, there is f.   93.7

fret: F. not thyself because of evil-doers   19.4

F. not thyself because of evildoers   282.1

fretting: Martha, Martha, you are f. and fussing
  282.8

friend: a f. of tax-collectors and sinners!   94.8

A faithful f. is the medicine of life   94.6

Faithful are the wounds of a f.   94.5

Forsake not an old f.   94.7

he received the name 'f. of God'.   94.11

Jesus said to him, 'F., do what you are   94.9

The Lord spake... as a man speaketh unto his f.
  94.1

there is a f. who sticks closer than a brother.   155.9

friends: F. always show their love.   94.3

God has made you his f., in order to bring you
  198.7

I speak to you as my f.   94.10

some f. are more loyal than brothers.   94.4

friendship: A friend shows his f. at all times   155.8

The f. of the Lord is for those who fear him   94.2

frightened: without being f. in any way by those who
  oppose   45.8

fruit: By contrast, the f. of the Spirit is...   119.37

go and bear much f., the kind of f.   95.5

He will bless the f. of your womb.   95.1

in me, and I in them, will bear much f.   95.4

Just as the branch cannot bear f. by itself   184.46

My Father's glory is shown by your bearing much f.
  95.4

Whoever remains in me, with me in him, bears f.
  31.31

fruits: Bring forth therefore f. meet for repentance.
  95.2

You will know them by their f.   95.3

full: dwelt among us, f. of grace and truth.   96.2

From his f. store we have all received grace   96.3

fullness: For in him the whole f. of deity dwells
  bodily   96.7

That you may be filled with all the f. of God.   96.5

The earth is the Lord's, and the f.   96.1

the f. of him that filleth all in all.   96.4

When the f. of the time was come, God   199.11

you have come to f. in him.   96.7

futility: for all is f. and a chasing of the wind
  57.11

G

gain: For all... are out for ill-gotten g.   56.4

What will you g., if you own the whole world   6.17

Galilee: Men of G., why stand there looking up
  144.61

gate: Enter through the narrow g.   144.23

gave: And he g. him tithes of all.   101.1

first of all they g. themselves to the Lord   101.8

For God so loved the world, that he g.   100.1

you g. them to me, and they have obeyed you.
  72.6

gaze: to g. on the beauty of the Lord   6.1

generosity: G. will be rewarded: 97.4

overflowed in a wealth of g. on their part.   97.8

You know the g. of our Lord Jesus Christ   265.11

generous: A g. person enjoys prosperity   265.1

God is a g. giver.   97.13

Sometimes you can become rich by being g.   97.4

generously: All goes well for one who lends g.
  97.3

anyone who sows g. will reap g. as well.   97.9

be ready to give g. and to share with others.   97.11

the righteous give g.   97.2

you obeyed it by sharing g. with God's people
  97.10

Gentile: let such a one be to you as a G.   33.2

Gentiles: A light to lighten the G.   98.3

a root of Jesse... to it shall the G. seek   98.2

Christ has made peace between Jews and G.   98.9

granted life-giving repentance to the G. also   98.6

the Holy Spirit... poured out even on G.   98.5

to make my name known to G. and kings   98.4

When G., who do not possess the law   98.7

When the G. heard this, they were overjoyed   205.6

gentle: the ageless beauty of a g. and quiet spirit   99.8

We were g. among you, like a nurse   99.5

wisdom from above is first pure, then... g.   99.7

gentleness: an apt teacher, patient, correcting   opponents with g.   99.6

Paul, appeal to you by the... g. of Christ   99.2

The fruit of the Spirit is love... g.   140.5

the fruit of the Spirit is... g.   99.3

gently: who live by the Spirit must g. set him right.   99.4

Ghost: by the Holy G. which is given unto us.   119.28

gift: As every man hath received the g.   1.12

Do not neglect the spiritual g.   100.10

each person has the g. God has granted him   28.2

Every good g. and every perfect g.   100.11

it is the g. of God.   100.9

Money paid to workers isn't a g.   52.11

not of yourselves: it is the g. of God.   108.15

Thanks be to God for his g.   100.8

the g. of God is eternal life   100.4

you will receive God's g., the Holy Spirit.   100.2

you will receive the g. of the Holy Spirit   31.24

you will receive the g. of the Holy Spirit.   119.22

gifts: Be eager to have the g.   100.7

Let us use the different g.   1.9

presented unto him g.; gold... and myrrh   135.65

the Spirit... decides which g. to give   100.6

There are different kinds of spiritual g.   100.6

We have different g.   100.5

give: Each one should g. as much as he has decided   101.9

G. to anyone who asks you   97.6

God exalted him... so that he might g.   100.3

If you g. to others, you will be given   97.7

If you g. to others, you will be given   101.6

It is more blessed to g. than to receive.   140.4

So when you g. something to a needy person   101.4

given: Do something to show that you have really g.   up   203.5

If you give to others, you will be g.   101.6

of thine own have we g. thee.   101.2

this poor widow has g. more than   101.5

Where someone has been g. much   188.4

giver: God loves a cheerful g.   101.9

gives: The Lord g. and the Lord takes away   35.18

giveth: All that the Father g. me shall come to me   72.3

All that the Father g. me shall come to me;   12.1

giving: the upright is generous in g.   52.3

their g. surpassed our expectations   101.8

There is more happiness in g. than in receiving.   117.6

glad: let us rejoice and be g. in it.   137.3

gladly: For ye suffer fools g.   91.12

I will boast all the more g. of my weaknesses   137.16

stand for those who receive the message g.   137.9

glorify: So now, Father, g. me in your own presence   102.8

glory: all have sinned, and come short of the g. of   God.   236.11

Ascribe to the Lord the g. due to his name   204.5

be with me where I am, to see my g.   3.3

before the presence of his g. with exceeding joy   31.41

beholding as in a glass the g. of the Lord   102.13

cannot compare with the g. that will be   102.10

come short of the g. of God.   102.9

crowning his head with g. and honour.   102.4

do everything for the g. of God.   102.11

earth shall be filled with the g. of the Lord.   102.2

For men to search their own g. is not g.   228.3

God's g. has left Israel   102.3

he reflects the image and g. of God.   102.12

he revealed his g., and his disciples believed   102.7

may be with me where I am, to see my g.   144.13

Moses prayed, 'Show me your g.'   102.1

Moses prayed, 'Show me your g.'   31.43

the g. that I had in your presence   102.8

The Son is the radiance of God's g.   13.9

The Son is the radiance of God's g.   102.14

when he comes in the g. of his Father   102.6

go: G. therefore and make disciples of all nations   278.5

G. and preach the good news to everyone   278.7

I g. the way of all the earth: 51.3

It is I, the Lord. Now, g.   2.1

God: A father of the fatherless... is G.   103.20

All scripture is inspired by G. and is useful   17.11

all the fullness of G. was pleased to dwell.   135.33

Alleluia: for the Lord G. omnipotent reigneth.
103.7

appears in the presence of G. on our behalf.
144.17

Be thou exalted, O G., above the heavens   103.60

Because of his great love for us, G.   103.54

Being therefore exalted at the right hand of G.
135.6

believeth that Jesus is the Christ is born of G.
18.14

By his blood we are now put right with G.   23.4

Can G. indeed dwell on earth?   103.58

Christ sitteth on the right hand of G.   135.103

Christ the power of G., and the wisdom of G.
135.24

definite plan and foreknowledge of G.   240.7

Did not one G. create us?   103.24

Elect according to the foreknowledge of G.   259.7

Eternal life... to know you, the only true G.   188.5

For G. so loved the world   135.56

For G. so loved the world, that he gave   100.1

For G. so loved the world, that he gave   103.48

For G. so loved the world, that he gave   31.21

For nothing will be impossible with G.   103.6

For us there is one G., the Father   103.29

gave he power to become the sons of G.   31.20

Give... to G. the things that are God's.   162.4

G. chose those who by human standards are fools
30.12

G. has publicly proved this by raising him   103.45

G. has sent into our hearts the Spirit of his Son
188.10

G. himself shall be with them, and be their G.
144.21

G. himself shall be with them, and be their G.
46.10

G. is not a human being, that he should lie
103.68

G. is spirit, and those who worship him   103.57

G. is wise and powerful! Praise him   103.72

G. made the earth by his power   103.12

G. said to Moses, 'I am who I am.'   103.55

G. sent his Son, born of a woman   135.57

G. treats everyone on the same basis   196.2

G. who called you is holy.   31.8

G. who made the world and everything in it
103.66

G., you are my G.   31.46

hast thou not heard, that the everlasting G.
103.10

he is able... to save those who approach G.
135.73

he is G. in heaven... there is none else.   240.1

He is G., not of the dead, but of the living.   144.50

He was in the form of G.   135.58

Herein is love, not that we loved G.   103.49

I delight to do your will, O my G.   135.86

I saw the dead, small and great, stand before G.
144.42

If G. is for us, who is against us?   12.6

In the beginning G.   103.8

In the past, G. forgave all this   31.26

In their case the g. of this world   58.8

It is G. himself who called you   103.17

Know therefore that the Lord your G. is G.   103.15

Know ye that the Lord he is G.   103.9

my G., and the rock of my salvation.   103.21

My G., my G., why have you forsaken me?
135.105

No one is good but G. alone.   103.34

Now unto the... only wise G., be honour   103.73

one G. and Father of all   259.6

one G. and Father of all, over all   103.31

Our holy G. lives for ever in the highest heavens
103.65

peace with G. through our Lord Jesus Christ
188.7

riches both of the wisdom and knowledge of G.!
103.2

sincerely ask you to make peace with G.   198.4

sword of the Spirit, which is the word of G.   17.7

temple of G., declaring himself to be G.   144.5

The glorious gospel of the blessed G.   106.15

the Lord, a G. merciful and gracious   103.50

the Lord your G. is the only G.   103.47

the love of G.... be with you all   259.5

the mysteries surrounding G. All-Powerful?   103.59

the only wise G., be honour and glory for ever
103.14

the powers that be are ordained of G.   218.10

the same G. who activates all of them   259.4

the sword of the Spirit, which is the word of G.
119.40

The word of G. is alive and active   17.12

they are before the throne of G.   144.19

Thomas said, 'My Lord and my G.!'   135.68

We must obey G. rather than any human   170.7

We must obey G. rather than any human authority
243.2

Who, though he was in the form of G.   135.43

Wonderful, Counsellor, the mighty G.   135.53

you were eternally G. and will be G. for ever.
103.13

Your G. is faithful and true   103.44

your G. was disciplining you as a father   103.18

your G. will be my G.   155.1

God's: failing to see that G. kindness   103.35

Now he is sitting at G. right side.   135.75

then it will be whole, like G. knowledge of me.
142.12

You are G. chosen and special people   31.9

godless: the g. is the ruin of his neighbour   104.5
the glee of one who is g. lasts but a moment!
 104.1
What hope is there for the g.   104.2

godliness: G. with contentment is great gain.
 162.6

gods: the worship of false g.   128.4
Thou shalt have no other g. before me.   283.1
Thou shalt have no other g. before me.   128.1

good: a g. man on behalf of sinners   216.20
Before the end comes, the g. news must be preached
 to all   278.6
cease to do evil, learn to do g.   215.8
created in Christ Jesus unto g. works   105.13
desires won't let me do anything that is g.   105.7
Do g. in thy g. pleasure unto Zion   105.3
Everything God created is g.   105.14
Find out for yourself how g. the Lord is.   103.32
For he is g., for his steadfast love   105.2
g. people will keep on doing right   215.14
Go and preach the g. news   278.7
God saw… and, behold, it was very g.   105.1
he has chosen me to bring g. news to the poor
 106.4
he went about doing g. and healing all   105.5
hold fast to what is g.   105.10
I bring you g. tidings of great joy   35.8
instead conquer evil with g.   105.11
know to refuse the evil, and choose the g.   215.10
let us do g. unto all men   230.8
No one is g. but God alone.   103.34
No one is g. except God alone.   105.4
O give thanks unto the Lord; for he is g.   103.33
that he may… distinguish g. from evil.   215.4
to testify to the g. news. of God's grace.   106.5
We know that all things work together for g.   105.8
We know that all things work together for g.   31.4
what it commands is holy and upright and g.
 105.6
ye may prove what is that g., and acceptable   105.9

goodness: arouse others to love and active g.
 140.7
The fruit of the Spirit is… g.   105.12

gospel: called you… and following a different g.
 251.6
Even if I preach the g., I can claim no credit   106.7
Even if our g. is veiled, it is veiled   106.10
For I am not ashamed of the g. of Christ: 106.6
Go out to the whole world; proclaim the g.   106.3
in a manner worthy of the g. of Christ.   106.14
Now, my friends, I must remind you of the g.
 106.8

repent ye, and believe the g.   106.2
that it announced the future g. to Abraham
 106.12
the g. I preach is not of human origin.   106.11
The glorious g. of the blessed God   106.15
to make known the mystery of the g.   278.15
to make known the mystery of the g.   106.13

gossip: A g. tells everything   107.3
G. is no good! It causes hard feelings   107.4
nothing so delicious as the taste of g.!   107.5

gossips: Stay away from g.   107.6
they learn to be g. and meddlers   107.12

government: the g. shall be upon his shoulder
 135.53

grace: Being justified freely by his g.   108.6
boldly approach the throne of g.   108.16
But where sin was multiplied, g.   108.8
For by g. are ye saved   108.15
For by g. are ye saved through faith   221.14
For ye know the g. of our Lord Jesus Christ
 108.10
God's act of g. is out of all proportion   84.4
great g. was upon them all.   108.4
Grow in the g. and knowledge of our Lord   108.17
it is by g. you have been saved.   108.14
keep on living in the g. of God.   108.5
My g. is sufficient for thee   35.52
My g. is sufficient for you   108.11
My g. is sufficient for you   2.8
Shall we continue in sin, that g. may abound?
 236.13
The g. of the Lord Jesus Christ… be with you all
 108.12
The Word was made flesh… full of g. and truth.
 108.2
to testify to the good news. of God's g.   106.5
we have access by faith into this g.   108.7
we have all received, g. upon g.   108.3
ye are fallen from g.   108.13
ye know the g. of our Lord Jesus Christ   135.42

grain: you have no money, come, buy g. and eat;
 90.9

grave: he made his g. with the wicked   135.16

great: Anyone who wants to become g.   149.5
do not take a place among the g.;   6.12
whoever wants to be g. must be your servant,   6.19

greater: G. is he that is in you, than he that   266.9
they will do even g. things   161.8

greed: Be on your guard against all kinds of g.
 56.5

Greek: There is neither Jew nor G.   98.8

grief: a man of sorrows, and acquainted with g.
 109.5
For my life is spent with g.   109.1
found them sleeping for sheer g.   109.10
I am worn out with g.   55.2
My heart is ready to break with g.   109.8
My heart is ready to break with g.   153.3

griefs: Surely he hath borne our g.   13.2
Surely he hath borne our g.   35.45
Surely he hath borne our g.   129.7

grieve: G. not the holy Spirit of God   119.38

groaning: He heard their g.   35.40

ground: I bring the first of the fruit of the g.   143.4
some fell on stony g.   81.7

growing: If you keep g. in this way   31.16

grumble: Do not g., as some of them did   41.5

guard: g. your heart, for it is the wellspring of life
 116.5

guide: he will g. you into all the truth   110.5
The Lord will always g. you   110.4

guides: The Lord g. people in the way they should go
 110.3

guilt: g. has departed and your sin is blotted out.
 111.5
you forgave the g. of my sin.   111.3

guiltless: not hold him g. that taketh his name in
 vain.   111.2

guilty: do not help a g. person by giving false
 evidence.   132.1
g. of committing adultery with her in his heart
 157.11
he is g. of breaking all of them.   111.8
he or she is g. of sin against the   111.7
Which one of you can prove that I am g. of sin?
 135.37

gulf: between us and you there is a great g. fixed
 144.27

H

Hades: I hold the keys of death and H.   135.104

hairs: the h. of your head have all been counted.
 192.8

hallowed: Father, which art in heaven, H. be thy
 name.   103.26

hand: do not stretch out your h. against him!
 253.2
Israel stretched out his right h.   147.1
put his h. upon the head of the burnt offering
 220.3
said unto my Lord: Sit thou at my right h.   135.44
thou shalt open thine h. wide unto him   97.1

handiwork: all of us are your h.   125.10

hands: Be in no hurry to lay h. on anyone   147.10
blessed you by placing their h. on you.   147.9
for Moses had laid his h. upon him   147.3
he cured a few sick people by laying his h.   147.4
He… put his h. upon them, and blessed them.
 147.5
He shall put both his h. on the goat's head   147.2
Pilate… washed his h. before the multitude   205.4
prayed and placed their h. on them.   147.6
teaching about baptisms and the laying on of h.
 147.11
they laid their h. on them and sent them   147.7
When Paul had laid his h. on them   147.8

Hannah: H. made this vow: 'Lord of Hosts   86.12

happy: H. is the one who does not take the counsel
 of   31.13
The Lord's followers in Antioch were very h.
 137.13

hard: By your h. and impenitent heart you are storing
 112.9
Moses permitted… because your hearts were h.
 112.5
their hearts have grown h. as stone.   112.11

harden: h. not your hearts, as in the provocation.
 112.12
I will h. his heart   112.1
thou shalt not h. thine heart   112.2

hardened: h. through the deceitfulness of sin
 236.33
Their minds were h. Indeed, to this very day
 112.10

hardship: In the world you will have h.   246.10
We are subjected to every kind of h.   57.16

harp: Praise the Lord with h.: sing unto him
 166.5

hart: As the h. panteth after the water brooks
 31.45

harvest: celebrate the H. Festival   27.2
h. is rich, but the labourers are few,   278.4
The h. of the Spirit is love, joy, peace…   95.6

hate: All who h. others are murderers   165.7
Do I not h. those who h. you, O Lord?   113.1

H. evil and love good, and establish justice   113.4
nations will h. you for your allegiance to me   113.5
People who do evil h. the light   113.6
The world cannot h. you, but it does h. me   113.7

hated: just remember that it has h. me first   113.8
you will be h. by people of all nations.   144.2

hates: If the world h. you   113.8
There are seven things that the Lord h.   113.2

hatred: Better... than a stalled ox and h. therewith.
    113.3

head: Christ is the h. of the church   33.7
gave him to be the h. over all things   135.7
He is the h. of the body, the church   135.33

heal: He sent his word to h. them   114.5
to h. every kind of disease and sickness.   114.7
will forgive their sin and h. their land.   114.3
will forgive their sin and h. their land.   212.1

healed: By his wounds you have been h.   13.10
pray one for another, that ye may be h.   114.10

healeth: who h. all thy diseases.   114.4

healing: h. people who had all kinds of disease
    114.6
Now I shall bring h. and care for her   115.9
the tongue of the wise brings h.   115.6
To another the gifts of h. by the same Spirit   114.9

health: h. to their whole being.   115.5
thy saving h. among all nations.   115.2

healthy: may your spirit, soul, and body be kept h.
    115.12
This will make you h., and you will feel strong.
    115.4

hear: be more ready to h., than to give the   152.4
h. me and you will have life.   152.6
he would have refused to h. me.   184.41
I h. from heaven, and will forgive their sin   184.39
if any man h. my voice, and open the door   152.13
if any man h. my voice, and open the door   184.17
prophets and kings wished to h. what you h.
    188.3
sins have hid his face from you... will not h.
    184.23
They have ears, but they h. not.   152.2
We are certain that God will h. our prayers   184.30
while they are yet speaking I will h.   184.13

heard: He h. their groaning and called to mind
    35.40
If thou hast h. a word, let it die with thee   107.8
the Lord h. him, and saved him   184.1

heart: A new h. I will give you   116.7
Blessed are the pure in h.:   116.8
closes his h. to him, how can the love of God
    228.13
For it is from within, from the human h.   186.4
from a person's h., come the evil ideas   116.10
From his h. shall flow streams of living   116.11
from the h. that evil intentions emerge   79.7
God, create a pure h. for me   116.4
guard your h., for it is the wellspring of life   116.5
have become obedient from the h.   116.12
I will take away your stubborn h.   163.7
love one another earnestly with all your h.   116.16
love the Lord thy God with all thine h.   116.1
my h. grew parched as stubble   55.4
Search me, O God, and know my h.   80.1
shalt believe in thine h. that God   116.14
Solomon... serve him with a perfect h.   163.2
The h. is deceitful above all things   116.6
The h. is deceitful above all things   163.6
the Lord has sought out a man after his own h.
    116.2
the Lord looketh on the h.   116.3
the Lord saw her his h. went out to her   249.8
When they heard this they were cut to the h.   43.5
Your h. will always be where your treasure   116.9

hearts: Beloved, if our h. do not condemn us
    116.17
I judge people by what is in their h.   29.1
Let the peace of God rule in your h.   116.15
the Lord always knows what is in our h.   163.5

heathen: Ask of me, and I shall give thee the h.
    98.1

heaven: After saying this, he was taken up to h.
    135.5
heard a great voice out of h.   144.21
Jesus who has been taken from you up to h.
    144.61
parted from them, and carried up into h.   135.2
the assembly of the firstborn who are enrolled in h.
    144.74
the highest h. cannot contain you   103.39
wait for our Saviour... to come from h.   144.16
when the Lord Jesus appears from h.   144.64
Whom have I in h. but thee?   31.47
Whom have I in h. but thee?   144.9

heavenly: set him at his own right hand in the h.
    places   135.7

heavens: Be thou exalted, O God, above the h.
    103.60
lo, the h. were opened unto him,   15.2
The h. declare the glory of God   210.1

When I consider thy h., the work of thy fingers
47.3

heaviness: the garment of praise for the spirit of h.
164.8

heir: His Son, whom he appointed h. of all things
135.34
his Son, whom he hath appointed h.   131.11

heirs: God will give you all that he has for his h.
131.6
h. of God and fellow-h. with Christ   131.3
H. together of the grace of life.   131.14
justified by his grace, we might become h.   131.10

hell: God, who can destroy both body and soul in h.
144.25
The wicked shall be turned into h.   144.67

help: God is… a very present h. in trouble.   117.2
H. to carry one another's burdens   117.10
he also chose some to… h. others.   117.8
I sought the Lord's h.   35.3
I will h. you to speak   2.1
I will make him an h. meet for him.   157.1
I will strengthen thee; yea, I will h. thee   35.36
My h. cometh from the Lord   117.3
our refuge and strength, a very present h. in trouble
35.4
she knelt down and begged, 'Please h. me, Lord.'
117.4
The Lord my God will h. you   1.6
to find grace when we are in need of h.   81.14
try to h. them by doing what pleases them.   265.5
When he arrived, he was a great h.   117.5
when you h. a needy person   101.4

helped: so the believers in Ephesus h. him by writing
117.5
Thus far the Lord has h. us.   117.1

Helper: The H. will come – the Spirit   119.18
The Lord is my h.   117.11

helping: As you also join in h. us by your prayers
117.9

helpless: Christ died… when we were h. and sinful.
104.8

herbs: Better a dish of h. when love is there   90.8

hesitate: Why did you h.?' he said. 'How little faith
66.5

hid: Adam and his wife h. themselves   84.1
because I was naked; and I h. myself.   232.1
I was afraid, because I was naked; and I h.   111.1
I went off and h. your talent   81.6
My way is h. from the Lord   66.3

highly: Don't be frightened! God thinks h. of you
59.7

holds: Whoever h. back his grain is cursed   228.1

holes: Foxes have their h. and birds their roosts
120.10

holier: for I am h. than thou   229.3

holiness: God did not call us to live… but in h.
118.7
perfecting h. out of reverence for God.   118.6
Pursue peace with everyone, and the h.   118.10
saving justice and h. and redemption.   222.5
so that we may share his own h.   118.9

holy: be h., for I am h.   118.3
Be h. in all that you do   31.8
by the H. Ghost which is given unto us.   119.28
God wants you to be h., so don't be immoral
222.6
he is h., innocent, undefiled   118.8
H., h., h., is the Lord of hosts: 103.36
H., h., h. is the Lord of Hosts   118.4
place where you are standing is h. ground.   204.1
place whereon thou standest is h. ground.   118.1
present your bodies a living sacrifice, h.   222.4
Remember the sabbath day, to keep it h.   118.2
the high and lofty One… whose name is H.
103.41
This will make you h. and will lead you   118.5
what h. and saintly lives you should be living
188.16
You are… a h. nation, God's own people   118.11
You shall be h., for I am h.   236.34

home: be at h. with the Lord.   51.17
He lets the barren woman be seated at h.   120.3
Martha welcomed him into her h.   120.13
may he grant each of you the security of a h.
120.2
My people will live in a peaceful h.   120.9
no one who has given up h., brothers or sisters
120.12
so is anyone who strays away from h.   120.8
that disciple took her into his own h.   120.14
they spent time… in one h. after another.   120.16
we would rather be… at h. with the Lord.   144.71
welcome strangers into your h.   124.3
When you go to a h., give it your blessing   120.11

homes: breaking bread in their h., they shared
120.15

homicide: Now this is the case of a h. who might flee
165.4

homosexual: No one who… behaves like a h. will
share in God's   121.5

nor h. offenders… inherit the kingdom of God.
231.5

honest: those who bring a good and h. heart
122.2

honor: A prophet is not without h., save in his own
country   190.4

fear God and h. the emperor.   204.16

give h. to the aged, and fear your God.   204.4

H. thy father and thy mother.   154.10

Thou art worthy, O Lord, to receive glory and h.
283.13

To h. the Lord is to hate evil   211.5

you… do anything else, always do it to h. God
205.8

honored: Marriage must be h. by all   157.8

hope: For in h. we were saved.   123.4

having no h. and without God in the world.   123.7

hold tightly to the h. that we say is ours   31.37

H. deferred makes the heart sick   63.9

h. maketh not ashamed   123.3

h. thou in God: for I shall yet praise him   35.29

h. thou in God: for I shall yet praise him   123.1

I pray that God, who gives h., will bless you   123.5

it is Christ among you, your h. of glory.   123.8

Keep alert and set your h. completely on   123.10

Now h. that is seen is not h.   123.4

three things that last for ever: faith, h.   123.6

therefore I will h. in him.   55.7

We have this h., a sure and steadfast anchor   123.9

We… rejoice in h. of the glory of God   123.3

hoped: Abraham believed and h.   123.2

horn: I saw a little h. coming up among the others.
10.1

This h. had human eyes and a mouth   10.1

horse: Be ye not as the h., or as the mule   225.1

Do you give the h. his strength?   9.6

hospitable: Be h. to one another without
complaining.   124.7

hospitality: A bishop then must be… given to h.
124.4

Do not neglect to show h.   124.6

showing h., washing the feet of the saints   124.5

host: we have not the strength to face this great h.
270.3

hour: And about the eleventh h. he went out
256.5

This is the h. to receive God's favour   256.11

hours: Jesus answered, 'Aren't there twelve h.
256.8

house: As for me and my h., we will serve the Lord.
86.11

come and stay at my h.   124.2

He that troubleth his own h. shall inherit   120.5

talk of them when thou sittest in thine h.   120.1

than share the h. with a nagging wife.   120.7

The curse of the Lord is in the h. of the wicked
120.4

household: We have a great priest set over the h. of
God.   188.14

human: although we are h., it is not by h. methods
271.3

being found in h. form, he humbled himself
135.43

h. being knows… except the h. spirit   242.9

On the day when God created h. beings   125.17

Sharing the h. lot, he humbled himself   135.90

the breath of every h. being!   125.4

the gospel I preach is not of h. origin.   106.11

We must obey God rather than any h. authority.
243.2

We must obey God rather than any h.   170.7

Who knows what a h. being is but the h. spirit
125.12

humble: be h. towards one another   126.6

God… gives grace to the h.   126.7

I will look, to the h. and contrite in spirit   126.1

If my people… h. themselves, pray   203.1

Whosoever therefore shall h. himself   126.3

humbled: being found in human form, he h. himself
135.43

humbly: to walk h. with thy God?   205.2

humility: all of you must clothe yourselves with h.
126.7

hunger: he that cometh to me shall never h.   41.4

hungry: When I was h., you gave me something to
eat   140.2

hurt: They shall not h. nor destroy   272.1

husband: A h. is the head of his wife, as Christ
86.7

if the h. dies, she is free to marry   275.8

the h. is supreme over his wife, and God   86.6

Your h. or wife who isn't a follower   86.5

husbands: h. must live with your wives with   86.8

hymns: sing… h. and inspired songs to God.
166.14

hypocrite: You h.! First take the plank out   127.2

hypocrites: When you pray, do not be like the h.!
127.1

Woe unto you, scribes and Pharisees, h.!   217.5
You h.! Isaiah prophesied rightly about you   127.3

I

idols: Little children, keep yourselves from i.
128.6
Their i. are silver and gold   128.3
turned away from i. to serve the true   128.5

ill: Lord, the man you love is i.   129.5

ill-gotten: No good comes of i. wealth   64.5

ill-treat: If you i. the poor, you insult your Creator
173.5

image: God created man in his own i., in the i. of
God   59.1
He… cast an i. of a calf   128.2
to be conformed to the i. of his Son   32.4

Immanuel: shall call his name I.   135.52

immoral: God wants you to be holy, so don't be i.
222.6
You may be sure that no one who is i.   56.6

immorality: Keep away from sexual i.   236.29

immortality: our mortality has been clothed with i.
77.12
this mortal must put on i.   35.25

imperishable: the dead will rise i., and we shall be
changed.   77.12
What is sown is perishable, what is raised is i.
144.53

impossible: For nothing is i. to God.   161.6

incorruptible: But you should search for… i. men
25.1

incorruption: For this corruptible must put on i.
35.25

inherit: flesh and blood cannot i. the kingdom of
God   131.5
i. the kingdom prepared for you   72.2
i. the kingdom prepared for you   131.1
so that you i. a blessing.   21.9
the wicked will not i. the kingdom of God?   131.4

inheritance: In whom also we have obtained an i.
131.7
riches of his glorious i. among the saints.   131.9
that Spirit is a pledge of the i.   131.8
to give you your i. among all the sanctified.   131.2

iniquities: Your i. have separated between you
236.6

iniquity: By mercy and truth i. is purged   236.25

the Lord hath laid on him the i. of us all.   236.5
Wash me thoroughly from mine i.   111.4

innocent: I am i. of the blood of this just person:
205.4
so be cunning as snakes and yet i. as doves.   235.5

insight: Beg for knowledge; plead for i.   263.2

inspired: All scripture is inspired by God and is
useful   17.11

instruct: I shall i. you and teach you the way to go
44.2

instruments: praise him with stringed i. and organs.
166.8

intercedes: Christ Jesus… i. for us.   12.6
Spirit i. with sighs too deep for words.   184.35

intercession: he always lives to make i. for them
135.73
made i. for the transgressors.   135.93

intercourse: women have exchanged natural i. for
121.4

interests: Look to each other's i.   228.10

interpreter: there is no i., the speaker should keep
quiet   258.11

intruders: For certain i. have stolen in among you
251.11

invisible: He is the image of the i. God   135.33

invite: When you give a dinner… don't i. your
friends   26.4
When you give a feast, i. the poor   26.4

Israel: And so all I. will be saved   133.7
anger down on I. by profaning the Sabbath   219.2
follow this as their rule and to the I. of God.
133.8
he come forth… that is to be ruler in I.   133.2
I. saw that great work which the Lord did   161.2
I., you are the chosen people of the Lord   108.1
Not all the offspring of I. are truly I.   133.6
sit on thrones, to rule the twelve tribes of I.   133.3
Thy name shall be called no more Jacob, but I.
133.1

Israelites: These are the stages in the journey of the
I.   136.2

J

Jacob: J. went on his journey and came into the land
136.1

jealous: I the Lord thy God am a j. God   134.1
Love… is not j.   134.6
the Lord, whose name is J., is a j. God.   134.2

jealousies: belongs to the unspiritual nature… j. 134.7

jealously: God yearns j. for the spirit that he 134.9

jealousy: Anger… is nothing compared to j. 134.3
For the ear of j. heareth all things   134.4
If at heart you have the bitterness of j.   134.8
no more lying or hypocrisy or j.   76.6

Jerusalem: A man was going down from J. to Jericho 140.3
that he must go unto J., and suffer   135.17
When the Lord brought us back to J.   145.5

Jesus: at the name of J. every knee should bend 167.14
be baptized… in the name of J.   31.24
Become a believer in the Lord J., and you will be saved   31.25
complete confidence through the blood of J.   23.8
'Do not cling to me,' said J.   135.4
find in Christ J.: 'He was in the form of God 135.58
For ye know the grace of our Lord J. Christ   108.10
For ye know the grace of our Lord J. Christ   135.42
From that time forth began J. to shew   135.94
God has given proof… by raising J.   31.26
God raised this man J. to life   135.96
If anyone acknowledges that J. is God's Son,   38.4
J. came into the world to save sinners   236.17
J. Christ is the same yesterday, today   135.35
J. cried aloud, 'Eli, Eli, lema sabachthani?' 135.105
J. drank the wine and said, 'It is finished!' 135.111
J. drew near and said to them   135.11
J. himself became like them and shared   135.62
J. increased in wisdom, in stature   86.21
J. knew that everything had now been completed 135.110
J. knew that the hour had come for him   135.81
J. of Nazareth, King of the Jews.   133.4
J. said unto him, Verily I say unto thee   135.107
J. said… Before Abraham was, I am.   135.32
J. saith unto him, I am the way, the truth   31.23
J. the Nazarene, King of the Jews   135.49
J. was talking about the Holy Spirit   135.3
J. who became for us wisdom from God.   277.16
J. who has been taken from you up to heaven 144.61
J. will overthrow with the breath of his mouth 144.6
live and reign through the one man, J. Christ   84.4
looking to J. the pioneer and perfecter of   31.38
'My food,' J. said… 'is to obey   135.88

shall give him the name J., for he will save   221.3
Sir, we would see J.   31.49
spirit which acknowledges that J. Christ   135.64
the blood of J. his Son cleanses us   23.11
The grace of the Lord J. Christ   259.5
the name of the Lord J. gained in honour.   167.13
Then said J., Father, forgive them   135.106
This is the prophet J., from Nazareth   135.77
time forth began J. to shew unto his disciples 135.17
we have a great high priest… J.   135.71
We see J., who was made a little lower   135.61
When J. had been baptized   259.2
When J. had cried with a loud voice   135.108
When J. saw his mother and the disciple whom 135.109

Jesus': Simon Peter saw it, he fell down at J. knees 135.67

Jew: here is neither J. nor Greek   125.25
Rather, a person is a J. who is one inwardly   133.5
There is neither J. nor Greek   196.4

Jews: Jesus of Nazareth, King of the J.   133.4
Turning to the J. who had believed him   31.30

joined: If you don't stay j. to me   85.6
What therefore God hath j. together, let not   157.3

journey: He himself went a day's j. into the wilderness   136.3
How long will the j. last   136.4
Jacob went on his j. and came into the land   136.1
Jesus, therefore, being wearied with his j.   136.9
my husband… has gone on a very long j.   136.5
'Take nothing for the j.,' he told them   136.7
These are the stages in the j. of the Israelites   136.2

journeying: After this he went j. from town to town 136.6

joy: Ask and you will receive, that your j.   137.12
everlasting j. shall be upon their heads   137.8
for j. in the Lord is your strength.   137.1
I have no greater j. than this   137.22
in thy presence is fulness of j.   137.2
Looking unto Jesus… who for the j.   137.20
May the God of hope fill you with all j.   137.15
more j. in heaven over one sinner who repents 137.10
my j. might remain in you, and that your j.   137.11
So you rejoice with a great and glorious j.   137.21
The fruit of the Spirit is… j.   137.17
The Lord has done… we are filled with j.   137.5
They that sow in tears shall reap in j.   137.6
With j. you will all draw water from the wells 137.7

joyful: Be j. in hope, persevere in hardship   35.48

judge: Are you not aware that we are to j. angels 144.37
He has given his Son the right to j.   135.13
Shall not the J. of all the earth do   103.43
those who sat… were given the power to j. 144.20
You should each j. your own conduct.   227.5

judged: he will have the world j. in righteousness 144.35
the world j. in righteousness by a man   135.97
whoever does not believe is j. already   193.5

judges: Let them sit as j. for the people at all times 149.1

judgment: but after this the j.   144.39
Final j. must wait until the Lord comes   144.36
For all of us must appear before the j. seat   144.38
On the day of j. Jesus will save us from God's anger. 8.9
The meek he will guide in j.   53.3
the rest exercise their j. upon what is said.   60.5
waiting for the fair j. that never comes   138.6

just: a j. weight is his delight.   122.1
how can a mortal be j. before God?   139.2
If we confess our sins, he is faithful and j.   103.46

justice: Give the king your j., O God   138.3
he will judge the whole world with j.   216.10
J., and j. alone, must be your aim   138.2
J. is driven away, and right cannot come   138.7
Let j. roll down like waters   138.9
Seek j., encourage the oppressed.   138.5
The Lord says, 'I love j.   138.8
there is no perversion of j. with the Lord   132.4
You are not to pervert j.   132.2

justification: was raised again for our j.   135.21

justified: Being j. freely by his grace   108.6
Being j. freely by his grace   139.7
j. freely by his grace through the redemption   13.4
now that we have been j. by his death   139.10
Therefore being j. by faith,   12.3
Therefore being j. by faith, we have peace   139.9
those whom he called he also j.   31.4
those whom he called he also j.   139.12
we have now been j. by Christ's sacrificial death, 12.4

justifies: It is God who j. Who is to condemn? 139.12
To one who without works trusts him who j. 139.8

justifieth: He is near that j. me; who will contend with me?   139.4

justly: do j., and to love mercy, and to walk humbly 138.10
that he may govern your people j.   215.4

K

keep: If ye love me, k. my commandments.   170.6
put him into the garden of Eden… to k. it.   279.1

keeper: Am I my brother's k.?   165.1

kept: dear to God the Father and k. safe   31.12
he k. him as the apple of his eye   154.2
Who are k. by the power of God   31.39

keys: I hold the k. of death and Hades.   135.104

kill: Do not be afraid of those who k. the body 144.25
You want something and you lack it; so you k. 56.8

killed: will be arrested, punished, and even k. 144.2

killer: the k. may flee to one of these cities and live 165.4

killeth: for the letter k. but the spirit giveth life. 242.12

kind: Be k. to one another, tender-hearted   140.6

kindness: it was really God's k. at work and not me. 108.9

king: Jesus the Nazarene, K. of the Jews   135.49
Look, your k. is coming to you!   135.47
See, your k. comes to you, righteous   135.41

kingdom: be born again, he cannot see the k. of God.   141.9
behold, the k. of God is within you.   141.8
Blessed are the poor… the k. of heaven.   141.1
Christ will… hand over the K. to God   141.14
For thine is the k., and the power   184.33
God's k. isn't about eating and drinking.   141.11
his k. is one that will never be destroyed.   135.46
inherit the k. prepared for you   141.5
'Lord, Lord' will enter the k. of Heaven   141.4
My k. does not belong to this world.   135.48
not receive the k. of God as a little child   141.7
Seek ye first the k. of God   141.3
the k. of God consists not in spoken words 141.12
the k. of God has come near; repent   141.6
The k. of the world has become the k. of   141.17

The k. we are given is unshakeable   141.16

the wicked will not inherit the k. of God?   141.13

through… persecutions… enter the k. of God.
141.10

Thy k. come. Thy will be done   141.2

Thy k. come. Thy will be done   144.11

transferred us into the k. of his beloved Son
141.15

kings: thanksgiving should be offered… for k.
218.12

The k. of the earth prepare for war   218.9

The k. of the earth stand up, and the rulers   104.3

knock: Behold, I stand at the door, and k.   184.17

k., and the door will be opened for you.   184.42

know: Be still, and k. that I am God!   142.3

Eternal life is this: to k. you   142.10

Eternal life is this: to k. you   188.5

For I k. that my redeemer liveth   142.2

I k. my sheep and they k. me.   142.9

I k. whom I have trusted, and am confident
142.16

it is given unto you to k. the mysteries   188.2

k. that we k. him, if we keep his commandments
142.17

Let us k., let us press on to k. the Lord   142.7

Let us strive to k. the Lord   224.11

My one desire is to k. Christ   32.9

That I may k. him, and the power of his   142.14

knowledge: K…. puffs a person up with pride
142.11

My k. now is partial; then it will be whole   142.12

Such wonderful k. is far above me.   142.5

the earth shall be full of the k. of the Lord   142.6

The heart of the prudent getteth k.   53.6

the tree of k. of good and evil.   142.1

To know the love of Christ that surpasses k.
142.13

We ask God to fill you with the k. of his will
142.15

known: For what can be k. about God is plain
210.6

knows: As the Father k. me and I know the Father
142.9

no one k. the Son but the Father   142.8

L

labor: Come to me, all you who l.   35.14

Except the Lord build… they l. in vain   279.5

in the Lord your l. is not in vain.   285.5

L. not for the meat which perisheth,   6.20

laborer: The l. deserves to be paid.   279.13

The l. is worthy of his hire.   279.9

laborers: The harvest is rich, but the l. are few
278.4

lake: book of life was cast into the l. of fire.
144.31

not found… was cast into the l. of fire.   144.42

second death in the burning l. of sulphur.   144.32

lamb: choose a l. or a young goat for his family to eat
174.1

Christ, our Passover l., has been sacrificed.   174.5

Christ, that spotless and innocent l.   23.10

he is brought as a l. to the slaughter   135.16

hide us… from the wrath of the L.   144.41

standing before the throne and the L.   144.18

The L. who was killed is worthy   135.69

Then the wolf will live with the l.   9.10

They overcame him by the blood of the L.   23.13

Worthy is the L. that was sacrificed   183.10

Your l. shall be without blemish   220.2

lamentation: there was widespread l. among the
crowd.   202.2

land: For six years you shall sow your l.   143.1

gave us this l., a l. flowing with milk   143.4

I will forgive them and make their l. fertile   143.6

proclaim liberty throughout all the l.   143.2

Your l. must not be sold on a permanent basis
143.3

lands: as many as owned l. or houses sold them
143.8

language: people from every nation, race, tribe and l.
98.10

languages: all races. and tribes, nations and l.
196.5

speaking whatever l. the Spirit let them speak
258.1

lasciviousness: the works of the flesh are manifest…
l.   231.7

laugh: A time to weep, and a time to l.   145.8

Blessed are you who are weeping… you shall l.
145.11

Sarah said, God hath made me to l.   145.1

she can l. at the day to come.   145.7

The righteous will look on… then l.   145.4

laughed: How we l., how we sang for joy!   145.5

So she l. to herself and said   66.1

laughing: you who are l. now: you shall mourn
145.11

laughs: He who sits enthroned in the heavens l.
145.3

laughter: A feast is made for l.   145.10
Choose sorrow over l.   145.9
Even in l. the heart finds sadness   145.6
He will yet fill your mouth with l.   145.2
Turn your l. into mourning and your gaiety   145.12

law: Do not.. come to do away with the L. of Moses
146.3
Do we then make void the l. through faith?   146.5
For I delight in the l. of God   31.50
For I delight in the l. of God   222.3
His delight is in the l. of the Lord   31.13
I may behold wondrous things out of thy l.   146.2
If ye fulfil the royal l.   146.18
In my inmost self I delight in the l. of God   146.9
L. does allow us to help someone on the Sabbath.
219.4
look into the perfect l., the l. of liberty   146.17
made under the l., to redeem them... under the l.
199.11
no one is put right... by doing what the L.   146.12
Now all the words of the l. are addressed   146.4
so love is the fulfilment of the L.   146.11
So the L. was in charge of us until Christ came
146.13
So then, the L. itself is holy   146.8
The l. contains but a shadow of the good   146.16
The L. of Moses cannot do this, because   146.10
The l. of the Lord is perfect   146.1
There is no l. against such things as these.   31.15
to redeem those who were under the l.   146.14
What then should we say? That the l. is sin?   146.7
ye are not under the l., but under grace.   146.6

lawless: the l. one is revealed,   10.4
Then the l. one will be revealed   144.6
then the l. one will be revealed,   10.5

lawlessness: who commits sin guilty of l.; sin is l.
236.21

laws: I will put my l. in their minds   146.15

Lazarus: And there was a certain beggar named L.
144.68

lazy: Besides, they will become l.   148.6
If you are l., you will meet difficulty   148.3
keep away from all... living a l. life   148.4
some people among you who live l. lives   148.5
We do not want you to become l.   148.7

leader: A church l. must be without fault   71.6
if a man is eager to be a church l.   71.6
The Lord said to Moses, Choose a l.   149.2

leaders: A country in revolt throws up many l.
218.3

Don't forget about your l.   71.9
Obey your l. and submit to their authority   71.10

leadership: If it is l., let him govern diligently.
149.6
To aspire to l. is an honourable ambition.   149.9

leadeth: He l. me beside the still waters.   110.1

left: All Jesus' disciples l. him and ran away.   153.4
I only, am l.; and they seek my life   153.1

leopard: Can... the l. his spots?   280.1

leper: There was a l. who came to him and knelt
129.8

leprosy: Immediately his l. was cleansed.   129.8

letter: for the l. killeth, but the spirit giveth life.
242.12

Leviathan: L. too! Can you catch him with a fish-
hook   9.7

liar: denies that Jesus... is nothing but a l.   156.9
Not only is he a l. himself   156.5

liars: are l. and there is no truth in them.   156.8
Save me, Lord, from l. and deceivers.   156.3

liberation: he has... secured an eternal l.   199.16
in him we have... our l.   199.8

lie: Ananias, why did... l. to the Holy Spirit   156.6
Do not l. to one another   156.7
God is not a human being, that he should l.
103.68
God is not a human being, that he should l.   156.2
'L. with me.' But he refused   231.4
you l. to the Holy Spirit   119.24

lied: You have not l. to human beings   156.6

lies: he is also the father of all l.   156.5
they have taught their tongues to speak l.   156.4

life: a man lay down his l. for his friends   265.4
and believes him who sent me has eternal l.
150.17
Because than thy lovingkindness is better than l.   150.6
breathed into his nostrils the breath of l.   150.1
breathed into his nostrils the breath of l.   18.1
but the righteous into l. eternal   213.6
but the righteous into l. eternal.   150.16
Christ gave his l. for us.   32.13
Eternal l. is this: to know you   77.9
Ezra said... To all of them you give l.   192.4
For as the Father has l. in himself   103.56
for the letter killeth, but the spirit giveth l.   242.12
gain the whole world but forfeit their l.?   150.14

guard your heart, for it is the wellspring of l.   116.5

he came…to give his l. to redeem many people.
  199.5

he laid down his l. for us   265.13

he that hath not the Son of God hath not l.   262.9

He that hath the Son hath l.   150.36

He that hath the Son hath l.;   12.12

he was brought to l. in the spirit.   31.29

I am the resurrection, and the l.   150.22

I am the way, the truth, and the l.   150.23

I am the way, the truth, and the l.   31.23

I give unto them eternal l.   150.21

I have come in order that you might have l.
  150.20

I have set before you l. and death   150.4

I shall satisfy him with long l.   150.7

if a person takes the l. of another   165.2

Jesus said unto them, I am the bread of l.   150.18

Lead a l. worthy of the Lord   283.11

leave this l. and be with Christ   51.20

Only God's Spirit gives new l.   18.11

proves that we have gone from death to l.   150.35

ruled by the Spirit, we will have l.   150.28

should not perish, but have everlasting l.   31.21

Take no thought for your l.   150.12

Take no thought for your l.   35.12

the Father hath l. in himself;   14.10

The gate to l. is narrow   150.13

the gift of God is eternal l. through Jesus   150.27

the good shepherd lays down his l. for the sheep.
  135.18

The l. of a creature is in the blood   23.1

the l. of Jesus may also be made visible   150.30

those who hate their own l. in this world   226.4

thou hast the words of eternal l.   150.19

through this faith you may have l. by his name.
  150.25

we will be raised to l. because of Christ   135.102

When Christ, who is our l., shall appear   150.34

Whoever follows me will have the light of l.
  151.12

whosoever will save his l. shall lose it   228.6

Would you like to enjoy l.?   284.2

You killed the author of l.   135.20

light: Arise, shine; for thy l. is come   151.7

Everything exposed by l. becomes visible   151.17

God commanded l. to shine in the dark.   151.14

God is l. and in him there is no darkness   151.21

God said, Let there be l.   151.1

He alone is immortal; he lives in the l.   151.19

He came as a witness… to the l.   151.10

his clothes became as dazzling as l.   102.5

I am the l. of the world,   151.12

I have made you a l. to the nations   278.13

I will also make you a l. to the nations   151.6

if we walk in the l. as he himself is in the l.
  151.22

If we walk in the l., as he is in the l.,   12.10

If you have l. for your whole body   115.11

In him was life; and the life was the l.   151.9

now as Christians you are l.   151.16

out of darkness into his marvellous l.   151.20

people preferred darkness to l.   151.11

so that they may turn from darkness to l.   151.13

The entrance of thy words giveth l.   151.4

the Lord God will be their l.   144.22

The Lord God will be their l.   151.23

The Lord is my l. and my salvation   151.2

The Lord is my l. and my salvation   221.1

The true l., which enlightens everyone   151.10

walked in darkness have seen a great l.   151.5

what communion hath l. with darkness?   151.15

Ye are the l. of the world.   151.8

Ye are the l. of the world.   31.2

Your l. must shine in people's sight   29.4

Your word is a l. to my feet   151.3

Your word is a… l. to my path   151.3

lighting: like stars l. up the sky.   151.18

like: when Christ returns, we will be l. him   32.12

likeness: I shall be satisfied, when I awake, with thy
  l.   32.1

we are being transformed into his l.   32.6

lilies: Consider the l. of the field   35.12

lion: Like a roaring l. your adversary the devil
  253.24

Like a roaring l. your adversary the devil prowls
  271.12

lips: keep watch at the door of my l.   107.2

keep watch at the door of my l.   241.2

openeth wide his l. shall have destruction.   225.3

listen: Anyone who has ears should l.!   152.8

Come to me and l. to my words, hear me   152.6

Don't l. to the lies of these false prophets   152.7

everyone should be quick to l. but slow to speak.
  152.10

everyone who knows God will l. to us.   152.12

he made me willing to l. and not rebel   152.5

l. and l., but never understand   42.3

not just l. to it and deceive yourselves.   152.11

not l. when I called, so I would not l.   184.25

This is my Son, the Beloved. L. to him.   152.9

to l. to him better than the fat of rams.   217.1

You will ask for my help, but I won't l.   184.20

listened: If I had… the Lord would not have l.
  184.19

listening: Speak, your servant is l.   152.1

listens: Anyone who l. to the Word and takes no action   152.11
The Lord… l. to their cries.   184.11
The wise ear l. to get knowledge.   152.3

live: Because I l., you also will l.   150.24
Choose life so that you… may l.   150.4
come unto me: hear, and your soul shall l.   150.9
For 'In him we l. and move and have our being'   150.26
For me to l. is Christ, and to die is gain.   150.33
For me to l. is Christ, and to die is gain.   172.10
He said to me, 'O man, can these bones l.?'   150.10
He said to me, 'O man, can these bones l.?'   212.4
If we l., it is for the Lord that we l.   205.7
It is in him that we l., and move, and exist.   192.9
put to death your sinful actions, you will l.   150.29
that ye may l., and that it may be well with you   115.1
those who have done good will rise and l.   144.51
though he were dead, yet shall he l.   150.22
though he were dead, yet shall he l.   144.52

lives: but it is Christ who l. in me.   135.26
God's Spirit now l. in you   119.30
None of us l. for himself only   205.7
ought to lay down our l. for our brothers.   265.13
we… must give our l. for our fellow-Christians.   32.13

liveth: For I know that my redeemer l.   150.5

living: He isn't the God of the dead, but of the l.   150.15
it is no longer I, but Christ l. in me.   150.31
what holy and saintly lives you should be l.   188.16
You are the children of the l. God!   150.11

loans: The Lord says l. do not need to be paid back   52.1

lonely: Lord, and be merciful to me… I am l.   35.34

longsuffering: The fruit of the Spirit is… l.   226.5

look: L.! He is coming with the clouds   144.66
they may l. and l., but never perceive   42.3

lord: as done for the L. and not for your masters   230.9
but the issue depends wholly on the L.   192.7
call upon the name of the L. shall be saved   31.27
calls on the name of the L. shall be saved   221.2
Come, see the place where the L. lay.   135.95
Do not l. it over the group   149.11

Find out for yourself how good the L. is.   103.32
For I am the L., I change not   103.69
For the L. himself shall descend from heaven   144.56
For the L. is full of compassion   103.52
For thou, L., art high above all the earth: 103.61
God… is himself L. of heaven and earth   103.66
Hear, O Israel: The L. our God is one L.   259.1
High is the L. above all nations   103.62
Holy, holy, holy, is the L. of hosts: 103.36
humans make plans, but the L. has the final word.   192.6
If the L. is God, worship him!   30.4
in the clouds, to meet the L. in the air   144.62
L., who doesn't honour and praise your name?   103.38
O give thanks unto the L.; for he is good: 103.33
O L., how manifold are thy works!   103.71
O L., you have searched me and known me.   103.1
One L. one faith, one baptism   15.10
one L., one faith, one baptism   259.6
Seek ye the L. while he may be found   31.17
so the Son of Man is l. even of the sabbath.   219.5
that I may dwell in the house of the L.   31.44
The days are surely coming, says the L.   135.45
The fear of the L. is the beginning of wisdom   277.2
The grace of the L. Jesus Christ   259.5
the L. chose you because he loves you   108.1
The L. created me the first of his works   135.30
the L. hath laid on him the iniquity of us all.   135.16
The L. is your mighty defender   103.44
The L. isn't slow about keeping his promises   203.18
the L. looketh on the heart   116.3
The L. said to me, 'Your son Solomon   103.19
The L. said to Satan, 'Very well   240.2
The L. said unto my L. Sit thou at my right hand   135.44
The L. says: 'My thoughts and my ways   103.64
The L., the L., a God merciful and gracious   103.50
the people feared the L., and believed the L.   161.2
The steadfast love of the L. never ceases   103.16
There is one L., one faith, one baptism   103.31
This is the word of the L.   103.42
Thomas said, 'My L. and my God!'   135.68
varieties of services, but the same L.   259.4
We will fall into the hands of the L.   103.53
we would rather be… at home with the L.   144.71
what does the L. your God require of you?   154.25
what doth the L. require of thee   205.2
When the L. saw her his heart   249.8

Why do you call me, 'L., L.,'   127.4
Yet it pleased the L. to bruise him   135.93
You took us and the L. as your model   32.11
You, L., are our Father.   103.23
you, L., are our Father; our Redeemer   103.22

Lord's: but the L. will is going to be done.   240.3
I sought the L. help; he answered me   35.3

loses: whoever l. his life for my sake   226.2

lost: he wants everyone to turn… no one to be l.
     203.18

lots: The l. may be cast into the lap   192.7

love: a curse on everyone who doesn't l. the Lord.
     154.31
Because of his great l. for us, God   154.8
Beloved, let us l. one another   154.22
But of these three, the greatest is l.   154.18
Can anything separate us from the l. of Christ?
     154.6
Consider how great is the l. which the Father
     31.11
continue ye in my l.   135.82
for his steadfast l. endures for ever.   159.5
For I desire steadfast l. and not sacrifice   159.8
God hath prepared for them that l. him.   154.30
God is l.   154.9
Greater l. hath no man than this   265.4
Herein is l., not that we loved God   103.49
Husbands, l. your wives, as Christ loved   154.20
I l. the Lord, for he has heard me   154.26
I say unto you, l. your enemies   154.13
If I did not l. others, I would be nothing   154.18
If ye l. me, keep my commandments.   154.27
It follows that when we l. God and obey his
     154.23
Keep yourselves in the l. of God   31.41
know the l. of Christ that surpasses knowledge.
     135.84
Lord, the man you l. is ill   129.5
l. of God is shed abroad in our hearts   188.7
l. one another; as I have loved you   154.16
l. them as you love yourselves.   154.12
l. your neighbour as yourself   154.11
No one can have greater l. than to lay down
     154.17
Nothing… can separate us from God's l.   154.6
nothing… can separate us from the l. of God
     135.83
Only to fear the Lord your God… to l. him
     154.25
Remain in my l.   31.31
The fruit of the Spirit is l.   154.19
the l. of God is shed abroad in our hearts   154.4

The steadfast l. of the Lord never ceases   103.16
The steadfast l. of the Lord never ceases   35.32
The steadfast l. of the Lord never ceases   55.7
things work together… for those who l. God
     154.29
those who l. God must love their brothers   154.33
Thou shalt l. the Lord thy God   154.24
Thou shalt l. the Lord thy God   205.3
With faithfulness and l. he leads all who keep
     159.2
Yet I shall not deprive him of my l.   159.4
You l. him, although you have not seen him
     154.32

loved: Christ l. us and gave his life for us   13.8
For God so l. the world, that he gave   103.48
For God so l. the world, that he gave   154.3
For God so l. the world, that he gave   31.21
he that loveth me shall be l. of my Father   154.28
Herein is love, not that we l. God   154.9
I would gain nothing, unless I l. others.   154.18
it was because the Lord l. you   154.1
Son of God, who l. me and gave himself for me.
     154.7

loves: God has shown us how much he l. us
     154.5
Think how much the Father l. us.   5.10

loveth: every one that l. is born of God   154.22
He that… keepeth them, he it is that l. me   154.28

loyal: be more l. to one than the other.   155.11
They were not l. to him in their hearts   155.5
who is more l. than David?   155.3

loyalty: Guilt is wiped out by l. and faith   155.7
What matters most is l.   155.10

lured: one's own desire, being l. and enticed by it
     253.11

lust: the l. of the flesh, and the l. of the eyes   56.9
the l. of the flesh, and the l. of the eyes,   6.23

lutes: the accompaniment of lyres, l., and cymbals.
     166.4

luxuriant: they are l., wide-spreading trees.   115.3

lyres: to the accompaniment of l., lutes, and cymbals.
     166.4

M

Majesty: he sat down at the right hand of the M. in
     heaven.   13.9

Maker: kneel before the Lord our M.   47.5

male: m. and female created he them.   125.1
m. and female created he them.   231.1
neither m. nor female: for ye are   196.4
there is neither m. nor female   125.25

males: m. behave indecently with m.   121.4
Three times a year all your m. must come   125.18

malice: as must every kind of m.   48.10

man: A m. should fulfil his duty as a husband
    231.3
As a m. is, so is his strength.   125.19
As by one m. sin entered into the world   4.3
before me was one like a son of m.   135.46
Christ is supreme over every m.   86.6
For the Son of m. is come… to save   221.8
Happy is the m. that hath his quiver full   86.14
he blessed them and called them m.   125.17
I found, that God hath made m. upright; but
    125.9
It is not good that the m. should be alone   125.13
It is not good that the m. should be alone   4.2
It was the woman who was made from a m.
    125.23
m. became a living soul   4.2
m. who marries her commits adultery also.   157.13
one like a son of m., coming with the clouds of
    heaven.   144.58
one mediator… the m. Christ Jesus.   135.70
So God created m. in his own image   4.1
So God created m. in his own image   47.2
So God created m. in his own image   125.1
So God created m. in his own image   196.1
the head of every m. is Christ   125.22
The Lord God formed m. of the dust   125.2
The Lord God formed m. of the dust of the ground
    4.2
The m. without the Spirit does not accept   262.4
the result of the obedience of the one m.   4.4
Therefore shall a m. leave his father   157.2
What is m., that thou art mindful of him?   125.5
What is m., that thou art mindful of him?   188.1

man's: The Lord saw how great m. wickedness
125.3

manager: There was a rich man who had a m.
245.2

Manasseh: his left hand on the head of M.   147.1

manna: He made you go hungry, and then he gave
you m.   150.3

mansions: In my Father's house are many m.
144.12

marital: but then resume normal m. relations.
231.3

marriage: M. must be honoured by all   157.8

marriages: m. must be kept undefiled   157.8

married: For m. people I have a command   157.15

marries: and m. another woman commits adultery.
157.14
making her commit adultery if she m. again
157.13

marry: if the husband dies, she is free to m.   275.8
In the resurrection men and women do not m.
157.4
others do not m. for the sake of the Kingdom   28.1
These liars will forbid people to m.   157.7

master: you and your slaves belong to the same M.
279.10

masters: as done for the Lord and not for your m.
230.9
No one can be the slave of two m.   53.10

mature: All of us who are spiritually m.   178.9
that we may present everyone m. in Christ.
178.10

maturity: to m., to the measure of the full stature
178.7

meat: have need of milk, and not of strong m.
178.13
He hath given m. unto them that fear him: 90.6
Ravens brought him bread and m. twice a day
90.4

meddling: nor should it be for m. in other people's
107.14

mediator: For this reason he is the m. of a new
    covenant   135.74
one m. between God and men… Christ Jesus.
135.59
one m…. the man Christ Jesus.   135.70

medicine: A merry heart doeth good like a m.
115.7

meditate: I shall m. on your precepts and keep your
    paths   158.6
you shall m. on it day and night   158.1

meditation: it is his m. day and night.   158.2
Let the words of my mouth, and the m. of   158.4

meek: Blessed are the m. for they shall inherit
31.14
I am m. and lowly in heart: 99.1

Melchisedec: a priest for ever after the order of M.
135.72

melody: making m. in your heart to the Lord.
183.8
Raise a m.; beat the drum   166.7

men: different reasons why m. cannot marry   28.1
I am made all things to all m.   274.11
pick seven m. of good repute   50.1

mercies: by the m. of God, that ye present your
bodies   159.13
his m. never come to an end; they are new   159.6
thy tender m. blot out my transgressions.   159.3

merciful: Be m. just as your Father is m.   159.11
Blessed are the m.   159.10
God, be m. to me, a sinner!   191.2
I am the Lord God. I am m. and very patient
159.1

mercy: for they shall obtain m.   159.10
Have m. upon me, O God, according to   159.3
Have m. upon me, O God, according to thy   92.2
he has pity and m. on anyone he wants to   72.9
I require m., not sacrifice.   220.7
Relying… on your great m.   159.7
to love m., and to walk humbly with thy God?
159.9

mercy seat: the cherubims of glory shadowing the m.
191.6

message: God is begging you to listen to our m.
278.14
God trusted his m. to the Jews.   17.6
keeps the m. of truth on a straight path.   17.10
the most important part of the m.   106.9

messenger: he is the m. of the Lord of hosts   14.1

messengers: people spoke as m. of God.   17.13

Messiah: from them by natural descent came the M.
188.8
kingdom of our God and the authority of his M.
135.51
Was it not necessary that the M. should suffer
135.1

Michael: At that time M. will arise   7.3

milk: have need of m., and not of strong meat.
178.13

mind: be ye transformed by the renewing of your m.
160.7
For who has known the m. of the Lord   160.8
For who hath known the m. of the Lord?   160.6
God's Spirit… knows what is in God's m.   255.6
Let this m. be in you, which was also in Christ Jesus:
32.8
Make your own the m. of Christ Jesus.   160.9
Those of steadfast m. you keep in peace   160.1
with all thy soul, and with all thy m.   160.2

mindful: He is ever m. of his covenant   201.3

minds: guard your hearts and your m. in Christ
Jesus.   160.10
keep our m. on the things that cannot be seen.
35.51
set their m. on the things of the flesh   160.5
their misguided m. are plunged in darkness.   160.4

mine: I have called thee by thy name; thou art m.
35.6

minister: God has chosen them to m. to him
187.4
m. the same one to another   1.12
the Son of man came not to be ministered unto, but
to m.   32.3

ministered: the Son of man came not to be m. unto
32.3

ministry: devote ourselves… to the m. of the word.
50.1

miracle: Jesus performed this first m. in Cana
161.7

miracles: by signs and wonders and various m.
161.13
perform m. and wonders in the name of   161.9
signs, wonders and m. – were done among you
161.12
To another the working of m.   161.11

mirror: glory of the Lord as though reflected in a m.
158.9
We all see as in a m. the glory of the Lord   32.6

misdeeds: put to death the m. of the body
237.10

mocking: men who guarded Jesus were m. and
beating him.   48.8

model: You took us and the Lord as your m.
32.11

money: cannot be the slave both of God and of m.
53.10
Do not live for m.   162.8
For the love of m. is the root of all evil.   162.7
If you love m. and wealth   162.1
must not love m.   162.5
should set their hopes not on m.   214.8

moon: the m. will not give her light   144.4

morning: Each m. he awakens me eager to   152.5

mortal: How then can a mere m. be justified in
God's   125.20

mortals: As for m., their days are like grass   125.7
he sees the whole race of m.   125.6

mortgaging: they were m. their fields, vineyards
52.2

Moses: By faith, M., when he was come to years, refused to be called   30.13

Do not think that I have come to do away with the Law of M.   146.3

M. hid his face; for he was afraid to look upon God. 88.2

M. prayed, 'Show me your glory.'   31.43

M. said, 'No, Lord, don't send me.   2.1

The law... given through M.; grace and truth came... 108.3

The Lord spake unto M. face to face   94.1

Then M. stretched out his hand over the sea 161.1

mother: he said to the disciple, 'Here is your m. 135.109

help his father or m.... 'This is Corban'   86.19

His m. stored up all these things in her heart 86.21

Honour thy father and thy m.:   86.9

Those who love their father or m. more   86.18

motive: does not spring from delusion or sordid m. 163.12

motives: but the Lord judges your m.   242.3

the Lord weighs up his m.   163.3

with false m. or true, Christ is proclaimed   163.11

mourn: a time to m., and a time to dance.   109.3

Alas... you shall m. and weep.   164.11

anointed me... to comfort all that m.   164.8

be sorrowful, m., and weep.   164.13

Blessed are they that m.; for they shall   164.10

m. with those who m.   35.23

that those which m. may be exalted to safety. 164.2

mourned: I was in sorrow and m., as I would for 164.4

They m. and wept, and they fasted till evening 164.1

mourning: a time for m. and a time for dancing. 164.5

Better to go to the house of m. than   164.6

I shall change their m. into gladness   164.9

Thou hast turned for me my m. into dancing 164.3

Turn your laughter into m.   164.13

your days of m. will be ended.   164.7

mouth: He that keepeth his m. keepeth his life 225.3

Lord, set a guard on my m.   253.13

Out of the m. of babes and sucklings   86.13

Set a watch, O Lord, before my m.   225.2

that I may open my m. boldly   278.15

this people draw near me with their m.   217.2

multitude: charity shall cover the m. of sins 154.21

murder: Do not commit m.   165.3

were told in the past, 'Do not commit m.   165.6

murdered: Cain attacked and m. his brother. 165.1

murderers: As for the cowardly, the faithless... the m.   165.8

you know that m. have not got eternal life   165.7

music: I shall sing to the Lord, making m. to the Lord   166.1

let the m. of our praises resound all our life   166.9

take charge of the m. in the house of the Lord 166.3

the people of Israel were playing m.   166.2

the young have given up their m.   166.10

musical: They performed their m. duties   166.3

musicians: the m., surrounded by young women playing   166.6

mystery: to make known the m. of the gospel. 278.15

to make known the m. of the gospel.   106.13

N

naked: they knew that they were n.   84.1

when I was n., you gave me clothes to wear.   140.2

name: A good n. is more to be desired than great 29.3

Anything you ask in my n. I will do   167.9

baptize them in the n. of the Father   167.7

baptizing them in the n. of the Father, and   259.3

blessed be the n. of the Lord.   35.18

calls on the n. of the Lord shall be saved   221.2

do all in the n. of the Lord Jesus   167.15

For where two or three come together in my n. 184.43

God... gave him the n. that is above every n. 135.8

God... gave him the n. that is above every n. 167.14

he... invoked the n. of the Lord.   167.1

His n. is the only one in all the world   167.12

Holy Spirit... the Father will send in my n.   167.10

I have called thee by thy n.   31.1

In the n. of Jesus Christ of Nazareth rise   167.11

Lord, in your n. even the demons submit   271.2

no other n. by which we must be saved   221.10

Our Father... hallowed be thy n.   167.5

Repentance... should be preached in his n.   167.8

tell them that the Lord, whose n. is 'I Am'   167.2
The n. of the Lord is a tower of strength   167.4
the n. of the Lord Jesus gained in honour.   167.13
Thou shalt not take the n. of the Lord thy God
     167.3
two or three are gathered together in my n.   167.6
Whatever you ask in my n. I will do   184.45
whosoever shall call upon the n. of the Lord   31.27

narrow: Try your hardest to enter by the n. door
     221.7

nation: a group of royal priests and a holy n.   31.9
people from every n., race, tribe and language;
     98.10

nations: all races and tribes, n. and languages
     196.5
before him shall be gathered all n.   144.34
From one ancestor he made all n.   196.3
Go therefore and make disciples of all n.   278.5
I have made you a light to the n.   278.13
the good news must be preached to all n.   278.6
the n. are as a drop of a bucket   103.40

nature: controlled by the old n., but by the Spirit.
     237.9

near: Draw n. to God, and he will draw n. to you.
     3.8
So let's come n. God   3.7
The Lord is n. to those who are discouraged   35.27

necessary: Was it not n. that the Messiah should
     suffer   135.1

necessity: For n. is laid upon me   285.4

need: all we n. and see one of our own people in n.
     214.10
lend him sufficient for his n.   97.1
We have everything we n. to live a life   31.16

needy: do not be hard-hearted… towards your n.
     181.2

neglect: How shall we escape, if we n. so great
     salvation?   221.18

neighbor: Love your n. as you love yourself.
     168.4
not bear false witness against thy n.   168.1
Thou shalt love thy n. as thyself.   205.3
Which one of these three people was a real n.
     168.3
You must love your n. as yourself.   265.2
you must love your n. as yourself.   168.2

neighbor's: Thou shalt not covet… any thing that is
     thy n.   168.1

neighbors: he asked Jesus, 'Who are my n.?'
     168.3

never-failing: Provide for yourselves… n. treasure
     81.9

new: God has promised us a n. heaven and a n. earth
     144.46
I saw a n. heaven and a n. earth   144.47
if any man be in Christ, he is a n. creature   169.4
you have put on a n. self which will progress
     202.11

news: For we brought the Good N. to you   185.8
he has chosen me to bring good n. to the poor
     106.4
he told him the Good N. about Jesus.   78.2
How beautiful are the feet of those who bring good
     n.!   185.5
This good n. of the kingdom   106.1
to testify to the good n. of God's grace.   106.5
went from place to place, telling the good n.   78.1

Nicodemus: N. saith unto him, How can a man be
     born   169.3

Noah: At the end of forty days N.   269.1

noble: my n. designs are swept away as by the wind.
     59.4

noble-minded: the Jews were more n. than those in
     Thessalonica   29.6

noise: Suddenly there was a n. from heaven
     144.14

nothing: it is certain we can carry n. out.   162.6
n…. can separate us from the love of God   135.83

O

obedience: He was humble and walked the path of o.
     126.6

obedient: Be o. to God, and do not allow your lives
     170.13
became o. to the point of death   170.10
because you have been o. to me.   170.1
he learnt through his sufferings to be o.   170.11
many of the priests became o. to the faith.   212.9
was o. even to the point of death   135.90

obey: Behold, to o. is better than sacrifice   170.4
Children… o. your parents.   247.3
Everyone must o. the state authorities   247.1
He asked the people to o. the Lord faithfully
     202.1
Holy Spirit… given to those who o. him.   170.8
I am the Lord your God… have refused to o.   65.2
if you o. the Lord your God   170.3
If you will not o. the Lord your God   65.1
It follows that when we love God and o.   170.15

'My food,' Jesus said to them, 'is to o.   135.88

not o. the Good News about our Lord Jesus   65.5

O. your father and your mother   86.22

ones who o. my Father in heaven will get in.
170.5

receive from him whatever we ask, because we o.
170.14

Slaves, o. your human masters   247.4

Surely, to o. is better than sacrifice   220.4

We must o. God rather than any human   170.7

We must o. God rather than any human authority.
243.2

obeyed: you o. the teaching you received from me.
170.9

obeying: do what the Law commands by o. the Spirit
146.10

obstinate: anger and sorrow at their o. stupidity
112.6

offense: Happy is he whose o. is forgiven   139.3

offender: if the o. refuses to listen even to the church
33.2

offering: lame or sick, and this you bring as your o.!
217.4

put his hand upon the head of the burnt o.   220.3

thou shalt make his soul an o. for sin   191.1

old: Do not cast me off when o. age comes 172.4

Show respect for o. people and honour them
172.1

that still bear fruit in o. age   172.6

There was a very o. prophet   172.8

older: Instruct the o. men to be sober, sensible
172.11

o. women to behave as women should   172.11

one: Are you the o. who is to come   66.4

being in full accord and of o. mind.   264.8

for ye are all o. in Christ Jesus.   125.25

for ye are all o. in Christ Jesus.   196.4

Hear, O Israel: The Lord our God is o. Lord.   259.1

o. Lord, one faith, one baptism   15.10

That they all may be o.   264.5

that they may be o., as we are o.   31.32

There is o. body and o. Spirit   264.7

they shall be o. flesh.   86.1

Onesimus: Perhaps O. was taken from you
208.15

open: I send you to o. their eyes   22.12

open-handed: they have shown themselves lavishly
o.   101.8

oppress: Do not o. widows, orphans, foreigners
173.8

You shall not wrong or o. a resident alien   173.1

oppressed: He was o., and he was afflicted   173.7

May the Lord be a tower of strength for the o.
173.3

O Lord, I am o.; be my security!   173.6

Save the o. from the hand of the oppressor   173.9

The Lord judges in favour of the o.   173.4

oppressors: Moreover, are not the rich your o.?
173.10

orders: After all, I am under o. to do so.   245.4

I have given the o. to all their array.   103.11

others: should each look after the interests of o.
265.7

ourselves: Christ… died so we would no longer live
for o.   228.9

outward: man looketh on the o. appearance, but the
Lord   116.3

They will hold to the o. form of our religion   217.7

over: respect those… who are o. you in the Lord
149.8

who work hard among you, who are o. you   71.5

overcame: o. him by the blood of the Lamb, and by
the word   23.13

overcome: be of good cheer; I have o. the world.
266.2

overseers: the Holy Ghost hath made you o., to feed
71.4

overwhelmed: Therefore is my spirit o. within me
57.9

own: All one's ways may be pure in one's o. eyes
229.2

For all seek their o.   228.11

ox: Is the wild o. willing to serve you   9.6

You shall not muzzle an o.   279.13

P

paid: not get out until you have p. the last penny
52.9

pain: P. borne in God's way brings no regrets
109.14

palms: I have graven thee upon the p. of my hands
35.37

panteth: As the hart p. after the water brooks
224.3

parables: Why speakest thou unto them in p.? 188.2

parade: Be careful not to p. your uprightness 163.8

paradise: To day shalt thou be with me in p. 144.69

Today shalt thou be with me in p.   135.107

pardon: our God, for he will abundantly p.   31.17

our God, for he will abundantly p.   203.2

parents: p. are the pride of their children.   86.16

parted: he was p. from them, and carried up into heaven   135.2

partners: who has called you to be p. with his Son 31.5

passions: God has given them up to shameful p. 121.4

Passover: and they prepared the P. meal.   174.4

everyone came to Jerusalem to celebrate P.   27.3

For our P. Festival is ready   174.5

now that Christ, our P. lamb, has been sacrificed. 174.5

This is the P. Festival in honour of me   174.1

went to Jerusalem for the festival of the P.   174.3

past: At my time of life I am p. bearing children 66.1

pastors: The gifts he gave were that some would be... p.   175.1

patience: do you despise the riches of his... p.? 176.4

The Spirit produces... p.   176.7

patient: be p.... for the coming of the Lord is near. 176.9

Be p. in time of trouble   176.5

God is p. because he wants everyone   203.18

I know... how p. you have been.   176.10

Love is p. and kind   176.6

We urge you... be p. with everyone.   176.8

You must be p., my friends, until the Lord comes 269.18

patiently: Be still before the Lord and wait p. for him 176.1

pattern: Take me as your p., just as I take Christ 32.5

pay: He shall p. for the lamb four times over 207.6

I will p. him back four times the amount.   207.11

The worker earns his p.   213.9

you must p. the owner double.   207.1

peace: effect of righteousness will be p.   216.4

For he is our p.   177.20

God does not want... but in harmony and p. 177.18

Having made p. through the blood of his cross. 23.6

He sent Christ to make p. between himself and us 198.4

His name shall be called... The Prince of P.   177.2

Hold thy p. at the presence of the Lord God   234.9

I did not come to bring p., but a sword.   177.7

I give you p., the kind of p. that only I can   177.12

If possible... live at p. with all.   177.17

it is my own p. that I give you.   35.10

Jesus... said to them, 'P. be with you.'   177.14

Let the p. of God rule in your hearts   177.23

lettest thou thy servant depart in p.   177.10

May the Lord of p. himself give you p.   177.24

no p. for the wicked, says the Lord.   177.4

on earth p. to all in whom he delights.   177.9

'P.! Be still!' Then the wind ceased   177.8

P. be with this house.   177.11

P. is what I leave with you   35.10

p. of God, which is beyond all understanding 177.22

set the mind on the Spirit is life and p.   177.16

spoken unto you, that in me ye might have p. 177.13

that in me ye might have p.   45.6

The fruit of the Spirit is... p.   177.19

The Lord gives perfect p. to those whose faith 177.3

The Lord... give thee p.   177.1

the p. of God, which surpasses all   35.16

we have p. with God through our Lord Jesus Christ. 177.15

we have p. with God through our Lord Jesus Christ: 12.3

Your feet shod with... the gospel of p.   177.21

peace-loving: If a p. person lives there, let your greeting   177.11

peacemakers: Blessed are the p.:   177.6

people: faithful p. who will be able to teach others 149.10

for he will save his p. from their sins.   221.3

he himself could tell what was in p.   125.11

It is God's p. who are to judge the world   144.37

Once you were nobody. Now you are God's p. 188.15

Such p. claim to know God, but   251.8

the one righteous act sets all p. free   4.4

the one sin condemned all p.   4.4

they shall be his p.   46.10

You are God's chosen and special p.   31.9

perfect: Be ye therefore p.   178.3
Be ye therefore p., even as your Father   29.5
for power is made p. in weakness.   108.11
If thou wilt be p., go and sell that thou hast   178.4
or have already been made p., but I press on
178.8
prove what is… p., will of God.   178.5
The law of the Lord is p.   178.2
the spirits of the righteous made p.   144.74
to make everyone p. in Christ.   6.7
we may present every man p. in Christ Jesus.
31.36
When he was made p., he became the source
178.12

perfected: For by a single offering he has p. for all
time   178.14

perish: Let the day p. wherein I was born.   55.1
they shall never p.   12.2

persecute: Before all this happens they will… p. you.
179.4
Bless those who p. you   179.9
If people persecuted me, they will p. you   179.5
pray for them which… p. you.   19.9
pray for them which… p. you.   179.2
Saul, Saul, why do you p. me?   179.7

persecuted: Blessed are they which are p.   31.14
Happy are those who are p. because they do
179.1

persecution: P. will indeed come to everyone
179.10
Shall tribulation, or distress, or p.   179.8
That day a bitter p. started   179.6
when trouble or p. arises   179.3

persecutions: through many p. that we must enter
248.6

perseverance: watching thereunto with all p. and
supplication   74.5

persist: For if we deliberately p. in sin   85.10

Peter: P. said, Silver and gold have I none   114.8
thou art P., and upon this rock   33.1
When Simon P. saw it, he fell down at Jesus' knees
135.67

Pharisee: Brothers, I am a P., a son of Pharisees.
180.10
The P. stood over by himself and prayed   180.8
When the P. saw this, he said to himself   180.6

Pharisees: because of the P. they did not talk about it
180.9
Now you P. clean the outside of the cup   180.7
One day when Jesus was teaching, some P.   180.4

The P.… complained to his disciples   180.5
The P. went off and made a plan to trap Jesus
180.2
Then the P. went out, and held a council   180.1
Woe unto you, scribes and P., hypocrites!   180.3

Philip: P. appeared at Azotus, and toured the country
136.10

Philistines: That is how the P. sent gifts to the Lord
207.5

Pilate: For in this city… Pontius P.   205.5
P.… washed his hands before the multitude   205.4

pilfer: they are not to answer back, not to p.
244.8

pit: He raised me out of the miry p.   35.28

pity: God, have p. on me! I am such a sinner!
159.12
in his love and in his p. he redeemed them   249.4
To him that is afflicted p. should be shewed   249.1

place: I go to prepare a p. for you.   144.12

plan: the definite p. and foreknowledge of God
240.7
whatever your hand and your p. had predestined
205.5

plants: All green p. I give for food   90.1

play: p. skilfully with a loud noise.   166.5
p. the tuneful lyre and harp.   166.7

plead: p. the case of the widow.   138.5

please: Even Christ did not try to p. himself.
265.5

pleased: Yet it p. the Lord to bruise him   276.2

pleases: when we ask for what p. him.   184.30

pleasure: p. of the Lord shall prosper in his hand.
276.2

pledges: had to give their sons and daughters as p.
52.2

ploughshares: they shall beat their swords into p.
198.1

pluck: neither shall any man p. them out of my
hand.   12.2
neither shall any man p. them out of my hand.
150.21

ponder: We p. your steadfast love   255.1

pondered: Mary kept all these things, and p. them
158.8

poor: anointed me to preach the gospel to the p. 181.9

Blessed are the p. in spirit: 126.2

Blessed are the p. in spirit: 181.6

for your sakes he became p.   181.11

give to the p., it is like lending to the Lord   181.5

Has not God chosen the p. in the world   181.12

He raises the p. from the dust   181.3

If you oppress p. people, you insult the God   181.4

Truly, I tell you, this p. widow   181.8

When you give a party, ask the p.   181.10

You must not deprive the p. man of justice   181.1

You shall not withhold the wages of p.   173.2

You will always have the p. with you   181.7

pour: After this I shall p. out my spirit   119.7

poverty: she out of her p. has put in everything 226.1

she out of her p. has put in everything she had 181.8

that ye through his p. might be rich.   181.11

power: abound in hope by the p. of the Holy Spirit 182.9

At that moment Jesus felt p. go out from him 182.5

being protected by the p. of God through faith 182.19

But you will receive p. when the Holy Spirit   31.3

Christ the p. of God, and the wisdom of God 182.10

face all conditions by the p. that Christ gives me. 182.16

for it is the p. of God unto salvation   182.8

for p. is made perfect in weakness   2.8

for p. is made perfect in weakness   108.11

for p. is made perfect in weakness   182.12

for p. is made perfect in weakness   266.7

For thine is the kingdom, and the p.   182.2

For thine is the kingdom, and the p.   184.33

hold to the outward... but reject its real p. 182.18

Holy Spirit comes... you will be filled with p. 182.7

How very great is his p. at work in us   182.13

Jesus returned in the p. of the Spirit   182.6

know neither the scriptures nor the p. of God. 182.3

Son of Man coming... with p. and great glory. 182.4

strong in the Lord, and in the p. of his might. 182.14

that the excellency of the p. may be of God 182.11

the good news, it was with the p. and assurance 182.17

the p. of Christ may dwell in me   2.8

to know Christ and the p. of his resurrection 182.15

to them gave he p. to become the sons of God 31.20

to them gave he p. to become the sons of God, 14.9

with a demonstration of the Spirit and of p. 119.33

with authority and p. he commands   135.12

You will receive p. when the Holy Spirit   119.20

powers: against principalities, against p.   54.9

He disarmed the cosmic p. and authorities   54.10

the p. that be are ordained of God   218.10

praise: Enter... into his courts with p.   183.3

his p. shall continually be in my mouth   183.1

Let us now p. famous men, and our fathers   183.6

Let us, then, always offer p. to God   183.9

offer p. to God as our sacrifice through Jesus 220.10

the garment of p. for the spirit of heaviness   164.8

the garment of p. for the spirit of heaviness   183.5

Whoso offereth p. glorifieth me   183.2

will receive from God the p. they deserve.   144.36

praises: This people... will proclaim my p.   183.4

praising: eating with glad and humble hearts, p. God 183.7

p. God, and enjoying the good will of   283.8

pray: If my people... humble themselves, and p. 184.39

p. that you will not fall into temptation   253.6

P. without ceasing.   184.16

Stay awake, and p. that you may be spared   184.34

This, then, is how you should p.   184.31

two of you... agree about anything you p. for 184.43

we do not know how to p. as we ought   184.35

When you do p. and do not receive   184.29

When you do p. and do not receive   184.8

When you p., do not be like the hypocrites 184.26

When you p., go to your room   184.14

prayed: Moses p. 'Show me your glory.'   31.43

p. for thee, that thy faith fail not   253.15

p. wrongly, wanting to indulge your passions. 184.8

Three times I p. to the Lord about this   184.4

prayer: have faith, everything you ask for in p. 184.44

in everything by p. and supplication   184.6

The effectual fervent p. of a righteous man   184.9

the p. of faith shall save the sick   129.9

This kind can come out only through p.   184.2

prayers: In your p. do not go babbling on   184.26
p., intercessions, and giving of thanks   184.37
the Lord would not listen to your p.   184.18
We are certain that God will hear our p.   184.30
We are certain that God will hear our p.   184.49
when ye make many p., I will not hear   184.22

praying: keep on p. and never lose heart.   184.15
P. always with all prayer and supplication   184.36
You co-operate by p. for us.   184.3

preach: But we p. Christ crucified   185.6
Go and p. the good news to everyone   278.7
P. the word; be instant in season   185.12
the gospel I p. is not of human origin.   106.11
the Lord hath anointed me to p. good tidings
    185.2
Whom we p., warning every man, and teaching
    31.36

preached: Repentance and remission of sins should
    be p.   185.3
the good news must be p. to all nations.   278.6

preaching: don't stop p. and teaching.   185.9
if they work hard at p. and teaching.   185.10
it pleased God by the foolishness of p.   185.6
p. the gospel gives me nothing to boast of   185.7

precept: fear toward me is taught by the p. of men
    217.2

predestinate: For whom he did foreknow, he also did
    p.   32.4

predestined: For those whom he foreknew he also p.
    72.8
those whom he p. he also called   31.4

prepare: If I go and p. a place for you   35.22

prepared: things which God hath p. for them that
    love   144.15

presence: we have the boldness to go into God's p.
    3.6
where can I flee from your p.?   103.4

press: I p. towards the finishing line   285.8

pressure: I am under daily p. because of my anxiety
    149.7

pretend: inside you are evil and only p. to be good.
    229.5

price: you have been bought at a p.   199.9

pride: evil intentions come... p.   186.4
P. goeth before destruction   186.2
the p. of life,   6.23
the p. of life, is not of the Father   56.9

priest: Every high p. chosen from among mortals
    187.9
For the high p. we have is not incapable   135.63
Ours is not a high p. unable to sympathize   135.38
was fitting that we should have such a high p.
    135.39
we have a great high p.... Jesus   135.71

priest's: Then they led Jesus away to the high p.
    house   187.6

priesthood: He holds his p. permanently   135.73
you are a chosen race, a royal p.   187.12

priests: Aaron, and his sons... to serve me as p.
    187.2
p. made their submission to the faith.   187.8
Since all p. must offer gifts and sacrifices   187.10
So Judas... spoke with the chief p.   187.7
the p. are to be given the shoulder, the jaw   187.3
The p. do their work each day   187.11
Then the p., the sons of Levi   187.4
You are a group of royal p. and a holy nation.   31.9
You will be to me a kingdom of p.   187.1

prince: appoint him p. over his people   149.3

principalities: For we wrestle... against p., against
    powers   54.9

prison: opening of the p. to them that are bound.
    93.1

prisoner: I therefore, the p. in the Lord   31.6
making me a p. under the law of sin   146.9

privilege: begging us earnestly for the p. of sharing
    188.9
I received the p. of an apostolic commission   188.6

prize: take hold of the p. for which Christ Jesus
    6.6
to win the p. of God's heavenly call in Christ Jesus.
    6.6

proclaim: how are they to hear without someone to
    p.   185.5

promise: Behold, I send the p. of my Father upon
    you   189.1
but it is the children of the p.   189.2
strangers to God's covenants and the p.   189.4

promised: for he is faithful that p.   189.6
God has p. us a new heaven and a new earth
    189.9
receive the crown of life that the Lord has p.
    189.7

promises: because it is based on p. of better things.
    189.5
God made great and marvellous p.   31.16

he has given us his very great and precious p. 189.8

in him every one of God's p. is a 'Yes'.   189.3
The Lord isn't slow about keeping his p.   189.9
The Lord isn't slow about keeping his p.   203.18

pronounce: he could not p. the word correctly 241.1

prophecies: But as for p., they will come to an end. 190.9

prophecy: be eager... above all for p.   190.10

prophesied: Lord, Lord, have we not p. in thy name? 190.3

prophesy: I will pour out... and they shall p. 190.6
You can all p., but one at a time   190.11

prophesyings: Despise not p. Prove all things 190.13

prophet: A great p. has risen among us!   135.78
A p. is not without honour, save in his own country 190.4
he will choose one of your own people to be a p. 135.76
The p. has spoken presumptuously   190.1
This is the p. Jesus., from Nazareth   135.77
This man was a p. and was considered by God 135.79
where... the false p. had already been thrown 144.57

prophetic: p. spirit is to be under the prophets control.   190.11

prophets: appointed in the Church are... secondly p. 190.8
During this time some p. from Jerusalem   190.7
false Messiahs and false p. will appear   190.5
I have persistently sent all my servants the p. 190.2
P. or interpreters of dreams may promise   251.1
the foundation laid by the apostles and p.   190.12
The p. did not think these things up   190.14

propitiation: God hath set forth to be a p. through faith   13.4
He is the p. for our sins   191.7
He is the p. for our sins: 13.12
sent his Son to be the p. for our sins.   191.8
Whom God hath set forth to be a p.   191.3

prosper: proud and evil people and to watch them p. 214.2

prospers: So he too p. in all he does.   31.13

prostitute: make it part of the body of a p.?
Impossible!   231.6

prostitutes: nor male p.... will inherit the kingdom of God.   231.5

protect: p. them in your name that you have given me   31.32

protector: The Lord is your p., and he won't go to sleep   26.2

proud: Do not be p., but be willing to   186.7
he hath scattered the p. in the imaginations   186.5
Knowledge makes us p. of ourselves   37.8
Love is... never jealous, boastful, p.   186.10

prove: P. all things; hold fast that which is good. 80.4
Which one of you can p. that I am guilty of sin? 135.37

provide: Abraham called that place 'The Lord will p.' 192.2
p. clothing for those who have none.   280.2
Whoever does not p. for relatives   279.12

provided: On the mount of the Lord it shall be p. 192.2

psalms: With gratitude in your hearts sing p 166.14

punish: because their power to p. is real.   193.8
p. me not for my sins and ignorances   38.8

punished: arrested and handed over to be p. 248.3

punishment: And these shall go away into everlasting p.   144.26
God's servants and carry out God's p.   270.9
Just think how much worse is the p.   193.10
These shall go away into everlasting p.   193.4
They will suffer the p. of eternal destruction   193.9

pure: Blessed are the p. in heart: 31.14
Blessed are the p. in heart: 194.3
keep yourself p.   194.4
the commandment of the Lord is p.   194.1
The wisdom from above is first p.   194.6
To the p. all things are p.   194.5
wisdom from above is in the first place p.   277.22
Your eyes are too p. to behold evil   103.37
Your eyes are too p. to behold evil   194.2

purified: by your obedience to the truth you have p. 194.8

purify: P. your hearts, you people   194.7

purpose: are called according to his p.   240.8
make you willing and able to obey his own p. 240.11

Q

quake: cause the nations to q. before you!   212.3

quarrels: What causes fighting and q. among you?
271.9

quench: Q. not the Spirit   119.41

quick-tempered: [Love] isn't q.   8.15

quiet: anyone with good sense will keep q.
195.10
Even fools seem clever when they are q.   234.5
he will q. you with his love   195.11
its imperishable quality of a gentle, q. spirit
195.13

quietly: A wise man speaking q. is more to be
heeded   195.6
q. wait for the salvation of the Lord.   195.9

quietness: Better is a dry morsel, and q. therewith
195.4
Better is an handful with q.   195.5
in q. and in confidence shall be your strength.
195.7
the effect of righteousness q.   195.8

R

race: people from every nation, r., tribe and language;
98.10

races: all r. and tribes, nations and languages
196.5

radiance: The Son is the r. of God's glory   135.34

rags: All our righteousnesses are as filthy r.   216.5

raised: be r. again the third day.   135.94
But Christ has been r. to life!   135.102
Christ has been r. to life!   35.24
God r. this man Jesus to life   135.96
He r. him from the dead   135.7
just as Christ was r. from death   135.99
that like as Christ was r. up from the dead   15.8
was r. again for our justification.   135.21
was r. again for our justification.   135.98

raising: assurance to all by r. him from the dead.
135.97

ransom: Christ Jesus, who offered himself as a r.
199.14
to give his life as a r. for many.   13.3

ransomed: The r. of the Lord shall return   199.3
You know that you were r. from the futile ways
199.17

reap: For they have sown the wind, and they shall r.
the whirlwind: 79.2

reasons: because you pray just for selfish r.
163.13

rebel: if ye refuse and r., ye shall be devoured
197.8
if you do not r. against his commands   197.3

rebelled: they have r. and gone their own way.
197.11
They will see the corpses of those who r.   197.10
You have r. against the Lord   197.2

rebellion: because you have preached r. against the
Lord.   197.12
For r. is as the sin of witchcraft   197.4
his eyes keep watch… to forestall r.   197.5
That day cannot come before the final r.   197.14
The wicked person thinks of nothing but r.   197.7

rebellious: I know how stubborn and r. you   197.2
This people has a r. and defiant heart   197.11
Woe betide the r. children! says the Lord   197.9

rebels: I will separate the sinful r. from the rest
197.13
r. must live in the bare wastelands.   197.6

rebirth: by means of the cleansing water of r.
272.12

rebuild: They will r. the ancient ruins   208.8

rebuilder: r. of broken walls, the restorer of houses
208.7

rebuke: As many as I love, I r. and chasten   62.5
be instant in season, out of season… r.   62.3

receive: If anyone will not r. you or listen   200.6
Whatsoever we ask we r. of him   184.48
will r. a hundred times more   213.5
you will r. the gift of the Holy Spirit.   119.22

received: As many as r. him   31.20
As many as r. him, to them gave he   5.4
He came unto his own, and his own r. him not.
200.8

recommends: the one whom the Lord r., who is to
be accepted.   37.10

reconcile: That he might r. both unto God in one
body   198.5
Through him God was pleased to r. to himself
198.6

reconciled: go and be r. with your brother first
198.2
we were r. to him through the death of his Son
198.3

we were r. to him through the death of his Son, 12.4

red: wine tempt you, even though it is rich r.   68.1

redeem: he came… to give his life to r. many people. 199.5
I will r. you with an outstretched arm   199.1
to r. them that were under the law   199.11
who gave himself for us that he might r.   199.15

redeemed: By becoming a curse for us Christ has r. 191.4
Christ has r. us from the curse   199.10
I have r. thee   31.1
I have r. thee, When thou passest through the waters 35.6
O Israel, Fear not: for I have r. thee   199.4

redeemer: For I know that my r. liveth   199.2

redemption: through the r. that is in Christ Jesus. 199.6
we wait for adoption, the r. of our bodies.   199.7

reed: A bruised r. shall he not break   35.31

refreshing: r. shall come from the presence of the Lord.   212.7

refuge: God is our r. and strength   35.4
Tell him all your troubles, for he is our r.   184.12
The eternal God is thy r.   35.41

refuse: You r. to come to me to receive life!   112.7

refused: Knowing God, they have r. to honour him as God   262.3

reign: they will r. for ever and ever.   144.22

reject: to punish those who r. God   65.5

rejected: Because you have r. the word of the Lord 200.1
Come to him, a living stone, though r.   200.10
He is despised and r. of men   200.4
The stone which the builders r.   200.2

rejecting: You have a clever way of r. God's law 200.7

rejects: if anyone r. me publicly, I will reject 144.33
There is a judge for anyone who r. me   200.9

rejoice: I r. in your promise like one who finds 137.4
Let all those that put their trust in thee r.   27.6
r. in hope of the glory of God.   137.14
R. in the Lord alway: and again I say, R.   137.18
R. with those who r.   35.23
yet I will r. in the Lord   35.46

rejoicing: come again with r., bringing his sheaves 137.6
there is r. among the angels of God   27.7

relations: does not make provision for his r.   86.26

religion: Be careful not to parade your r.   229.4
will hold to the outward form of our r.   127.5

remain: Happy are those who r. faithful   74.10
R. in my love.   31.31

remember: I r. the days gone by   158.7
Let all the ends of the earth r. and turn   201.4
My dear friends, r. the warning   201.17
R. me when you come into power!   201.12
R. now thy Creator in the days of thy youth.   201.8
R. that Jesus Christ of the seed of David   201.15
R. the former things of old   201.9
R. the marvels he has done   201.5
R. the Sabbath day and keep it holy.   201.1
R. the whole way by which the Lord your God 201.2
They only asked us to r. the poor   201.14

remembrance: bring all things to your r.   201.13
my body given for you; do this in r. of me.   201.11
The righteous shall be in everlasting r.   201.6

remission: declare his righteousness for the r. of sins 13.4

remorse: he was struck with r.   40.1

rend: r. your hearts and not your clothing.   203.4

render: What shall I r. unto the Lord   52.4

renew: fall away, to r. them again unto repentance 202.13
Lord… r. our days as in times long past.   202.6
r. a right spirit within me.   202.3
wait upon the Lord shall r. their strength   202.5

renewal: r. in the Holy Spirit.   202.12

renewed: more it is r. in the image of its Creator. 202.11
yet the inward man is r. day by day.   202.9
you must be r. in mind and spirit   202.10

renewing: let the r. of your minds transform you 202.8

renounce: in later times some will r. the faith   85.8
wants to be a follower of mine must r. self   226.2

reparation-offering: he must bring to the Lord as his r. a ram   207.2

repay: Do not think to r. evil for evil   209.3
he, if caught, will have to r. sevenfold   207.9

repent: Be earnest, therefore, and r.   285.12
remove thy candlestick… except thou r.   203.19
r., and do the first works; or else I will   203.19
'R.', said Peter, 'and be baptized   31.24
R.! Turn away from all your offences   203.3
R. ye therefore, and be converted   203.12
Unless you r. you will all perish as they did.   203.8

repentance: God has given even to the Gentiles the r.   203.13
God's kindness is meant to lead you to r?   203.16
I have not come… but sinners to r.   203.7
life-giving r. to the Gentiles also.   98.6
R. and remission of sins should be preached   203.11

repents: more joy in heaven over one sinner who r.   203.9

replace: if you cannot afford to r. the animals   207.1

reprove: be instant in season, out of season; r.   62.3
I r. and discipline those whom I love 285.12

reproves: for the Lord r. the one he loves   2.4
for those whom the Lord loves he r.   62.1

requests: let your r. be made known to God.   184.6

require: what doth the Lord r. of thee, but to do justly   205.2

resentful: he must be kind to everyone… not r.   19.12

resist: R. him, steadfast in your faith   253.24
R. the devil, and he will flee from you.   271.10

resisted: you too have always r. the Holy Spirit   119.25
you too have always r. the Holy Spirit!   112.8

respect: each wife should r. her husband.   204.12
Have r. for everyone   204.16
Have the greatest r. and affection for them   204.13
r. to the one to whom r. is due   204.11
R. your father and your mother   204.2
They will surely r. him!   204.8
We know what it means to r. the Lord   211.11

respected: A gracious woman will be r.   204.6

respecter: I perceive that God is no r. of persons   204.9

rest: Come to me… and I will give you r.   206.2
Come with me… and r. a little.   206.3
I will give you r.   35.14
I will give you r.   31.18

In returning and r. shall ye be saved   206.1
they will r. from their labours   144.76
those who receive that r. which God promised   206.4

rested: will rest from their own work, just as God r.   206.4

restitution: He must… make r. in full   207.4
until the times of r. of all things   144.44
will make r. for it: a life for a life.   207.3

restoration: whom heaven must keep till the universal r.   208.13

restore: Ben-Hadad said, 'I shall r. the towns   207.7
For I shall r. you to health   208.9
God, r. us, and make your face shine on us   208.5
I will r. to you the years that the locust   208.10
If the wicked r. the pledge   207.10
R. our fortunes, Lord, as streams return   208.6
R. to me the joy of your deliverance   208.4
R. unto me the joy of thy salvation   35.30
then the Lord your God will r. your fortunes.   208.1
they will r. the ruined cities   208.8
We will r. them, and will require nothing   207.8
ye which are spiritual, r. such an one   208.14

restored: Buildings long in ruins will be r.   208.7
He touched their eyes… and their sight was r.   208.11
his flesh was r. like the flesh of a young boy   114.2
his hand was r. whole as the other.   208.12

restores: When the Lord r. his people's fortunes   208.2

restoreth: The Lord is my shepherd… He r. my soul.   208.3

resurrection: attaining the r. from the dead.   32.9
Jesus said… I am the r., and the life   144.52
Jesus said… I am the r., and the life   35.21
So it is with the r. of the dead   144.53

retribution: The r. of his wrath awaits those who are   193.6
who warned you to flee from the coming r.?   8.4

return: let him r. unto the Lord   203.2
R. to the Lord, your God, for he is gracious   203.4
The day of the Lord's r. will surprise us   144.46

returns: But we do know that when Christ r.   32.12

reveal: anyone to whom the Son chooses to r. him.   210.3
those to whom the Son chooses to r. him.   142.8

revealed: a salvation ready to be r. in the last time. 221.19

But God hath r. them unto us by his Spirit.   210.7

flesh and blood hath not r. it unto thee   210.4

He was r. in flesh   135.60

It was Jesus Christ himself who r. it to me.   210.8

revenge: do not take r. on someone who wrongs you 209.4

I am the one to take r. and pay them back.   209.5

reverence: an acceptable worship with r. and awe. 211.14

as it lived in r. for the Lord.   211.9

perfecting holiness out of r. for God.   211.12

Ye shall keep my sabbaths, and r. my sanctuary 204.3

yet do it with gentleness and r.   211.15

reviled: my name r. increasingly all day long   20.2

revive: O Lord, r. thy work in the midst of the years 212.6

O Lord... In our own time r. it   202.7

Wilt thou not r. us again: 212.2

reward: a great r. is kept for you in heaven.   213.4

Abram: I am... thy exceeding great r.   213.1

fear the Lord... your r. shall not fail.   213.3

I am thy shield, and thy exceeding great r.   35.1

in keeping of them there is great r.   213.2

the builder will receive a r.   213.8

You will then have a great r.   213.7

rewarder: he is a r. of them that diligently seek him. 213.10

rich: Come now, you r. people, weep and wail 214.9

Instruct those who are r.   214.8

the r. he hath sent empty away.   214.4

There was a certain r. man   214.5

There was a certain r. man, which was clothed 144.68

riches: A good name is more to be desired than great r.   29.3

O the depth of the r. both of the wisdom   277.14

The unsearchable r. of Christ.   214.7

right: By his blood we are now put r. with God 23.4

Can you find one person who does what is r. 149.4

do what is r. are acceptable to him.   215.11

Doing what is r. and fair pleases the Lord   138.4

everyone did what was r. in his own eyes.   215.2

good people will keep on doing r.   215.14

He did what was r. in the eyes of the Lord   215.5

He has given his Son the r. to judge   135.13

I shall show you what is r. and good   215.3

If you had done the r. thing   215.1

Now he is sitting at God's r. side.   135.75

Our purpose is to do what is r.   122.4

the tax collector... was in the r. with God   139.6

righteous: effectual fervent prayer of a r. man 184.9

Happy the r.! All goes well with them   115.8

Noah was a r. man   216.1

so the result of one r. act is acquittal   84.4

the spirits of the r. made perfect,   144.74

There is none r., no, not one.   216.12

trusted in themselves that they were r.   229.6

righteousness: A harvest of r. is sown in peace 216.19

and r. like a never-failing torrent.   216.6

Blessed are they which do hunger and thirst after r. 6.2

Blessed are they which do hunger... after r.   216.7

For therein is the r. of God revealed   216.11

he counted it to him for r.   139.1

he counted it to him for r.   216.2

he has covered me with the robe of r.   139.5

He that walketh uprightly, and worketh r.   29.2

he will have the world judged in r.   144.35

in him we have our r.   216.15

Now the r. of God without the law is manifested 216.13

R. exalteth a nation: but sin is a reproach   216.3

Seek ye first the kingdom of God, and his r.   216.9

Stand... having on the breastplate of r.   216.17

The effect of r. will be peace   216.4

the r. of God which is by faith   216.13

unless your r. exceeds that of the scribes   216.8

we might be made the r. of God in him.   139.13

righteousnesses: All our r. are as filthy rags   216.5

rise: Martha saith... I know that he shall r. again 144.52

risen: If ye then be r. with Christ., seek those 135.103

rivalry: springs from r. between one person and another.   76.3

rivers: heart shall flow r. of living water   272.10

road: narrow is the gate and constricted the r. 273.8

Wide is the gate and broad the r.   273.8

robe: Each of them was given a white r.   144.75

robed: were r. in white and had palm branches 144.18

rock: he set my feet on r.   35.28
upon this r. I will build my church   33.1
You are my mighty r., my fortress   82.2

rocky: The seeds that fell on r. ground stand for
137.9

roll: a little longer, until the r. was completed
144.75

rule: thy husband, and he shall r. over thee   84.2
you twelve followers… sit on thrones, to r.   144.43

ruler: come forth unto me that is to be r. in Israel.
218.5
Don't speak evil of me or of the r.   218.1
God, the blessed and only R. of all   218.13
Many seek audience of a r.   218.4
When thou sittest to eat with a r.   218.2

rulers: among the gentiles the r. lord it over them
218.6
be made known to the r. and authorities   7.10
One of the r. put this question to him   218.8
r. of darkness and powers in the spiritual   218.11
Remind your people to obey the r.   218.14
the r. join together against the Lord   218.9
the r. of the darkness of this world   54.9
there cometh one of the r. of the synagogue   218.7

Ruth: R. said… wherever you go, I shall go   155.1

S

Sabbath: If you treat the S. as sacred   219.3
Remember the s. day, to keep it holy   219.1
so the Son of Man is lord even of the s.   219.5
The s. was made for humankind   219.5
What if… it falls into a deep hole on the S.?   219.4
You're making the S. unholy.   219.2

sacred: This is a s. day, so don't worry or mourn!
27.5

sacrifice: Christ also was offered in s. once   144.65
Christ… for all time a single s. for sins   220.9
I require mercy, not s.   220.7
offer praise to God as our s. through Jesus   220.10
present your bodies a living s.   220.8
Surely, to obey is better than s.   220.4
there can be no further s. for sins.   85.10
To obey is better than s.   217.1
ye present your bodies a living s.   283.9

sacrificed: Christ s. his life's blood   23.5

sacrifices: Noah built an altar where he could offer s.
220.1

offering again and again the same s.   220.9
The s. of God are a broken spirit   220.5

said: remind you of what I s. while I was with you.
17.4

sake: everyone who has left… for my sake   213.5

salt: Ye are the s. of the earth   31.2

salvation: a s. ready to be revealed in the last time.
221.19
How shall we escape, if we neglect so great s.?
221.18
kept by the power of God through faith unto s.
31.39
leads to s. through faith in Christ Jesus.   221.17
Restore unto me the joy of thy s.   35.30
S. belongs to our God…   221.21
see, now is the day of s.!   221.13
The Lord is my light and my s.   35.2
The Lord is my light and my s.   221.1
There is s. in no one else   221.10
Work out your own s. with fear and trembling
205.9
You must work out your own s.   221.15

Samaritan: a S. while travelling came near him
140.3

same: Jesus Christ is the s. yesterday, today
135.35

sanctification: as slaves to righteousness for s.
222.2
For this is the will of God, your s.   276.7
through s. of the Spirit, unto obedience   222.8

sanctify: S. them through thy truth   222.1
The very God of peace s. you wholly   222.7

sanctuary: a man-made s. which was merely a model
144.17
free to enter the s. with confidence   188.14
then takes s. in one of these cities   165.5
With such longing I see you in the s. and behold
31.46

sandals: Take off your s.   204.1

Sarah: S. was like that; she obeyed Abraham   86.8

Satan: After the thousand years are over, S.   144.8
I watched S. fall from heaven   271.2
Lest S. should get an advantage of us   58.7
S. accused our people in the presence of God
58.16
S. himself masquerades as an angel of light.   58.9
The Lord said to S., 'Very well   253.2
the work of S. displayed in all kinds of counterfeit
10.5
Turn… from the power of S. to God   58.6

satisfy: If you… s. those who are in need   140.1

The Lord will… s. your needs in parched places   41.2

save: Christ Jesus came into the world to s. sinners   236.17

for he will s. his people from their sins   236.8

for he will s. his people from their sins.   221.3

For the Son of man is come… to s.   221.8

He will… s. those who are waiting for him.   144.65

S. yourselves from this corrupt generation.   73.1

saved: But for those of us who are being s.   221.12

call upon the name of the Lord shall be s.   31.27

calls on the name of the Lord shall be s.   221.2

faithful right to the end, you will be s.   221.5

For by grace are ye s. through faith   221.14

God our Saviour, who wants everyone to be s.   221.16

Harvest is past… and we are not s.   57.13

it is by g. you have been s.   108.14

it is by grace you have been s.   169.5

no other name… by which we must be s.   221.10

s. us, not because of any works of righteousness   169.6

shall we be s. by his life!   12.4

Sir, will there be only a few s.?   221.7

Sirs, what must I do to be s.?   221.11

Sirs, what must I do to be s.?   31.25

that the world through him might be s.   221.9

that the world through him might be s.   281.4

Who hath s. us, and called us   31.7

'Who, then, can be s.?' they asked.   221.4

saves: he s. those who have lost all hope.   35.27

savior: Father sent the S. to be the Saviour of the world   221.20

Father sent the Son to be the S. of the world   221.20

For unto you is born this day… a S.   221.6

God our S., who wants everyone to be saved   221.16

say: When you did all this, I didn't s. a word   234.4

scandalmongers: The older women, similarly, should be… not s.   107.13

scapegoat: sending it into the desert as a s.   236.1

scars: Thomas said to them, 'Unless I see the s.   66.8

schooled: I might be s. in your statutes!   2.3

scribe: A s. came up and said to him, 'Teacher   223.4

They told the s. Ezra to bring the book   223.1

scribes: chief priests and the s. saw the amazing things   223.5

crowd with swords and clubs, from… the s.   223.7

far better than the s. and Pharisees   223.2

He taught them… unlike their own s.   223.3

scripture: All s. is inspired by God and is useful   17.11

All s. is inspired by God and is useful for   210.9

It was because s. foresaw that God   106.12

scriptures: You search the s. because you think that in them   17.3

searched the s. daily   17.5

search: I the Lord s. the heart   163.6

If you s. for him, he will let you find him   224.1

S. me, O God, and know my heart: 80.1

s., and you will find   184.42

s., and you will find   224.12

Silently s. your heart as you lie in bed.   158.3

you will s., but you won't find me.   184.20

searched: s. the scriptures daily   80.2

searches: God who s. our inmost being knows   80.3

whoever s. eagerly for me finds me.   224.7

season: For everything there is a s.   256.3

seasons: God said… let them be for signs, and for s.   256.1

seduce: not to let these unprincipled people s. you   236.36

see: hath shut their eyes, that they cannot s.   22.8

Happy the eyes that s. what you are seeing!   188.3

Sir, we would s. Jesus.   31.49

seed: between thy s. and her s.   135.15

seek: at all times s. his presence.   224.5

believe that he… rewards those who s. him.   184.27

I s. you eagerly with a heart that thirsts   31.46

If ye then be risen with Christ, s. those   135.103

Let all who s. you be jubilant   224.2

rewards those who s. him.   224.14

see if there were any that… did s. God.   224.4

S. the Lord and his strength, s. his face   184.10

s. them not.   6.15

s. ye first the kingdom of God   35.12

S. ye the Lord while he may be found   31.17

S. ye the Lord while he may be found   224.8

They were to s. God in the hope that   224.13

to s. him in his temple.   6.1

When you s. me, you will find me   224.9

With all my heart I s. you   224.6

seekest: S. thou great things for thyself?   6.15

seeketh: The Lord is good… to the soul that s. him. 224.10

self-centred: in the last days… People will be s. 228.12

self-control: add… s. to knowledge, fortitude to s. 225.14

An open town… such is anyone who lacks s. 225.5

but the Spirit of power and love and s.   225.9

Tell the young men to have s. in everything. 225.10

The harvest of the Spirit is… s.   225.8

The Spirit produces… s.   252.2

self-controlled: you must lead s. and sober lives. 225.13

selfish: Love isn't s.   265.9

Nobody should be looking for s. advantage   228.8

shepherds who ill-treat… for s. gain.   228.4

with every s. person who rejects the truth   228.7

sell: If thou wilt be perfect, go and s.   284.8

send: And I said, 'Here am I; s. me!'   278.2

Moses said, 'No, Lord, don't s. me.   2.1

sent: As you s. me into the world, I have s. 278.10

The one who s. me is with me.   135.89

the sign for you that it is I who s. you   230.1

separate: Can anything s. us from the love of Christ? 63.12

nothing… can s. us from the love of God   135.83

Who will s. us from the love of Christ?   35.47

Who will s. us from the love of Christ?   12.6

separated: s. from the presence of the Lord 144.28

sepulchres: ye are like unto whited s., which indeed appear   217.5

serpent: Now the s. was more subtil than any beast 84.1

Now the s. was more subtil than any beast   58.1

servant: For you will not… suffer your faithful s. 135.92

If you want to be great, you must be the s.   230.4

let him be your s.   32.3

no s. [ranks] above his master.   230.3

so that my s. will be with me where I am.   230.5

wants to become great among you must be your s. 126.4

serve: If it is serving, let him s.   230.7

It is written… him only shalt thou s.   230.2

the Son of Man did not come to be served but to s., 13.3

Whoever wants to s. me must follow me   230.5

You cannot s. both God and money.   155.11

serves: my Father will honour anyone who s. me. 230.5

Whoever s. must do so with the strength   230.10

service: which is your reasonable s.   283.9

serving: do it… as though you were s. Christ. 247.4

sexual: If a man has s. relations with another man 121.2

No man is to have s. relations with another   121.1

not right that any matters of s. immorality   231.8

s. impurity for the degrading of their bodies   121.3

the man who is guilty of s. immorality sins   231.6

sexually: Neither the s. immoral nor idolaters 231.5

shame: endured the cross, despising the s.   232.7

I hid not my face from s. and spitting.   200.3

not be put to s. before him at his coming.   232.9

share: a brother is born to s. troubles.   155.8

In so far as you s. in the sufferings of Christ   89.9

to be allowed to s. in this generous service   101.8

Yours was the only church to s. with me   89.8

shared: he himself likewise s. the same things 135.29

he himself… s. the same things   35.11

sharing: When we drink… s. in the blood of Christ? 89.4

shedding: without the s. of blood there is no forgiveness   23.7

sheep: All we like s. have gone astray   236.5

I am sending you out like s. among wolves   235.5

shepherd: He shall feed his flock like a s.   233.2

I am the good s.; the good s. lays down his life 135.18

I am the good s., who is willing to die   233.8

I shall set over them one s.   233.5

I shall strike the s. and the sheep   233.6

our Lord Jesus, that great s. of the sheep   233.9

The Lord is my s.; I shall not want.   233.1

they were… helpless, like sheep without a s. 135.80

When Christ the Chief S. returns   233.11

you have returned to the one who is your s. 233.10

you have returned to the one who is your s.   42.8

shepherds: Look after the flock of God whose s. you are   26.8

prophesy against the s. of Israel   233.4

The s. returned, glorifying and praising God   233.7

their s. have led them astray   233.3

shibboleth: they said, 'All right, say "S."'   241.1

shine: Let your light so s. before men   151.8

Wake up, O sleeper… Christ will s. upon you.   151.17

You must s. among them like stars   151.18

shining: Now God is s. in our hearts   151.14

shone: his face s. like the sun   102.5

show: Moses prayed, 'S. me your glory.'   31.43

sick: Is any s. among you?   129.9

The Lord will help them when they are s.   129.6

When I was s., you took care of me   140.2

sight: I have come… to give s. to the sightless   22.11

sightless: I have come… to give sight to the s.   22.11

sign: the s. for you that it is I who sent you   230.1

signs: God added his testimony by s. and wonders   161.13

s., wonders and miracles – were done among you   161.12

will produce great s. and wonders to mislead   161.5

silence: a time to keep s., and a time to speak.   234.6

there was s. in heaven for about half an hour.   234.13

silenced: the wicked will be s. in darkness.   234.1

silent: Everyone, be s.! The Lord is present   234.10

if my disciples are s. the stones will shout   234.11

let all the earth be s. in his presence.   234.8

O Lord my rock; be not s. to me   234.3

silver: He that loveth s. shall not be satisfied with s.;   6.13

Simon: S., S., behold, Satan hath desired to have you   253.15

simple: The Lord preserveth the s.   235.2

The Lord's instruction… makes the s. wise.   235.1

your word unfolds… even the s. understand.   235.3

simplicity: corrupted from the s. that is in Christ.   235.11

that in s. and godly sincerity   235.10

you simple fools be content with your s.?   235.4

sin: and does not do it commits a s.   237.13

As by one man s. entered into the world   84.3

As by one man s. entered into the world   236.12

Be sure your s. will find you out.   236.2

Be sure your s. will find you out.   193.2

But where s. was multiplied, grace   108.8

dead to s. and alive to God in Christ   135.100

Everyone who commits s. is guilty   236.21

everyone who sins is a slave of s.   236.10

For our sake he made him to be s. who knew no s.,   13.7

For the wages of s. is death   236.14

God is their Father, they cannot continue to s.   236.22

hardened through the deceitfulness of s.   236.33

he made him to be s. who knew no s.   31.28

How shall we, that are dead to s.   253.16

I will remember their s. no more.   92.5

If we confess our s., he is just   236.20

If we say, 'We have no s.,'   237.14

law brings only the consciousness of s.   146.4

no more I that do it, but s. that dwelleth in me   237.8

regard yourselves as dead to s.   236.28

Shall we continue in s., that grace may abound?   236.13

that I might not s. against thee.   236.24

thou shalt make his soul an offering for s.   191.1

was through one man that s. entered the world   237.7

When I acknowledged my s. to you   38.6

who takes away the s. of the world   236.9

sinful: Depart from me; for I am a s. man, O Lord.   43.3

every word that passes my lips is s.   43.2

his own Son in the likeness of our s. nature   237.9

I live among a people whose every word is s.   43.2

s. from the time my mother conceived me.   237.2

The mind of s. man is death   237.10

sinfully: Whoever lives s. belongs to the devil   215.13

sing: Judith said… s. unto my Lord with cymbals   166.12

S. out in praise of God our refuge   166.7

S. unto him a new song   166.5

When you meet together, s. psalms, hymns   166.13

singers: The s. come first   166.6

singing: s. with grace in your hearts to the Lord.   283.12

sinless: If we claim to be s., we are self-deceived
236.20

sinned: Against thee, thee only, have I s.   111.4
Against thee, thee only, have I s.   236.3
Against you only have I s.   43.1
all have s., and come short of the glory of God.
237.6
Christ never s.!   236.15
death passed upon all men, for that all have s.
236.12
Father, I have s. against heaven   203.10
For all have s., and come short   236.11
for that all have s.   84.3
If any of you have never s., then go ahead   237.5
If we say, 'We have never s.,'   237.14
inasmuch as all have s.   237.7
we have s. against you.   85.3

sinner: God, be merciful to me, a s.!   191.2
God treated him as a s.   236.15

sinners: a good man on behalf of s.   216.20
Christ died for us while we were still s.   13.5
Christ Jesus came into the world to save s.   236.17
I have not come… but s. to repentance.   203.7
while we were s. Christ died for us.   135.22

sinning: No one… upright to do good without ever
s.   237.4

sins: charity shall cover the multitude of s.   154.21
Christ died for our s., in accordance with   135.25
Christ died once for our s.   13.11
Christ too suffered for our s. once and for all
31.29
Christ… for all time a single sacrifice for s.   220.9
for he will save his people from their s.   236.8
for he will save his people from their s.   221.3
He carried our s. in his own person   13.10
He is the propitiation for our s.   191.7
He is the propitiation for our s.:   13.12
He was bearing our s. in his own body   236.19
I know my misdeeds and my s. confront me   43.1
If one of my followers s. against you   62.2
If we confess our s., he who is faithful   38.11
Keep back thy servant also from presumptuous s.
253.12
poured out for many for the forgiveness of s.   23.2
sent his Son to be the propitiation for our s.   191.8
shedding of blood there is no forgiveness of s.
236.18
show that you have really given up your s.   203.5
Though your s. are like scarlet   236.4
when we were dead because of our s.   237.12
you were dead in your transgressions and s.
236.16

your s. have hid his face from you   184.23
your s. have hid his face from you   236.6

sit: Allow us to s. with you in your glory,   6.18

skill: all who have ability, whom I have endowed
with s.   1.1

skilled: artisans without number, s. in working gold,
1.4
the s. workers are prepared   1.6

skills: Lord has given to Bezalel… the s.   1.2

skin: Can the Ethiopian change his s.   280.1

slave: did not come to be a s. master, but a s.
230.4
everyone who sins is a s. of sin.   236.10

slavery: I put myself in s. to all people   265.6

slaves: s. are not better than their master.   32.2

sleep: Give light to my eyes lest I s. the s. of death
238.3
he who provides for his beloved as they s.   238.5
How long wilt thou s., O sluggard?   238.7
I s. and wake up refreshed   238.1
I will both lay me down in peace, and s.   238.2
If you s. all the time, you will starve   238.8
nor allow myself s., until I find a sanctuary   238.6
Now it is high time to awake out of s.   238.12
The labourer's s. is sweet   238.9
them also which s. in Jesus will God bring   144.73
we must not s. like the rest   238.13
Why s. ye? rise and pray   238.11

sleeps: The guardian of Israel… never s.   238.4

sluggard: Go to the ant, thou s.; consider her ways
148.1
How long wilt thou sleep, O s.?   148.2

smiters: I gave my back to the s., and my cheeks
200.3

snake: Yes, that old s. and his angels   58.16

snares: S. and pitfalls lie in the path of the crooked
236.26

sober: form a s. estimate based on the measure of
faith   37.6
think with s. judgement, each according   186.6
we belong to the day. So we must stay s.   252.3
Your minds, then, must be s.   225.12

sold: Esau, who for one morsel of meat s. his
birthright   131.12

soldier: a s. does not triumph because of   270.5

solitary: have become like a bird s. on a rooftop.
35.35

Solomon: God gave S. very great wisdom,
discernment   277.1

S. in all his glory was not arrayed like   35.12

son: a virgin shall conceive, and bear a s.   135.52
About the S. he says, 'Your throne, O God   135.50
Even though he was God's S., he learnt   135.91
For the S. of man is come… to save.   221.8
God sent his S., born of a woman   135.57
he gave his only begotten S.   135.56
He has given his Son the right to judge   135.13
he that hath not the S. of God hath not life   262.9
If anyone acknowledges that Jesus is God's S.   38.4
my S.; today I have become your Father'?   135.34
no one knows the S. except the Father   210.3
one like a s. of man, coming with the clouds of
heaven.   144.58
one who loves his s. brings him up strictly.   86.15
She brought forth her firstborn s.   135.54
so the S. of Man is lord even of the sabbath.   219.5
S. of Man has authority on earth to forgive sins
135.10
The S. is the radiance of God's glory   13.9
the S. of Man coming on the clouds of heaven
144.59
The S. of Man will die in the way that   240.4
those who love their s. or daughter more   86.18
time was come, God sent forth his S.   199.11
When the S. of man shall come in his glory
144.34
when the S. of Man sits on his glorious throne
144.43
Woman, here is your s.   135.109

song: Sing unto him a new s.   166.5

songs: When you meet together, sing… spiritual s.
166.13

sons: power to become the s. of God   5.4
power to become the s. of God   18.10
to them gave he power to become the s. of God
31.20
who are led by the Spirit of God are s. of God.   5.5
you shall be my s.   5.6

sorcery: Do not practise divination or s.   171.1
Simon had practised s. in the city   171.8

sores: he afflicted Job with running s.   129.2

sorrow: How long will s. fill my heart day and night?
55.3
in s. thou shalt bring forth children   84.2

sorrowful: My soul is s. to the point of death.
246.8
S., yet always rejoicing.   109.13

sorrows: borne our griefs, and carried our s.
35.45
He is despised… a man of s.   109.5
Surely he hath… carried our s.   129.7

sorry: Jesus felt s. for them and touched their eyes
249.7
When he saw the crowds he felt s. for them   249.5

soul: Bless the Lord, O my s.   239.3
Every living s. belongs to me   239.4
He restoreth my s.   239.1
He shall see of the travail of his s.   135.93
man became a living s.   18.1
man became a living s.   125.2
My s. doth magnify the Lord   239.8
My s. is exceeding sorrowful, even unto death
239.7
so panteth my s. after thee, O God.   31.45
so panteth my s. after thee, O God.   224.3
the s. of the child came into him again   114.1
who kill the body but cannot kill the s.   239.5
Why art thou cast down, O my s.?   35.29
Why art thou cast down, O my s.?   239.2

souls: I also saw the s. of those who had been
executed   144.20
you will find rest for your s.   239.6

sown: have s. the wind… reap the whirlwind   79.2

sparrow: not one s. falls to the ground without
192.8

sparrows: you are worth much more than many s.!
192.8

speak: s. the word only,   14.3
We were sent to s. for Christ   278.14

speaking: S. the truth in love   241.7
we cannot stop s. of what we… have seen   278.12

special: This is a s. day for the Lord   27.5
You are God's chosen and s. people.   188.15

speech: Let thy s. be short, comprehending much
241.5
Let your s. be alway with grace   241.9

spend: I will very gladly s. and be spent for you.
265.12

spirit: After this I shall pour out my s.   119.7
Afterwards I will pour out my S. on everyone
212.5
All of them were filled with the Holy S.   119.21
Be filled with the S.   119.39
blasphemy against the S. will not be forgiven.
119.11

Blessed are the poor in s.   242.4

but by my s., saith the Lord of hosts.   119.8

But the Advocate, the Holy S.   119.17

but the human s. within him?   125.12

By contrast, the fruit of the S. is…   119.37

Eagerly follow the Holy S. and serve the Lord.
119.32

Except a man be born of water and of the S.
119.14

Except a man be born of water and of the S.   272.7

Father give the Holy S. to them that ask him?
119.13

Father, into thy hands I commend my s.   135.108

fellowship of the Holy S. be with you all.   259.5

For if I pray in a tongue, my s. prays   258.6

For it has seemed good to the Holy S.   110.7

for the letter killeth, but the s. giveth life.   242.12

For the S. explores everything   119.34

G. is spirit   242.7

God is s., and those who worship him   103.57

God's S. now lives in you   119.30

Grieve not the holy S. of God   119.38

he saw the S. of God descending like a dove   259.2

he will baptise you with the Holy S. and fire   119.9

I have filled him with the divine s.   119.2

I will put my s. in you   119.6

I will put my s. within you   169.2

I will send the S. to you. The S. will come   119.19

if I pray in an unknown tongue, my s. prayeth
242.11

It is the decision of the Holy S.   119.27

Jesus was talking about the Holy S.   135.3

Let me inherit a double share of your s.   242.1

Likewise the S. helps us in our weakness   119.31

Likewise the S. helps us in our weakness   184.35

no one comprehends… except the S. of God.
242.9

Not by might, nor by power, but by my s.   271.1

Now he said this about the S.   119.15

Peter, filled with the Holy S., addressed them
119.23

Quench not the S.   119.41

renew a right s. within me.   169.1

renew a right s. within me.   242.2

set their minds on the things of the S.   160.5

so is every one that is born of the S.   240.5

take not thy holy s. from me.   119.4

the Holy S. told them, 'Appoint Barnabas   119.26

The Holy S. will come on you   119.12

The particular manifestation of the S.   119.35

The sacrifices of God are a broken s.   220.5

the s. is willing, but the flesh is weak.   184.34

The s. is willing, but the flesh is weak.   242.5

the S. led Jesus into the desert to be tempted
253.4

the S. of God coming down on him like a dove.
119.10

The S. of God moved upon the face of the   119.1

The s. of the Lord came upon him   119.3

The s. of the Lord shall rest upon him   119.5

the S. of truth; whom the world cannot receive
119.16

The S. produces love, joy, peace, patience   31.15

the s. who is now at work in those who are   58.10

the S., who reveals the truth about God   119.18

The S. will teach you everything   17.4

the sword of the S., which is the word of God.
119.40

the sword of the S., which is the word of God.
271.6

The way to recognize the S. of God   135.64

they were all filled with the Holy S.   212.8

those who live in the S. have their minds   119.29

through sanctification of the S.   259.7

under the control of the Holy S.   119.42

varieties of gifts, but the same S.   259.4

When the Holy S. comes upon you,   278.11

Where can I go from your s.?   103.4

where the S. of the Lord is, there is freedom.
119.36

will worship the Father in s. and truth   242.7

with a demonstration of the S. and of power.
119.33

you lie to the Holy S. by keeping part   119.24

you received the S. of adoption   242.8

you too have always resisted the Holy S.   119.25

You will receive power when the Holy S.   119.20

you will receive power when the Holy S. comes
31.3

you will receive the gift of the Holy S.   31.24

you will receive the gift of the Holy S.   119.22

you will receive the gift of the Holy S.   15.4

spirits: Any man or woman who consults the s.
171.3

not go for advice to people who consult the s.
171.2

Saul… advice from a woman who talked to s.
171.5

the s. of the righteous made perfect,   144.74

The unclean s. too, when they saw him   54.4

spiritual: The s. man makes judgments about all
things   242.10

spiritually: he cannot understand them, because they
are s.   262.4

spoke: To Job they s. never a word   234.2

spoken: account of every useless word he has ever s.
241.6

Hath in these last days s. unto us by his Son
210.10

spots: Can… the leopard his s.? 280.1

spring: will be a s. of water within him 272.8

stand: able to s. against the wiles of the devil. 253.18
access by faith into this grace wherein we s. 3.4
S. therefore, and fasten the belt of 271.6
Who may s. in his holy place? 3.1

standing: Deacons… are entitled to high s. 204.14

star: Bright morning s., how you have fallen from heaven, 6.14

stars: the s. will fall from the sky 144.4

state: Everyone must obey the s. authorities 243.3

stay: come and s. at my house. 124.2
Stop here, and s. awake with me. 153.3

staying-power: It strikes no root in him and he has no s. 74.2

steal: If you s. an ox and slaughter or sell it 207.1
Let him that stole s. no more 122.5
Thou shalt not s. 244.1
Ye shall not s., neither deal falsely 64.1

stealing: Out of your heart come evil thoughts… s. 244.4

steals: When someone s. an ox or a sheep 244.2

stewards: as good s. of the manifold grace of God 1.12
as good s. of the manifold grace of God. 245.7
s. are required to show themselves trustworthy 245.3

still: after the fire a s. small voice 195.1
Be s. and acknowledge that I am God 195.2

stilled: the waves of the sea were s. 195.3

stony: some fell on s. ground, 81.7

storeroom: he brings out the wind from his s. 192.5

stranger: I was a s., and ye took me in. 130.5
I was a s., and ye took me in. 124.1

strangers: Be sure to welcome s. into your home 130.6
s. to God's covenants and the promise 189.4
s. to the covenants of promise 262.8
The Lord watches over the s. 130.4
welcome s. into your home. 124.3

strength: for my s. is made perfect in weakness. 35.52

God is our refuge and s. 35.4
God is the s. of my heart 35.43
He has given me the s. for my work 1.11
the Lord is the s. of my life 35.2
the Lord stayed with me and gave me s. 35.39
the mighty s. which he used when he raised Christ 182.13
wait upon the Lord shall renew their s. 182.1
will not let you be tested beyond your s. 253.17

strengthening: S. the disciples and encouraging them 31.34

strikes: s. him a fatal blow, and then takes sanctuary 165.5

strive: S. to enter in at the strait gate: 6.3

striving: s. towards the goal of resurrection from the dead. 6.6

strong: Finally, my brethren, be s. in the Lord 182.14
have need of milk, and not of s. meat. 178.13

stubborn: 'How s. you are!' Stephen went on to say. 112.8
If you are s., you will be ruined. 112.3
Make these people s.! 112.4

stumble: anything that makes your brother or sister s. 252.1

stumbling: I have said… to keep you from s. 85.7
my feet were on the point of s. 76.2
There are bound to be causes of s. 253.7

stupid: Don't be s. Instead, find out what the Lord 263.9
The Lord says, 'My people are s. 263.5
The s. give free rein to their anger 225.6

subject: Be s. to one another out of reverence for Christ 247.2

submit: Obey your leaders and s. to their authority. 204.15
Obey your leaders and s. to them 247.5
S. yourselves therefore to God. 271.10

suffer: For ye s. fools gladly 91.12
If one member suffers, all s. together 248.9
It is now my joy to s. for you 248.11
s. many things… and be killed 135.94
the more you understand, the more you s. 246.4
Was it not necessary that the Messiah should s. 135.1
Was not the Messiah bound to s. in this way 248.5

suffered: Christ himself s. for you 31.10

suffering: if you endure s. even when you have done right   31.10

in the knowledge that it is the same kind of s.   248.12

sure that what we are s. now cannot compare   248.8

we know that s. is a source of endurance   246.11

sufferings: in so far as you share in the s. of Christ   2.9

though he was God's Son, he learnt through his s.   135.91

sufficiency: our s. is of God.   265.10

sufficient: My grace is s. for you   108.11

Not that we are s. of ourselves   265.10

sun: the s. will be darkened   144.4

the s. will be darkened, and the moon   144.59

support: exert ourselves in this way to s. the weak   117.6

ye ought to s. the weak   140.4

sure: I am s. that he can guard until the last day   12.8

So I am s. that God,   12.7

We are s. that we live in union with God   12.11

surrender: S. to God! Resist the devil   247.6

sweat: In the s. of thy face shalt thou eat bread   279.2

sweet-smelling: gave his life as a s. offering and sacrifice   13.8

sword: separate us from the love of Christ?... or s.?   270.8

the s. of the Spirit, which is the word of God.   119.40

sympathetic: Finally: you should... all be s.   249.14

sympathy: fellowship in the Spirit, any warmth or s.   249.11

I had hoped for s., but there was none   249.3

They expressed their s. and comforted him   249.2

T

tabernacle: Behold, the t. of God is with men   46.10

Behold, the t. of God is with men   144.21

Tabitha: 'T., get up.' Then she opened her eyes   161.10

tale-bearer: for want of a t. a quarrel subsides.   107.7

talebearer: Thou shalt not go up and down as a t.   107.1

talent: I went off and hid your t. in the ground.   81.6

talents: To one he gave five t.   1.7

tales: Have nothing to do with... old wives' t.   107.11

talk: Stop all your dirty t.   241.8

tambourines: young women playing t.   166.6

task: Whatever your t., put yourselves into it   230.9

tax: The t. collector, standing far off   191.2

the t. collector... was in the right with God   139.6

taxes: Is it lawful to pay t. to the emperor   162.4

Pay... t. to the one to whom tax is due   52.13

pay them your personal and property t.   243.3

teach: faithful people who will be able to t. others as well.   149.10

Go ye therefore, and t. all nations   250.3

I shall instruct you and t. you the way to go   44.2

t. Jacob thy judgments, and Israel thy law   187.5

T. me, Lord, the way of your statutes   250.2

T. them to your children.   250.1

The Spirit will t. you everything   250.5

What I t. is not my own teaching   250.4

teachers: God has put... in the third place t.   250.8

The Pharisees and the t. of the Law   223.6

teaching: All inspired scripture has its use for t.   250.10

in opposition to the t. that you have learned   251.5

proclaiming the message to you and t. you   250.7

t. and admonishing one another in psalms   250.9

t. for doctrines the commandments of men.   251.3

through their t. will come to believe in me.   278.10

Whom we preach, warning every man, and t.   31.36

tears: And God shall wipe away all t. from their eyes   35.56

And God shall wipe away all t. from their eyes;   144.47

My t. have been my meat day and night   55.5

tell: I will t. you what to say   2.1

T. him all your troubles, for he is our refuge   184.12

yet don't do what I t. you?   280.4

temper: a hot t., you only show how stupid you are.   8.11

better control one's t. than capture a city.
8.13

temperance: The fruit of the Spirit is… t.   226.5

temperate: Women likewise must be… t.   252.4

tempers: Hot t. cause arguments,   8.12

temple: beauty of the Lord, and to inquire in his t.
31.44

I pine… for the courts of the Lord's t.   31.48
your body is the t. of the Holy Spirit   24.3

temptation: Lead us not into t.; but deliver us
253.5

pray that you will not fall into t.   253.6
Those who want to get rich fall into t.   56.7
you think you can stand up to t., be careful   186.9

temptations: count it all joy when ye fall into divers
t.   253.21

tempted: Because he himself suffered when he was t.
253.19

lest thou also be t.   253.9
No one, when t., should say, 'I am being t. by God
253.11

the Spirit led Jesus into the desert to be t.   253.4

tenants: When the t. saw the owner's son   204.8

tent: For in this t. we groan, longing to be   172.9

test: do not be surprised at the painful t.   35.55
do not put us to the t.   236.27
God will not let you be put to the t. beyond   74.4
in the wilderness to humble and t. you   253.1
Put yourselves to the t.   227.4
t. the spirits to see whether they are   80.5
when God put Abraham to the t.   253.10

tested: God… will not let you be t. beyond your
powers   35.49

one who has been t. in every way as we are
253.20

will not let you be t. beyond your strength   253.17
your faith… is t. by fire   253.22

testimony: God added his t. by signs and wonders
161.13

testing: do not be taken aback at the t. by fire   2.9
don't be surprised… you are going through t.
253.23

No t. has overtaken you that is not common
253.17

thank: T. God, then, for giving us the victory
254.4

thanked: prostrated himself at Jesus' feet and t.
254.3

thankful: With t. hearts offer up your prayers
254.9

thanks: do all… giving t. to God and the Father
283.12

give t. unto the Lord; for he is good: 103.33
Giving t. always for all things unto God   254.8
I have not stopped giving t. to God for you.   254.6
In every thing give t.: for this is the will   254.10
It is good to give t. to the Lord   254.2
Rather you should give t. to God.   254.7
T. be unto God for his unspeakable gift.   254.5

thanksgiving: Offer unto God t.   254.1

thief: Anyone who was a t. must stop stealing
64.14

cared about the poor, but because he was a t.
163.9

He said this… because he was a t.   244.5
the Day… come like a t. in the night.   144.63
The day… will surprise us like a t.   144.46
The t. must give up stealing   244.7
The t. shall make restitution   244.2
You deserve to suffer if you are… a t.   244.9

thieves: Neither… t. nor the greedy   244.6
ye have made it a den of t.   244.3

things: all t. have their proper place   192.11
For all t. come of thee   192.3
He alone does these wonderful t.   161.4
I am made all t. to all men   274.11
they will do even greater t.   161.8
to be thoughtful and to do helpful t.   280.10
Upholding all t. by the word of his power.   192.12
We know that all t. work together for good   35.47

think: I t. about all that you have done   158.7
if there be any praise, t. on these things.   255.9
What t. ye of Christ? whose son is he?   255.5

thinking: do not be children in your t.   255.7

third: be raised again the t. day.   135.94

thirst: he that believeth on me shall never t.   272.9
he that believeth on me shall never t.   41.4

thirsteth: My soul t. for God, for the living God:
31.45

thirsty: he said: I am t.   135.110
when I was t., you gave me something to drink.
140.2

Thomas: T. said, 'My Lord and my God!'   135.68

thorn: a t. was given to me in the flesh   248.18
I was given a t. in my flesh   186.11

thou: for I am holier than t.   229.3

thousand: with the Lord one day is like a t. years 256.15

thought: I t. on my ways   227.1
we take every t. captive   255.8

thoughts: Fix your t. on that higher realm   160.11
For my t. are not your t.   210.2
For my t. are not your t.   255.4
How mysterious, God, are your t. to me   255.2
Let your t. be on things above,   6.22
The Lord says: 'My t. and my ways   103.64
try me, and know my t.   255.3
understandeth all the imaginations of the t.   163.2

throne: About the Son he says, 'Your t., O God 135.50
boldly approach the t. of grace   35.53
come bravely before the t. of our merciful God. 184.7
his seat at the right hand of the t. of God.   31.38
I saw a great white t., and him that sat on it 144.42
set down at the right hand of the t. of God.   35.54
the t. of God and of the Lamb will be in it   144.22
then shall he sit upon the t. of his glory   144.34
Thus saith the Lord, The heaven is my t.   144.10
who is seated on the t. will shelter them.   144.19
Your t., O God, will last for ever and ever   135.34

thrones: Then I saw t., and those who sat on them 144.20
twelve followers… sit on t., to rule… tribes of Israel 144.43

throng: After that I looked and saw a vast t. 144.18

tidings: I bring you good t. of great joy   35.8
the feet of him that bringeth good t.   185.1

time: a t. to be born, and a t. to die.   256.3
always make good use of the t.   256.14
carefulness bringeth age before the t.   256.4
For me the right t. has not come yet   256.7
Redeeming the t., because the days are evil. 256.13
The t. has arrived; the kingdom of God   256.6
When the right t. finally came   256.12
When the t. came for me to show you favour 256.11

times: It is not for you to know about dates or t. 256.9
My t. are in thy hand.   172.3
Whom the heaven must receive until the t.   256.10

tire: Let us never t. of doing good   257.7

tired: Jesus, t. out by the journey   257.5
So let us not become t. of doing good   285.6

tithe: Bring the full t. into the storehouse   101.3

tithes: And he gave him t. of all.   101.1

today: t. is the day to be saved!   256.11

together: Can two walk t., except they be agreed? 264.3
were t. and had all things in common.   89.2

tolerant: Be t. with one another and forgiving 32.10

tolls: t. to the one to whom t. are due   52.13

tongue: For those who speak in a t. do not speak 258.5
Guard your t. from evil   241.11
If anyone speaks in a t.   258.11
no one has ever been able to tame the t.   241.10
not so many as have fallen by the t.   241.4
One who speaks in a t. should pray for   258.6

tongues: followed by those who… speak in strange t. 258.3
is greater than one who speaks in t.   258.10
'strange t.' are not intended as a sign   258.8
than ten thousand words in a t.   258.7
they spoke in t. and prophesied.   258.2
Though I speak with the t. of men and of angels 258.4
Yet another has the gift of t. of various kinds   258.9

tormented: All who do this will be t. in fire and sulphur   144.29
they wandered about… afflicted, t.   48.12
will be t. day and night for ever and ever   144.30

tower: The Lord is a mighty t. where his people 35.5

town: A blessing on you in the t.   143.5

train: T. up a child in the way he should go   86.17

trance: As the sun was going down, Abram fell into a t.   267.1

transfigured: There in their presence he was t.: 102.5

transformed: be ye t. by the renewing of your mind 222.4
we are being t. into his likeness   32.6

transgressions: But he was wounded for our t. 13.2
For I acknowledge my t.   111.4
he removed our t. from us.   92.3
I acknowledge my t.   38.9
you were dead in your t. and sins   236.16

transgressors: he was numbered with the t.
135.93

travail: He shall see of the t. of his soul   13.2

traveled: So they set out and t. from village to village
136.7

traveling: Continually t., I have been in danger
136.13

While he was t. to Damascus   136.11

treasure: Do not store up for yourselves t.   162.2

sell everything… you will have t. in heaven   214.6

t. my commandments in your heart.   201.7

treat: t. others as you would like them to t. you
154.14

tree: He is like a t. planted beside water channels
31.13

t. of life also in the midst of the garden   150.1

trials: if you have to go through many hard t.
248.20

tribe: people from every nation, race, t. and language;
98.10

tribes: all races and t., nations and languages
196.5

tribulation: For then shall be great t.   248.4

knowing that t. worketh patience.   248.16

tribulations: We glory in t.   248.16

triumphing: public example of them, t. over them in
it.   271.7

trouble: can comfort those in any t. with the comfort
248.17

Each day has enough t. of its own.   282.7

God is our refuge and strength, a very present help in
t.   35.4

our t. which came to us in Asia   246.12

when t. or persecution arises   248.2

Yet man is born unto t.   248.1

troubled: We are often t., but not crushed   248.10

troubles: comforts us in all our t.   248.17

These little t. are getting us ready for   35.51

true: You, Lord, are the t. God   260.1

trumpet: at the last trump: for the t. shall sound
144.54

Praise him with the sound of the t.   166.8

trust: Though he slay me, yet will I t. in him
35.42

Though he slay me, yet will I t. in him   2.2

t. in him, and he will act.   82.3

T. in the Lord and do good   82.3

T. in the Lord and do good   41.1

T. in the Lord with all thine heart   82.4

trusted: followers who can be t. to tell others.
83.9

trustworthy: Who, then, is the wise and t. servant
83.4

truth: by the open statement of the t. we commend
122.3

Everyone who lives by the t. will come to   260.4

having your loins girt about with t.   260.11

Jesus saith unto him, I am the way, the t.   31.23

Jesus saith unto him, I am the way, the t.   260.6

keeps the message of t. on a straight path.   17.10

know the t., and the t. will make you free.   260.5

Pilate said, 'What is t.?'   260.9

rightly explaining the word of t.   260.13

Sanctify them through thy t.: thy word is t.   260.8

Sanctify them through thy t.   222.1

speaketh the t. in his heart.   29.2

Speaking the t. in love   260.10

T. abides and remains strong for ever.   260.2

the pillar and support of the t.   260.12

the Spirit of t.; whom the world cannot receive
119.16

the Spirit, who reveals the t. about God   119.18

The Word was made flesh… full of grace and t.
108.2

When the Spirit of t. comes   260.7

tune: t. unto him a new psalm: exalt him   166.12

turn: announce the Good News, to t. you away from
42.5

everyone everywhere must t. to him.   31.26

he commands all… to t. away from their evil
203.14

I gave solemn warning that they should t.   203.15

So that they may t. from darkness to light   42.6

T. away from your sins and believe   203.6

T. back to me, and I will t. to you.   85.4

turned: like your ancestors before you, have t. away
85.4

stubborn people have… t. your backs on me.
200.5

turning: I am astonished to find you t. away
251.6

U

unbelief: boy's father cried: 'I believe; help my u.'
261.5

unbelievers: Be ye not unequally yoked together with u.   262.6

The god... has blinded the minds of u.   262.5

unbelieving: O u. and perverse generation   261.3

none of you has a sinful, u. heart   261.10

undefiled: marriages must be kept u.   157.8

understand: By faith we u. that the worlds were prepared   263.11

Do you u. what you are reading?   263.8

I tried to u. everything that happens here   246.4

u. what the will of the Lord is.   276.6

When anyone hears the word... and does not u.   263.7

understanding: Be ye not as the horse... which have no u.   225.1

Do not be like a horse or a mule, without u.   263.1

from him come knowledge and u.   263.2

give me u., so that I may know your teachings.   142.4

I shall light a candle of u. in thine heart   263.6

knowledge of the Holy One is u.   263.4

lean not unto thine own u.   263.3

like foolish children; they have no u.   263.5

The peace of God which is beyond our u.   263.10

the spirit of wisdom and u.   60.2

with the knowledge and complete u.   60.6

you k. all about me. You k. when I am resting   142.5

understood: u. and seen through the things he has made   210.6

undivided: give an u. heart to Solomon my son   155.4

unfairly: How long will you keep judging u.   132.5

unfruitful: ye shall neither be barren nor u. in the knowledge   29.11

ungodliness: wrath of God is revealed... against all u.   104.7

ungodly: Christ died for the u.   135.22

were designated for this condemnation as u.   251.11

united: The whole group of believers was u.   264.6

unity: every effort to maintain the u. of the Spirit   264.7

how pleasant... to dwell together in u.!   264.1

universe: He is the one through whom God created the u.   281.3

unjust: the u. knows no shame.   132.8

unmarried: An u. man concerns himself with the Lord's work   28.3

unrighteous: the u. man his thoughts: 104.6

unrighteousness: Woe unto him that buildeth his house by u.   132.7

unsophisticated: u. about all that is evil.   235.8

unspeakable: Thanks be unto God for his u. gift.   254.5

uphold: I will u. thee with the right hand   35.36

upright: acts uprightly is u., just as he is u.   215.13

You have been u. in all that has happened   215.7

uprightly: He that walketh u., and worketh righteousness   29.2

uprightness: in him we might become the u. of God.   216.16

urging: u. you to live the kind of life that pleases God.   175.2

Uzziah: In the year that King U. died I saw   267.6

V

vain: not hold him guiltless that taketh his name in v.   167.3

not take the name of the Lord thy God in v.   20.1

vainglory: Let nothing be done through strife or v.   37.13

vanity: this is also v.   6.13

vengeance: V. is mine, and recompense   209.2

You shall not take v. or bear a grudge   209.1

victorious: uphold you with my v. right hand.   266.1

victory: He gives us v. through our Lord Jesus Christ.   266.5

prisoners when he celebrated his v.   266.8

v. over the world by means of our faith.   266.10

vine: I am the v., you are the branches.   31.31

viper's: the young child dance over the v. nest   9.10

vision: As I, Daniel gazed at the v.   267.9

During the night a v. came to Paul   267.16

For the v. is for its appointed time   267.11

He fell sound asleep and had a v.   267.15

I the Lord will make myself known... in a v.   267.2

Is it not a false v. that you prophets   267.7

King Agrippa, I did not disobey the heavenly v.   267.17

Lord spoke to me in a v. during the night   267.12

not speak, and they knew he had seen a v.   267.13
That night Paul had a v.   67.9
there was no outpouring of v.   267.3
they had also seen a v. of angels   267.14
Where there is no v., the people perish.   267.5

visions: In dreams, in v. of the night   267.4
your young men see v.   267.10
your young men shall see v.   67.7

visit: For years I have wanted to v. you.   136.12

voice: a v. from heaven said, 'This is my Son   259.2
after the fire a still small v.   195.1
I heard a great v. out of heaven saying   144.21

void: it shall not return unto me v.   17.1

vow: Hannah made this v.: 'Lord of Hosts   86.12
If you make a v. to the Lord your God   268.2
Then Jacob made a v. to the Lord   268.1
to make a v. and then have second thoughts.   268.5

vows: I will pay my v. before them that fear him.   268.3
O Judah, fulfil your v.   268.6
pay thy v. unto the most High.   268.4

W

wages: Do not hold back the w. of someone   138.1
For the w. of sin is death   193.7
For the w. of sin is death   236.14

wait: able to w. for it with persevering confidence.   269.16
Be still before the Lord and w. patiently   158.5
blessed are all they that w. for him.   269.9
It is good to w. in patience   269.11
Rest in the Lord, and w. patiently for him.   269.5
They that w. upon the Lord shall renew   269.10
They that w. upon the Lord shall renew   176.3
w. continually for your God.   269.12
w. for the Lord to deliver you.   269.8
w. in patience until the early and late rains   269.18
W. on the Lord: be of good courage   269.3
W. seven days until I join you   269.2

waited: Patiently I w. for the Lord   269.6
We have w. eagerly for the Lord   269.4

waiting: After w. seven more days, he released the dove   269.1
he was also w. for God's kingdom to come.   269.14
w. for the consolation of Israel   269.15

w. to see what would happen to Nineveh.   269.13
With all my heart, I am w., Lord, for you!   269.7

walk: name of Jesus Christ… rise up and w.   114.8

wandered: You had w. away like sheep.   42.8

want: not what I w. but what you w.   2.6

wanting: You have been… found w.   81.5

war: avoid bodily desires which make w. on the soul.   271.11
The Lord is a man of w.   270.1
though w. should rise against me   270.4
When you go out to w.   270.2

wars: You will soon hear about w. and threats of w.   270.7

wash: you also ought to w. one another's feet.   230.6

washed: After he had w. their feet   230.6
if your Lord and teacher has w. your feet   126.5
w. his hands before the multitude   205.4

water: after making it clean by washing it in w.   272.11
by means of the cleansing w. of rebirth   272.12
Come for w., all who are thirsty;   90.9
Except a man be born of w. and of the Spirit   119.14
Except a man be born of w. and of the Spirit   272.7
heart shall flow rivers of living w.   272.10
I baptize you with w., for repentance   272.6
I will sprinkle clean w. upon you   272.5
our bodies washed with pure w.   272.13
people will get w. from the well of victory.   272.2
Philip and the eunuch, went down into the w.,   15.5
Whoever drinks the w. I shall give   272.8

waters: every one that thirsteth, come ye to the w.   272.3
The Lord, the fountain of living w.   272.4

way: by the new and living w. that he opened   273.11
For the Lord knoweth the w. of the righteous   273.2
he instructs sinners in the w.   273.3
I go the w. of all the earth: 51.3
I worship the God… by following that W.   273.10
Jesus saith unto him, I am the w.   273.9
Jesus saith unto him, I am the w., the truth   31.23
My w. is hid from the Lord   273.6
one who has been tested in every w. as we are   253.20

some fell by the w. side,   81.7

There is a w. which seemeth right unto a man
273.4

This is the w., walk ye in it   273.5

to destruction, and many enter that w.   273.8

when it is their own w. that is not just.   273.7

ways: The Lord says: 'My thoughts and my w.
103.64

turn back, turn back from your evil w.   273.7

weak: but the flesh is w.   274.4

by such work we must support the w.   274.5

For when I am w., then I am strong.   274.13

God hath chosen the w. things of the world   274.9

Lord, and be merciful... I am lonely and w.   35.34

Strengthen ye the w. hands   274.1

the Lord's followers whose faith is w.   274.8

those who are w. in the faith fall into sin   274.10

To the w. became I as w.   274.11

Welcome those who are w. in faith   274.7

weakest: You were the w. of all nations   108.1

weakness: for my strength is made perfect in w.
35.52

for power is made perfect in w.   2.8

it is sown in w.; it is raised in power.   274.12

the Spirit comes to the aid of our w.   274.6

the Spirit helps us in our w.   119.31

we who share his w. shall live with him   274.14

weaknesses: I am most happy, then, to be proud of
my w.   274.13

is not incapable of feeling our w. with us   81.14

wealth: Do not wear yourself out in quest of w.
6.11

he who gives you power to get w.   214.1

You cannot serve God and w.   162.3

weariness: much study is a w. of the flesh.   257.1

weary: Come to me, all who are w.   246.6

Come to me, all who are w. and whose load is
31.18

Come to me, all you that are w.   257.4

speak a word in season to him that is w.   257.3

weep: A time to w., and a time to laugh   109.3

w. with them that w.   249.9

weeping: every night my bed is damp from my w.
55.2

there shall be w. and gnashing of teeth.   109.7

there shall be w. and gnashing of teeth.   144.24

welcomed: as you might have w. Christ Jesus himself.
26.5

you w. me as if I were an angel of God   26.5

well: that you are as w. physically   115.13

wearied with his journey, sat thus on the w.   136.9

wellspring: guard your heart, for it is the w. of life
116.5

wept: Jesus w.   109.12

Jesus w.   164.12

Peter went out, and w. bitterly.   109.11

when he saw it, he w. over it   109.9

whirlwind: have sown the wind... shall reap the w.
79.2

whole: thy faith hath made thee w.   115.10

wholeness: the partial vanishes when w. comes.
178.6

wicked: Do not follow the path of the w.   253.14

Let the w. forsake his way   104.6

see if there be any w. way in me   80.1

The w. shall be turned into hell   144.67

the w. shall die in their iniquity   193.3

widow: a poor w. came up and put in two coins
275.5

A w. who is all alone, with no one   275.9

he relieveth the fatherless and w.   275.3

He secures justice for the... w.   275.1

plead the case of the w.   275.4

was a very old prophet, a w. named Anna   275.6

widows: prefer that the younger w. get married
275.11

their w. were being neglected   275.7

to care for orphans and w. in their distress   275.12

w. in your towns, may come and eat their fill
275.2

wife: A capable w. is her husband's crown   86.2

A capable w. who can find?   86.4

A w. is bound as long as her husband lives.   157.5

cleave unto his w.: and they shall be one   157.2

do not let anyone be faithless to the w.   157.12

He who finds a w. finds a good thing   86.3

the husband is supreme over his w., and God   86.6

Your husband or w. who isn't a follower   86.5

will: after the counsel of his own w.   240.10

all things after the counsel of his own w.   192.10

except I drink it, thy w. be done.   135.87

For this is the w. of God, your sanctification   276.7

good, and acceptable, and perfect, w. of God.
110.8

He made known to us the mystery of his w.   276.5

he that doeth the w. of God abideth for ever.
276.9

I delight to do thy w., O my God   276.1

In every thing give thanks: for this is the w.   276.8

My food is to do the w. of the one who sent me   276.3

not my own w. but the w. of him who sent me.   265.3

prove what is that good… w. of God.   276.4

Thy w. be done, in earth   2.5

to w. and to work for his good pleasure.   205.9

understand what the w. of the Lord is.   276.6

Who can resist God's w.?   2.7

willing: the spirit is w. but the flesh is weak.   184.34

win: to w. the heavenly prize   285.8

wind: have sown the w., and… reap the whirlwind   79.2

sound of a mighty w.! It filled the house   144.14

The w. bloweth where it listeth   240.5

wine: come, buy w. and milk, not for money   90.9

Don't let w. tempt you   68.1

Jesus took a cup of w. in his hands   36.4

use a little w. for thy stomach's sake   252.5

w. that maketh glad the heart of man   90.5

wisdom: choose seven… full of the Holy Spirit and   w.   277.13

Christ Jesus, who became for us w. from God.   277.16

For after that in the w. of God the world   277.15

God gave Solomon very great w., discernment   277.1

Happy are those who find w.   277.3

hid all the treasures of w. and knowledge.   277.20

If any of you lack w., you should pray to God   110.9

If any of you lacks w., he should ask God   277.21

It is the Lord who gives w.   263.2

Learn where is w., where is strength   277.7

may give unto you the spirit of w.   277.19

O the depth of the riches both of the w.   277.14

The basis of w. is to fear the Lord.   277.6

The fear of the Lord is the beginning of w.   277.2

the spirit of w. and understanding   277.4

The true beginning of w. is the desire to learn   277.5

The w. from above is in the first place pure   277.22

The w. I proclaim is God's hidden w.   277.17

To one is given… the utterance of w.   277.18

Yet w. is justified by her deeds.   277.10

wise: Be not w. in thine own eyes   37.2

be ye therefore w. as serpents   277.9

Jesus became w., and he grew strong.   277.11

like a w. man who built his house on rock.   277.8

Now unto the… only w. God, be honour   103.73

the w. wait for it to cool.   225.6

Those who are w. shall shine   144.49

Woe betide those who are w. in their own sight   37.5

wisely: the unjust steward, because he had done w.   277.12

witchcraft: Now the works of the flesh are… w.   171.10

Some who had been practising w.   171.9

withhold: You shall not w. the wages of poor   173.2

witness: he will bear witness to me.   278.9

one must be appointed to serve with us as a w.   11.2

you will bear w. for me in Jerusalem   31.3

witnesses: And you also are my w.   278.9

we are surrounded by so great a cloud of w.   31.38

ye are w. of these things.   278.8

you will be w. for me in Jerusalem   278.11

wives: W. should always put their husbands first   86.7

you w. must submit to your husbands   86.8

woe: I said: 'W. is me! I am lost   109.4

wolf: Then the w. will live with the lamb,   9.10

woman: a w. should fulfil her duty as a wife   231.3

and the head of the w. is the man   125.22

God sent his Son, born of a w.   135.57

I permit no w. to teach   125.26

It was the w. who was made from a man   125.23

she shall be called W.   125.13

Unto the w. he said, I will greatly multiply   18.2

Unto the w. he said, I will greatly multiply   125.14

W., here is your son.   135.109

women: w. should be silent in the churches.   125.24

wonders: perform miracles and w. in the name of   161.9

signs, w. and miracles – were done among you   161.12

word: A w. fitly spoken is like apples of gold   241.3

accepted it not as a human w. but as… God's w.   17.9

every idle w. that men shall speak   107.9

he could not pronounce the w. correctly   241.1

In the beginning was the W., and the W. was   135.31

in Thessalonica… they received the w.   17.5

Let the w. of Christ dwell in you richly   283.12

Let the w. of Christ dwell in you richly   17.8

Man is not to live on bread alone, but on every w. 17.2

my w. be that goeth out of my mouth   210.2

So shall my w. be that goeth forth out   17.1

speak the w. only,   14.3

sustaining all things by his powerful w.   13.9

sword of the Spirit, which is the w. of God.   17.7

the sword of the Spirit, which is the w. of God. 119.40

The w. of God is alive and active   17.12

The W. was made flesh, and dwelt among us 135.55

The W. was made flesh, and dwelt among us 260.3

The W. was made flesh… full of grace and truth 108.2

Your w. is a lamp to my feet and a… Light   151.3

words: by thy w. thou shalt be condemned.   107.9

W. of thanksgiving and cursing pour out   241.10

Write: for these w. are true and faithful.   144.47

work: always abounding in energy for the Lord's w. 280.7

At w. in all these is one and the same Spirit   240.9

Do your w. as slaves cheerfully   279.10

God is always at w. in you   240.11

I am sure that God, who began this good w.   31.35

may be proficient, equipped for every good w. 280.9

that great w. which the Lord did   161.2

Then people go out to do their w.   279.4

there is no w., nor device, nor knowledge   279.7

This is the w. of God, that you believe   280.5

to hire some men to w. in his vineyard.   279.8

W. out your own salvation with fear   205.9

Whoever refuses to w. is not allowed to eat.   148.5

You have six days to labour and do all your w. 279.3

You must w. out your own salvation   221.15

worked: Instead, we w. and toiled.   122.6

worketh: w. all things after the counsel of his own will.   240.10

working: w. with his hands the thing which is good 122.5

we worked and toiled; we kept w. day and night 148.4

workmanship: his w., created in Christ Jesus unto good works   280.8

works: it is the gift of God: Not of w.   280.8

seeing your good w., they may give praise   29.4

so faith without w. is also dead.   280.14

that they may see your good w., and glorify   280.3

What must we do to perform the w. of God? 280.5

world: but also for the sins of the whole w.   191.7

but that the w. through him might be saved. 221.9

Christ Jesus came into the w. to save sinners 236.17

Father sent the Son to be the Saviour of the w. 221.20

For God so loved the w.   281.4

For God so loved the w.   31.21

For God so loved the w., that he gave   103.48

for the sins of the whole w.   13.12

God sent not his Son into the w. to condemn the w. 221.9

God who made the w. and everything in it   281.2

he will show the w. how wrong it was   43.4

If the w. hates you, just remember   281.5

Love not the w.   281.8

Now I am no longer in the w.   31.32

Now I am no longer in the w., but they are   281.6

the light has come into the w.   151.11

the w. by wisdom knew not God   277.15

the w. through him might be saved.   135.56

They are not of the w., even as I am not   281.7

What did we bring into the w.? Nothing!   41.7

who takes away the sins of the w.   236.9

Ye are the light of the w.   31.2

you loved me before the foundation of the w. 144.13

worried: Don't be w.! Have faith in God   282.10

So don't be w. or afraid.   282.11

worries: When I was burdened with w.   246.2

worry: But when you are arrested, do not w. about 35.13

Do not w. about anything   35.16

don't w. about how you will defend yourselves 282.9

Don't w.! You are now well   45.5

I am telling you not to w. about your life   282.6

Never w. about anything; but tell God   282.12

Rid yourself of all w. and pain   282.5

So do not w.; do not say, 'What are we to eat? 282.7

W. makes a heart heavy   282.4

W. makes a heart heavy.   246.3

worship: got out of the habit of meeting for w. 33.8

If the Lord is God, w. him!   30.4

It is written, Thou shalt w. the Lord thy God 283.6

kindness shown to the poor is an act of w.   181.4

O come, let us w., and fall down   283.3

This people w. me with empty words   283.4

w. him day and night within his temple   144.19

w. the Lord in the beauty of holiness.   283.2

worshipped: young child… and fell down, and w. him   283.5

worshippers: true w. will worship the Father in spirit   283.7

worthless: they are too w. to do anything good.   251.8

worthy: W. is the Lamb that was sacrificed   183.10

wounds: By his w. you have been healed   13.10

wrath: For the great day of his w. is come   144.41

For the great day of his w. is come;   8.10

For the w. of God is revealed from heaven   8.7

in w. remember mercy.   8.3

let not the sun go down upon your w.   8.17

the w. of God abideth on him.   8.6

the w. of the Lamb: 8.10

wrestle: For we w. not against flesh and blood   271.5

writing: no prophetic w. is a matter for private   17.13

wrong: All of us do many w. things.   81.15

done w. and lied from the day you were born.   237.3

He did what was w. in the eyes of the Lord   215.6

What credit is there… when you have done w.?   215.12

you did the w. thing, and now sin is waiting   215.1

wrongdoing: you cannot look on w.   236.7

wrongly: for you acted faithfully, while we did w.   215.7

Money w. got will disappear   64.7

Y

years: days of our y. are threescore y. and ten   172.5

let them be for… days, and y.   256.1

with the Lord one day is like a thousand y.   256.15

yeast: with bitter herbs and thin bread made without y.   174.1

yoke: For my y. is easy, and my burden is light.   206.2

I broke the bars of your y.   59.3

young: How can y. people keep their way pure?   284.3

I write to you, y. people   284.12

Let no one underrate you because you are y.   284.10

When we are y., it is good to struggle hard.   284.7

younger: the y. of them said to his father   284.9

yourself: Do not say to y., 'My power and the might   186.1

not to think of y. more highly than you   186.6

You seek great things for y.   228.5

youth: Avoid the passions of y.   284.11

Remember now thy Creator in the days of thy y.   284.5

youths: Even the y. shall faint and be weary   284.6

Z

Zacchaeus: Z. stood his ground and said to the Lord   207.11

zeal: As to z., a persecutor of the church   285.7

but their z. is not based on knowledge.   285.2

Z. for your house has consumed me   285.1

zealous: be z. therefore, and repent   62.5

people of his own who are z. for good deeds.   285.9

Zion: Woe to them that are at ease in Z.   214.3

ACKNOWLEDGMENTS

Scripture quotations are from the *Contemporary English Version* copyright © 1991, 1992, 1995 American Bible Society. Used by permission/Anglicizations copyright © 1997 British and Foreign Bible Society.

Scriptures quoted from the *Good News Bible* published by The Bible Societies/ HarperCollins Publishers Ltd, UK copyright © 1966, 1971, 1976, 1992 American Bible Society. Used with permission.

Extracts from the Authorized Version of the Bible (*The King James Bible*), the rights in which are vested in the Crown, are reproduced by permission of the Crown's Patentee, Cambridge University Press.

Extracts from *The Revised English Bible* copyright © 1989 Oxford University Press and Cambridge University Press.

Extracts from *The New Jerusalem Bible* published and copyright © 1985 Darton, Longman and Todd Ltd and Doubleday and Co., Inc.

Extracts from *The Book of Common Prayer* of 1662, the rights of which are vested in the Crown in perpetuity within the United Kingdom, are reproduced by permission of Cambridge University Press, Her Majesty's Printers.

Scripture quotations taken from the Holy Bible, *New International Version*, copyright © 1973, 1978, 1984 International Bible Society. Used by permission of Hodder and Stoughton Ltd. All rights reserved. 'NIV' is a registered trademark of International Bible Society. UK trademark number 1448790.

Quotations from *The New Revised Standard Version* of the Bible, copyright © 1989 the Division of Christian Education of the National Council of the Churches of Christ in the USA. Used by permission.